INDIVIDUALISM RECONSIDERED

INDIVIDUALISM

David Riesman

RECONSIDERED

AND OTHER ESSAYS

The Free Press, Glencoe, Illinois

TO MY WIFE

Contents

Preface

IN MAKING the selection of essays for this book, I decided to omit **all** articles published before 1946 when, having given up law teaching, I came to the University of Chicago. I have included most of my articles contributed to fifteen journals and half a dozen symposium volumes between 1947 and 1953. I am indebted to all these original sources for permission to reprint as well as for their original hospitality and in some cases, notably *Psychiatry* and *Commentary* and my article in *Years of the Modern*, helpful editorial criticism. I am also indebted to Reuel Denney, who took a major share in the research and writing on the football article, for his consent to its reprinting here; likewise to Nathan Glazer for allowing me to reprint, in a single revised piece, two articles we had jointly written on public opinion. My wife is co-author of the article on "Movies and Audiences," and her help at every step of the making and editing of these articles has been extensive.

The articles appear, for the most part, as they did originally, with a few cuts here and there and an occasional word changed or phrase clarified.

Mrs. Claudia Kren helped prepare the manuscript for the publisher and the latter, my friend Jeremiah Kaplan, did much to encourage this book and clarify its purposes.

D. R.

Chicago, Illinois
October, 1953

I

INTRODUCTION

IN ONE of his speeches Justice Holmes remarks that he would like before he dies to comment on all the great questions of the law, while all he could encompass are some thousand cases, many of them petty. To be sure, he used some of those cases for obiter dicta on some burning philosophical and social issues, but he was still hedged in by the passivity of the role of the judge, who must await what litigants bring before him and decide, if he is conscientious (as Holmes wasn't always), at retail rather than wholesale. At the same time, the occasions provided by litigants may widen a judge's scope, may take him in the course of his occupation away from his preoccupations. As I looked over my own essays and reviews, including unpublished ones buried in files, in preparation for this volume, I was at first dismayed by the "scatter" of so many tentative themes begun and not returned to—some of them occasioned by specific requests which I should have had the strength to dismiss.

What I have written, for the most part, seems linked less by topic than by a certain attitude, best summed up in "Values in Context." That article concluded with the motto of William Blake I have adopted as my own: "When I tell any Truth, it is not for the sake of Convincing those who do not know it, but the sake of defending those that do." This implies a defense of people from themselves, as well as from outside pressures. To do this I must know something about the audiences reached by what I say. For instance, when I published in 1942 a monograph on "Civil Liberties in a Period of Transition," in which I criticized a number of traditional civil liberty assumptions (such as the "clear and present danger" test), I was writing for those already on the side of civil liberties, not for the unenlightened. And so I was very happy when I learned that the American Civil Liberties Union had distributed copies to its board; but when asked to debate with Roger Baldwin in a public meeting I declined because I felt that before a large lay audience I would prefer to support Baldwin on certain major issues rather than to attack him on minor ones. Indeed, I believe that when issues are complex, one must write for a special audience, because one can't say everything at once.

Not long ago *The Lonely Crowd* brought me a critical letter from a woman in North Dakota; she wrote:

"I am not a Dr. I never went to college, I have not even finished High

School, I am only a nurses aid, and I like things simple and clear. All really great things, characters and thoughts are simple and clear. . . ."

Lack of clarity may sometimes be the result of confused ideas. But it may also be the result of an attempt to speak to some audiences to the exclusion of others. A writer may pitch his discourse at a certain level, in a certain vocabulary or metaphoric language for that purpose. Indeed, for reasons just given, there have been times when I regretted that *The Lonely Crowd* was not more inaccessible. Thus, there is a section in it dealing with tendencies in a now traditional sort of progressive education: I criticize the frequent "groupiness" of teachers, their lack of concern for intellectual content, their preoccupation with watery, presumably tolerance-breeding "social studies." As it happened, publication of the book coincided with a renewed drive against "Dewey-ism" and progressive education generally; I was dismayed to find myself quoted (or misquoted) by angry people in their all too easy onslaught against "new-fangled" notions in the public schools. Dismayed because, of all occupational groups, school teachers are among the most vulnerable; under attack, often from virulent reactionaries, they were hardly in a mood for truly critical self-examination. Despite what seemed to me reasonable caution, I had furnished *outside* ammunition against them. In his book *Persecution and the Art of Writing*, Leo Strauss argues that political philosophers and other writers have engaged in a form of concealed exposition to avoid either punishment for their views or their spread in untoward quarters. Whether Strauss' interpretation is correct or not in any particular case, the problem he deals with is real enough for me, less because of the tyranny of the powerful, who probably do not read me, than because of what might be deemed "the tyranny of the powerless" over their group—the tyranny of beleaguered teachers, liberals, Negroes, women, Jews, intellectuals, and so on, over each other. These are my principal audiences and the power of these audiences to intimidate their own constituencies is a theme of many of the papers in the next two sections.

Naturally, I do not alter my critical appraisals of contemporary schools because reactionaries are also on the warpath; rather, I try to present my views in such a way as to carry challenge to the complacency of reactionaries if they should chance upon them. Unlike some of the men whom Strauss discusses, I do not a priori divide mankind into an elite which can understand, and a mass which needs to be fobbed off, and I am hostile even to the best excuses for censoring ideas.

"Individualism Reconsidered," the essay which has lent this book its title, may also serve to exemplify my contextual view of the intellectual's role. If one should compare it with the essay on civil liberties just mentioned, one would find in the latter (as well as in "Equality and Social Structure," also published in 1942) an effort to show some of the limitations of laissez-faire liberalism and individualism in the realm of ideas. Both of the earlier essays emphasize the cultural conditioning of thought; both aim to put civil liberties doctrines in the perspective of the sociology of knowledge. To some extent I have changed my views since then; to some extent, the world has changed, and "groupism" become ever more of a danger; but also, to some extent, my audiences have changed. The earlier essays were written when I was still a law professor, addressing colleagues who appeared slow to recognize the social-psychological roots of opinion—colleagues, often enough, still immured in the heavenly city of the eighteenth-century philosophers. In contrast, "Individualism Reconsidered," like most of the essays in this volume, was written with an audience of social scientists (including historians and philosophers) mainly in mind—groups which, as I see them, have sometimes been all too inclined to overemphasize the values of collective or folkish life and to damn the individualism they find rampant in bourgeois, industrial, urban society.

Towards my lacunae of training and erudition, my new-found colleagues, the social scientists, have been more generous and hospitable than I should have expected. Though I first dipped into the study of the social sciences as a law student (attending Carl J. Friedrich's courses as well as those of some Harvard economists), I have learned much of what I have put into these essays from my colleagues at Chicago. Moreover, my students at Chicago, free of immediate vocational aims, have been willing to join me in learning how to study society—though to be sure many of them, bent on immediate reform, have been impatient with my skepticism, which they considered a form of delaying tactics. The atmosphere is different from that even of the best law schools where both students and faculty are after the "straight dope" (though they define it differently) and are all too clear as to how to get it. While my legal colleagues had been eager to facilitate my research, the diversity of aims had made difficult the sort of colleagueship that I found on leaving the law. In coming to Chicago, I was in search of colleagues with whom it would not be necessary to spend time explaining and justifying one's indulgence in what Veblen termed "idle curiosity," colleagues who are heirs of a longer tradition of cosmopolitan disinterestedness. A number of my articles also reflect my training in psychoanalysis (primarily with Erich Fromm, and to a very minor extent with Ernest Schachtel and the late Harry Stack Sullivan of the Washington School of Psychiatry). Much of my work is in the "neo-Freudian" tradition of these analysts. Only briefly represented in the final section of this book, it has involved the effort to relate social structure to character structure, and to bring such psychoanalytic methods as the "depth interview" and interpretation of dreams and folk tales out of the consulting room and into the study of large-scale social systems. And, needless to say, this effort is part of a vast movement under way for several decades in social anthropology, social psychology, and sociology.

Implicit in what I have said is the belief that social science can no more be divorced from values than from other contexts. Much as I defend "idle curiosity" against other imperatives for research, I know this value too is contextual and that it takes effort if one is to become aware of one's biases and to make use of them in what one undertakes. No artist or scientist needs to seek "engagement" when he cannot help it: a measure of disinterestedness is, indeed, one of the great and fragile values which the Western world has achieved.

A generation ago, however, when social science was still struggling to free itself from theology and social work (from socialism, too), even the oversanguine efforts to establish a "value-free" social science made good pragmatic sense.[1] Social scientists, finding their professional passion to lie in casting a cold eye, could in this way disassociate themselves from American reformism and the optimism about the social process it usually implied. To get rid of the old fuddy-duddy moralists aroused the zest of the Young Turks who marched under such banners as "operationalism." Their work was essential in freeing American social science from much sentimentality and highly ethnocentric preaching.

For my part, I want to make my evaluative position clear, or at least to flag the reader with my prejudices. (Even so, scrupulousness in self-revelation can very well run into all the ambiguities of "sincerity" which I take up in "Values in Context.")

Some social scientists have sought escape from terms which common usage has loaded with values, escape into manufactured symbolism so lacking in overtones as to avoid connotations of praise or

1. When I read Max Weber's influential discussions of the place of values in the selection but not the treatment of problems, there comes to my mind the picture of an imposing German professor bewailing Versailles and urging his students to patriotic hysteria—it is against such that Weber contended. In this country, outside the ex cathedra context in which Weber wrote, his fine-spun distinctions are correspondingly less useful: in so pluralistic a country as ours, and in one so unlikely to be swayed by professors, there may perhaps be less danger than in Germany from their succumbing to a particular political program and smuggling it into their work.

blame. In the spirit of certain schools of logical positivism, they want to make only "meaningful" statements and only purely denotative ones. But, in my opinion, the relation of social science to its subjects, who are also its audience, forbids any such easy undialectical answer to the problem of the researcher's ethical judgments. Terminological opacity will itself be taken as a judgment upon the world, perhaps a manipulative, frightened, or unsympathetic one. Deadpan symbols may symbolize a deadly determinism in the researcher. Literate peoples are going to read what is said about them, no matter how many verbal formulae are set up as barriers, and what they cannot understand they may aggressively misunderstand. Communication involves "noise," redundancy—and overtones. And beyond these problems of misunderstanding lies the further point that all our understanding of society is in my opinion metaphorical or analogical in some sense. Among our most fruitful intellectual tools are those metaphors which remind us by their very nature—even their very outrageousness, as for instance Freud's metaphoric use of Greek mythology—that we are abstracting and selecting (not simply "inducting" and not simply model-building). Contrary to the situation of a generation ago, we live, I am inclined to think, in an era of a "safe and sane" Fourth of July and a "safe and sane" sociology, though the world itself has hardly got safer and saner in the interim. Even my own obscurities of thought, my unresolved judgments and uncontrolled overtones, reflect in part a necessary and inevitable tension between life and reportage.

II

INDIVIDUALISM AND ITS CONTEXT

IN ESSAYS on the "nerve of failure," written in 1946-7 ("We Happy Few," "Community Plans and Utopia," and "'Minority' Living"), I am still persuaded that Americans are dominated by the success ethic; I am thinking of people who are jockeying for wealth and power. The self-abasement of avant-garde intellectuals that I criticize in "We Happy Few" struck me a few years ago as a minority reaction, not yet influential in American culture at large. That is, my picture of what was going on in the United States carried some hangover from the 20s and 30s. And of course it should, for the country has not changed overnight. Nevertheless, my later writings are less acrid and satiric; there is a somewhat more sanguine attitude toward American culture.

Throughout the articles in this and the following section I am defending individualism (of a certain sort) and being critical of conformity (of a certain sort). Yet I am perfectly sure that I would not be attacking "groupism" in America if I could not rely on its durable achievements—it is just these that make individualism possible. I attempt to deal with such shifting contexts of judgment in "Values in Context," the first article in this section. It was delivered as an address at a conference on Science and Human Values at Mt. Holyoke College.

"Individualism Reconsidered" and "The Saving Remnant" try to grapple in brief compass with intricate questions of salience and causation in the shaping of the modern temper. I feel that in this whole area we profit from many different interpretations. We know neither what produces autonomy in individual children nor independence in the social order; it is easier to locate blockages than to propose practicable remedies.

It is to this very issue that the paper on "Community Plans and Utopia" is directed, for there I ask why we have allowed ourselves to focus so exclusively on our social fears rather than our social hopes —a focus not entirely explained by the grim events reported in any day's press (more accurately, the reports themselves are a selection, and their availability reflects as well as shapes our times).

In this essay, I suggest that the utopian tradition has gone sour because of collectivist, especially Communist, abuse, and gone stale (especially in America) because so many of our earlier hopes for equality and abundance have been attained—leaving us either to try to put meaning back into outdated struggles or to find a political agenda not in planning for a better future, but in postponing a worse one. Many writers and statesmen have pointed out that America now has world responsibilities for the less fortunately situated countries, but it also needs pointing out that we have responsibilities to ourselves, to improve the quality of our own daily life, even while we concern ourselves with the miseries of the less fortunate parts of the globe. Otherwise, all we shall succeed in doing is to level down. Similar issues, of course, face the Socialists in Britain and in Scandinavia, for whom the old-time Fabian and social-democratic slogans have so patently worn thin.

1. Values in Context

LYMAN BRYSON, examining a few weeks ago the papers submitted for the annual [1952] Conference on Science, Philosophy and Religion, observed that only four out of forty-five dealt with values in any concrete and empirical way; the rest were hortatory, many of them assuming that the academicians there assembled understood each other and needed only some formula of belief to impose values on a world that had presumably lost them. Reading a number of these same papers, I also was struck by the frequent assumption that values in general, not merely some values or the speakers' values, had gotten lost or dissipated; moreover, that without consensus on values, our democratic society would not hold together. I see no convincing evidence for either of these assumptions. It seems plain to me that men cannot live without values, without preferences and choices, without the vocabulary of motives that we partly learn and partly teach ourselves. Those who bewail the loss of values seem disingenuously to bewail the loss—that is, the replacement—of their own values; and in many cases I believe this applies quite literally: for many of the men whom I find to be most hysterical about the loss of values appear to me to lack confidence in their own ongoing processes of valuation; they do not enjoy making choices, and their effort to escape from freedom is writ larger than life in their overly subjective appraisal of the society as a whole.

Something of this sort, I think, must lie behind the second assumption also, namely, that agreement on fundamental values is essential for democratic functioning. The attempt to enforce such agreement seems to me a good way to bring on civil war; and it is important to study those institutions in our society which allow society to function precisely in the face of profound disagreements on fundamentals. One of these institutions, I suggest, is the city bosses and their machines: these act as brokers among competing urban values, based as they are on religious, ethnic, regional, occupational and other identifications. These bosses can trade a park in a middle-class section for a symbolically important Italian judgeship, and otherwise keep a tolerable peace by appropriate pay-offs from the spoils of American productivity. The current attempt to unify the country against municipal patronage and bossism seems to me dangerous, because by enforcing an ideological unity on politics we threaten with extinction a few men, soaked in gravy we can well spare, who protect our ideological pluralism.

To be sure, there is a fundamental value underlying my own view, which is that men should not be forced by the needs of society to give more than conditional co-operation to specific, short-term goals. Thus, I think we can ask people to be vaccinated, but not to believe in its efficacy, or in science, or in long life. And on the whole I prefer that we win people's co-operation by offering concrete advantages—including such personal growth as they may gain from the co-operation itself—without asking them what their fundamental values are. (Incidentally, the Communists in our midst have made this program difficult, not only because their fellow-workers in the usual front organizations naively assume that since the Communists share the work they also share the liberal and humane values alleged to be involved in the joint enterprise, but even more because the country at large assumes that it is always the fellow-workers and never the Communists who are the dupes: the fact often is that the Communists are gulled into doing the work on the improvident speculation that they will win converts or make some other gain.) To put the matter another way, I believe it a fallacy to assume that people can co-operate only if they understand each other (this is the illusion of many semanticists), or if they like each other, or if they share certain preconceptions. The glory of modern large-scale democratically-tending society is that it has developed the social inventions—such as the market, the practices and skills of negotiation, and the many other devices which allow us to put forward in a given situation only part of ourselves—which allow us to get along and, usually, not to kill each other while retaining the privilege of private conscience and of veto over many requests made of us by our fellow men. No doubt, for this to occur there has to be some *procedural* consensus, some shared values of a very general sort like due process, and among sufficient people in strategic locations, some less-than-fanatical attitude toward compromise and even corruption. But this is far from saying that we would be better off if we could go forward by going back to some partly mythical state of value-agreement based on choicelessness.

§ II.

THE PSYCHOANALYTIC psychologist can come at this same problem in another way. His clinical work makes him aware that in an individual values are contextual, with each value-element having a very different loading depending on the *Gestalt*, on the whole. It did not,

of course, take Freud to teach us that, for instance, the morally indignant person is often a sadist whose own impulses were his first
victims. But the analytic method does allow us to delineate such
observations in more detail and in more complexity. Let me take as
an illustration the virtue of sincerity, which is becoming a salient
and unquestioned value, so far as I can see, among a whole generation
of young people. One gifted boy of fifteen, whose interview I have
analyzed in detail elsewhere, stated that his best trait was sincerity,
and proved the point by a gallant effort to be totally frank with the
interviewer. It did not occur to him that such sincerity puts pressure on others in a social situation to be equally sincere: it is coercive, and tends to break down etiquettes which we use to protect
our emotional life from strangers, from over-inquisitive relatives and
friends, and at times from ourselves. Nor did it occur to him that his
very frankness concealed some of its driving motives, not only this
coercive one but also another equally coercive insistence that he be
regarded and valued for his truth-telling. He tells us everything about
himself without reserve—everything but what he doesn't know, namely,
that he wants the credit, or at least some response, for this very
frankness.

In this connection, it is interesting to note the study of values
made in Vienna some years ago by Else Frenkel-Brunswik. She
asked people what values they thought they possessed and then asked
their associates to rank them on the same values. And she discovered,
for example, that people who said they were sincere were not thought
to be so by their friends; rather, those who said "I try to be sincere
but I am often insincere," were regarded by others as sincere. Such
observations confirm my feeling of wanting to be particularly cautious when meeting someone who says, "I am going to be frank with
you."

But of course it would be going much too far to say that the
contemporary cult of sincerity is simply negative, a regression from
the superior age of manners. The *opportunity* to be sincere, particularly between men and women, is a tremendous achievement over the
past; the *opportunity* to convert a stranger into a friend in a Pull-
man car or academic convention is an American blessing; the growth,
through the practice of sincerity, of the One Big Union, the union
of sinners, has lifted intolerable burdens of moral underprivilege
from the isolated and the inarticulate. Moreover, in a big rich country, lifted above the needs of peasant guile and tenement-house suspiciousness, millions of us can afford sincerity, just as in many parts
of the country we can afford to leave our cars unlocked and would
in any case suffer—unlike the Italian victims of *The Bicycle Thief*

—only moderate discomfort from an instance of misplaced confidence.

My point rather is to show how a trait like sincerity must be studied in the life-plan of given individuals and of society as a whole before we conclude that it is a value we want to encourage or discourage. My own guess is that sincerity is today so much taken for granted as an unequivocal blessing that it becomes important, as it never was at an earlier historical point, to discover some of its ethical ambiguities and limitations. To do so may help curb the tyranny of the self-styled sincere over the rest of us.

§ III

I WANT to turn now from the problem of appraising the values of an individual or of an age to the analogous problem of evaluating the ethical positions of the great thinkers of the past and present. For here, too, I believe a contextual analysis is necessary if we as intellectuals are to live in some productive tension with our times and not merely to ride the waves of the past or of the future. Let me begin by taking as an illustration the great controversy opened up by the debate between Condorcet and Godwin on one side and Malthus on the other. The former, trusting to the increasing ability of science to make nature produce, believed that an age of abundance was dawning on mankind, and that the march of history was a march of progress toward human perfectibility. Malthus lacked trust. He was more impressed with the ability of fecund, improvident men and women to produce children than with the possibilities of technological advance. The only way he could see out of nature's trap was an ascetic "moral restraint," and sociological invention, and for this way he had scant hopes. Moreover, he was perhaps the first economist to foresee that depressions might be permanent. For him there was no question about perfectibility: man had his choice between late and frugal marriage, coupled with intensive work, and the various miseries from war to pestilence by which in the past the adult population was periodically aborted. His book on population was written as a reply to Godwin, Condorcet and the other utopians of his day.

Now it seems to me, though I may well be mistaken, that Godwin and Condorcet, though in their personal lives badly treated, were to a considerable extent in line with late eighteenth-century ideas: they might be vilified, but they did not stand alone. By contrast, Malthus, whose personal fortunes were much more secure, was heretical; and, indeed, his views on depressions remained so for many years. Trying to look at these thinkers in terms of their own day, I respect and admire both sides, and do not feel called upon to take a stand with one and against the other: each made a decisive and stimulating contribution to our understanding. However, when the argument shifts to our own day, my attitude shifts to some extent also. Moving in circles where Malthus is greatly esteemed, and Condorcet and Godwin, if regarded at all, sneered at as childish Enlightenment utopians possessed with *hubris*, my tendency in teaching and writing is, without derogating Malthus, to emphasize the courage which Condorcet and Godwin also had, and the importance today of faith that nature, including human nature, is not a trap, though we can make it one. On the other hand, where complacency still rules, there one would want to stress Malthus, and some of the neo-Malthusians are probably quite useful in this direction. But where, as in so many intellectual circles, there prevails an anti-Enlightenment temper which prides itself on its realism, its refusal to share any dreams of man's potentially fine future, there a reappraisal of Godwin and Condorcet is desirable—taking account, however, of all that Malthus and his followers have taught us.

§ IV

I MUST now confess—in an effort to communicate and to be relevant more than to be sincere—that what I have to say here has been guided in some part by a similar feeling for context. When I received this invitation, I assumed—perhaps unfairly—that the balance of opinion and assumption here would turn out not to be too radically different from the one that Lyman Bryson reported on for the Conference on Science, Philosophy and Religion; and I also assumed that I had myself been asked because the planners were themselves pluralists, at least to start with. So I felt it incumbent on me to stress that side of my thought which is skeptical about absolutes and, in a day when very few admit being relativists, to illustrate some of the possible advantages of a relative approach to values. By the same token, I would have done somewhat differently had I been asked to talk on scientific method before the American psychological or sociological societies; there, confronted with many who still believe in a value-free social science and a deceptively neutral operationalism, I might have stressed not only the importance of the study of values, but also the inescapable and creative role of values in the scientific process itself.

When I conduct myself in this way, a host of problems immediately arises, and in discussing them I may be able to clarify somewhat our elusive topic. In the first place, I may be mistaken about my audience: I may be hardening their prejudices when I am seeking to be liberating. I try to cope with this by insisting, when I discuss such matters, that there be an extended question period, or its sublimation in a panel like ours here; the question period may help correct my misapprehensions about the audience and simultaneously their misapprehensions about me. But it is not enough to know the audience; one must also know *their* context. They may be so buffeted by their adversaries that they need, at least temporarily, to have their prejudices confirmed rather than shaken. For instance, girl students at some of our liberal universities need occasionally to be told that they are not utterly damned if they discover within themselves anti-Negro or anti-Semitic reactions—else they may expiate their guilt by trying to solve the race question in marriage. But even that judgment has to be made in terms of the wider social context— in this case, a judgment that the lot of Negroes, let alone Jews, in America is not always so utterly desperate as to call for the ruthless sacrifice of protective prejudices. And, as I have indicated, each of these judgments of context, from the audience out in widening circles, may be mistaken.

In the second place, I may be mistaken about my own motives as a speaker. What may on the surface appear to me as my courageous choice of an unorthodox and unpopular position may turn out on closer examination to be a form of exhibitionism. Or I may be more conciliatory than is warranted because I want to be liked. More probably, I may be falling into the all-too-common academic pitfall of finding and clinging to a pet heresy, proud of my intransigence, while failing to realize that it has become, if not a popular orthodoxy, at least the vested heresy of an in-group. I must therefore try to keep up with myself, as I develop, as well as with my audience, and to watch for any symptoms showing that I prefer to shock or startle people rather than to enlighten them. At another level, I cannot help but be aware that a shifting position which takes a stand only against the need to take a stand on many exigently argued issues may have terrible moral pitfalls in convenient uncommitment—I say I cannot help this awareness because all my adult life I have been besieged by people who wanted to convert me to their loyalty and thought me cowardly for refusing to join. It has taken me a long time to recognize the possible values, including courage, behind such refusals. But still, this issue too has to be re-examined. To complicate matters further, I know that ambiguity is fashionable today in the literary world, so my plunging into it as a pedagogic device may not be entirely disinterested. Let me hasten to add, however, that I don't think I or anyone else need be faultless before opening his mouth, for the history of thought teaches us how many men were productive for the "wrong" or at least very neurotic motives, and vice versa.

Discussion may help somewhat, as I have said, to clarify an audience for me and me for an audience. Even so, someone is likely to ask me: "Don't you think so-and-so is true, irrespective of time and place? Isn't taking your audience into account a complicated form of lying?" A somewhat more subtle questioner may ask: "Don't you place yourself above your audience, and even above the ideas you deal with, by making yourself into a governor or thermostat for the society, trying to prevent its going to extremes? Can't 'extremes' be right? And doesn't this conduct make you, after all, a servo-mechanism, dependent for your own motion on that in the larger society?" All I can do now is to begin an answer to some of these questions—to deal with all of them would mean to discuss the function of intellectuals in our society; the possibilities of democratizing that function so that any number can play; and indeed a discussion of the play itself, of the play of the mind, of what Veblen termed "idle curiosity." But I can say right off what is perhaps already clear, that I do not take a relativist position on *all* issues—that would be another absolutism—but only on some. Santayana said of James that he didn't think any questions were ever settled, whereas for me some questions are settled, some positions are indefensible. I cannot, for instance, agree that Plato, or anyone else, makes a tenable argument, in any context I can conceive of, for banishing poets. And while I can see that sadism when incorporated into certain personality types can be socially useful, for example if sublimated into a surgeon's work, I react negatively to the trait even in ameliorative contexts, and violently against it in destructive ones. In fact, destructiveness in its grosser and its subtler forms—when, for example, I see students' confidence that they can learn something being undermined by teachers or classmates or parents—so arouses my combativeness that, like Karl Popper in his book *The Open Society and Its Enemies*, I tend to become a fanatic crusading against fanaticism. The very position I have described to you here is taken partly because I want no possibly liberating voice in the thinkers of the past to be wholly lost by destruction of the psychological roots in us enabling us to sympathize with it.

Thus, there are issues on which I am a relativist and issues on which I am an absolutist and those in which I am in doubt as to what I am, or should be. Such moral experimentalism, while it has the perils I have already outlined and others I know not of, is essential if we are to meet life flexibly, listening to the ancestor within and the friend without, but not bound to obey either.

Let me add that I don't posit this as some sort of middle way: what *is* the middle is a contextual problem in itself, and extremes may be right. Nor would I quite define my role as that of a thermostat or other simple feed-back mechanism. For I define the context as including not only what is "really" there, as your self-styled realist would see it, but as including what is potentially there, given what my intervention may evoke in others and theirs in me. To find out this potential, one has to take risks, and one may be disappointed; but the only alternative is to condemn society to an endless regress in which each thermostat is reacting to each other thermostat or to a Generalized Thermostat of some sort.

To put this another way: I believe that the processes of communication are inherently ambiguous, since we understand other people's symbols in terms of our own character and the experience it has let us have. Therefore even those people who are sure they know what the truth is may not succeed in communicating it, but something quite the opposite, as the history of every reform movement testifies. Perhaps in America communication is especially ambiguous, for reasons already partly indicated. I think, for instance, that the wild exaggeration and tall tales so characteristic of American humor may reflect, among other things, the speaker's fear that unless his stretching of the truth is highly visible, he may run the risk of being believed. On the whole, to our loss, we have had few gentle satirists, and the *New Yorker*'s development of some gentle cartoonists may signify the beginnings of a common culture among its readers.

Some will take this complexity of communication to American audiences as further evidence that we should seek lowered ambiguity through value-uniformity. But is it not better, while admitting that there are losses involved, to take heightened ambiguity as an indication of the great variety of experience available to Americans in the face of all standardizing tendencies? At any rate, I prefer to come to grips with this ambiguity directly, as the psychoanalyst uses his patient's resistance as a very central part of his cure, and to seek to develop values in the very process of discussing them. For I think we do well to take advantage of the fact that we live, as Albert Camus puts it, in *la civilisation du dialogue*, whence arises the problem of sincerity, and also the need upon occasion to interiorize and perhaps even to transcend the dialogue, in such recesses of privacy as we can make for ourselves, even at some cost in sincerity.

§ V

TO RETURN now to the beginning: I suggest that the anxiety manifested by so many intellectuals about values, especially other people's values, may be on the point of being overdone. Having watched what happened when the experimentalist progressive education of John

Dewey, via the patronage networks of various teachers' colleges, was installed in many ill-equipped schoolhouses throughout the country, I am not attracted by the picture of a crusade to implant self-consciousness about values in all the pious and platitudinous teachers of America: I would rather have them teach languages and algebra and biochemistry. Movements of thought, it seems to me, do not so much reflect the society in which they arise as take account of what that society appears to have left out of account—to emphasize individualism when mercantilism reigned, or groupism when laissez-faire did. But as society becomes more highly differentiated, and as the audiences among whom intellectuals talk become more stratified, it becomes more and more difficult to know whether, let us say, a preoccupation with values is at fruitful odds with the times or a cruel addition to its excesses. In this, as in other cases, it may begin as the one and end as the other. I think that ways of observing our society with some detachment, such as literature and social science, offer us the chance to understand these dialectical relationships better than we now do, and to safeguard our judgment as to what intellectual tasks need doing; some tasks, of course, are hardy perennials. And then when we communicate what we have observed back to these audiences, we will find that the same pluralism which exists in the society exists in many of its individuals, and that we are talking to one part of a person and against another. For such a situation, I like the motto of William Blake: "When I tell any Truth," he wrote, "it is not for the sake of Convincing those who do not know it, but for the sake of defending those that do."

2. Individualism Reconsidered

Since such terms as "society" and "individual" tend to pose a false as well as a shifting dichotomy, I must anticipate misunderstanding; if I succeed in being suggestive to at least a few, I shall be satisfied. We live in a social climate in which, in many parts of the world and of the United States, the older brands of ruthless individualism are still a social danger, while in other parts of the world and of the United States, the newer varieties of what we may term "groupism" become increasingly menacing. Actually, we can distinguish conceptually between the needs of society (as a system of social organization) and those of the environing groups (as a system of psychological ties and expectations). As so defined, society, the larger territorial organization, often provides the mechanisms by which the individual can be protected against the group, both by such formal legal procedures as bills of rights, and by the fact that large-scale organization may permit the social mobility by which individuals can escape from any particular group. Prior to the rise of passports and totalitarianism, the modern Western city provided such an asylum and opportunity for many, while the existence of this safety-valve helped alleviate the pressure of "groupism" everywhere.

§ I

Just as a self-proclaimed "realist" is a different fellow in the Middle Ages, in the Enlightenment, and in modern America, so also the meaning of "individualism" depends on the historical setting. And it is worth tracing here the paradoxical development which, in the course of the modern era, freed Western men progressively from many previous restraints while at the same time developing a seemingly individualistic character-type enclosed within new psychological restraints. Men of the emerging middle classes, after the Renaissance, were turned loose in an economic order freed from the supervision of mercantilism, in a political order freed from the supervision of an hereditary aristocracy, in a religious order freed from the supervision of ecclesiastical hierarchy. To many observers of this process, whether radical or reactionary, these men who were freed of external restraints under the slogans of laissez-faire economics, utilitarian philosophy, and so on, appeared fiercely and viciously individualistic and competitive.[1] But if we look at these new men from the inside, so to speak, we can see that it was precisely their internalization of a great deal of restraint that allowed them to become free of the group sanctions that might have been arrayed against their "individualism." They could disregard the religious anti-money-making attitudes that had survived from the medieval and early Reformation period only because (as Max Weber pointed out) their Puritan religious ethics provided them with stern justification and with a shell of protection against the shocked attitudes of their contemporaries.

Today, with some old evils behind us, we can admit that the hardy men who pioneered on the frontiers of production, exploration, and colonization in the last three hundred years were usually men who acted according to a code and who, though of course there were many pirates like Daniel Drew and the slave traders among them, were more likely to subscribe to high moral principles (e.g. the elder Rockefeller). These men were bound by a character orientation I have termed "inner-direction": they were guided by internalized goals and ideals which made them appear to be more individualistic than they actually were. Often, they were men who walked in the imagined footsteps of idealized parents—and this gave them their seven-league boots, and their feeling of having a personal destiny. And since the ideals that were internalized included many vestiges of older traditions, they were frequently paternalistic men, who, despite nominal belief in free enterprise, helped ameliorate the worst abuses brought about by their innovations. They shared, then, more than appears of the ethics of their anti-individualistic critics, from Owen and Marx to Karl Mannheim and Tawney. Evidence of this may be found in comparing these Western enterprisers with their counterparts in other countries, such as South America or China or the Soviet Union, where when traditional restraints on ruthlessness broke down, fewer internalized restraints were available to take their place. In sum, it proved possible in the West in early modern times to carry individualism to its limits of usefulness—and, in some cases, far beyond these limits—because a fair amount of social cohesiveness was taken for granted. . . .

Moreover, the same sort of moral compulsions which many of these "freedmen" carried within themselves, as the result of their socialization in a patriarchal family, were also turned loose upon the society at large. Individualistic "promoters" turned up not only in business and colonization, but in the many zealous reform movements

---

1. To Werner Sombart, these men appeared free of "scruples"—that is, free from such traditional obligations as those of guild morality. The fighting slogans were, of course, often blatantly individualistic.

of the last several hundred years. These movements fastened new restraints on a society that was shaking loose from old ones—how effectively, we can see by contrasting the attitudes towards law and society in India today, as the legacy of British rule, with the attitudes in neighboring countries which were not compelled to internalize the "white man's burden." In the West, the nineteenth century witnessed the triumph of the Victorian way: a triumph of legal and orderly justice, of honesty in business and government, of greater concern for women and children, and so on. (Inclined as we are today to patronize the Victorians, we generally see the seamy side of their attainments and emphasize their hypocrisy, failing to observe that this hypocrisy was itself some evidence of their success in driving corruption, vice, and social sadism underground.) In the eighteenth century it was impossible to walk unarmed in many English cities, let alone in the country; public and private violence abounded; corruption was taken for granted; the slave trade was thriving. By the middle of the nineteenth century, the lower orders had been freed, the lower impulses (as well as some higher ones) subdued. The development in America ran parallel, but was never, of course, as complete or as spectacular; as we all know, lawlessness reigns in many areas of American life today.

Nevertheless, anti-individualist writers such as Tawney, while they may have neglected the dangers of collectivism out of their disgust with their acquisitive society (and their failure to appreciate that medieval society was in some ways more acquisitive still), do express a very common mood of dislike for the cash nexus—a mood which appears in more astringent form in Veblen. It is hard for people to find satisfaction in a society whose best defense is that it is a lesser evil than some other social form. People can become greatly attached only to a society which takes account of their longings for connection with each other, and they may even opt for totalitarianism because it pretends to satisfy these longings and to get rid of the felt indecency of the cash nexus. To the degree that capitalist individualism has fostered an ethic of callousness, the result has been to undermine all forms of individualism, good and bad.

§ II

IN THE PERSPECTIVE of hindsight, we can see how Darwin's *Origin of Species* came to be so completely misinterpreted when it first appeared, as a brief for struggle to death *among individuals*. We can see, as the pendulum has swung towards groupism, that Darwin's book might just as well be interpreted as demonstrating the need for social solidarity or symbiosis within and among given species in order to achieve survival; thus (as Kropotkin pointed out) the book has much to say about cooperation as a technique of competition.

But the hardy Victorians, who had freed themselves from external restraints on economic competition and who were at the same time still sensitive, as I have indicated, to anti-moneymaking ethics, welcomed their interpretation of Darwin as a support in their continuing polemic against restraints—a polemic carried out also within themselves. One can, for instance, almost watch William Graham Sumner trying to stamp out, with the aid of Darwin, any softness and tenderness towards those who were pushed aside in the competitive struggle; he would have been less violent towards "do-gooders" if he had not feared their echo inside himself.

Today the argument against Sumner, and against this nineteenth century variety of individualism, seems very dated. We have come to realize that men who compete primarily for wealth are relatively harmless as compared with men who compete primarily for power (though, to be sure, there are violent, even totalitarian, implications in the treatment of labor, at home and abroad, as a commodity). Nevertheless, we are still inclined to use the word "bourgeois" as an epithet; we are well aware of the vices of the money-grubber, and perhaps less sensitive to the meannesses of spirit that develop in a monastery or a university where wealth as a goal is minimized. Even so, the centuries-old campaign against the middle class should not have hidden from us the advantages of a social system in which some men seek wealth (including wealth through power), pretty much for its own sake, and others seek power (including power through wealth), pretty much for its own sake, thus establishing a dichotomy of drives in which protective separation of specifically political powers can take its stand.

I recall Walter Duranty talking some twenty years ago about the Soviet abandonment of the "New Economic Policy," the policy by which, in the early twenties, a moderate capitalism had been encouraged in Russia. He spoke of the horror with which the ascetic Communists had reacted to the champagne parties and lovely ladies of the burgeoning NEP-men who were speculating in commodities, and making fortunes overnight by methods hard to distinguish from black-marketing. I felt then, and still feel, that if these Communists had been more historically minded and less morally indignant they might have seen that the NEP policy offered the only chance of curbing the totalitarianism which sets in when only power, and not money, talks. (The Communists were like those farmers who, in their hatred of varmints, get rid of the very creatures on whom the whole ecological balance depends.) At the same time, we can see that if the

Russian capitalists had not allowed moral restraint to be monopolized by the Communists, they might have aroused less of this sort of antagonism. (Today, it is the top Party functionaries—and occupation troops—who have access to champagne and ladies!) And we also see that economic control through the "impersonal" market mechanism (Adam Smith's "invisible hand"), where this is at all possible, is decidedly preferable to the all too visible and personal hand of the state or private monopolist.

§ III

IN THE EPOCH when "money talked," the conception of human nature underwent a series of changes quite as ironical as the social developments themselves. The view of man as naturally cooperative runs through the writings of a number of otherwise quite diverse nineteenth century thinkers: St. Simon and Comte, Kingsley and Marx, Durkheim and Bellamy, Kropotkin and Ruskin. All these writers, more or less explicitly, reject competitive capitalism in favor of a medieval type of guild harmony and order, while differing in their attitudes towards the machine and in their remedies for the diseases of industrialization.

Likewise, the view of man as naturally antagonistic has given rise to a number of diverse solutions to the problem of the social order thus presented. Freud, for example, deeming men innately aggressive, thought that a strong elite, with a monopoly on the capacity for being reasonable, would have to compel the majority to cooperate in the tasks of civilization, at once demanding submission from the masses and providing them with consolation. In Elton Mayo and in other recent writers, one can find a similar elitism and a similar concern with the formation of group consensus through strong leadership.

All these writers thus arrive at positions in which they become advocates of what I have labelled "groupism," whether they start from reactionary or revolutionary political positions, or from Rousseauistic or Freudian and even Hobbesian views of human nature. That is, whether one begins with the assumption that cooperation is man's natural state, which he is prevented from attaining by a reactionary social order, or with the assumption that the "state of nature" is one of war of all against all, one can readily end by focussing on forcing or allowing men to define themselves entirely as social animals. (To be sure, in the early Marx, and even in Bellamy, one finds more anarchistic strains; and some thinkers of the last century and of this one, such as John Stuart Mill and Bertrand Russell, have worried less about order than about liberty.)

Obviously, the preoccupation with the desires and needs of men for group affiliation testifies, often enough, to the actual presence of disorder in the society. But it often testifies also to the obsessive feeling on the part of some intellectuals that disorder in itself is a terrible thing. Furthermore, one of the themes that unifies many of these writers is their attitude towards the disorderly trait of "selfishness"; in true medieval fashion, they denounce it and welcome, if not always altruism as such, then at least a class or national consciousness that submerges individual self-interest. The confidence in self-interest that ran from Mandeville through Smith to Sumner, seems to have been almost utterly defeated among influential thinkers by the end of World War I; it is still assumed that self-interest is natural —and sometimes, indeed, that an "enlightened" self-interest is called for—but on the whole, reliance is placed on concern for the needs of the group.

This altruism might have worked during the 1900-1950 shift toward emphasis on the group, if those group needs had themselves been clear. In that case, people might have developed a pattern of obedience to the group in certain limited spheres (regarding the group demands as a kind of tax collection), while retaining individuality in other spheres. If this had happened, the shift from the preceding attitudes of subtly socialized individualism would hardly have been noticeable. But in fact, the group needs have not been clear; moreover, they have been constantly changing. There has developed today a great preoccupation, less with specific needs, than with group mood —a feeling on the part of individuals that they wanted or felt they had to spend their energies, first in making a group, and second, in attending to and improving its morale.

This groupism, which rests not on obvious group emergencies but on the vague disquietude of lonely individuals, is probably strongest in America, where people appear to be most vocally concerned about the problems of group participation and belongingness. Americans have devoted less scientific attention to the measurement of group needs and potential wants through market research techniques (save in the most obvious commercial forms) than to what we might term "mood engineering" in work, play, and politics. Mood engineering leads not so much to specific "altruistic" behavior as to a general readiness to participate in the given group activities of the moment, even if their only purpose is to help other people pass the evening. As Margaret Mead has pointed out, Americans feel selfish if they stay at home when they might be amusing people who are "underprivileged" in the skills of self-amusement.

It would take us too far afield even to begin to try to explain the reasons for the psychological changes which have occurred at least as rapidly as those in social and political organization. For example, shifting patterns of child socialization are important: among other things, parents today face the responsibility of "making a group" with their children—are on the defensive vis-a-vis their children's moods—in a way quite different from the attitude of parents in an earlier day. Not all the developments towards groupism are to be deplored. Groupism rests in part on an increasing sensitivity to subtle states of feeling, and this is an advance. Only, as always, such advances bring with them a dialectical train of new perplexities and limitations. We must skeptically question the demands for greater social participation and belongingness among the group-minded while, on another front, opposing the claims of those who for outworn reasons cling to individualism as a (largely economic) shibboleth.

§ IV

IT IS NOT EASY, for obvious reasons, to discover the actual state of this conflict in Soviet Russia today. We do not know, for instance, to what extent people have become cynical and apathetic as a way of resisting an enforced group belongingness. However, occasional arguments appear in the press which, by claiming that the issue is settled, show that it is not settled. Thus, in 1940 there was a discussion of a psychology textbook which was attacked, not only for its "objectivity," but for its failure to realize that the whole science had undergone a profound change in the Soviet Union. "The tragedy of the loneliness of the individual," it was asserted, "which characterizes a society founded on classes, has been liquidated. The conflict between the individual and the community has disappeared. The interests of the Soviet people are harmoniously identified with the interests of Soviet society." Furthermore, theories about "unchanging human nature" are damned as bourgeois (an issue not absent from American social science polemics)—it would seem that Lysenko-ism operates in the field of psychology too.[2]

---

2. A poignant newspaper story from Warsaw indicates that the Poles may be maintaining some resistance to the Stalinist extremes of groupism. A young Polish girl loosed a flood of abuse and correction on herself by writing a letter to the newspaper *Standard of Youth* declaring that "my private life does not concern anyone." She continued that the ideal member of the Union of Polish Youth was a "creature with wings . . . wearing a long and clean cloak of sackcloth. When it meets a pal it discusses only Marxism. It does not push in tramways nor spit on the floor and walks only on the right side of the street. . . . According to you we should wear only a spotless uniform of our organization, straight hair and, of course, no trace of makeup . . .—all, in order to discuss the development of education in the New China! . . . I am young and lucky enough to have survived the war and have a right to live as I like. Z.M.P. meetings, discussions and some artistic shows are not enough for me."

To be sure, it is no adequate answer to Western advocates of groupism to show how the idea has fitted so well into the totalitarian pattern (which eventually serves to destroy all local groupings). In fact, the advocates of an anti-individualist position use the seeming success of the dictatorships to buttress their views (not seeing to what extent the dictatorships, beneath their ideology, are seeking to imitate *us*), pointing out that men welcome social solidarity even if they must pay, in the loss of freedom, a high and terrible price for it; and that actually they want demands made on them—a point to which war experience also testifies—rather than to be left alone and forced to direct their own efforts. Still other voices argue that, in order to defeat the USSR, we must evoke our own spirit of sacrifice and devotion to the group: our alleged anarchy will be our undoing in the war of the two worlds. And still other, though few, voices would like to see international anarchy put down by an all-powerful world state.

What strikes me in many of these proposals is an ascetic uninventiveness reminiscent of the discussions which bored the Polish letter-writer quoted in the footnote. We assume that all possible forms of human relatedness have already been experienced, so that if present forms are unsatisfying, then better ones must be looked for in our own past, in wartime comradeship, or in the grisly present of the Soviet Union. Ironically, the very people who extol groupism, whether as an inexorable necessity or as desirable in its own right, usually do not themselves lead parochial and "groupy" lives; they draw sustenance from all the continents and all of history; they have friends everywhere, just as their material needs, through the modern division of labor, are met from everywhere. But like Plato and many other unhappy intellectuals since, they believe that those others, the masses (obviously, the very term "masses" is heavily value-loaded), can be saved from a Durkheimian anomie only by an enforced groupism and its concomitant ideology.

We can see, moreover, other forces than a simple nostalgia, or even simple elitism, at work. Anti-urbanites, for example, argue among themselves, in the guise of instructing the "masses." Unable to stand alone, lacking the "nerve of failure," they tend to project onto others their own uneasiness and frequently their own contempt for intellectuality. I do not mean, of course, that there is no malaise in our great middle and working classes in urban life; but rather, on the one

---

For this display of "selfishness," the writer was termed demoralized by war and occupation, said to "almost sanction(s) debauchery," and informed that "exceeding the production target . . . is happiness. Work in the organization provides happiness certainly greater than that gotten out of dancing or making up."

hand, that the intellectuals greatly underestimate the terror, misery, and disorder of the "status society" of the past which they so much admire, while underestimating, on the other hand, the tremendous achievements of modern men in making themselves comfortable in the face of the novelty of a fluid industrial society.

Americans of the more mobile classes have not only adapted themselves to a fluid society, but have also begun to adapt the society to their own needs. They have achieved an extraordinary ability to make judgments about, and friends with, a great variety of humankind. Whereas more traditional societies have an etiquette to govern the relation between people of different age, class, and sex groups, these Americans have abandoned etiquette for a more individualized and personalized approach. And while we are familiar with the negative aspects of this development—its enforced joviality of the "greeter" and glad-hander, its enforced politeness of the Helen Hokinson type— we may in our self-contempt be less ready to see its great adventurousness: the liberation of people and their movements from the chain mail of etiquette.

In the arts of consumption as well as in the arts of production, Americans have moved so fast that, in architecture and design, in moving pictures and in poetry and criticism, we are living in what I believe to be one of the great cultures of history. It is not fashionable to say this. Yet we may ask, as Crane Brinton does in *Ideas and Men*: What is there in Pericles' famous praise of Athens that does not apply to us, in some or even in extended measure?

Sensitive Americans—and they are more in number than each individually is apt to think—have become exceedingly allergic to anything that smacks of chauvinism; this very symposium is in part a testimony to this development. Vis-a-vis Europe, we have lost the defensive aggression of Mark Twain, though his was a needed corrective; vis-a-vis Asia, we were until recently taken in by the image of the peaceable, unaggressive, technologically-unseduced Chinese. It now seems likely that we shall fall for the idea that the Russians have more to offer the Far East than we; and that they have unequivocally convinced the peasants that this is so. While this attitude stems in part from our disenchantment with machine civilization and our failure to use machinery as a means to greater, more creative leisure, it would appear ludicrous to that part of the world which needs machines before it can realize the possibility of becoming disenchanted with them!

One of the interesting semantic expressions of our own disenchantment is that of bewailing our society as "impersonal." What would the member of the village group or small town not give at times for an impersonal setting where he was not constantly part of a web of gossip and surveillance? Furthermore, this use of the term "impersonal" is a way of deprecating our great human achievement of turning over productive routines to machinery and to formal organization. One result of this attitude is clear enough: the sphere of work tends to come increasingly under the supervision of the engineers whose concern is less to reduce the time and strain of the worker, than to render the workaday world "meaningful" in terms of shared emotions reminiscent of the guilds, or perhaps of our nostalgic image of the guilds.

A contrary attitude would assume that we should be grateful to find, in our work, areas of freedom from people, where the necessary minimum of productive activity could be accomplished without the strain and waste of time involved in continuous concern for the morale of the working group. If men were not compelled to be sociable at work, they could enjoy sociability in their leisure much more than they often do now. In fact, while men in the nineteenth century may have underestimated their satisfactions from solitary occupations, hobbies and other pursuits, we tend today to reverse these extremes and to forget that men can enjoy, let us say, the physical rhythms of work or the private fantasies of leisure even when they are for long periods deprived of social comradeship at work and play. What is necessary is some sort of balance which will find room for quite idiosyncratic individual desires to be, variously, alone and with others. The flexibility of modern industrial organization, no longer bound geographically to rail lines and power sites, the steady decrease of hours of compulsory work which our abundance allows, and our increasing sensitivity to the psychic as well as physical hazards of the different occupations—these developments permit us to move towards the reorganization of work so that it can offer a greater variety of physical and social challenges and stimulations. But work should never be allowed to become an end in itself simply out of a need to keep ourselves busy.

§ V

APART FROM the everpresent threat of war—not seldom used as a rationalization to sop up our "excessive" comforts, leisures, and painfully-attained easy-goingnesses—most of our social critics cannot imagine a society being held together without putting organized work in the forefront of its goals and agendas. Their efforts to restore the participative significance of work, allegedly enjoyed in earlier social stages, show the same poverty of imagination as their belief in the inevitable need for the parochial group as the only conceivable build-

ing block of society. When we turn to formal politics, we see that
the same fundamentally reactionary ideology leads to a demand for
national unity and a distrust of the chaos of democratic politics and
of the war among the so-called "special interests."

The notion that there must be "agreement on fundamentals" in
order that democratic politics may go on is an illusion. Carl J. Friedrich, in *The New Image of the Common Man,* provides a discriminatory critique. While it is true that people must be prepared to accept
the fact of a vote or election going against them, and to accept certain legal and juridical minima of the same sort, this is not what is
meant when agreement on fundamentals is asked as the price of
national unity and survival. What is meant is actually a surrender of
special interest claims, whether these grow out of ethnic loyalties,
church affiliation, regional, occupational, or other ties. What is
meant is agreement that democracy itself (defined to mean more,
much more, than the legal minimum) is a good thing; agreement on
equality of races; agreement to put American needs ahead of any
foreign loyalty. Yet the fact is that our democracy, like that of
Switzerland, has survived without securing such agreements. In our
country, this has been attained by a party system that serves as broker
among the special interest groups: the parties do not ask for agreement on fundamentals—certainly, not on ideological fundamentals—
but for much more mundane and workable concessions. At the
same time, our expanding economy (and concomitantly expanding
state services) has made these concessions possible without bank-
ruptcy and, on the whole, with a steady reduction in hardship and
injustice.

Those who would like to see the parties "stand for something,"
and those who have framed their own image of the future in terms
of some Armaggedon of proletarian revolution or overthrow of the
"interests," feel unhappy and misgoverned under such a system. To
them it seems simply a lack of system. Thus, we are in part the victims of ideals of polity which turn our virtues into vices and which
have confused the Western world since Plato's *Republic,* if not before.
What we need are new ideals, framed with the future rather than
the past in mind—ideals closer to the potentialities actually realizable
under the impetus of industrialization.

One of the elements in such a new ideal would seem to be a relaxation of the demand for political dutifulness now made by many citizens who are worried about apathy. Apathy has many meanings. Its
expression today may be one of the ways the individual—in the Soviet
zone or Franco's Spain, no less than here—hides from ideological
pressures, hides from "groupism." Lacking an active counterfaith in

individualism, or any way of meeting up with others who share his resentments, he falls back on apathy as a mask behind which he can protect the remnants of his privacy. If it were widely recognized that not all people in a democracy need concern themselves continuously with public affairs (or with the union, or with the PTA, or what not), but that all should have a "right of veto" of which to make sparing, residual exercise, they might more readily agree to comply with the minimal demands for information and participation that such a veto would need for its effectiveness. And with politics no longer regarded as a continuous duty, people might feel less resistance to participation.

§ VI

IF THE INTERNATIONAL (and hence domestic) outlook continues to be as grim as during recent months [written in early 1950], readers may wonder whether this advocacy of "irresponsible" individualism is not sheer escapism. It would be insufficient to answer that "escape," like "compromise" or "appeasement," has become a bad word to the crusaders for political and group commitment. It would perhaps be a better answer to observe that if America is to be saved from destruction or self-destruction, it will be by preserving, as part of our armory of significant escapes, our humor and creativity and sense of perspective.

I recognize, of course, that many Americans feel guilty about their "luxuries" if others are forced to fight and suffer, and so would welcome a kind of edited hardship as an alleviation of their guilt. But though this is understandable and, in many ways, desirable, it provides the privileged countries and groups with much too limited and hence too easy a morality. The present international dangers menacing America (real enough in the view I hold of Stalinism) can obviously be used by many people in America to rationalize their partiality for the shared hardships of war against the solitary hardships of developing their individuality in time of peace.

Again, it should be obvious to the reader that I speak in a social context in which anarchy and "unbridled" individuality are much less likely prospects (except on the international scene) than the all-too-evident danger of the "garrison state." This danger must make us particularly sensitive to the fact that we depend for advance, in morals no less than in physical science, on individuals who have developed their individuality to a notable degree. We must give every encouragement to people to develop their private selves—to escape from groupism—while realizing that, in many cases, they will use their freedom in unattractive or "idle" ways. Our very abundance makes it possible for us, even in the midst of war, to take the minor risks and losses involved in such encouragement as against the absolutely certain risks involved in a total mobilization of intellect and imagination.

Yet in these remarks I find myself, as a final irony, addressing the defense of individualism to some presumed director of unselective service: I am using, Adam Smith style, group-survival arguments to justify the "selfish" living of an individual life. (Much of the same irony overtakes many devout people who "sell" religion as a variety of group therapy—because it is good for morale rather than for morals.) Possibly I am thereby revealing my own arguments against my own guilts. But I think more is involved. I am trying to answer Dostoevsky's Grand Inquisitor in terms that he would understand, as well as in the transcendent terms that his interlocutor, Jesus, understands. I am insisting that no ideology, however noble, can justify the sacrifice of an individual to the needs of the group. Whenever this occurs, it is the starkest tragedy, hardly less so if the individual consents (because he accepts the ideology) to the instrumental use of himself. . . .

Social science has helped us become more aware of the extent to which individuals, great and little, are the creatures of their cultural conditioning; and so we neither blame the little nor exalt the great. But the same wisdom has sometimes led us to the fallacy that, since all men have their being in culture and as the result of the culture, they owe a debt to that culture which even a lifetime of altruism could not repay. (One might as well argue, and in fact many societies in effect do, that since we are born of parents, we must feel guilt whenever we transcend their limitations!) Sometimes the point is pushed to the virtual denial of individuality: since we arise in society, it is assumed with a ferocious determinism that we can never transcend it. All such concepts are useful correctives of an earlier solipsism. But if they are extended to hold that conformity with society is not only a necessity but also a duty, they destroy that margin of freedom which gives life its savor and its endless possibility for advance.

3. The Ethics of We Happy Few

WE HAPPY FEW[1] is the ironic title of Helen Howe's study of an academic community. The community happens to be Harvard, and the English Department. But both Miss Howe and her readers have insisted that this is merely coincidental, and that the same sort of self-centered behavior is to be found on other campuses and in other departments. It is a study of intellectuals, and my interest in it here is in the representative character of its ethical attitude towards them.

The central character of *We Happy Few* is Dorothea Natwick, accomplished daughter of a liberal New England family. In observing the Natwicks, Miss Howe has seen through the conventionalities of people who seek desperately to be unconventional. "To *épater* the bourgeois both of the faculty of St. Cuthbert's and the countryside around Constable was the crusade into which Mrs. Natwick was forever flinging herself, while from her tilted lance fluttered the pennant of the good, the true, the beautiful, and the 'interesting.' And the greatest of these was the 'interesting.'" When Mr. Natwick dies, Mrs. Natwick holds a service in her barn: "Isn't it too good to be true?" she announces gaily to Dorothea, "I've got the Gordon String Quartet to say they'll play. I thought the Mozart Clarinet Quintet would be just right. . . . Then there's a chapter from Fabre's *Life of the Fly* which your father was particularly fond of. . . ."

The picture of the Harvard faculty into which Dorothea marries is drawn in the same spirit. Everything is "interesting"; nothing is serious—nothing, that is, except the bitter rivalries for prestige and place. There is a terrible striving always to be *avant-garde*: to "discover" Henry James, T. S. Eliot, Melville or the more obscure modern English poets. There is a standing rule for admission to the happy few, who call themselves "The Little Group": *never to be taken in* by any person, idea or emotion.

So far, very good. Miss Howe has had the nerve to tackle not the easy targets of the Babbitts or the Hucksters, the Sammy Glicks, et al., but people who are far above the average, even among intellectuals and academes, in intelligence, sensitivity, and breadth of view. She has not been taken in by the self-deceptions of the élite of culture. She has their number with the wit of a Helen Hokinson, but with a mordancy of her own.

---

1. Helen Howe, *We Happy Few*, Simon & Schuster (1946).

The main sin of The Little Group is pride, meaning self-centeredness. Dorothea symbolizes arrogant unconcern for ordinary people, ordinary emotions and ordinary events. The war news annoys her. She finds Basic English more interesting than the RAF. Miss Howe's criticism of these "selfish" attitudes and preoccupations becomes clearer by contrast with the brave, unselfish males in Dorothea's life. The males—Dorothea's suitor, husband, son, and father—are completely uninterested in themselves. The suitor is a gauche Idaho crusader who becomes a fighting liberal Senator. Uncultivated and inhospitable to the play of ideas, he is out of sorts in the Natwick atmosphere. He is a sterling democrat from the great open spaces. He gets things done. He finally rejects Dorothea because she is too snobbish, frivolous, and unworthy. The husband, John, is immersed in the study of seventeenth-century England as Dorothea's father had also been immersed in his teaching, his research, and his hobbies. John, despite Dorothea's pushing, refuses to angle for the mastership of "Bromfield House," one of the swank Harvard Houses. When war comes he enlists in the British Navy, quietly, without fuss or feathers. When Dorothea consoles herself with a lover, he is not jealous, but only concerned lest Dorothea be wounded. He dies at sea. Their son, Johnny, is exempt from service as a medical school student and is fascinated by his work. But he, too, is unselfish. Again quietly, without fuss or feathers, he seeks to enlist and finally gets Dorothea's permission to do so. Even Dorothea's lover, a wonderfully sketched portrait of the slick success-boy who makes women and money for the love of making, comes off at least no worse than The Little Group. Since he is uncomplicated and unintellectual his selfishness is undisguised. He debunks the academic airs, and is billed as a more intrepid and successful lover than any Harvard professor could possibly be. Except for him, then, the men close to Dorothea and thus contrasted with her and The Little Group, are models of unselfishness, devoted to their work, their cause, or both. They are not always looking out for number one.

§ THE ETHICS OF INDIVIDUALITY

IF WE LOOK at The Little Group and Dorothea, we must grant the charge of selfishness. But we must grant it from a quite different critical position, namely in terms of Erich Fromm's distinction between selfishness and self-love.[2] Fromm points out that a "selfish" person has no real self, and no fondness for the self; therefore, he must continuously seek security in terms of conquests and power to

---

2. See "Selfishness and Self-Love," *Psychiatry*, (1939) 2:507-523. I am also indebted to his forthcoming book, *Man For Himself*.

compensate for his lack of "self-love." In other words, the selfish person is not interested in himself, but only in others' evaluation of himself. He shines in their reflected light—he is their satellite, even when he dominates them. On the other hand, the self-loving person is confident of his own self-evaluation. He does not need others for psychic security, but is capable of loving them as he loves himself. He has an erotic attitude towards the world, not a greedy one. Dorothea and all The Little Group were selfish and lacking in self-love as thus defined. Dorothea depended on the Group for admiration, and won it; the Group basked in its conviction of superiority over the less esoteric and advanced. Lacking any conviction of their individuality, they needed constantly to appear "original" and "interesting"; the war on banality was a major problem. Lacking ambition for personal quality and distinction, their aims were necessarily petty. Their fault was not an excess of pride but a deficiency of it.

"Moralists are constantly complaining," De Tocqueville observed in 1834, "that the ruling vice of the present time is pride. This is true in one sense, for indeed everybody thinks that he is better than his neighbor or refuses to obey his superior; but it is extremely false in another, for the same man who cannot endure subordination or equality has so contemptible an opinion of himself that he thinks he is born only to indulge in vulgar pleasures. He willingly takes up with low desires without daring to embark on lofty enterprises, of which he scarcely dreams.

"Thus, far from thinking that humility ought to be preached to our contemporaries, I would have endeavors made to give them a more enlarged idea of themselves and of their kind. Humility is unwholesome to them; what they want most is, in my opinion, pride."[3]

Pride in De Tocqueville's sense, like self-love as Fromm uses the term, is an essential ingredient of true individuality, which is based on an awareness of, and liking for, one's self in its particularity and uniqueness. The individuality of the members of The Little Group was factitious—a put-up job with differentness cultivated for its ability to create status. The Little Group is liberal-minded, but its method of achieving individuality resembles that of the reactionary Uncle Jules, in Sartre's "Portrait of the Anti-Semite," whose one claim to fame was that he could not stand the English. Thus true individuality goes together with pride, while a want of individuality frequently appears in our culture as selfishness.

§ THE ETHICS OF COLLECTIVISM

A SELFISH PERSON, then, if he is to change, needs to cultivate above

---

3. *Democracy in America*, (Phillips Bradley ed., 1945), Vol. II, p. 248.

all else a feeling of pride, and an understanding fondness for his own individuality. As is evident, Miss Howe's therapy for Dorthea's selfishness is just the opposite. Dorothea finds in suffering and humility the cure for her Little-Groupish pride, and in the collective activities made available by the war the cure for her Little-Groupish individualism. With the war, Dorothea suffers a series of losses and defeats: husband, lover, son, and maid abandon her in one way or another; Bromfield House and Basic English also fall away. Then she is put through a number of "experiences" which bring her close, physically at least, to the troubles and pains of ordinary folk. Becoming a nurse's aid, she meets other nurse's aids socially; they are fine and dull. Traveling to Coeur d'Alene to be near her son in training, she "sees" America: in the stench of the ladies' room, the sadness of platform partings, the good-heartedness of Middle-Westerners. The townsfolk of Coeur d'Alene are another "experience"; they, too, are fine and dull. At the end, Dorothea returns to Cambridge a sadder and wiser woman: her pride is gone, and she has learned humbly to admire the great open spaces and the open sentiments usually associated with them in song and story.

Suffering and physical discomfort, however, do not always succeed in submerging one's individuality, though they are among the most useful weapons. Nor are feelings of identification with others, whether in Coeur d'Alene or elsewhere, adequate; such feelings are quite consistent with a strong feeling of individuality and personal value. So Dorothea, following the penances set out for her by Miss Howe, must further submerge her own self by the device of self-belittlement: in order to build up the common man, she must learn to run herself down. This lesson of submersion begins, rather mildly, when Dorothea discusses with her mother, Mrs. Natwick, the "original" arrangement for burying Mr. Natwick at the cheery barn funeral already described.

"Even Dorothea," Miss Howe writes, "found herself wondering if it might not have been 'simpler' to accept the common lot, and to take death with all the other trappings and the suits of woe decreed by the organized morticians, along with millions of other anonymous human beings who had never hoped to assert an individuality in life and certainly would not have the temerity to storm the ramparts of eternity on their own momentum." Is there any greater virtue in bowing to the pressure of the organized morticians than in bowing to the private need to be "original"? At least the Natwick style of life was an attempt at individuality, even if it failed as too external a "creation."

Dorothea has absorbed this anti-Natwick lesson of acceptance by the time her own husband dies. At the service "the beautiful words of the Burial of the Dead engulfed her. It was comforting to lose oneself in their blanketing anonymity. *The burden of being one's own arbiter of taste and feeling had been removed.* John was not narrowed into a gifted young man, with nice tastes and a knowledge of the seventeenth century. He had become enlarged, enfolded. He was simply one more 'man that is born of woman who hath but a short time to live.' . . . One must go with it, accept it, believe that some transubstantiation was wrought, beyond our power to understand."[4] Where have we heard before of loss of oneself in blanketing anonymity? Of the burden of taste and choice? Of one's duty to accept what one neither likes nor understands? Is not that the essence of the denigration of the individual in the reactionary ideology—none the less so because here put in the context of John's anti-fascism?

Dorothea continues learning the lesson of self-belittlement. After John's death, her lover deserts her. Dorothea is overwhelmed with shame for having slept with him, for having given way to her desires. "She had been dethroned by her own flesh." As a result, she feels she has no right to condemn Japanese atrocities; she had finally "made up (her) mind that (she) was not one bit better than the meanest of earth." She says to herself caustically: "What insufferable hypocrisy and arrogance that she should dare to hand out moral judgments. . . ."

Having been dethroned by the flesh, Dorothea must mortify it; hating illness and filth, she is taunted into becoming a nurse's aid by a fellow-traveling and wholesome member of The Little Group who has already joined. "Don't tell me the lady has an idea she's somebody!" is the friend's irrefutable comeback to Dorothea's protest that the work would not make use of her special gifts. Dorothea's education continues; she learns that: "What makes a good nurse is simply the power to forget yourself—completely." Staggering through the agonizing days at the hospital, she learns in her few off hours to enjoy Schumann as well as her beloved Bach and Mozart: "Her aesthetic as well as her human taste was stretching, too—cruder, possibly, but warmer and more inclusive." In other words, whatever makes for individualization and idiosyncracy in taste requires "stretching"; in compensation for this, she makes herself believe that "quintessential beauty is to be found at the very heart of human pain." How convenient! *Ad astra per aspera.*

The pain, submission, and self-belittlement which put an end to Dorothea's efforts to achieve individuality are symbolized by her change of attitude towards Harvard. No longer is it a subject for

---

4. Italics mine—D. R.

jokes, or for Natwick insouciance. Listening to Churchill's speech at Harvard in September 1943, she glows with thoughts of sacrifice: "Here, in this dark, mellow, sanctified hall was the distilled essence of values worth dying for." The institution, too, is sanctified: Dorothea concludes that "Harvard College—like any community of men dedicated to a goal higher than themselves—was greater than the sum of its parts."

At the end, in a touching scene, Dorothea shows that she is "cured," she has learned her lesson well. She is taking leave of her son Johnny at Coeur d'Alene; he is about to be shipped out. He is a gifted, sensitive lad, just eighteen. He is also Dorothea's one remaining human tie with life, and she is genuinely devoted to him. But now she sees him, "for the first time, as only part of the general whole—no longer anything special or remarkable or favored—just one more American gob." Again, how convenient! These are precisely the sentiments of passivity and resignation which make it possible for the underlying population to take the miseries of war with a minimum of fuss and feathers. But why should people not weep, protest? Why should they so easily be reconciled?

Dorothea's soul is "saved" by the most humble and uncritical surrender. Her surrender must be humble, in Miss Howe's ethics, because her claims at the beginning of her career were regarded as so proud. It is the very American morality of the higher they come the harder they fall.

§ THE ETHICS OF AFFIRMATION

ARE "LITTLE GROUPS" of intellectuals, then, more proud than most people, or more selfish? As Miss Howe is aware, frantic concern about status is to be found in almost all groups, little and big. The notion that sensitive and educated people are more conceited or more vicious than the average is a romantic fiction; and, like romantic fictions generally, serves a social function. That function is to justify attack on a weak and powerless minority: the intellectuals. They are, Miss Howe says, detached from America. But what does this mean, except to say that they are weak; otherwise, one might claim that America is detached from them, and that is too bad for America.

I do not, of course, intend to deny that the intellectual, like everyone else, faces a staggering problem of relating himself genuinely to other people and other problems than his own. How can he give up selfishness for self-love, in a culture which practices selfishness and preaches self-abasement? How can he maintain a feeling of belonging in the world, of having just claims on life, if the world ignores or rejects him? Miss Howe lets us and herself down into the one easy answer which we know to be false. That is also the judgment of Diana Trilling, whose brief, brilliant review of *We Happy Few* stimulated my own attempt at a more extensive analysis. "Miss Howe is scarcely alone among current novelists," Mrs. Trilling writes, "in regarding democracy—or the proletariat, or the fight against fascism, or a sweeping view of the multitudinousness of American life—as if it were a medicine especially prepared to cure the sick soul of the modern individual. One recalls, as an extreme instance, the novel of a few years ago in which a young woman was cured of neurosis by giving visas to refugees; or the more recent example in which the heroine was saved from nervous collapse by joining the movement for cooperatives. As a matter of fact, asked to name, on the evidence of the novels I read, the one dominant trend of our progressive literary culture, I would probably specify this mechanical notion that the individual finds himself by losing himself in some larger social manifestation."[5]

In fact, we can observe the same trend in writers of such different backgrounds from Miss Howe, of such tremendous power, and of such exceptional awareness of the issues, as Koestler and Silone. In *Arrival and Departure*, Koestler is frightened by his own mocking of contemporary liberal and democratic values, mocking which he puts into the mouths of Bernard the fascist and the woman psychoanalyst. He is unwilling to face his fear, and to take the responsibility for his mockery, for if he dealt with them in their own terms he might be defeated. His answer? A symbolic plunge into "affirmation." Peter, the hero, is parachuted into enemy territory, a dangerous war exploit; by his act, he seems to reject the mockery, which nevertheless remains verbally persuasive and unanswered. He drowns the self-doubts with which the analyst has filled him in violent, unreflective anti-fascism.

Silone's recent play *And He Hid Himself* is a good deal more ambivalent in its conclusions; yet it contains a similar lesson. Murica, a revolutionary student who has been living beyond his psychological means, under pressure betrays his comrades to the Fascist police. No one knew; no one would know; he is safe. But he finds it intolerable to be alone in the sense of being detached from the revolutionary movement, and also in the sense of having no one to submit to. He is tormented by remorse and confesses, first to his girl, then to Don Benedetto, a sympathetic cleric, and finally to Pietro Spina, the socialist leader who has disguised himself as a priest. By these confessions he risks his life, for he knows the law of the underground:

---

5. 163 *The Nation*, 50, 51, 1946.

traitors are assassinated. However, Spina forgives him, permitting him to rejoin the movement; Murica remains unpunished until, at the end of the play, he is captured and tortured to death by the authorities. He dies without betrayal but instead with psychological solvency. Silone treats this final act of heroism as redeeming not only Murica but also the peasants whose revolutionary ardor and hope it stimulates after they had become cynical and apathetic.

The play throughout is framed in Christian imagery. The priestly robes in which Spina hides himself are more than make-up for a getaway: they represent an effort to combine Socialist and Catholic traditions. And though the allegory is not, for me, quite clear, it seems that Murica's sacrificial return to the illegal movement symbolically resembles that of Christ, who also took upon himself the guilt of the suffering poor. Thus, while Silone has wonderful things to say about the virtue of pride, he nevertheless is also, with part of himself, on the side of those who believe that man is redeemed from weakness and neurosis by "taking punishment" and by joining, through submission, the hierarchies of Church and Party.

§ THE NERVE OF FAILURE

NONE OF THESE AUTHORS means to be popular. They do not intend to join the chorus, and they are certainly unaware of doing so. They believe themselves to be daring and heretical. What, then, is going on in them? Sidney Hook has referred to the contemporary "failure of nerve" among intellectuals.[6] The concept is significant and correct, but it is only part of the story. It assumes that, if there were no failure of nerve, the intellectuals might win battles, might save themselves from defeat, from the rout of democratic and liberal values. But such defeat, for the time being, seems inexorable. Hence, the other part of the story is the courage to accept the possibility of defeat, of failure, without being morally crushed. This courage I would call "the nerve of failure." The "failure of nerve" concept looks at the problem primarily from outside; it assumes there is no failure but that of nerve. The "nerve of failure" concept looks at the problem primarily from the inside; it assumes there is no nerve but that of failure. Plainly, little nerve is required on the winning side: nerve has no meaning except when we must face the possibility, today the probability, of failure.

What is feared as failure in American society is, above all, aloneness. And aloneness is terrifying because it means that there is no one, no group, no approved cause to submit to. Even success—the seeming opposite of failure—often becomes impossible to bear when

6. 10 *Partisan Review*, No. 1 (1943).

it is not socially approved or even known. This is perhaps why successful criminals often feel the need to confess, that is, to submit to the community's judgment, represented in the person to whom the confession is made. They will confess, as Murica did, even under circumstances where this will probably, if not certainly, endanger their previous success: proof, I think, that aloneness is more intolerable than mere failure. For mere failure, provided it is found in company, can rather easily be borne; many ideologies have the function of making it possible for people to digest the worst miseries and even death. Under the sway of the ideology, they do not feel the impact of their failure; they are in the grip of an authority, even if it lets them down. On the other hand, one who is alone lacks this solace which can make even failure comfortable.

Of course, this problem of aloneness existed before democracy and before fascism. It is part of the problem of man's relation to the world and to other men which intellectuals today face with such specialized acuteness. The nerve of failure is needed to face the fact that the problem remains unsolved, and the possibility that it is insoluble. Thus we may experience defeat in our personal life-goals as well as in our social aims. Franz Kafka expressed these problems in his writing. He had the "nerve of failure"; he faced failure without illusion and without affirmation.

§ THE USES OF GUILT

KAFKA WAS VIRTUALLY ALONE. Most writers—writers of the sort we have been discussing—lose their nerve of failure by allowing themselves to succumb to feelings of guilt. Such feelings are accompanied by the need to submit to others and to affirm others' affirmations. An intellectual today, simply by virtue of being an intellectual, has perhaps a harder time than most people to escape such feelings of guilt. He is weak; he is despised; he has no assured social role and status; he is out of step. In a culture which values strength and power, the weak and powerless are easily made to feel that there is something wrong with them. What is taken to be wrong, of course, are all their individual defects which they share with other men. But beyond that material which is always available, the intellectual can focus on those very elements which differentiate him from the majority. Do I prefer Bach to Schumann? Do I prefer sensitive and cultivated people to squally brats on trains? Do I fail to thrill to mass ceremonials in Sanders Theatre? Then I must be guilty; I am impious. But this is only the beginning. What is really differentiating and most valuable in the intellectual is his gift of sharply and critically seeing through many conventional values, "democratic" as well as fascist, "wholesome" as well as treacherous. Since he cannot help, given his originality, having a critical attitude toward the dominant culture, he either represses those insights which detach him from that culture, or mixes them, as we have just now seen, with penances of "affirmation." What kind of authority has laid down the rule that it is wrong to be critical or negative if one cannot also be constructive? It is the same kind which favors the yes-man and yes-woman in business, politics, and domesticity. It is the same kind which, long ago, alleviated and manipulated guilt by inventing the confessional and coupling it with a system of penances.

In the conventional judgment, confession is regarded with approbation; it is good for the soul. We are invited so to regard it, although with qualifications, in Silone's play. Yet confession is often more immoral than the original act which is confessed, because it means that the person is unwilling to bear the responsibility for his actions; by confession they become no longer *his*, but are shared. Penance serves to destroy the last vestige of aloneness. Had Murica, for instance, been a moral person, able to stand alone, he would have felt neither remorse nor the need to confess; he would have recognized his betrayal as *his*, not to be shifted, not to be wiped out in the bookkeeping of the heavenly authorities. He would have decided what he was, and wanted to become, on the basis of his potentialities for the future, rather than on the basis of the judgment of his past made by outsiders.

Of course, the intellectuals and the novelists who represent them and speak for them are not Muricas; they are not dissembling traitors. Yet they, or the characters with whom they identify, go in heavily for self-accusation. Dorothea becomes expert at accusing herself. Koestler luxuriates in the guilty self-doubts which assail Peter, through the words of Bernard and the psychoanalyst. Silone's *mea culpa* is more complicated and more ambiguous; it deserves greater respect. Yet is has led him from the wonderful irreverence and humor of *The School for Dictators* (1938) and the early novels, to the sticky piety of some parts of *And He Hid Himself* (1945).

It is, I think, guilt which lies behind this sticky piety which is, in turn, the trade-mark of all these writers' "affirmations." Consequently, while talent and passion enliven their satire and criticism, their affirmations turn out to be "negative" and "unconstructive." *And He Hid Himself* ends lamely with the once-disillusioned and apathetic peasants uniting for new revolutionary action, although nothing in their character makes this turnabout convincing. Koestler concludes *Arrival and Departure* with a Hollywood trumped-up ending, also disguised as anti-fascist heroism. Such an ending shows a lack of respect for the previous seriousness of the book. In Miss Howe's book the ironic contradiction is even more striking, because so much of the book is devoted to Dorothea's discovery of American democracy, common or garden style. As Mrs. Trilling observes: "It is the lesson of democracy that finally cuts Dorothea down to size. The only flaw is that, with her, democracy itself also gets cut down to size—Miss Howe's firmest intentions to the contrary notwithstanding. *We Happy Few* ends with the wide American panorama presenting itself as little more than a series of small-spirited, harassed, and unhappy people who in their uneducated fashion are just as egotistical as the well-educated Dorothea. The commonalty of man, therapy for a poorly balanced emotional nature, shows itself to be largely a matter of helping make sandwiches with the other ladies or holding a neighbor's crying child. . . . It is as if the eye and ear that can catch the subtle nuances of the first section of *We Happy Few* cannot but go on to betray Miss Howe's formulation of conscience. While Miss Howe's program calls for Dorothea's regeneration through contemplation of some vast body of corporate virtue called the United States of Democracy, her literary senses feel out all the petty snobberies and prides that are bound to inform a nation of human beings. . . . Because draughts of solemnity taste so bad, we deceive ourselves that they are our eye-openers instead of our newest opiates."

To answer serious questions with trivial "solutions" is deceptive. For it puts the weight of the writer's earnestness, ethical conviction, and insight into the business of telling the reader that *his* doubts, too, are "negative" and bad. The reader is only too ready to believe this, and to indulge in his own orgy of identification with the pride of a Dorothea and the fall that follows. He, too, convinces himself that he is guilty, and thus rationalizes climbing on the bandwagon and stifling his critical uniqueness. There results a failure to develop his potentialities and, in Fromm's terms, an "escape from freedom." Readers, like writers, need support of their "nerve of failure" not anaesthesia. The ethical convictions that they lack are the belief in their own values, and the belief that only in their differences from others will they find their identity with them.

I trust no one will misunderstand me as saying that anti-fascist or pro-democratic activity is worthless or immoral. My point is that many people engage in such activity without ever deciding whether it has real meaning for them, and without the realistic judgment as to the practical possibilities which cannot be made in the absence of the nerve of failure. Instead, collective activity appears affirmative, sustains illusions, assuages doubt, and finds guilt useful; these are some of its attractions for powerless and isolated intellectuals.

§ THE ETHICS OF EXPERIENCE

THERE IS, however, another side to this powerlessness and isolation. The intellectual believes that he wishes to submerge his pride—i.e. his independence—in the fate of common humanity. In Silone's play where Murica offers himself up to almost certain death; in Koestler's novel where Peter returns to the wars despite conduct which should make him feel entitled, if any one ever did, to a passage to America and relative peace; in Miss Howe's book where Dorothea gives up her intellectual life and shares the hardships of a hospital, of war-time travel, of the camp-followers of servicemen, the motives appear noble. To a large extent they are. But there are other aspects of this type of behavior which are not noble at all. In many cases, the attempt to share wider human burdens and situations is a disguise for the greedy cult of experience, an anxious fear of missing those experiences which others have had or claim that they have had. Dorothea doesn't want to let any pitch of life go by. But the "experience" is not given raw by nature; we really experience only what we as individuals can interpret and assimilate as our own. In the phoniness of "sharing" common experiences, there is masochism of two sorts, one obvious, one indirect. The obvious masochism is that the experience is usually painful and humiliating, as in Dorothea's case. (In an earlier generation of novelists who were less religious and less ideological, the experience was generally supposed to be pleasureful, e.g., sleeping around or getting drunk.) The more concealed masochism lies in submission to the experiences everyone is supposed to have. It is really easier to do this than to experience one's course of life directly, let us say as an intellectual; for this latter requires an individuality of interpretation: the interpretation is not given by the culture. Dorothea does not ask herself what she, as a unique person, can uniquely experience in the very process of living; rather she welcomes being overwhelmed by what might be called the collective experience. "The burden of being one's own arbiter of taste and feeling had been removed." Her son loses his poignant closeness to her to become "just one more American gob." . . .

§ THE ETHICAL ELITE

THIS SUBMISSION to generally shared interpretations of experience is the most self-effacing form of the intellectual's response to his feelings of social weakness. Often, however, if not usually, his response disguises a strong desire for power and status. In joining the common man, the intellectual really wants to lead him; he feels called upon to save society. Apparent submission to the common lot and the common work—rather than the specialized work called for by his gifts—conceals delusions of grandeur. The intellectual is not willing to accept himself as he really is, with his unusual assets and their compensatory drawbacks, but he must be an "operator"; he must be "versatile"; he must be "practical." Coupled, therefore, with the masochism of pain and of rejection of the person's own talents and values, there is an even more concealed desire for domination, in which great claims are covertly staked out for leadership in the day-to-day social scene. Such a person privately feels that he has his finger in the dike against fascism, or whatever other evils threaten, and that if this finger were removed, but only then, the flood would overwhelm us. (Of course, situations can arise where this fantasy will be true; but where there is no "nerve of failure," judgments of social need and personal capacity cannot be realistic.) Thus the intellectual who professes to engage in the activities of ordinary folk only partially wants to lose his individuality in the collective whole; since he believes with Dorothea that the whole is greater than the sum of its parts, he wants the difference for himself. That is, he makes the secret stipulation that he is not really lost but will become one of the élite.

The form this stipulation takes in *We Happy Few* is subdued. Miss Howe demands of Dorothea, of her class, and perhaps of her sex, that they suffer more pain, become more unselfish, more humble, and in general lay claim to higher, more altruistic standards of behavior. Dorothea is harder on herself for sleeping with Gordon than she is on Gordon, or than she probably would be with one of the girls in Coeur d'Alene. This in itself may conceal pride—the arrogance of the member of the élite who must be a hero, or at the very least, an "example." Dorothea begins her mature life by rejecting marriage with the Idaho crusader. In this rejection there are some elements of snobbery: she laughs at his crudity and lack of sophistication. In her later encounter with him she feels herself inferior to him—this time he has rejected her. He is so much nobler and finer; his lack of aesthetic sensitivity, his simple moralistic sureness, become assets in her eyes. Dorothea, it is plain, has learned to value his differentness from her, but also to undervalue her differentness from him. If she does not belong among the happy few, he surely must. Our culture lives by these judgments of superiority and subordination, and differences among races, classes, and individual personalities are largely made use of to place oneself and others in the social hierarchy. In feeling unworthy, just as in feeling superior, Dorothea practices not the ethics of democratic equality but those of the collectivist discrimination between élite and mass.

This feeling of unworthiness, this need to rank herself, brings us back to the role of the romantic myth mentioned earlier: that intellectuals, that is, the self-conscious people, are more vicious than ordinary folk. Others are of course glad to hear this, for it means that demands are not to be made on them, but on the intellectuals who had the nerve to challenge them. And their envy is assuaged by learning that intellectuals are not only immoral but unhappy. More generally, this teaching means that people who are aware of the problem of choice are morally inferior to those whose choices are largely made for them by the culture. If this is so, a rational individualistic ethics becomes impossible. For where is new moral insight to come from, if not from the self-conscious few, from the morally perceptive Helen Howes and Koestlers and Silones? It is not likely to come from the "shared values" of some collective enterprise.

§ THE ETHICS OF SACRIFICE

CATHOLICISM is older than the answers of the Koestlers and the Howes, and it is illuminating to compare the attitude of Miss Howe towards Dorothea with the virtually identical attitude of the Catholic nuns towards the heroine, Nanda, of Antonia White's novel *Frost in May*. This is a very moving story, plainly autobiographical, of a young girl growing up in a convent school. At the school, one finds precisely the same feeling as in *We Happy Few* that pride, in the form of self-love, is the most intolerable sin. When one of the school girls really enjoys her excellent performance as Beatrice in *The Inferno*, she is removed from the role, lest she become vain. And Nanda is told by a nun: "It is a hundred times better to knit a pair of socks humbly for the glory of God than to write the finest poem or symphony for mere self-glorification."

Nanda is warned not to choose her friends "for such superficial attributes as cleverness and humour, and even for the still more unworthy and frivolous reasons of mere 'good looks' and a social position . . ." but instead for "solid piety" and a lower social status.

Beauty is, in fact, a great temptation: "A saint said it was dangerous to walk through a beautiful wood." For it means that things, and people, are looked at for their own sakes rather than as manifestations of collective purposes, in this case called God. When thirteen-year-old Nanda begins to write an adolescent novel, she is brutally expelled, and the head nun explains: "God asks very hard things from us, the sacrifice of what we love best and the sacrifice of our own wills. That is what it means to be a Christian. For years I have been watching you, Nanda. I have seen you growing up, intelligent, warm-hearted, apparently everything a child should be. But I have watched something else growing in you too—a hard little core of self-will and self-love. I told you once before that every will must be broken completely and re-set before it can be at one with God's will. And there is no other way. That is what true education, as we understand it here at Lippington, means." In return for this sacrifice of self, the convent offered collective security. If one did penance for one's own individuality, one was deprived of "the burden of being one's own arbiter," and permitted to feel at one with God.

The nuns were especially severe with Nanda for two reasons: she was remarkably sensitive and gifted, and she was not of an old wealthy Catholic family. It is always the individually gifted and socially weak who are the first to be asked to give themselves up. The same point might even be put more strongly. It is a truism that certain qualities or behavior traits are differently valued, depending on the social position of their possessor. What is offensive arrogance in an underling is charming insouciance in a lord. What is squirming subservience in the lower middle class is lovable modesty in the upper. At Miss Howe's hands, Dorothea's pride comes off more shabbily than that of Mrs. Calcott, the "true" aristocrat into whose family Dorothea climbs by matrimony. Likewise, the galling pride and independence of the intellectual is impressive in a "temperamental" movie star or ball player. Conversely, Nanda had, from the nuns' viewpoint, too many stubborn intellectual gifts for her sex and station.

Nanda escapes the nuns, very probably because she was ejected for rebellion, which was scarcely conscious and not at all planned. And it is generally not too difficult to escape the nuns, for their Puritanism—the especially virulent Puritanism of the Counter-Reformation—is other-worldly and is out of fashion. But, as Max Weber pointed out, the western world has closed the monasteries and turned earth itself into a nunnery. It is very much harder to resist the diluted but pervasive Puritanism of sacrifice and subservience which takes modern and "progressive" forms. It is harder for Dorothea to resist the "education" given her by what her society calls "life"—as in the phrases "that's life," "that's how things are"—than for Nanda to resist the "education" of antiquated Lippington.

Intellectuals today do have a hard time resisting their education, resisting attack. They need to be defended not attacked, if they are to succor their "nerve of failure." Miss Howe, a member of the class, attacks the "Happy Few" for their selfishness and pride. As we have seen, the intellectuals turn against themselves because they are few, and because they are not happy enough; that is, they have not enough love for themselves, or pride in what they are. "We ought to have our

own class-consciousness," William James declared in his 1907 speech
The Social Value of the College Bred.[7] " '*Les Intellectuels!*' What
prouder clubname could there be than this one, used ironically by
the party of 'redblood,' the party of every stupid prejudice and passion, during the anti-Dreyfus craze, to satirize the men in France who
still retained some critical sense and judgment!"

---

7. *Memories and Studies* (1911) p. 323, quoted in 2 Ralph Barton Perry,
The Thought and Character of William James (1936) p. 299.

4. A Philosophy for "Minority" Living

THE "NERVE OF FAILURE" is the courage to face aloneness and the possibility of defeat in one's personal life or one's work without being morally destroyed. It is, in a larger sense, simply the nerve to be oneself when that self is not approved of by the dominant ethic of a society.

In America, "success" is central; we are provided with a catalogue of what is success and what is failure, and nothing matters except achieving the first and avoiding the second. Whoever accepts the prevailing social standards of our times is not alone, not morally isolated; even if he is a "failure" he remains related, if only in fantasy, to the dominant theme. Such a person has no more need of the "nerve of failure" than a gambler who has had a bad day at roulette: for him life is centered on the wheel, and he remains related, though anxious and miserable, so long as he can go on watching the others who are still in the game. The "nerve of failure" is needed only for really heretical conduct: when one renounces even the company of misery and takes the greater risk of isolation—that is, the risk of never rejoining the company.

The "nerve of failure" is akin to the traditional virtue of "courage in defeat," praised in a number of ethical systems. But it differs in this sense: it comes into play before defeat is actual, when it is only a possibility. To be sure, one may have a good deal of the "nerve to fail" and still be cowardly in extreme situations. But, on the other hand, while many can find courage in defeat only when others are defeated too, those endowed with the "nerve of failure" have the capacity to go it alone.

A man may maintain a lonely course by other means. He may not realize that he is heretical—Rousseau, the "primitive" painter, seems to have thought he was painting just like everybody else. He may be more or less crazy, constructing an elaborate system to justify himself—as did Fourier and Comte. He may attach himself to nature and to imagined transcendental forces—as did William Blake. He may overestimate his personal influence and the extent to which others are listening to what seems to him self-evident and reasonable —as did Robert Owen, the English manufacturer and utopian socialist, whose later life was on the surface one long series of failures. He may

convince himself that history, or science, is inevitably on his side—
as did Karl Marx. He may protect himself from aloneness by remaining conventional in many spheres—as Darwin did. He may surround
himself with a small body of ardent disciples and limit his contact
with contemporaries—this also was Comte's way. Only very rarely
will an individual with enough originality to disturb society be able,
without such adventitious aids, to face his situation realistically and
yet be unshaken by what the majority considers "failure."

These moral attitudes in the face of frustration and defeat become
even more complicated, enormously more so, in the life of groups
lacking material power, whether domestic "minorities" or small nations. Negroes, Jews, intellectuals, and women as domestic "minorities"; Poles, Irishmen, Italians as small nations coping with big powers
—all feel the need of protecting themselves in one way or another
from the moral impact of power. In different historical periods they
develop different means and modes of coping with this problem. If
I discuss the fate and problems of the Jews here, it is because, despite
all differences, they still provide one of the most suggestive paradigms
of the relatively powerless group.

§ I

FOR THE LAST two thousand years the Jews have been a minority;
before that, it may be suggested, they were a "small power," a buffer
state.[1] But until recent times, many Jews did not have what we might
today regard as a typical minority outlook. Their ethical regime was
quite defiantly Ptolemaic, revolving about the small group of Jews,
not the larger Gentile group—and, accordingly, they learned to
remain unimpressed by Gentile temporal power. Being unimpressed
did not mean being unafraid—material power might beat or starve one
to death; it did mean refusing to surrender moral hegemony to the
majority merely because it had power. Instead, the Jews saw through
power by observing its blindness in comparison with the vision possible to the weak. A saying of Nahman of Bratzlav exemplifies this
outlook: "Victory cannot tolerate truth, and if that which is true is
spread before your very eyes, you will reject it, because you are a
victor. Whoever would have truth itself, must drive hence the spirit
of victory; only then may he prepare to behold the truth."

In other words, since the Jews' ethical scheme placed no great
premium on material power, on material success, the majority was not

---

1. I am indebted to Dr. Erich Fromm for calling my attention to the relations between Jewish power and ethics in their historical changes. The reader
will recognize, of course, how difficult it is to generalize about Jewish ethics,
as about anything else concerning "Jews"—or indeed any group.

looked up to with envy and admiration; hence its verdicts, both as to the ends of life and as to the value of the minority itself, did not echo in the Jews' self-consciousness.

A related attitude was expressed in the belief—which kept the Jews Jews and not Christians—that the Messiah was still to come. To be sure, many Jews during the dark periods between the 11th and 17th centuries were deceived at times into believing that the Messiah had indeed come. But these aberrations were limited in scope and time: Jews in general continued to have faith in the continuance into the future of the process of revelation and to be unimpressed by contemporary events and the would-be Messiahs who, consciously or unconsciously, exploited these events. If we do not take this belief, that the Messiah will yet come, too literally, we can see that one of its meanings is an attack on the powers that be, and an emphatic statement that justice and peace shall some day—as they do not today—prevail everywhere among men.[2]

Jewish ethics, though not devoid of authoritarian strains, is, like Greek ethics, based primarily on reason, although reason has sometimes descended to casuistry. It is an ethics of reason both in its ends, which are human and earthly, and in its means, which are argumentative rather than dogmatic. Even the casuistry seems often to have been turned to the humanizing of authoritative texts, as a lawyer might "interpret" a statute or decision in order to reach a more humane and reasonable result.

Such an ethical pattern as the one just described would seem admirably fitted to the psychic situation of a powerless minority which —unlike, let us say, the Republican party during recent years—has no chance of soon becoming a majority. But, as we know, ethical systems are not developed in the abstract; though they have a momentum of their own, Jewish ethical patterns arose in connection with given social and economic conditions; and they were embroidered by complex, demanding rituals and racial myths.

Occasionally, the group's "nerve of failure" was supported by the notion that its very powerlessness proved the Jews to be in fact the Chosen of God. In this way, defeat itself could strengthen the faith of the "saving remnant" of Jews. On the other hand, we should recognize that the spiritual forces that gave the Jews their immense moral resistance in the ghetto rested on a material base that, though often pre-

---

2. There are many Messianic, or as we should say, utopian elements in Christianity, of course; but the established institutionalized churches have always tended to play down these disturbing notions and to treat revelation as a completed or at least a centralized process. Dissenting sects have tended to restore the Messianic faith.

carious, had considerable solidity. The Jews were part of the medieval order, which gave them, like everyone else, a relatively fixed psychic place, even though theirs was that of pariah. (See Daniel Bell, "A Parable of Alienation," *Jewish Frontier*, November 1946.) Within the medieval order, moreover, the Jews developed a near monopoly of certain skills, in artisanship as well as in trade, which were handed down, as in the guilds, from father to son.

Thus, the ghetto walls buttressed the Jewish ethical walls.

§ II

THE RISE of modern capitalist society and the levelling of ghetto walls may be said to have started an uneven dialectic of change in the spiritual and material bases of Jewish life. Many Jews in the main Western countries surrendered their inherited ethical system in return for a chance to participate in the wider world, thus losing their special sources of spiritual strength. Sometimes this was done out of opportunism; more often than not this drive was mixed with more idealistic motives. For among the forces that broke down ghetto barriers from the outside was the Enlightenment. Liberty, Equality, and Fraternity were a set of values with great moral appeal—as well as with many parallels in Jewish ethics.

The Enlightenment was impious towards authority, utopian about the future, and hospitable to reason. What then could have been more attractive to many of the most ethically sensitive Jews, especially at a time when the ghetto tradition itself seems to have become somewhat impoverished in Western Europe? Such Jews could move from a religious to a political minority position with hardly any change in ethical attitude.

The great Jewish intellectual and political leaders of this period represented, in highly individual ways, mergers of Jewish and Enlightenment ethics, and the retention of the "nerve of failure." At the same time, certain skills and attitudes nurtured by ghetto life became useful and rewarding assets in the modern world. In the expanding era of international finance and international markets, the developed financial and commercial skills of a Rothschild, as later of a Rosenwald, were important: some Jews, that is, had a head-start. Jewish cultivation of a particular type of intelligence, moreover, could be turned to account in modern managerial, professional, and intellectual capacities; while the Jewish view of an open future (the Messiah still to come) was well adapted to leaders of progressive political or labor movements. In sum, many Jews gained personal power and self-confidence during the free capitalism that lasted until the close of the 19th century.

In those days, Jewish self-contempt did not exist in its characteristic contemporary forms. While rising Jews often shared the attitudes common to parvenus, they had confidence in their ultimate social acceptance, or that of their progeny; consciously or unconsciously, they felt they had something of particular value to offer. Likewise, those Jews who took a direct share in the struggles of the Enlightenment felt no insecurity or self-belittlement as Jews; they could be wholeheartedly indignant at discrimination since they had confidence in the ultimate triumph of the ideals of the Enlightenment. They, too, felt that they had something to offer—namely, a social program that the majority needed and would learn to want.

During this period, therefore, the consequences of Jewish acceptance of a largely Gentile ethics were positive: both because that ethics was rational and progressive and because the role and material power of Jews were on the increase.

§ III

HOWEVER, HISTORICAL DEVELOPMENTS soon began to undermine the material position of the Jews and give a different meaning to their new ethical position. As heavy industry grew in importance, it gradually freed itself from the free market. Jewish family and group "trade secrets" soon became common property. "Fair trade" acts and similar autarchic limitations on the free market came to restrict Jewish merchandising talents (while permitting, however, the marginal survival of many small Jewish shopkeepers). Though Jews shared in the growing managerial and professional openings of the "new" middle class, they began to be faced with increasing competition.

This lessening of the Jew's sense of economic value, and of his self-confidence in the possession of a special skill, helped lessen his feeling of ethical security, and made him increasingly a psychological victim of the dominant social and economic systems of the modern world.

But this is also a fate that, both in its economic and its psychological aspects, has overtaken vast numbers of the less "successful" classes in our new society, and condemned them to "alienation." For them, as for Jews, the relative security of a social role fixed by skill, family, age, and sex has vanished. One must now "show one's stuff" in a competitive market, and one's stuff is one's "personality," an externalized part of the self, and not primarily one's matter-of-fact skill. (See Erich Fromm, *Man for Himself* pp. 67-82.) In other words, it is not the genuine self that is put on the market in the race for success, or even economic survival, but the "cosmetic" self, which is free of any aroma of personal, non-marketable idiosyncracy as it is free of "B.O." or last year's waistline. If this artificial self succeeds, then doubts may be temporarily quieted. However, since self-evaluation has been surrendered to the market, failure in the market, or even fear of failure, is translated into self-contempt. (The market in this sense includes all spheres of life—business, politics, art, love, friendship.)

For the dominant groups—those that, by birth or temperament or luck, have been able to make the grade—the subjection of all values to the test of the market is convenient. It justifies their own existence in what amounts to moral rather than merely power-political terms. In a market situation pervaded by what Karl Polanyi has termed the "market mentality" (*Commentary*, February 1947), control of the economy will carry with it, to an unusual degree, control of the ethical regime. And the market, we must remember, has had perhaps a more complete sway in America than elsewhere.

Now, add to this the fact that America happens to have colonials —Negroes and other ethnic minorities—within its borders, and that we have developed a racialism not to be found in Europe. Upon the Jewish minority, this situation operates with special force, as can be seen in the encounter between Jewish traditions and the melting pot.

The melting pot had, especially in its early days, valuable elements: a kind of Whitmanesque equalitarian vigor and a seeming hospitality to cultural diversity—but it increasingly became a form of internal imperialism in the interest of the earlier arrivals. Its aim was narrowed to producing "Americans all" of a starched uniformity, freed of all cultural coloring, maladjustment, or deviation. The main burden was on the minorities, while few demands were made by the ethical system of the Protestant majority. (Protestantism and modern capitalism, having grown up together, have always been congenial.)

Even today, the typical Protestant businessman still makes money as a by-product of his devotion to his work and his organization; the money, as Max Weber pointed out, serves as a proof of fulfilment of ethical duty, of having found one's "calling," one's proper—and therefore prosperous—social niche. But there is no such compatibility between non-Protestant ethics and modern capitalism; hence the moral disorientation worked by the latter among Mexicans and South Americans generally, Eastern and Southern Europeans, and Treaty-Port Chinese. The same moral disorientation was produced among these people when they emigrated to America, affecting not only Jews from pre-capitalist Eastern Europe, but also Italians, Greeks, Mexicans. For these non-Protestants, business was not originally the expression of their religion, but a by-product of the need for money, status, or family security. For the dominant groups, the Protestant—or, more accurately, the Puritan—strain in our culture permitted a development of a kind of ethics intertwined with business. "Mere" money-making, for example, was open to criticism when not accompanied by an ethos of business as "calling" or as service. The non-Protestant, on the other hand, was often led, both by the special pressures of modern capitalism upon him and the strangeness of the Protestant market ethic to his own, to discard his own values without assimilating prevailing values. As a result he often became a caricature of the American careerist.

In this process, certain elements in Jewish ethics—the attitude towards power, towards the future, and towards reason—often tend to become distorted. The irreverent attitude towards power becomes contempt for what remains of the Puritan ethics of business and professional enterprise, which is interpreted as softness or hypocrisy. Irreverence towards authority degenerates into an indiscriminate disrespect for convention, whether that convention is an exploitative device or a crystallization of decent standards of personal intercourse. This Jewish irreverence may also appear as a cynicism that seeks money and power without the conviction that they represent the fruits of virtue or that they are genuinely important ends—or even the means to such ends.

Similarly, the Jewish attitude towards the future, with its Messianic devaluation of present reality, can be fitted, by distortion, all too nicely into the American success tradition, where—as the Lynds have remarked—people live "at" the future, eternally "on the make," either awaiting a lucky break for themselves, or planning for one for their offspring.

Finally, the Jewish attitude towards reason can also suffer a change. "Pure" reason for its own sake, what we might call Talmudic intelligence, is at a discount in America: it is not "practical." On the other hand, manipulative intelligence is exceedingly useful; in fact, the entire Jewish constellation of intelligence, humor, and charm is often humiliatingly exploited—for instance, by so many Jewish comedians—as entertainment and self-ingratiation.

Jews in America, like other Americans, go in for hero-worship; and it is possible to trace, in the types they frequently select for admiration, patterns of compromise between the American Protestant tradition and their own. Though they can afford to admire the "impractical" Einstein because he has been such a world-famous success, they tend more to bestow their medals on intelligent operators like Brandeis and Baruch. Though these men have the ear of presidents, they are not mere "court Jews": they are quite outspoken; moreover, they are old and white-haired, appropriate to the Jewish reverence for aged wisdom—yet they are also energetic and eupeptic, in keeping with the American worship of dynamic youth.

It goes without saying that—like Jewish ethics—American Protestant ethics contains many divergent themes, and that the Enlightenment still lives in its best representatives. However, the Jew emerging from the European ghetto was not met at Ellis Island by the representatives of enlightenment. At most, he was given a choice between accepting the melting pot and the ethics of success—as interpreted by earlier immigrants often bent on exploiting him economically or psychically—or trying to retain his traditions as a transient in a voluntary ghetto. If he took the latter course, he was seldom stimulated towards any effort to reinterpret the meaning of his ethical background in terms of the American context; rather he tended to freeze defensively in his memories and rituals. If he took the former —perhaps more typical—course, he altered his ethical and intellectual inheritance so that it could be turned to account in the struggle for success, just as a neurotic makes use of his illness, or a cripple his misery, for fragmentary advantages.

However, the same recent social and economic changes that have weakened the material position of Jews have also tended to alter the meaning of success as such. The mere matter-of-fact achievement of high economic or even political position no longer satisfies. Since we market our personalities, it is imperative that we be popular, accepted; and handicapped ethnic minorities are not popular. The Jew who plays the power and success game can hardly help viewing himself through the eyes of the more successful players.

Bernard Marx, a character in Aldous Huxley's *Brave New World*, despises himself because he is short. The majority, stunted lower-caste people, are also short, but he compares himself with the tall top-caste to which in other respects he "belongs," and to which, though with some ambivalence, he surrenders his ethical judgment. That is, he accepts from them the same cultural emphasis on height that sells Adler Elevator Shoes (the sexual reward being, as so often, a symbol for the reward of status). Since his society puts a high value on science, Bernard Marx's shortness is explained in seemingly rational terms by the rumor that some alcohol accidentally got into his feeding solution when he was a bottled embryo (alcohol being intentionally used only to stunt the lower castes). In any rational ethics, of course, there would be no correlation between height and human value. Yet Bernard does not quite dare look behind the "scientific" social judgment, and so must turn the blame upon himself. Among Jews, this relation between physical appearance and ethical valuation is seldom quite so obvious (there is more of this among Negroes, who tend to rate each other according to lightness of skin and other white characteristics); nevertheless, the Jewish devaluation of Jewish physiognomy is not confined to Hollywood, as the flourishing state of plastic surgery in Manhattan would testify.

§ IV

IF A MINORITY accepts the majority's definition of good looks, we would expect that the majority's definition of good conduct would be likewise accepted. And so it turns out. But is the Jew who sharply criticizes the behavior of his fellow-Jews accepting the majority's standards, or is he not simply exercising his human privilege—from which it would be anti-Semitic to exclude him—of disliking certain kinds of behavior? We cannot tell at first glance, though we may wonder why, amid all the evil in the world and all the examples of vicious and mean conduct, he fastens on the Jews. Moreover, even when the traits he selects for attention are not so obviously differentiated according to race—where, for instance, a Jew claims to despise Italian and Greek as well as Jewish manners—we may ask the same sort of question: why is he preoccupied with differences in manners and not, let us say, with differences in coldness and warmth, gloominess and wit? Has he not accepted the majority's judgments as to what is important and the majority's criteria of good and evil?[3]

However, the Jew whose focus of criticism is the poor behavior of his fellow-Jews may urge that, far from accepting the majority's standards, he feels merely threatened by them: he is worried by the menace of anti-Semitism if Jews do not conform, and is being "realistic." Here we may ask why, among the many "causes" of anti-Semitism, he selects primarily those over which Jews themselves seem to have some control. Perhaps better manners on the subway would mitigate anti-Jewish feeling; perhaps if Jews did not appear in public at all—no Frankfurter on the Supreme Court, no Dubinsky in the labor movement—they would not be noticed. But in advocating such things, has this timorous Jew done anything more than accept the majority's anti-Semitic stereotype, as well as their rationalizations for refusing to accept Jews as individuals on their own merits? Is this Jew really concerned about the daily quality of direct personal contacts between Jews and non-Jews, which might, in the long run, have some marginal effect on anti-Semitism?

---

3. I don't mean to enter here upon complicated questions of national character and to examine whether Jewish manners are characteristically undignified, or British behavior is really lacking in warmth; I am raising the problem rather of the way in which majority ethics gives rise to a process of stereotyping and selection in which certain traits are valued, others devalued, still others ignored.

But ordinarily I think it can be shown that the threat such a Jew feels is that of being himself caught, in his own deeper consciousness, in the majority stereotype of "the Jew." This involves not only contempt for "the other Jews," but his own self-belittlement. The real cause of his concern with the behavior of his fellow Jews is the moral retreat he has made in servilely accepting the majority's ethics, not the so-called undesirable Jewish traits that provoked his anxiety. And if he wanted to do something about anti-Semitism—and if he understood what in the face of fear is difficult to understand—he might begin with his own moral subservience, where he has at least a real chance to change things, instead of trying to reform the manners or career choices of his fellow-Jews.

If we confined our attention to such instances of the acceptance of majority judgments as these (and of course we are selecting a particular segment of majority opinion and not the entire spectrum), we might underestimate the extent of present-day Jewish ethical bondage. However, since many Jews, especially in recent years, have tried to repress their tendencies towards group-belittlement of themselves, evidence of this self-belittlement—where not covertly released in gibe or gesture—is less obvious since it issues in reactions that are seldom fully conscious.

Apologetics as a reaction to attack hardly needs discussion in these pages. It surrenders the ethical initiative, for it permits the anti-Semite to frame the issue of debate and the norms of criticism. Denials that Jews are rich, radical, or rude concede to the anti-Semites that it is a crime to be rich, radical, or rude.

Another reaction is self-denial, in which Jews deny as Jews that there are such things as Jews. Sometimes this self-denial is a "liberal" reaction, an insistence that there are no anthropological (racial) differences, out of a fear that such differences would be exploited. Sometimes this self-denial is rationalized as a "radical" reaction, by the insistence that there is no "Jewish question" whatsoever, but only some other question, such as the question of capitalism. Jews who take this latter course do at least identify themselves with a submerged group larger than their own, but they run the risk of carrying the position to extremes in believing that the Jewish problem, despite cultural and historical differences, is in all respects similar to—let us say—the Negro problem, or the problem of the working class as a whole. In this way, the specifically Jewish overtones are lost; but indeed this is precisely what the self-denier wants.

Still a third reaction occurs as a revulsion against all traits associated with the majority stereotype of "the Jew." Are Jews pushing? Very well, we will be retiring. Are Jews over-critical? Very well, we will swallow our protest.[4] The minority group actually expects more from itself than from the rest of the population; that is, it applies the majority ethics but with a double standard.

It is evident that this timid double standard is very different from the feeling of *noblesse oblige* of certain ruling classes. These classes have no doubts of their right to rule, even when they are far from perfect; in contrast, the "double-standard" Jews seem to say that Jewish claims for full equality are invalid if Jews are merely human.

In all these instances Jews try to cope with American anti-Semitism in terms of majority stereotypes, which by their very irrationality prevent both minority and majority from making any fresh approaches to reality.

§ V

RECENT EVENTS have brought still another aspect of Jewish self-doubt to light. I think that exaggeration of the uniqueness of the crime committed by the Nazis against the Jews may sometimes be read as betraying an unconscious doubt as to the ethical justification of the Jewish case. When some Jews claim that no injustice was ever so great, nor any dictator the peer of Hitler, they are not always simply venting an understandable grief. They are afraid that the very enormity, the irretrievable quality, of the killing of the Jews must prove something about them, something in fact against them. For there is no way that a success ethics can cope with unavenged material defeat. Some may try to still the doubt—whether, after all, Hitler was not right—by racist vindictiveness against the German people. What seems to be lingering in the minds of so many is the notion that Hitler somehow won a victory over the Jews.

On the other hand, a Jew who has found his way to an independent ethics would say with Rabbi Johanan: "All distress that Israel and the world bear in common is distress; the distress confined to Israel alone is not distress" (From *In Time and Eternity*). On the ethical side, he would find little to choose between the Nazi murder of Jews and of Poles, or between the concentration camps

---

4. Some Jews indulge in what looks on the surface like just the opposite reaction. They aggressively play up what they accept as Jewish traits; sometimes they select the very ones that are detested in the majority stereotype; sometimes they indiscriminately fasten their affection on those traits, good or bad. Are Jews pushing? Very well, pushing is nice, and we will push. Are Jews critical? Very well, let us exploit this fine cultural resource. Some young Negroes, too, play this pathetic game, accepting the whites' judgments in the very act of making an issue with them. Likewise, many middle-class intellectuals spend their lives reacting against middle-class standards and values, for instance in bohemianism, as if this were the only ethical contrast to what they conceive as the middle class.

of Hitler and Stalin; on the political side, he would be free to perceive that the slaughter of the European Jews was to some extent a
historical accident in which they happened to become material game
and spiritual symbol for a congeries of reactionary forces.

Victory and defeat, success and failure, are facts. But they are
facts in the world of power, subject to an evaluative judgment in
which defeat may become victory and victory defeat. Who "really"
won in the war between Athens and Sparta? It is conventional today
to decide in favor of Athens. What, for example, about Weimar
Germany? Are many of its critics, who attack its experimentalism,
its pacifism, its artistic and intellectual "irresponsibility" and lack of
consensus only disapproving of these tendencies because they did
not ward off political defeat? Many generations hence, may not
people look back with admiration on the cultural and even some of
the political and social achievements of that brief period between
1919 and 1933, and pay little attention to all our elaborate explanations
for its "failure," explanations which, as in the case of the slaughtered
Jews, consciously or unconsciously subordinate ourselves to an ethics
of success pure and simple, and overemphasize what was wrong with
the victim?

Even such devastating defeats as those of the last decade the truly
moral man must find the courage and the capacity to face with the
nerve of failure.

§ VI

OF COURSE, it would be applying a double standard to expect Jews
to have the nerve of failure when other groups do not. Moreover, it
would be as unfair to blame Jews for losing their traditional ethics in
the melting pot, as to blame them for not emerging from it as Anglo-
Saxon gentlemen. But the opposite error, which tolerantly understands all minority behavior as the inevitable consequence of persecution, is not helpful either. The real question is, what choices do
the Jews now have?

There is no want of proposed solutions, many of which seem to
me to repeat or exacerbate the circular problems in which a minority
is so often caught. One is a plea for a return to the ritual and religious
elements historically linked to the ethical resources of Jewish life.
It is not surprising that this same plea for what amounts to a medieval
revival is also being made at this time by many non-Jews as a general
therapy for modern alienation.

The usual criticism of such efforts to restore psychic security and
dignity is that they are impractical, since the change from medieval
to modern times cannot be reversed. But another criticism can be

made from the standpoint of the very Jewish ethics which one wants
to recapture. That ethics contains a fervent claim for a more decent
future, a claim that takes the form of Messianic hope. Though the
glories of biblical Palestine are looked back upon with pride and
sorrow, utopia lies in the future, not in the nostalgic past. To seek
restoration of an earlier time is to confess intellectual and ethical im-
poverishment. The "nerve of failure" implies the ability to face the
possibility of failure, but it is rooted in the assumption that past and
present failures need not mark the limits of human powers. To be satisfied with something no better than that which medieval Jewry had—
assuming, in defiance of all reason, that this could be attained—is a
surrender of that demand typical for Jews (though of course not
exclusively theirs) for a more decent future for Jews and non-Jews
alike.

The surrender of utopian claims is one of the most revealing
symptoms of the current state of minority ethics. Despite differences
in shading, such claims are a part of Judaic, Christian, and Enlightenment ethical systems. But they are very much at a discount today.
The powerful do not need visions; they either fear or scorn them.
Their response to such claims is: "If you don't like it here, why don't
you go back where you came from?" Some minority representatives
aggressively propose to do just that, to go back—in time. Whereas
the older success game permitted many minorities to be easily satisfied with petty gains in the American scene, the newer religious
revival would satisfy them with petty dreams from the past.

Political Zionism is another suggestion proposed as a means of
obtaining psychic as well as physical security for Jews. Jewish nation-
alists seem to be even more impressed by worldly power than Jews
who urge a religious revival; they have given up the success game
on the domestic scene only to transfer it to the international sphere;
this entails a complete acceptance of majority attitudes towards force
and *raison d'état*. Thus they abandon the critical attitude which subjects to principle and to reason all claims of power and all demands
for loyalty—an attitude which I believe to be among the significant
contributions of Jewish ethics to the general problem of the powerless
minority and the small nation.

If Jews are to avoid self-defeating courses of action, it would
seem necessary to clarify the themes in their ethical tradition that fit
the problem of the powerless, and then to separate these from their
cultist and ritualistic trappings. The way food is prepared or the
style of beards are locally various and ethically quite indifferent matters—questions of taste and not of value. To attach one's love and
admiration to them is to risk putting the superficial or parochial as-

pects of Jewish culture in the center of affection, rather than its ethically significant elements. And it is this sort of love that so easily runs over into fondness for, or defensiveness about, even the weaker sides of Jewish life in America. This sort of chauvinism is particularly easy to rationalize today, just because the Jews seem at the moment a defeated people on the world's stage. It would be well, however, to recall Nietzsche's advice not to love a defeated nation. (Nietzsche seems to have meant that an honorable person finds it harder in defeat than in victory to detach himself from his nation —witness German nationalism after the First World War.)

The concept of minority ethics suggested here is not meant as an invitation to minority fanaticism or as a condemnation of all majority ethics as such; the minority position in itself is no guarantee of ethical superiority. Rather, it points out that the Jewish minority in America must discover what are the ethically significant themes relevant to its present situation, which in turn requires reinterpretation of Jewish tradition.

Such a reinterpretation of tradition would in itself do something to overcome Jewish self-belittlement by giving the past meaning without mystery. But the more direct function of this reinterpretation would be to foster a Jewish self-image counterposed to the majority ethics. Adherence to majority ethics may be a help in social climbing, or in rationalizing one's acceptance of the values of the culture that happens to be dominant. But the experience of many Jews in America must be that this adherence is emotionally precarious, and that it easily becomes self-destructive once things do not go well for oneself or one's group. There are more ways of acquiring a feeling of "belonging" in the American scene than the alternatives of melting pot or parochial separation.

Yet is it not merely wishful to ask that Jews today, of all people, be reasonable men looking for guidance in their personal and political lives to a rational, and therefore experimental and tentative, ethics? No matter how ethically inadequate the ritualist, racialist, and nationalist therapies may be, does not their very existence prove that the vast bulk of Jews cannot be expected to defend themselves morally against power without the encompassing support of daily ritual observances, or without the *ersatz* program of Palestinian terrorism? Is not one of my own arguments—that Jewish ethics has been closely related to Jewish material circumstance—proof of the impracticality of any therapy that begins with ethics and not with environment? I would answer that movements of thought among a people are never entirely determined by the material setting. On the contrary, an ethical and intellectual feature—such, for instance, as an eloquent tradition of utopian thought—may itself become one of the institutional forces of the environment. In the case of the Diaspora history of the Jews, utopian thought was even a decisive force. Of course, such a program does not pretend to "save" the Jews; its goal is moral independence from the majority, not physical survival or a solution of "the Jewish problem." Its gains would largely be in the happier lives of Jews and other powerless folk. Nevertheless, a reduction of Jewish self-contempt and an increase in the Jewish "nerve of failure" is bound to make for more realistic, as well as attractive, behavior by individual Jews and Jewish agencies, and so reduce those minor, pointless tensions and self-defeating patterns that Jews themselves may create.

Specific groups of Jews in America are meeting widely different problems and experiences. There is room for research into the intricate relations between their ethics and their attitudes toward themselves, research that would test and refine such hypotheses as those suggested here. Such work has meaning for minority groups in general. At the same time American Jews have much to learn from other minority experiences and traditions—from Negroes in America and South Africa; from anti-fascists in Mussolini's Italy, Hitler's Germany, Franco's Spain, Peron's Argentina; from intellectual and cultural dissenters from modern capitalism and Stalinist Communism; and so on. Moreover, the utopian traditions of Christian sects, of the Enlightenment, of America itself—these have contributions to make to the development of a minority ethics. In fact, is not such development enjoined on almost all of us by our human situation? For who does not face at some time—at least as a child—a conflict between his own values and those of a stronger and oppressive power? Until a time when power is no longer used oppressively, minorities will have a compelling need of the nerve of failure to defend an independent view of the self and of what life holds.

5. Some Observations on Community Plans and Utopia

A REVIVAL of the tradition of utopian thinking seems to me one of the important intellectual tasks of today. Since we live in a time of disenchantment, such thinking, where it is rational in aim and method and not mere escapism, is not easy; it is easier to concentrate on programs for choosing among lesser evils, even to the point where these evils can scarcely be distinguished, one from the other. For there is always a market for lesser-evil thinking which poses immediate alternatives; the need for thinking which confronts us with great hopes and great plans is not so evident. Yet without great plans, it is hard, and often self-defeating, to make little ones. Such utopian thinking requires what I have termed "the nerve of failure," that is, the ability to face the possibility of defeat without feeling morally crushed. Without this sort of courage, any failure implies a personal defect, and brings feelings of intolerable isolation; to avoid this fate, people tend to repress their claims for a decent world to a "practical" point, and to avoid any goals, personal or social, that seem out of step with common sense.

Curiously enough, however, in a dynamic political context, it is the modest, common-sensical goals which are often unattainable—therefore utopian in the derogatory sense. I do not mean, of course, that "anything can happen"; I do mean that the self-styled realist tends to underestimate the strength of latent forces because he is too impressed by what he "sees." To take only one example, it often seems that the retention of a given status quo is a modest hope; many lawyers, political scientists and economists occupy themselves by suggesting the minimal changes which are necessary to stand still; yet today this hope is almost invariably disappointed; the status quo proves the most illusory of goals. To aim at this goal requires little nerve, for many people share the same hope; so long as things appear to go well, anxiety is stilled; and even when things go badly, many people will join in providing rationalizations for the failure: misery will have company.

The problem of how individuals can fortify themselves, without insanity, to the point at which they will believe their own, isolated imaginations, is of course a very old one. It is this problem that Spinoza deals with when he discusses how the Biblical prophets attempted to assure themselves of certainty:

"For instance, Jeremiah's prophecy of the destruction of Jerusalem was confirmed by the prophecies of other prophets, and by the threats in the law, and therefore it needed no sign; whereas Hananiah, who, contrary to all the prophets, foretold the speedy restoration of the state, stood in need of a sign, or he would have been in doubt as to the truth of his prophecy, until it was confirmed by facts. 'The prophet which prophesieth of peace, when the word of the prophet shall come to pass, then shall the prophet be known that the Lord hath truly sent him.' "[1]

Today in America, at least in intellectual circles, the Jeremiahs share a widespread, and in that sense comforting, defeatism; there are few Hananiahs who prophesy restoration and peace. The recent book *Communitas: Means of Livelihood and Ways of Life*,[2] by Percival and Paul Goodman, is therefore particularly welcome; it is avowedly utopian, both in its critique of earlier community plans and in its presentation of new ones. I propose in this article to indicate some of the Goodmans' contributions to utopian thinking; but first to place these in perspective by a review, necessarily sketchy, of the present state of such thinking in America.

§ I

A HUNDRED YEARS AGO, in the *Communist Manifesto*, Marx and Engels welcomed the criticisms which their so-called utopian predecessors, such as St. Simon, Fourier, and Owen, had made of capitalist society, but they rejected the peaceable methods of these men for achieving socialism. Their label "utopian" (expanded in Engels' *Socialism: Utopian and Scientific*) stuck as a derogatory term. Moreover, having taken their polemical position, they were themselves bound by it, and carefully avoided setting forth more than fragmentary views on what the classless society might look like: this refusal became a mark of realism and orthodoxy—and a great convenience to left-wing politicians and writers. While some Europeans, such as William Morris and Theodor Hertzka,[3] continued to work in the older utopian tradition as late as the '90's, the masses were soon recruited either for Marxist "scientific," *i.e.* hard-headed socialism, or for Fabian and Social-Democratic versions of practical, unmessianic politics.

In the rough and ready America of the last century, a serious interest in utopian thought found other obstacles than Marxism. However,

1. *The Philosophy of Spinoza* (Ratner ed.), p. 51.
2. University of Chicago Press. All quotations are from this source unless otherwise indicated.
3. For discussion and bibliography see Lewis Mumford, *The Story of Utopias*.

the country itself seemed to be a functioning utopia to peoples else-where, and it was the scene of most of the utopian experiments of the period, as in Oneida and New Harmony. Immense enthusiasm greeted Bellamy's *Looking Backward* (1888); during the same period, huge audiences in the Midwest were inspired by the utopian prophecies of Ignatius Donnelly.[4] All this ferment has vanished. The appeal of such writers as Bellamy appears to have declined just about the time that the socialism of Debs and DeLeon began to make some headway in America. But since this type of socialism, too, has died out (of course, economic determinism has always been influential in America, from the Founding Fathers on down), we must look for deeper causes at work.

The idea of a dialectical opposition between "ideology" and "uto-pia" is suggested by Karl Mannheim's book, though I use the words here in a somewhat different sense from his.[5] A "utopia" I define as a rational belief which is in the long-run interest of the holder; it is a belief, not in existing reality, but in a potential reality; it must not violate what we know of nature, including human nature, though it may extrapolate our present technology and must transcend our pres-ent social organization.[6] An "ideology" I define as an irrational system of belief, not in the interest of the holder. It is sold to him by a group which has an interest in swindling him; he accepts it because of his own irrational needs, including his desire to submit to the power of the vendor group. An ideology may contain elements of truth; these serve to lend plausibility, rather than to open the eyes and increase the awareness of the recipient. Contrariwise, a utopia may contain ele-ments of error, initially less significant than its truth, which assist its later conversion into an ideology: in this way, the utopias of one age tend to harden in a distorted form into the ideologies of the next, taken on faith rather than rationally rediscovered.

The America of the last century, I suggest, made room for a lim-ited amount of utopian thought and experiment because, among many other factors, the capitalism of that period was singularly unconcerned

4. The early chapters of Dorfman, *Thorstein Veblen and His America* evoke and document this atmosphere.

5. Mannheim, *Ideology and Utopia* (translated from the German by Wirth and Shils). See also Mannheim, "Utopia," in 15 *Encyc. Soc. Sci.*, p. 200.

6. These features distinguish utopian thinking from, on the one hand, a mere dream, and on the other hand, a mere description of existing facts. In other words, "utopia" is a place—in contemporary terms, a plan—that now is nowhere, save maybe for pilot models, but that may someday be somewhere, so far as science can say; thus, heaven is not a utopia in my sense, while the Boston of *Looking Backward* is one. An element of ambiguity remains in these, as in Mannheim's definitions, perhaps reflecting the complexity of the topics them-selves. For a thoughtful discussion, see Kenneth Burke, "Ideology and Myth," 7 *Accent*, p. 195.

about propagandizing itself as an ideological system. Perhaps this is because it was so much taken for granted that it did not need verbal defense, though Southern writers continued to attack its Northern version. The system was written into the landscape, so to speak; it did not need to be written into books. After the Civil War, a dominant capitalism got brutal, but it did not get especially articulate; its critics, from Mark Twain to Veblen, treated it with an impiety and irreverence which we seldom find today. A few preachers continued to mumble grace over the economic system, but their combination of theology and economics was on the wane, while the new one of Social Darwinism coupled with laissez faire seems to have made little impression before William Graham Sumner started writing such essays as "The Absurd Effort to Make the World Over."[7] Throughout the period, to be sure, Eastern capitalists met resistance from the Populists, and perhaps the gold standard should be called an ideology; but on the whole dissent could be bought off without too much debate, *e.g.*, by homestead rights, or by subventions to the appropriate political rings.

By the turn of the century, however, many developments, including tremors of socialism, put the capitalists on the defensive; they could no longer quite so freely use Pinkertons; they began to talk, to bargain collectively "through instruments of their own choosing." Then, a whole new class of university-trained demi-intellectuals began to find jobs and status in doing the talking: personnel men, trade-association men, organization-chart men, lawyers, economists, house-organ men, advertising men, etc. Meanwhile the school system had taught almost everyone to read. Thus both the quantity of and the receptivity for capitalist ideology grew enormously, most of it paid for—as Veblen pointed out in his article on "The Breadline and the Movies"[8]—by the underlying population, which subscribes to the mass media.

Business enterprise in America has, however, always tended to disguise its ideological pressures under a coating of apparently utopian aims, such as the promise of a chicken in every pot or a car in every garage. These promises, when made in U. S. A., can scarcely be called utopian. First, given our resources, it is not difficult to fulfill them; they are, in very fact, just around the corner. Second, attainment of these goals would not make the great mass of well-fed Americans noticeably happier. The fulfillment of utopian aims, on the other hand, is a revolutionary affair; it makes substantial demands on the community, and promises substantial gains in human happiness. While in the Age of Liberalism, capitalism was associated with just such great

---

7. 17 *Forum*, p. 92, reprinted in *Sumner Today*, p. 99.
8. An editorial in *The Dial*, reprinted in *Essays in Our Changing Order*, p. 450.

human aims, it has become distanced from them in its later phases of complacency, ideology, or reaction. But the utopian coating referred to has tended to satisfy masses of people with spurious social goals, while many thoughtful folk rebelled by doubting the whole Enlightenment concept of gradual progress towards a liberal utopia.

With minor exceptions, moreover, the large-scale anti-business movements in America have tended more and more to copy business methods in covering an essentially ideological approach with a few utopian trimmings. Populism, for example, was ambivalent: it included not only ancient rural hatred for city slicker "usury" but the scarcely veiled "me too" cry of the farmers, unions, small businessmen and small debtors to be cut in on the big money. The New Deal added to these Populist aims (expressed in the Holding Company Act and other anti-Wall Street measures) the goal of achieving the Social Democratic attainments of the Continent, such as social insurance, a minimum wage, and public assistance in housing; none of these measures promised a fundamental change in the quality of American life. The T.V.A., some F.S.A. projects, and a few housing ventures such as Arthurdale and Greenbelt—these pushed beyond relatively easy attainment towards utopian goals; the T.V.A. particularly serves as a pilot model for a new way of life, a new community plan. But the general poverty of aim of the New Deal is shown by the fact that, by 1937, it had reached its own limits, a point obscured by its continuing ideological competition with "The Interests." The war provided a welcome agenda for avoiding insight into this impasse; the government ideologists sold war bonds (or "unity") by the same sort of specious arguments as had sold N.R.A.'s blue eagle.

The more recent political developments which have tended to engender disillusion with all systematic thinking—ideological and utopian alike—hardly need review. The positive goals of both world wars were oversold; peace movements have seemed so futile, and have been in such bad company, as to be discredited among all but the most courageous and independent (or religiously-supported) thinkers. Marxian Socialism, once a branch of bourgeois Enlightenment utopianism despite its founders' assertions to the contrary, has tended, like capitalism, to degenerate into an ideology, notably, of course, in Communist hands. In fact, the Stalinist bureaucracy has brought Russia under the sway of the most leaden and impenetrable of ideologies; its propagandists continue to make utopian claims which conceal from the faithful the actual abandonment of those utopian advances, as in the treatment of women, which the Old Bolsheviks had fought for. As hypocrisy is the tribute vice pays to virtue, so ideology pays tribute to utopian thought. But as hypocrisy revealed discredits the very possibility of virtue, so people who are disillusioned find it hard not to reject the utopian aspirations as well as the ideological pretense.

While these disillusionments are general, the fear of being intellectually out of step, of belonging to a political party with no chance of immediate power, seems to be considerably greater here than in Europe; this was true even in the nineteenth century, as Tocqueville and Bryce observed. In the absence of a tradition of respect for independent thinking, many Americans have found only one workable defense against the pressure of their ideological environment, namely apathy, often touched with humor, or a self-protecting cynicism. This attitude resembles the way in which many adolescents cope with the ideological authority of their parents: they brush it off as the mouthings of the "old man" or the "old lady," and largely disregard it in practice, without ever taking the genuine risks of commitment to an untried and independent ethics. This is the way soldiers dealt with the ideological output of the Information and Education branch of the Army; and it is the way in which many civilians cope with the public-relations staffs of business, government, and labor.

However, these amiable defensive aspects are not the whole story: apathy and cynicism—and a kind of self-deprecating humor which is often attractive—also serve the function of gaining status through toughness or slickness, or through the smoother type of indifference to enthusiasm of the well-bred. These attitudes are so strong in America that decent, constructive people, too, come to fear being taken for suckers, or enthusiasts; from childhood on, boys especially have been made ashamed of their own impulses towards warmth, commitment, generosity. Among intellectual groups, one fears to be accused of the "bourgeois" virtues; or more fashionably today, fears lest some humane reaction escape one which might be translated in the Freudian dictionary, where, e.g., "justice" may be read simply as "envy." It is a characteristic of utopian thinking, however, that it springs from humane enthusiasm; those whose greatest fear is to be gullible, serious, or "soft" are immune. But, as we know, those who fear most to be taken in, while they will escape utopia, are in fact among the easiest prey for ideology. Astrologers, anti-Semites, editors of the *Daily News,* and other confidence men make their living from the very cynics who will fall for the craziest story or ideology, if only it appears sophisticated, brutal, illegal or mysterious.

These seem to me to be among the many factors which have contributed to destroying the market for utopian thinking in America. The increasing division of labor characteristic of an industrial society has meantime played a part in inhibiting the production of such thinking which by its very nature requires a broad approach to the problems of the society as a whole. Specialists shrink from this task; being "in the know" as to a particular set of details, they are suspicious of the injudicious who make large plans without such knowledge. Indeed, a whole theoretical analysis, typified by Von Hayek, holds that large-scale planning is a human impossibility without a compulsory limiting of choices, on the ground that no planner can know enough to do the job if choice remains free. Where scholars and men of superior intellectual training fear to tread, cranks and charlatans—e.g., Howard Scott of Technocracy—fill what market there is for big, bold, bad plans.[9] More sedate is the work of men like Ralph Borsodi, and the Southern Agrarians; while seemingly just the opposite of the Technocrats, these nostalgic writers are quite as insouciant in prescribing for the power-relations of modern industrial society.

These writers, moreover, can hardly be called utopian, in the sense in which I use the word. For utopia is time-located in the future: it is a social order which has not yet been tried, though it is a realistic possibility, not a mere idle dream. But the agrarians and anti-industrialists generally seek to restore something—their picture of the earlier age is usually distorted by convenient historical amnesias—without too much serious attention to limiting technological factors. Thus their writings have often an uneasy similarity to dream-work on a more popular level, like the cults of California.

If we turn to the universities, we shall not completely escape such literary restoration movements. However, American social science has in general sought escape from ideological pressures—where this is not guaranteed by specialization—by means of ethical relativism, a value-free attitude which might be thought of as the academic counterpart of popular cynicism. (Curiously enough, Sumner represents both tendencies: the hardening of capitalist ideology and the beginning of a relativism which would have revolutionary implications vis-à-vis capitalist as well as other mores and ethnocentric prejudices.) In recent years, under the influence of thinkers such as Dewey and the Lynds, this sort of relativism has been under attack, and properly so. However, the insistence on an immediate plan-for-action and a somewhat Puritan distrust of "idle" curiosity and "irresponsibly" speculative scholars have tended to bring utopian as well as relativist-descrip-

---

9. Of course, such writers often make slashing, though hardly original, criticisms of contemporary society, but what they would substitute for it is left vague. For instance, a recent issue of *Technocracy Briefs* has the running-head: "Technocracy Engineers Have Designed a Blue Print for A 'New America,'" which appears in the repeated injunction to "Think North American!" and in such statements as: "Not 'Dictatorship of the Proletariat,' but Dictums of Technology; Not 'Equality of Birth,' but Equality of Opportunity; Not 'Geopolitics,' but Geotechnics; Not 'Sovereign States' but Mechanics of Area Operations."

tive thinking under condemnation.[10] Both academic movements—value-free and action-oriented schools—are reinforced by a stereo-typed notion as to what constitutes research. Research is organized either about the methodological framework of the existing disciplines or about "problems." But the problems are those things which we know bother us, such as poor administration, too much employment or too little, race and international tensions, etc. Researchers do not go looking for other problems which we ought to have, and indeed do have; in any case, the problems we are aware of are so urgent that they are felt to provide not only a necessary, but also a sufficient agenda.

By and large, the people whose function it is to think, under the division of labor, are over-impressed by what they think about. That is, they are over-receptive to their data, which they take at face value; even where they are not ethical relativists, they are terribly concerned with "what is." On the other hand a few intrepid heirs of an older tradition try to impress themselves on their data, without too much respect for "what is," *e.g.*, Spengler, Sorokin. These latter, therefore, come closer to the cranks and poets already mentioned for whom "what is" is to be found inside their heads; the aggressiveness of such thinkers towards the facts, the enormous empirical material they deal with, may perhaps be related to the reactionary *content* of their approaches to questions of social reorganization. Few scholars achieve the kind of sensitive and friendly relation in reality which is necessary for utopian creation—a relation in which one respects "what is" but includes in it also "what might be" and "what ought to be."

One small group in our society, the architectural fraternity, has continued to produce and to simulate thinking in the utopian tradition—thinking which at its best combines respect for material fact with ability, even enthusiasm, for transcending the given. (Perhaps the architects are in a good position to do this since they have had so little building to do!) Veblen was mistaken in hoping for great things from the engineers; the unideological matter-of-factness which he thought their work-a-day tasks would encourage usually succumbs to a pedestrian acceptance of the prevailing ideologies—a more un-critical acceptance, often enough, than that of their businessmen or governmental bosses. Architects, however, are engineers with a dif-ference: their profession would have no future if there were no dif-

---

10. In view of the reactionary onslaughts against Dewey today, I wish to make plain that I speak here only of a tendency in his thought (something of the same sort can be said of Lynd's *Knowledge for What?*), which is not actu-ally central to it. In fact, Dewey is not nearly so narrowly "pragmatic" as his enemies often assume; on the whole, he is certainly a "utopian thinker."

ference. Architects, that is, are paid to dream—paid even to waste, Veblen would say—but they must not ignore engineering requirements if they wish their structures to stand. Of course, most architects do not dream; they are simply businessmen, and their "waste" is of a most prudent kind, since their customers buy just the right amount of it to qualify for the social status they want. There remains a minority: *e.g.*, Wright and Le Corbusier; Behrendt and the Bauhaus group; the young editors of *Task* magazine; also there are community planners, such as Lewis Mumford, Charles Ascher and Catherine Bauer, who have worked with architects and have learned to relate their social thinking to this form of technological experience. This minority, despite the fundamentally reactionary character of Wright's and Le Corbusier's types of planning,[11] has helped to keep alive the utopian tradition both in the drawing of plans and in the experimental demonstration of new possibilities for living.

However, the architectural utopians have generally remained isolated from other forms of technological experience and analytical tools (classical economics and social psychology, for example); they have indulged, like most isolated men, in fanaticism and wars of sectarian annihilation, as in Wright's assault on Le Corbusier; we might even suggest that such eccentricities and blindnesses were necessary to preserve their "nerve of failure," their courage to be different and to stand alone.[12] The book *Communitas* is one attempt to break down this intellectual isolation. One author, Percival Goodman, is an architect and city planner; the other, Paul Goodman, a novelist and social critic. They have studied, not only the physical plans of some predecessor architects, but the intellectual constructions of some predecessor utopians. Their effort is ambitious to see what man is and may become, what society is and may become.

---

11. For Wright see, e.g., *The Disappearing City; When Democracy Builds;* and the remarkable interchanges between Wright and a group of English architects in *An Organic Architecture.* For Le Corbusier see, e.g., *When the Cathedrals Were White.*

12. Since writing the foregoing, I have read the brilliant review by Meyer Schapiro of *Architecture and Modern Life* by Baker Brownell and Frank Lloyd Wright. "Architect's Utopia," 4 *Partisan Review.* Mr. Schapiro argues that the utopias of such contemporary architects as Wright serve no constructive function but rather operate as reactionary middle-class ideologies, glossing over class relations by the use of words like "organic," "construction," "framework," which mix metaphors taken from architecture and from social thought. He sees the architects, especially of the depression period, as just another underemployed profession with delusions of its central role; these men, contemplating architecture as the mirror of society, fail to grasp those social realities which cannot be read directly from the physical forms. I am persuaded by Mr. Schapiro that there is less difference between architects of this stripe and engineers than I had supposed.

§ II

AS UTOPIANS, the authors' ethical and moral platform rests on a scientific psychology only hints of which are given in the text. It is a psychology which sees man as fundamentally good, capable under proper social and physical arrangements of enjoying work, family life, nature, privacy and cooperation—and alternating, temperamentally varied, rhythms between them. They see their fellow-Americans as, by and large, an unhappy folk, trapped in their competitive production and competitive consumption, strenuously passive, sourly emulative. They believe them, even now, to be capable of more spontaneous pleasures and more democratic cooperation. Thus, they have not fallen into the contemporary mood of a gloomy, Niebuhrian view of man, but have remained attached to more optimistic Enlightenment traditions, as represented in such various men as Godwin, Owen, Kropotkin and Dewey; like these thinkers, they see "what external conditions have grown inordinately large and are obstructing the harmony of society and the internal freedom of the people"; like them, they look for counterforces, for unmanipulative leverage, especially education. To hold this view today takes, I think, a certain amount of courage, more so, paradoxically, than to confess defeat at the outset. For the person who has the "nerve of failure" takes the risks of failure but also the risks of an improbable success; he dares to look at life in all its contingency. It is easier, and also more fashionable, to play the Cassandra role, and thus to reap from each new atrocity and impasse in world affairs new moral assurance and confirmation for one's position—like Prince Bagration in Tolstoy's *War and Peace* who gave the appearance of calm mastery by looking wise at each bit of catastrophic news from the battle as if he had not only foreseen but planned it just that way.

In one way or another, the Goodmans feel, most contemporary city planners avoid any responsibility for the ultimate values which their plans will freeze, destroy or serve. Believing that planning only makes sense on the assumption of peace, with its economic surplus and political choices, they are critical of those planners who are concerned simply with finding methods to minimize atomic destruction though this might become the easiest kind of planning to sell.[13] They

---

13. Lewis Mumford writes of an earlier city planner, who faced somewhat similar problems: "Leonardo da Vinci . . . dealt in his notebooks with the city proper, suggested the separation of pedestrian ways from heavy traffic arteries, and went so far as to urge upon the Duke of Milan the standardized mass production of workers' houses. But despite these pregnant suggestions, his contributions to the art of city building remain poor and meager compared with his extraordinary zeal in improving the art of fortification and assault." *The Culture of Cities*, p. 86.

are also critical of those more modest plans which aim at no positive good, but merely at the minimizing of lesser evils than atomic war: for instance, the relief of traffic congestion, or of unemployment (community development subordinated to make-work and pump-priming). For they feel that the planner, by virtue of his position and skill, has a responsibility to see, not only what people think they want, or have been persuaded to want, but what they might want, if they knew of its possibility. Unlike many utopian radicals, however, they sympathize with those planners who limit themselves to what can be realized at any given time, provided that the choice of evils, or of small gains, is informed by larger aims, and a full realization of the social consequences of amelioration.

It is also clear that the Goodmans do not think of utopian planning as a kind of exercise in legislation, in which the planners fit people to their theory; rather, it is an exploration of alternative possibilities. It is, therefore, a piecemeal approach: there is no one plan, no philosopher's stone. Technologies of scarcity, such as the Orient, pose entirely different alternatives than technologies of surplus, such as the U.S.A. Each geographic region, each cultural constellation, each stage of industrial development, presents material for exploiting quite different optima. This sounds like relativism or eclecticism, but it is not; among the utopias they sketch, the authors have reasoned preferences which are grounded in a systematic ethics; the same ethics leads them to dismiss as immoral still other alternatives—such as an improved Garrison State—which are conceivable, even probable.

The Goodman brothers evaluate those great city and community plans of the recent past which, on the basis of the attitudes just indicated, they feel to be of continuing importance. They ask of each plan: what does this tell us about the architect's underlying assumptions as to the ends of life? How, for instance, does he feel about modern industrial work—is it something to be belted off from the wives and children? In the design of the suburb, what are his implicit attitudes towards cultural variety—is he freezing in his plan the one-class, one-race, one-outlook ghettos which, as Catherine Bauer has observed,[14] are increasingly fostered by government and philanthropic planners and builders today? In the location and design of the factory, is his only value the goal of more commodities—and even within the limits of this goal, has he been taken in by current conventions, technologically outdated, as to the efficiency of mass production and the limits of machine-analysis of parts and subcontracted assemblies? In the design of the home, and landscaping, how does he feel towards

---

14. Bauer, "Good Neighborhoods," 242 *Annals*, p. 104.

children—is it, for instance, more important for them to have a work-shop and climbable trees than, since choices must be made, for their parents to have standard plumbing and a white picket fence? In this fashion, by looking at the plans—the book is full of drawings and sketches—the Goodmans read off from them the implicit social values of the planners and those for whom they worked: in their hands the recent history of architecture becomes a record of evaluations and ideas. It is also a dialectical process in which the avoidance of some evils has brought others, usually unanticipated, and in which the commitment of social resources in physical form has its own logic, opening some possibilities and foreclosing others.

We may compare the Goodmans' method to that of a psycho-analyst who examines the unconscious choices, and values which have crystallized in the posture, the gestures and the character struc-ture of a given individual. His task is to help the individual bring these values into conscious awareness and then to see what other structures can be built from the materials already given. This type of study owes much, in my opinion, to Mumford's writings; he has seen the interconnectedness of city shape, city movement, and city values;[15] the Goodmans, however, do not deal either with his analyses or with his own plans, such as those for Honolulu or post-war England.

The Goodmans feel that the central problems for the modern planner are posed by the Industrial Revolution. Is the planner revolt-ing against its coal and iron slums, like the creators of Garden Cities and Greenbelts (e.g., Ebenezer Howard,[16] Unwin, Stein)? Is he concerned with its economic insecurity, its Frankenstein qualities, like Frank Lloyd Wright? Or is he, on the contrary, fascinated with capitalist technology, anxious to speed the Industrial Revolution and plunge us all at once into a World's Fair kind of city, like Le Corbusier? Does he think primarily of consumption values, like Buck-minster Fuller, or of production values, like the planners of the Soviet state farms, or is he concerned with restoring the relation be-tween consumption and production which preceded the Revolution, like Borsodi? Or does he have his eye primarily on the possibilities of economic surplus given by the Revolution, and on the alternatives

---

15. See especially *The Culture of Cities* and *City Development*. I am indebted to Mr. Mumford for a number of helpful references and suggestions.

16. The Goodmans view the work of Howard too narrowly. Like them, he made plans not to divorce, but to reunite, work and residence. Far from espous-ing bigger and better suburbias, he insisted on the integration of industry, agri-culture, and dormitory along regional lines which took account of local re-sources and cultural patterns. Significantly, he was inspired by Bellamy. See Giedion, *Space, Time and Architecture*, p. 509.

in production and consumption offered by these in turn, like the planners of the T.V.A.? To illustrate the Goodmans' analyses, I shall select their treatment of Buckminster Fuller and of the T.V.A.

Most readers will remember Fuller's Dymaxion House as a pre-fabricated mushroom—a mobile hexagonal house on a mast, one of the absurd technocratic dreams of the depression days. Fuller (who was trained not as an architect but as an engineer) called it a machine for realizing the "Eternal Now," without commitment to site, cities, or tradition. Fuller also roams all fields, untroubled by the division of labor. His "economics" rests on "automatic minimum existence credits selectively contractable . . . based on foot-pounds per hour of physical effort, with time study credits for labor-saving contributions of individual activity . . . plus sex-segregated main-tenance of anti-social laggards," combined with a system of mass spec-ulation in 10¢ industrial shares. His "politics" is abbreviated by se-curing, through patents and city services (though what role these would play in the self-contained Dymaxion House is not clear), world control for the Universal Architects, a self-effacing elite "after the manner of the Ford planning department." His "religion" is a new phase of Christianity where, through mass-production and divorce from material concerns, especially landed property, men will again become (rather curiously isolated) brothers. His "psychology," starting from the child's fear of noise and falling, analogizes the structure of the House to the structure of the human body (how-ever, in the World War II version of the House, the functions of "fueling" and "refusing," *i.e.* elimination, are put on one side rather than in the central shaft).

One might dismiss all this as a mad pot-pourri, including Fourier-ist, money-crank, and possibly fascist bits. The Goodmans, however, take Fuller seriously both for what he says and what he symbolizes. They note the importance of the Dymaxion House's freedom from ground rent and public utilities (this is an as yet unimplemented aim: Fuller's proposed machine for using sun-power has not yet been in-vented; perhaps a little atomic pile will do instead). And the Good-mans see in the utter convenience of the House, its drive for complete consumer's effortlessness—no furnace to fix, no garden to putter in, no screens to hang—a symbol of the current craze for photoelectric doors, button-lowered car windows, and other magic-carpet fan-tasies. I find this search a very puzzling phenomenon, since the effort which is saved, for instance of cranking a car window, is not actually unpleasant; on the surface it appears to be a pathological laziness, but the people who go in for it probably play golf or go bowling. The Goodmans do not try to give a complete explanation, but they observe that the consumer, by the proliferation of these magic, fool-proof devices, becomes progressively enslaved and helpless in the hands of the "Universal Architects" who, in Fuller's scheme, monopolize all creative and decisive steps in the productive process.

In some respects, the T.V.A. may be thought of as a complete contrast to Fuller's work, though the Goodmans call attention to the Dymaxion-like section-trailers developed by the Authority for its mobile construction workers. For the T.V.A. does not divorce production from consumption; in its efforts at grass-roots democracy, as in its use of electric power, the two are brought into novel and multiple relations. The T.V.A.'s success rests on the adaptation of its plan to the logic of the man-nature pattern in the Valley: to keep the dams from silting up, it is necessary to prevent erosion, the land must be fertilized, and some restored to grass; to get these grass-roots, it is necessary to teach good land-use practice and to make possible a more intensive cultivation of the plowland; this requires encouragement of the cooperative movement, the sale of cheap fertilizer, and the easing of the farmer's tasks by cheap power and cheap appliances; and so on. People are freed from their primary, archaic relationship to the land; but are then enabled to relate themselves to the land and their neighbors on it in a more abundant, though more complicated, way. The authors, in their brief treatment, do no more than hint at the full meaning of the T.V.A. experience; they say little that is concrete; they move altogether too quickly from T.V.A.'s achievements to the issues it has not so far touched: "the problems of surplus and leisure, of the relation of culture and work, the role of great cities." For the solution of these, they turn to their own model plans.

§ III

THE AUTHORS PRESENT three such models. Each chooses to solve one problem to the exclusion of the others. The first model aims to increase leisure and the consumable surplus; the second, to reintegrate culture and work; the third, to reduce to a minimum both economic regulation and economic insecurity while maintaining large urban concentrations. The authors believe that the great plans of their predecessors expressed mixed aims; and they realize that any conceivable plan would likewise blend patterns from each of their three separated goals. In their logical abstractness, the plans are "ideal types" in Max Weber's sense; but they are also ideal types in the vernacular sense of something to be striven for, something utopian. Thus, the models, or, as the authors call them, paradigms, may be thought of as tools for analysing any existing plan; but in their statement, they are also efforts at analysing the conflict of aims in contemporary America.

The latter purpose comes out most clearly in the first plan, which rather sardonically assumes that there is to be no change in dominant American cultural values and socio-economic organization and raises the question: how can such values be unequivocally represented in the plan? Here the authors present a paradox in Veblen's thought: Veblen wanted to remove the archaic and pecuniary fetters on production by applying the matter-of-fact logic of the engineer; however, having stepped up production, he also wanted to step down consumption by getting rid of leisured waste and emulative luxury; would not the result be still greater mass insecurity through "over-production?"[17] The Goodmans feel that this paradox is not solved by Keynesian methods, both because, short of building pyramids, there are not sufficient objects of public spending to sop up the excess production, and because such public works do not give sufficient incentive, including psychological incentive, to profit. Their "solution" in this case is therefore an advertising man's dream: *city planning for efficient consumption of luxury goods.*

This requires the following physical arrangements: (1) Metropolises, large enough to permit mass production of luxuries, and to encourage the sway of emulation and thereby the insatiability of desire. Buildings will be crowded together to lower distributive costs, so that even more resources may be devoted to production, shopping, and consumption. (2) The center of the city becomes a huge shell of a department store; the shell also provides room for offices, entertainment and other light industry, and hotels; the corridors of the department store are the streets, so that no one may walk without being tempted to buy; and of course people are forced to walk— they need not and cannot drive their cars in these corridors. By thus merging streets and corridors (Bellamy suggested enclosable streets in *Looking Backward*), and building a cylindrical 21-story skyscraper one mile in diameter, the authors calculate that they could include all the non-residential facilities for the population of Manhattan—and New York of course comes closest as it is to their model. A tremendous gain in servicing and construction efficiency would ensue. But the most important gain would be in the opportunities for display and advertising—a world's fair every day and everywhere. (3) In their irony, the planners naturally fear lest the poetry of the great writers compete with the poetry of advertising. Hence the universities, museums, and other great institutions of non-popular culture are zoned—like any nuisance—outside the central cylinder; how-

---

17. The authors realize that Veblen did not live to see the present potentialities for abundance in America.

ever, by visits there, people weary of the fashion-show at the City Center, weariness which would be economically disastrous, may renew themselves for further bursts of consumption. (4) A somewhat similar renewing function is served by planning a zone of open country, a real "escape," quite near, perhaps five miles from the concentrated Center, beyond which would lie a further zone of state parks and adult camps. (5) Since the authors believe that the true alternative to the city is country, not suburbs, the residence zone is not a satellite town of free-standing homes, but an encircling ring of apartment houses. The apartments, however, are merely service shells, permitting the individual occupants to partition and decorate their space to taste—and emulation.

At the time of spring inventory, by a revival of carnival practices, there would be a season of immense idleness, with bonfires of outmoded furniture, a crescendo of waste—in preparation for the next organized spurt of highly efficient consumption.

The reader of this abstract, as of the text, may not always be sure here what is sexy but serious satire (as in Huxley's *Brave New World*), what plain silliness, and at what point the authors are stating their own genuine goals. In general, however, the moral of the plan comes through without ambiguity: it is a criticism of popular culture, with its drive for less work, more pay and more play; it is also an effort to reveal certain hidden elements of moral worth in modern capitalism. The criticism—the air-conditioned nightmare theme—is familiar enough among radical writers, who sometimes tend to attack with equal fervor the worst abuses, such as lynching, and the most venial foibles, such as radio commercials. But the implicit ethical defense of capitalism on the ground of its provision of bounteous consumption is seldom found outside Chamber of Commerce circles. Sophisticated people who defend capitalism do so either on lesser-evil grounds, or as an interim system, or as a support for political and intellectual freedom; they tend to be apologetic about its encouragement of consumer self-indulgence, if not about consumer values generally.

This general attitude springs, it seems to me, from a growing intellectual hostility to the values of consumer free choice.[18] It is not simply a question of poverty, for many people do not even enjoy window shopping. The left-wingers feel the choice is immoral, because unequally distributed; many, Puritan at heart, would prefer to distribute scarcity. Social hygienists feel it is bad for people: they

18. For discussion of the percolation of consumer attitudes into all spheres of life and the overreaction against those attitudes, see my article, "The Cash Customer," 11 *Common Sense*, p. 183.

eat too much rich food (a feeling often rationalized by reference to starving people elsewhere in the world), go to too many movies, etc. Snobs, especially in the older Seaboard cities, react against popular emulative consumption—and the growing cult of effortlessness referred to above—by cultivating an indifference to material things; driving Fords, for instance, until they, too, became designed for comfort, rather than more plushy "petit bourgeois" cars such as Oldsmobiles. Those influenced by Veblen or theorists of functionalism in design are hostile to "waste," to conspicuous consumption, and to competition in sale and display. And many people seek to assert their individuality, not by enjoying choice among available consumption products, but by making an issue of resistance to all salesmanship and advertising. Indeed, it has become fashionable even for advertising men to attack advertising.

These attacks are indiscriminate: the joys of consumption, of free consumer choice, of "waste" and frivolity and excess, are thrown out along with the obvious evils of inequality and of anxious emulation. Yet while we are waiting for a better social order, or more meaningful job-opportunities, it would be a mistake to overlook this freedom and the available chances for making it still more free.

This, if I understand them, is one of the points the Goodmans have in mind in their "City of Efficient Consumption." The efficiency they seek is of two sorts. On the side of production, they follow Veblen in seeking to eliminate waste, for instance excessive distribution costs, in order to increase, while lowering hours, the total annual consumable product of goods and services. But on the side of consumption, the "efficiency" is of a different order: it is an effort to heighten waste and emulation in order to make sure that everything produced is consumed, lest the economy be choked by its own superlative productiveness; the pump to be psychologically primed is that of the individual spender. Perhaps, too, the Goodmans seriously feel that by enhancing the efficiency of consumption of the population as a whole, it might be possible to avoid the economic, maybe even political need for periodic creation of an enlarged class of professionally-efficient consumers, namely the armed services. If by consuming luxuries, we could avoid "consuming" armaments, most of us would settle for their City, any day. But it is intended rather as a caricature than as the best of their possible worlds.

In their second model or paradigm, the Goodmans present their own values explicitly. There they try to deal with the divorce of production from consumption in modern industrial society, and to recreate forms of work which will be meaningful without a futile attempt at full retreat to handicraft production. But unlike most of the writers from Marx on who discuss this problem, often in terms of modern man's "alienation," they are fully aware that the impersonality of work today has certain advantages, even if these advantages are analogous to the "secondary gains" of a neurotic illness. They see, for example, that punctuality on the job, which seems to enslave man to the clock, "makes the work itself much more tolerable; for it establishes it in an impersonal, secondary environment where—once one has gotten out of bed early in the morning—the self has already resigned all claims." At work, one is "relieved" of one's family; by the same token, after hours one is "free" of work. Nevertheless, it is, humanly speaking, a crazy divorce, which is simply made smoother by those planners of suburbs who shield the residential area from any contact with the productive economy. The Goodmans try to see what utopian reunions are possible.

To reunite workshop and home, they advocate restoring some work to the home, as domestic industry or subsistence farming, while taking out of the home, and into the larger economy, some domestic services. As to the former, they point to the decentralization made possible by electricity and the new types of small machine tools; as to the latter, they rearrange the home itself, and the role of children.

What the Goodmans are suggesting here is a program which, by increasing the self-sufficiency of the home, the city, and the region, will both lend variety and meaning to work and provide the economic basis for freedom. In this, they follow Frank Lloyd Wright on the physical side and Kropotkin on the social and political; they insist that each producer must have a say in the distribution of "his" product. They believe that the solution of the problem of political power in an industrial economy lies in planning for farm-factory units on a regional basis, where each unit will have enough self-sufficiency to defend itself in bargaining against other like units. This involves "the close integration of factory and farm workers—the factory hands taking over in the fields at peak seasons; farmers doing factory work in winter; town people, especially children, living in the country; farmers making small parts for the factories." But the self-sufficiency must not go too far; each farm, each unit, each region will be integrated into the national and international market as to some of its dealings; there is to be none of the "wilful provincialism that is so nauseating in movements of regional literature and art." Education on and off the job, and frequent changes of job, are to give the producers the knowledge to support their control of distribution, and the world-minded outlook which will guide trading of their regional surpluses for surpluses from elsewhere.

The Goodmans say nothing as to how such a redistribution of resources is to be set up, nor how it will differ in operation from certain patterns of bargaining we have at present, when, let us say, Montana trades its copper for Pennsylvania's coal. In their effort to create a kind of internal balance of economic power, they are up against the same sort of problem which is faced in the Acheson-Lilienthal report on atomic energy: namely, how to find the leverage to distribute economic (or war) potential in such a fashion as to prevent either raids or autarchy. Those who now have the potential (in the atomic case, the United States) hesitate to surrender it, even for the hope of peace; those who lack it (in the atomic case, the U.S.S.R.) hesitate to surrender the chance of getting it, even for the fear of war.

The authors are more instructive in their psychological analysis of the problem of bringing productive work back into human scale. They see the problem as even more difficult, since they see man as even more complex, than many of the industrial psychologists who have been influenced by Elton Mayo. To illustrate: they do not insist, as the Mayo group does, that most workmen want always to work in teams, but rather that men want both group and individual work, both city and country work, both supervision and apprenticeship. Now, since it is undeniable that many factory workers today do not seem to want such diversity, but prefer their accustomed routines and their cluster of associates, we would have to say that this is not what they might want under a different social structure and a different educational system. While many industrial psychologists attempt to adjust workers as they find them to their malaise, as by seeing that they have "recognition" from management and agreeable team-mates, the Goodmans, being utopian, are more interested in adjusting the factory-system to their vision of what man is "really" like. For instance, adolescents would spend five months in general education, two in study-travel, and four in productive work, divided between farm and factory; older workers would shift around less, but would still work on a rhythmic basis with some time devoted either to supervision or to work at their highest technical skill. The jobs themselves would be reanalyzed, not with an eye to technical efficiency, either for production or consumption, but with an eye primarily to joy in work and the assurance of freedom: "Any end is prima facie suspicious if its means, too, do not give satisfaction."

"Supposing one of the masters, away on his two months of individual work, drafting designs for furniture, should decide—having studied the furniture of the Japanese—to dispense with chairs!

"It is problems like this that would create a bitter struggle in the national economy."

It is important to observe, in this otherwise idyllic passage, that the Goodmans do anticipate "bitter struggle" even in Utopia. This is an advance on the work of Bellamy as well as earlier utopians (including Marx) who, focussed on the sordid struggles which spring from capitalist relations, were not sufficiently attentive to clashes of temperament and interest which would spur the making of new utopias even when theirs had been achieved.

The Goodmans illustrate their plan—which they term "The New Commune: the Elimination of the Difference between Production and Consumption"—with drawings of the farmhouses in which families with children will be living. The farms are to be diversified, and zoned quite near to the smallish (200,000) urban nuclei. All children will do farm chores and thus enter "the economy" at a point where it is most comprehensible; the family-sized farms, aided by cooperative marketing and mechanization, will develop a cultural tone which can compete with, rather than submit to, the metropolitan culture.

The metropolitan milieu itself is to recapture something of the quality of leisureliness and sociability of the medieval city square. In their illustrative plan for "Printers' Square," for example, there would be a place for causerie among the gathering workmen, more typical of the French cafe than of the American tavern or coke-bar. Fronting on the Square is the printing factory, with its attached technical school of printing and engraving; a library with terrace-tables for drinks and snacks; some shops; an apartment for urban (childless) dwellers, whose meals are home-cooked after the dirty-work of vegetable washing and peeling, etc., has been communally done. The concept of the Square is, however, rather artificial. Printing happens to be a noisy industry, though not perhaps inevitably so; its relation to the rest of the activities that front on the Square seems tenuous: mere ecological proximity will not produce the kind of local color and culture which the Goodmans seek. Any utopian planning faces the problem of visualizing the intangibles that would give social meaning to physical form and layout. The problem is symbolized by the authors' puzzle as to what kind of public monument they should locate in the Square. A church? Hardly, though Frank Lloyd Wright, despite the idiosyncratic character of his own religion, plunks one down in his plan for Broadacre City. The Goodmans half ironically suggest a Sir Patrick Geddes Regional Museum as the focal point of their Square.

Bellamy's *Looking Backward*, published 60 years earlier, gives us, I think, a more imaginative glimpse of the social and domestic life of a utopian city which in spaciousness and cultivation resembles the more fragmentary picture of the "New Commune"; however, Bel-

lamy's handling of the problems of work and economic life generally
is about as different as can be from the Goodmans'. Unlike so many
of his contemporary utopians, Bellamy did not turn his back on the
Industrial Revolution; he welcomed the increasing pace of mass production and trustification; under his plan, industry was to be "efficiently" run on a national scale, under the direction of the generals
of the Industrial Army. All youth were to serve a three-year term at
common labor in the Army (rather like a compulsory C.C.C.); those
who lacked the ability or desire to specialize would stay on in its
lower ranks. The political leaders were to be chosen from among
the top administrators who had risen in the Army; in fact, politics
was to be largely the process of industrial administration. In some
senses, then, Bellamy was a precursor of the theorists of the "managerial revolution."

Since consumption goods and services were to be equally distributed, without regard to rank in the Army (invalids, too, would receive
an equal share), Bellamy was particularly concerned to meet the
charge of capitalist critics that there would be no "incentive" either
to work or to rise—this old, but ever renewed charge based on man's
alleged innate laziness. He met this argument partly as the Goodmans
do, by an effort to make work meaningful and pleasureful in itself
and by encouraging feelings of benevolence and human fellowship
in work, but also by reluctant though heavy reliance on the love of
praise and the fear of censure. Men were to be educated to seek glory
through their industrial ardor, and to avoid being held in contempt for
ducking their social responsibilities; officers would rise on the basis
of the zealous performance of their underlings.

It seems plain today that production can all too easily be organized
on such an emulative and centralized system (compare the "socialist
competition" of the Russians); in fact, the motives of hunger and
gain which are supposed to operate our market economy have been
very largely dispensed with even there.[19] Bellamy, it seems, was not
quite utopian enough. One reason is that, though he foresaw the possibility of abundance, if the nationalized industries were properly organized and competitive and distributive wastes abolished, he did not
foresee—who could have?—the possibilities of overabundance, the
bountiful surplusage of means of production. Equality, and a comfortable, unostentatious standard of living had therefore to be his
principal goal, not joy and freedom in work.

Moreover, as we have just observed, the earlier socialists and uto-

19. Karl Polanyi's *The Great Transformation* raises the question whether
hunger and gain were actual motives as well as approved ones to any large extent,
even in the heyday of the market.

pians, including Bellamy, believed that politics would disappear, once
the community owned the means of production; and that universal
peace would reign, once people were no longer educated to meanness and fear by the ruthlessness of the capitalism of their day. Today,
an Industrial Army would give us nightmares; our awareness of
totalitarian dangers leads the Goodmans to turn to regionalist and
syndicalist writers as against the authoritarian-nationalist Bellamy for
suggestions how to limit the power of the managerial bureaucracy.
But as indicated above, their suggestions do not meet the issues.

On the side of the manner of living, however, life has not caught
up with Bellamy to the same degree; if we judge by the Goodmans'
work, he is still utopian here. The city pictured in *Looking Backward*
has about as much sociability and amenity as the Goodmans' "New
Commune."[20] There is ample leisure; there are goods enough to satisfy all "genuine" needs (Bellamy even foresaw the radio); domestic
life is urbane, with the lot of women improved by communal services. A citizen who is willing to settle for a somewhat lower standard
of living is permitted after a time to avoid industrial service, and to
devote himself to study, the arts, or whatever he pleases—a suggestion
which is also made in the Goodmans' book. Above all, human relations
are to be friendly and unexploitative; women are the companions and
equals of men (though organized for work in a separate hierarchy);
and the individuality of children is respected; in fact from early years
on, children are encouraged to develop their taste and their vocational
bent. What is similar here to the quality of the Goodman's Commune
is the emphasis on quiet happiness, as against excitement, as the aim
of life. There is to be neither war nor economic competition; the
excitement of the chase, of sadism, of exploitation will be disapproved;
the city plan calls for contemplative, easy-going, and cultivated joys.

The Goodmans do not really hope that we could move directly
to such a utopia, when our values are so very largely the excitement-
values of the "City of Efficient Consumption." They offer, therefore,
a third plan which they term an interim measure: its purpose is to
minimize economic regulation, and thus to permit once more a choice
of economic goals.

Over-regulation in our surplus economy arises, the Goodmans
argue, because "overproduction" jeopardizes the jobs of the poor and
the profits of the rich; the government is forced to interfere to assure
full employment, thus making employment itself—in all its modern
meaninglessness—the very end and aim of the community's political

20. In his sequel, *Equality*, Bellamy dealt more fully with decentralization;
Manhattan was to have 250,000 people.

activity. Then the free market, one of the few remaining freedoms, becomes entangled in regulation (private, of course, as well as governmental) and taxes (private, of course, as well as governmental) to raise funds to subsidize, insure, and otherwise shore up the economy. The authors propose: that the problem of subsistence be divided off from the problem of luxury; the subsistence market, occupying a small fraction of the country's resources, would be government-controlled, with some scheme akin to rationing providing everyone with his basic needs; while the luxury market would be free of control and entitled, since no one would starve in any case, to its privilege of boom and bust.

"The retrenchment might go very far, relaxing kinds of governmental regulation that are now indispensable; for, where the prospective wage earner has a subsistence independently earned, the conditions under which he agrees to work can be allowed to depend on his own education rather than on the government's coercion of the employer."[21]

The industrialist would then lose the subsistence market and its labor force; the worker, unless in post-adolescence he could afford a paid substitute, would be coerced for the fraction of his time (recall again Bellamy's conscription) needed to produce the subsistence goods and services.

The authors believe that such a pattern (its economic details, obviously complex, are barely sketched) would commit the community to less irreversible change, in architecture and layout, than is demanded by the present type of Keynesian-New Deal methods for insuring full employment. They fully realize, however, that the basic question "what is subsistence?" is a cultural, not a medical problem, and that its solution requires a decision as to how much in consumers' emulative goods (the "standard of living") we are willing to give up in order to gain a greater measure of freedom from regulation. The Goodmans assume that much of our expenditure on clothing, cars, etc., is really forced on us by a competitive race, failure in which threatens even the minimum of self-support. The subsistence economy will, accordingly, provide food, clothing, and prefabricated shelter which is adequate but not varied or stylish. On the other hand, since people are to be freed for such work in the luxury economy as they want, they must be assured, as part of their subsistence, more physical and psy-

---

21. By giving those who want to pursue wealth an entire economy to themselves, insulated from the subsistence economy, the plan retains one of the chief advantages of nineteenth-century capitalism, where power was divided because some men sought it directly in the political sphere while others went primarily after money. Thus, unlike the modern managerial state, politics and economics were not entirely overlapping spheres; the result was some freedom in the interstices and a lessening of ideological pressures.

chological mobility than at present; hence, full transportation (and medical service) are handled as subsistence items also.

The most difficult political and economic questions arise in attempting to relate the two economies, the free one and the subsistence one. (It is here, as the authors point out, that similar attempts—Robert Owen's plan for New Lanark, Louis Blanc's Workshops, the FSA and the WPA—have failed.) To keep the subsistence economy non-competitive, its standards cannot be permitted to rise; to keep the private, free economy from oppressing it, for instance by control of facilities such as transport that both would use, the government might have to use its power over the labor supply. In times of prosperity, demand for subsistence products such as clothing and shelter will diminish, since almost everyone will be able to afford the greater variety of offerings on the private, free economy; in times of crisis, the subsistence demands will rise—but this very pattern will tend to mitigate the business cycle. By the (admittedly) very roughest of calculations based on national income and production figures, the authors guess that no more than one-seventh of the available resources (in labor-time or money) would be required to produce subsistence for all Americans; and that this figure is less than that to which the country, in pursuit of the same security goals, is already committed. Obviously, these calculations, financial and political, would need refinement before one could be pretty sure that the plan of the Goodmans would be any less fragile than the Keynesian approach which they attack.

Most interesting on the architectural side are the elevations and layouts for the residences of the subsistence workers. The Goodmans, unlike Mumford, have faith that prefabrication can produce really cheap mass housing. Many of their trailer-type houses would not need public utilities; others would operate with community kitchens and showers; families could combine their allotments to secure more commodious quarters. The subsistence houses are not meant to be especially inviting—though, as drawn, they look better than millions of rural and urban slum dwellings—for if one wants better housing, one must work in the free economy to pay for it: the subsistence economy's purpose is freedom, not luxury.

Once the obligations to the subsistence economy have been met, one would not have to work at all; whatever one needed, within the subsistence limits, would be free (again compare *Looking Backward*). But do we really want freedom?

"Suddenly, the Americans would find themselves rescued from the physical necessity and social pressure which alone, perhaps, had been driving them to their habitual satisfactions; they might suddenly find the commercial pleasures flat and unpalatable, but they would not therefore suddenly find any other resources within themselves.

"Like that little girl in the progressive school, longing for the security of the grownup's making her decisions for her, who asks: 'Teacher, today again do we have to do what we want to do?' "[22]

Escape from bored freedom into compulsive activity and excitement might become a powerful political movement, until education had been able to nourish the instinct of workmanship, of spontaneous creativity, the capacity for happiness as against excitement, which the Goodmans, along with their utopian teachers, believe to exist in everyone. Perhaps, they suggest, there would be a revival of small business ventures (in fact, we have actually seen this among the veterans, who today come closest to having a subsistence claim devoid of moral strictures); "for the risk of fundamental insecurity of life has been removed, and why should one not work to amass a little capital and then risk it in an enterprise that was always close to one's heart?" In any case, there would be renewed emphasis on the problem of one's "calling," one's true vocation, when all have behind them the security and experience of the subsistence economy and can take their time, as only the rich can now do, before choosing one's work in the free enterprise economy. (Again, a theme from Bellamy.) Or, one might choose not to choose, but to travel or study, a modern (and therefore quite different) Thoreau.

The Goodmans, however, share values with Thoreau (and Frank Lloyd Wright) but also with Marx, who spoke of the "idiocy of rural life"; they do not want to dismantle the metropolis. But trailers will not work in a large city; even a city slum will be too dear for the subsistence economy—as, indeed, the poor today cannot afford big city housing where there is no direct or indirect subsidy. So, then, a man must pay for his metropolitan advantages by work in the private economy, without thereby securing exemption from his subsistence duties. Thus many might desert the metropolis for the subsistence centers, and the Goodmans realize that this problem is not fully solved in their theoretical structure. But, since the purpose of their plan is security with minimum regulation, it cannot be said to leave most big city dwellers worse off than today. Especially if they want freedom.

§ IV

IT HAS NOT BEEN my purpose in these pages to criticize the Goodmans'

---

22. Bellamy had observed: "The fact that all the world goes after money saves a man the necessity of anxiously debating what his life is for." From the unpublished papers of Bellamy, quoted in Arthur E. Morgan, *Nowhere Was Somewhere*.

own models, nor their discussion of earlier community plans. The real value of their book lies not in this or that detail but in their explicit attachment to the now-languishing tradition of utopian thought. Their text, like a physical plan, does not render up all its meaning at first glance: an innocent-looking phrase may conceal a whole philosophy; I hope that they and others who are qualified will proceed with the necessary follow-up. The sort of imaginative courage, the sort of detail-work, which is required to plan today even for the development of a single city or region, is no news to the readers of this Law Journal, since the Yale Law School was one of the first institutions to recognize that community planning demands both a policy goal and a novel integration of the sciences.[23] But it may be news to the many community planners, at least of the older generation, who view their work as just another specialty. This problem of interdisciplinary cooperation may be illuminated by a brief comparison with a bold contemporary plan which is [1947] being put into effect, the Plan for the community of Warsaw. What follows is based on a conversation in the spring of 1946 with Szymon and Helen Syrkus, the former being one of the principal architects (now a director of the National Ministry of Reconstruction) and the latter an executive of the Plan.

Long before 1939, a small group of architects, city planners, social scientists and social workers had begun, in isolation from the dominant soddenness of the Polish government, to develop rather utopian conceptions of community planning. To a large extent, they seem to have been inspired by Robert Owen. They had an opportunity to build a "pilot model," a spacious though inexpensive cooperative in Racasiewicz, a Warsaw suburb; then the War came. After the bombing and capture of the city, members of the group continued to meet secretly to make plans for the rebuilding of the capital after the War. As they proceeded, they drew into their circle additional scientific collaborators. They discovered, for instance, that proper residential layout required an analysis of how far children could comfortably walk alone—for this they went to the child psychologists and social workers. From the economists, they secured data as to the cost to the community if private automobiles had to be provided for. From the data of the engineers, the group concluded what factories still had to be treated as nuisances under modern conditions, and what other fac-

---

23. See Lasswell and McDougal, "Legal Education and Public Policy: Professional Training in the Public Interest," 52 *Yale Law J.*, pp. 217-32; Directive Committee on Regional Planning, Yale University, *The Case for Regional Planning*. On the diversity of interests and skills required of the community planner, see Martin Meyerson, "What a Planner Has to Know" in *Proceedings, Annual Conference on Planning* (1946), p. 167. I am indebted to Mr. Meyerson for helpful suggestions.

tories due, for instance, to the type of skill employed, might add to
the culture and amenity of the city; they proceeded with zoning on
this basis. Architects and landscape architects worked on the problem: what sort of vistas, what sort of décor, create what sort of social
and psychological attitudes in people; they wanted the walls and
roofs and other shapes to say to people: "what's your hurry?" (The
subtlety of this problem is such that it seems hardly to have been
touched scientifically; the Rorschach test provides certain clues to
its investigation, as Schachtel's work has shown.)[24]

On the basis of these and other studies, the cooperating architects
then began to draw the detail plans for post-war Warsaw. Most of
the group were eventually killed by the Nazis; the Syrkuses were
among the few who managed to survive the wounds they suffered in
concentration camps; many of the plans also survived. But after the
isolation of the War, the survivors felt the need to see what had been
learned elsewhere in their field; they journeyed to Sweden, to Russia,
to the United States to find out.

It is my impression that they discovered little (save a few technical points such as new types of building materials) which their
interdisciplinary group had not already explored. Reading *Communitas* fifteen months later, it was striking to see the resemblances between the Warsaw plans and those of the Goodmans' favorite utopia,
the "New Commune," both with respect to some of the social values
implicit in the plans and with respect to their physical features. The
Warsaw residences are to be formed in super-blocks, but without the
monotonous regularity of most of our own urban redevelopments;
rather, with an eye to vistas, the paths will wind; the walk-up apartments will be variously grouped. At the calculated radii there will be:
trees and play-yards for small fry; schools and libraries and meeting
halls for the older folk; shopping centers will be on the through high-
ways no further away than a mother can easily walk with a small
child. Since the women are to be freed as much as possible from domestic drudgery, laundries, crèches, cooking will be communal; there
are rooms where they can park their children at night to attend political meetings or go to the library with their husbands. But since
women also enjoy cooking, when they are not compelled to it, and
gain a feeling of status from the quality of a particular soup or casserole, the Polish planners insisted that each apartment have a private
kitchen too, even though they were trying desperately to save on

24. Ernest Schachtel, "The Dynamic Perception and the Symbolism of Form:
With Special Reference to the Rorschach Test," 4 *Psychiatry,* p. 79; "On Memory
and Childhood Amnesia," 10 *id.,* p. 1.

plumbing and all dispensable expense. In this decision, they expressed their own values, and also, they felt, those of the people.

Interdisciplinary cooperation and scientific surveys, however, will not solve the problems which arise when the planners' values diverge from those of the general community. This point was raised by my question: suppose a family prefers the amenity of an automobile to the amenity of a kitchen, or would even sacrifice for it the minimum standards as to square feet of space per person that the planners had fixed upon; how could the family exercise consumer free choice and make its preference felt? The Syrkuses replied that, apart from obvious economic obstacles in present-day Poland, the example of America had convinced them that the automobile will spoil the best of urban residential plans; moreover, the factories and even open country will be within easy walking or bicycling distance from the homes; there will be a rapid transit system and a highway net along the River outside the City (I suppose, for common carrier and military traffic). They also added that the appropriate legislative bodies had enthusiastically approved the Plan. I was not entirely satisfied with this explanation.[25] Abstract as the question was in 1946, I had the impression that the planners might be freezing the shape of the City against private cars, perhaps without fully acquainting their constituents with the meaning of the choice being made in their behalf. Yet since health and the general welfare are clearly involved in minimum housing standards, I asked myself if the question really differed from the forcible vaccination of individual recalcitrants by public health authorities. Anyhow, the car question came to symbolize for me the whole issue of coercion in utopian community planning.

The very gap that separates the thinking of the advanced planner from that of his clients tends to lead him to dictatorial measures. For his work teaches him that he can do little to achieve his goals by verbal persuasion: if the walls and streets and vistas, the cars and subways, the kitchens and showers—if these say "hurry, hurry," how can his message of communal quiet and calm possibly be heard, or, if heard, emotionally understood? If people are drugged with excitement, will they not crave more of the same, like any addict, especially when the whole economy would flounder if they failed to respond? Must not the planner at least jazz up his plans and elevations? I suggest that

---

25. Before the reader becomes too skeptical of the Polish dictatorship—on *this* score—let him recall that rent subsidies, multiple dwelling laws, etc., compel the renter in American cities to buy space and fixtures where he might prefer to spend his share of the social income on something else. A group of American architects and city planners, visiting Warsaw, recently commented on the "extremely humanistic" and undoctrinaire quality of the Poles' physical planning. N. Y. Times, Sept. 13, 1947, p. 6, col. 3.

the true utopian errs if he allows himself to be seduced by such arguments. The moment he begins to manipulate (let alone use physical coercion)—even if the manipulation only consists in the use of reasoning which does not convince *him* but which he feels may "sell" his audience—he leaves the realm of utopia for that of ideology. Thereby he demonstrates, in many cases, his lack of the "nerve of failure." For it is not always his benevolence which leads him to force or manipulate people to do what is in their objective interest. It is his doubt as to his own correctness, which can be assuaged only by securing confirmation in plans and behavior he will live to see—these are his prophet's "sign."

The Goodmans quote Daniel Burnham who lived at a time (the turn of the century) when, or so it appears to us, faith was a less difficult virtue:

"Make no little plans; they have no magic to stir men's blood and probably themselves will not be realized. Make big plans: aim high in hope and work, remembering that a noble, logical diagram, once recorded, will never die, but long after we are gone will be a living thing, asserting itself with ever growing insistency."

So might the Warsaw underground planners have thought, who later perished in the concentration camps, or in the city's battles of liberation. Their diagrams did survive. But this strikes us as somewhat accidental, a rather insubstantial ground for faith. The real question is one about people, not plans: are they really hopeless addicts or can they, enough of them, appreciate what a good community plan would be like even when they have grown up under a bad plan? The utopian's faith is that the answer is affirmative, though its timing—here he can learn from Marx and Engels—depends on a congeries of social forces. That faith is supported by the very tradition of utopian thinking in which the planner works, and which is a record of just such human ability to transcend the ideologies provided by the culture and to add something new to the small precious stock of social ideas.

6. The Saving Remnant:
An Examination of Character Structure

In 1794 THE MARQUIS DE CONDORCET, in hiding from the French Revolutionary Terror, ill and near death, wrote his *Sketch of an Historical View of the Progress of the Human Spirit*, a great monument to faith in human power to shape human destiny. Condorcet refused to be dismayed either by his own experience of human meanness and savagery or by his wide historical reading in the annals of cruelty and error. For he rested his hopes, not only on "observation on what man has heretofore been, and what he is at present," but also on his understanding of the potentialities of human nature.

It has proven more difficult than he had perhaps supposed to develop those potentialities. Today we are aware that the raw material of human nature is shaped by what we call culture into the organized force of a particular character strucure; that this character structure tends to perpetuate itself from parent to child; that, largely determined by early experience, it determines in turn the adult modes of life and interpretations of new experience. The combination of character structure and social structure in a given culture is therefore relatively intractable to change. Though in America we are near Condorcet's dream of the conquest of poverty, his dream of the conquest of happiness seems ever more remote. It has become fashionable to sneer at him and other philosophers of the Enlightenment for lacking a sense of the human limitations on improvement. The sneer, however, is unimaginative. Condorcet's scientific, empirical method urges us to see precisely how recent changes in character structure, as well as in the conditions that gave rise to them, have helped to deny utopia. His philosophy then invites us to apply human reason and effort to the improvement of the human condition as thus understood.

My purpose here is to advance such understanding by tracing a shift I believe to have occurred in very recent times in this character structure of modern man: a shift from the predominance of a type I have called "inner-directed," whose source of guidance in life is an internalized authority, to a type I have called "other-directed," dependent on external authorities. We shall further explore the relationship between these two types of character and the changing feelings in people as to their power to resist social pressures. For obviously, given the objectively identical social pressure, the individual's feeling and experience will depend upon his character, in which his previous life-experiences, especially those of mastery and submission, have been crystallized.

While our helplessness in the world is historically the condition of every advance in our mastery of it, the feeling of helplessness may today be so overpowering that regression, and not advance, ensues. But only when we have understood those forces that make for helplessness can we assay the probable outcome, and see what might be required for the new leap to security and freedom envisaged by Condorcet. One requirement is a type of character structure that can tolerate freedom, even thrive on it; I call persons of such type "autonomous," since they are capable of conscious self-direction. The very conditions that produce other-direction on the part of the majority today, who are heteronomous—that is, who are guided by voices other than their own—may also produce a "saving remnant" who are increasingly autonomous, and who find strength in the face of their minority position in the modern world of power.

§ I

THROUGHOUT MOST of history, people have lived in the bosom of nature, and at her mercy. They have sought a kind of defensive power and command of nature through magic and animism, by which they attempted to personalize and to propitiate the environment. The Pueblo Indians of the American Southwest, for instance, still cope with fear of drought by preoccupation with word-perfect rituals of rain making—and by very practical communal organization of the available water supply. These tribes quiet their anxiety over the weather by substituting for it anxiety over the ritual, which remains in their control. In such a society, as in the feudal past, people live on a relatively unawakened level, with limited life-expectations and limited potentialities for choice. An over-all balance is struck between helplessness and power; institutions mediate this balance, and character structure builds upon it.

This balance altered radically in the West during the age that opens with the Renaissance and closes, to set an equally arbitrary date, with the virtual cutting off of immigration from Europe following World War I. During this period, men were forced to face a world of changed dimensions, changed social relations, and changed meanings. As a result, some felt increasingly helpless and alone: the Calvinist doctrines appealed to them because those doctrines stressed man's helplessness to secure grace, the "chosen" being predestined by a terrifying and inscrutable God. The practical Calvinist, however, did not merely wait for the day of judgment; he tried to force God's hand by a ritual. This ritual, unlike the Pueblo Indian's rain making, was symbolized by hard work in the worldly processes of production—even though the ultimate aim was otherworldly. The result for many was success in mundane pursuits—which was regarded as a sign of election. Thus both hard work and its practical fruits assuaged the feeling of helplessness in the new conditions of life and led to the attainment of a new balance between power and weakness.

This period was the age of the early physical and industrial frontiers—the frontiers of expanding industry and trade, as well as expanding geographical frontiers. This age also enlarged the frontiers of intellectual and emotional discovery, excavating man's past and acquainting him with other cultures. To pioneer on a frontier, whether an external one—at the edge of a white settlement—or an internal one —at the edge of the known in science, art, or industry—requires a somewhat new type of character that is, to a degree, capable of self-piloting, a type that can act when the guidance of custom breaks down or when a choice must be made among several different sets of customs.

I call this type inner-directed, since the source of direction is internalized. By inner-direction, however, I do not mean genuine autonomy, but rather obedience to an internal psychic "gyroscope" which, installed in childhood, continues to pilot the person as he struggles to master the exigent demands of the frontier. This gyroscope is set going by the parents, or rather by their subconsciously internalized ideal image; or by heroes or great men of antiquity or revered elders taken as models. Driven by these internal voices, the inner-directed person is often ambitious—for fame, for goodness, for accomplishment in the world; and this is as true of the bold men of the Renaissance as of the hard, ascetic Puritans. By their own efforts at self-discipline and self-development, these men often helped to "produce" their own characters; the conquering of this internal frontier was accompanied and rewarded by mastery over others and over nature.

In all I have said, I speak primarily of the middle classes, for it was among them that inner-directed types arose; the lower classes moved more slowly out of feudalism. In time, as the doctrine of predestination became attenuated or forgotten, these middle classes developed an ideology of liberalism and individualism that proclaimed for all men the values of freedom and self-reliance compatible with characterological inner-direction. The inner-directed person came to *feel* free and to *feel* self-made: in his psychological innocence, he was not aware how many of "his" choices had been made for him already by his parents and his conditioning generally. He might have read the famous phrase of Heraclitus—"Character is fate"—to mean that he, as an individual, possessed his own fate, working in him through his own self-mastery; while we today would read the same sentence to mean that our own character is not truly ours, but is produced by our social environment, our "fate" of living in a particular place and time —a new, more sophisticated doctrine of predestination. Moreover, the inner-directed person, living in a time of expanding frontiers, could in fact achieve a small degree of the freedom that he felt. Many inner-directed persons achieved a measure of psychic autonomy and independence as theocratic controls declined in the eighteenth and nineteenth centuries.

§ II

THIS SECURITY of character was reinforced by the experience of a world which itself appeared to be inner-directed. Adam Smith and other late eighteenth-century thinkers saw society as operating "gyroscopically" in a beneficent direction. In general the men who established the industrial revolution in England and America were as unaware of their countries' good luck[1] as of the forces shaping their own characters. A world that seemed to be running on schedule was, of course, an illusion.

A number of great thinkers during this period did not, however, share the widespread optimism of the rising inner-directed middle class.[2] Of these, Malthus is one of the most interesting. He insisted on the entirely temporary quality of any victory over nature, and, contrary to Condorcet, Godwin, and other progressive thinkers, warned that the natural bounty of the earth—now, so it seemed, thoroughly explored—stood in danger of being turned into parsimony by the "natural" growth of population. Yet even Malthus was, by modern standards, optimistic; for he saw the world, not as a bad joke on man, but as a meaningful obstacle race designed to develop man's capacities for rational self-restraint. In our terminology, though not of course in his, he advised people to become inner-directed as the sole means of keeping population in line with subsistence: that is, he advised them to plan ahead, to work hard, and to postpone marriage —thus accumulating wealth without accumulating children. Thus, in

---

1. Karl Polanyi well describes in *The Great Transformation* the series of happy accidents that made liberal capitalism work in the period before 1914.

2. Most of these thinkers—Brooks Adams, for example, in America—were isolated men. Matters stand very differently today, when the prophets of despair are more popular.

effect, he proposed a way out of nature's trap by characterological change.[3]

We can see now, with the advantage of hindsight, that such a program never really had much chance of success. Inner-direction was never very widespread, but rather represented the ideal model toward which people strove. We have evidence that many people of that era tried desperately to conduct themselves in the approved inner-directed way, but were unable to conform. Thus, in Vermont of the eighteenth and nineteenth centuries many more people started diaries and account books—perfect symbols of inner-direction of which Malthus would have approved—than kept them up. Such people must have felt helpless in their efforts at self-mastery, particularly since they took as models those pre-eminent men, from George Washington to Andrew Carnegie, who then stood unshaken by disciples of Marx and Freud. Thus, in a very special sense, the feelings of potency were monopolized by those whose inner-direction was relatively stable and successful in the public mind, while a reservoir of hidden impotence existed. Yet for many of the unsuccessful, failure never seemed quite final, and so long as the future beckoned, or the belief in grace persisted, helplessness could be staved off.

§ III

INDIVIDUAL HELPLESSNESS and collective power play leapfrog with each other throughout history. Today, the helplessness foreseen by a few thinkers, and sensed even in the earlier age of frontiers by many who failed, has become the common attribute of the mass of men. We turn now to discuss some of the factors responsible for this development: in economic and political life, in methods of child-rearing, and in their consequences for character structure.

When immigration from Europe was cut off in 1924, a great symbol of hope in the Western world was destroyed. The "no help wanted" sign had been posted on the American frontier in 1890, but it was now hung out along our borders for all to see. Today, in the advanced industrial countries, there is only one frontier left—that of consumption—and this calls for very different types of talent and character.

The inner-directed type fitted the conditions of an essentially open capitalism, which rewarded ability to envisage new possibilities

---

3. Malthus' non-ecclesiastic successors substituted birth-control for chastity—which required less, but still something, in the way of character change. Actually, as far as food supply goes, Godwin, with his high hopes for technological change in agriculture, has turned out to be the better prophet. But, to complete the irony of the account, only for those industrialized countries where inner-direction—and Malthusian attitudes toward life—actually made great strides!

for production, and zeal to realize those possibilities. To a degree, this is still the case. Nevertheless, it would seem that, on the whole, contemporary society, especially in America, no longer requires and rewards the old enterprise and the old zeal. This does not mean that the economic system itself is slowing down: total production may continue to rise; but it can be achieved by institutionalizing technological and organizational advance, for instance in research departments, management counsel, and corporate planning staffs. The invention and adoption of new improvements can be routinized, built into the system, so to speak, rather than into the men who run the system. Therefore, the energies of management turn to industrial and public relations, to oiling the frictions not of machines but of men.

Likewise, with the growth of monopolistic competition, the way to get ahead is not so much to make a better mousetrap but rather to package an old mousetrap in a new way, and then to sell it by selling oneself first. People feel they must be able to adapt themselves to other people, both to manipulate them and to be manipulated by them. This requires the ability to manipulate oneself, to become "a good package," to use a phrase current among personnel men. These pressures are, of course, not confined to business, but operate also in the professions, in government, and in academic life.

As work becomes less meaningful and intense, however, leisure grows and men who are discarded as workers are cultivated in the one role that still matters, that of consumer. This is not an easy role, and people become almost as preoccupied with getting the "best buys" as they once were with finding their proper "calling" in the production economy. They turn, then, to the mass media of communication for advice in how to consume; at the same time, these media help make them anxious lest they fail in the role of consumer. I speak here not merely of "keeping up with the Joneses"—this is part of an older pattern—but rather of the much more unsettling fear of missing those leisure-time experiences, including sex, love, art, friendship, food, travel, which people have been induced to feel they should have.

These changes in the nature of work and leisure have made themselves felt most strongly among the middle classes of the American big cities in the last twenty-five years or so. It is here that the character type that I call other-directed appears to be concentrated, a type whose source of direction is externalized. The clear goals and generalized judgments of the inner-directed types are not implanted in the other-directed person in childhood. Rather, he is taught, vaguely, to do the "best possible" in any given situation. As soon as he can play with other children, he is made sensitive to the judgments of this play group, looking to it for approval and direction as to what is best. Parents and other adults come to value the child in terms of his ability to live up to the group's expectations and to wrest popularity from it.

The adult never loses this dependence, but continues to live psychologically oriented to his contemporaries—to what sociologists call his "peer group." Of course, it matters very much who these others are: whether they are his immediate circle of the moment, or a higher circle he aspires to, or the anonymous circles of whose doings he learns from the mass media of communication.[4] But the great psychological difference from inner-direction is that this modern type needs open approval and guidance from contemporaries. This new need for approval goes well beyond the human and opportunistic reasons that lead people in any age to care very much what others think of them. People in general want and need to be liked, but it is only the other-directed character type that makes others its chief source of direction and its chief area of sensitivity and concern.

These differences in the source looked to for direction lead to different modes of conformity in the two types. The inner-directed person will ordinarily have had an early choice made for him among the several available destinies of the middle-class child. What holds him on course is that he has internalized from his elders certain general aims and drives—the drive to work hard, or to save money, or to strive for rectitude or for fame. His conformity results from the fact that similar drives have been instilled into others of his social class. As against this, the other-directed person grows up in a much more amorphous social system, where alternative destinations cannot be clearly chosen at an early age. The "best possible" in a particular situation must always be learned from the others in that situation. His conformity to the others is thus not one of generalized drives, but of details—the minutiae of taste or speech or emotion which are momentarily "best." Hence, he internalizes neither detailed habits nor generalized drives, but instead an awareness of and preoccupation with the *process* of securing direction from others.

We can find exemplars of the other-directed character in leisured urban circles of the past, where the preoccupations were those of consumption, not production, and where status depended on the opinion of influential others. What is new is the spread of such an out-

---

4. These are some of the "anonymous authorities" of whom Erich Fromm has written in *Escape from Freedom* and *Man for Himself*.

look over large sectors of a middle class that was once inner-directed. Elements of this outlook, moreover, have now filtered down in America to many members of the lower-middle class.

It is my tentative conclusion that the feeling of helplessness of modern man results from both the vastly enhanced power of the social group and the incorporation of its authority into his very character. And the point at issue is not that the other-directed character is more opportunistic than the inner-directed—if anything, the contrary is true. Rather, the point is that the individual is psychologically dependent on others for clues to the meaning of life. He thus fails to resist authority or fears to exercise freedom of choice even where he might safely do so.

An illustration may clarify my meaning. I have sometimes asked university students why they come to class so regularly day after day, why they do not—as they are technically free to do—take two or three weeks off to do anything they like on their own. The students have answered that they must come to class or otherwise they will flunk, though the fact is that many students get ahead when they finally do break through the routines. It has become apparent that the students cling to such "rational" explanations because, in their feeling of helplessness, freedom is too much of a threat. They fail to see those loopholes of which they could take advantage for their own personal development; they feel safer if they are obeying an authoritative ritual in sympathetic company. Their attendance at class has much the same meaning as the Pueblo Indian's rain-making dance, only the student has less confidence that his "prayer" will be heard. For he has left "home" for good, and all of modern thought teaches him too much for comfort and too little for help.

We can, of course, find more drastic illustrations of the loss of individual self-reliance by looking to the field of political theory and practice. We may, for instance, compare the attitude which Hobbes held toward state power in the seventeenth century with the attitude of some nineteenth and twentieth century advocates of tyranny. Hobbes, in the *Leviathan*, held that the only intelligent recourse of the individual in a world of power was to surrender to it and to form with his fellows an all-powerful state that could repress internal violence and resist external foes. Above all an individualist, Hobbes saw the state as a necessary evil, useful only so long as it delivered physical security, but without any *ideological* claims. He wrote that a state was entitled to obedience only so far as its strong arm reached, but he did not think kings ruled by divine right nor would he have been deceived today by the equivalent superstition of nationalism. Hobbes believed people needed a strong state as a physical umbrella, not as a psychic altar. For example, he defended the individual's privilege against self-incrimination: the state, he wrote, had every right to kill a subject, with or without reason, if it had the power; but it could not expect cooperation from the victim, who had every right to resist. In his whole outlook, Hobbes spoke for the individual, whose interests, he felt, could be protected in a time of anarchy only by strong, tyrannical rule.

In the last hundred years, many thinkers have echoed Hobbes' desire for a strong, centralized state. But until very recent years their concern has been primarily with an attempt to satisfy psychological cravings—their own or those of the masses—for the sake of unity and emotional cohesion. Comte, for instance, desired a secular state that would match the medieval Church in evoking men's devotion. Freud, who resembles Hobbes in his view of man's aggressiveness, believed this aggressiveness could not be curbed by appeals to self-interest, but only by providing leaders with whom and through whom men might establish emotional ties. (See his *Group Psychology and the Analysis of the Ego*.)

In general—this is not true of Freud—modern reactionary thinkers begin with the society and not, like Hobbes, with the individual. Their fastidious distaste for disunity and "chaos"—their uneasiness in the open rough-and-tumble of democratic politics and capitalist economics—leads them to a blind worship of group solidarity and the "leader." Modern totalitarianism, however, exploits these psychological attitudes and fosters an internal as well as international anarchy far worse than that which plagued Hobbes. Only on the surface can a totalitarian movement provide solidarity and emotional cohesion even for its own following. The struggle for power goes on inside the movement, and the reactionary thinkers who abetted the seizure of power are among the first to become disillusioned—and dispensable.

During the last war, the British and Americans captured a number of Russians who had been taken prisoner by the Nazis. Most of these men were quite sure that they would be killed if they returned to Russia. This is not surprising, but what was striking to us was their apparent lack of indignation at the prospect. Some simply took it for granted; others even justified it. One man, a schoolteacher, said that Stalin would be entirely justified in killing him or anyone else who had been in the West, for such a person could never again be completely satisfied in Russia. The *Leviathan* of Hobbes stands outside the individual and tells him to join, or else suffer the consequences; but these Russians carried *Leviathan* inside them.

This modern nationalism has a very different psychological mean-

ing from that of the businesslike nationalism of Hobbes. It also differs
from the more progressive nationalisms of the pre-totalitarian era,
which date from a time when the state did not exist, or was weak,
and had to be created by individual effort. *Modern* nationalism, on
the other hand, insists on emotional submission to a power that is
already armed with unbeatable military force and with immense economic and propaganda powers. Shortly before his death, Largo Cabal-
lero, former Republican premier of Spain, said:

I would like to see every bricklayer go to work with his rifle slung on
his shoulder. Then I know that nothing could exist in Spain except the
will of the great mass of Spaniards.

For us, in "the years of the modern," the statement has an archaic
ring. We happen to live at a moment when, as Hannah Arendt has
pointed out, the state is so overwhelming that even martyrdom—the last
despairing appeal of the individual human spirit against the group—
is no longer possible.

Americans may feel that all this does not apply to them, but only
to the totalitarian states. The latter, to be sure, are extreme instances,
but Americans are perhaps not sufficiently aware of the current changes
in the quality of their own nationalism. For many people, the program of their lives is determined by fear of a fifth column, and what
the Russians or their allies do is an urgent and an all-embracing preoccupation. To such persons there is little identification with America
in terms of positive aims, but rather a neurotic clinging to a shadow-
war in which our national Superman is engaged.

We may conclude that while the state, through technological and
organizational change, has become immensely powerful, the individual, through characterological change, has become less capable of
psychological resistance to his contemporaries. Modern man feels
helpless, and justifies this feeling by looking at the frightening world
around him. Like a hypochondriac, he uses the undeniable threat of
real danger to rationalize an even greater anxiety than a balanced view
might warrant. During the long Victorian period, people assumed as
the norm of life an existence in which a few external dangers, such
as germs and foreigners, would soon be vanquished; possibly our
present hypochondria comes in part from learning the falseness of
that assumption. People of a different history have often lived comfortably in the face of impending misery.

§ IV

LET US EXAMINE several further factors that have robbed the middle-
class individual of his defenses against the pressure of the group. We
shall deal in somewhat more detail with changes in the nature of

private property, of work, and of leisure, all of which at one time functioned as defenses.

In the feudal era, the individual was attached to property, largely land, by feudal and family ties. The breakdown of feudalism meant helplessness for many peasants, who were thrown off the land; but for the middle class the result was a gradual gain in consciousness of strength. A new type of relationship between persons and property developed: the person was no longer attached to property, but attached property to himself by his own energetic actions. Property, including land, became freely alienable; at the same time, it was felt to be an individual, not a family, possession. And property was satisfying, substantial—an extended part of the self. Inside the shell of his possessions, the inner-directed person could resist psychological invasion.

Today, however, property is not much of a defense. Taxes and other state activities, inflation and the panicky desire for liquid assets, have made it factually friable. Moreover, the fears of property-holders outrun the actual dangers. Thus, even powerful groups in America feel more frightened of Communism than its actual power warrants. Property no longer represents the old security for those who hold it, and the fear that it may vanish any day makes it as much a source of anxiety as of strength. The rich no longer dare flaunt wealth, but tread softly, guided by considerations of "public relations." Wealthy students often act as if ashamed of their wealth; I have sometimes been tempted to point out that the rich are a minority and have rights, too.

The change in the meaning of work is even plainer. For the inner-directed person, work seemed self-justifying: the only problem was to find the work to which one felt called. As we have seen, the age of expanding frontiers provided the individual with an inexhaustible list of tasks. Work, like property, moreover, was considered a mode of relating oneself to physical objects, and only indirectly to people. Indeed, the work-hungry inner-directed types of this period sometimes found that they were cut off from family and friends, and often from humanity in general, by their assiduity and diligence. And work, like property, was a defense against psychological invasion, a "do not disturb" sign guarding the industrious man of the middle class.

Today the meaning of work is a very different one, psychologically, though in many professions and industries the older modes still persist. To an increasing degree, the self is no longer defined by its productive accomplishments but by its role in a "friendship" system. As the isolate or rate-buster is punished and excluded from the work force in the shop, so the lone wolf is weeded out of management; up-to-date personnel men use deep-probing psychological tests to eliminate applicants, whatever their other gifts, who lack the other-directed personality needed for the job.

To be sure, out of anxiety, a lingering asceticism, and a need for an impressive agenda, the professional and business men and women of the big cities continue to work hard, or more accurately, to spend long hours in the company of their fellow "antagonistic cooperators": "work" is seen as a network of personal relationships that must be constantly watched and oiled. Increasingly, both work and leisure call on the same sort of skills—sociability, sensitivity to others' feelings and wants, and the exercise of taste-preferences freed from direct considerations of economic advantage. Work in this case has a certain unreality for people, since it has almost floated free from any connection with technical crafts. The latter have been built into machines, or can be easily taught; but people must still go to the office and find ways of keeping, or at least looking, busy. Thus in many circles work and leisure are no longer clearly distinguished—as we can see by observing a luncheon or a game of golf among competitors.

The feeling of powerlessness of the other-directed character is, then, the result in part of the lack of genuine commitment to work. His life is not engaged in a direct struggle for mastery over himself and nature; he has no long-term goals since the goals must constantly be changed. At the same time, he is in competition with others for the very values they tell him are worth pursuing; in a circular process, one of these values is the approval of the competing group itself. Hence, he is apt to repress overt competitiveness both out of anxiety to be liked and out of fear of retaliation. In this situation, he is likely to lose interest in the work itself. With loss of interest, he may even find himself little more than a dilettante, not quite sure that he is really able to accomplish anything.

From this it follows that this type of other-directed person is not able to judge the work of others—for one thing, he is no longer sufficiently interested in work as such. He must constantly depend on specialists and experts whom he cannot evaluate with any assurance. That dependence is an inevitable and indeed a valuable fruit of the division of labor in modern society; but the inability even to dare to pass personal judgment is a defect rooted in the character of the other-directed person.

When we turn from the sphere of work to the sphere of leisure, we see again that roles in which the individual could once find refuge from and defense against the group have become stylized roles, played according to the mandates and under the very eyes of the group. The individual in the age of inner-direction had little leisure; often he was so work-driven he could not even use the leisure given him. On occasion, however, he could escape from the pressures and strains of the workaday world into a private hobby or into the resources of culture, either high-brow or popular. In either case, the stream of entertainment and communication was intermittent; to come into contact with it required effort. Leisure, therefore, by its very scarcity, provided a change of pace and role. Moreover, beyond these actual leisure roles stood a group of fantasy roles—roles of social ascent, of rebellion against work and inhibition, dreams of world-shaking achievement; the individual was protected against invasion at least of his right to these dreams.

Today, leisure is seldom enjoyed in solitude, nor is it often used for unequivocal escape. Hobbies of the older craft type seem to have declined, and a baseball game is perhaps the only performance where the mass audience can still judge competence. The torrent of words and images from radio, the movies, and the comics begins to pour on the child even before he can toddle; he starts very early to learn his lifelong role of consumer. The quantity of messages impinging on the child becomes increasingly "realistic"; instead of "Just-So Stories" and fairy tales, children are given "here and now" stories of real life, and escape into imaginative fantasy is therefore held at a minimum.

Likewise, movies, fiction, and radio for adults increasingly deal with "here and now" problems: how to handle one's relations with children, with the opposite sex, with office colleagues away from the office. Story writers for the better woman's magazines are instructed to deal with the intimate problems faced by the readers, and soap opera is one long game of Going to Jerusalem: when one problem sits down, another is left standing. Indeed, to put it paradoxically, there is no "escape" from leisure. Wherever one turns, in work or in popular culture, one is faced by his peers and the problems they present, including the pressure they put on one to "have fun." A kind of ascetic selflessness rules much of the greatly expanded leisure of the other-directed person: selflessness disguised by the craving for comfort, fun, and effortlessness, but ascetic nonetheless in its tense use of leisure for preparing oneself to meet the expectations of others.

Thus, the newly reached horizons of leisure and consumption made possible by our economic abundance have not been as exhilarating for the individual as the realized horizons of work and production proved to be for many in the age of expanding frontiers. On the

frontiers of consumption, limitless in quality and almost equally so
in quantity, men stand anxiously, haunted by the fear of missing some
consumption-experience which they are supposed to have enjoyed.
Young men and women today, for instance, in some urban middle-
class circles, often feel they must walk a tightrope in their sex lives:
they must have "experiences," yet they must not become involved
emotionally on any deep level of human tenderness and intimacy.
And the while they are worried lest they are incapable of loving
anyone. The word of the "wise" to the young—"don't get involved"
—has changed its meaning in a generation. Once it meant: don't get,
or get someone, pregnant; don't run afoul of the law; don't get in
the newspapers. Today the injunction is more deeply psychological;
it seeks to control, not the overt experience, but its emotional interpretation in terms of smooth, unruffled manipulation of the self. This
transformation is characteristic of the change from inner-direction,
with its clear and generalized mandates, to other-direction, with its
emphasis on the process of receiving from others very detailed stage
directions in the work-play of life.

To sum up, the inner-directed person had a sense of power as
he faced the group because of his relationship to property, to work,
and to leisure; and because both he and the group accepted certain
specific rights that encouraged any individual to be himself. Such
persons often became men of substance and men of the world—they
made the world *theirs*. If we look at the portraits of the more emi-
nent men in a centuries-long gallery stretching from Holbein to
John Singer Sargent, we can see that they were indeed solid citizens. Today the solid citizen has given way to the "solid sender," the
"good Joe," not solid enough to risk offending anyone and afraid of
disobeying the subtle and impermeable injunctions of the contemporary peer group to whom he looks for approval. He is a sender and
receiver of messages in a network of personal ties which, unlike the
personal ties of a folk society, neither warm nor protect him.

On the surface, it might appear that the individual today feels
powerless because he finds no protection from the hazards of war
and depression. He feels weak because he has no control over these
vast matters that are decisive for him; to avert war or internal catas-
trophe he cannot even turn to a ritual. Yet, granting these objective
reasons for anxiety and weakness, we must nevertheless ask, why is
war so likely, when few people want it? I suggest that one reason—
certainly not the only one!—is simply that great numbers of people
do not in fact enjoy life enough. They are not passionately attached
to their lives, but rather cling to them. The very need for direction
that is implied in our phrases of inner-direction and other-direction

signifies that one has turned over one's life to others in exchange for an agenda, a program for getting through the day.

To be sure, the abdication is not complete. But the fact remains that the person who is not autonomous loses much of the joy that comes through strength—through the effort to live one's life, not necessarily heroically, but, come what may, in full commitment to it. Modern life, for many people, is full of tense and anxious relationships to people, to production and consumption; therefore, these people are prepared to resign themselves to war which does, after all, promise certain compensations in group companionship and shared meanings.

Thus, we have come full circle from Hobbes' view of man. For him, people risked war because they were selfish individualists, and he reasoned with them that they were better off in the *Leviathan*. Modern man does not want to risk war, but allows it to come with astonishingly little protest because, fundamentally, he is not an individualist. It is tractable men who operate the intractable institutions that now precipitate war, and when it comes, it is they who conduct it.

§ V

I DO NOT MEAN to imply that our society "produces" other-directed people because such people are in demand in an increasingly monopolistic, managerial economy. The relations between character and society are not that simple. Moreover, neither character nor society changes all at once. But it would take us too far afield to trace the many formative agencies in the still far-from-complete shift from inner-direction to other-direction in the middle classes.

Furthermore, I must guard against the implication that I think inner-direction is a way of life preferable to other-direction. Each type has its virtues and its vices: the inner-directed person tends to be rigid and intolerant of others; the other-directed person, in turn, is likely to be flexible and sensitive to others. Neither type is altogether comfortable in the world. But in different ways each finds the discomforts it psychologically needs in order, paradoxically, to feel comfortable. The inner-directed person finds the struggle to master himself and the environment quite appropriate; he feels comfortable climbing uphill. The other-directed person finds equally appropriate the malaise that he shares with many others. Engrossed in the activities that the culture provides, he can remain relatively unconscious of his anxiety and tonelessness. Moreover, the character type must always be judged in context. Many persons who are inner-directed and who, in an earlier age, would have gone through life in relative peace, today find themselves indignant at a big-city world in which they have not felt at home. Other-directed persons also may not feel at home, but home never had the same meaning for them. It would appear to the envious inner-directed observer, that the other-directed manage their lives better in a mass society. Conversely, the other-directed may envy the seeming firmness of the inner-directed, and look longingly back on the security of nineteenth-century society, while failing to see that firmness was often merely stubbornness and security merely ignorance.

§ VI

WHAT I HAVE SAID about the loss of the individual's defenses is recognized by many thinkers who, however, feel that through voluntary associations people can attain security analogous to that which family and clan provided in the era of primary ties, and for which work and property made additional provision in the days of expanding frontiers. They see labor unions as giving a feeling of solidarity to the working class, and even to increasing numbers of white-collar employees; they see racial minorities protected by their defense organizations, and farmers by their cooperatives; they see "group belongingness," in some sort of informal association, available to all but the most depressed. The advocacy of this as the chief remedy for the loneliness of the individual is an admission of his weakness. But it is more than that. It bolsters another set of power-combinations, only slightly democratized by individual participation. And it adds to the pressure on the individual to *join*, to submerge himself in the group—any group—and to lower still further not only his feeling that he can, but that he has a right, to stand on his own.

Conceivably, these associations in the future will succeed in strengthening the individual's feeling of his own powers by providing him with defenses, political, economic, and psychological, and by encouraging him to gain, outside his work, a variety of skills, encounters, and experiences. In the meantime, however, with the balance between helplessness and power tipped in favor of the former, the "voluntary" associations are not voluntary enough to do this job.

I turn now to examine another voluntary association, that between the sexes, whose nature, in our age as in any age, provides a profound clue to the state of subjective feelings of power and helplessness. In this context, the rapid change I discern in the denigration by American women of their own sex seems ominous. Eighty years ago, John Stuart Mill (turning to a theme touched on by Condorcet's *On the Admission of Women to the Rights of Citizenship*) wrote *The Subjection of Women* in order to show how attitudes toward this "minority" poisoned all social life; how both men and women suffered from the power-relations that prevailed between them; and how women's potentialities, even more than those of men, were crushed by social pressure. He observed that "the greater part of what women write about women is mere sycophancy to men." But he was gentle with women for he added, "no enslaved class ever asked for complete liberty at once. . . ."

In the intervening period, women did not attain "complete liberty," but they came a long way toward equality with men. In the years after 1890 and until recently, American young women of the middle class insisted on sharing with men the tasks and excitements of civilization. Today there is some evidence that many women of this class have retreated; they have again become enemies of emancipation of their sex; as the weaker power, they judge each other through the eyes of men.

Women today feel under almost as great a pressure to get married as did their pre-emancipation ancestors. In a certain way, they are under greater pressure, since all sorts of psychological aspersions are cast at them if they stay single too long.[5]

Perhaps all this means simply that women have won the battle of emancipation and can relax. I am inclined, however, to think that there is an increasing submissiveness of women to what men want of them, and to the world as men have largely made it. I interpret this, in part, as testimony to the fact that men today are far too anxious, too lacking in psychological defenses against each other, to tolerate critically-minded women. The women they want must be intelligent enough to flatter their vanity but not to challenge their prerogatives as men. Men once complained to their mistresses that their wives did not understand them; now they would complain if they did. For in their own competitive orientation to the world, men would interpret understanding from the side of women as still another, and underhanded, form of competition. This is partly because, since Mill's day, the economic and social power of women has grown; they can no longer be so obviously kept in their places. Hence their gifts, their critical powers, can no longer be patronized by powerful men, but must be subtly destroyed by anxious ones and their willing allies among the women themselves. Men and women, in their weakness, act like those minorities who throughout history have kept each other in subjection in the face of an oppressive power.[6]

---

5. Indeed, men, too, feel under pressure to get married early—among other reasons, lest they be thought homosexual.

6. Something of the same transformation has occurred in the relation between parents and children. Even as men are worried lest they might not pass the test with women, so parents are afraid that their children will not approve of them— a problem that would hardly have troubled the person of inner-directed char-

In sum, men and women eye each other not as allies, but, at best, as antagonistic cooperators. In their roles as parents, they are uncertain of their children and whether they will be liked by them; in turn, this anxiety is absorbed by the children. In earlier epochs of history, events outside the home were interpreted, often somewhat narrowly, through the perspective of family needs and family morality. Today, the situation is reversed, and the home must be adjusted to the values of the outside. As with the state, "domestic policy" and "foreign policy" are interdependent, and the conflicts and strains of each sphere add to weakness in the other.

We come, then, to a conclusion that would seem paradoxical: certain groups in society have grown weaker, but others have not gained in strength at their expense; rather, weakness has engendered weakness. And the state, the beneficiary of individual weakness, is ruled by men who are themselves no less weak than the rest. Even the dictators and their henchmen only seem strong under the imagery of modern propaganda. While the savage believes he will gain in potency by drinking the blood or shrinking the head of his enemy, in the modern world no individual gains in strength of character from the weakness of his fellows.

§ VII

NEVERTHELESS, even under modern conditions, and out of the very matrix of other-directed modes of conformity, some people strive toward an autonomous character. An autonomous person has no compulsive need to follow the other-direction of his culture and milieu— and no compulsive need to flout it, either. We know almost nothing about the factors that make for such positive results; it is easier to understand the sick than to understand why some stay well. It hardly helps to repeat that man's helplessness is the condition for his every advance, because this generalization tells us too little about individual cases. However, it seems that the helplessness of modern man in a world of power has been one element in the genesis of some of the extraordinary human achievements of our age. Some of these achievements are the physical and literary productions of men's hands and

---

acter. While parents appear to be terribly concerned to give their children approval—as they are told by all the textbooks to do—this disguises the parents' own dependence on being approved of by the children, who stand, as Margaret Mead has noted, for the New, for Youth, for the American Way—or, as I might say, for better other-direction. Moreover, parents assume the role of advisors and managers of their children's competitive struggles. This new family constellation is in fact one of the changes that may partly account for the formation of the other-directed character.

minds, but other achievements lie in the internal "productions" of men—their characters; it is of these that I speak here.

There were autonomous people of course, in the era of inner-direction, but they were made of sterner stuff; the barriers they encountered were the classic ones: family, religion, poverty. On the other hand, the person who seeks autonomy today in the upper socio-economic levels of the Western democracies is not faced with the barriers that normally restricted him in the past. The coercions against his independence are frequently invisible. An autonomous person of the middle class must work constantly to detach himself from shadowy entanglements with his culture—so difficult to break with because its demands appear so "reasonable," so trivial.

For my study of autonomy, I have drawn freely on Erich Fromm's concept of the "productive orientation" in *Man for Himself*. Fromm shows the orientation of a type of character that can relate itself to people through love, and to objects and the world generally through the creative gift. The struggle for a productive orientation becomes exigent at the very moment in history when solution of the problem of production itself, in the technical sense, is in sight.

All human beings, even the most productive, the most autonomous, are fated, in a sense, to die the death of Ivan Ilyitch, in Tolstoy's "The Death of Ivan Ilyitch," who becomes aware only on his death-bed of his underlived life and his unused potentialities for autonomy. All of us realize only a fraction of our potentialities. Always a matter of degree, always blended with residues of inner-direction or other-direction, autonomy is a process, not an achievement. Indeed, we may distinguish the autonomous by the fact that his character is never a finished product, but always a lifelong growth.

I speak of autonomy as an aspect of character structure, and not in terms of independence of overt behavior. The autonomous person may or may not conform in his behavior to the power-requirements and conventions of society; he can choose whether to conform or not. (The Bohemians and rebels are not usually autonomous; on the contrary, they are zealously tuned in to the signals of a defiant group that finds the meaning of life in a compulsive non-conformity to the majority group.) Yet the separation of "freedom in behavior" from "autonomy in character" cannot be complete. Autonomy requires self-awareness about the fact of choice, about possible ways of living. The autonomous person of today exists precisely because we have reached an awareness of the problem of choice that was not required among the Pueblos, or, for the most part, in the Middle Ages, or even in the period after the Reformation, when the concepts of God's will and of duty confined choice for many within fairly narrow bounds.

The very fluidity of modern democratic social systems, that, for the mass of people, results in anxiety and "escape from freedom," forces those who would become autonomous to find their own way. They must "choose themselves," in Sartre's phrase, out of their very alienation from traditional ties and inner-directed defenses which inhibited true choice in the past. However, I think Sartre mistaken in his Kantian notion that men can choose themselves under totalitarian conditions. If most of the choices that matter are made for us by the social system, even if it is in appearance a democratic system, then our sense of freedom also will atrophy: most people need the opportunity for some freedom of behavior if they are to develop and confirm their autonomy of character. Nevertheless, the rare autonomous character we have been describing, the man of high, almost precarious, quality, must arise from that aloneness, that helplessness of modern man, that would overwhelm a lesser person. It is in this quality, and in the mode of life he is groping to achieve, that he has made a contribution to living in a somewhat unstructured world. Often, in vanity, we judge our own era as the most advanced or the most retrograde, yet the type of perspective on the world and the self that thousands of people have today was probably matched in the past by only a few.

The people I speak of live under urbanized conditions in every land, but they are world citizens in thought and feeling. Sensitive to wide perspectives of time and space, they have largely transcended prejudices of race or time or class. Their guides are diverse, and they feel empathy and solidarity with their colleagues across all national boundaries. There have been cosmopolitans before, but their horizons were limited by want of knowledge, and their view of man was necessarily abstract. There have been internationalists before, but they have been restricted by class and region. The contemporary autonomous person has all the sensitivity to others of the other-directed type: he needs some interpersonal warmth, and close friends mean much to him; but he does not have an irrational craving for indiscriminate approval.

In one relationship, that between the sexes, the men and women who are striving for autonomy are seeking an equality that takes account of differences, an equality of which Mill would have approved. Here women are not the subtle slaves of men, nor do they flatter them as the feminists did by seeking to adopt men's particular privileges and problems. Though we have as yet to attain a new model of marriage, grounded neither in contract nor in sex alone but in mutual growth towards autonomy, we see new sets of roles developed by people who have achieved relationships to which both partners contribute from their productive gifts. It is unlikely, however, that beyond such families, and small groups of friends or colleagues, there exist any sizeable institutions or organizations predominantly composed of autonomous folk. It is hard to imagine an autonomous society coming into being now, even on a small scale, or perhaps especially on a small scale.[7]

The fact is, moreover, that the autonomous are hardly aware of others like themselves. Those who are to some degree autonomous may not always reveal themselves as such, preferring to conform overtly out of conscious choice. As a result, the potentially autonomous often do not discover each other, though they would in that very process strengthen and defend their own autonomy.

Indeed, the potentially autonomous person tends to bewail as a tragedy his isolation from the masses and from power. He neglects the opportunity of his lot—an opportunity to develop his individuality and its fruits in art and character. Hence he wishes he could undergo a metamorphosis and rid himself of the problem of choice, indeed of his very autonomous strivings; he wishes he were like the others—whose adjustment he often overemphasizes—thus revealing his own other-directed components. By these very tendencies to betray himself and his partially achieved autonomy, he becomes weaker and less autonomous.

The autonomous few can do little enough to reduce the strength of atom bombs and of the hands that now hold them, but some can at least defend their own and others' individuality, and pioneer in various ways of living autonomously. They will enjoy this pioneering to a degree, though it will be held against them by the envious and frightened ones who have abandoned the effort toward autonomy.

If these conjectures are accurate, then it follows that, by a process of unconscious polarization which is going on in society, a few people are becoming more self-consciously autonomous than before, while many others are losing their social and characterological defenses against the group. The latter, though politically strong, are psychically weak, and the autonomous minority, by its very existence, threatens the whole shaky mode of adaptation of the majority.

Nevertheless, joy in life has its own dynamic. I have said that people today are not sufficiently attached to life. We have traced this to their other-directed character structure, and this in turn to large-

---

7. Mary McCarthy describes with humor and insight the fate of an imaginary enclave of intellectuals seeking autonomy in her novel *The Oasis*.

scale social changes. Yet character structure is not completely fixed for the individual, so long as life lasts, or for the group. Men have some control over the fate by which their characters are made. By showing how life can be lived with vitality and happiness even in a time of troubles, the autonomous people can become a social force, indeed a "saving remnant." By converting present helplessness into a condition of advance, they lay the groundwork for a new society, though, like Condorcet, they may not live to see it.

III.

MARGINALITY, MINORITIES, AND FREEDOM

IN THIS SECTION the theme of individualism is viewed from a perspective slightly different from that of the preceding one. Yet the placing of individual essays in one or in the other section is somewhat arbitrary. Thus, in "The Ethics of We Happy Few" I examined some consequences for the intellectuals of their minority status, while in the first essay herein, "Some Observations on Intellectual Freedom," I probe some of the ways in which intellectuals, in fighting for freedom against McCarthyism, can endanger their individuality in a "united front" interpretation of the contemporary scene. Likewise, in "A Philosophy for 'Minority' Living" in the preceding section I used the situation of American Jews to illustrate my treatment of the alternatives open to the lone individual, while in "The 'Militant' Fight against Anti-Semitism" I discuss how the Jewish minority, in response both to Hitler and to the generic problems of ethnic newcomers to America, has tended (like the intellectuals) to embrace victim-psychology and to adopt its enemies' tactics in trying to censor hostile communications, or those believed to be such.

The political pressures of intellectuals upon each other with which my article on intellectual freedom deals are, however, relatively mild in comparison with the pressures American Jews have lately put upon each other to support Israel and the various other idols of the Jewish party line. "The 'Militant' Fight against Anti-Semitism" was delivered as an after-dinner speech to a meeting (in April, 1949) of the National Community Relations Advisory Council, a coordinating group of Jewish agencies concerned with defense, propaganda, and race relations at national and local levels.

I return to the Jews as a source of illustrative material in the first of the two articles on "Marginality"; the life of the Negro, Richard Wright, furnishes illustration for the second. Both were given as lectures, and here again something should be said about the audiences in order to indicate context. "Some Observations Concerning Marginality" was presented to graduate students in an introductory course at the University of Chicago on "Society, Culture, and the Individual"—at the time, they were reading excerpts from Robert Park's *Race and Culture*; more important, they were reading anthropological writings critical of modern urban society in comparison with the "folk society"—of course, they would hardly need to read anything so specialized to encounter a very widespread nostalgia for preliterate times. This is one reason for my emphasis in the lecture on certain positive aspects of marginality and for my all too brief critique of current ideals of the "integrated" personality and of the "integrated" culture which provides no discontinuities in the life-cycle of its members.

The second article, "Marginality, Conformity, and Insight," carries both these matters a bit further, though it is far from constituting a satisfactory critique of contemporary personality ideals. It was first presented as the Billings Lecture at Smith College. Needless to say, some remarks in a lecture (and both of these on marginality were recorded, and retain much of their oral chattiness and meandering) can only begin discussion of such exigently argued issues.

Whether in these papers I deal with women, Negroes, Jews, intellectuals, or such unorganized minorities as the physiologically overprivileged or underprivileged, my concern is continuously with the individual. It is his freedom, rather than the freedom of the group as a whole, to which I address myself; and again I write in context, for I know that many are preoccupied with Negro rights against whites, or women's rights against men, and so on, whereas I speak for the individual against, if need be, the very group that protects him. And this brings us back to the discussion, in "The Saving Remnant," of whether the voluntary associations which have done so much for a pluralistic freedom in America, so much to establish what Galbraith terms "countervailing power," are as voluntary as they appear to be, when looked at from within their constituencies. Negroes who want to "resign from the race" are violently criticized as self-haters, but Negroes who can't admit having such a wish may be as badly off as self-deceivers. Insight, it seems to me, and with it a certain measure of freedom, comes when one can face and question one's marginalities rather than simply accept them as given by the order of nature or of the group to which one "belongs."

7. Some Observations on Intellectual Freedom

> And if the ice was really to be broken, laughter and jest must be introduced into the consideration of the matter. In politics or business it would be obvious enough that one could not achieve a realistic view of what was happening if one was debarred from discussing principles or acts save in terms of respectful solemnity. Fun and ridicule must be allowed to play their part in the analysis of the motives or characters or doings of the principal actors; otherwise political discussion would remain at an unrealistic level, and those who discussed them would have a sense of servitude.
> —R. F. Harrod, *The Life of John Maynard Keynes*

VAGUE AND HORTATORY ARTICLES and speeches about the crisis of our age are a sign of the "respectful solemnity" we ethnocentrically reserve for *our* problems. I myself have sinned by entitling a monograph "Civil Liberties in a Period of Transition," falling too uncritically in with the comfortably disquieting supposition that the time in which I happen to be alive is by definition such a period! Such rhetorical grandiosity may illustrate Tocqueville's observation that, as a result of living in a democracy, the American's "ideas are all either extremely minute and clear, or extremely general and vague; what lies between is an open void."

This article is an effort to enter, in a somewhat dialectical fashion, into the open void, and to do so without the sense of servitude that characterizes much contemporary talk and writing about the fate of the intellectuals. I shall discuss some new-found conformities that seem to be emerging among many people who claim, often with good right, the mantle of liberalism; I am also curious about general tendencies influencing the position and self-confidence of intellectuals. Archibald MacLeish's article on "Loyalty and Freedom" is therefore the occasion compelling me to set down observations long accumulating. If, in what follows, I sometimes refer to his piece, I do so because it provides a ready illustration; many others could be found. I want to make it clear that I respect Mr. MacLeish's integrity and generosity; his motives recall Yeats' lines: "All things can tempt me from this craft of verse. . . . The seeming needs of my fool-driven land. . . ." If, to a person of my trade and training, certain poets and other artists appear at times politically naive when they make proclamations (while I must appear naive in another sense to them), this naivete doesn't bother me and doesn't require an "answer"; I will

fight with any censor for the right of such people to go on being
naive and "irresponsible." At best, my article is intended not to
engender a debate, but to qualify a tone and thereby the better to
represent the pluralism which is one of the glories of liberalism.

§ I

INTELLECTUALS TRY TO COPE with their anxiety by telling each other
atrocity stories about America. When this is done in science fiction,
as in *Galaxy's* serial "Gravy Planet" (recently republished in a pocket
book as *The Space Merchants*), it can be be witty and even revealing.
But when it is done with seriousness and portentousness, the consequences can only be anti-intellectual, can only stultify thought in the
listener who, bemused at once by guilt and by self-righteousness,
murmurs "Amen," "how true."

Other than as the expression of a current mood of a priori despair,
the tales about America currently in circulation are often not entirely
true. When, for instance, America's justly criticizable follies and
excesses are compared with the systematic and calculated terror of the
Soviet Union and the Nazis, the double standard applied misleads us
in our estimation of events on both sides of the Iron Curtain. Totalitarianism, though it draws on attitudes and on techniques of organization available in the Western, and perhaps the whole world, becomes
in its totality something new as soon as it seizes power; as Hannah
Arendt has observed, we quite fail to understand totalitarianism when
we simply extrapolate from (or back to) societies where the party
system and its ideological competition still function, however badly.
In my opinion totalitarian societies, once in power, dispense to a large
extent with group or national loyalty (which involves danger of
overadherence to principle), much as they dispense with ideological
propaganda for internal consumption (replacing it with instructions
in what the "line" now is, and who has hold of it). If many writers
appear to overestimate the loyalty engendered under totalitarianism,
they also fail to count their blessings when they attack the apathy,
that is, the lack of loyalty to ideals, of many Americans. For this very
apathy has its positive side as a safeguard against the overpoliticization
of the country: the apathetic ones, often not so much fearful or faith-
less as bored, may be as immunized against political appeals, good or
bad, as against much commercial advertising. Though, of course,
there is much pressure for an undiscriminating chauvinistic loyalty
and belongingness to a wide variety of groups, including the nation,
I am impressed by the fact that among GIs there is far less nationalism
than in the first World War—indeed, the pressure for loyalty may be,

among other things, one, often unconscious, form of the battle between older and younger generations.

Moreover, the conflict between loyalty and freedom may be quite absent from the minds of many politically apathetic people who appear to be "followers" of Senator McCarthy: they see him in terms of the drama of his career: has he found a gimmick that will get him ahead? The meaning they see in him resembles what they find in figures of the entertainment world or the underworld who have risen to the top without gentility, without connections, and apparently without education. Some of those who have this dramatic view of what on the surface operates as an "anti-Communist crusade" are quite prepared to continue to befriend neighbors who have been called, as ex-Communists, before congressional committees; because for them the salient issue is not one of loyalty, or politics at all, they may even be a bit proud to know somebody who got into the papers. I don't know how widespread this apolitical reaction is, but I do know it is terribly difficult to interpret what Mr. MacLeish refers to as "our silence as a people"—European intellectuals can make very little of it either, perhaps because American cynicism and European cynicism exist in very different contexts. When we try to deal with so big and stratified a country as ours—so big it often cannot hear the talk of the articulate—we ought not begin by reading into others our own fears and idealisms.

Something of a double standard is also employed in many conventional comparisons of the American present with the American past. If, despite the Know-Nothings, a rough toleration has at times been maintained within our country, fears and hatreds have found outlets against Indians, Mexicans, Spaniards—and Japanese (wars often fought, or prolonged, for social-psychological reasons after the enemy had virtually capitulated). Moreover, to exalt the Founding Fathers as having faith in man, as Mr. MacLeish does, would certainly come as a surprise to crusty John Adams, and to Madison; Jefferson might be willing, periodically, to accept the accolade. The Constitution exists, and is the magnificent job it is, in large part because the Fathers had so very limited a faith in man that they sought to protect us from our own and each other's weaknesses wherever possible. The more we know about American 18th-century thought the more complex it appears: strands of religious pessimism persisted from the Great Awakening; the Enlightenment itself was no single-voiced adventure in optimism (recall Diderot's *Rameau's Nephew*); much talk of Reason took account not of all men but only of the educated; and so on. I am inclined to think we have, with a few exceptions, much more faith in man than the Fathers had, and I think this is in some respects a sign of our progress.

Very likely, however, we do not have as much faith as our parents did: we know a bit more, we have seen a lot more, and our aspirations are hardly less. The New Deal and World War II gave many intellectuals and academic people a pleasant feeling of being close to the seats of power, of being in on big doings. To some extent, this feeling was delusive—an aspect of the amiable come-on Franklin Roosevelt practiced with many different groups, from Groton graduates to Hollywood stars. Correspondingly, for all too many intellectuals it drew a connection between being influential and having self-confidence, a connection any even temporary fall in the "market" might sever; in the process, enjoyment of study and intellectual functioning for their own sakes became too much devalued. The post-War inflation which has raised the level of living for organized workers, many small businessmen, and other groups has relatively squeezed our financial security at the same time that, still prominent but no longer so politically protected, the intellectuals have faced a new (but I am hopeful to think presently receding) wave of loyalty oaths, investigations, and other marks of special suspicion and special attention.

Even so, I am inclined to think that many intellectuals today, so far as I can judge their views, overestimate the monolithic power of Reaction. Peter Viereck once remarked that anti-Catholicism is the anti-Semitism of the intellectuals. Certainly in many strata people like to exaggerate the Church's power as in less educated circles they enjoy exaggerating the power of the Jews; very seldom can one hear or read much discussion about the cleavages within American Catholicism or read analyses of the great reservoirs of decency there, analyses which show understanding of the role of the Orders, of missionary parishes, etc.

Likewise, gloomy talk about the "fascist menace" in America overlooks the fact that all efforts of fascist groups to join forces have in the past come to nought because the very suspiciousness and paranoia which are the fascist leader's stock in trade make it well-nigh impossible for him to cooperate with other salesmen on his side of the street—splinter movements seem endemic to "true believers." Moreover, our ethnic diversity, our regional and religious pluralism, our vested corruptions, all tend to confine a fanatical leader to "his" people and section. While only the smug would assert "it can't happen here," it does seem reasonable to assert that it is unlikely, and that the Nazi parallels that undoubtedly exist can be overdrawn. We are neither a small, nor a defeated country.

The naming of evils, intended as a magical warding-off, can have the opposite effect. It is easy to imagine a group of academic people or civil servants, sitting about in the hot summer of 1953, and swapping stories about who got fired from the Voice of America because he subscribed to *The Nation,* and how so-and-so was not rehired at Benton College because his wife had once joined the League of Women Shoppers—each capping the other's whopper of the reactionary menace. What is the consequence? A stiffening of spines? A clearing of the mind and will for action? I doubt it.

I often suspect [if I may quote an earlier article of mine[1]] that the people who tell such stories are, unconsciously, seeking to create a climate which will justify in their own minds the concessions they are making— or, sometimes, a climate which, being worse in those they have spoken to and convinced, is better "inside" than "out." That is, the person who tells such stories (and, as I've indicated, it doesn't matter that they are true stories, one must distinguish between the weight and purpose of different truths) can feel he is bowing to strong pressures when he himself for instance drops a friend who might be suspected of an undue interest in racial equality. . . .

In short, intellectuals who, for whatever reason, choose to regard themselves as being victimized contribute to the very pressures they deplore. These pressures are not so strong as alleged; thinking them strong helps make them so.

§ II

IN A WAY, the attention that intellectuals are getting these days, though much of it is venomous and indecent, testifies to the great improvement in our status over that of an earlier day. What might not Henry Adams have given for such signs of recognition! In his day the intellectual was no threat to anybody: whether clergyman or scholar, he had to defer to the "practical" men, the men of business and affairs. It is almost inconceivable today that a father should say "Where Vanderbilt sits, there is the head of the table. I teach my son to be rich." In the much more fluid and amorphous America of our time, the writer, the artist, the scientist, have become figures of glamour, if not of power. It is harder to say where the head of the table is. The practical, non-intellectual man feels uneasy with these changes; he resents the fact that his own importance, as well as his own understanding of the world, are threatened by the intellectual and the intellectual's ability to change ideas. There is a tendency for the older "class struggles," rooted in clear hierarchical antagonisms, to be replaced by a new status warfare: the groups which, by reason of

---

1. "Some Observations on the Limits of Totalitarian Power," *Antioch Review,* XII (1952), at p. 156. [Reprinted below, p. 414.]

rural or small-town location, ethnicity, or other parochialism, feel threatened by the better educated upper-middle-class people (though often less wealthy and politically powerful) who follow or create the modern movements in science, art, literature, and opinion generally.[2] In other words, anti-intellectualism has increased in this country in proportion to (though not only because of) the growth of intellectualism. City slickers are no longer only bankers, lawyers, and drummers—they are drummers of ideas, that is, professors, teachers, writers, and artists.[3]

The reaction of many intellectuals to Stevenson's defeat may be taken as an illustration of my point about their real strength despite their professed weakness. They acted throughout the campaign as if *they* were up for election: they identified themselves with Stevenson's pathos as well as with his lovely wit. They saw the campaign through his eyes as an Oxford Union debate in which the opposition mulishly refused to answer "points" or explain contradictions. The same over-ideological outlook allowed them to be bemused by the notion, so strenuously promulgated by F. D. R., that the Democrats were the party of virtue and progress, the Republicans of reaction. Surprised, as I hardly think they should have been, that Ike swept the country, they felt they had been rejected. In their despair, they neglected the impressive fact that their man, their identity, had garnered over 27,000,000 votes against one of the most appealing candidates ever put up, and in spite of all the inherited handicaps of the Democrats. Perhaps, like any rising class, we do not feel we are rising quite fast enough, and momentary setbacks unduly dismay us.

§ III

AS ONE MOVE toward greater differentiation, we should review some case-histories of people who have refused to make concessions urged upon them, and consider whether and to what extent they have suffered for it. I think that such a study would show how, for instance, a professor can call and be called names and survive unscathed. An account of the detailed reasons why Harvard, Sarah Lawrence, Chicago, and many other places have not succumbed to the first trumpet blasts of investigating committees would seem to me both more illuminating and more important than to add to the well-rehearsed

2. Cf. Eric Larrabee's discussion of the Gathings Committee majority and minority reports in "Obscenity and Morality," address to the American Library Association, Los Angeles, June 1953.

3. Many of the humanists are in a paradoxical position, for they suffer the vulnerabilities without attaining the glamour and glory of other academics—one reason, possibly, for their frequent very great resentment of their colleagues who lay claim, justified or not, to the mantle of Science.

choruses of academic degradation. Without doubt, liberals as well as fellow-travelers are under attack in many parts of this country. But are these places where they were formerly secure?

I do not overlook the fact that liberals teaching in small colleges in fundamentalist or reactionary communities are still less secure now.[4] And such people do need succor and defense. Articles in Mr. MacLeish's tone may give such people succor through recognition, if not clarification, of their plight: through giving labels to their mood. But by and large I would assume that the *American Scholar* circulates, not in these areas, but in the larger centers where, in sizeable groups, views such as Mr. MacLeish has expressed are not news. In these latter groups, there seems to exist a blind fright and frenzy about "witch-hunts," all committees and their membership being lumped together in a composite caricature.

From the Hiss[5] case we may perhaps date the beginning not only of the excessive power and renown of many Johnny-come-lately anti-Communists but also, on the other side, of what might be thought of as a new united front in some liberal colleges and universities, admission to which is gained by denouncing "witch-hunts" and refusing to cooperate with them. Much as the Communists were forgiven their earlier treacheries when they joined in the Resistance against the Nazis in occupied Europe, and indeed fought their way to leader-

---

4. A balanced estimate would have to take account of shifts in the issues, manifest and covert, to which the community is sensitive. In 1890, Veblen was refused a post at St. Olaf's College because he "does not see the difference between science and religion," and "would treat the historical content of the Bible as he would handle an old document that one might find in China." (See *Scandinavian-American Studies and Records*, XV, 1949, pp. 128-9.) Neither such views nor sexual irregularities would cause a professor similar trouble today. In our time, professors may have become conformists in many respects—there may be fewer "characters" among us—but I am struck with how many, provided they are anti-Communist, have held on to Marxist views without being vilified or pressured.

5. I believe Hiss, in his arrogant treatment of Chambers and the Congressional Committee, was doing the country a far more serious disservice than in his earlier, very likely inconsequential espionage and other efforts to influence foreign policy. If he had told the Committee, as less publicized witnesses have done since, how it happened that a more or less idealistic and successful young lawyer could get involved with the Communist Party, he would have contributed to clarification instead of mystification, and perhaps partially disentangled the knots of identification binding so many decent people to him and hence to the view that he was being victimized. It might have been revealed that his case had special elements (special guilts, special arrogances, special impatiences) and that therefore, despite appearances, it was not a generation on trial but a fringe. Perhaps Hiss thought he could brazen it out. As the square-jawed, clean-cut hero of the two he would have a comic-strip advantage. Perhaps he was ashamed to disillusion his non-Communist friends and preferred to drag them down with him.

ship, so in the new American front the menace of McCarthy helps bring about a similar factitious solidarity among those who are sympathetic to, or apologetic about, or opposed to Communism. In some colleges, professors who testify before the Velde or Jenner committees with dignity and restraint (often educating committee members in the process, as Hiss so notably failed to do) are slandered as appeasers. To the extent that Communists, by such tactics, can get non-Communists to claim the Fifth Amendment, they too can pass off their men as martyrs to principle. This is the general confusion that let Odysseus out of the giant's cave; and in the scramble, the chief ethical problem—to what extent one should tell the committee not about oneself but about others—is obscured. The very term "witch-hunt" is obscurantist.

It may be true that, as this new-found front gains momentum, in AAUP chapters and elsewhere, it will shift the context into which such articles as Mr. MacLeish's fall. While the view of America they bespeak is so dispiriting that in some circles a kind of internal neutralism may be encouraged—why defend freedom if it is already beaten?—in united front circles these writings may well stiffen resistance to loyalty investigations, and thus in some degree serve to strengthen academic freedom. But this might turn out to be an ambiguous dividend, won only because many professors will have become afraid of being thought scared, and because many who share Mr. MacLeish's premises will have concluded that any intra-academic dissension is treachery. However, in my opinion achievement of this airless conformism under the banner of non-conformity would be a confession of academic defeat and vulnerability.

Even critics of articles like Mr. MacLeish's may fall in with this kind of "don't wash dirty linen" clannishness: they may fear that his attitude would encourage European and Asian neutralism. Doubtless, many Europeans are already too inclined to accept some American intellectuals' estimate of their own situation. (In our tradition, what is critical often seems more plausible than what is approbatory.) And since the Soviet Union, Red China, their satellites and mass parties remain the chief threat to freedom, such writers as Mr. MacLeish may be criticized for giving indirect aid and comfort to the foreign foe. But at this point, I would come to their defense and say that we are not so weak as to need a unity chorus at home to persuade intellectuals abroad to love and admire us! Since I share Mr. MacLeish's enthusiasm for freedom of thought and expression, I gladly take the risks of Europeans or Indians overhearing our conversation, and drawing their own conclusions—not the ones, I feel sure, that Mr. MacLeish would expect them to draw.

§ IV

IT IS CHARACTERISTIC of our times that we raise public relations considerations, if only to reject them. I agree with the implication of Mr. MacLeish's article that we are not the men our ancestors were—we tend to be less rigid, more agreeable, more cooperative and conciliatory. In an earlier, less "other-directed" age, polemics could be carried on, as they still are among Europeans, with fewer restraints based on one's resonance with the other, one's awareness and sympathy and misgiving. Such "weaknesses," when judged by an older standard of intransigent self-righteousness, are among those that Mr. MacLeish would perhaps like to see expunged in favor of the Spartan virtues he attributes to an earlier America. In Lionel Trilling's novel, *The Middle of the Journey*, we can see the power of such virtues, in Mrs. Croom or in Maxim, as against the hesitant and conciliatory Laskell in whom all voices echo.

Yet if we are to find our way out of the tricky personal and social perils peculiar to our day, as well as out of those that afflict any given day, it does not profit us to strive for the moral athleticism and heroism that not even a William James could drill into us. We must work with the psychological tools available to us, and not waste time bemoaning the loss of those blunter ones our forefathers possessed. We know today, for example, that all communication is problematic, a trap of serried ambiguities and obscure consequences. One must always bear in mind—can hardly help bearing in mind—for whom one is writing, even if one violently disagrees with Sartre's theory of "engagement." (I am aware that I am writing this for the *American Scholar*, not *Life*, the new *American Mercury*, or even *The New Leader*.)

However, a writer may make mistakes both about his audience and the pressures they are under: in aiming to challenge complacency wherever he finds it, he may instead strengthen it, or he may further harass people too wounded to listen.[6] I have often been in just this dilemma, as a result of the domestic repercussions of the cold war, in my relations with students and audiences. For instance, when I speak, usually on non-political topics, in the Midwest or in smaller communities in the East, someone is almost sure to ask out of the blue what about Owen Lattimore or don't I think America is going fascist or something of the sort. Often, he turns out to be a *Nation* reader, isolated and bereft, decent and dogmatic, frozen in middle life into what may earlier have been a less spiky carapace of liberalism. He has been waiting eagerly for the coming of light and learn-

---

6. For fuller discussion of this problem see my article, "Values in Context," *American Scholar*, XXII (1952), p. 29, at pp. 34 et seq. [Above pp. 21-25.]

ing from the University of Chicago to help lift the siege he has been laboring under among his townsfolk: he wants to be told that he isn't crazy, but that the others are. What am I to do when I share his associates' opinions of his opinions, if not of his character and motives? Am I to add one more blow to his self-esteem? To deny my own principles to support his? The mixture of therapy with education is characteristic of our time, and we have no easy answer for a problem that would not have bothered the Victorians.

With students, similar problems arise. Before World War II, I had moderate good luck in getting totalitarian-minded students to chuck some of their stereotypes about America, even if they did not accept mine. When very little penalty, and often even kudos, befell the members of the Party-dominated student groups, I could attack their criticisms without seeming to attack them as individuals; one can do this with the young—their ideas are not affixed to them but are part of a diffuse process of development and discovery; individually, I could encourage them not to be intimidated by the fear of being thought bourgeois. They would not suspect me of worrying about the reputation of my university. Now, as I need hardly say, all that is changed. Radical-minded students have learned in high school or even earlier to be wary of adults; afraid of being seduced by expediency, they have put a kind of intellectual chastity belt around their views. Since some of the nobler-spirited young still want risk and emancipation from parents, the educator who offers them a less clear and less violent set of ideas tends to be fanatically resisted.

Another curious kind of situation arises when the question of the books one uses in teaching comes under the scrutiny of an investigating committee. One of the general education courses in the College at Chicago was criticized by the Broyles Committee of the Illinois legislature because it assigned the *Communist Manifesto* and other writings of Marx and Engels. Before that, some of us had felt these works to be inappropriate for the particular course—for one thing, because the students had not yet had any historical background to understand the portrait of English industrial misery in the 1840's; for another, because we felt the course already too overweighted on the side of the "great books" as against more empirical or experimental materials. But ever since the investigation, the *Manifesto* has been frozen into the course: to replace it now would be regarded as a symbol of knuckling under to egregious, ill-meant criticism; and we and our students have become to that extent a captive audience.

While perhaps a majority of students in this course find Marx dull—in a way, they feel they know all that, and it's irrelevant—a minority feels called upon to speak up for or about Marx, lest they conclude they have betrayed themselves. I hesitate to put students into a position where they must make such a choice (our course is required), but would prefer to have them select their Armageddons at their own time and place. And this is one reason among many why I am opposed to most teaching of social studies in the high schools or earlier, for neither students nor teachers can be protected there against at least some kind of inquisition; the result will either be mushy piety or muddled bravado: in neither case will it be critical understanding. The schools, I think, would do better to teach subjects less vague and less inviting to censorship, leaving the social studies until later or for independent student exploration.[7] But again, the context makes it difficult to say this, or for the schools to do anything about their curricula, without being put in the position of seeming to bow to reaction, or to the intemperate attacks on John Dewey and progressive education. Thus, captive audiences spring up all around, precisely in the most advanced sections of the intellectual community.

I recall in this connection a conversation with the energetic editor of a liberal periodical who had suggested in one of his articles that there was something to be said for the investigating committees: they were not all vicious, and after all Communist conspiracies had existed. As a result, he was bombarded by letters charging that now he, too, was betraying the cause, was giving in to hysteria, was leaving his loyal readers in the lurch. He *did* give in to hysteria—to his readers' —and decided to publish no more such articles. Who can blame him, for where will he find another audience if he alienates his present one?[8]

In sum, the current atmosphere tends to inhibit thought in ways other than those generally recognized. United fronts for political action are one thing: intellectuals need lobbies and pressure groups just as other minorities do who in that way contribute to the pulling and hauling of American politics; but united fronts for intellectual understanding are as impotent as for artistic creation. In that area, each of us must go it alone, and, on occasion, even muster the courage not to take a stand.

---

7. It is an ironic symptom of the vulnerability of the school system that even Mr. MacLeish, in search of an explanation for our "escape from freedom," turns at the end to attacking education! "The underlying failure," he writes, "is a failure of education." Educators are fond of this kind of boasting, which so greatly over-estimates our role in the total culture.

8. In her otherwise admirable article, "The Menace to Free Journalism in America," in *The Listener*, May 14, 1953, p. 791, Mary McCarthy goes too far, in my judgment, in seeing such instances of editorial subservience as typical. It has even become the formula of many magazines to provoke or needle their readers; and certainly many seek to stay ahead of them.

§ V

BUT I WOULD also maintain at the same time and in the same connection, that the effort to rid ourselves utterly of cowardice is inhuman (it is analogous to the effort to rid the country utterly of corruption, Communism, or McCarthyism). We must learn to fight battles while admitting our fear of the enemy, as the American soldier has increasingly learned to do. Otherwise, we encourage a needless martyrdom in some, and an excessive self-contempt in those many valuable people who cannot live up to the courage and stern morality our ancestors represent for us. A friend who recently visited some members of the New Deal government-in-exile in Washington wrote me that his own high spirits were taken as a kind of physiological affront. To be gay or glad about anything in these days is considered by many who share Mr. MacLeish's views to be a sign of idiocy, ill-will, or both.

To be sure, the guilt for being well-off (or well-to-do) is a notable and not wholly negative feature of the American educated classes—we feel it vis-à-vis our own poor and vis-à-vis the ill-nourished of the rest of the world. Likewise, those of us who are reasonably safe from attack by school boards or investigating committees because, out of good luck, timidity, good judgment, or whatnot, we never flirted with Communism, and because the hatred with which we have regarded Communism is now widespread—we, too, do not feel quite happy in our security, even if we do not share the widespread conviction that liberals as well as Communists and their fellow-travelers in general are being victimized. As intellectuals, we the "Pollyannas" inevitably and properly ask ourselves if we can be right, when the country is in some rough measure with us—and so many respected intellectuals are against us. In any case, we cannot but be sympathetic with the many decent people who are anguished, even if their anguish appears to us frequently self-defeating and the source for a monotonous style of talking about America.

But I regret that they do not see that we in America now live in what in many ways is a great age. Terrible things are happening but wonderful things too, and the former do not cancel out the latter any more than they do in one's personal life. The sudden rise to relative affluence of millions of people has intensified the struggle—no new thing in America—between the "old," Eastern-oriented merchant and professional middle classes and the "new," half-educated small business and small-town-manufacturing middle classes. In this confrontation, an astonishing number of the latter seek culture or worldliness in a benevolently energetic way—the heroine of *South Pacific*, for an exotic instance. But another group, as I have indicated, feels put upon and dominated by the intellectuals who seem to control or at least understand the respectable and influential people, media, and opinions; the very ferocity with which these anti-intellectuals sometimes try to outlaw the worldly and the educated is a sign of their resentment of their inferior status in the traditional hierarchies of prestige and comprehension. We are witnessing, not only a tremendous increase in the number of intellectuals in the occupational structure, but an anxious resurgence of some aspects of Populism. This springs not merely from rural areas, so greatly diminished, but also from the half-urbanized and far from urbane city folk for whom nationalism provides an identity of sorts when all else shifts.

And not only nationalism but other narrower groupings. The Pole in Cicero who has helped build a family, a parish, a neighborhood which Negroes threaten to invade, evicting him (and where shall he begin over again?), may find in a crusade against intellectuals some surcease for his own guilt for his inability to sacrifice much of the status he has precariously erected to the values of tolerance and charity the respectable teachers, media, and pastors urge upon him. The violence of his response makes him at least momentary prey for politicians who refuse to abide by the orderly rules of their body, just as he wants to smash the orderly rules of property and mobility which permit anyone with the money to buy a house, and hence school his children, anywhere. Increasingly, Congress and our state legislatures have become more democratic, more representative and less corrupt; they often speak for these previously under-privileged millions, and less often for the "wise, the good, and the [very] rich." By continuing to think of our country as banker-ridden or boss-ridden, we have sought not to recognize these sometimes tenuous changes in the sources of social and personal control of violence and impulse, or to find scapegoats in "demagogues" who whip up "the people," otherwise innocuous. Doubtless, demagogues play a part in "legitimizing" frictions within and among Americans—and how should there not be frictions with vast new populations entering the market for goods and ideas in little more than a decade?

These large-scale and scarcely understood changes and resistances to change in the bases of American life and allegiance are likely to have far greater long-run effects on the climate of freedom in America than the tendencies to conformism within liberalism to which this article has mostly been devoted. We should not allow short-run rises or falls in temperature, even while we suffer from them or oppose them, to obscure these climatic changes. But by the same token, we cannot predict the outcome of the complex, sometimes silent, sometimes vocal struggle against the influence and prestige of intellect and education, nor is there any course we can take which will guarantee victory to the scholar. However, in personal or political life I think there are limits to the usefulness of speculation on ultimate outcomes for oneself, one's group, one's nation, the white race, the Western world, or even the planet. Defeat is not the worst fate. The Athenians were "defeated." So were many other great civilizations. We must recognize the tragedy of every loss, every defeat, without banking too much on the quantifiable measure of longevity as proof of value. To become too fascinated by eventualities of destruction is not only not the way to ward them off but a way to distract ourselves from equally important questions about America: Why, for instance, are Americans often so anxious and unhappy, when Europeans, who live much closer to military or economic disaster are so sanguine in their personal lives, often expressing philosophies of despair with exuberant arrogance? Why are American young people so frequently aimless, lacking private passions and pursuits, when a greater variety of skilled careers are open to them than ever before? Why in intellectual circles is there so much malice, when there are jobs and prestige and tasks enough for everybody and to spare? The American culture, high, low, and middle, nearly always lacks the gamut of qualities our best and most creative spirits have evoked and represented, and the list of reasons for our not having become the promised land is endless—not to be dealt with by such general terms as "loss of faith" or "growth of reaction." Since small actions can have large consequences, the future of America is as bewilderingly open as the present is opaque. Nevertheless, it seems to me that individuals in America have still an undiminished potential for good and great, rich and fortunate lives. In living up to this potential, we express our freedom.

§ POSTSCRIPT

AS THE FOREGOING ARTICLE implies, it represents one side of a debate staged in the pages of *The American Scholar* (the official organ of Phi Beta Kappa) between Archibald MacLeish and me. I had, as a member of the *Scholar's* editorial board, opposed our running an address by Mr. MacLeish entitled "Loyalty and Freedom," for I felt that the views expressed in it were not news to our readers, did not illuminate the issues, and—whatever value these views might have in magazines not read by people like ourselves—would, in the context of other articles previously published in the *Scholar*, only contribute to an atmosphere of resignation, depression, and misunderstanding of the intellectuals' plight. The article was, however, accepted, and I was encouraged to write a reply (something I would have refused to do in any more public forum not only because Mr. MacLeish has suffered greatly from patrioteers but also because our differences, as far as the great anti-intellectual world goes, are marginal and intra-academic). Mr. MacLeish in turn wrote a brief reply to me, chiding me for lack of passionate concern for intellectual freedom and for a social scientist's presumed preference for cold analysis over eloquence and rhetoric.

Very much the same argument arose between me and Professor Laurence Sears of Mills College when I drew on this article in giving a lecture there. This argument attracted the attention of local papers and was reported in a distorted fashion, especially by the Hearst press: the argument itself could scarcely be understood from the reports, but the pleasure outsiders always take in seeing insiders fighting each other was evident enough. I had been trying to talk to liberal intellectuals and thoughtful college students, but was overheard by reactionary editors to whom I was not talking, to whom I would have said something very different. But of course one irony inside this irony is that it is very difficult to get across to people outside the academic world any such complex intention: such people want to know whether something is so or isn't so, and can't see any harm in broadcasting a debate especially if it encourages them to feel superior about professors! At the same time, as my article declares, I have never been willing to accept the "don't wash dirty linen" position, which implies that a group under attack must stop talking unless all exits are sealed. If we are not to succumb to overwhelming "inside" pressures, we have to take a good many chances.

Even so, I must add that when I wrote this article (in the spring and early summer of 1953), I did so with a good deal of misgiving lest it comfort those intellectuals, rather rare in my own circles but no doubt plentiful, who might take it as an excuse not to worry. At times, even the most intrepid among us may secretly long for excuses for inaction, and I was aware that, in criticizing the panic doctrine that America is on the road to fascism (my opinion in part based on the none too hopeful ground that we have always had illegality and violence in this country), I might leave some readers even more smug than before. I now think that I did not pay sufficient heed to my own misgivings, for some reactions favorable to my article have had this smug quality; on rereading what I wrote, I feel I should have emphasized more some of the impalpable erosions of intellectual freedom that are related both to the general pressures hostile to individualism and to the specific tensions and irritabilities of the cold war.

Certainly, since my article was written, I have encountered painfully little evidence of the willingness of American intellectuals, let alone businessmen, lawyers, broadcasters, and government officials, to come out swinging in the old free-hand way, not only against McCarthy but against the careful, excessively fine-spun arguments of many of those whom McCarthy has attacked: the latter, if innocent of Communist ties, are often deferential and conciliatory, expressing neither firmness and conviction nor making use of the traditional American pattern of political villification for one's own protection. What is involved here is perhaps not so much the rational fear of people for their careers; rather, people fear public embroilment with a bully, which can become an unbelievably harrassing and time-consuming job. Many of us can recall, or prefer not to recall, our dismal encounters with bullies in high school or earlier; being Americans, unprotected by arrogance of class or family, we could not be sure we were in the right if we lost or ran away from such a fight. Thus, in dealing with a demagogue, we often lack assurance and are unprepared for virulence and bad faith; at times, we fall back on argumentative weapons deemed weak by a sports-loving public. And this weakness would seem especially grave when one is dealing with Senator McCarthy, whose sales appeal to the newly well-paid but socially uneasy strata in his constituency is as much his outspoken contempt for all symbols (such as Harvard, England, the State Department, or Army brass) of older and better educated strata, as is his opportunistic and picayune domestic anti-Communism.

Moreover, I sense among many members of the intellectual community an understandable tendency to establish our patriotism, our incontrovertible loyalty and anti-Communism, as a kind of public-relations gesture. And we are likely to argue that we are better fighters against Communism at home and abroad than McCarthy or *Counter-Attack*. These declarations are true, yet they have an air of enforced piety about them, like the declarations of some comic-book and pocket-book publishers who, instead of ridiculing the Gathings Committee's hypocrisy and denouncing its unfairness and mistrust of freedom, proclaim their own desire to avoid "obscenity" in cover and content. The fact that we feel such politic declarations must be made, that we cannot have our virtue (or the viciousness of our critics) taken for granted, is one of the many signs of the increasing pressure against freedom that I think now I did not take sufficiently into account in this article.

8. The "Militant" Fight
Against Anti-Semitism

I T WAS NOT so long ago that Jews sought to defend themselves against anti-Semitism by discreet and persuasive apologetics and by the quiet intercession of their "best people" with the authorities. Though these methods survive, the past two decades have tended to replace them by pressure-group tactics in which Jewish organizations take the offensive—by means of picketing or boycott, or the threat of these weapons—against books (*The Merchant of Venice*), movies (*Oliver Twist*), teachers (City College's Knickerbocker), performers (Gieseking, Furtwängler), and exhibits (the German Industries Fair) that are thought to promote or condone anti-Semitism. It must be at once conceded that much has been accomplished by these methods in the last years in the field of civil rights and fair employment practices. Yet the new "militancy" has brought with it new problems, at once ethical and practical.

The classic American pattern encourages personal self-reliance, hitting back as an individual against attack, but Jews have scarcely felt themselves more free to do this than the Negroes in the South have. This situation promotes smoldering resentment and repressed aggression, which often seek release through the channels of Jewish organizational life. So, for example, a Jew who in private life puts up with mildly anti-Semitic friends, or has changed his name, may support an organization whose public "militancy" assuages his own private discomfort. At the same time, the "leader" of such an organization, afraid of losing his following to still more militant leaders, may be far more outspoken in his public "militancy" vis-à-vis non-Jews than he is in private life.

Whatever the effect of pressure-group tactics in reducing anti-Semitism in the larger American community, they do seem to have gone a long way toward enforcing unanimity among Jews themselves. Though only a small minority of Jews would seem to be what Alfred Kazin has called "mindless militants," this group has steadily gained a disproportionate power, often enabling them to intimidate the community, so that many Jewish "leaders" are actually the captives of the most violent and intemperate of their "followers." When a part of this article was presented in an address to a meeting of the National

Community Relations Advisory Council (April 30, 1949), a number of people told me they agreed with my views but were in no position to say so publicly. Apparently, they were afraid of being called "scared Jews."

Just as liberals in the days of the Popular Front could often be forced to take extremist positions in order to prove that they were not "petty bourgeois," not "enemies of the working class," so today the more comfortably situated Jews, who are very likely a numerical majority, can often be brought into line to support ill-advised policies which are justified by picturing the Jews (in America as well as elsewhere) as an oppressed group—a picture that plays much the same role in these tactics as the Stalinist picture of the workers as members of a "proletariat." Thus, many American Jews who feel guilty about having been untouched by the Nazi holocaust, guilty about their "assimilation," guilty perhaps about not being Palestinian soldiers or pioneers—in addition to all the other guilt-feelings they have as middle-class Americans—are easy ideological victims of Jews with more aggression and (frequently) lesser social standing, whom, in an earlier day and for equally bad reasons, they would have snubbed. In fact, in order to "prove themselves," the most assimilated occasionally become the most militant. Every threat or presumed threat to Jews anywhere in the world can be converted into a lever for the "militant" minority of Jewish organizational life, much as Russian threats to American interests anywhere reinforce the power of our self-proclaimed militant anti-Communists to put a blanket of "unity" over American life as a whole.

§ II

IT SHOULD, however, be noted that there are factors not peculiar to the Jews that motivate similar cycles of "appeasement" and "militancy" among many other ethnic groups in America.[1] The first generation of immigrants enjoyed an improved lot. They had come to this country, or migrated within it, in order to find greater economic and social opportunity, and they had found it. The standard of comparison was always with the old country—an old country assumed to have remained unchanged.

The second and third generations apply a different standard of comparison. For they are sufficiently Americanized, which means sufficiently middle class, to judge their experience in terms of a creed of complete equality of opportunity. While the older generations were glad to get into a college, the more recent ones are terribly hurt

---

1. I owe much to Professors Oscar Handlin and Everett C. Hughes for my understanding of this cycle.

if they do not get into a fraternity; while the older generations were happy to achieve economic security and civic equality, the younger generations find exclusion from the Racquet or Hunt Club a grievous burden. Sensitive to rebuffs to which their parents would have given scant heed, they turn in their disillusionment and resentment towards ethnic nationalism. National revivals—Irish, Polish, Czech, Italian— are thus mainly the prerogative of the native-born; in this sense, ethnic nationalism is paradoxically a sign of Americanization. Those American-born Jews who today seemingly reject America's promise in favor of Israel have been shaped by American schools, American economic institutions, and American culture in general: their very effort and style of protest against America proceeds mainly along American lines, even though colored by specifically Jewish factors, and testifies to their "assimilation."

In terms of most objective indexes of discrimination, it is undeniable that the position of Jews has substantially improved in the last generation. There are many more Jews in the universities, and on the whole there is considerably less prejudice. Though indeed it is still a long way towards complete equality, I would guess that there is today, both in the fields of law and academic life,[2] more discrimination against women than against Jews. Yet, the improving situation of Jews in America corresponds to a mounting sensitivity by Jews to all manifestations of prejudice.

§ III

FURTHER UNDERSTANDING of the psychological complex behind the need of many American Jews to assert themselves aggressively can be found if we look at some of the targets against which Jewish groups have recently directed their fire. Almost invariably, these targets have been weak ones. In some cases, those attacked (or "pressured") have been movie exhibitors or movie lords—"lords" who tremble so readily before an archbishop or a Hearst or a Congressional committee. Another target is the public school boards, so often submissive to whoever in the community can make a big noise. Jewish bigots cooperated with Catholic bigots years ago to deny Bertrand Russell a chair at City College in New York. In descending on Pro-

---

2. In the field I know best, that of academic life, the situation has changed very much, even in the last ten years. I recall that when in 1938 and 1939 I tried to find places for Jewish refugees in American law schools, as the executive secretary of a committee headed by John W. Davis, I found my efforts hampered not only by anti-Semitism but also by well-intentioned persons who felt that Jews had so little chance in academic or professional life that they had best go into business. Today the men our committee succeeded in helping find very few of the old obstacles: they teach in the top law schools and have jobs in the government and in Wall Street law offices.

fessor Knickerbocker at the same institution, Jewish organizations had of course a rather different case, since he was charged not only with anti-Semitic opinions but with actual discriminatory practices in running his department. But what about the assumption apparently made in this case that if he could be proved to have made anti-Semitic remarks he should be fired—as if private anti-Semitism in City College (of all places!) is the menace that it might be, say in Congress, or in the utility industries.

Still another target for American Jews is supplied by all things German. Although Germany is, of course, potentially strong, she has been weak since the war in the important sense that American educators, trust-busters, and others have found it easier to influence (or at least make a fuss about) American policy in Germany than about comparable problems on the domestic political scene. Just as anti-Semites portray Jews as powerful, in order to justify attacking them under the code of fair play, so the anti-German Jews have utilized allegations of "the German danger" to justify notions as cruel and crazy as the Morgenthau Plan. To be sure, the American Jews have probably not been strong enough to affect appreciably the course of events in Germany, either for good or ill. But they have been strong enough to keep Gieseking out of the country—and to harden in the Jewish community the picture of a solidly unregenerate German people, as openly and intensely anti-Semitic today as were the Nazis, thus inhibiting any serious discussion of German realities. This last is yet another example of the attempted *Gleichschaltung* of Jewish organizational life.

In the case of Germany, Jewish concern is often rationalized in terms of fighting alleged resurgences of anti-Semitism there. Actually, however, it would seem to be motivated by a natural desire to remind the world of the slaughter of fellow Jews. It is probably inevitable that those who have not suffered should feel a certain guilt about that very fact, especially if one feels that not all was done that might have been done to rescue the doomed—and if one also has to combat one's own desire to forget and gloss over what happened. But the sensitive person should need no reminders: he lives all too constantly with the memory of history's crimes and disasters. Conversely, the insensitive person may react negatively to reminders, especially if he feels that they are sometimes a form of moral blackmail. At the same meeting at which my own address was delivered, another speaker who had been concerned with Jewish affairs in Germany mentioned how, when he would lay his complaints before a certain American general, the latter would say, in a friendly tone, "Now, don't throw the six million at me again."

True, the American Jews who attack weak and easy targets in this country, or who applaud such tactics at home and abroad, certainly do not interpret their action as bullying or blackmail; and they would be horrified to be classified with those groups who use force or threats of force to censor art, or to suppress free discussion. And let us grant that there may be some warrant, emotionally at least, in viewing a Furtwängler or Knickerbocker as a symbol both of the European massacre and the worldwide threat of political anti-Semitism. Nevertheless, while any instance of anti-Semitism *may* testify to a fascist potential, there is a grave danger of distortion when a hotel's restriction, a chance remark, or a silly book come to be automatically identified with Nazi cruelties, and call forth a reflex action of violent indignation and an effort at aggressive suppression. A kind of fantasy is built up which, though it has much more justification behind it, curiously resembles that of the anti-Semite who sees in the acts of an individual Jew the systematic conspiratorial intentions of a whole race.

In coping with anti-Semitism, Jews have a problem similar to that with which all Americans are faced in coping with the Russians. As Americans we have to learn to live with relative comfort and self-control in a state of cold war that in all likelihood will go on for many years. If we get panicky, and unable to keep our heads in the face of even serious hostility, we can bring disaster on ourselves as well as on the world. Thus, for instance, if Americans were to concentrate on hating the Russians, we should already be reduced by them part-way to their own level. As Jews we have even less choice. We are going to be able at best only to contain anti-Semitism in America, to prevent its spread, to prevent violent incursions and active discrimination; we have no chance whatsoever of wiping out anti-Semitism by force, although maybe some Jews, underneath fantastic fears, nourish even more fantastic hopes. But since this is so, those Jews who are over-alert to anti-Semitism and go to all lengths to lash out at any and every sign of it are likely to waste too much of their time and resources. And they will tend to neglect the things that might be done to better the lot and widen the horizon of all Americans, including Jews.

Perhaps Jews, looking at the European experience, consciously or unconsciously feel that no dividing line separates an anti-Semitic remark from an extermination camp. This is to assume more or less that there are no social and psychological barriers between thought and action, and between moderate action and extreme action. And it also assumes that Americans are not bound by specific traditions and habits. We Americans, Gentile and Jew, like big talk, and much that passes for anti-Semitic expression is big talk, with no thought or dream behind it of real action. And, happily, it is a fact that Americans draw a line between anti-Semitic remarks and actual persecution, and it is by virtue of this distinction (and the political and social institutions built upon it) that Jews in America have little more occasion for anxiety as Jews than for anxiety as Americans.

§ IV

SO FAR I HAVE ASSUMED that the books and movies Jews are attacking are in fact anti-Semitic. But is this really so? Who will deny that there have been Jewish Fagins? And are these the worst men to be found in the gallery of literature and life? If these things are the worst that can be said in serious literature about Jews, they are surely no worse than what can be said about other people. Indeed, as I recall *Oliver Twist*—the book, I mean, since I haven't been permitted to see the film—Dickens never makes Fagin's Jewishness an excuse for general charges against the Jews.[3] And Shakespeare in *The Merchant of Venice* puts into the mouth of Shylock one of the most eloquent pleas for the humanity of Jews that has ever been written.

But even if I were wrong about these particular works, it still would not change my view. There are violently anti-Semitic writers, such as Ezra Pound or Louis-Ferdinand Céline, who have the right to say what they please, just as Montherlant, Farnham, and Lundberg have the right to say what they please about women. When Jews try to suppress such writers, they act as if they had something to hide. My own feeling is that Jews have nothing to hide, either in literature or in life. At one time I thought it might be practicable to draw a line between group-libel of the Jews which included false statements of fact—such things as are now peddled by Curt Asher and William Dudley Pelley—and works of art in which Jews are dealt with perhaps unsympathetically, but as part of a whole picture of life. But in time, my studies convinced me that there were virtually insuperable administrative difficulties in drawing such a line, and in entrusting it to public officials and juries, and that the dangers outweighed the possible benefits. Suits for libel by individual Jews and replies in the forum of public discussion are, of course, another matter entirely, though hardly one of great importance. My general feeling is that our tradition of civil liberty is the best defense we have for individuals

3. Since writing the above, my British-born friend, John Seeley, has informed me that Fagin does make a profound impression on British boys as to what happens when a Jew "reverts to type"—just as Bligh is what happens when an Englishman does. And Fagin, he adds, by virtue of the very humanity with which he is portrayed, is made to seem far more human, near, and threatening than Bligh.

and for minorities; and Jews have every interest, as Jews and as Americans, in seeing that this tradition remains strong and vital.

In view of what happened in Europe and of the existence of anti-Semitism in America, it is not surprising that Jews feel weak and therefore lack confidence that full and free discussion will be just to them. Nevertheless, I feel that we should encourage such discussion. Jews are, after all, much more interesting to talk about than anti-Semitism. And I think it best that we should be prepared to take our chances in such a discussion, only making efforts to see that it is stimulating and abundant.

At present we may distinguish four levels of talk about Jews in America, four levels that hardly mix or meet. At the top level are the intellectual and artistic circles, of Jews and non-Jews, where there is at the same time curiosity and matter-of-factness about things Jewish. The pages of *Commentary* are an excellent illustration of this kind of discussion. There one finds reporting of Jewish life without a fearful concern for public relations; philosophic and sociological debate about what, if anything, it means to be a Jew; and, in the department "From the American Scene," occasional pictures of the fabulously interesting, rich, and varied life of Jews in America. On this level, one can also find literature that is not a tract against anti-Semitism but an exploration of Jewish consciousness and unconsciousness; there comes to mind Saul Bellow's fine novel, *The Victim*.

Our second level of discussion is in the liberal middle class, both Jewish and non-Jewish, the class responsible for putting car cards about brotherhood in the New York subways. A friend of mine claims to have heard a radio jingle over a New York station, "He's no Jew, he's like you." I suspect him of satire. But if it didn't actually happen it might well have, given the notion of "defense" prevailing in many advertising minds. It is here that a mythical world is constructed in which Negroes and whites, Jews and non-Jews—and, for that matter, men and women—are "really" alike; such differences as there still are, being expected to wither away like the Marxist state. On this level Jews fail to see that it is their very difference which may be both worthwhile and appealing. This insistence on denying differences, or on seeking to eradicate them, identifies "American" with "Americanization"—and insists that for people to be treated as equals they must have more than their humanity in common.

The chief quality I sense in discussion about Jews on this second level is piety, a kind of dreary piety, filled with platitudes about unity, amity, democracy, and so on. This piety, it seems to me, as it spreads throughout "official" culture, through our churches, schools, and many voluntary associations, has two consequences. On the one hand, in the obedient circles it tends to stultify observation and thought. On the other hand, it enables those rebellious souls who refuse to subscribe to it to appear as terribly dashing and bold and "militant." The violent anti-Semites and those Jews who throw eggs at Bevin both achieve an easy victory for their image of the Jew over the official picture. Just this appearance of toughness is, I think, one of the great attractions of the Chicago *Tribune* and even more of the New York *Daily News*: such organs appear to monopolize daring and impiety. The only way to combat this is by open and honest discussion about Jews, to make people aware that Jews are *real*, and to make an effort to talk about them as they are.

The third level of discourse about Jews is on what we might call the Catskill-Broadway plane, in which there thrives a form of culture spread throughout America by the press, film, and radio. Perhaps we find its beginnings in *Abie's Irish Rose*. Danny Kaye, the Goldbergs, Eddie Cantor, Billy Rose—day by day and night after night they exploit aspects of Jewish life and Jewish character. Many non-Jewish comedians play the same circuit; perhaps they have Jewish gag-writers. I wish I knew what Billy Rose's readers in Dubuque and Dallas, Charleston and Seattle, have made of his accounts of life and love at Lindy's; and I wish I knew what America makes of Milton Berle. Does this add to that identification of Jews with big-city life which —as Arnold Rose has observed—is so powerful an element in modern anti-Semitism? Do the lower-middle-class non-Jewish audiences of this Catskill culture have personal contacts with Jews of their own and other social levels, or is their only "contact" through these images of stage and screen? What is the attitude of these audiences towards the Jewish comic or, for that matter, the Jewish Winchell—are these performers patronized as something exotic and foreign? Are they felt to be Jews at all? I expect we would find a good deal of ambival-aspect of Jewish culture that he symbolizes. The same listener, for ence, a mixture of emotions, both towards the performer and the instance, may both despise and be fascinated by Winchell. I would like to know a lot more about this whole area for the sake of the light it would shed on both the myths of the Americans and the myths of and about the Jews.

The fourth level of discussion about Jews I would locate primarily in the working class, but with ramifications in the lower-middle-class. These people have little opportunity to express their own attitudes except through conversation—on the workbench, in the bar, on the street corner. The only medium of publication available is the walls of toilets. Even apart from the question of interstate commerce, group-libel laws—such as those being pushed by the Commission on Law and Social Action of the American Jewish Congress —can hardly be effective here! These toilet walls, indeed, are the distorted reflection of—and rebellion against—middle-class piety in respect to the two things, race and sex, that so many Americans find both indecent and alluring. If this level is reached at all by the propaganda of the dreary pietists, the principal effect might perversely be only to make Jews seem even more mysterious than before—and official culture more mendacious and mealy-mouthed. Working-class anti-Semitism is very strong indeed, if I may judge from recent studies of prejudice conducted under the auspices of the Scientific Department of the American Jewish Committee. Whether much of it is anti-Semitism that yearns for action or just big talk and griping, I do not know. . . .

§ V

SO FAR, I HAVE MADE clear my conviction of the futility of much that passes for militancy and—the other side of the coin—much that passes for sweet, pious reasonableness. I want now to draw a few needed distinctions.

First, I think Jewish attacks on anti-Semitism should aim at its containment, not its extirpation. In general, human efforts to eliminate vice totally, rather than to contain it within tolerable bounds, run the risk of a total "politicization" of society. That is, there are totalitarian implications in permitting political measures to encompass all of private, academic, and literary life.

Second, I think Jews go beyond the legitimate containment of anti-Semitism when they seek, as a pressure group, to limit freedom of teaching and expression. Naturally, a Jew need not himself support anti-Semitic expression; why should he? If a Jew resigns from a welcoming committee for Gieseking, he stands on his personal dignity. So does a Jew who declines to read or to place advertising in an openly anti-Semitic newspaper. But just as soon as such Jews band together and try to prevent other people from reading a paper or hearing a pianist, then they are no longer exercising a personal privilege but interfering with the personal privileges of others. In the present context of American society, freedom of expression is one of the great safeguards for Jews and all other minorities subject to prejudice. As we know, this freedom needs to be protected not only against government, but even more against private censorship—whether by Legionnaires, businessmen, unions, the Legion of Decency, or the Commission on Law and Social Action. Above all, freedom needs active support and encouragement from its friends, as well as protection from its many powerful foes.

Third, I would suggest that Jews are on the whole wisely advised not to spend their lives as anti-anti-Semites. We suspect that the vice crusader probably enjoys pornography and perhaps the anti-anti-Semite is fascinated by what he fights.

In any case, paradoxical as it may seem, Jews could become more at ease if they accepted the fact (I believe it to be a fact) that their fate as Jews in America is largely beyond their control. As many realize, Jewish well-being depends on the health of society as a whole, and only anti-Semites will claim that Jews are powerful enough to save or sink America. And it is relatively futile for Jews to address themselves to hardened anti-Semites as an audience: why should the anti-Semite listen to the Jew, especially when the latter speaks, not as one human being to another, but through the mass media of communication? We are always better off in devoting ourselves to talking to people who, at least in part, want to hear us.

Since, therefore, Jews waste their time when they spend it all trying to impress or repress their enemies, their very lack of power becomes an invitation to devote their major energies to self-development. This, too, may involve combat, but of a different sort and with a different goal, for the focus would shift away from the question as to what menacing things are being said about Jews to more challenging questions: What kind of better, more creative Jewish communities and American society would we like to see in the future? What are the arts that give us pleasure and enrich our lives, and how do we go about encouraging them? What will make America a more interesting and lively place to live in?

There are, I will agree, times so desperate in the life of a society, that repression of a totalitarian movement on its way to power may be required. That is not, in my opinion, the situation now—and if it were, as I have said, the Jews would not be the ones most able to do much about it. But Jews, like other Americans, can always find the situation they are in to be grim and desperate if they look hard enough, and can thus rationalize their failure to concern themselves with the possibilities of a more abundant life.

The policy I propose, as should be evident, is motivated not by a fear that in a contest of strength and fanaticism the Jews are bound to suffer because they are fundamentally weak, but rather by a fear of the evil Jews inflict on themselves and on other Americans by interfering with freedom of expression. We seem to be building a society in which any reasonably well-organized minority group can get itself a limited veto over the mass communications industries and, with some exceptions, over public political debate. Let us return to the movies as a prime example. The focus on the problem of repression that the organized Jews share with other organized groups tends to give us movies in which disagreeable things cannot be shown about doctors, veterans, Jews, morticians, priests, labor leaders, Negroes, Marshall Plan countries, and so on; only lawyers, gangsters, night-club operators, and Russians lack effective Hollywood lobbies. Curbed on these scores, and also on the score of open sex, the movies cater to sadism—even movies which are "good for race relations" do this. Perhaps if Jewish energies were spent, not in adding to the list of taboos, but in trying to free the mass media and the public mind from taboos, they would not get very far. But the advantage of choosing freedom as an ally is that, while it may sometimes be defeated, it is always a more interesting and agreeable side to be on.

A dangerous disregard and contempt for artistic work is evident in the easy condemnations of allegedly anti-Semitic movies, books, and performers by the militants. But a more subtle contempt also appears in those who view every act from the standpoint of real or imaginary "others" and therefore would like to use the arts to promote "better race relations." Indeed, we find that while the militants profess scorn for tactical considerations, they are in agreement with these public-relations-minded Jews in their view of culture as a mere expendable. Recently, for instance, a producer's representative, typical of the latter group, wanted me to go on record in favor of *Home of the Brave* on the ground that it was "good for race relations." When I asked him (the somewhat ironic question) whether he thought *Symphonie Pastorale* was good for race relations, he did not understand me—what did this movie about a pastor's family tragedy have to do with race relations? In his attitude, he patronized both his own craft of movie-making and the movie audience: he assumed that people get out of a movie a message as simple as the fortune-teller's printed slip in a penny arcade. The notion that the art form itself, over a period of time, could affect the quality of American life, and hence of its race relations, is forgotten in anxious concern for the presumed immediate results. This producer's representative did not ask himself what kinds of movies he himself enjoyed seeing, but looked at his product from the stance of an outsider —this is the hallmark of the public-relations approach. But it is evident that a person who seems only to patronize others also patronizes his own human reactions and, while he thinks he manipulates the emotions of the audience, also manipulates, and eventually causes to evaporate, his own emotions.

In fact, it is on a platform of contempt and distrust for people
that the militants and the public-relations-minded groups, whatever
their internecine quarrels, can unite. While the militants assume that
most Jews not of their faction and all non-Jews except their certified
"friends" are anti-Semitic, and sally forth to fight them, the public-
relations-minded people assume that Americans are governed only by
expediency and sally forth to cozen them. Instead of defending in
their own membership and among its allies the best traditions of
American freedom, they devote themselves to specious arguments
with which to manipulate the indifferent mass.

An instance of the latter practice is the argument against racial
discrimination frequently advanced by Jewish organizations—and
not only by them, of course—that restrictive covenants and other discriminatory practices are economically expensive. Or, in another form,
the argument says that racialism makes trouble for our foreign policy.
People are hardly going to like Jews and Negroes better because
hating them costs money or looks bad in Indonesia! The people who
put out such arguments do not "believe" them; that is, the arguments
are true enough, but it is not because of them that the arguers were
themselves won over to the cause of racial justice and equality. To
offer arguments that do not have weight for oneself is, I think,
patronizing and arrogant. Wishing, each in his way, to be "realistic"
and hardboiled, the militants and the public-relations people both
are apt to forget that people need ideals and that the human passion
for freedom is one of the recurrent experiences of mankind.

§ VI

INDEED, to defend freedom by appeals to public-relations considerations is, in a fundamental sense, to weaken it. One reason why the
American tradition of freedom is perhaps less vital now than a hundred years ago is precisely that it has become enmeshed in piety and
propaganda. This, of course, is not something the Jewish defense organizations have done; it is part of a long historical development in
which freedom and democracy have become schoolbook words, have
been linked with reactionary economic programs, and have been made
available for the export trade. To see what has happened we need only
compare the kind of writing about American democracy current in
Jefferson's day with that of our own. From Jefferson to Mark Twain
and Veblen there was a bite and vigor in American letters that is
seldom dared today. Our various official doctrines of unity—the
phrase, "the" American way of life, is revealing—and our various
pressures of censorship are both symptoms and causes of the shift.

The picture of America which gets through the censorship is a stereotype, and not a very interesting one. During the last war, we experimented with an effort to create a stereotype both of America and of the GI, and to sell this to the soldiers through advertising, radio, and the military indoctrination agencies. The soldiers resented it, but took their resentment out in swearwords and apathy, since they lacked the resources and encouragement to develop their own picture of themselves and what they were doing. Today, we seem to be marketing to the civilian population a picture as spurious, as lacking in complexity and savor, as the GI Joe myth. Jews in America, like the other minorities who make up the majority, will not thrive on such stereotypes, even though severally favorable to racial tolerance—if freedom is the price, tolerance comes too high. But, in fact, this is an unreal alternative, since minorities thrive, not on a colorless uniformity but on diversity, even conflict—including diversity and conflict among themselves.

Many Americans have lost faith in freedom and have lost hope in the future. Many Americans have imitated the methods of their totalitarian enemies and have swung away from complacency and over-timidity in the direction of paranoia and over-aggression; still others have swung away from tolerance as a fighting faith to tolerance as a public-relations maneuver. Many Americans are attracted by force and repression, many by the veiled (and hence in many ways preferable) force of manipulative public relations. The "mindless militants" among the American Jews, and the public-relations soothsayers, have therefore plenty of company, though not good company. But what is particularly sad and ironic in this development is that those very Jews who often violently attack the policy of "assimilation" and who make much of their Jewish consciousness seem to have been completely uprooted in America from the mainstream of Jewish values. For in the past Jews learned to depend for life, liberty, and the pursuit of happiness on very formidable weapons of another order: namely, good judgment, the free exercise of reason, and hospitality to intellect and hatred of force, traditions which go back almost three thousand years.

Since analogous developments have overtaken many Jews and many Americans, we may suppose that the explanation for the historical shift in Jewish attitude lies less in the miseries peculiar to Jews than in those that they share with their fellow Americans. Specifically, as I have already indicated, many Jews, like many other Americans, do not know how to be happy—do not even know how to become aware of whether they are happy or not. Despite, as things go, a fair degree of security, despite very considerable material abundance, we find it somehow easier to be miserable. In our private lives, we look for, or easily fall into, agendas—ways of getting through the day and the evening. In our public lives, we live under a sense of menace and doom, create a context of chronic emergency, and are drawn to crusades against enemies, real and imaginary, because our lives are not sufficiently rewarding in their own terms. We think we would be happy in a world free of anti-Semitism and such evils, but I doubt it.

Any programs of "action" that rob us of any part of our intellectual heritage, that inhibit our curiosity and wonder about the world and the people in it, or that substitute the miasma of "piety" for the élan of truth, cannot make for happiness. And a life filled up with activities, aggressions, and anxieties is not my conception of a full life.

9. Some Observations Concerning Marginality

THE PREVAILING ATTITUDE toward marginality on the part of social scientists, it seems to me, is one of dislike for it (it is sometimes called "alienation"). They would like to see us go back to a social system in which every one was supposedly rooted, in which there were no marginal people; everyone had a place and knew it. Now it has occurred to me that this attitude, which is so prevalent here [at the University of Chicago], might have something to do with the fact that we live in the city of Chicago, and that current uneasiness about this city might have given its particular tinge to some of the more recent discussions of urbanization and migration.

What I have in mind is that it has become fashionable to dislike Chicago, to view it as the very model of the "impersonal," sprawling, and disorganized metropolitan blob. The older, Sandburgian attitude of admiration for the steel plants, the packing houses, the railroads, and the other majesties of the city seems almost to have disappeared, and with it the studies of an earlier day which explored the city with fascination, even awe, and a certain touch of romance.

I propose in these remarks to take up first two kinds of marginality, which I shall call "open" and "secret"; then to turn to a brief case study of the Jews; and, finally, to make some comments about the ethical aspects of marginality.

§ I

"OPEN MARGINALITY" is the kind that we read about in the writings of Robert E. Park, that we are familiar with: the situation created when we have the educated Negro, the self-made man, the woman engineer, all the various kinds of marginality which have become, so to speak, institutionalized, defined. And they become institutionalized and defined for many reasons, for one thing because people in our society can make a living by these definitions: that is, by giving roles to marginal people. This seems to me one of the important functions of such organizations as the National Association for the Advancement of Colored People, the American Jewish Congress, the Portia Society of women lawyers, even on occasion the Rotary Club —all these groups, and in a way social scientists too—include those who make a living by defining other people's marginalities for them.

153

Now in the case of all these open, defined, institutionalized marginalities, we find people who are marginal to their marginality: that is, people who exist in one of the groups as defined and yet do not feel the group protest quite fits them, or their feelings. They do not feel as they are supposed to feel as inhabitants of that margin. And if that is true, then they join the ranks of those whom I would like to speak of as the bearers of a "secret" marginality. These are the people who subjectively fail to feel the identities expected of them. Obviously this dichotomy that I am suggesting between open and secret marginality cannot be made too sharp.

Let us look at some instances of secret marginality. The most obvious is the case of the passer. And we must think of the passer not only in the color ranks, but also in the status ranks and in the "brow" hierarchy. We may define the passer, drawing from Professor Hughes' article on "Social Change and Status Protest" (*Phylon*, X, First Quarter, 1949, 59-65), as a person who can identify with his new group in every attitude it has except its attitude towards the group he has left. And it is this sore point, of course, which makes his passing a problem of psychological marginality, rather than simple espionage. While this is the most discussed, it is perhaps the least important or prevalent of the kinds of secret marginality. For instance, there is the girl in Samoa, as Samoan culture is described by Margaret Mead, who feels more passionately, who has more jealousy, than she is expected to have. She feels marginal in a way which the culture does not allow her to credit, to recognize, to label, to give a name to, and therefore, in a way, to feel comfortable with. Or, to take a recent example that came to my notice, a girl came to see me, a university co-ed, who felt that she was quite crazy. When I tried to find out why she felt crazy, it came out that it was because she felt guilt about sexual adventures. That is, she had the feelings that would have been perfectly normal in earlier decades, but she had been convinced that it was wrong for her to feel the least bit troubled or problematic about sexual experience—she should be "cool" —and therefore she felt somewhat alienated from her group as she interpreted it, and felt marginal in a way that the youth culture did not define.

We may ask what are the factors that lead to this kind of secret marginality? I think that these factors arise from the "shape" we are in, from all the variety of human character and temperament and physique which separates us from others, which makes us individual; likewise, our position in the family, and many other individualizing experiences. Think, for instance, of the problem of the beautiful girl. Some years ago a friend of mine met a celebrated beauty-contest winner. She spent all her time trying to tell him how much she admired Harvard; she wanted to be thought of as a great brain and not as a great body; and she felt furious with the brutal, as she thought, qualities of the publicity men who moved her around the country. Contracted to appear at an exposition as sponsor of a House Beautiful, she felt all this as vulgar and materialistic. This is a well-known problem, yet we are inclined to be so envious that we cannot be quite sympathetic enough with the plight of the beautiful girl whose role is defined in a way which does not fit her as she feels herself to be; she cannot avail herself of the strategy of hiding behind her mask, because her mask is too much of a cynosure. I have known girls in this position to try to appear less beautiful than they are, for instance by wearing glasses (before these, too, became sexy), or ill-fitting clothes, or by, so to speak, wearing their body in an ill-fitting way, as some tall, big, handsome men also do.

All these people who do not fit, who do not hang together in the way that they are supposed to, who do not feel the identities they are supposed to feel, are unorganized. They have nobody to define them. They lack both the advantages and the dangers of the cultural compartmentalizers, who make their living by defining others' marginalities for them.

We must compare with this the concept of the invisible church: the union of people who, without organization, that is, formal organization, but through piety and through print (the Bible) feel close to one another and feel they "belong" through some invisible set of bonds which are irontight. They are as sure of the existence of this church as a spy is sure of the writing he has just done with invisible ink; in both cases, the future will reveal the presence of the now-invisible. But the group of people who are secretly marginal seldom have this confidence that there are recognizable others who share their situation and feeling; rather, they feel isolated because the marginalities that are talked about are precisely those they cannot bring themselves to share.

§ II

THOSE OF YOU who are familiar with the concepts of inner-direction and other-direction that my collaborators and I have developed in *The Lonely Crowd* will perhaps be in a position to raise the question whether characterological marginality may not be spreading with the spread of other-direction. Perhaps I can put this in best and clearest form by a reference to the concept of marginal differentiation. Marginal differentiation is a term I have developed from the economists who sometimes speak of "marginal" and sometimes of "product" differentiation under conditions of monopoly. What they have in mind is that each product in a monopolistic economy differentiates itself from other products by slight deviations in brand name and packaging. Each sector of the economy in this way is isomorphic, that is, tries to be similar—yet at the same time to be different. (I recently heard that one of the leading textbook publishers has the slogan, "We will sell books that are new, but not too new," and I think that puts the slogan of marginal differentiation very well.) Now with the spread of psychological other-direction in the upper-middle class, people themselves go in for marginal differentiation of personality. In order to do this they must be sensitive enough to themselves and each other to know how they appear to others, and to be aware concerning the degree to which they are different from others without being too different. This is an anxious, precarious business, to look at it negatively; it can be sensitive and comradely, to look at it positively, because it keeps people in touch both with themselves and with others. It creates a kind of attitude towards oneself which was absent in the earlier era of inner-direction, when conformity was in some ways perhaps more rigid, and in which people were less aware of these nuances of personality difference.

This awareness, this radar-like sensitivity to how one is navigating in the social world, and this tendency to make that navigation into an end of life as well as a means—these seem to me to be characteristic of the psychological type I have termed other-directed. By the same token, the idea can be advanced that the spread of this type will carry with it the spread of awareness that one is different, in secret and subtle ways. That is, we become so greatly interested in interpersonal relations, in our own sociometric location on friendship charts, and so on, that we are enabled to realize discrepancies between our internal states and those we sense in others. Moreover, as our growing economic abundance allows us to rise above the problems of sheer subsistence, we have time and energy to speculate about our fitness in the interpersonal scheme of things.

There is, furthermore, a connection between these characterological developments of our day with respect to marginality and certain social changes. On the social side what we see is a group of new hierarchies springing into existence, under which the older, relatively clear hierarchies of class and caste become amorphous and diffuse. We find, for instance, problems arising as to who rates whom, as between intellectuals and businessmen; we find problems of protocol in all walks of life, which imply that we can no longer easily speak of someone as marginal to a defined class or a defined caste. Instead, we are witnessing the rise of all kinds of, so to speak, brown and mulatto societies, groups who, with various shadings of slight difference from each other, occupy a place in the social system, not clearly distinct from other places. This confusion as to location is one of the reasons for the development of other-direction as a psychological trait, and in addition, one of the reasons why marginality may be on the increase in the sense that secret marginality (undefined marginality) is dependent on situations which are not yet fully understood and recognized by the participants. There is no union of the people who have, let us say, not quite the *New Yorker* attitude toward life, whereas they have the economic and educational position which would permit or require them to have this attitude, this being a more subtle differentiation than the older ones of sheer economic and social class. As a matter of fact, we can think of Lloyd Warner's work, with its emphasis on consumption values, as, in a way, a symptom or indication of the change in hierarchies; and all the arguments which go on so tiresomely, as I think, between Warner and the Marxists, seem to me an argument as to which status system runs the country when, in fact, neither does.[1]

§ III

WE HAVE TO THINK of marginality in terms of the social function of the marginal man before we can make any adequate inquiry into his psychology and ethics. Pirenne describes the man who, in the late Middle Ages, began to move around in the burgeoning cities and ports where one's position, as Pirenne says, instead of being measured by social status depended only on intelligence and energy. Now the court Jew is one of the most famous examples of this type of person, and he begins to take a prominent place in the society sometime after the period with which Pirenne deals, when the rise of absolute monarchy begins. The court Jew, with his international connections, is the banker of the embryo king, trying to help the king to do what the king wants to do. But the court Jew is not a marginal man at all in Park's sense; that is, he does not have the psychological consequences Park describes, be-

---

1. Perhaps a word of explanation should be added here concerning the challenge in this paragraph to some prevailing theories of social stratification in America. I am inclined to believe that researchers, by their very techniques, tend to "prove" their assumption that everyone, and not only a large number of people, is aware of his class membership (as against simply sharing values and behavior with others who are aware of the class cues of those values and behavior). Moreover, the problem of class has been investigated largely in the smaller communities where the number of parallel hierarchies is at a minimum; matters may stand very differently in large metropolitan clusters where people cannot establish a single common basis for ratings. This is not to be read, of course, as one of the now conventional criticisms of the stimulating and important explorations of Lloyd Warner and his coworkers, without which we would not be able to move on to these further complications which research has not yet found a way to handle.

cause there is little questioning on his part as to what his mission is, and there is no break on his part with the traditional Jewish values. He lives amid those values, though he moves in court circles, quite as comfortably as the British civil servant often lived amid his traditional values in India or Egypt. The British civil servant is out among strange people, but they do not exist for him except as objects to be organized, to be manipulated—the detachment of a Lord Cromer in Egypt is a good example. In the same way, the court Jew is very much a Jew: still orthodox, still tribe-connected, still the leader of the other Jews by virtue of his role in the non-Jewish economy, and using whatever power he has in that other economy simply to better the position of the Jews (in much the same way that the Rothschilds are reported to have improved the position of the Jews in Frankfort through intercession with Count Metternich).

Since, then, this kind of court Jew has a definite function both in the Jewish and the non-Jewish worlds, he does not have the psychological outlook of the bearer of either open or secret marginality. Likewise, the Jewish rebel who found his way to a political and intellectual role in the nineteenth century lacked many of the psychological consequences of social marginality; lacked some of the misery of Heinrich Heine. One good clue to this, I think, is the fact that such Jewish rebels as Marx or Börne could be violently yet not uncomfortably anti-Semitic, both in polarization from the court Jew on the one hand and from the Jewish masses on the other. For these rebel Jews of the nineteenth century found their security, found the end of their seeming marginality, in their clear vision of a future when no irrational margins of class, or ethnic group, or caste, would be left; rather than finding security, as the court Jew did, in past values. They held only to the future, with such tenacity that they could be violently anti-Semitic without self-hatred; ironically, they had some assistance here from the Messianic trend in Jewish thought itself.

The position of the Jew as marginal man really develops when he no longer has either his economic function as the court Jew or his political function as the socialist rebel.[2] Then only his marginality is his function. To a very considerable degree this is what has happened to the Jewish intellectual in the period of the last fifty to seventy-five years. (It is this which is described brilliantly in Hannah Arendt's book, *The Origins of Totalitarianism*.) The society Jew, welcomed

---

2. As one would expect, there are marginal cases to any statement one can make about a group. Thus, Ferdinand Lassalle, Marx's great contemporary, sought not only to climb in the class system as a social, but also as an ethnic parvenu. Tied securely neither to the past nor to the future, he was vulnerable to aristocratic aspersions on his Jewishness.

into the salons of the Faubourg Saint-Germain, as Proust relates, has nothing to sell in the way of an economic function; once democracy gets established, there is no longer a court for the court Jew to attend, and the Jew is not needed to finance the republic since taxes are so much more effective. Instead of goods and services, the society Jew is selling his Jewishness. In a sense, he is selling his marginal differentiation in which he claims to be different from the other Jews; and at the same time, if he were not a Jew, there would be no peculiar mutual attraction between him and the anti-Semitic aristocracy. For it is precisely because the aristocracy is anti-Semitic that he is drawn to it, as this keeps out the other Jews, while the aristocracy in its turn enjoys playing with "vice": Proust observantly describes how Jewishness and homosexuality play the same role because both are vices of the aristocracy. In the extraordinary study called the "Portrait of the Anti-Semite," Sartre recognizes something of this, and sees that the Jew in modern France, at least the emancipated Jew, is in a way created by the expectations of the anti-Semite, toward which he reacts, and against which he may sometimes later polarize himself.

We all know that it is possible to enjoy skating on thin ice, and so we must not be too sorry for some of these Jews who may have enjoyed the very risks of their marginality—the point is important because we tend all too often in social science to look only at the punishing aspects of such phenomena as alienation, marginality, and social mobility. Think, for instance, of the enjoyment some theologians derive from skating on the thin ice of their orthodoxy, while at the same time embracing avant-garde movements of thought; such men seem almost to have consciously sought out the most precarious margins one could find in the society; they are challenged, as well as tortured, by the intellectual reconciliations they must constantly make. . . .

§ IV

I WANT NOW to turn to a theme touched on at the outset, namely the contemporary influential view that marginality is some sort of disgrace, which should be abolished in all well regulated social and psychic systems. One evidence for this, to continue with our example of the Jews, can be taken from contemporary efforts, from both sides of the ethnic line, to erase Jewish marginality wherever found, to "normalize" the Jewish situation. Whereas once such efforts were manifested by plastic surgery on "Jewish" noses, they are now manifested by psychic efforts on "Jewish" souls, taking such forms as Zionist nationalism, the religiosity of the self-Judaizing Jews, artificially sustained Jewish and Yiddish usages, and so on. The chauvinistic and normalizing Jews are in turn quite aggressive against the "homeless

cosmopolitan," that is, the margin-hugging Jew who owes his existence to the Enlightenment—some Zionists here employ a similar vocabulary to that of the Soviet Union today and show the prophetic
quality of Veblen's fear that the loss of marginality might also mean
the loss to Western culture of the distinctive Jewish achievements in
intellectual life. These Jewish efforts are abetted, in America, by those
non-Jews who are so afraid of being thought ethnocentric that they
overeagerly welcome all signs of Jewish folksiness from their Jewish
friends, much as jazz was welcomed as so beautifully Negro by some
white Bohemians.

A further example of the attempts to abolish marginality by psychic surgery can be found if we examine the compulsion put on many
rapidly self-emancipating people to erase any feelings of prejudice
they may have against those of different class and ethnic background.
On this campus, for instance, students sometimes fail to realize that
they are being asked to cross both class and ethnic lines at the same
time—the situation appears to them to involve only the ethnic line.
A middle-class boy from a small Midwestern town may be confronted
with a Jewish boy from Brooklyn who is of working-class parentage,
but the former may define the encounter as a test of his ability to
shed any latent anti-Semitism; he fails to see that class and rural-urban
differences may be much more important. Or again, an upper-class
white girl may meet a lower-middle-class Negro boy and be horrified
at what she thinks is her own race prejudice, since all the marginalities
in the meeting have been packaged under the single ethnic label.
People may even break down—I have seen such cases—out of a feeling
of inadequacy to rise to such demands put on their tolerance of differences, because they do not realize how great and many-sided those
demands are. Here, as I have stated, the psychic surgery operates on
the member of the group which, in the society at large, is the dominant one—of course, such situations are probably confined to fairly
small cultural enclaves.

Reflection on such examples has increasingly forced upon me the
feeling that children have the right to be prejudiced and to move at
their own pace across class and ethnic lines; that they should not be
compelled by psychic surgery to move at a pace not of their choosing. I realize this view creates many problems to which I have no
ready answer, because one might say that they do not choose their
prejudices either; if they are given their prejudices they may be
frozen in them and unable to move or to be liberated. Nevertheless I
think we can do things which set up the educational system in such
a way as to make young people aware of what is being asked of them,
so as to reduce the loss of identity by children who are being invited

to normalize in their own proper persons relations which are a product of history, often centuries of history.

I feel this most clearly in the case of the relationship between men and women. What seems to me to be going on today is that the marginality which always exists between the sexes—because men are not quite men and women are not quite women, and wish in each case that they were surer which they were—leads under conditions of coeducation to confusion in which men are not able to establish their identity as men without being forced at once to polarize themselves against women, and much more strongly is this so for women. Men are deprived today of the latency period; they must take girls to proms from the age of—well, the sixth grade or the seventh grade on. When older, they are deprived of taverns, country clubs, and factories as sanctuaries against women. They tend to retaliate by trying to lock all women up in the suburb so as to avoid the dilemmas of confronting them outside; thus being able to meet them at their own pace and timing, without the women being aware that there are other paces and other timings.

In sum, the person who is on the other side, on the majority side, on the dominant side, of the sexual, ethnic or class line, may be forced to move rapidly, and with little awareness, across all these lines under the imputation that if he is not prepared to do so gracefully and at once he is bigoted or unemancipated.

This raises a question as to what the relation is in a given case between the life-cycle of an individual and the race-relations or sex-relations cycle in which he happens to live. It may be that the problem I am discussing is a problem of a temporary sort because it happens there is a concurrence between the particular phase of the race-relations cycle in our liberal upper-middle-class culture with the life-cycle of some of you. But I suggest that the life-cycle, even in the best of cultures, involves some marginality. We are all of us going to live too long for somebody else, though not long enough for ourselves, and I sense a tendency in contemporary social science to ascribe to marginality and to all the things that have brought marginality about—mixing of peoples, urbanization, and the rest—the problems which are the dilemmas of living in any culture. While the discovery of marginality as a concept and a topic for investigation is recent, the problem of marginality must be about as old as organized social life.

§ V

LET ME IN THIS CONNECTION say a word about the attitude of many social scientists and intellectuals today that a socially mobile person is punished and hurt by his drives to climb in the class system, by the ambiguities and marginalities of his ever-changing position. The implication is, even among thinkers who feel in the abstract that an open society is a good thing, that such mobility is hard on those who strive for it; they would be happier if they stayed put. And of course this view operates much more strongly among those increasingly active voices who sing the charms of the static society. Here it is thought that marginality can be eliminated largely by operations on the social structure, to ensure its rigidity (an utterly futile ideal, I think, but that is not my point here), though there will also be operations on psychic structure to eliminate the "anal" motivations which impel to climbing.

What appears to be left out in such views is the possibility that people use the mobility the system gives them in part to minimize the discomforts of secret marginalities, of which often they may not be aware. A lower-class person may actually feel more at home with middle-class people, not just because they have higher status—in fact, this higher status is one source of his sufferings at their hands—but because they are actually "his kind" of people. Some Negroes may actually feel more comfortable in white society. In both cases, movement which is "up" is also movement into the larger pool, and of course into a pool whose members differ from the members of the lower pool in many ways other than "upness."

What looks like the climbing of the parvenu may also be simply movement as such, or the search for challenge, or the desire for a greater amount of "social space." Conversely, we should not frown on those who want to "climb down"—a motive which is perhaps sublimated in some anthropologists and sociologists who, in their romantic belief that the lower classes or the Negroes or the preliterates have more fun, manage to spend most of their time with them. In neither case should we make people feel guilty about their desire to find new associates, or stigmatize as "uprooted" or "mobile" a person who does not care to be sedentary or parochial. Save for the rarely fortunate person who happens to be born and to live among his true peers (and is this always so fortunate?), most of us need to move around to find peers as we mature. We should not be intimidated from seeking liberation by the fear of becoming marginal both to the groups we leave behind and the groups to which we aspire. Most of the punishments meted out to the mobile person come, not from either old or new associates, but from within—from his own interpretations of what he is doing.

§ VI

MY OWN VIEW, it should be clear, springs from the ethical postulate that for a rational system of conduct one needs insight and the possibility of choice. So our problem becomes one of seeing what positions in society are conducive, more or less, to insight and choice. Whether marginality fosters insight and choice depends, of course, on the given case. Marginality can freeze people with anxiety or nostalgia, while the absence of marginality can give people so much power that they need not choose, but can make all the other people choose. That is, if one is powerful, one may be marginal in a quantitative sense, but not in a social and psychological sense. The English ruler of India did not need to choose: the Indians were the ones who had problems in dealing with him, like Aziz in *A Passage to India*.

On the other hand we must not assume, contrariwise, that powerlessness is always conducive to ethical superiority. While the powerless need insight to avoid being impressed by power, precisely because they are powerless they may not have the opportunities for insight which they need. They may not have the position, the mobility, even the marginality which they need in order to be aware of other ways of living and therefore of the possibility of choice. We must not, incidentally, assume that the upper class in America is necessarily powerful in the sense I have spoken of. If we think of the marginality of Henry or Brooks Adams or of Santayana, we will realize that in this country the upper class since perhaps the Eighties of the last century, has been in many ways quite as marginal as any other sector. This, indeed, is an aspect of the lack of clear class structuring on which I commented earlier.

To put all this another way, I am saying that the intellect is a controller of the consequences, an interpreter, of marginality, and that the intellect is at its best, and its ethical insights are at their best, when one is in a marginal position that is not too overpowering—just as one may have one's best ideas when one is on the margin between sleep and waking.

Now, finally, we might end with some questions about the implicit ideals of human life and of human society in the minds of those intellectuals and social scientists who are hostile to marginality. Park used to tell a story of an old ex-slave whom he met in Alabama. The old man was poor, and undoubtedly worse off in all material respects than under slavery. In fact, he used to boast about what a good life he had had under his old master. Park asked him whether he was not sorry about having been emancipated, and the old man replied that, no, he liked freedom—for, he said, "There's a kind of looseness about this here freedom." I myself feel that a certain looseness and disorderliness and variety of attitude are a part of the good life. One might ask, why do I have to take my stand on every issue? Why need I be all of a piece? . . .

Much the same might be said about continuity. The integrated life is connected with the straight career line, with life in the integrated neighborhood, with lack of discontinuity between the stages of the life cycle, and so on. Yet it seems to me that in taking this attitude, we patronize the skills of people in handling discontinuities. We tend to patronize the primitive when we think of him as someone who cannot move into the industrial culture. We certainly patronize the child when we think he is hard up if he has to move sometimes to a new neighborhood. We patronize the rural person when we think that he is so rural he cannot move into an urban way of living. And in our patronization we prove ourselves right. In all this it seems to me that our very gifts, especially, perhaps, in America, our ability to move in different directions, to be unintegrated to a degree, to operate on discontinuities of life and career, come to be regarded as liabilities, at least if they exceed the tolerated margin of marginal differentiation.

Plainly, this problem of ideals for human life is immensely complex, and terms such as "integration" are traps of ambiguity—I would not quarrel with someone who defined my kind of unintegrated, loosely ordered life as a form of integration on a higher level! At any rate, we can be fairly sure that the intellectuals who, in their dislike for marginality, would erase the sources of their intellectuality, are not likely to be successful in reforming society as a whole: life will continue to create both secret and open marginalities and secret and open defenses for them.

Park, in his essay on "Personality and Culture Conflict," is aware of this; he writes:

Considering that man lives so largely in the minds of other men, and is so responsive to the attitudes and emotions of those about him, it is nevertheless true that he is rather less dependent upon his environment . . . than other animals. He maintains, as over against other individuals—their attitudes and their claims—a certain degree of reserve. It is only in states of exultation and of ecstasy that he lets himself go completely, and yields himself wholly to the occasion and to the influences of the persons about him.

Ordinarily he is able, by means of his rationalizations, his cynicism and his casuistry—

And you see Park treats these, as I would, as at least in part valuable traits,

to defend himself against the psychic assaults which the presence of other persons makes upon him. He can, when he chooses, make his manners a cloak and his face a mask, behind which he is able to preserve a certain amount of inner freedom even while mingling freely with other persons. He can withdraw from the world on occasion, and men have always consciously and unconsciously devised means for maintaining social distances and of preserving their independence of thought even when they were unable to maintain their independence of action.

And, incidentally, it is just this that is one terrifying thing in totalitarian society: that it may bring this possibility to an end.

And this fact is just as significant and as charactristic a trait of human behavior as is the opposite disposition to respond to every change in the social atmosphere of the world about him.

It is for this reason, as much as for any other, that man invariably builds himself somewhere and some time a home, a retreat, a refuge, where, surrounded by his family and his friends, he can relax, and, so far as it is possible for so gregarious a creature, be wholly at home and at ease, and in more or less complete possession of his own soul. This is no more than to say that most men and some women possess a sales resistance which not even the magic of the new salesmanship can always overcome.

10. Marginality, Conformity, and Insight

LET ME WARN YOU in advance that I am not going to talk about this massive topic by laying out for you a scheme or typology of analysis, or by presenting interview material or projective test protocols, and so on. Rather, I propose to get at my subject by indirection and by implication. I shall raise many questions to which I have no answers. I shall deal heavily and designedly in ambiguities. Else Frenkel-Brunswik, Donald Campbell, Rokeach, and various other psychologists have made experiments to demonstrate the relationships between nonconformity and tolerance for ambiguity—willingness to look at a picture without having to decide at once whether it is a this or a that. Just such tolerance will be required if you are to follow me without discomfort in a mutual effort at understanding. Among other things, I shall discuss the ways in which several well-known literary men—Edmund Gosse for one, and Richard Wright for another, both of whom were brought up in extremely doctrinaire homes in which there was no other extravagance than that of doctrine—found their way to a measure of nonconformity, fruitful both for them and for society. Members of minorities in the society, they also grew up as minorities of one within the home. One of my objectives will be to emphasize that a minority position can be a blessing as well as a curse, and particularly that a marginal position—not quite in the minority, not quite outside it—may be a superior vantage point for understanding and for self-development.

§ I

LET ME BEGIN, then, with the episode in Edmond Gosse's *Father and Son*, in which Gosse as a boy experimented with idolatry, a sin severely condemned by his zealously religious father, a leader in a Puritanical sect known as the Plymouth Brethren:

All these matters drew my thoughts to the subject of idolatry, which was severly censured at the missionary meeting. I cross-examined my Father very closely as to the nature of this sin, and pinned him down to the categorical statement that idolatry consisted in praying to any one or anything but God himself. Wood and stone, in the words of the hymn, were peculiarly liable to be bowed down to by the heathen in their blindness. I pressed my Father further on this subject, and he assured me that God would be very angry, and would signify His anger, if any one, in a Christian country, bowed down to wood and stone. I cannot recall why I was so pertinacious on this subject, but I remember that my Father became a little restive under my cross-examination. I determined, however, to test the matter for myself, and one morning, when both my parents were safely out of the house, I prepared for the great act of heresy. I was in the morning-room on the ground-floor, where, with much labour, I hoisted a small chair on to the table close to the window. My heart was now beating as if it would leap out of my side, but I pursued my experiment. I knelt down on the carpet in front of the table and looking up I said my daily prayer in a loud voice, only substituting the address "Oh, Chair!" for the habitual one.

Having carried this act of idolatry safely through, I waited to see what would happen. It was a fine day, and I gazed up at the slip of white sky above the houses opposite, and expected something to appear in it. God would certainly exhibit His anger in some terrible form, and would chastise my impious and wilful action. I was very much alarmed, but still more excited; I breathed the high, sharp air of defiance. But nothing happened; there was not a cloud in the sky, not an unusual sound in the street. Presently I was quite sure that nothing would happen. I had committed idolatry, flagrantly and deliberately, and God did not care.

The result of this ridiculous act was not to make me question the existence and power of God; those were forces which I did not dream of ignoring. But what it did was to lessen still further my confidence in my Father's knowledge of the Divine mind. My Father had said, positively, that if I worshipped a thing made of wood, God would manifest His anger. I had then worshipped a chair, made (or partly made) of wood, and God had made no sign whatever. My Father, therefore, was not really acquainted with the Divine practice in cases of idolatry.

It is clear that Edmond Gosse had trapped his father in the latter's own theology. But he is not entirely happy about it; indeed, the incident remains in his memory all his life long.

For us, the episode can serve to recall an age when parents and children dealt with each other, so to speak, at arm's length; an age when parents, either with conscious or unconscious hypocrisy, sought to exclude their children as much as possible from the social and sexual know-how of adult life. Yet this marginal and excluded position of children was not without advantages for those who were not completely crushed or swindled by parental authority. The slight furtiveness of the boy making the prayer seems not unconnected with the development of his understanding of adults—to get round his father became for him almost a matter of life and death. In many Victorian novels, one gets a similar sense that the child struggles for identity through a fog of parental moral obfuscation—in *The Way of All Flesh,* the father is again a very pious man, while in *David Copperfield* he is that dream of Victorian parental neglect, the stepparent, who forces David into what seems on the surface like servitude but what turns out in the long run to be independence.

In Freud we can find explicitly the lesson we have teased out of the Victorian novelists. He writes (in his *General Introduction to*

Psychoanalysis): "The feeling of having been deceived by grown-up people, and put off with lies, contributes greatly to a sense of isolation and to the development of independence." While in this passage and quite generally he had in mind sexual life and where babies come from, he elsewhere equates lies on this topic with religious illusions and sees both together as an effort by authority to keep mankind in subjection. But his genius lay in seeing that deception isolates people and so may strengthen them, or at least those who survive and do not succumb to neurosis.

The domineering parent or teacher, as in Gosse's case or Richard Wright's, may force the child into a rebellious or sly independence —but he is quite as likely to crush the child entirely. Conversely, in a general atmosphere of permissiveness, the friendly or relaxed parent or teacher may smother children in a mood of amiable camaraderie. This may be done in the name of encouraging criticism, and in my portrait of a hyper-progressive school in *Faces in the Crowd*, I have sketched some of the ways in which nonconformity itself can become a uniform, cramping the child into an uncritical tolerance (in certain areas) and a sort of Stalinoid pessimism. The nonconformity which I admire may be defined as a map of the world made from where the given individual sits, not from where somebody else sits—an individualized map but not a crazy one, since it has some basis in reality, including social reality. We know almost nothing about the conditions in home and school and street which encourage such map-making —a therapeutic milieu does not necessarily produce it, or adversity eliminate it.

Apart from these larger questions raised by Freud's statement, I think we may take it as a good thing that sexual mysteries are today no longer the great divide between teachers and pupils, parents and children. For with secrecy the premium on a merely sexual initiation was so great that many Victorians defined maturity in terms of getting married and starting a family. Their portraits give us a sense that after adolescence they grew old—or as old as they ever did grow— quite young; unlike many people today, they were not very concerned about continued development in middle life. In fact, Freud's concept of the "genital" character as the final stage on life's way, after one has passed successfully through what he termed the oral, anal, and phallic stages, symbolizes this sudden accretion of final maturity and insight. By, let us say, the age of twenty, Freud assumed that the individual contained no more inner worlds to conquer if he had sexually joined the ranks of the grown-ups and been initiated into the secrets of the tribe.

We should bear in mind these constricting features of regularized

initiation rites, as well as the obvious emancipating ones, before we
grow too nostalgic over the simplicities, virilities, and easy conformities of an era in which, at a certain age, a young man put on his first
long pants and smoked a pipe to the accompaniment of his mother's
sobs while, at another certain age, a young woman put on her first
party dress. Lacking these compartmentalizations, our young people
are in some ways much more knowing and precocious, if less independent, than their predecessors were in Freud's day; and their initiation into life, while less sharp, may last longer, not stopping with the
acquisition of sexual or theological enlightenment. While there are undoubted losses in the fact that parents in our time want very much
to be pals with their children, to keep no secrets from them, or barriers against them, the parents may themselves be kept more alive by
this interaction with their growing children.

What seems to have happened, among many other things, is that
parents in the educated classes today have become terribly, even ter-
rifiedly, aware of their power to make or to mar their children's fates
and fortunes. They can no longer oppress children with a good conscience, and then blame the child's bad impulses or the mother-in-
law's poor heredity if things do not turn out well. The twentieth
century is not likely to be the Century of the Common Man, but it
may well be viewed as the Century of the Child, this being actually the
title of an influential book by Ellen Key written at the turn of the
century. Since children have remained small powers in a world of big
powers—a point brilliantly underplayed by the New York *Herald-
Tribune's* comic strip, "Small World"—it is parental concession and
not child rebellion which is responsible. The child has been brought
into the United Nations, given access to news and opinion, and permitted to make his voice heard long before he himself is ready to arm
himself and take on adult occupational, preoccupational, and procrea-
tional roles. The paradoxical result is that one can go into many modern
homes and get the feeling that it is the parents, and especially the fathers,
who are marginal, who are in a precarious position, who are the frightened conformists, while the children hold the strategic initiative. Like
the willing self-subordination of the British Tories in the last generation, this parental abnegation is one of those rare historic cases where
power has not shut off insight into the situation of the weaker classes,
but has actually facilitated it, even to the point of weakening the power.

§ II

ORDINARILY, of course, if one has power one does not feel the need
of insight; it is up to others, the powerless ones, to obtain insight as a
means of anticipating the wishes of the power-holder. That is one

reason why the possession of power and being shackled by a rigid conformity—an undifferentiated map of the world—often go together. Thus, we can see in the South that the amiably prejudiced white who feels that he "knows" Negroes is continuously deceived by Negroes who know him much better than he knows himself. They are in a marginal position and their livelihood, even perhaps life, depends on the acuteness of their responses, their often highly graceful ability to know what the "boss-man" wants before he wants it, while at the same time appearing insouciant and stupid. Their surface conformity is a form of nonconformity. To be sure, the white has some awareness of being deceived, just as he knows that the Negro maid is taking "totings" from the ice-box to her friends and family. But the awareness of a little deception and sabotage comforts him by establishing complicity and by demonstrating his power, just as the falsely friendly greetings he receives demonstrate his power. He is, however, not aware of the full extent to which he is seen through, manipulated, and controlled in many ways by those he believes himself to dominate. He resembles in this the husband who likes to boast that the "little woman" makes all the decisions, because he really feels, contrary to the much more ambiguous fact, that he is truly boss, bearing, if not the *white* man's burden at least the white *man's* burden; we would expect in such a case that the wife would know her husband much more coolly and unsentimentally than vice versa. The fiction that Negroes and women are sentimental is, it seems to me, plainly wishful thinking by people who do not have to know any better.

Actually, however, there are limits to the sort of knowledge the powerless person can gain in this way, for this knowledge is too close to cynicism to fit all cases. The Negro is protected by his cynicalness from an over-ready response to the white liberal, whose generosity he mistrusts as an unsentimental woman will mistrust a Don Quixote, a noble-minded man. In many cases, the suspicion of nobility is well-founded; it prevents one from being disillusioned, saves one from involvement in reform movements which will get nowhere. But a rule of thumb, no matter how useful, is not insight, and it is my judgment that the person who is completely powerless is seldom able to rise above animal cunning. And such cunning cannot cope with wholly novel, unanticipated situations. It is again an undifferentiated map, not individualized, and hence no matter how rebellious the individual may feel himself to be, he is incapable of fruitful nonconformity.

While I was reflecting on this problem, I had occasion to leave my office building at an unaccustomed mid-afternoon hour—I am living now in Kansas City. The old Negro janitor was standing outside in the sun, unconcernedly whistling a tune, when I came up from behind him. He was at once aware of my presence and, without an instant of guilt or gear-shifting, he was in the middle of the old Darky act, mumbling "yassir," "yassir," his eyes vacant, his feet shuffling. Even in his sleep such a man is instantly ready for vacuous inaction, for an uninnocent innocence of regression to childhood. Kansas City appears to retain enough of a Southern exposure not to threaten this janitor with a great deal of resentment from fellow-Negroes who would tease him as an "Uncle Tom," although to be sure the editors of the alert Kansas City Negro weekly, *The Call,* have very different ideas as to how Negroes should behave. Even so, however, the janitor's instantaneous, near-automatic response deprives him of the perplexities many Negroes confront in Northern communities, where not only other Negroes but other whites would be displeased by the actions of a handkerchief-head. In that sense, such a Negro is not marginal enough to have to make choices among complex alternatives, and to gain in the process more insight than simple sight and smell of the color white.

§ III

OFTEN, SUCH INCIDENTS bring me back to Richard Wright's remarkable autobiography, *Black Boy.* For this book can be of great help to us in understanding the subtle relations between marginality and insight. As man and boy, Wright has found it, as it seemed to him, physically impossible to respond in an automatic conformist fashion. In job after job that he held as a youngster, when he desperately needed money, his eyes would not be vacant enough when a white man was looking at him; try as he might, he could not suppress the critical nonconforming look of an equal. Angry white men would say, "What you looking at, black boy?"; friendly whites would take him aside and urge him to conform, at least while he was still in the South. As a bellboy in a hotel, he had to enter a bedroom to bring whiskey on a white man's order, and on one occasion he found a man naked on the bed with a woman. Other bellhops in such a situation could always appear not to see anything. Or they could enter into the bawdy yet subservient camaraderie of poor whites and poor blacks of the sort movingly portrayed in James Agee's book, *Let Us Now Praise Famous Men.* But Wright could not veil his frank curiosity —curiosity of the sort that, in one of the most revealing of adages, is death on cats. During all his time as bellhop, Wright feared some slip would cost him his life.

One job he held was in an optical company, making lenses. The boss was a Northerner who appreciated Richard Wright and wanted him to get on. But the two white lens-grinders for whom Wright ran errands and carried water no more liked the way he watched them work than the man in the hotel room did; they feared he would steal their trade secrets, which in his area of the South were white secrets. To amuse themselves, they set Wright to fighting against a black boy in another shop, but finally, afraid of their own boss' sympathy for Richard, they threatened to kill him if he did not quit the job. In this situation, his white protector was as helpless as he, and resignedly let him go.

I should add that, far from admiring him for his intransigence, the Negro world in which he moved was much less sympathetic than this white employer. Some tried very hard to help him cotton on to the ways of the white world, ways which to them came easily as second nature so as almost to seem like original nature: they could not grasp what it was that Wright found difficult, much as a good dancer cannot understand why anybody, having once watched him do a step, cannot do it in turn. The Negro school principal and other Negro intellectuals sought to teach him how to gain what seemed to be his ends without antagonizing the benevolently influential whites as well as the menacing if uninfluential ones. But his own uncle and other relatives, and many of his school-fellows and work-mates, hated him for putting on airs—which is how they interpreted his inability to "act right," as they termed it, in inter-racial situations. They did not realize that he wanted nothing so desperately as to "act right," to know the ropes; how little he thought of himself and how little he sought any friction or provocation!—as little as a new waiter who, out of trembling fear to hold his job, drips gravy down the back of the hostess. Not until much, much later, when he was becoming known as a writer and finding in the Communist Party certain recapitulations of his experiences in the South, did he encounter people who respected the very qualities in himself which he had vainly sought to destroy.

In *Black Boy,* as in other personal documents, our job is to try to understand the author better than he understood himself—in this case, to see if possible some of the sources of Wright's inability to conform to his "own" family, to his bellhop peers, and eventually to his Communist cellmates in Chicago. Again and again, in *Black Boy* and in the chapter Wright contributed to the book by former Communists, *The God that Failed,* we find him missing a cue that all the others got. His failure to understand something everybody around him took for granted seemed endemic. Thus, in childhood, he took the word "white" literally and could not understand why his light-colored grandmother was socially defined as Negro. This is the first example, perhaps, of Wright's problem in "looking through" a person, a problem which was interpreted by him and all his associates simply as a form of blindness. He was confused by his grandmother's being physically white. And, though he does not himself observe this, we can assume that in her ways, too, she was white in the sense of following lower-middle-class Puritanical norms. She and all the Wright family were Seventh Day Adventists, a sect which celebrates the Sabbath rather than Sunday and is in other respects much more strict than most of the denominations to which Negroes belong. Separated in many ways from other Negroes, the colored Adventists come as close as one can without "passing" to resigning from the race.

I can illustrate this by a story a friend of mine tells about a Seventh Day Adventist maid they had in their Chicago apartment. The maid was indubitably dark. But she acted "white" in her way of maintaining distance from the other colored maids in the apartment house; in her religion there are no races, and this theology influenced her posture, her manners, her whole behavioral set. It is not irrelevant to this that she would be going to church on the day, Saturday, that is the festive day for others. Finally, one of the maids next door could not stand the confusion any more and one Saturday knocked on the door to ask our friends whether that maid of theirs was colored or not. For she, like most whites, had been trained to look at the social uniform a person wears and not at the underlying color. And we may suppose that Richard Wright, having a grandmother who was both an Adventist and physically white, had a double reason for confusion. One source of his later creativity would seem to lie in his inability as a boy to put an easy end to his confusion and bewilderment.

Yet we know that other members of his family were not confused; why was he? We have no way of fully understanding this. But it seems to me that Wright's great intelligence, his artistic power and a certain unconscious stubbornness made it difficult for him to acquire cultural understandings which, in the most literal sense, were superficial. Consciously, he experienced these qualities when he was a boy as "stupidity," which is how his behavior was interpreted by others; since he could not see what they saw, he became convicted in his own eyes of being a dope. And of course once such a process of interaction with one's social environment begins, it may be cumulative; since he *is* a dope, others do not give him even such cultural understandings as he might grasp, and what begins as a slight and marginal nonconformity to the group ends up as a more sharply differentiated one.

§ IV

I HAVE CHOSEN Richard Wright as an example because he has so brilliantly described his experiences; but it is no news that these processes are universal and not confined to poor Negroes in the American South. I could as well have chosen Stephen Spender's semi-autobiographical novel, *The Backward Son,* in which the hero is defined, at home and school, as "backward" in comparison with an older brother who is "forward"—a brother to whom everything comes easily. Spender was made to feel stupid, as we now can see, because he was more alive, more sensitive, more inquisitive than his school-fellows. He was marginal to his group in ways nobody—least of all himself—could recognize; there was no definition of schoolboy intellectual at his public school. It was only much later, when he could move around the globe, that he could find people like himself and feel, instead of backward, that he was avant-garde—so much so that, like Wright, he ended up as an ex-Communist and a contributor to *The God that Failed!*

Spender comes of an upper-middle-class British intellectual family; for him, travel came naturally, once he was out of school. But Wright desperately needed the railroad fare, which he finally partly stole, in order to escape from the South. Yet in each case it often seems like an accident whether or not the step is finally taken by which the subconscious observations such a person is making all the while he is berating himself for not understanding anything—whether these observations are recognized and validated by others—consensually validated, as Harry Stack Sullivan liked to say. No matter how deeply buried, an element of irrepressible personal confidence appears to be involved. But, as with some unrecognized geniuses, a too hopeless and hapless marginality gradually shuts out experimental behavior and nonconformity, replacing it with craziness or apathy. Only in the rarest and greatest instances, that is, can one individual's inner, generative power lift him by his own bootstraps, and give him enough energy to combat the overwhelming atmospheric pressure of the total culture. By the same token, however, such power, once it has been confirmed in use—once it has established some contact with the world—becomes strengthened still further. Richard Wright tells the story in *Black Boy* of his mother's sending him as a very small youngster to shop for groceries; on his way a gang of boys beat him up and stole his money. When he came back and told his mother this, she did not comfort or protect him, but locked the door on him and gave him a stick—he was not to come back without the groceries. Even more terrified of his mother than of the boys, when he had to face their attack again, his frenzy lent him strength, and laying about him wildly with his stick he chased them off and brought home the bacon; he was never again molested.

But frenzy, while it can be momentarily salutary, is not insight; it does not help us draw a working map of ourselves or the world, nor does it have cumulative life-giving adequacy. The way out that Wright seems to have found as a non-fighter was through print; newspapers and books gave him access to a wider universe; through his literary imagination he could make contacts that surmounted the gang. At first, *any* newsprint would do: hair-raising fantastic tales, love stories, any amount of "trash" he could get hold of. The unreality of such tales, their lack of direct bearing on his situation, on race relations, on the economy—all this was probably to the good. For Wright was surrounded by people who "knew" what reality was, who had definite views on race relations, and who, like the school principal, did not lack dialectical skill in argument. Even to argue against them on the "realistic" plane would have been a kind of submission to the overriding Puritanism of the whole Negro middle-class world which brought him up and schooled him. By what was defined as "self-indulgence" in such bootless reading, and later in trying to write such far-fetched stories himself, Wright actually came in contact with a self for which the Seventh Day Adventist code made no provision. (We must remember that the middle-class Negro, eager to appear sober in the eyes of the whites, and to distinguish himself from the lower-class Negroes with their permissive, promiscuous ways, is apt to be far more inhibited than the middle-class white of the same epoch, more like a throwback to the middle-class white Puritan of an earlier day.)

When, years later in Chicago, Wright came in contact with another Puritan code, that of Communism, he finally broke from it on what amounts to the same set of issues. For he insisted again on "self-indulgence" in imagination; he refused to allow himself to be swallowed up in "agit-prop" work. He wanted to write fictionalized biographies of the South Side Negro Communists, and he frightened his less wide-ranging cell-mates by probing into details of their lives they believed to be irrelevant to the Cause. And once again Wright was defined as "stupid"; he did not seem to understand the rules of the Party, its manipulative use of writers, its internal intrigues. He tried as hard to conform to the Party code as he had to the race etiquettes of the South; he tried to suppress his curiosity and his individuality.

Eventually, however, he learned from the response of a wider, indeed an international, audience to appreciate his own qualities; no longer only as a reader of print but as a writer he could find support outside the cells in which he had previously been imprisoned. And he could begin to accept as his own insights what he had previously experienced as mere backwardness and confusion. He could win his way to the courage that is surely no less important in human affairs than physical courage: the courage of his free associations with both ideas and people.

§ V

WHEN WRIGHT encountered the Communist Party, its "line" was, and I assume still is, to use such experiences as he had had as a source of organized "minority" animus against American capitalism. To do this, it had to interpret his sufferings as due to his being a Negro first of all, an unhappy proletarian besides. That is, it had retroactively to "re-educate" his memory so that all his confusions and misgivings appeared to fall into a schematized theory of oppression of ethnic minorities, and of the working class. In turn, much as an oil company expects us to buy gas at its stations because it has given us a road map, the Party demands of people that they do its bidding because it has given them a map describing (in color) the places they have been and where they are going. And since it is simpler to navigate with a map, even if it is a distorted one, a great many people have accepted such assistance as part of a tie-in sale of ideological commodities. It is a rare person who, like Richard Wright, rejects the map in order to grope his own way.

The Communist Party, with its now-defunct plans for a Black Republic, is only an extreme instance of an organization whose existence depends on interpreting for people the source and the internal and external meaning of the discomforts they have experienced. The NAACP, the Chicago *Defender*, and other Negro "defense" agencies and media exist by defining for their constituencies the meaning of what happens to them as individuals and to the colored group in the wide white world. If, unlike Richard Wright's white-complexioned grandmother, one is obviously Negro, one can fall back on what Myrdal termed "the advantages of the disadvantages," including an ability to organize one's life around a status protest which serves as an explanatory key. And status protest can become a way of life, furnishing one not only with an alibi for the past but an agenda for the future.[1] . . .

I recall the outburst of a Negro student in a college class last fall at the University of Chicago, who said he was sick and tired of having to hear about every incident in the worldwide struggle of color,

---

1. Everett C. Hughes, "Social Change and Status Protest: An Essay on the Marginal Man," *Phylon* (First Quarter, 1949), 58-65.

no matter how trivial or distant. He could not pick up a Negro paper, he said, without having to discover the story of a Negro who had failed to have his windshield wiped by a station attendant in West Virginia, or a Negro hockey player who had been fouled, or a new pronouncement by Premier Malan. The more vocal students in the class were shocked at this, and asked him if he was against the progress of his own race, which was being won by just such agitation. They acted as if he had betrayed the cause of the oppressed merely for the sake of a little peace and comfort—a cause in which many of them were also engaged. Thus, if I had not intervened, they would have forced him to admit his guilt, as he was ready to do, for objecting to a daily diet of atrocities, and would have deprived themselves of the insight into the individual who becomes marginal to the very marginality which has previously been organized on his behalf. In some ways, I think it is more oppressive to be a minority within a minority than to be a minority within a more loosely organized and defined majority group.

§ VI

ONE WAY of looking at what I have said is to realize that every institution or label brought into being to define human experience is out of date almost as soon as created. Every sect tends to become a church; every noncomformist idea, an orthodoxy. People, therefore, are constantly under pressure to accept social definitions which do not apply to them in their ever-renewed individuality, and the resistance to these definitions is apt to generate uneasiness and guilt. . . .

I believe that social organizations draw much of their energy from unavowed and hidden marginalities. Marginality and nonconformity can, so to speak, be sublimated, much as Freud reasoned that sexual energy could be. And this is an aspect of the broader observation that people tend to systematize and rationalize their feelings in terms of socially-provided vocabularies of emotion. To be sure, such social provision must operate with certain limits given by the human condition. There are physiological as well as cultural reasons for the fact that we can discriminate many more shadings of color than of taste, which makes things difficult for those who write labels on wine bottles as well as those who seek to experience what intimations of dryness or nuances of asperity the label talks about. (In this connection, the Chinese dishes which are called "sweet and sour," such as sweet-and-sour pork, have always appealed to me semantically, for there are sweet-and-sour things which taste at once sweet and sour, as there are sweet-and-sour people and sweet-and-sour swing music.) In the same way, there is apt to be some physiological or temperamental base to the differences among people that a given culture can exploit, a theme Margaret Mead has thoughtfully explored. And all other differentiating factors, either those arising from the "shape" we are in, or from our intellectual and imaginative endowments, or from individualizing experiences such as position in the family or unique encounters, can serve, depending on circumstance, to set us apart from people or to force us together with them for protective coloration, or can leave us on some margin between belonging and not belonging. Insight and a creative rather than sterile nonconformity, I would argue, depend on one's ability to accept one's differences from others and one's similarities to them, without an artificial forcing of identity, without, that is, accepting entirely the definitions as to "who am I" and "who are we" that every family, clan, ethnic group, class and nation seeks to furnish to, and fasten on, its members. . . .

We are afraid of a chaotic situation in which people do not know their own "names," their own brand names, that is. In fact, under the mantle of cultural pluralism we often intensify these tendencies, by telling the Polish girl in Cleveland, for instance, who does not really feel very Polish, that we want to see her country's folk-dances and to put a Christmas tree in the Public Library which she will decorate after the Polish customs she has had to look up in a book. And it is evident that we are able to face these more subtle problems of identity because we have moved away from the earlier quite ferocious practices of "Americanization," when newer arrivals in this country were subjected to a kind of hazing on the part of the older arrivals. It always happens in the dialectic of social advance that the solution or abandonment of older problems has given us the fortune of newer ones. . . .

CULTURE: POPULAR AND UNPOPULAR

"LISTENING TO POPULAR MUSIC" was written as an interim research memorandum in 1947: it was intended simply as a prologue to more systematic research in musical tastes and their meanings. This, however, was one of the projects interrupted by my taking leave from Chicago to do some research at Yale. Only in this last year have I been able to return to the sociology of music, this time as consultant to a study being undertaken of the patronage of the Philharmonic Orchestra (and the relation of the Philharmonic to the whole musical culture) in Kansas City, Missouri, and I have had once again to confront the challenging and nearly insuperable difficulties of interviewing people about their musical interests and relating what they say to other relevant data about them.

I should report, in fact, that, in a seminar on "popular culture" which Reuel Denney and I gave for the Committee on Communications at Chicago in 1950, musically literate students who sought to establish correlations between preferred musical form and personality type got nowhere; the same fate has met analogous efforts elsewhere. Perhaps music in its setting contains too many subtleties for our still crude methods, for of course we do know that listening to music is the outcome of a great variety of influences, social and idiosyncratic. "Listening to Popular Music" may be read as an essay on these methodological conundrums, and perhaps as a demonstration of the virtues as well as the limitations of the small-scale project—a theme to which I return in the concluding section devoted to research method. For I firmly believe that fifteen interviews—even one—if properly understood can teach us a great deal.

The second essay in this section, "Movies and Audiences," touches lightly on analogous questions and suggests explicitly (what is implicit in the music study) that humanistic criteria of taste and judgment may help focus scientific research aims in the field of mass communications. This of course is highly controversial: many social scientists will insist that all audience behavior must be viewed relativistically, without preferring more independent reactions to stereotyped ones—or passing such judgment only in terms of social "function." But the fact remains that the most stimulating audience researches

—Robert K. Merton's *Mass Persuasion*, for example—have come out of passionate if controlled preferences for critical as against passively manipulated response. Indeed, both articles included here—on music and on movies—as well as "Bookworms and the Social Soil" and "How Different May One Be?," could just as well have been put in the preceding sections on individualism and minorities, concerned as they are with the opportunities of the audience to individuate responses to canned, mass-distributed products.

If social scientists find these articles controversial because they make qualitative judgments of the contents and consequences of the media, and do not stop with describing them, some humanists (in the narrow sense of many who call themselves that) may find just these judgments unpalatable. Many of the humanists feel on the defensive vis-à-vis the social sciences (as symptoms of all that they fear and dislike in the modern world). And they are ready to excommunicate colleagues who refuse to share their contempt for TV, opinion polls, Hollywood movies, swing music, Kinsey, and other forms of what they regard as vulgarized mass taste. While the highbrow gamesmanship of finding savor in lowbrow tastes has become fairly common in recent years, English and art departments in some universities remain refuges for those who judge a culture entirely by its traditionally packaged products, such as poetry and easel painting, and dismiss all newer forms as base and "commercial." In one sense, I respect this attitude because of its refusal to give in to sheer numbers, though often it gives in to the localized pressure of "near numbers." Those who are imprisoned by it miss a lot. They also fail to evaluate a culture properly, because they fasten on one or two conventional indices, and these may not be adequate: thus, novels may decline in quality while films rise; music may wither while architecture improves; manners may dwindle while understanding rises; and so on.

A number of my essays, in making such general appraisals, are somewhat more hopeful than the article on popular music—the same shift in my perspective I have noted earlier in this volume. Yet my sanguinity is very tentative. It is based in part on the personal experience that the culture of an earlier, more aggressively highbrow generation of Americans—my parents' generation—was thin and donnish. The very lack of a strenuous dialectic vis-à-vis lowbrow and middlebrow culture made the possession of correct taste too easy and complacent a matter. Few of the refined Americans of this period, as I meet them in person and print, seem to me as interesting and various as a great many of my own contemporaries and still younger people, even if the earlier group had more assured taste. At the same time, I recognize that there is a lot to be said for the position held by the critic

Clement Greenberg and many others that the social mobility of the middlebrow—the rise of a great culture-hungry but undisciplined group—has damaged and deranged high culture.

This same rise of a new, enormous leisure class in need of tutelage has been one of the factors responsible for the development of new professions engaged in taste leadership and education for leisure. From the sponsors of book clubs and home decoration magazines to travel agents and cruise directors, occupations have altered and originated to cope with unoccupied time. My article on "Recreation and the Recreationist" is at once an analysis of the motives behind professionalization and a warning against the dangers of a narrowing of the means and ends of play through well-meant supervision. In suggesting, for example, that a new supermarket might do as much for a community's leisure as a new park—indeed, that "chores" can often be redefined as play—I was urging my audience of professionals to examine critically conventional judgments as to the worthiness of play.

What is work for the recreationist is presumably play for his clients. In "Football in America: A Study in Culture Diffusion," Reuel Denney and I sought tentatively to indicate some of the ways in which collegiate football had become not only a highly speculative big business for the schools involved but a route of career ascent and career training for one after another of America's ethnic groups, whose mobility is reflected in the increasing degrees of movement within the game itself. Since the game was imported from England, it is possible to trace the detailed steps by which the English rules were modified to reflect different folkways among audiences and players alike; that is why we wanted, for a non-anthropological audience, to emphasize the theme of diffusion of cultural patterns.

Naturally, no simple and heavy-handed conclusions are to be drawn, such as that football is a mere reflection of American assembly lines and industrial teamwork. All we can do is to suggest certain compatibilities between the changing game, the changing factory, and the changing class mores of the country. It is one of a series of studies of sports and audiences which Mr. Denney has stimulated. I am in Mr. Denney's debt in less palpable fashion for many of the ideas in the two articles which deal with changes in leisure attitudes and standards. The first of these was presented to a group of school superintendents at the Harvard Summer School in 1952, under the auspices of the Harvard School of Education; the second was one of a series of appraisals of changing standards in contemporary American life which Professor Basil Rauch arranged at Barnard College.

The two concluding pieces in this section, "Bookworms and the

Social Soil," and "How Different May One Be?," deal with more or less high culture and defend it from middlebrow enemies. The former grew out of the Conference on Reading Development called by the American Book Publishers Council to examine the fate and future of reading in America. I found myself among some people who seemed more concerned with adjusting books to people than vice versa; my own view is that a certain amount of social maladjustment might be a small price to pay for the glories of literature. When, in "How Different May One Be?," I restated this point with reference to a hypothetical girl whose passion for music separated her somewhat from her age-mates, I was surprised to get letters from angry mothers insisting I must be an old-fashioned Simon Legree, prepared to sacrifice a child's happiness, at worst, to parental pride, and, at best, to the advance of the musical arts. Indeed, it was very hard for some readers of the article, bemused by mothers who wanted to push their child prodigies, to realize that more "permissive" and less insistent mothers might also harm a child's development, by anxious concern for the child's day-to-day adjustment rather than her long-run happiness. To be sure, I am not prepared to imprison any given child beneath the weight of its talents—to turn it into a cultural asset at its own developmental expense; nevertheless I am quite prepared to bore a number of children with difficult or classical subjects for the sake of the few who will profit from them. Again I am an individualist, but one who believes that, for most people, competent exercise of one's talents leads in the long run to a happy life.

11. Listening to Popular Music

THE STUDY OF POPULAR CULTURE—radio, movies, comics, popular music, and fiction—is a relatively new field in American social science. Much of the pioneering in this field has been done by or on behalf of the communications industry to prove to advertisers that it can influence buying habits, and to pre-test its more expensive productions, such as potential best sellers and movies. At a more theoretical level, a good deal of current interest in popular culture springs from the motives, seldom negligible in scientific investigation, of dismay and dislike. Gifted Europeans, horrified at the alleged vulgarization of taste brought about by industrialization, left-wing critics in the traditions of Marx or Veblen who see popular culture as an anti-revolutionary narcotic, high-brows who fear poaching on their preserves by middle-brow "culture diffusionists"—all these have contributed approaches, and sometimes methods as well, to the present state of research in this field.

In using Harold Lasswell's formula—"who says what to whom with what effect"—the question of effects has proved most intractable to study, being at the same time in my opinion the most important and rewarding area. By its very nature, popular culture impinges on people unceasingly; it is part of their environment, part of the background noise, color, and verbal imagery of their lives from the age at which they can first listen to the radio, watch television, or "read" comics. The researcher has two courses open to him. He can either question listeners and readers to see what uses they make of popular culture materials, or he can study the materials themselves and make guesses about the uses made of them. He is usually pushed by the difficulties of interviewing toward the latter procedure, that is, toward some form of content analysis. This is especially the case where he wants to discover the effects of nonverbal materials such as music and paintings. For he will find that, on the whole, people can talk more readily about their responses to words than about their responses, say to a tune. Yet this very readiness to talk, this availability of a critical vocabulary, may hinder as well as help the researcher; words about words may screen rather than reveal underlying meanings. The current preference for the Rorschach test or the Thematic Apperception test ("inkblot" or pictorial stimuli) as a way of getting at underlying character is evidence that verbal responses to verbal cues are likely to be stereotyped and conventionalized.

I do not mean to deprecate content analysis where this is used to suggest possible audience effects. T. W. Adorno's essays on radio music[1] and recently the Wolfenstein-Leites' book on the movies[2] indicate how suggestive such work can be, where it is informed by a grasp of the social structure into which and out of which the content comes. We must be on guard against a tendency to sniff at library or arm-chair research as against field work; certainly the quickest short cut to understanding what popular culture does for people—and hence to understanding a great deal about American culture as a whole—is to make oneself the relevant audience and to look imaginatively at one's own reactions. But the danger exists then of assuming that the *other* audience, the audience one does not converse with, is more passive, more manipulated, more vulgar in taste, than may be the case. One can easily forget that things that strike the sophisticated person as trash may open new vistas for the unsophisticated; moreover, the very judgment of what is trash may be biased by one's own unsuspected limitations, for instance, by one's class position or academic vested interest.

While field work may not cure this attitude, it may chasten and modify it, provided that we can find the vocabulary to talk to people about experiences which are not particularly self-conscious ones. My judgment is that the same or virtually the same popular culture materials are used by audiences in radically different ways and for radically different purposes; for example, a movie theater may be used to get warm, to sleep, to neck, to learn new styles, to expand one's imaginative understanding of people and places—these merely begin an indefinitely expansible list. What these various ways and purposes are, we can scarcely imagine all by ourselves; we must go out and talk to various sorts of people in various moods to get at them. It may then appear that it is the audience which manipulates the product (and hence the producer), no less than the other way around.

This is a particularly important consideration in the field of popular music, where the music industry, with its song pluggers, its jukebox outlets, its radio grip, seems to be able to mold popular taste and to eliminate free choice by consumers. The industry itself may like to think it can control matters, even at the price of feeling a good deal of guilt over trashy output or dubious monopolistic practices. Nevertheless, there seems to me no way of explaining by reference

1. T. W. Adorno, "On Radio Music," in *Studies in Philosophy and Social Science* (New York: Institute of Social Research, 1941), vol. 9, and "A Social Critique of Radio Music," *Kenyon Review*, vol. 7, p. 208 (1944).
2. Martha Wolfenstein and Nathan Leites, *Movies: A Psychological Study.*

to the industry controllers the great swings of musical taste, say, from jazz to sweet in the last decade; actually the industry ignores these swings in consumer taste only at its peril. Even in the field of popular music, there is always a minority channel over which less popular tastes get a hearing, eventually perhaps to become majority tastes.

These, then, are some of the very general assumptions which guided me in setting down the following hypotheses about a majority and a minority audience for popular music among teen-age groups. These hypotheses were directed to the Committee on Communication of the University of Chicago as a tentative basis for research, and in the period since their drafting several students have been working in this area. They have, as was to be anticipated, come up against the great methodological obstacles already indicated: how to isolate music from the influences of other media; how to understand the relations between musical conventions and the conventions of the peer-groups (the groups of age-mates); how, in the case of popular tunes, to separate the mélange of words and music, performer and piece, song and setting.

It has proved easy enough, through *Billboard, Variety,* and other trade sources, to establish popularity ratings for hits; through a study of juke-box preferences in particular neighborhoods to get an indication of class and ethnic, sex and age differences; through an analysis of chord progressions or arrangements to get clues to what musical patterns and conventions might be common to a group of hit tunes. But to move from there to the more basic problems of the use of music for purposes of social adjustment and social protest, or the role of music in socializing the young, teasing the adolescent, and quieting the old—such things as these loom on the far horizon as unsolved problems.

§ II

BEARING THE DIFFICULTY of these problems in mind, I venture to suggest, nevertheless, that one role of popular music in socializing the young may be to create, in combination with other mass media, a picture of childhood and adolescence in America as a happy-go-lucky time of haphazard clothes and haphazard behavior, jitterbug parlance, coke-bar sprees, and "blues" that are not really blue. Thus the very problems of being young are evaded—the mass media also furnish comparable stereotypes for other deprived groups, such as Negroes, women, GIs, and "the lower classes." I do not mean to suggest that in thus presenting the young with a picture of Youth drawn by adults there is conspiratorial intent—rather there is a complex interplay of forces between the adults who are the producers and the young who are the consumers.

Most teen-agers, though much more "knowing" than the picture gives them credit for being, do not think about this situation at all. Among those who do, some are aware that their group standards are set by outside forces. But their loss of innocence has made them cynical, not rebellious; and they are seldom even interested in the techniques of their exploitation or its extent.

A small minority is, however, not only aware in some fashion of the adult, manipulative pressure but is also resentful of it, in many cases perhaps because its members are unable to fit themselves by any stretch of the imagination into the required images. Such a "youth movement" differs from the youth movements of other countries in having no awareness of itself, as such, no direct political consciousness, and, on the whole, no specialized media of communication.[3] If we study, for instance, the hot rodders, we see a group of young (and pseudo-young) people who, in refusing to accept the Detroit image of the automobile consumer, create a new self-image though one in turn liable to manipulation. Likewise, the lovers of hot jazz, while not explicitly exploring the possibilities of how youth might take a hand in formulating its own self-images, do in fact resist certain conventional stereotypes. But they do so by making a differential selection from what the adult media already provide.

Thus, we may distinguish two polar attitudes toward popular music, a *majority* one which accepts the adult picture of youth somewhat uncritically, and a *minority* one in which certain socially rebellious themes are encapsulated. For the purposes of this analysis, I shall disregard the many shadings in between, and also neglect the audiences of hillbilly and "classical" music.[4]

---

3. This is of course not intended to deny that there are certain very small groups in the United States who follow the patterns of European youth movements. Many teen-age followers of Henry Wallace and young left-wing Zionists preparing for emigration to Palestine seem to have all the emotional paraphernalia of European movements, whether nominally "right" or "left."

4. Actually, both these areas are very important ones. It would be interesting to study urban fanciers of hillbilly music as possible exemplars of the many city folk who, though they depend on the city for income, friends, and entertainment, despise or pretend to despise it and long nostalgically for the very rural life from which they or their parents may have fled; perhaps for such people to define themselves as country folk in their musical and other leisure tastes is the only way they can accept the city. As for "classical" music, it is worth observing that people who tell the interviewer that they like, or "don't mind," classical (or "symphonic") music almost invariably in my own experience mean Tchaikovsky, sometimes Chopin, and occasionally Brahms. People of serious musical taste almost never describe their interests by means of a rubric, but rather by reference

§ III

MOST OF THE TEEN-AGERS in the majority category have an undiscriminating taste in popular music; they seldom express articulate
preferences. They form the audience for the larger radio stations, the
"name" bands, the star singers, the Hit Parade, and so forth. The
functions of music for this group are *social*—the music gives them
something to talk or kid about with friends; an opportunity for
competitiveness in judging which tunes will become hits, coupled
with a lack of concern about how hits are actually made; an opportunity for identification with star singers or band leaders as "personalities," with little interest in or understanding of the technologies
of performance or of the radio medium itself. Thus I assume that the
psychological functions of this medium for most of its audience include those that Herta Herzog has found in the radio daytime serial
or the quiz program and that Leo Lowenthal has found in popular
biographies.[5]

It is not easy at this stage to state the precise way in which these
indiscriminate listening habits serve to help the individual conform
to the culturally provided image of himself. To discover this is one
of the tasks of research. And to this end some further lines of inquiry
suggest themselves.

First, it has often been remarked that modern urban industrial
society atomizes experiences, isolating each experience from other
experiences. Does this same pattern operate, as T. W. Adorno suggests, in the auditory experience of popular music? Such music is
presented disconnectedly, especially over the radio—where it is
framed by verbal ballyhoo and atomized into individual "hits"—like
the disparate items on a quiz program. Can it be established that this
mode of presentation reinforces the disconnectedness often associated
with modern urban life?

Second, by giving millions of young people the opportunity to
share in admiration for hits, hit performers, and the hit-making process, are identifications subtly built up which serve to lessen the effects

---

to specific composers or, perhaps, distinctive musical epochs. It is striking that
some of the new, big, hundred-selection jukeboxes will have a "classical" section,
which is apt to include some Tchaikovsky (in an André Kostelanetz version)
along with music from *Oklahoma!* or other similar shows (in an André Kostelanetz
version). Indeed, "classical," for this sizable audience, might be defined as whatever music Kostelanetz will arrange and play.

5. Herta Herzog, "Professor Quiz—A Gratification Study," *Radio and the
Printed Page*, Paul F. Lazarsfeld, ed., and "On Borrowed Experience," *Studies in
Philosophy and Social Science*, vol. 9 (1941). Leo Lowenthal, "Biographies in
Popular Magazines," *Radio Research 1942-43*, Paul F. Lazarsfeld and Frank
Stanton, eds.

of social conflicts and to sustain an ideology of social equality?[6]

Third, does the music tell these people, almost without their awareness, how to feel about their problems in much the same way that the daytime serials package their social lessons?

Fourth, since this music is often dance music, does it help to create and confirm postural and behavioral attitudes toward the other sex? Does the facial expression assume the "look" the music is interpreted as dictating? Is the music felt as inculcating the socially right combination of "smoothness" with stylized "spontaneity," of pseudosexuality with reserve? Do these psychic and gestural manifestations then carry over from the dancing situation to other spheres of life? We should not be surprised to find that such molding of the body-image and body responses affects girls more powerfully than boys; as the subordinate group, with fewer other outlets, girls can less afford even a conventionalized resistance.

It is not unlikely that we will discover that the majority role represents in many of its aspects a pattern of "restriction by partial incorporation."[7] That is, the majority is continuously engaged in the process of adapting elements of the minority's musical outlook, while overtly ignoring or denigrating minority patterns. Jazz itself,[8] many of the dance steps, and lyrical images are almost entirely minority products to begin with. But they undergo significant changes in being incorporated into the majority style, just as radical intellectual and ideological developments are modified by academic acceptance.

§ IV

THE MINORITY GROUP is small. It comprises the more active listeners, who are less interested in melody or tune than in arrangement or technical virtuosity. It has developed elaborate, even overelaborate, standards of music listening; hence its music listening is combined with much animated discussion of technical points and perhaps occasional reference to trade journals such as *Metronome* and *Downbeat*. The group tends to dislike name bands, most vocalists (except Negro blues singers), and radio commercials.

The rebelliousness of this minority group might be indicated in some of the following attitudes toward popular music: an insistence on rigorous standards of judgment and taste in a relativist culture; a preference for the uncommercialized, unadvertised small bands rather

6. Cf. my article "Equality and Social Structure," *Journal of Political and Legal Sociology*, vol. 1, p. 72 (1942).

7. See Harold D. Lasswell, *World Politics and Personal Insecurity*.

8. Cf. Kurt List, "Jerome Kern and American Operetta," *Commentary*, vol. 3, p. 433 (1947).

than name bands; the development of a private language and then a flight from it when the private language (the same is true of other aspects of private style) is taken over by the majority group; a profound resentment of the commercialization of radio and musicians. Dissident attitudes toward competition and cooperation in our culture might be represented in feelings about improvisation and small "combos"; an appreciation for idiosyncrasy of performance goes together with a dislike of "star" performers and an insistence that the improvisation be a group-generated phenomenon.[9]

There are still other ways in which the minority may use popular music to polarize itself from the majority group, and thereby from American popular culture generally: a sympathetic attitude or even preference for Negro musicians; an equalitarian attitude toward the roles, in love and work, of the two sexes; a more international outlook, with or without awareness, for example, of French interest in American jazz; an identification with disadvantaged groups, not only Negroes, from which jazz springs, with or without a romantic cult of proletarianism; a dislike of romantic pseudosexuality in music, even without any articulate awareness of being exploited; similarly a reaction against the stylized body image and limitations of physical self-expression which "sweet" music and its lyrics are felt as conveying; a feeling that music is too important to serve as a backdrop for dancing, small talk, studying, and the like; a diffuse resentment of the image of the teen-ager provided by the mass media.

To carry matters beyond this descriptive suggestion of majority and minority patterns requires an analysis of the social structure in which the teen-ager finds himself. When he listens to music, even if no one else is around, he listens in a context of imaginary "others"— his listening is indeed often an effort to establish connection with them. In general what he perceives in the mass media is framed by his perception of the peer-groups to which he belongs. These groups not only rate the tunes but select for their members in more subtle ways what is to be "heard" in each tune. It is the pressure of conformity with the group that invites and compels the individual to have recourse to the media both in order to learn from them what the group expects and to identify with the group by sharing a common focus for attention and talk.

Moreover, many factors, including the youth orientation of the culture generally, lower the age at which children venture into the

---

9. This combination of respect for group cooperation along with individual spontaneity can be found here in both unconscious preference and explicit formulas. Sometimes hot jazz constitutes a satire on sweet or corny music, hence of the attitudes that go with them.

"personality markets" to be judged by their success in terms of popularity. As high schools adopt the social customs and listening habits
previously postponed until college, so the grammar school tends to
ape the high school in dating patterns, proms, and so on. At the same
time, the personalities of the popular music industry have every reason to cultivate the child market and are quite willing to "rob the
cradle." This convergence of forces means that children are compelled to learn how to respond to music, in a fashion their peer-group
will find acceptable, at increasingly earlier ages. Under these pressures, music can hardly help becoming associated with both the
excitements and the anxieties of interpersonal relationships.

§ V

SO FAR, I HAVE OBTAINED some fifteen long interviews with young
people about popular music. Since these interviews were in the nature
of a limited pre-test, simply part of the long process of developing
a questionnaire which could then be used on a selected sample, I
made no effort to obtain a sample but engaged in random house and
street interviewing in white (and Nisei) South Side Chicago, seeking
to vary only sex, age, and economic standing in a very rough way.
The respondents ranged from fourteen to twenty-two and from probably upper-lower to middle-middle class. In addition, I sought data
on the higher social strata from the always available "sample" of
traditional social psychology—namely, my students—and data on the
Negro community from a few discussions with Negro students and
musicians.

One advantage in interviewing teen-agers about their music
listening habits is that—as compared, for instance, with interviewing
on politics—one meets little resistance (save for an occasional over-
protective mother), since all do listen and like to talk about their
tastes; if the interviewer had cards with hits listed on them, they
would doubtless enjoy ranking the cards and then explaining their
rankings. However, the group as a whole—as compared with housewives—tended to be inarticulate, even if not shy; a good deal of
direction was needed in some portions of the interview, and this ran
the obvious risk of tilting the responses.[10] After introductory questions concerning the respondent's age, schooling, family data (for
example, siblings, father's occupation, residential mobility, and, where

---

10. I have also found that dual interviewing, in which my colleague Reuel
Denney participated, can help to establish easier rapport and deeper probing and
can allow much closer analysis of the interviewing process itself. Here one of
the pair of interviewers can take notes—or fend off the baby—while the other chats
with the respondent; of course, the two interviewers have to be sensitive to
each other's cues if they are not to get in the way.

possible, socio-economic status and mobility strivings), I turned to general questions about radio listening habits: length of time, place (that is, where, and with whom, listening occurs), favorite types of programs, and the like. Then came the questions about music. (Depending on the rapport, the order was sometimes reversed.) The schedule was long and open-ended, pointing toward the problems indicated in the analysis above.[11]

One question which sometimes led to illuminating answers was this: "How do you and they (your friends) decide what is a good or bad piece?" One seventeen-year-old girl, the daughter of a railroad telegrapher, said, "If it's popular we go for it; if it's played on the Hit Parade." Her answer to whether her social life would be affected if she hated music was, "That's all there is to do for kids our age." Yet the time she craved music most was when she was alone; the somewhat sultry love ballads that were her favorites were perhaps vicarious company. Like virtually all the other respondents, she vigorously denied attending broadcasts or having any desire to meet her favorite performers. "I don't swoon over anybody," she said.

I also discovered that respondents generally felt much safer in stating their musical dislikes than their musical likes; the former were volunteered readily, while the latter came out only if approval for the preference seemed in the offing. That is, many would quickly reject a whole area: "I hate hillbilly," or "I can't stand fast music," or "Negroes are too jumpy." More rarely something specific was rejected: "I dislike Tommy Dorsey; he has no rhythm, just blasting of horns." Or, " 'Bubble Gum' is the craziest song." Many said they disliked commercials and several that they would not buy anything that was advertised. As in high-brow circles, so in middle-brow and

---

11. A few sample questions: favorite tunes (and how far back these, and the lyrics, can be recalled); favorite bands; perhaps a discussion about the shift from swing to sweet and the reasons for it; what the hit-making process is and what effect a disclosure of such information has on the respondent; questions about the function of popular music in the peer-group, e.g., for dancing, kidding around, appearing sophisticated, and what would be the effect on his popularity —or on his more general feelings of "belonging" to the community—if the respondent could no longer listen (where I went into this, and the respondent was willing to make the experiment of thought, he said, in effect, "I would be isolated," or "I would be lost," or sometimes, "It would make no difference"); attitudes toward Negro musicians; favorite movie stars and fan attitudes generally; feelings about people with different musical tastes (often revealing within a family constellation, either vis-à-vis adults or vis-à-vis siblings); attendance at radio broadcasts; possible relations between mood and amount and type of music listening. Of course it often turned out that a whole congeries of questions was irrelevant for the participating respondent, or he was incapable of answering them; further interviewing should sharpen the questions that can be asked and shed further light on those that provoke anxiety, sudden awareness, sudden rapport, and so forth.

low-brow ones, enthusiasm would seem to be a greater social danger than negativism: the fear is to be caught liking what the others have decided not to like.

Among these young people, music seemed to be one of the principal areas for peer-group training in the appropriate expression of consumer preferences; by learning to talk about music, one also learned to talk about other things. Yet the vocabulary used to discuss music, as it turned up in the interviews, was in the majority of cases not a very differentiated one, but rather the "swell," "lousy," "I go for that," and so on which signify preferences for other cultural commodities, tangible and intangible. Indeed, one differentiation, as already indicated, between my hypothetical majority and minority wings lies in the latter's development of strict and often highly articulate standards for judging jazz.

This leads us to a final paradox. The hot jazz lovers are protesters. They are individualists who reject contemporary majority conformities. In the very process, however, do they not in many, perhaps most, cases simply move into another peer-group which holds them fast, and adopt a new conformity under the banner of nonconformity? While my handful of interviews in white South Side Chicago brought to light only a single hot-jazz fan, there have been a number of such fans among the students at the University of Chicago. Sometimes these are young men—strikingly enough there are very few hot-jazz girls, save in an occasional "symbiotic" relation to a hot-jazz boy—who grew up as somewhat rebellious individuals in a small high school group where they stood almost alone in their musical orientation. Then, when they came to the university, they found many other such people and for the first time experienced the security and also the threat of peers who shared their outlook.

What happens then, when this discovery is made, is something we are far from understanding; obviously, the problem touches on the whole congeries of issues connected with social and intellectual mobility, the American *rites de passage*, the role of big cities and intellectual centers. We may perhaps assume that the hot-jazz fan can employ his *musical* deviations (from the standpoint of the great majority) to conceal from himself other surrenders he makes to his peer-group. Or, he may find within the field of jazz further possibilities of protest by taking a still more esoteric stance, for example in favor of "pure" Dixieland or of some similar now-frozen cult. But what if his peer-group, conceivably as the result of his own initiative, moves with him there also? Does popular music itself offer him enough variety to permit him to use it alternatingly to establish prestigeful social distance from others and needed ties to them? And how does it compare in this respect with other cultural products, such as books, movies, art, and modern furniture?

Difficult as these questions are, it seems to be easier to understand the uses of music in this sociological sense than it is to understand the variations in what people of different psychological types actually hear when they listen to music. Is it foreground noise for them or background noise? What is it, precisely, that they "perceive?" Ernest Schachtel has made a brilliant beginning on the question of what meaning physical forms have for people, through seeing what they make of Rorschach inkblots. Experts in auditory perception have not succeeded, so far as I know, in finding an auditory stimulus as useful as the Rorschach test in circumventing cultural stereotypes. Our problem is to reach the people for whom music or plastic art or the movies are appealing in part just because they are more comfortable with sounds and images than with print and words. We are brought back to our problem of how to communicate with them.

§ VI

WHILE THE INTERVIEW GUIDE I developed on the basis of these research suggestions covered movies, magazines, and favorite radio programs as well as music, it did not explore the whole range of popular culture activities (and inactivities such as just sitting), or pay sufficient attention—though it did pay some attention—to hobbies, pets, dating, and other leisure pursuits. I am convinced that we cannot understand the role of any communication medium in isolation from the other media and from other leisure activities, any more than we can understand individual manipulation of the materials in the media without understanding the group which the individual belongs to, wants to belong to, or wants to be set apart from.

This truism led me to the further conclusion that one cannot hope to understand the influence of any one medium, say music, without an understanding of the total character structure of a person. In turn, an understanding of his musical tastes, and his use of them for purposes of social conformity, advance, or rebellion, provides revealing clues to his character, to be confirmed and modified by a knowledge of his behavior and outlook in many other spheres of life. . . . Plainly, we cannot simply ask "who listens to what?" before we find out who "who" is and what "what" is by means of a psychological and content analysis which will give us a better appreciation of the manifold uses, the plasticity of music for its variegated audiences.

12.   Movies and Audiences*

It is said by film critics (Gilbert Seldes, for example) that older people stay away from movies because the latter are not sufficiently adult and mature. (We know that the "average" moviegoer is 19, and that comparatively few people over 30 are to be found in the film audience.) The facts, however, may be just the reverse: films are too mature, move too fast, for older people to catch on to and catch up with. The same may be true of other newly-developed media whose conventions and emotional vocabularies the American young have learned as a mother tongue. Possibly realization that the old have to learn the new language of films (or TV) would be a first step toward appreciating some of the ambiguities of communication in which the movies and other media are involved—ambiguities related to the tensions between the generations, between the social classes, and between character types.

§ I

AN EFFORT TO UNRAVEL some of the ambiguities hidden in the term "escape," often used in connection with films and other media, may be a good place to begin. It seems to us that association of movies with the concept of escape may be a way of playing down the revolutionary or insubordinate rôle of the media, for one's children, or the lower strata, or even the childlike or less responsible parts of oneself. Children and adults often toss off a movie as "just a show," as if it made no more impression on them than the popcorn did which they ate there. But parents are right to suspect, in moments when they do suspect, that there is more to movies than that, though the nature of that "more" seems to have been changing over the years.

In the studies of the movies made under the Payne Fund twenty years ago, much evidence was gathered concerning use of the movies by young people who wanted to learn how to look, dress, and make love. What has changed since then, perhaps, is the kind of enlightenment that is sought. The young people whose reactions were studied by the Payne Fund investigators were often of lower-class origin; in the films they were suddenly brought face to face with sex and splendor, with settings and etiquettes remote from their own experience and observation. Today, however, American audiences are, with

---

* With Evelyn T. Riesman.

the rising standard of living, less remote from splendor, and with the rising standard of education, less remote from etiquette and social know-how generally.

While the movies are still a place where social class-learning goes on, the mixture of messages has become a more complex one; many other, less palpable skills are taught in addition to the linguistic lessons which enabled Eliza Doolittle to be received among those whose passport was their control of R.P.—"received pronunciation." Though the evidence is tantalizingly little, we have the impression that young people of, let us say, sixth grade level and up resort to the movies today, not so much to have a look at an exotic and make-believe world (though of course, as in the films of DeMille, these older patterns survive), but increasingly in order to understand complex networks of interpersonal relations. . . . Children who meet each other in the shifting peer-groups of city high schools are driven, somewhat more even than children of an earlier time, to depend on a precarious popularity as their main security. Athletic prowess may be declining as an unequivocal assurance of status, and certainly no other prowess can substitute for interpersonal competence as a guarantor of social success.

There have been analogous developments in the occupational world, and middle-class adults, with the loss of older certainties, religious and secular, look to their contemporaries for cues as to what in life is worthwhile. The flood of "peace of mind" books is one illustration. To take another example, audiences at race relations "problem" films may take the movie, not in terms of getting worked up themselves about racial injustice, but as a cue concerning proper race-relations attitudes in a group in which they may want to move. Or they may take it as a cue to "interesting" experiences they might want to have with Negroes or Jews. An advertisement for *No Way Out* in the New York papers (August 15, 1950) declared it to be "an ADULT picture . . . it challenges your own ability to experience the emotions of others."

§ II

TO PUT THIS another way, the "problem" film may be a far wider category in fact than it is in popular belief. Not only do the movies portray scenes that duplicate or foreshadow the audience's own leisure-time problems in dealing with people, but the movie-going itself increasingly becomes an experience-with-people, one which makes demands on the audience for having the proper reactions. This focus may be beyond the grasp and even the interest of those who grew up in a more "inner-directed" era. Although on one level—and, to be sure, for many people entirely—the movie fills in between people who go in company, so that they avoid any demand for conversational or sexual gambits, on another level the performance is not simply a way of killing time: it makes the demand that it be appraised. A doctoral thesis by Eliot Freidson on children's attitudes towards the media shows how early they place themselves on a critical "taste-gradient," with a peer-oriented vocabulary for describing the comics, TV shows, and movies; these children are often very critical critics indeed, in terms of documentary detail if not of ultimate values. In their feeling, they are seldom alone at the movies; rather, the films are a place to show sophistication. At another age and class level, movie audiences coming out of a "little" or "art" theatre are even more concerned with their reactions and criticisms, and how these affect the company they are with. On a more abstract level of research, the degree to which contemporary movie *content* may be seen as involving common interpersonal angles and triangles can be seen in the psychoanalytic interpretation of plot-themes in the Wolfenstein-Leites book *Movies: A Psychological Study.*

§ III

IT IS IN this context of shifting meanings—based both on shifts in movie form and content, and concomitant shifts in audience situation and mood—that cultivated upper-middle-class parents and teachers today carry on their battle against their children's and charges' addiction to the media. It sometimes seems that they object to all "passive" forms of recreation, and are angry that their children do not play out in the open air, or go folk-dancing, or learn handicrafts. That this cannot be the whole story becomes evident when these same adults accuse the media of destroying children's reading habits, at least for "good" books. The fact is, that parents feel about these newer media much of the way paternalistic employers have felt about union organizers—strangers who are coming in with strange gods to break up the one big happy family. For these parents can share the culture of books with their children, but often cannot share the culture of comics, movies, or TV; the personalities of the latter appeal to children over the heads of parents, much as the Pied Piper of Hamelin did.

Occasionally, the parents band together in PTA groups or otherwise to bring pressure on movie exhibitors and others. More often, they succeed in convincing their own children that their (the parents') tastes and values are superior. But the results of such a victory are not always happy. When Katherine Wolf and Marjorie Fiske of Columbia's Bureau of Applied Social Research made their pioneering study of child comic-book readers, they discovered that those children who did not read comics (or who strongly felt, though they did read, that they shouldn't) were often oppressively and neurotically under parental domination, pathetic imitators of adult attitudes. Unable to invent counter-stimulations for their children, these parents had had to resort to manipulative intimidation, as those did who convinced their children (shades of the crusade against masturbation!) that comic reading was bad for the eyes.

To be sure, social class is one of the main factors determining parental stances towards the media as Margarete Midas shows in her article, "Without TV," in a previous issue of *American Quarterly*. There, interviews done immediately in the wake of a controversial advertisement for television sets, in which Angelo Patri testified that children without TV were likely to be left out of the popularity game, showed that only in the better educated strata was there any parental concern about children's media habits; in the working classes, of whatever income level, TV was taken for granted as part of the furniture, as pleasant and as apt to be shared as a sofa.

It is perfectly possible that working-class insouciance toward children is superior to middle-class anxiety. But to draw this conclusion would be to accept too readily the prevalent versions of urban pastoral. The working class, both as price and asset of its position, avoids by greater or lesser degrees of passivity some of those ambiguities in the dialectic between children, peers, parents, and media that the middle-class person cannot avoid who aims, in Ortega y Gasset's phrase, to "live at the height of the times." Middle-class parents, however, have been too ready to conclude that the media are in the trough rather than the height of the times (a judgment Ortega himself would share). They have therefore taken a defeatist or a censor's attitude toward the products of Hollywood and Madison Avenue.

§ IV

CENSORSHIP ALMOST ALWAYS miscarries when it is merely negative— in the media it has ironically (as G. Legman has so carefully documented in *Love and Death*) helped substitute sadism for sex. Censorship either of the act of looking at movies, TV, etc., or of the quality of the media looked at can best be avoided by providing something even better. But this is difficult to accomplish at a time when parents feel they have lost influence over their children. Indeed, the media are blamed for all our ills because by chance they have developed at the historical moment when the philosophy about bringing up children has been to leave them to their own devices. "Their own devices" have been the media, and parents have begun to beat a retreat from laissez-faire, without as yet arriving at a well-administered domestic economy. If they had more conviction about making their children practice music, for example—less misgivings both about music and their own authority rôle—they might have less objection to other things that their children did in their "free" time. But nobody is going to find for parents the films and other media performances which are as sure cross-generational bets as *Huckleberry Finn* or *Treasure Island;* in order to guide children, parents must first make an effort to understand them and the media —as already indicated, the one presents no fewer problems of acculturation than the other.

Let us take as illustration the movies of W. C. Fields. We don't suppose that Sam Goldwyn would contend that they are problem films. Yet in a society where we are frequently urged to be tolerant of others and to understand them, and where the others are presented as amiable, if manipulative, the huge suspiciousness of Fields may be liberating. It may allow children to come to terms with their own paranoiac though unacknowledged fears, and parents to recollect their own, and thus move closer to their own childhood. We may also learn from Fields to acknowledge our inhumanities—and thus paradoxically to become more human. Yet our critical conventions may lead us to deny these virtues in Fields and to see him (unaware that clowns are never simple) simply as a clown.

§ V

SUCH CONSIDERATIONS lead us to raise questions about the various levels of movie criticism both by the audiences and by the reviewers. The children studied by Eliot Freidson knew that *Born Yesterday* had won an Academy Award—indeed, for many who were Catholics, this seemed to legitimate the film at least as sound entertainment despite the ban on it pronounced by the local priest. But in general the children's judgments were cramped by a narrow "realism"—"why is it that cowboy heroes never get killed?" or "how could he fire seven shots out of a Colt six-shooter?"—although they did move, as they grew older, away from the excitement of "exciting" films (cowboy, gangster, etc.) to the subtler pleasures of supposedly adult films (*Bird of Paradise*). Yet perhaps this gradient itself is a sign of "realism": they know what is becoming to their age-grade. They were, perhaps, preparing to make the same sort of judgment later on that many of our friends made about *King Solomon's Mines,* whose complaint that "Hollywood *would* have to put in the love interest" and "keep Deborah Kerr looking too well-groomed for a safari" nearly spoiled their pleasure in an excellent movie. For they, too, in their purism, were misled by a very rigid idea of "realism."

From the side of the reviewers and critics, we all know that it has become standard operating practice to urge Hollywood to cope with real-life "problems." These people, however, are frequently all too sure what the "problems" of American life are, in all our great variety of subcultures; in this sense, even the problems are comforting in their timelessness and stereotypy. It takes imagination to look for problems that are not recognized as such, and films can remain a resource for such imagination only if children and adults alike are taught—or not untaught—to reject the gloss finish of "realism" and to appreciate what the literal-minded might reject as fantastic. Possibly the vogue of science-fiction testifies to an effort to blend both tendencies; but there is all too little fiction in most of it, indeed only banal extrapolative predictions of things to come.

On a more general level, it seems to us that many of the older generation who find films vulgar and shallow simply miss what is there. If we look at movies even ten years old, we see how quickly naunces of expression and phrasing replace the (as it now seems) strident and stilted acting of the earlier sound films. Thus, the "good-bad girl" heroine, as Wolfenstein and Leites describe her, is a tissue of ambiguities compared with the clear outlines of vamp or good girl in less sophisticated films of the 20s and 30s. While the young are often also unable to appreciate these ambiguities—and certainly to verbalize them they can take such movies in their stride without any feeling of alienation from contemporary usage and convention.

We have almost no movie criticism concerned with such questions. After seeing and greatly enjoying the film of *The Great Gatsby*, we examined some of the critical reactions to it. The fan magazines carried such comments as "a terrible vehicle for Alan Ladd"—made by those who wanted Ladd to stay typed as a private eye or something like that. In the daily press, the comments on the film were as conventional as these "program notes" usually are. In the occasional mentions of the film in the critical reviews, it was also panned as a poor vehicle for Ladd—this time in terms of sacrilege to Fitzgerald's memory. The actual directorial achievement with Ladd, the gifted casting of Betty Field and Shelley Winters, and the many subtle qualities in the film—these, as it seemed to us, were not recognized by any of the critical notices at any "brow level." And if we are even half-way right, the makers of the film must have felt that their intentions failed to communicate to any significant sector of their audience—certainly not to the motion picture exhibitors who wrote in to their trade journals about the "poor biz done by this stinkeroo."

It goes without saying that anyone who sought to discuss "Gatsby" in terms of stage and literary traditions—or, for that matter, to adapt the book to the film medium in overdeference to those traditions—would overlook many of the very themes which might illuminate the understanding of films and so create modes of criticism in which older and younger generations might eventually converse. (To be sure, in any such cross-generational effort there are timing problems involved: the young have time to see films they don't have time to understand, while adults have time to understand films they don't have time to see!) In all likelihood, any improvement of the grown-up audience of films would encourage those in Hollywood who must now feel that only "message" films get a message across. The failure of quality in the movies that is now so endemic might then become less frequent.

To be sure, the reactions to *Gatsby* may be a poor example; and in any case there are some fine media critics—James Agee, the late Otis Ferguson, Mark Benney, John Crosby come to mind—who are developing an independent tradition of media criticism.

In saying this, however, we realize that any substantial increase in critical awareness for films and other popular culture products may tend to reduce still further their limited function as avenues of escape. While there is much to be said for teaching young and old an understanding of film art, we are all too aware of the ambiguities of the educative process, the dangers of overseriousness and over-preciousness and overcompetitiveness. Any declaration that American films can be taken seriously means guilt for many that they had missed this, and strenuous efforts to climb this newly revealed gradient of taste. On the other hand, such a declaration may liberate some from a prejudice which virtually forbade them to enjoy American films—and made others feel secretly guilty for falling for "corn." Parents and children who seek to come together in terms of mutual appreciation of the newer media will doubtless often find themselves facing similar dilemmas.

§ VI

WE HAVE DONE little more than open up discussion of some of the complex relationships which exist between movies (and other media), parents, children, and critics. Actually, students know almost nothing about these various audiences. This is so in part because movie audience-research (having the "Hooper" of the box-office) has lagged behind radio audience-research (where it was needful to show advertisers that radio, and now TV, do have effects). It is also because we have looked too much for the overt "messages" the movies bear and too little for the ways in which different audiences shape their experiences of the movies in terms of their character structures and daily-life situations. Moreover, the influence of films may lie in seeming irrelevances—in the handling of shape and color, for instance—and not in what they "say." But this remains in the realm of the speculative. The painstaking studies of film-effects by the Research Branch of the Army (see Carl Hovland *et al., Experiments in Mass Communications,* 1949) indicate how terribly difficult it is to come up with valid quantifiable results even where, as under Army conditions, we can shift audiences and create control groups with some freedom and resourcefulness of method.

Yet we suspect that the difficulties in qualitative analysis of the effects of films are not unconnected with the present low state of criticism of the movies as an art form. While the translation of esthetic experience into verbal form presents in any case an almost insurmountable problem—how much music criticism is there, for example, which is more than gossip or pedantry?—the movies have hit us so suddenly that we have not had time to begin a tradition of appreciation on which a tradition of research might build. Here, then, is one of the places where humanists and social scientists, equally at a disadvantage, might come together to see what each set of skills might contribute to heighten the awareness of Americans of all ages for the imaginative qualities of their best films. As it took the Romantics to "invent" the beauty of mountains, so it may take an analogous effort to "invent" the beauty of "the Hollywood hallucination."

13. Some Observations on
Changes in Leisure Attitudes

> . . . our sole delight was play; and for this we were punished by
> those who yet themselves were doing the like. But elder folks' idle-
> ness is called "business"; that of boys, being really the same, is
> punished by those elders; and none commiserates either boys or
> men. For will any of sound discretion approve of my being beaten
> as a boy, because, by playing at ball, I made less progress in studies
> which I was to learn, only that, as a man, I might play more unbe-
> seemingly? and what else did he who beat me? who, if worsted
> in some trifling discussion with his fellow-tutor, was more embit-
> tered and jealous than I when beaten at ball by a playfellow?
> —*The Confessions of St. Augustine*

TEN YEARS AGO, I sat as a member of an international committee
engaged in drawing up a Bill of Rights to be presented to some
presumptive postwar agency. Among the rights proposed was one
stating that all men and women had a right to "reasonable leisure,"
and that it was the duty of governments to make this right effective.
In the ensuing debate, this was dubbed (by a Harvard professor)
"Riesman's freedom from work" amendment, and, though the amendment carried, many of the hard-working delegates regarded it as a
concession to the modern cult of effortlessness. Others thought the
issue irrelevant, on the ground that, until the right to work was
secure, the right to leisure could wait. This was my first introduction
to the discovery that many people are uncomfortable when discussing leisure: as with sex, they want to make a joke of it. And there
is no doubt that most of us feel vulnerable in a milieu that increasingly asks us whether we are good players as well as good workers—
a problem St. Augustine's serious-minded, self-deceiving elders do
not appear to have faced. For us, at any rate, there is nothing easy
about effortlessness. I want here to trace some of the sources of vulnerability.

§ I

IN HIS NOVEL, *The Bostonians*, written about seventy-five years ago,
Henry James describes a week that his hero, Basil Ransom, passed at
Provincetown on the Cape. He smoked cigars; he wandered footloose
to the wharves; perhaps he read an occasional book; it does not
appear that he swam. He was, *pro tem*, a "gentleman of leisure." It
may be that a few fossils of the species are preserved in the Athenaeum,

but I rather doubt if they can be found in Provincetown. At least my impression is that people who go to such places for the summer appear to lead strenuously artsy and craftsy lives: even if they lie on the beach, they are getting a competitively handsome tan, but most of the time they appear to be playing energetic tennis, taking exhausting walks, entertaining children and guests by that mixture of grit, insects, and tomatoes known as a picnic; and in the evening attending lectures, the experimental theatre, and colloquia in private houses. While they may be less systematically engaged than many students in laying by credits, they are gainfully improving themselves in body and mind; and, perhaps unlike many students, they are subject to the additional strain of having to feel and to claim that they are having a good time, being victims of that new form of Puritanism which Martha Wolfenstein and Nathan Leites in their book *Movies* have termed "fun-morality."

All this in a country in which the average industrial work-week has declined from 64 hours in Henry James' day to around 40 in ours, not including the mid-morning coffee break and the other sociabilities which have crept into the hours which the census registers as working ones. We are in the ambivalent position described by Lynn White, Jr., President of Mills College, commenting on a roundtable on "leisure and human values in industrial civilization" of which he was chairman at the Corning Conference a year ago:

> We said, "Ha, ha, I have no leisure; why am I involved in this?" It was a sense of guilt and, at the same time, a sense of pride. In other words, we feel leisure is a cultural value. Theoretically we would rather like to participate in it, but we are sort of proud that we are such responsible members of society that we really have no time for leisure.[1]

Our responsibility extends, in fact, to a concern for how other people —our children, our pupils, our union members, the community at large—are spending their leisure. In fact, those of us who are in the education industry and its allies, such as the library industry, have developed quite substantial interests—vested interests—in other people's leisure. We see their loose time, as others see their loose change, as our problem and our responsibility. This is, I suggest, one reason why the "gentleman of leisure," whose portrait Thorstein Veblen drew so sardonically in the '90's, is obsolete today. Instead, we are all of us—that is, almost all—members of the leisure class, and face its problems. As Eric Larrabee pointed out at Corning, the expansion of the leisure "market" has brought "friction" in its wake.

---

1. For this and later quotations, see *Creating an Industrial Civilization: A Report on the Corning Conference*, Eugene Staley, ed. I have drawn on the materials prepared for this conference by Reuel Denney and myself.

It is, of course, characteristic of American life that our bonanzas, our windfalls, whether treasures of the soil or treasures of the self, have been interpreted by the most sensitive and responsible among us as problems. I'm not sure but that the hue and cry against Puritanism isn't beginning to be overdone, and that we won't come to realize that our moral seriousness—in fact, our fun-morality—is not wholly negative. At the Corning Conference, the Wellesley-educated Hindu author, Miss Santha Rama Rau, scolded us; she commented:

I am wondering why leisure is a problem at all. Surely, nowhere else in the world do people fuss about what to do with their spare time. I think it is rather sad that some kind of guilt has been built up in this particular society so that people feel that they should be productive in their spare time. . . . What is wrong with lying on the beach and relaxing?

I suppose one, perhaps unfair, answer to her is to be found in the six- and seven-year old Indian children standing guard over their families' fields all night long, lest a sacred bull trample the crops down and leave the family to starve. It is Puritanism that, in considerable part, has brought us to the point where leisure is or can become a problem for the vast majority. In fact, so great is the sheer quantity of our available leisure and leisure resources, that I do not think we can find very helpful models in other countries.

Recent reading and reflection, and discussion with Mark Benney of the London School of Economics (now visiting lecturer at the University of Chicago), has convinced me that this is true enough, at any rate, for England, from which we once derived our working model of the gentleman of leisure, and from which, too, I suspect the Hindu aristocrats such as Miss Rama Rau have learned more than many will admit. The English remain torn between the aristocratic leisure pattern, which is rural, sportsmanlike, casual, and on the edge of such quasi-criminal activities as cock-fighting, and the middle-class leisure pattern, dating from the sobersides of the Puritan revolution, which is urban, uplifting, strenuous. (The urban working-class pattern, as represented in the London music hall and a vivid "street culture," is pretty much dying out.) A recent extensive survey by Seebohm Rowntree and G. R. Lavers, entitled *English Life and Leisure*, was evidence to me that the English today on the whole know even less than we how to spend leisure—that there is a sameness and lack of imagination about their pastimes and pursuits. The English aristocrats with their natural allies, the lower class, have won the day in the sense that the Victorian middle-class morality appears to be almost dead in England, and sexual intimacy seems the chief leisure resort after puberty. But while the young people are uninhibited, they are not joyful. They have to watch every penny they spend on liquor, but again seem to take no great pleasure in it. They gamble, but often with desperation. The truth is that they can no longer afford the aristocratic vices which are now, with the decline of religious sanctions, psychologically available to them. And the middle-class values of self-improvement are still strong enough so that many are dissatisfied with the aimlessness of their lives; I recall one young middle-class girl, for instance, who told the interviewer that she slept with young men who asked her to, but wished she could find something better to do.

What, then, do Rowntree and Lavers, who are distinguished students of English social life, recommend? They plug the old middle-class model, only more of it. After touring the Scandinavian countries to study leisure practices there, they urge more folk-dancing, more hobbies, more adult education, better books—and, I need hardly add, fewer Hollywood movies.   ,

In fact, their attitude towards Hollywood may be regarded as symptomatic of the attitude of a great many students of leisure—"recreationists" perhaps we'd better call them—here and abroad. In their view, Hollywood is a source of disruptive leisure patterns, of vulgarity, spendthrift living, and false values generally. You know the indictment, I'm sure—an indictment which includes most of our popular culture, radio, TV, and bestsellers as well. Rowntree and Lavers put themselves up, as many school officials have, as angry competitors with this commercial popular culture, waging a losing fight. If they can offer nothing better, I am afraid that both the old aristocratic pattern, which is too expensive, and the old middle-class pattern, which is too didactic, will evaporate from England, leaving nothing of much quality to take their place.[2]

§ II

NOW IT IS MY OPINION that Hollywood movies not only are often shoddy but are often profoundly liberating and creative products of the human imagination. And I am not referring to so-called "message" films, pleas for better race relations or labor relations. I refer rather to such films as *The Asphalt Jungle*, or *All About Eve*, or *An American in Paris*, or *The Marrying Kind*, or *The Great Gatsby*, and many others without any patent social message; some successful, some not; movies which take us out of ourselves or force us back in; movies which open a window on life, and movies which exhibit a nightmarish

---

2. Mr. Benney believes that English leisure is not quite so dreary as this book indicates: the interviewers seem to concentrate on the activities that shock them and, indeed, to encounter a high proportion of rather sad and isolated people; moreover, nothing appears in the book about such gregarious leisure pursuits as political meetings and dart matches in the pubs.

fantasy. If English leisure is sterile and mean-spirited, I doubt if such movies have made it so. Rather, I think English, and American life also, would be enriched if people learned to understand and appreciate the movies, and could enjoy them in the spirit, at once critical and friendly, with which people at different times and places have enjoyed literature. The thought occurred to me some years ago that our schools and colleges, and particularly our altogether too pious adult education ventures, might begin experimenting with courses on movie appreciation, and popular culture appreciation generally— a movement which would require us to develop something we have not yet got in this country: a corps of gifted movie and radio and TV critics. The beginnings are evident in the work of John Crosby, for instance; what is lacking is any program for developing such critics, operating in the different media and at different levels of irony and sensibility. I argued that such a program might help close the gap which now separates the literary culture of the schools—the culture which such men as Rowntree and Lavers narrowly regard as the only true and genuine culture—from the popular culture of RKO and CBS.

I argued too that such a program might help us get rid once and for all of the current distinction between active and passive recreations—"active" being such things as sports, hobbies, and square dancing, and "passive" such things as movie-going, TV-watching, and other things parents and teachers wish their children wouldn't do. For I am convinced that this is not a real distinction: much leisure which appears to be active may be merely muscular: its lactic acid content is high, but there may be little other content, or contentment. And conversely, such supposedly passive pursuits as movie-going can obviously be the most intense experience, the most participative. Indeed, Hollywood movies could hardly corrupt England and Europe if they were as passive and as pacifying as is charged! And so I wanted to teach people to enjoy the movies as participants in a fine performance, and not merely as a place to pass the time out of the old folks' reach. In fact, I was particularly eager to develop courses just for the old folks in the understanding of popular culture, thinking in this way not only to open up to them a wide range of imaginative experience but also of helping to close the gap which separates the young, who have been raised with movies, comics, radio, and now TV, from the old who have come to them late if at all. . . .

But now I am not so sure that the problem I have in mind can be solved by courses, or possibly by any sort of conscious social program. I vividly recall my experience a few years ago when, asked to talk informally at a men's dormitory at the University of Chicago, I chose the movies as my topic, and started to say some things about the contemporary tendency among educated Americans to regard the movies as "just a show," to be "taken in" when one has nothing better at hand. I was talking to an audience most of whom devoutly believed that Hollywood movies other than Chaplin and the early Griffith are without exception junk, and that only England, France, and Italy make movies seriously worth seeing. I was trying to rebut this prejudice by saying something about the differing film conventions on the Continent and in this country: how, for example, we had had a convention of a happy ending which our more arty directors were now tending to exchange for an equally conventional, though Continental, unhappy ending, and that no necessary superiority lay in one convention rather than another, any more than in one sonnet form rather than another. Likewise, I sought to show how the undoubted inanities of the Production Code often resulted in a movie treatment—the so-called Lubitsch touch, for instance—which was a creative surmounting of the constricting forms. And then suddenly I stopped in the middle of my lecture, and for a while could not continue.

For I had realized, as I looked at the intent faces of the students, that I might well be engaged in closing off one of the few casual and free escape routes remaining to them; that I might be helping to inaugurate a new convention: namely, that one had not only to attend Hollywood movies but to understand and appreciate them. I might be imposing on a group of students already zealously engaged in self-improvement, in social and intellectual mobility, still another requirement—and this in the very act of seeking to liberate them from a common prejudice against American movies. I could continue my lecture only after I had made some of these misgivings explicit, and had indicated that I came to offer some of them an opportunity, not another extra-curricular curriculum.

I realized the problem here was not so much mine of becoming a possible taste-leader, as it was one for the students who were looking for such leadership, if not from me, then from somebody. Contrary to the situation in my own undergraduate days, when we were, at least for external consumption, stoutly individualistic, these students were more malleable, more ready to be told. One reason for this is that the general level of teaching has improved, despite all the attacks currently being made against our educational system. Not only has the teaching improved, but the teachers have changed their pace and style; we try to get close to our students, to be good group leaders rather than platform ham actors, and to concern ourselves with more aspects of student life than simply classroom performance. We are perhaps today less distant from the student than we once were, both in terms of social class position and in terms of intellectual attitude. . . . The students I was talking to, were ready to shift their leisure behavior at a moment's notice; I could envisage a group of them going to a Sam Goldwyn movie and, coming out, being very self-conscious as to how they ought to respond to it, whereas earlier they would have gone to it with the excuse that they needed to relax a bit before hitting the books again. Since so much of their leisure was already highly self-conscious, I hesitated to add to the burden. All planning for other people's leisure has to face this fundamental ambiguity, a form of the ever-present problem of the unintended consequence.

To be sure, leisure is a burden of the sort I am describing only among the educated, among the great many high school and college graduates who have some aspirations towards culture; men and women who, in the absence of any visible aristocratic model of leisure in American life, look to their fellows for clues, look to the magazines and the press, and the "how to" books. For the working class, there is leisure now too, and often money to spend, but it is not usually a burden, not perhaps a burden enough. Hunting and fishing and bowling; puttering about the house, garden, or car; watching television with and without discrimination; playing the numbers—these are recreations, not so very different from those turned up by Rowntree and Lavers in England, which my students have observed among steelworkers in Hammond and Gary. To be sure, there is considerable aspiration towards improved taste on the part of some of the younger wives, who read the women's service magazines. And the unions make sporadic efforts to give political education to the men; you will hardly be surprised to hear that some of the leaders blame the mass media for seducing the rank and file away from meetings— a charge which Mark Starr, educational director of the Ladies Garment Workers' Union, leveled at David Sarnoff of NBC at the Corning Roundtable. I think the charge is quite unjust, for I see no reason why people should spend their leisure in political activity unless that is their form of sport and they enjoy it, save in those cases where conditions are really so terrible that every good man has to come to the aid of the party—and, contrary to what is so widely urged, I believe such conditions are rare in this country.

One reason why the steel workers have so few problems with their leisure is that their work today is itself often quite leisurely and gregarious. It was not like that even thirty years ago when, as we know, there were ten- and twelve-hour shifts, and when the work was so hot and heavy that many men, on returning home, lay exhausted on the kitchen floor before they could get the energy to eat and tumble into bed. Now at the big sheet and tube mill in Gary the men often take naps on mattresses they have brought in, and cook meals on burners attached to the fiery furnaces; if a new foreman doesn't like the practice, production is slowed down until he does like it. Think here, too, of the extent to which the schools train young people in this kind of comradely slow-down against the teachers and against the system generally, so that I sometimes think of school teachers as foremen who conspire with their pupils, the workers, to conceal the true state of affairs from top management, the principals, and from the parents who are the absentee stockholders, who grouse now and again about their dividends. At any rate, since work has now become so relatively lacking in strain—though it is not nearly so routinized in feeling as it may seem to be to observers of factory life—the worker leaves the plant with a good deal of energy left, which carries him readily through his leisure hours.

By contrast, the professional and business person is apt to leave his work with a good many tensions created by his reactions to interpersonal situations, and as a result his leisure "needs" may have to be satisfied before he can rise above the level of needs—before he can rise from the level of re-creation to the level of creation. But it is just this very person on whom fall most of the demands for participative, active, constructive leisure which we have been examining earlier; and he may move from a job, where he is constantly faced with others and their expectations, to leisure pursuits, again in the company of others, where workmanlike performance is also expected of him. While he may nominally have a short work-week—though in many middle-class occupations such as medicine and teaching, hours are as long or longer than ever—he has not got much time which is not filled with stress. As my colleague, Nelson Foote, likes to put it, he has very little reverie as a balance to his sociability.

§ III

LET US LOOK at a concrete example. A friend and former colleague, Professor John R. Seeley, is now engaged in directing a large research project on the relations between school and community in a wealthy, upper-middle-class suburb. It is a suburb which has one of the finest public school systems on this continent, one which is often held up as a model to others; in fact, the magnificent new modern high school dominates the community, even physically, as the cathedrals did in the Middle Ages. The very fact that this elaborate research is

going on there—it is to take a period of at least five years before any
final conclusions are reached—is indicative of the alertness of the
school officials, the school board, and the other community leaders.
Yet, from my own very limited observation and from what has been
reported to me, it is plain that the community, despite all material
advantages, is not happy. The parents have neuroses; the children
have allergies; and the teachers—well, I don't know. What has gone
wrong?

If we follow the life of the children after school, we can perhaps
get some clues. They are being prepared now for their later careers
and their later rather hypothetical leisure. Their parents want to
know how they have fared at school: they are constantly comparing
them, judging them in school aptitude, popularity, what part they
have in the school play; are the boys sissies? the girls too fat? All
the school anxieties are transferred to the home and vice versa,
partly because the parents, college graduates mostly, are intelligent
and concerned with education. After school there are music lessons,
skating lessons, riding lessons, with mother as chauffeur and sched-
uler. In the evening, the children go to a dance at school for which
the parents have groomed them, while the parents go to a PTA
meeting for which the children, directly or indirectly, have groomed
them, where they are addressed by a psychiatrist who advises them
to be warm and relaxed in handling their children! They go home
and eagerly and warmly ask their returning children to tell them
everything that happened at the dance, making it clear by their
manner that they are sophisticated and cannot easily be shocked. As
Professor Seeley describes matters, the school in this community operates a "gigantic factory for the production of relationships."

Since, moreover, the same interpersonal concerns dominate life
within this "plant" and outside it, there is no sharp change of pace
between work and play, between school and home activities. The
children and their mothers—the fathers who work in the city at
least make a geographical shift and also something of an emotional
one—are characterized by a pervading anxiety. This is connected, I
think, with the fact that the older, clear goals of achievement have
been called into question, and these family units must decide not
only how to get what they want but also what it is they should want.
To answer this question, the community makes much use of professionals—the school principals and teachers themselves, who have
a very high standing; child guidance experts and mental hygienists;
and the packaged professionalism which can be bought in books or
over the radio. The result is a well-known paradox: here is a suburb
devoted to the arts of consumption and leisure, where these arts are

pursued with such dogged determination that leisureliness as a quality of life is very largely absent. While all the appurtenances of
variety are present, life is monotonous in the sense that it is steadily
gregarious, focussed on others, and on the self in relation to others.
As I have observed among some students, at Harvard and elsewhere,
even casualness can be an effortful artifact.

§ IV

YET IT IS all too easy to deride these parents and children and assorted
experts, to urge them—as some people are now doing in the anti-
progressive education movement—to drop all this new-fangled nonsense and get back to hard work and traditional curricula and nineteenth century or classical "values" generally. It is perhaps not
surprising that both aristocratic and working-class stances towards
leisure combine in this derision. When, for example, this suburban
community was recently discussed in my seminar on leisure, many
people, both faculty and students, took the position that what these
suburbanites needed was more direct and uninhibited aggression,
more toughness and less talkiness. They compared the community
unfavorably to a working-class community where, for reasons I indicated a moment ago, leisure is undoubtedly more casually dealt with.
What they admired was aristocratic or artisan insouciance, as against
upper-middle-class anxiety and preoccupation. Yet I do not know by
what standard of value one prefers a broken nose to asthma, or lum-
bago or gout to ulcers. There is no doubt that the suburb in question,
and others like it, is anxious and vulnerable, individually and collectively; otherwise, it would not be quite so receptive to a team of researchers. But I think that overadmiration for toughness is part of a
romance which the middle class, in Europe as well as in America, has
been carrying on with the lower class for a good many years. . . .

Thus, I think we can look at the people of this suburb rather
differently from the way I have been doing so far, or from the way
my seminar reacted to them. We can see them, for one thing, as
explorers. Whereas the explorers of the last century moved to the
frontiers of production and opened fisheries, mines, and mills, the
explorers of this century seem to me increasingly to be moving to
the frontiers of consumption. They are opening up new forms of
interpersonal understanding, new ways of using the home as a
"plant" for leisure, new ways of using the school as a kind of community center, as the chapel of a secular religion perhaps. But frontier
towns are not usually very attractive. And frontier behavior is awkward: people have not yet learned to behave comfortably in the
new surroundings. There is formlessness, which takes the shape of

lawlessness on the frontier of production and of aimlessness on the frontier of consumption. In both instances, the solid citizens who stayed home are likely to feel superior, both to the formlessness and to whatever may be emerging from it, just as most Europeans of the educated strata have felt superior to most aspects of America throughout most of our history. The move to the suburb, as it occurs in contemporary America, is emotionally, if not geographically, something almost unprecedented historically; and those who move to any new frontier are likely to pay a price, in loneliness and discomfort. When the physical hardships are great, as they were for earlier generations of pioneers, the psychological hardships may be repressed or submerged—though we cannot be too sure even of that, for (as Oscar Handlin makes clear in his book on immigration to America, *The Uprooted*) the most devastating strains on the newcomers were in fact the emotional ones, rough though the physical conditions were.

To carry my analogy further, I do believe that discoveries are being made on the frontiers of consumption. Take the American diet, for instance. Once upon a time, and still in many quarters, this was in charge of the nutritionists, the exponents of a balanced meal, adequate caloric intake and colonic outlet, and plenty of vitamins. These good people bore the same relation to food that recreationists do to leisure: they want it to be uplifting, salubrious, wasteless. But now, among the better income strata at any rate, their work is done: it is incorporated into the formulae of bakers, into the inventories of chain-stores, the menus of restaurants and dining cars. We have, as I sometimes like to put it, moved from the wheat bowl to the salad bowl. In consequence, in the suburb I have been describing, and elsewhere throughout the country, there is an emphasis, which was once confined to small sophisticated or expatriate circles, on having the right responses to food, on being a gourmet. Save for a few cranks, the housewives are not concerned with having enough wheat-germ, but with having enough oregano, or the right wine—and more than that, with having the right enjoyment of the wine. In the middle of the shopping center in this suburb is a store which stocks a stupendous array of delicacies, spices, patisseries, delicatessens, and European gadgets for cooking; the casserole replacing the melting pot!

Now, as I have indicated, the residents of this suburb are anxious about food and their attitudes towards it. They want to be knowledgeable about it and also to enjoy it, but they are not yet easygoing in the matter. Among men particularly, the demand that one must enjoy food, and not simply stow it away, is relatively new, and again these pioneers are awkwardly self-conscious. (Let me make clear in passing that I am not talking about old-fashioned conspicuous consumption. I am not talking about the hostess' fear of making a gastronomic *faux pas*, or fear that her children's table manners will disgrace her; no doubt these fears may still exist, although greatly muted, in the group I am describing. No, these parents are afraid that they are missing some taste experience, which in turn reveals the lack of a basic personality attribute.) We are observing these families, it appears, in a time of transition, when they have left old food-conventions behind and are exploring, without settling on, new ones. They are, in effect, paying the society's cost of research and development.

And can there be any doubt but that the result will be—in fact, has already been—an addition to the stock of American leisure bounties and benefits? The self-service supermarket, with its abundance of foods capably displayed, where the shopper's caprice and imagination can roam without interference from officious clerks or sabotage from indifferent ones, seems to me as significant an invention on the side of consumption as the assembly-line on the side of production. But the invention would be meaningless without a group of experimentalist families prepared to develop new eating patterns, new combinations of color and taste. And here enters still another service industry: the cookbook and recipe industry, which has ransacked the world's cuisines and produced a host of books and newspaper columns, as well as those restaurants which serve as pilot plants. I think there can be no doubt that the children of the children now growing up in our demonstration suburb will be reasonably free of fears, guilts, and awkwardness about food prepared as a matter of course for the pursuit of happiness in this area of existence. In fact, I see only one caveat: the return of the nutritionist ghost in the craze for reducing, which makes not only women but men choose between food and figure, with one eye on mortality tables and the other on the way one appears in the hall of mirrors which is society! Even so, the reduced diets on which these figure-chasers bravely live are, item for item, unquestionably superior to anything known before in the American provender—which a generation ago made our food, like our bootlegging, an international joke. Moreover, the cult of one's figure, as of one's dress and one's coiffure, is certainly not an illegitimate one for one's happiness and aesthetic sense.

In other fields of consumption such as music, painting, and literature; in the whole subtle field of sociability and conversation; in sports; in the changing style of vacations I think the pioneers are also paying a high price in emotional outlay, particularly in anxiety. I have already raised the question of whether our intellectual and literary culture is not too severe and derisive about the middle-class vice of anxiousness, compared with its benign tolerance for the aristocratic and lower-class vices of brutality and indifference. Such very general questions of value judgment are of great importance in determining contemporary attitudes towards leisure. I think, for example, that we make life and leisure harder for the already anxious person—whose anxiety is in fact thoroughly understandable in the light of our discussion so far—by making him also anxious about his anxiety, so that we heap on him a cumulative burden. . . .

Teachers also feel it compulsory not to be anxious, but to be always easygoing, warm, and relaxed—what a burden this puts on teachers in the better public and private schools!—whereas lack of discipline and firmness would have worried teachers in an earlier day. I am inclined to think we should form a union of the anxious ones, to defend our right to be anxious, our right to be tense, our right to aspirin and to our allergies. I was shocked when one of my colleagues remarked, after our seminar had had a description of life in the suburb I have here used as a case, that children were worse off there than they had been under the *ancien régime*. Historical amnesia had blinded him, as it blinds many now-fashionable critics of progressive education, to the brutalities and savageries in the treatment of children a hundred years or so ago. Then children were harnessed to the engine of society with often little concern for their own development. Many were too frightened or too cowed to be anxious.[3] . . .

§ V

I HAVE STRESSED as much as I have the conflicts in our attitudes towards the proper use of leisure, and the kind of training children should get with their later lives of leisure in mind, because I feel that a recognition of ambiguity at the very heart of our problem is a first step towards perspective and a certain necessary detachment. I can't emphasize enough how rapidly our country is changing, and how hard it is even for the wisest among us to grasp what is going on.

Let me give just two illustrations: Recently a friend of mine who works for one of the pocket book companies visited an Ohio Valley city of about 75,000. There is no bookstore in the town, but a few books are kept, along with stationery and oddments, in the main department store. My friend asked at the department store why

---

3. Stephen Spender's novel, *The Backward Son*, and George Orwell's account of his schooldays, "Such, Such Were the Joys" (which appeared in *Partisan Review* since the above was written), can remind us that even a generation ago the English public school could still treat the sensitive young with ferocious bullying. Likewise, the fictional hero of Salinger's *Catcher in the Rye* might have profited from some of the humaneness and sensitivity introduced by the now maligned progressive educators.

they didn't put in a real bookstore, and was told, "Well, this is a steel town. People here don't read; they just look at television or go to the taverns." Yet over three-quarters of a million pocket books were sold in this same town in 1951 at restaurants, at newsstands and in drugstores, many of them in the Mentor line of modern classics. This is well over a book a month for those old enough to read. I wish we had some knowledge and understanding of what these citizens made out of all they read: the Faulkner novels, the Conant *On Understanding Science*, the Ruth Benedict *Patterns of Culture*, along with the Mickey Spillane and other mixtures of sadism with sex. But studies of this kind in the field of leisure have not yet been made, as far as I know.

I draw my other illustration of the laggard state of our knowledge even of the basic data from an article by Gian-Carlo Menotti which appeared in a recent issue of the New York *Times Sunday Magazine*. As you know, Menotti is a gifted and widely hailed young composer who, after some twenty years residence here, considers himself an American. He was complaining about the precarious position of the creative artist in American life, particularly in the field of music. Here, he points out, we bestow all our adulation on the performer: the glamorous conductor or singer, the Menuhin or Serkin or Reginald Kell, who interprets music but does not create it, while the modern composer, unless he writes for the movies or gets some help from a foundation or a rich wife, will starve (as Bela Bartok did)—and is certainly not in any case featured in the billing along with the star performers. And he goes on to say that many parents in America are ashamed if their sons choose an artistic career; not only do they fear they will not make a living—even if they (the parents) could afford to support them—but fear, too, that they will be sissies; fathers try to force their sons to becomes businessmen or doctors or something else equally reassuring. Now I am sure that Menotti has a very good case about the plight of the composer, who seems so much worse off than the painter or writer, having more impresarios standing between him and his public. However, it seems to me that Menotti does not take account of the rapid and widespread change which has been going on in just the attitudes he is attacking. Through amateur chamber music groups and through the fabulous growth of the long-playing record industry, many thousands of Americans are today discovering modern music with a rush, just as they are discovering wine and other pleasures that were once confined to a small cultivated indigenous group and a somewhat larger group of immigrants who brought this culture with them from the old country. Likewise, it seems to me unlikely that millions of middle-

class parents would not in 1952 be pleased if their sons exhibited artistic gifts and interests, even if not commercially promising. . . .
When I said as much, however, at the Corning Conference, Miss
Rama Rau and others said I was mistaken: parents would only accept
art if it was advertised in *Life* magazine. . . . I would be greatly
interested in comments on this topic, for I feel that here again we
simply do not know.[4]

§ VI

SO FAR we have been looking at our culture from inside. We have
asked ourselves some questions about what is going on, about what
attitudes are prevalent towards it, what models of competent use of
leisure exist, what differences there are among different social strata,
and so on. But there is another way of going at our problem which
is to ask, not what play and leisure are like, or were like, in our
culture but what they are like in any culture. Is there, for instance,
any natural or biological basis for leisure or is it entirely conventional? *Homo Ludens,* a book by the late Dutch scholar Huizinga,
offers some interesting clues to this. Huizinga points out that every
language he examined had a word for play which is different from
the word for work, and that many cultures have a pattern of sport,
of noneconomic serious and yet playful competition. Many if not all
cultures, moreover, operate on a periodic or seasonal rhythm between heavy work and heavy play—and I might add that many
societies also have feasts even if they do not suffer from famines.
That there is a cross-cultural solidarity of play may be indicated by
a well-known example. Our Army advised soldiers and aviators to
always carry a piece of string with them and when downed in a
Pacific jungle to start playing cat's cradle if a suspicious native approached; the native would sometimes start to play, too.

All this must rest on something basic in the biological substratum of man and many animals. We know of course that children
play even without instruction, provided certain basic minima of
security are met. Thus, while children's play has aspects of artifice
which the ever-renewed child's culture elaborates, much of it is

---

4. In discussion [at the Harvard Summer School], it was argued that parents
will now often accept art as a glamorous stairway to quick success, but that this
makes it even harder than earlier for a youngster whose interest in art cannot be
readily commercialized: his parents are impatient with him, not because he is an
artist or composer—which would lead to a total break and a relatively good conscience on the artist's part—but because, being in a glamorous field, he has not made
his way; since the youngster in part also wants success, he finds it harder to cut
himself off from his parents' values and anxieties. For thoughtful discussion of
this problem, and a critique of the art schools which cash in on this craving for
success, see Lyman Bryson, *The Next America.*

simply given. In fact, work and play are not yet, for the child, independently organized; and what he makes of play as he develops depends to a very considerable extent on the society's interpretation of his play—is it regarded as "child's play," as useless, as preparation for life, or is it disregarded?

I think we can say, indeed, that the child's play serves as the principal model for all later efforts to free leisure time from its burdens and to cope with its puzzling ambiguities. We all of us know, if we think about it, that children's play is by no means always free and spontaneous; it is often filled with terror and morbidity; but at its best it is surely one of the unequivocally good things of this earth, and no wonder we try to recapture it as Paradise Lost. But if we look closely at children's play we can observe something else which may even give us a clue as to how that recapture can, in part, be achieved, namely that the child's greatest satisfaction appears to arise from experiences of mastery and control. As Erik H. Erikson has noted in imaginative detail, the developing body provides a graded set of experiences; anyone can observe this who watches children play with their new-found mastery of walking or running or talking or diving. Play seems to reside in a margin, often a narrow one, between tasks which are too demanding, and those which are not demanding enough to require the excited concentration of good play. A child or adult who is simply going through the motions is not engaged in play or leisure as we have been talking about it here, however the society may define it. But without some social forms for leisure and play, forms which have to be broken through, yet have to be there to be broken through, I do not think we will have much play either. For the demand that play be constantly spontaneous, unchanneled by social forms, is too overwhelming; spontaneity, as we have already seen, is lost if we strive too hard for it. Thus, play would seem to consist in part of giving ourselves tasks, useless in any immediate sense, which challenge us but do not overwhelm us —tasks which allow us to practice our skills on the universe when not too much is at stake. Some of us, who lose this ability in our waking lives, retain it (as Erich Fromm points out in *The Forgotten Language*) in our dreams, which can be astonishingly witty, brilliant, and artistic—an indication, perhaps, of the child still buried within us, not so much in Freud's sense of the vicious child but rather of the child natively gifted with the capacity for imaginative play.

I have spoken of mastery of tasks, but I do not want to be understood as implying that this necessarily means physical activity—that is only one example. The child in the front of a subway train who intently watches the motorman, the signals, and the tracks may be quiet, but is undoubtedly playing, and may be playing very well—a point Reuel Denney eloquently voiced at the Corning Conference. When we speak of "role-playing," we should have something of this sort of vicariousness in mind. And this leads me to the complicating point that many of our workaday tasks as adults can be handled with a certain quality of leisure if we are able to regard work as a series of challenging tasks to be mastered, where the net of expectations surrounding us is at the same time not too frightening. On the other hand, we can be playful at work as a way of *evading* demands, sometimes by being one of the boys, pretending to ourselves and others that, if we really worked, we would get to the top. Students often play such games with themselves. But this is not really carrying out in adult life the effort at competence which is our lesson learned from the play of the child. That requires that we work at the top of our bent, while at the same time enjoying the very processes of accomplishment—enjoying our awareness, for example, of all that is going on in a classroom; enjoying our understanding of a technical problem; enjoying ourselves, in other words, as functioning and effective human beings.

We get here, it is apparent, into very deep waters indeed, where the boundaries between work and play become shadowy—as I think, for other reasons, they are tending to become in our society anyway —waters where we are looking for a quality we can only vaguely describe: it is various and rhythmical; it breaks through social forms and as constantly recreates them; it manifests itself in tension, yet not too much of it; it is at once meaningful, in the sense of giving us intrinsic satisfaction, and meaningless, in the sense of having no pressing utilitarian purpose. It is some such model as this, I suggest, which haunts us when we consider leisure and judge its quality in ourselves and others. It is a model which has been elaborated in our culture, and yet which transcends most, and perhaps all, given cultures.

14. New Standards for Old: From Conspicuous Consumption to Conspicuous Production

In a recent column, John Crosby affectionately quoted a remark of Sylvester L. Weaver, vice-chairman of the board of NBC: "The kids," said Weaver, "are already getting the full picture. 'The kids running around in space suits are smarter than the adults who are laughing at them.'" The parents' imagination, Weaver implied, is localized, whereas that of their children floats free even of planetary boundaries. A recent story in the science-fiction magazine *Galaxy* preaches a similar moral. It is a tale of two children, aged ten, who take off on a Moebius ring for other times and places. These children, at home in an Einsteinian universe, patronize their parents, are sorry for them, and obey them, not out of fear or favor, but lest they cause them pain. The parents are bound to a specific time and place, a specific job, whereas the children, free of chores for the most part both at home and school, are not hindered, as they would have been in an earlier day, from rapidly overtaking and surpassing their parents' know-how on the frontiers of consumption. It would be my guess, for instance, that more children than parents today favor "modern design" not only in space suits but in cars, bars, houses, and furniture.

Margaret Mead and others have pointed out that immigrant parents in America have always been on the defensive, because their children were more "American" than they. But the tendencies I am discussing seem to extend beyond this country, for they are the consequences of industrialization and urbanization and the growing leisure that, in later stages, accompany these developments. Indeed, when countries without a long Christian and Puritan heritage adopt the techniques of modern industry, they may appear more "American" than America in their readiness to slough off older ideologies of thrift and workmanship; they may hanker for leisure and consumption before they have solved the problems of production. The Coca Cola bottlers, the Hollywood film distributors, and other consumption missionaries preach a gospel that may be premature in Thailand or Egypt. But whatever the gospel, it is doubtless the young—lacking the trained incapacities of their elders—who catch on to it most quickly, but at times, as I myself think may be true with space suits, most shallowly.

§ II

I AM GOING to illustrate some of these matters by referring to a play many of you have doubtless seen: *Death of a Salesman*. Whereas in 19th-century literature, children often fear that their parents will catch them out in some frivolity, it is Willy Loman, the father in *Death of a Salesman*, who is caught out by his son in a hotel room. And the other son, Happy Loman, openly ridicules his father as a fool for working hard; Happy—how meaningful his nickname!—has latched on to American consumption know-how at its most garish: his eyes are on the pleasure frontier while his father's are still on the production-achievement frontier. Not that Biff or Happy escape defensiveness towards their father—today as in an earlier day sons are still trapped by the irrelevance of their parents' hopes and fears for them—but the initiative is certainly changed.

The changes that have taken place can scarcely be fitted into a simple chronology of parent-child relations. Too many other factors are involved. The east coast is different from the middle west—and the differences, despite our stereotypes, are not well understood. There are very great differences in social class. It has been said that the upper class is oriented to the past, the lower class to the present, the middle class to the future. The upper class therefore tends to be strongly family-centered—think of the social memories of the Apleys, cemented by estates, portraits, memoirs, family names, and other impedimenta, as these are portrayed in Marquand's novel. Willy Loman, by contrast, seems to live always in the future, even though he spends much time listening to voices out of the past which point him to a future he didn't take or that didn't take him. Willy, in fact, appears to have no past, which is part of his pathos. . . . And Willy faces the problem that he is not really identified with salesmen but—as happens among some particularly outstanding salesmen—with the customers. It is often taken for granted that the good salesman should identify with the customers on whom he is dependent. Actually, the motives of men in business are more complex, and ambivalence towards the customer is common. Recently, a friend of mine, a market researcher, told me how a shaving lotion manufacturer stubbornly refused to alter his product, even to meet complaints of customers: it was the best on the market, and that was that. Similarly, another client, a pie-mix maker, while steadily losing business, would not agree to change his advertising to suit what market research had uncovered as to its effects: if potential customers who read his copy were "biased," that was their hard luck. Here, strikingly enough, resentment of the customer survives in firms highly dependent on sensitivity to consumers, companies which go so far as to employ market researchers but not far enough to cater to what they regard as customer prejudice. . . .

Willy Loman, however, failed to establish such emotional distance from his clients, and lacking support from his own occupational group, he became something of an anomaly among salesmen, exceptionally vulnerable, without the occupation's long-built-up defenses against the demands of work. In his ignorance of the ropes, Willy again strikes me as unusually deracinated—something Arthur Miller mislocates, I suggest, in the intangible nature of the occupation.

§ III

SO MUCH may be regarded as an overture to a somewhat more systematic account of why some of these developments have come about, why our work and leisure have changed so considerably. Naturally, such an account must be speculative and abbreviated; I will have to confine myself to institutional changes and to such intellectual currents as *Babbitt* or *Death of a Salesman* represent.

Let me emphasize, first of all, that such changes are never wholesale. Thus, the attitude towards the middleman in *Death of a Salesman* is nothing new. The idea that the middleman doesn't produce anything can be found in medieval thought and in the Reformation; the idea was very strong in 19th-century American populism. Populism, though it appears to have vanished, has left its mark. For example, nostalgia for a rural past is still very strong in America. Even so urban a writer as Arthur Miller is obsessed in *Death of a Salesman* with the fencing in of a once-rural Brooklyn and with the virtuousness of working with one's hands close to the soil. What is interpreted as "close to the soil" is, to be sure, partly a matter of cultural definition; thus, in Kansas City the leading annual social event, at which debutantes are presented, is the American Royal, a stock show at which grain traders and cattle buyers parade around under huge Stetsons—perhaps believing for a moment that they can identify with ranch life although they make their living as down-town brokers, and although ranchers themselves would seldom wear such head-gear. These identifications, as they become ritualized, have much more influence on our conceptions of our work than anything "intrinsic" to that work (such as the soil itself) or to man's biological potentiality for work and for avoiding work.

An illustration of the slow way in which cultural definitions change lies in the fact that, as Americans have sloughed off to a considerable extent the Puritan's exalted valuations of work, we have nevertheless not on the whole sought jobs that would provide a maximum of income with a minimum of work. Rather, what has happened is that our aims have become more complex: we now seek "the right kind" of work, including the right blend of leisure with work and inside work. For instance, a recent series of articles in *Fortune* indicates that we are witnessing the death of our salesmen in general: companies are finding it more and more difficult to recruit salesmen, even or especially when they work on a commission basis. The old-fashioned salesman set his own pace; he had a great deal of leisure, and, if he was good and business was good, he could make money. But today such opportunities seem often to go begging, and corporations engage in all kinds of semantic niceties, such as redefining sales jobs as sales engineering to get around the problem; they try to replace direct selling by advertising, and by using the retail store as the point-of-sale as in the Supermarket. College graduates today want jobs in personnel work or other "service" occupations, rather than in the exposed and isolated position of the salesman. For one thing, their wives make more demands of them than Willy's wife did: they want them home, and free of ulcers—and these new-style wives are more help to their men than the neutral misery of Mrs. Loman was any comfort to Willy. In the old days, Biff might have become a salesman without afterthought, but his ambitions are confused by some of the newer currents.

One reason for this is that young people seem to be increasingly choosing the role of an employee in a large organization, with pensions and perquisites, rather than the chance to make a quick killing by commission selling or other risky and entrepreneurial job. One company reported to *Fortune* that they now look for salesmen among Greeks—an ethnic group not yet acculturated to the newer American values; another, that they do their recruiting for sales in Texas and Oklahoma—states where also old-fashioned crazy millionaires can still be found. Sometimes people refer to high income taxes as a determining factor, but I think taxes, though certainly an element, are frequently used as rationalizations by men who don't want to take risks. Taxes are simply part of the managerial climate in which enterprise is now carried on, in which innovation is entrusted to a research and development staff trained at the Columbia School of Industrial Management and the Harvard Business School—men who take courses which deal with human relations in order that they will be able to get along with their colleagues in the office, or at least to discuss problems of human relations at American Management Association meetings.

And this leads me to a further reflection on *Death of a Salesman*. You will remember the terrible scene in which Howard Wagner fires Willy, while listening to an idiotic recording. Some of my colleagues at Chicago have recently been studying retirement practices and find that one reason many companies have a firm rule compelling retirement at, let us say, 65 is that people today are too soft-hearted to fire other people. At one large steel company, a number of older men have jobs which are make-work because no one can bring himself to discharge them. A retirement rule locates the responsibility elsewhere, makes it impersonal. This is true of the retirement regulations in universities also. Indeed, wherever I have observed such matters—in business, in government, in academic life —I have noticed the lengths to which people will go before firing somebody. Howard Wagners are hard to come by. (Now again you will notice that I am criticizing the play on the basis of a sociological estimate, but I must say that the play invites such criticism by its own effort at documentary realism.)

§ IV

SO FAR, I have spoken as if fear of risk was the chief factor in the actual dearth of entrepreneurs and of salesmen in the American economy at present. But there is also a growing desire to be serviceable to others—this is one reason for the current high prestige of the medical profession. The attraction of personnel work for many college graduates rests on their urge to work *with* people (the fact is, they more often work with files—but that is in a way beside the point) rather than, as they interpret selling, *against* people. People want to be part of a team, part of a group. Work is done in groups, research is done in groups. It is this security which is often more important than pension plans. (I am discussing at such length the problem of work and the salesman today, because in order to see clearly the changes in the standards for judging consumption, we have to see how work itself has changed. For work and play seem to be fundamental dualities in culture, like day and night, male and female, parent and child, self and not-self.)

It may be that the changes I have been discussing are partly kept from clearer view by the American belief that men must be tough, not soft and sentimental; thus, we tend to conceal from ourselves as well as from others our conciliatory attitudes, our moods of fearing success and display, our sensitivity to envy. And so we continue to talk about free enterprise, about getting ahead—about all the older values which the Loman family, in its several ways, has taken so literally. But often this talk is big talk, or whistling to keep up our courage.

Such interpretation of contemporary talk, in fact, requires us to go back historically and raise the question whether in the 19th century, underneath all the Horatio Alger talk and the Samuel Smiles talk, similar ambivalences towards an all-out individualism were not present. The Christian values which are so strong in Mr. Gosse's group of Plymouth Brethren not only helped to spur the rise of a competitive, individualistic capitalism, but also moderated that capitalism by feelings of social responsibility, of concern for the other—after all, they were called "Brethren." And Christianity always contains the latent dynamic of a potential return to the values of the early Christian era, before the Church became a great going concern; in other words, there is always the available material for a reformation—within Catholicism as well as within Protestantism. Christianity may have become something of a shell in the 19th century, for many pious frauds, but it was always more than that and was not for long successfully allied with the more ferocious forms of competitiveness. Bruce Barton's notion of a generation ago that Jesus was really a big advertising man would hardly go over today among people of Babbitt's station, let alone among the advertising men who relish Mead's satiric *How to Get Ahead in Business without Really Trying.*

By the same evidence, we may conclude that there *have* been changes, very profound ones, although their origins can be traced back to an earlier day. Values once confined to a small elite group, or to an elite place within the hearts of many people—a kind of Sunday rather than weekday place—have now become much more widespread. For example, we can see this in attitudes towards conspicuous consumption. Veblen noticed in his book on the leisure class, published in 1899, that some small groups among the very rich were learning to be offended by conspicuous display, they were going in for "natural-looking" estates, "natural-looking" contrivances, and presumably "natural-looking" dress, too. He realized that when a leisure class gets large enough, and sufficiently in touch with itself, it can depart from grossly vulgar display—it can whisper rather than shout. And he saw how renewed attitudes of "workmanship," as against the earlier "wastemanship" at the top of the social pyramid, could spread downwards, as more people gained leisure, and as more came in contact with leisure class values.

Yet even he, perhaps because of his farm origin and midwest experience, did not see fully the extent to which nonconspicuous nonconsumption (or, as one of my friends more appropriately terms it, "conspicuous under-consumption") was already a powerful American pattern. He seems to have escaped contact with Boston Unitarians or Philadelphia Quakers whose display was much more veiled. Although in Henry Adams' novel, *Democracy*, we are treated to an inauguration ball more gaudy than the un-top-hatted one of a few weeks ago [January, 1953], when we read Henry James's *The Bostonians*, which appeared in 1876, we are confronted with wealthy young women who were plain of dress and disdainful of display. For them, good intangible causes took the place of good commodities.

I should add, in fairness to Veblen, that he saw some of this. But he largely overlooked the possibility that these attitudes were being shaped by intellectual as well as by merely technological currents. Thus it would not have occurred to him that his own books would influence people's attitudes towards consumption, that he would be the godfather of the consumers' movement—that, indeed, a whole series of books, including his own and coming right down to Marquand's novels or *Death of a Salesman*, have helped inter certain American values with irony and sarcasm. For him, as for Marx, men always conform eventually to economic necessity, not to cultural or ideological necessity.

Nevertheless, Veblen's *Theory of the Leisure Class* fitted not too badly the American scene from the gay 90s to the not quite so gay 20s. The hero in the novel *Jefferson Selleck* who suffers agonies on his wedding night because he is of lower social origin than his bride; the drama of *The Great Gatsby*, and the miseries of Charlie Gray in *Point of No Return* and of Mary Monahan and her intimidated Beacon Street lover in the *Late George Apley*, are so many testimonies to the Veblenian cruelties of the American status system, with its unmerry emulative chase. And yet the last novels I mentioned are testimony also to a newer note in American life and literature, that of the failure of success, rather than, as in *Death of a Salesman*, the failure of failure.

§ V

IT HAS, I BELIEVE, been the bounteousness of modern industry, especially in America, which has done more than almost anything else to make conspicuous consumption obsolete here. It would go much too far to say that consumption bores us, but it no longer has the old self-evident quality; it no longer furnishes our lives with a kind of simple structure or chronology of motives, as it did for William Randolph Hearst, for instance. To collect objects in Hearst's manner required a certain confidence, even arrogance, a certain imperviousness to ridicule and criticism. Hearst's "whim of iron" appears to be a thing of the past.

It is not only or primarily, however, that our interest in goods has been drowned by the boundless cornucopia of goods, by analogy with Engel's law that food consumption declines proportionately as income rises. The same expansion of the economy has created new fortunes much faster than their possessors could possibly be tutored by the old rich in the proper consumption values of the latter. No mere "400" located in a single city can any longer dictate appropriate leisure-class behavior in terms of what estates, houses, furniture, and so on to collect. The absence of titles in America, and of many old-family names equivalent to titles (judging by names, many Negroes and onetime Kabotskys belong to some of the best families), also makes such hegemony very difficult—indeed, from the point of view of an Italian count (unfamiliar with American distinctions even in the days of Daisy Miller), a Dallas oil heiress in seven figures and Neiman-Marcus clothes may be preferable to a Saltonstall in six figures and Jordan Marsh clothes. In this situation, the more established wealth and its auxiliary leaders of high taste have sought to fight back, not by a futile outspending, but by a conspicuous underspending. A Hearst has been ridiculed, not only for poor taste in *what* he bought, but *that* he bought in such quantity.

No doubt, universal education—itself part of our bonanza of good fortune—has exposed many people who later have come into means to tasteful critiques of working-class extravagance. The mass media, too, carry along with the prodigality of their advertising the relative emaciation of their judgments on expenditure: the *Vogue* style of restrained elegance is made an accessible model for millions. However, the movement of style has not only been from the top down—and how could it be when people can't tell, for reasons already indicated, where the top is? A relaxation of standards has spread upwards: the new rich gentleman needs no longer to struggle into a dress suit to hear Mary Garden at the Opera House, nor need he learn to ride to hounds or to send his sons to Groton or St. Marks. All he has to learn to do—and this, as Robert L. Steiner and Joseph Weiss point out in "Veblen Revised in the Light of Counter-Snobbery," is not easy for him—is to mute the wish for wild and gaudy spending that he learned as a lower-class lad, the very wish that may have helped propel him into the millionaire ranks. Frictions on this score are indicated by the concern of the Cadillac people with the consequences for their older clients of the fact that the Cadillac (rather than, as some years ago, the Buick) has become "the" car for well-off Negroes.

Today, men of wealth, fearful of making a wrong move, harried not only by taxes but by public relations and their own misgivings, are apt to give over the now-dreaded responsibilities for spending to a foundation, which then on their behalf can collect research projects or artistic works—protected by bureaucratic organization and corporate responsibility from imputations of extravagance. (As I write this, however, the big foundations such as Ford and Rockefeller are under Congressional Committee scrutiny—there seems to be no escape from money save anonymity!)

Another form of putting spending at arm's length is to delegate it to one's children. Whether for toys or for schools, for space in the home or advice on child management, more money is being spent on children and by them than ever before. The trouble with children, of course, is that they grow up—unlimited amounts cannot be spent on them. Before too long, in the same strata that Veblen and Arthur Miller have influenced, the children now grown up are denouncing advertising and disdainful of waste and extravagance. The parents, of course, can have more children, and as you may know, this is what has happened to the country in the last decade, much to the bewilderment of the demographers, who thought that the American urban middle classes would continue to have fewer and fewer children and more and more commodities. Demographers do not know, and I do not know, why the shift has occurred; doubtless the causes are complex and ramified—the same thing has happened in France and elsewhere. But I do suspect that the changes in value-patterns we have been discussing have been among the factors. I started several years ago reading college class books for the light they might shed on subtle shifts in attitude. I was struck by the emphasis on the family that began to appear in my own and other college classes of a few years back. People in writing about themselves no longer started off by saying they were Vice-President of Ozark Air Lines and a director of the Tulsa National Bank, and so forth; they began by telling about the wife and five kids and how they had a home in the suburbs where they all enjoyed barbecues in the back yard. The occupational achievement was played down; the family scene, with its pastoral virtues, played up. Since then I have found similar tendencies in other groups. This would seem to hang together with the devaluation of individual success we have been discussing: children are a kind of unequivocal good in a world of changing values, and we can lavish on children the care and emotions we would now feel it egotistical to lavish on ourselves. The younger age at which people are marrying today is a further factor; having started to go steady at fourteen, they want to settle down at twenty. Whereas a generation ago a career man and a career girl would have considered marriage an obstacle to their work aims, today marriage and children are in a way part of the consumption and leisure sphere, the side of life currently emphasized.

§ VI

THUS, CHILDREN ABSORB some of the surplus and foundations some more of it. Especially the biggest foundation of all—the federal government. Conspicuous consumption has been socialized, and appears of necessity largely in the form of weapons, with something left over for national parks. When we speak of government spending for armaments, it is clear that the line between consumption and production is hard to draw, and the much more general point I want to make is that with the decline in conspicuous consumption—a relative rather than an absolute decline perhaps—has come a great rise in what we might call conspicuous production.

As I have implied earlier, the company for which Willy Loman worked did not engage in conspicuous production—else they would have kept him on, finding a place for him in overhead. The companies that do engage in it begin by locating and designing their plants and offices for show as well as for "efficiency" in the older sense of nearness to suppliers, distributors, and other facilities. It would be interesting to know to what extent the immense tax-facilitated rebuilding of American industry since World War II has been influenced by management's desire to have a plant that looked like the *Fortune* ads of the Austin Company and other designers of low-slung, "streamlined" factories. To be sure, if such factories are good for morale, they are by definition efficient, but the Hawthorne experiments are some evidence that workers respond more to interest taken in them than to lighting, cooling, or other circumambient factors— very likely, such factories are good for executives' and directors' morale. (These experiments were made nearly a generation ago.)

Conspicuous production takes a great variety of forms. If a company leads the procession in granting paid vacations or in providing some new service for employees—that may be partly conspicuous production. Many additions to overhead both constitute such production and spend time advertising it—even some incumbents of the president's chair may have that as their principal role. Officials, who would no longer be as eager as their predecessors were to buy their way into an exclusive country club, suburb, or resort, are most eager to have their companies' ads appear in the pages of *Business Week, Fortune,* or on television, whether or not their market research can wholly justify each instance of space- or time-buying. I understand that some large companies have issued manuals to their officials on how to live up to their expense accounts, and we may properly regard such manuals as successors to all the educative literature by which previous ruling groups have been taught to spend—something which, strange as it may seem to some of you, needs always to be learned.

Professor Richard Hofstadter has suggested that these practices should be called conspicuous corporate consumption rather than conspicuous production. Certainly, it is as difficult to distinguish one from the other as to distinguish work from play among many of the managerial work-force. It would take a very close scrutiny of factory lay-out, for instance, to be sure what changes were the result of desires for corporate prestige rationalized as cost-cutting methods, and to know whether to allocate the costs of prestige itself to the production or the consumption side of the ledger. The aesthetics of the machines of production, factories and plants express a slightly different kind of conspicuous production. It is only when we adopt an "economizing" point of view that we can distinguish, in the activities centered around the economy, between the end of maximizing the product and the other ends, ceremonial, religious, prestige-laden, that are contextually being pursued. The conspicuousness of these other ends is the result, as Professor Martin Meyerson has pointed out to me, of our taking for granted as the sole end of work that of maximizing product—from that distorted, if traditional, perspective other ends embedded in the context of social life appear out of order, even garish. Men who in the 19th century or today seem to be pursuing wealth or efficiency as a single uncomplicated goal were certainly self-deceived as to their total gamut of motives. Nevertheless we can say, I think, that corporate consumption, in which each company goes into business as a junior welfare state, does currently rearrange our motives in a new configuration.

One factor, as I have already indicated, is the increasing professionalization of management, a development which has had consequences rather different from those Brandeis or Taylor hoped for. The 18th- and 19th-century industrialist came out of a rural background or ideology: he regarded his firm as a farm, and his work-force as hired hands, often transient and easily replaced, or as a small-town business, paternalistically run. He did not think of himself as having to be an expert on human relations—that could be left to the clergy, the main professionals in his purview. Feeling, moreover, some doubt as to where he stood socially, vis-a-vis the clergy and vis-a-vis Eastern aristocrats, he built a big feudal castle of a house for himself to show everybody that he had arrived, as if to declaim that he was personally worthy by visible evidences of his net worth: if he could not outshout the clergyman and the statesman, he could at least outshine them. And his wife, lacking the cultural tutelage of aristocratic wives and excluded by patriarchal convention from any contact with the workaday world, had nothing more to occupy her than to act as his deputy in conspicuous spending, his ambassador to the dominions of culture he was too busy and too bored to bother with.

Such an industrialist, when he met his competitors, frankly regarded them as such, and whatever conviviality he might show, he kept his secrets of production to himself. He met with others, that is, in terms of money, not in terms of a specialized profession which freely exchanges its own secrets while keeping them from the lay public. Today, the communication of industrialists and businessmen with one another is frequently quite different. Meeting as professionals, the former individuality which distinguished the American businessman is rubbed off. He seeks status in his ability to run a smooth, attractive, and pleasant social and technological organization. Unions obviously have done something to encourage this, and so has government, in its tax and labor policy, but the desire of businessmen themselves to become professionals in human relations seems to be a major element.

And their wives, too, have changed. If they are college trained, it isn't enough for them to spend their husband's income. Often they have had jobs themselves; they may be professionals in their own right, or potential professionals. They want to become pals and companions of their business spouses—sleeping partners, so to speak—aware of what goes on at work, and vicarious consumers of corporate conspicuousness, flaunting not so much their own now-standardized fur coats but their husband's firms—a more indirect display. Both husband and wife are urban, not small-town and rural, in their orientation; and they tend to view the factory work-force as a human collectivity in which there are roles to be played and maneuvers to be made. The earlier 19th-century horrors of rapid urbanization, in which human relations tended to become depersonalized and older social groupings disintegrated, now appear to be giving way to new institutional forms adapted to the conditions of contemporary city life. The presence of women on this scene, in fact or in feeling, helps alter the atmosphere, introducing a consumption mood into work relations, with its refreshing congeniality of association as contrasted with a male society of tycoons.

The divorce of corporate ownership from control and the consequent disenfranchisement of the stockholders (plus federal tax policies) have put responsibility for spending the corporate surplus on the executive in his capacity as an official, for corporate savings are only to a limited extent distributed to stockholders but are increasingly retained in depreciation funds or other concealment or reserve accounts. Business management schools play a part in deciding what it is that the corporation should now spend money for—whether it is for training directors, or market research, or philanthropic activity (which now supports much "pure" research)—all the multifarious forms of conspicuous corporate consumption.

In general, I think it can be said that many of the motives which were in earlier decades built into the character structure of individuals are now built into the institutional structure of corporate life. On the whole, I would rather see our surplus used to allow individuals a still greater amount of leisure, so that each of us would work, let us say, a four-hour day, than keep us at work eight hours so that our large organizations can generously spend the difference. And yet, in making such a judgment, I know I must continuously keep in mind the complex and stratified nature of the changes going on in our American life. If I had to choose between having Lever Brothers spend the American surplus on its beautiful Park Avenue offices and having the Happy Lomans and Glenn McCarthys spend it, I could easily come down on the side of Lever Brothers. Corporate consumption may be, as it has often been in architecture, a pleasure in its own right and sometimes a model for individual consumption.

15. Recreation and the Recreationist

As I was reflecting on our coming meeting, there came into my hands an article by Aileen Ross on the development of philanthropy in a Canadian city, which showed how from small amateur beginnings, the running of campaigns had become a professional job handled with increasing skill and cynicism on the part of the insiders—the designers of letterheads; the spearheads of the Special Gifts Committee; the full-time planners of other people's short-time bursts of energy and masochism—and with increasing apathy by the rank-and-file. I was thinking, too, about the notion, put forward in a recent book by Kenneth Boulding, that the most significant invention of modern times is the invention of the full-time organizer. The organizer moves in with his trained energy and skill, reminds people of identities and of needs they had only barely felt before, and builds a job for himself or somebody else as executive secretary. The full-time organizer is the answer our society has given to the problems created by rapid social change; the formula might be put this way: where the organizer is, disorganization was.

The trouble with the full-time organizer, however, is that he is apt to want not only a full-time job for a short time, but a life-time career. This means that he has a stake in the dependency of those he organizes. In the recreation field, he may want to do more than make facilities available to people, through books, magazines, and other media as well as in person; he may want to establish a group of clients who can't get along without him. I have watched this happening in the "field" of old age where, instead of trying to help young and middle-aged people prepare for old age by widening their leisure horizons, many spend much energy painfully organizing Golden Age clubs which turn the existing group of elderly people into the first wave of a permanent clientele. And we have all seen what has happened to teaching when the teachers' colleges and professional bodies forced those who entered it to make a career commitment, which has meant expulsion from teaching of those gifted amateurs for whom it could be a way-station on the road to something else, and has also meant that those who were in it for good were highly vulnerable to colleague pressures for conformity and not stirring up anything. It would be tragic if the still embryonic field of recreation should similarly become so professionalized that, for instance, able sociology graduates couldn't take a hand in it for a time, and then go on to something else (as my colleague Everett Hughes worked for the Chicago Park District while a student and learned thereby some of the ways in which different ethnic and class groups in Chicago like to amuse themselves, get married, and fight). Since recreation at its best depends a great deal on adaptability, spontaneity and enthusiasm, the field needs particularly to remain open at both ends, so that people can leave it and do something else, without feeling that there must be a loss of all ties, and can enter it either early or late in life without encountering restrictive barriers. The full-time organizers in the field can perhaps question the wisdom of giving up all claim to amateur standing, and come to think of themselves as a semi-permanent cadre, constantly bringing in short-term people.

§ II

THE FULL-TIME ORGANIZER, however, not only solves the problems of others but is a problem for himself. In this he is simply human. He wants to have people around who share his professionalization and the detachment this gives him, and with whom he can discuss his most intimate career concerns, share his "trade secrets," and get the news and gossip of colleagues. Since his clients constitute his major source of headaches, he can obviously not talk over his concerns with them; with them, he must maintain a front of piety, or permissiveness, or omniscience, or whatever else is the going mode of impressing clients in that line of work. He may find an audience in his wife, but she is not likely to fully understand a new business such as the one he is in, and he may in any case want to bring her his problems of play rather than his problems of work. Thus, the drive for professionalization among full-time organizers is in part a drive to regularize a colleague grouping, a drive to create a setting in which one is "understood."

But there is another sense in which the professional wants to be understood, in which what he really wants is to be appreciated, to have recognition and status for what he does. It is not only that he wants to impress clients, but he wants to impress himself, to feel he belongs, has a place; that he really exists and is not a figment of his own fertile imagination. When we are very young, we are apt to be asked: "How old are you, little man," and when we get out of school, we are asked: "What do you do for a living?" We want in the second case as in the first to make a self-evident answer, so that if, for instance, we reply that we are "in group work," we won't be asked, "Well, what the hell is that?" Recognition is, in fact, something to which the full-time organizer has every reason to be preternaturally sensitive, since he has to make his way not within a traditional going concern but within the very area which is to employ him and give him scope. He needs recognition outside the community in which he works in order to strengthen his hand inside, and so he devotes part of his effort to organizing his colleagues horizontally as well as his clients vertically.

The question still remains, however, as to who is to be admitted to, and who excluded from, the colleague group. How is one to draw the line between recreation as the "recreationist" sees it and the many different "industries" which contribute to the recreational side of life? Let me take, as an illustration, a traveling organizer of Columbia Concerts, or some similar service, who goes out to communities and organizes their previously dormant musical interests so that they will support a winter series of six or eight concerts. This person is adding to the recreational facilities directly and indirectly; for instance, many women will be led to spend their leisure as local volunteer helpers to put the concerts over; and the concerts may themselves stimulate local musical enterprises. Such concerts typically involve as many family members as can be persuaded to go, and the music offered is geared to a set of compromises between the musical tastes and fancies of young and old. The concerts may stimulate record sales—and vice versa—and perhaps the owner of the record shop should be viewed as a recreationist.

To take another example, the local movie theatre owner is certainly a recreationist, and if he is intelligent and public-spirited, he can play a not inconsiderable role in providing films for the family as a unit. With the ban on block-booking, he has come to have not inconsiderable power over the choice of individual films. I once knew a theatre manager in Brattleboro, Vermont, who regularly showed "art" and moderately highbrow films which he knew would lose $500 a run, because as he said he got tired of the usual stuff and figured he owed this to himself. Many of the films he got in this way provide a tight conversational web between parents and children, whereas other types of films either stratify the audience age-wise (and also, of course, in other respects) or bring the parents simply as bored guardians of the children or bring the children because the parents couldn't find a sitter. (I might express here in passing my prejudice against the drive-in theatre. It seems to me to have contributed to recreation within the family at the expense of the communal quality of an audience, being in this much like television. In a hall, one is aware of others being there. The quality is different; it is more festive. In the same way, I prefer to eat at restaurants rather than have food brought out to my car—but perhaps in this I am being merely old-fashioned.)

The theatre manager has another kind of power, in the voice the exhibitor has over the studios and the large distributing chains. He is the grass root which Hollywood sucks, and his comments are taken very seriously. If he says that Katie Hepburn in a film on tennis is box-office poison, he is going to make it hard for directors to make Katie Hepburn films, or they will try to change Katie Hepburn's style. And he in turn is vulnerable to local pressures. One theatre manager in Chicago told me that he was going to show no more Italian films because a local American Legion post had protested that it was "un-American." The recreationist who has a vision of the total leisure culture of his area will want to try to make an ally of this exhibitor, and to support him against both his own worst impulses and those of the pressure groups around him.

I am sure that a careful inventory would discover that any number of recreationists exist who do not realize their membership in a larger fraternity. And I think there is a good deal to be gained by the non-commercial recreationists from bringing them in. I belong to one professional group, the American Association for Public Opinion Research, whose meetings are worth attending because they bring together in one organization academic and governmental and business people concerned with opinion. To have market researchers and professors in the same outfit is stimulating to both—provided mutual defensiveness is not too great. The professors get to be a little more worldly, the market research people a little more curious about long-run developments. It may be that the analogy does not hold, and that camp directors and playground supervisors would find too little in common with the bowling-alley proprietor, the movie operator, the concert business manager, the bookseller, the sports promoters and pros.

I recall in this connection the feeling many educational broadcasters seem to have towards commercial radio and TV. Instead of looking for allies there, and finding here and there a program which, though not piously billed as "educational," actually stimulates the imagination and liberates a round of good family talk, they see the commercial broadcaster as the enemy almost by definition. Not recognizing in many cases the forms taken by their own commercialism under the disguise of an anti-commercial crusade, they draw an artificial line between private and public. . . . These are at least some cautionary themes which I would bear in mind before getting the profession of recreationist organized in such a way as to cut itself off from people who are not on a governmental or philanthropic payroll, but whose potentialities for a creative view of their work should not be underestimated.

§ III

NOW I WANT to turn to another set of misgivings, which are based less
on the problem of professional boundaries as such and more on the
ambiguity of the relation between recreation and public supervision.
The recreationist, when he looks at other people's play, finds it hard
to escape some of the biases the social worker is apt to have when he
looks at other people's budgets, or the housing official when he looks
at other people's accommodations. The latter, for example, when designing new housing or setting up standards for old tenements, is likely
to give more space to cleanliness and less to cooking than a lower-
class Italian or Polish family might choose if left to its own devices.
He may without knowing it cramp the family's recreation, traditionally
stove-oriented, in favor of the bathroom. (I don't mean to overlook the
value of the bathroom as a cubicle of privacy in our society, provided
the planner knows his clients' needs in this respect.) The social worker
may feel it is extravagant for a slum family to buy a TV set on time,
and fail to appreciate that the set is exactly the compensation for sub-
standard housing the family can best appreciate—and in the case of
Negroes or poorly dressed people, or the sick, an escape from being
embarrassed in public amusement places. Likewise, the recreationist—
especially if he comes out of a sports and camping background—may
insist too much on getting families out to play in the open, and stress
too little the solidarity a family can gain simply by dining out. Any
of you who have seen a whole family, in its Sunday best, fighting away
at lobsters at a seafood place with a sawdust floor, will recognize what
I mean; such feasts may be no less important as a family ritual—and the
similar feasts held at home—than the more muscular activities organized
by school and park people.

At the same time, I believe that recreation people need to be very
careful lest they place too much of a premium on families being together
as such. John Crosby remarked in a recent column (about the TV
program "Private Secretary"): "This is what is known as family
entertainment, which I guess means it's designed to bore the whole
family rather than entertain one section of it." We should not assume
that keeping the family together for recreation is a good to be gained
at the sacrifice of sharpness and vitality. However, there are, of course,
ways it can be done that do not have this watering down effect. I
think, for instance, of the Decca album of some years ago called
"Saturday Night at Tom Benton's," a pot-pourri of Tom, his wife,
and son playing the harmonica, guitar, and flute respectively, to the
accompaniment of a harpsichordist, folk singers, and other stray in-
strumentalists. It is all the more entertaining and dramatic as a family
experience because others are present, allowing each member of the

family to see the other in new and inventive roles. And this includes the little daughter, Jessie, who, in Tom Benton's cover for the album, stands looking on at all the doings—a recreationist might not define her as an active participant, but she is surely taking it all in.

In this connection, perhaps one main problem of the recreationist, as of the teacher, is to see that children and parents are neither brought together nor pulled apart in their leisure behavior by undue adult moralizing. If there is too much pious censorship of film-fare, some of the family are going to get their fancy fantasies somewhere else, perhaps surreptitiously. If the culture of the school and the culture of the street connect in no way with one another, the children are likely to find the street unduly exciting and the school a fraud. Certainly, some dichotomy there will always be. The family never can, and never should, become a "company town" controlling all aspects of its members' lives and budgets. It is a question of degree, the degree to which adult and child worlds can communicate—even communicate hostility— in the dramatized forms of recreational activity. I am pretty sure that the movies made by the Stephen Basutow group, such as "Gerald McBoing Boing" and "Mr. Magoo," have bridged parent-child hiatuses in a way that neither party alone could have done, just as I have found films and novels that could tell my children things which I am glad I don't have to.

Very likely, the best thing we can do for many families is to give its members vacations from each other, by introducing them to wider friendship constellations, or helping them form what Nelson Foote terms "quasi-families," those groupings of elected uncles and grandparents and cousins who are so characteristic of a mobile, urban society. There is a lot to be said for putting children fairly young into boarding school, or sending them to camp or on visits and trips, if for no other reason than that when they come home the reunion is both gay and intense; moreover, teen-agers can sometimes reveal themselves by letter-writing as they cannot do orally. And by the same token, I am inclined to think there is much to be said for periodic separation of sexes, in school and camp and later life; for here, too, reunions can be glamorous and more highly ritualized. I suspect that this goes against the grain of such a group as this, which prides itself on its informality and an easy familiarity between all sexes and all ages. But I am not convinced that good family life depends more on familiarity than it does on novelty and rhythm in relationships.

On the whole, it is probably easier for the recreationist to deal with people in groups, whether family groups or peer-groups. They take up less room, and perhaps need fewer facilities. But these considerations of material may be strengthened by the recreationist's own bias in favor of groups as such—he is apt to think of himself as a group worker, a facilitator of group enterprises and skills: after all, he has chosen a profession that means "working with people." In dealing with the many underorganized sectors of American life—the many isolated adults and deprived children—this professional bias is useful, but it needs to be guarded against in those sectors of American life where play outside the group is already under extreme pressure. We can perhaps remind ourselves how great this pressure is by asking whether such a poem as the following could be written today (at least without leading to a therapist's door!), and whether something very important in the valuation and protection of privacy is not now in danger:

> The "last man"—so I've heard it said—
> Will find his situation frightful;
> With all the other people dead;
> But *I* should think twould be delightful;
> There's nothing I'd enjoy
> Like being the last boy.

> That candy-store just up the street—
> I wouldn't lose a single minute
> In choosing what I'd like to eat,
> And spending several hours in it;
> With nobody to say
> I mustn't do that way.

> I'd go and visit all the shops,
> And fill my pockets—fill them, mainly,
> With little guns, and kites, and tops,
> And other things I've teased for vainly,
> And nobody would care,
> If nobody was there!

> I'd never go to bed—for then
> There'd be no horrid nurse to take me;
> I'd never go to school again:
> There wouldn't be a soul to make me:
> There's nothing I'd enjoy
> Like being the last boy.

> From *Slate-and-Pencil People*
> Verses by Emma A. Opper
> Frederick A. Stokes and Brother
> New York, 1885

§ IV

ONE MORAL of all this for me is that the recreationist needs to think of himself, less as the vanguard of a movement for the more participative use of leisure—long-term developments in our economy and culture are taking care of that—and more as a facilitator and stimulator, encouraging tie-ins with already existing activities. Thus, he may be living in Kansas City and discover that a TV show in Chicago is creating interest in the art galleries, and he may want to persuade the TV station in Kansas City to use that show in cooperation with the Art Museum; a telephone and a letterhead may be all the equipment he needs. On the whole, I should think it a good rule of thumb that the smaller his personnel budget and capital budget the better, lest he get a vested interest in a passing phase of play and recreation—an area whose very virtue lies in its fluidity. It may turn out that the community needs a tavern with tables for husband and wife groups more than it needs an adult education center; or a good supermarket more than a swimming pool. In fact, one of the most striking developments in family life in recent years appears to be the practice of husband and wife shopping together for groceries and staples, as one can see them of a Saturday morning, or of an evening in those shopping centers that have sparked and followed the new trend by staying open until nine or ten or even until midnight. Involved in this change are many things: the husband's shortened hours, and lengthened pocket-book (which has also influenced the superior design of the store itself) which makes purchasing an exercise in prodigality rather than in consumer's research; the self-service supermarket which does not demand good connections with the clerk to get waited on or with the butcher to get steak; ease in parking, which permits the family to come for the price of one; above all, perhaps, the modern middle-class families' re-arrangement of pleasures and duties which encourage bringing the husband in on what used to be the wife's private preserves. It would, I am inclined to think, be a muscle-bound recreationist who would think these evening or week-end shoppers were not engaged in recreation because the facilities they patronized were not labeled as a resort or park or camping-ground.

§ V

I AM NOT SAYING THIS, it should be clear, to urge the recreationist to follow majority vote, and if more dollars vote for a supermarket than a park, not to build or staff a park. There are many situations, many communities, where the majority can take care of itself, and where facilities for the minority may be the significant area of influence for the recreationist. It is a form of unrewarded sell-out for the public receationist—or librarian or broadcaster—to worry too much about how many people patronize his facility. I know that librarians, for instance, are often under pressure from their boards as well as from their own success-ethic, to turn the library into a kind of road-show, hauling customers in by public-relations stunts and catering to the large mystery-reading public (who could just as well buy pocket-books) at the expense of the few active library-users in town who depend on the library for their emotional lifeblood. I remember talking to the chief librarian of a small Western city about this. Her board judged her effectiveness by a traffic-count of the number of people she could entice into her premises, while it seemed to her that it was a more important function to sustain the intellectual life of the few ranchers and professional people who depended on books for communication with the great world beyond. Of course, if there is money enough to go round, such choices do not have to be made, but for the time being—I needn't tell you!—the budget will compel clarity in evaluating alternative facilities. And I suggest that we be not too frightened of the label of snobbery when we insist on providing leisure funds for those who want to do the rare and infrequent thing, whether that means taking out the book that is seldom used, or going to the camping spot accessible only to the young, spry, and moderately well-off. Indeed, so fast do American leisure habits change that what is rare today becomes a mass activity tomorrow, as we have seen happen in our generation with horseback riding, tennis, boating, record-collecting, painting, gourmandizing, ballet dancing, and a host of other pursuits.

The matter of budgets for leisure raises one final consideration. Such economists as Colin Clark have espoused the view that as an industrial society moves into a plateau of high mechanization and high labor productivity, more and more of the workforce comes to be employed in what he terms the "tertiary" industries—the service trades, including those catering to leisure. Those require, in comparison with manufacturing and transport, little capital plant but many workers. Think, for instance, of the beauty shop, both in terms of what it does for recreation—for the housewife who can escape from her children, telephone, bill-collectors, and sit under a dryer with her conscience appeased by the ads that make beauty a duty—and what it does for employment. Economists are now concerned with what may happen to the national income if and when military spending tapers off; they emphasize the vast increase in capital plant and the great rise in installment buying as indicating that private spending cannot easily take up the slack. Here is the point at which an Office of Recreation might come forward with plans for a great increase in recreational facilities and personnel, as a means at once of maintaining reasonably full employment and reasonably full family life. I am inclined to think, as I've already indicated, that these facilities and personnel should perhaps preferably not be public, but privately owned and publicly encouraged; although in a severe recession it may turn out that a "Play Progress Administration" rather than a WPA will be necessary to spend the money fast enough. Consequently, while some of us will remain as private tutors in effective spending, I am inclined to think it makes sense for others to make their voices heard when decisions are being made as to how to spend the national surplus no longer on the common defense of life and liberty but on the common pursuit of happiness.

16. Football in America: A Study in Culture Diffusion*

* With Reuel Denney.

§ I

ON OCTOBER 9, 1951, Assistant Attorney General Graham Morrison instituted an anti-trust action against a number of universities on account of their efforts to limit TV broadcasts of their games—efforts dictated by the terrible burdens of what we might speak of as "industrialized football." This action occurred only a few weeks after the scandal of the West Point student firings, which, along with the William and Mary palace revolution, indicated that football was indeed reaching another crisis in its adaptation to the ever-changing American environment. Small colleges such as Milligan—a church-supported school in the mountains of Eastern Tennessee—were discovering that football was now so mechanized that they could no longer afford the necessary entry fee for machinery and personnel. Last year, Milligan spent $17,000, or two-thirds of its whole athletic budget—and did not get it all back in the box-office net. Football had come to resemble other industries or mechanized farms, into which a new firm could not move by relying on an institutional lifetime of patient saving and plowing back of profits, but only by large corporate investment. The production of a team involves the heavy overhead and staff personnel characteristic of high-capital, functionally rationalized industries, as the result of successive changes in the game since its post-Civil-War diffusion from England.[1]

It would be wrong, however, to assert that football has become an impersonal market phenomenon. Rather, its rationalization as a sport and as a spectacle has served to bring out more openly the part it plays in the ethnic, class, and characterological struggles of our time—meaning, by "characterological struggle," the conflict between differ-

---

1. The growing scale of college football is indicated by its dollar place in the American leisure economy. In 1929, out of $4.3 billion recreation expenditures by Americans, the college football gate accounted for $22 million. In 1950, out of $11.2 billion in such expenditures, it accounted for $103 million. While something less than 1% of the total United States recreation account, college football had ten times the gross income of professional football. The 1950 gate of $103 million suggests that a total capital of perhaps $250 million is invested in the college football industry. The revenue figures, above, of course, do not include the invisible subsidization of football, nor do they hint at the place that football pools occupy in the American betting economy.

ent styles of life. The ethnic significance of football is immediately suggested by the shift in the typical origins of player-names on the All-American Football Teams since 1889. In 1889, all but one of the names (Heffelfinger) suggested Anglo-Saxon origins. The first name after that of Heffelfinger to suggest non-Anglo-Saxon recruitment was that of Murphy, at Yale, in 1895. After 1895, it was a rare All-American team that did not include at least one Irishman (Daly, Hogan, Rafferty, Shevlin); and the years before the turn of the century saw entrance of the Jew. On the 1904 team appeared Pierkarski, of Pennsylvania. By 1927, names like Casey, Kipke, Oosterbaan, Koppisch, Garbisch, and Friedman were appearing on the All-American lists with as much frequency as names like Channing, Adams, and Ames in the 1890's.

While such a tally does little more than document a shift that most observers have already recognized in American football, it raises questions that are probably not answerable merely in terms of ethnic origins of players. There is an element of class identification running through American football since its earliest days, and the ethnic origins of players contain ample invitations to the making of theory about the class dimensions of football. Most observers would be inclined to agree that the arrival of names like Kelley and Kipke on the annual All-American list was taken by the Flanagans and the Webers as the achievement of a lower-class aspiration to be among the best at an upper-class sport. The question remains: what did the achievement mean? What did it mean at different stages in the development of the game? Hasn't the meaning worn off in the fifty-odd years, the roughly two generations since Heffelfinger and Murphy made the grade?

There are many ways to begin an answer to such questions, and here we can open only a few lines of investigation. Our method is to study the interrelations between changes in the rules of the game (since the first intercollegiate contest: Rutgers, 6 goals—Princeton, 4 goals, in 1869) and to analyze the parallel changes in football strategy and ethos. All these developments are to be seen as part of a configuration that includes changes in coaching, in the training of players, and in the no less essential training of the mass audience.

Since football is a cultural inheritance from England, such an analysis may be made in the perspective of other studies in cultural diffusion and variation. Just as the French have transformed American telephone etiquette while retaining some of its recognizable physical features, so Americans have transformed the games of Europe even when, as in track or tennis, the formalities appear to be unaltered. Even within the Western industrial culture, there are great varieties.

on a class and national basis, in the games, rules, strategy, etiquette, and audience structures of sport. In the case of college football—we shall leave aside the symbolically less important professional game—the documentation of sportswriters (themselves a potent factor in change) allows us to trace the stages of development.

§ II

A STUDY OF Anatolian peasants now under way at the Bureau of Applied Social Research indicates that these highly tradition-bound people cannot grasp the abstractness of modern sports. They lack the enterprise, in their fatalistic village cultures, to see why people want to knock themselves out for sportmanship's remote ideals; they cannot link such rituals, even by remote analogy, with their own. These peasants are similarly unable to be caught up in modern politics, or to find anything meaningful in the Voice of America. Nevertheless, football itself, like so many other games with balls and goals, originated in a peasant culture.

Football, in its earliest English form, was called the Dane's Head and it was played in the tenth and eleventh centuries as a contest in kicking a ball between towns. The legend is that the first ball was a skull, and only later a cow's bladder. In some cases, the goals were the towns themselves, so that a team entering a village might have pushed the ball several miles en route. King Henry II (1154-89) proscribed the game, on the ground that it interfered with archery practice. Played in Dublin even after the ban, football did not become respectable or legal until an edict of James I reinstated it. The reason was perhaps less ideological than practical: firearms had made the art of bowmanship obsolete.

During the following century, football as played by British schoolboys became formalized, but did not change its fundamental pattern of forceful kicking. In 1823, Ellis of Rugby made the mistake of picking up the ball and running with it towards the goal. All concerned thought it a mistake: Ellis was sheepish, his captain apologetic. The mistake turned into innovation when it was decided that a running rule might make for an interesting game. The localism, pluralism, and studied casualness of English sports made it possible to try it out without securing universal assent—three or four purely local variants of football, football-hazing and "wall games" are still played in various English schools. Rugby adopted "Rugby" in 1841, several years after Cambridge had helped to popularize it.[2]

---

2. A commemorative stone at Rugby reads as follows:
                                  THIS STONE
                    COMMEMORATES THE EXPLOIT OF

This establishment of the running or Rugby game, as contrasted with the earlier, kicking game, had several important results. One was that the old-style players banded themselves together for the defense of their game, and formed the London Football Association (1863). This name, abbreviated to "Assoc," appears to have been the starting point for the neologism, "Soccer," the name that the kicking game now goes by in many parts of the English-speaking world. A second result was that the English, having found a new game, continued to play it without tight rules until the Rugby Union of 1871. As we shall see, this had its effects on the American game. The third and most important result of Ellis' "mistake," of course, was that he laid the foundations for everything fundamental about the American game between about 1869 and the introduction of the forward pass. (The forward pass is still illegal in Rugby and closely related football games.)

§ III

IN THE COLONIAL PERIOD and right down to the Civil War, Americans played variants on the kicking football game on their town greens and schoolyards. After the war, Yale and Harvard served as the culturally receptive importers of the English game. Harvard, meeting McGill in a game of Rugby football in 1874, brought the sport to the attention of collegiate circles and the press—two identifications important for the whole future development of the game. But if Harvard was an opinion leader, Yale was a technological one. A Yale student who had studied at Rugby was instrumental in persuading Yale men to play the Rugby game and was, therefore, responsible for some of Yale's early leadership in the sport.

It happened in the following way, according to Walter Camp and Lorin F. Deland.[3] The faculty in 1860, for reasons unknown, put a stop to interclass matches of the pre-Rugby variety. "During the following years, until 1870, football was practically dead at Yale. The class of '72, however, was very fond of athletic sports, and participated especially in long hare and hound runs. The revival of football was due in a large measure to Mr. D. S. Schaft, formerly of Rugby School, who entered the class of '73 and succeeded in making the

WILLIAM WEBB ELLIS
WHO WITH A FINE DISREGARD FOR THE RULES OF
FOOTBALL, AS PLAYED IN HIS TIME,
FIRST TOOK THE BALL IN HIS ARMS AND RAN WITH IT,
THUS ORIGINATING THE DISTINCTIVE FEATURE OF
THE RUGBY GAME
A. D. 1823

3. Walter Camp and Lorin F. Deland, *Football.*

sport popular among his classmates, and eventually formed an association which sent challenges to the other classes."

Soon after the period described by Camp, it became clear that American players, having tasted the "running" game, were willing to give up the soccer form. It became equally clear that they either did not want to, or could not, play Rugby according to the British rules. "The American players found in this code [English Rugby Rules] many uncertain and knotty points which caused much trouble in their game, especially as they had no traditions, or older and more experienced players, to whom they could turn for the necessary explanations," says Camp. An example of such a problem was English rule number nine:

"A touchdown is when a player, putting his hand on the ball in touch or in goal, stops it so that it remains dead, or fairly so."

The ambiguity of the phrase "fairly so" was increased by the statement in rule number eight that the ball is dead "when it rests absolutely motionless on the ground."

Camp's description of these early difficulties is intensely interesting to the student of cultural diffusion not only because of what Camp observed about the situation, but also because of what he neglected to observe. Consider the fact that the development of Rugby rules in England was accomplished by admitting into the rules something that we would call a legal fiction. While an offensive runner was permitted to carry the ball, the condition of his doing so was that he should *happen* to be standing behind the swaying "scrum" (the tangled players) at the moment the ball popped back out to him. An intentional "heel out" of the ball was not permitted; and the British rules of the mid-nineteenth century appear to take it for granted that the difference between an intentional and an unintentional heel-out would be clear to everyone. Ellis' mistake became institutionalized— but still as a mistake. This aspect of Rugby rule-making had important implications for the American game.

British players, according to tradition as well as according to rules, could be expected to tolerate such ambiguity as that of the heel-out rule just as they tolerated the ambiguity of the "dead" ball. They could be expected to tolerate it not only because of their personal part in developing new rules but also (a point we shall return to) because they had an audience with specific knowledge of the traditions to assist them. In America it was quite another matter to solve such problems. No Muzafer Sherif was present[4] to solidify the perceptions of "nearly so," and the emotional tone for resolving such question

---

4. Cf. his *An Outline of Social Psychology*, pp. 93-182.

without recurrent dispute could not be improvised. Rather, however, than dropping the Rugby game at that point, because of intolerance for the ambiguities involved, an effort was undertaken, at once systematic and gradual, to fill in by formal procedures the vacuum of etiquette and, in general, to adapt the game to its new cultural home.

The upshot of American procedure was to assign players to the legalized task of picking up and tossing the ball back out of scrimmage. This in turn created the rôle of the center, and the centering operation. This in turn led to a variety of problems in defining the situation as one of "scrimmage" or "non-scrimmage," and the whole question of the legality of passing the ball back to intended runners. American football never really solved these problems until it turned its attention, in 1880, to a definition of the scrimmage itself. The unpredictable English "scrum" or scramble for a free ball was abandoned, and a crude line of scrimmage was constructed across the field. Play was set in motion by snapping the ball. Meanwhile Americans became impatient with long retention of the ball by one side. It was possible for a team that was ahead in score to adopt tactics that would insure its retention of the ball until the end of the period. By the introduction of a minimum yardage-gain rule in 1882, the rulemakers assured the frequent interchange of the ball between sides.

The effect of this change was to dramatize the offensive-defensive symmetry of the scrimmage line, to locate it sharply in time ("downs"), and to focus attention not only on the snapping of the ball, but also on the problem of "offside" players. In the English game, with no spatially and temporally delimited "line of scrimmage," the offside player was penalized only by making him neutral in action until he could move to a position back of the position of the ball. In the American game, the new focus on centering, on a scrimmage line, and on yardage and downs, created the need for a better offside rule. From that need developed offside rules that even in the early years resembled the rules of today. American rulemakers were logically extending a native development when they decided to draw an imaginary line through the ball before it had been centered, to call this the "line of scrimmage," and to make this line, rather than the moving ball itself, the offside limit in the goalward motion of offensive players. At first, lined-up players of the two sides were allowed to stand and wrestle with each other while waiting for the ball to be centered; only later was a neutral zone introduced between the opposing lines.

Even with such a brief summary of the rule changes, we are in a position to see the operation of certain recurrent modes or patterns of adaptation. The adaptation begins with the acceptance of a single pivotal innovation (running with the ball). The problems of adapta-

tion begin with the realization that this single innovation has been
uprooted from a rich context of meaningful rules and traditions, and
does not work well in their absence. Still more complex problems of
adaptation develop when it is realized that the incompleteness of the
adaptation will not be solved by a reference to the pristine rules. In
the first place, the rules are not pristine (the English rules were in
the process of development themselves). In the second place, the tradition of interpreting them is not present in experienced players. In
the third place, even if it were, it might not be adaptable to the social
character and mood of the adapters.

Let us put it this way. The Americans, in order to solve the heel-
out problem, set in motion a redesign of the game that led ultimately
to timed centering from a temporarily fixed line of scrimmage. Emphasis completely shifted from the kicking game; it also shifted away
from the combined kicking and running possible under Rugby rules;
it shifted almost entirely in the direction of an emphasis on ball-
carrying. Meanwhile, to achieve this emphasis, the game made itself
vulnerable to slowdowns caused by one team's retention of the ball.
It not only lost the fluidity of the original game, but ran up against
a pronounced American taste for action in sports, visible action. There
is evidence that even if players had not objected to such slowdowns,
the spectators would have raised a shout. The yardage rule was the
way this crisis was met. This, in turn, led to an emphasis on mass
play, and helped to create the early twentieth-century problems of
football. But before we consider this step in the game's development
we must turn to examine certain factors in the sport's audience reception.

§ IV

A PROBLEM posed for the student of cultural diffusion at this point
can be stated as follows: What factor or factors appear to have been
most influential in creating an American game possessing not only
nationally distinct rules, but also rules having a specific flavor of
intense legality about many a point of procedure left more or less up
in the air by the British game?

We can now go beyond the rule-making aspect of the game and
assert that the chief factor was the importance of the need to standardize rules to supply an ever-widening collegiate field of competition, along with the audience this implied. The English rule-makers,
it appears, dealt with a situation in which amateur play was restricted
to a fairly limited number of collegians and institutions. The power
of localism was such that many an informality was tolerated, and
intended to be tolerated, in the rules and their interpretation. Ameri-

can football appeared on the American campus at the beginning of a long period in which intercollegiate and interclass sportsmanship was a problem of ever-widening social participation and concern. Football etiquette itself was in the making. Thus, it appears that when early American teams met, differences of opinion could not be resolved between captains in rapid-fire agreement or penny-tossing as was the case in Britain. American teams did not delegate to their captains the rôle of powerful comrade-in-antagonism with opposing captains, or, if they did, they felt that such responsibilities were too grave.[5]

Into just such situations football players thrust all of the force of their democratic social ideologies, all their prejudice in favor of equalitarian and codified inter-player attitudes. Undoubtedly, similar considerations also influenced the audience. Mark Benney, a British sociologist who is familiar with the games played on both sides of the Atlantic, points out that, whereas the American game was developed in and for a student group, the English game was played before quite large crowds who, from a class standpoint, were less homogeneous than the players themselves, though they were as well informed as the latter in the "law" of the game. Rugby football was seldom played by the proletariat; it was simply enjoyed as a spectacle.

Held by the critical fascination the British upper strata had for the lower strata, the audience was often hardly more interested in the result of the game than in judging the players as "gentlemen in action." "The players," Mr. Benney writes, "had to demonstrate that they were sportsmen, that they could 'take it'; and above all they had to inculcate the (politically important) ideology that legality was more important than power." The audience was, then, analogous to the skilled English jury at law, ready to be impressed by obedience to traditional legal ritual and form, and intolerant of "bad form" in their "betters." The early Yale games, played before a tiny, nonpaying audience, lacked any equivalent incentive to agree on a class-based ritual of "good form," and when the audiences came later on, their attitude towards upper-class sportsmanship was much more ambivalent —they had played the game too, and they were unwilling to subordinate themselves to a collegiate aristocracy who would thereby have been held to norms of correctness. The apparent legalism of many American arguments over the rules would strike British observers as simply a verbal power-play.

---

5. "Fifty years ago arguments followed almost every decision the referee made. The whole team took part, so that half the time the officials scarcely knew who was captain. The player who was a good linguist was always a priceless asset." John W. Heisman, who played for both Brown and Penn in the 1890's, quoted in Frank G. Menke, *Encyclopedia of Sports*, p. 293.

Such differences in the relation of the game to the audience, on this side of the Atlantic, undoubtedly speeded the development of the specifically American variant. Native, too, are the visual and temporal properties of the game as it developed even before 1900: its choreography could be enjoyed, if not always understood, by non-experts, and its atomistic pattern in time and space could seem natural to audiences accustomed to such patterns in other foci of the national life. The mid-field dramatization of line against line, the recurrent starting and stopping of field action around the timed snapping of a ball, the trend to a formalized division of labor between backfield and line, above all, perhaps, the increasingly precise synchronization of men in motion—these developments make it seem plausible to suggest that the whole procedural rationalization of the game which we have described was not unwelcome to Americans, and that it fitted in with other aspects of their industrial folkways.

Spurred by interest in the analysis of the athletic motions of men and animals, Eadweard Muybridge was setting out his movie-like action shots of the body motion (more preoccupied even than Vesalius or da Vinci with the detailed anatomy of movement)[6] at about the same time that Coach Woodruff at Pennsylvania (1894) was exploring the possibilities for momentum play: linemen swinging into motion before the ball is snapped, with the offensive team, forming a wedge, charging toward an opposition held waiting by the offside rule. In Philadelphia, the painter Eakins, self-consciously following the tenets of Naturalism and his own literal American tradition, was painting the oarsmen of the Schuylkill. Nearby, at the Midvale plant of the American Steel Company, efficiency expert Frederick Winslow Taylor was experimenting with motion study and incentive pay geared to small measurable changes in output—pay that would spur but never soften the workman.[7]

Since we do not believe in historical inevitability, nor in the necessary homogeneity of a culture, we do not suggest that the American game of football developed as it did out of cultural compulsion and could not have gone off in quite different directions. Indeed, the very effectiveness of momentum play, as a mode of bulldozing the defense, led eventually to the rule that the line must refrain from motion before the ball is snapped. For the bulldozing led, or was thought to

---

6. Sigfried Giedion, *Mechanization Takes Command*, pp. 21-27.

7. In view of the prejudice against "Taylorism" today, shared by men and management as well as the intellectuals, let us record our admiration for Taylor's achievement, our belief that he was less insensitive to psychological factors than is often claimed, and more "humane" in many ways than his no less manipulative, self-consciously psychological successors.

lead, to a great increase in injuries. And while these were first coped with by Walter Camp's training table (his men had their choice of beefsteak or mutton for dinner, to be washed down with milk, ale, or sherry), the public outcry soon forced further rule changes, designed to soften the game. After a particularly bloody battle between Pennsylvania and Swarthmore in 1905, President Roosevelt himself took a hand and insisted on reform.[8]

Camp's colleague at Yale, William Graham Sumner, may well have smiled wryly at this. Summer was exhorting his students to "get capital," and cautioning them against the vices of sympathy and reformism—a theme which has given innumerable American academes a good living since—while Camp was exhorting his to harden themselves, to be stern and unafraid. In spite of them both, the reformers won out; but the end of momentum play was not the end of momentum. Rather, with an ingenuity that still dazzles, the game was gentled and at the same time speeded by a new rule favoring the forward pass. But before going on to see what changes this introduced, let us note the differences between the subjects of Sumner's and Camp's exhortations on the one hand, and Taylor's on the other.

Frederick Taylor, as his writings show, was already coming up against a work force increasingly drawn from non-Protestant lands, and seeking to engender in them a YMCA-morality, whereas Camp was inculcating the same morality into young men of undiluted Anglo-Saxon stock and middle- to upper-class origins. Not for another fifty years would the sons of Midvale prove harder, though fed on kale or spaghetti, and only intermittently, than the sons of Yale. Meanwhile, the sons of Yale had learned to spend summers as tracklayers or wheat harvesters in an effort to enlarge their stamina, moral toughness, and cross-class adventures.

---

8. "In a 1905 game between Pennsylvania and Swarthmore, the Pennsy slogan was 'Stop Bob Maxwell,' one of the greatest linesmen of all time. He was a mighty man, with amazing ability to roll back enemy plunges. The Penn players, realizing that Maxwell was a menace to their chances of victory, took 'dead aim' at him throughout the furious play.

"Maxwell stuck it out, but when he tottered off the field, his face was a bloody wreck. Some photographer snapped him, and the photo of the mangled Maxwell, appearing in a newspaper, caught the attention of the then President Roosevelt. It so angered him, that he issued an ultimatum that if rough play in football was not immediately ruled out, he would abolish it by executive edict." Frank G. Menke, *Encyclopedia of Sports.*

Notice here the influence of two historical factors on football development: one, the occupancy of the White House in 1905 by the first President of the United States who was a self-conscious patron of youth, sport, and the arts; two, the relative newness in 1905 of photographic sports coverage. Widespread increased photographic coverage of popular culture was the direct result of the newspaper policies of William Randolph Hearst, beginning about 1895.

Nevertheless, certain basic resemblances between the purposes of Taylor and those of Sumner and Camp are clearly present. In contrast with the British, the Americans demonstrated a high degree of interest in winning games and winning one's way to high production goals. The Americans, as in so many other matters, were clearly concerned with the competitive spirit that new rules might provoke and control. (British sports, like British industry, seemed to take it more for granted that competition will exist even if one does not set up an ideology for it.) Much of this seems to rest in the paradoxical belief of Americans that competition is natural—but only if it is constantly recreated by artificial systems of social rules that direct energies into it.

Back of the attitudes expressed in Taylor, Sumner, and Camp we can feel the pressure not only of a theory of competition, but also a theory of the emotional tones that ought to go along with competition. It is apparent from the brutality scandals of 1905 that President Roosevelt reacted against roughhouse not so much because it was physical violence, but for two related reasons. The first and openly implied reason was that it was connected with an unsportsmanlike attitude. The second, unacknowledged, reason was that Americans fear and enjoy their aggression at the same time, and thus have difficulty in pinning down the inner meanings of external violence. The game of Rugby as now played in England is probably as physically injurious as American football was at the turn of the century. By contrast, American attitudes toward football demonstrate a forceful need to define, limit, and conventionalize the symbolism of violence in sports.

If we look back now at England, we see a game in which shouted signals and silent counting of timed movements are unknown—a game that seems to Americans to wander in an amorphous and disorderly roughhouse. Rugby, in the very home of the industrial revolution, seems pre-industrial, seems like one of the many feudal survivals that urbanization and industrialization have altered but not destroyed. The English game, moreover, seems not to have developed anyone like Camp, the Judge Gary of football (as Rockne was to be its Henry Ford): Camp was a sparkplug in efforts to codify inter-collegiate rules; he was often the head of the important committees. His training table, furthermore, was one of the signs of the slow rise in "overhead" expense—a rise which, rather like the water in United States Steel Stock, assumed that abundance was forthcoming and bailing out probable, as against the British need for parsimony. But at the same time the rise in costs undoubtedly made American football more vulnerable than ever to public-relations considerations: the "gate" could not be damned.

§ V

THIS PUBLIC RELATIONS ISSUE in the game first appears in the actions
of the rules committee of 1906—the introduction of the legalized forward pass in order to open up the game and reduce brutal power
play. Between 1906 and 1913 the issue was generally treated as a
problem centered about players and their coaches, and thus took the
form of an appeal to principles rather than to audiences. However,
the development of the high audience appeal that we shall show unfolding after 1913 was not autonomous and unheralded. If public
relations became a dominant factor by 1915, when the University of
Pittsburgh introduced numbers for players in order to spur the sale
of programs, it had its roots in the 1905-13 period. The rules committee of 1906, by its defensive action on roughhouse rules, had already implicitly acknowledged a broad public vested interest in the
ethos of the game. Let us turn to look at the speed with which football
was soon permeated by broad social meanings unanticipated by the
founders of the sport.

By 1913, the eve of the First World War, innovation in American
industry had ceased to be the prerogative of Baptist, Calvinist, and
North of Ireland tycoons. Giannini was starting his Bank of America; the Jews were entering the movies and the garment hegemonies.
Yet these were exceptions, and the second generation of immigrants,
taught in America to be dissatisfied with the manual work their
fathers did, were seldom finding the easy paths of ascent promised in
success literature. Where, for one thing, were they to go to college?
If they sought to enter the older eastern institutions, would they face
a social struggle? Such anxieties probably contributed to the fact that
the game of boyish and spirited brawn played at the eastern centers
of intellect and cultivation was to be overthrown by the new game of
craft and field maneuver that got its first rehearsal at the hands of two
second-generation poor boys attending little-known Notre Dame.

The more significant of the two boys, Knute Rockne, was, to be
sure, of Danish Protestant descent and only later became a Catholic.[9]
During their summer vacation jobs as lifeguards on Lake Michigan,
Rockne and Gus Dorais decided to work as a passing team. Playing
West Point early in the season of 1913, they put on the first demonstration of the spiral pass that makes scientific use of the difference
in shape between the round ball used in the kicking game and the oval
that gradually replaced it when ball-carrying began. As the first players to exploit the legal pass, they rolled up a surprise victory over
Army. One of the effects of the national change in rules was to bring

---

9. "After the church, football is the best thing we have," Rockne.

the second-generation boys of the early twentieth century to the front, with a craft innovation that added new elements of surprise, "system" and skull-session to a game that had once revolved about an ethos of brawn plus character-building.

With the ethnic shift, appears to have come a shift in type of hero. The work-minded glamor of an all-'round craftsman like Jim Thorpe gave way to the people-minded glamor of backfield generals organizing deceptive forays into enemy territory—of course, the older martial virtues are not so much ruled out as partially incorporated in the new image. In saying this, it must not be forgotten, as sports columnist Red Smith has pointed out, that the fictional Yale hero, Dick Merriwell, is openly and shamelessly represented as a dirty player in the first chapters of his career. But the difference is that his deviation from standard sportsmanship consisted largely of slugging, not of premeditated wiliness. In fact, the Yale Era, even into Camp's reign, was characterized by a game played youthfully, with little attention to the players' prestige outside college circles. Again, the second-generationers mark a change. A variety of sources, including letters to the sports page, indicate that a Notre Dame victory became representational in a way a Yale or Harvard victory never was, and no Irish or Polish boy on the team could escape the symbolism. And by the self-confirming process, the Yale or Harvard showing became symbolic in turn, and the game could never be returned, short of intramuralization, to the players themselves and their earlier age of innocent dirtiness.[10] The heterogeneity of America which had made it impossible to play the Rugby game at Yale had finally had its effect in transforming the meaning of the game to a point where Arnold of Rugby might have difficulty in drawing the right moral or any moral from it. Its "ideal types" had undergone a deep and widespread characterological change.

For the second-generation boy, with his father's muscles but not his father's motives, football soon became a means to career ascent. So was racketeering, but football gave acceptance, too—acceptance

---

10. One of us, while a Harvard undergraduate, sought with several friends to heal the breach between Harvard and Princeton—a breach whose bitterness could hardly be credited today. The Harvards believed Princeton played dirty—it certainly won handily in those years of the 20's—while Princetonians believed themselves snubbed by Harvard as crude parvenus trying to make a trio out of the Harvard-Yale duo. The diplomatic problems involved in seeking to repair these status slights and scars were a microcosm of the Congress of Westphalia or Vienna—whether the Harvard or Princeton athletic directors should enter the room first was an issue. A leak to the Hearst press destroyed our efforts, as alumni pressure forced denials of any attempt to resume relations, but the compromise formulas worked out were eventually accepted, about the time that the University of Chicago "solved" the problem of the intellectual school by withdrawing from the game altogether.

into the democratic fraternity of the entertainment world where performance counts and ethnic origin is hardly a handicap. Moreover, Americans as onlookers welcomed the anti-traditional innovations of a Rockne, and admired the trick that worked, whatever the opposing team and alumni may have thought about the effort involved. One wonders whether Rockne and Dorais may not have gotten a particular pleasure from their craftiness by thinking of it as a counter-image to the stereotype of muscle-men applied to their fathers.

It was in 1915, at about the same time that the newcomers perfected their passing game, that the recruitment of players began in earnest. Without such recruitment, the game could not have served as a career route for many of the second generation who would not have had the cash or impetus to make the class jump that college involved.[11]

The development of the open and rationalized game has led step by step not only to the T formation, but also to the two-platoon system. These innovations call for a very different relationship among the players than was the case under the older star system. For the game is now a coöperative enterprise in which mistakes are too costly —to the head coach, the budget, even the college itself—to be left to individual initiative. At least at one institution, an anthropologist has been called in to study the morale problems of the home team, and to help in the scouting of opposing teams. To the learning of Taylor, there has been added that of Mayo, and coaches are conscious of the need to be group-dynamics leaders rather than old-line straw bosses.

Today, the semi-professionalized player, fully conscious of how many people's living depends on him, cannot be exhorted by Frank Merriwell appeals, but needs to be "handled." And the signals are no longer the barks of the first Camp-trained quarterback—hardly more differentiated than a folkdance caller's—but are cues of great subtlety and mathematical precision for situations planned in advance with camera shots and character fill-ins of the opposing team. James Worthy and other advocates of a span of control beyond the usual half-dozen of the older military and executive manuals might find support for their views in the way an eleven is managed. Industrial, military, and football teamwork have all a common cultural frame.

Yet it would be too simple to say that football has ceased to be a game for its players, and has become an industry, or a training for industry. In the American culture as a whole, no sharp line exists between work and play, and in some respects the more work-like an activity becomes, the more it can successfully conceal elements of

11. See George Saxon, "Immigrant Culture in a Stratified Society," *Modern Review*, II, No. 2, February 1948.

playfulness.[12] Just because the sophisticated "amateur" of today does *not* have his manhood at stake in the antique do-or-die fashion (though his manhood may be involved, in very ambivalent ways, in his more generalized rôle as athlete and teammate), there can be a relaxation of certain older demands and a more detached enjoyment of perfection of play irrespective of partisanship.

The rôle of football tutor to the audience has been pushed heavily onto radio and TV announcers (some of whom will doubtless be mobile into the higher-status rôle of commentators on politics or symphony broadcasts). The managerial coalescence of local betting pools into several big oceans has also contributed to the audience stake in the game. Yet all that has so far been said does not wholly explain alumnus and subway-alumnus loyalties. It may be that we have to read into this interest of the older age groups a much more general aspect of American behavior: the pious and near-compulsory devotion of the older folks to whatever the younger folks are alleged to find important. The tension between the generations doubtless contributes to the hysterical note of solemnity in the efforts of some older age groups to control the ethics of the game, partly perhaps as a displacement of their efforts to control youthful sexuality.

And this problem in turn leads to questions about the high percentage of women in the American football audience, compared with that of any other country, and the high salience of women in football as compared with baseball imagery (in recent American football films, girls have been singled out as the most influential section of the spectators). The presence of these women heightens the sexual impact of everything in and around the game, from shoulderpads to the star system, as the popular folklore of the game recognizes. Although women are not expected to attend baseball games, when they do attend they are expected to understand them and to acquire, if not a "male" attitude, at least something approaching companionship on a basis of equality with their male escorts.[13]

For all its involvement with such elemental themes in American life, it may be that football has reached the apex of its audience appeal. With bigness comes vulnerability: "inter-industry" competition is invited, and so are rising costs—the players, though not yet unionized, learn early in high school of their market value and, like Jim in Huckleberry Finn, take pride in it.[14] The educators' counter-reforma-

---

12. Compare the discussion of Freud's playful work, pp. 331-333, below.

13. Anthropologist Ray Birdwhistell convincingly argues that football players play with an eye to their prestige among teammates, other football players, and other men.

14. Their pride varies to some extent with their place on the team. Linemen, with the exception of ends, have lower status than backfield men. Many players

tion cannot be laughed off. With the lack of ethnic worlds to conquer, we may soon find the now-decorous Irish of the Midwest embarrassed by Notre Dame's unbroken victories. Perhaps the period of innovation which began in 1823 at Rugby has about come to an end in the United States, with large changes likely to result only if the game is used as a device for acculturation to America, not by the vanishing stream of immigrants to that country, but by the rest of the world that will seek the secret of American victories on the playing fields of South Bend.

---

believe that backfields are consciously and unconsciously recruited from higher social strata than linemen.

17. Bookworms and The Social Soil

IN THE BRINGING UP of children today there seems to have been a definite shift in the attitude toward what books should and do mean to a child. Ever since Lucy Sprague Mitchell started writing the "Here and Now" books, parents and teachers have been told that imaginative books and fairy tales are bad and disturbing; that they may impart false values; that in dealing with princesses and giants they are trivial and unreal. In place of such fare it is said that children should have books that will enlighten them about the world, about reality. Reality turns out to be how things work, how water gets into the bathtub, for instance, or milk onto the doorstep; the human meanness of ogres and stepmothers is definitely not reality.

More recently parents have been told that children should not read too much, that it is better for them to learn through experience and to spend their time with other children—as if life were long and varied enough to find out very much about people without the aid of the social storehouse of books and other artistic works. There has been engendered a real fear of books among the very social groups that once upheld standards of cultivation, on the grounds that books may interfere with a child's development. A psychologist recently wrote in his daily newspaper column that "a child's main interest should be in doing things not in reading about them," and he added, "Living too much in the realm of imagination retards the development of his ability to distinguish reality from daydreams." Parents are also advised not to allow children to become bookworms—they will grow up lacking personality.

In the earlier years of settlement of this country many parents had just the opposite fear. Moving from Europe or from the cultivated seaboard to the frontier, they feared that their children would become illiterates; they struggled desperately to see that their children were taught to read and that a few books, including of course the Bible, would be part of their sparse furnishings. Perhaps, indeed, it is a sign of American abundance that we can now take literacy virtually for granted and can discover some of its ambiguities for personal adjustment. But such tendencies easily become self-confirming, and if psychologists tell us that a bookworm will lack personality we will have fewer bookworms and those we have will feel on the defensive.

To be sure, not only books can disturb "adjustment." Once, doing a study of teen-age attitudes towards music, I talked with the mother of a fourteen-year-old boy. "John likes to practise [the piano]," she told me, "but I don't let him play more than an hour a day. I want to keep him a normal boy." Possibly a daughter would have been allowed somewhat more freedom in this as in other areas of genteel accomplishment, though on the whole girls even more than boys would seem to be defenseless against the demand that they be adjusted. At any rate, when they grow up they do not take upon themselves the duty of reading books on behalf of the whole society; after leaving school both boys and girls in nine cases out of ten drop anything that could be called serious reading.

The bookworm, then, is the one person in ten who reads 70 per cent of the books, including the pocket-size books, that are sold or shelved in the United States. I am inclined to view these bookworms as performing something of the same service in aerating our society that earthworms perform for the soil. Yet worms and other invaluable contributors to the earth's ecology are sometimes considered "varmint" by farmers, despite all the Soil Conservation Service can do—very much as even adult bookworms are considered to be poor personalities by some personnel managers. Fortunately, the Committee on Reading Development has set itself up as a kind of Soil Conservation Service for the field of ideas and has gone to bat on various fronts to defend the bookworm's interests, including not only the stimulation of research but also a lobby in Congress.

One thing seems pretty clear, namely, that books remain the least censored of media. This is in part, I suggest, precisely because of the smallness of their audience; as pocket books somewhat widen the market the problem of censorship is bound to grow more acute. But print has an old tradition to defend—older than that of movies and radio—and it has had for many reasons less intimidated defenders. True, minds may be closed to new ideas even if books are not. But since people are seldom all of a piece books can usually get into their crannies and use parts of them for leverage to open up the rest. Books, that is, can be disturbing, disintegrating forces in people and in society.

There is actually little evidence that the people who read the most books have in general the fewest social contacts and hence suffer for performing the bookworm function for the community at large. Most studies of the audience for books and other media serve rather to demonstrate the principle of "the more, the more." The more books one reads, the more magazines one reads, too, the more movies one is apt to see, and the more organizations belonged to, and so on. Books,

in spite of all I have said, still carry enough of a prestige tag so that
many non-readers will tell the interviewer: "I would love to read
but I have no time." Freudian implications to the contrary, if they
do not have time to read they are also apt not to have time for much
voluntary leisure activity of any sort.

On the whole I cannot feel that by allowing children to be bookworms one is providing for the aeration of the social soil at their
emotional expense; reading is one of those functions where tragic
contradictions between social and individual interest are at a minimum.
But obviously this judgment depends in part on my view that "adjustment" is one of the sadder fates which can overtake a child in
our society and that "integration" of personality is a somewhat doubtful ideal as usually defined—that contradiction and discontinuity of
personality have to be part of any ideal which is not merely wan and
flaccid.

Some people who have given thought to the problem contend that
a short way to get rid both of the allegedly high price of books and of
any ambiguities in being a bookworm is to go over completely to
pocket books, which could be disposed of without a pang or trace as
readily as a magazine, and beyond that to substitute transmission of
information by facsimile for books altogether. Apparently, it is now
technically feasible to scan entire libraries electronically, so that by
pushing a button a "reader" could have flashed onto a television
screen a series of moving images containing the capsulated information or amusement that he wanted. When these prospects struck horror into some of the more cultivated members of the publishing
fraternity one of the Conference experts urged us to abandon any
sentimental attachments we might have to the moss on the bucket
which had previously dragged up ideas and to focus our emotional
eye only on the bucket's content.

Yet it is precisely on the good-sized, hard-cover book that the
bookworm is nourished. He cannot bury himself in a moving image
or even, unless he is very small, in a pocket book. He is a creature
who needs wide margins. For he tries to create amid all the pressures
of contemporary culture a kind of "social space" around himself, an
area of privacy. He does this by tying himself in his thinking and
feeling to sources of some relative permanence—hence impersonal—
while remaining somewhat impermeable to the fluctuating tastes, panics,
and, most menacing of all, the appeals to be "adjusted" from his contemporaries. Hard-cover books are essential as protection for our all-
too-small tribe of "hard-cover men."

There can be no doubt that many publishers do take very seriously
their crucial mission in the defense of the hard-cover men. It is often

this that leads them to be troubled by the rising break-even point of hard-cover books which makes it difficult to take chances with those first novels and non-fiction not entirely sure-fire. However, in view of the social and psychological pressures generally operative against becoming a bookworm it seems doubtful that the high price of books is one of the more serious deterrents to good reading (though, as just indicated, it may be a deterrent to new, creative writing). Rather, the fact that books are *believed* to be high-priced would seem to be a sign of public hostility to books and reading: the publishing industry is one of the few whose costs and prices create comment on the outside and guilt on the inside of the industry. The question seems worth raising as to why publishers as compared with other manufacturers should be deprived of the American right to a reasonable inefficiency and a reasonable Hotel-Algonquin-style expense account.

In fact it is my impression that the large, streamlined publishers of textbooks are somewhat more "efficient" and feel less guilt—but should feel more. Textbooks are hard-cover books which often lack—or even in the long run destroy—the hard-cover function. (In the short run a great many of the important ideas in society appear to be spread by textbooks rather than by more current writings: this is where ideas end up to pasture, after a few runs at Belmont Park.) Textbooks increasingly associate reading with "government issue," something which is handed out rather than bought. In some college towns bookstores carry only texts and students do not learn to browse among books or how to collect and cherish them. (I should add, of course, that this development is not so much the responsibility of the publishers as of my own teaching profession, whose occasional monopolistic practices in the promotion of texts make use of quite a few of the devices, such as tie-in sales and captive markets, that the FTC has condemned.)

This all too brief consideration of whether textbooks are really books leads into an even more difficult question: what is a good or a serious book anyway? What kinds of books should publishers feel responsibility to publish and readers to read? It is my own impression that much that is forced upon people as good reading may turn them against reading as a chore and help create a protective apathy against all ideological appeals. The "Here and Now" books have been followed by the waves of Little Golden Books such as "Let's Go Shopping," and "Scuffy the Tugboat"; similar developments have taken place in the adult world where books about international relations and race relations, whether fiction or non-fiction, are promoted because they are intended to awaken people to "reality," to the various critical issues of today such as foreign policy.

All this assumes that we know more than we do know about the consequences of reading one or another sort of book. There is always an element of indeterminacy in art; in the relation of a reader to a book many things—many unintended things—can and do happen. It seems possible to argue, for instance, that "Huckleberry Finn" is a more serious book on race relations than any of the recent crop, among other reasons because of the artistic ambiguities in the reflections of Huck on the problem of helping Nigger Jim escape. Likewise it seems possible to argue that people need to read less that deals with the present and more that deals with the past and future. The very expense and solidity of the hard-cover book—its quality as furniture—may bear some relation to the long-run timetable of its impact, as compared with those media that cannot as readily be preserved, annotated, reread, or inherited. And among such things it is perhaps precisely the more "escapist" ones which for many can nourish the longer perspectives and the detachments that this country with its abundant resources of people and goods can afford even—or especially —in wartime.

True, there is no necessary conflict in principle between the "escape" book which is a craftsmanlike treatment of literary themes and the topical book which is a tract for the times. It follows from what I have said that what is a liberating book for one person may not be for another—a point often overlooked by those who, nostalgically overestimating the uncorrupted tastes of an earlier day, assume that all those who read good books in the eighteenth century or saw Shakespeare's plays in Elizabethan days found the good things in them. (In her excellent historical study, "Fiction and the Reading Public," Q. D. Leavis does present some evidence, such as material from letters and diaries as well as analysis of best sellers, to indicate a decline of English taste in the last century and a half, but it is terribly difficult to be sure of any such judgment about a dead audience when we cannot even tell much about a live one.) In the "Road to Xanadu" John Livingston Lowes traced some of the kaleidoscopic influences which had seeped into the mind of Coleridge, but similar detective work has not been done to trace the impact of books in the lifespan of less notable figures. Beyond the well-thumbed indexes of reading by age, sex, and previous condition of social-class servitude, research, I must repeat, can so far tell us very little about the subtle interplays between books of different kinds and people of different kinds. Reading a sheaf of book reviews is evidence enough that any book of moment can be interpreted in a fantastic variety of ways.

I recall, for example, the hue and cry among many parents and teachers, already leery of comics, when the story appeared about the boy who had jumped from an apartment-house window wearing a Superman cloak and been killed. It was naturally assumed that children identify themselves with Superman and with other heroes of the newer media. But a careful study of comics readers—one of the very few sophisticated studies we have of any sort of reader—shows that perhaps the majority of children do *not* identify themselves with Superman or other potent wizards of the comics. . . . The reader's fear of being a sucker; the fear of seeming to make ambitious, envy-arousing claims; the here-and-now interest in aviation coupled with disinterest in imaginative "flying"—all these things may inhibit the child's power and willingness to identify with a fictional hero.

Much in the same way, I suggest, readers do not learn in school to identify themselves with writers, that is, to identify themselves actively with great literary achievement. Such identification is, obviously, not the same as that which is encouraged by gossip columns about authors as "personalities." Anyone can identify with a personality in this sense. He can wear the same Superman cloak, he can drink the same coffee, drive the same make of car. But the writing of books of the sort we are concerned about would seem to thrive only where readers can identify with the author as craftsman, as performer— where they are capable of an objective identification with performance as such. This doesn't mean, of course, that they have to be able to write themselves but I do suspect that schools might do more for reading if they worried a bit less about pupils' reading skills and tastes and a bit more about their writing.

Of course everyone damns the schools for the crushing of literary talents and enthusiasms; indeed, this may be one reason why the schools have tended to abandon the classical tradition in favor of social studies and other supposedly less spinsterly and more true-to-life topics—topics, however, which can seldom be taught "realistically" and honestly to school children. The schools in turn tend to shift the blame for the dissatisfaction of the book-reading minority—about the fact that they *are* a minority—onto the shoulders of the mass media.

However, just as we are in no position to declare what is a serious book for every type of reader so we cannot assume offhand that books are inevitably more liberating than the newer media. Furthermore, the school-teacher who feels TV as unfair competition with Jane Austen not only fails to realize that Jane Austen's audience may not have gotten out of her what the teacher herself would hope to get across; more important, the teacher may also be unaware of how much she could do for a gifted and sensitive child or two if she was not afraid of boring a hundred others. Or her attack on TV may be based on her own succumbing to the very values she deplores (often unfairly) in TV; she is apt to accept somehow the inverse snobbery and class romanticism of the prevailing assumption that the non-readers have more fun and are closer to the "natural" and to "life" than the rare gifted bookworms are. It is when she feels she must reach everybody that she compares the Hooper rating of books with that of the supposedly competing media.

The result of all this is neither to make TV more interesting and artistic nor to create social space for the minority of bookworms but rather to make the use of leisure from childhood on a matter for anxiety, inter-generational tension, and concern for social status. I notice among my own students, who are moving up to the top of the "brow" hierarchy, an all-too-ready tendency to adjust to this new set of tastes and to diminish to a safe point the total number of risky enthusiasms for books. They are not worried about being conspicuous for a Superman stunt but for liking a "middlebrow" best seller. (It is safer, of course, for intellectuals to have low tastes than middling ones.) They worry, let us say, that they like Dylan Thomas less than Stephen Spender.

For them the problem is not whether to read or not to read (as it is for the average textbook student mentioned earlier), but how to have read "everything" by the age of twenty-four. This kind of self-demand is historically new in American education and is due to the quiet revolution in standards of teaching which has occurred in the last decades in the more active colleges and universities. Around these students the social space is often small because they want in a few years to fill in an area that took earlier generations of students a lifetime. A small minority even within the small minority of bookworms, they indicate in their own way how haunted and unleisurely our leisure often is.

Yet Americans, despite their ability to make themselves unhappy by efforts to achieve the right amount of adjustment (or, depending on the group, of maladjustment), are an inventive people. I think it quite possible that there exist new and as yet unknown ways by which people may protect their privacy and social space for liberation through books and other mass media even against all the obstacles presented by their peers and by the society at large. When for such suggestions I am accused of fostering "escape" I usually ask: is the world so wonderful, then, that you can think of no better 'ole, even in a book? The world is what it is in considerable measure because of the books that have been written and read. Likewise, any hope of finding a better world—and therefore of making one—rests on books and on other imaginative productions of some permanence. But until moving day comes and we go to our new utopian quarters I think we have every right to insist on our prerogative of escape.

The question comes back to the quality of that escape, as the problem of the mass media comes back to their quality, for their variety of audiences, in all the concreteness of their impact. And it is here, partly because we are so much in the dark, that we tend to engage in polemics and in admonitions. We need neither to praise escape nor to blame it but to differentiate it. It is even conceivable that only the escapists will turn out to be living in a real world—while the ascetic promoters of serious and dutiful reading are inhabiting some other planet of their own fantasy!

18. How Different May One Be?

. . . IN AN EARLIER DAY, parents and other authorities held out to children certain objective goals: they should get rich, for one thing, or become great scholars, or maybe even become president. And parents drove their children toward these goals. The traits of character which mattered were such things as diligence, honesty, and thrift—the injunctions of Ben Franklin's Almanac. If the child delivered the goods according to these reasonably clear criteria, it mattered rather less what he was like as a person; parents neither knew enough to observe his psychological make-up nor were they very interested in it. As a member of society's work-force the child would be expected to produce, rather than to be a particularly well-adjusted or even happy person. Thus both his character, with its implanted goals, and his situation, as he turned to make his living or his mark, combined to intensify the demands made on him as a producer, while the demands made on him as a person were slight. This gave him a certain freedom to be different, provided he did his work adequately.

What matters about the individual in today's economy is less his capacity to produce than his capacity to be a member of a team. Business and professional success now depend much more than ever before on one's ability to work in a team in far-flung personnel networks; the man who works too hard or in too solitary a way is, by and large, almost as unwelcome in the executive offices, the universities, or the hospitals of urban America as he would be in a union shop. He cannot satisfy society's demands on him simply by being good at his job; he has to be good, but he has also to be cooperative. When translated into child-rearing practices, this means that parents who want their children to get along and to succeed will be quite as concerned with their adjustment in the school group as with their grades or with their industry on an after-school job.

I don't mean to suggest that parents consciously calculate their children's job-chances and train the youngsters accordingly. Rather, the same great and still not fully understood social changes that have altered the nature of attitudes toward work and the worker have also influenced the home (the parents, or at least the father, are also workers), the school, the movies and radio and other institutions which divide among themselves, in none too friendly a fashion, the tasks of defining the goals for modern children.

266

These goals are no longer clear-cut. The older goals—such as sheer money-making—were often shallow and have been to a considerable degree abandoned. New goals—such as a full and happy life —have not yet had a chance to become more than vague mandates that cannot guide a parent or a child from day to day. Consequently there is every opportunity for one goal, namely popularity, to outstrip all others in importance. This is a means of rating the child when there is no other means available. Parents can no longer prefer to have a child who is diligent to a child who is "one of the gang." So parents, too, though perhaps with some misgivings, share the concern with popularity. Unlike their predecessors of the Victorian Age, they know—from the teacher, the P.T.A., their own children—what the popularity score is.

Matters would be relatively simple for parent and child if the market demanded complete conformists. Then, at least, expectations would be clear—and rebellion against them equally clear. But matters are not simple. What is expected of children and adults, in the middle and upper educated strata at least, actually *is* difference—but not too much. That is, one must be different enough to attract attention, to *be* a personality, to be labeled and tagged. . . .

Progressive parents, taught for the last several decades to "accept" their children, have learned to welcome a certain amount of rebelliousness or difference. Likewise, business and the professions, especially perhaps in the growing number of fields catering to consumption and leisure, welcome a certain amount of eccentricity, if this goes together with a cooperative team spirit. Thus children often find themselves in the paradoxical position in which their "difference" is simply evidence that they are conventional and up-to-date. Perhaps more important, they are compelled to learn to find their way among exceedingly subtle expectations on the part of others. They are expected both to be spontaneous and not to disrupt the mood of a particular group; to a degree they must conform and yet maintain the personality they have already built up. . . .

And the parents themselves become concerned and anxious, and understandably so, if the child's age-mates reject him; they fear his differences are of the wrong sort, and perhaps, too, that their differences from their neighbors are of the wrong sort. Are they to defend their child's differences, then, at the cost of his undoubted present and possible future misery?

I think the answer to this crucial question depends at least in part on whether the parents are secure enough and capable enough to provide the child with an environment that will give him some protection against the expectations of his peers. They must offer him a way of life which will help him suffer less from his loneliness and his fear of it. They do this in part by altering the valuation put on loneliness and in part by encouraging interests that, while making his adjustment to his present group no easier, make his adjustment to a future group no more difficult.

Let me take a specific, wholly imaginary case. It is, perhaps, not a very frequent case. It may be less frequent than that of parents who push their children into academic or aesthetic pursuits beyond the children's potential gifts and interests, injuring the children's self-esteem (since they cannot live up to adult expectations) and sacrificing their present happiness to an impossible future goal. But it is a case of a sort that, I believe, occurs more often as parents are taught the gospel of "adjustment to the group" and apply it both in their own lives and in their concern for their children.

Isobel is very gifted musically. Her parents and teachers eagerly encourage her musical zealousness. Already in her early teens her passionate preoccupation with music begins to set her apart somewhat from the other girls, not to mention boys, in her group who have no such individual interests. Isobel takes music lessons while the other girls go to the movies; she practices while others gab in a friend's house.

But Isobel's problem arises not only, if at all, from the time taken out of play by her musical interests; it arises because a concern with music, regarded in the group as too highbrow, goes beyond the limits of marginal differentiation in her circle. Gradually, without her full awareness of what is happening, Isobel is labeled as "different" (that is, as *too* different); and in the ceaseless game of friendship-ratings that the other girls play, she is left near the bottom or put to one side.

Meanwhile Isobel has become devoted to her music teacher, who encourages her to go on with music as a career; but Isobel's parents and schoolteacher—and Isobel herself—become worried that she may diverge from the path of a "normal" girl. . . . Isobel's mother may even feel guilty that she has allowed Isobel's musical interests to develop to this point.

What are some of the alternatives that may be open to Isobel's mother in this situation? Certainly, I do not expect her to make decisions that will press Isobel toward martyrdom to some once-existent ideal. But I think that Isobel's mother and teacher might be making a mistake if they concluded that acceptance in the group was more important for Isobel than music. For one thing, it is easy for parents and children to believe that they want mere acceptance, whereas what they really crave is popularity going far beyond acceptance. (This confusion is all the easier to make because of the clique structure of many school classes where, indeed, there may be no midpoint between popularity and ostracism.)

But the real question is whether popularity or even acceptance is a goal worth the sacrifice of precious, genuine musical talent. What the group offers is attractive but precarious and evanescent; music is a delight and an endless resource. In due time Isobel will be old enough to journey to an environment where there will be other girls and boys who care more passionately about music than about anything else—perhaps even than about *anybody* else. While our society has done an extraordinary job in the cultivation of the social skills, these must never be allowed to become ultimates of existence; they are far from being the only skills from which people can derive pleasure and profit. Some social skills Isobel will have to learn as part of her musical training, but this can wait.

And, indeed, it really is the ability to wait that is involved here. Parents never ask themselves what will give their child (or themselves, for that matter) pleasure at the age of sixty or seventy. While our life-expectancy has lengthened, our life-timetables have shortened considerably; and our flattened perspective makes it hard for us to see our children suffer, even for a short time, let alone to be the cause of this suffering ourselves. Yet thousands of parents throw away their children's special gifts—which can best be cultivated during youth—in return for gifts of social adjustment to a particular group at a particular time and place. Though certainly an unhappy childhood is not desirable, it is true that many unhappy children do grow up to be happy, productive, befriended adults.

For Isobel's mother to make such a choice as to let her daughter suffer now in anticipation of her future satisfactions would require that she herself believe that music, no matter what its momentarily estranging qualities may be, is worth a child's devotion. She is likely to doubt this, despite the evidence of her own child's attachment, if her own reactions and values are largely influenced by the opinions and values of relatives, friends, and neighbors, for then she will look to the other children for cues as to what is "normal" adjustment.

How can she defend Isobel against the others, if they are taken as the norm? Indeed, she is likely to fail to defend Isobel if she cares too much whether Isobel likes her, for there will be times when Isobel will deeply resent her mother for permitting her to be "different," even if Isobel herself, pushed by her gifts and her music teacher, takes the first steps in this direction. Isobel's mother has some power to define the values in the home in such a way that a child's loneliness is not regarded as the worst possible fate, while a failure to develop potentialities is felt as a real tragedy. Thus, gradually Isobel may learn to defend herself against the expectations of any particular group, and can move toward genuine autonomy—toward the ideal, which we humans seek but never fully achieve, of cultivation of our genuine differences as these develop from our unique capacities and life experiences.

Furthermore, Isobel's parents are not only members of a particular family but members of a particular community. If they want to protect Isobel's future they are not entirely confined to giving her marginal guidance in the direction of marginal differentiation. As members of a P.T.A., for instance, they can insist that schools concern themselves not only with children's social adjustment, with forming them into tolerant, amiable members of a cooperating group, but with children's skills, musical, linguistic, mathematical, or whatnot. They can raise the question whether we may not have gone too far in de-emphasizing academic performance, thus concentrating the teachers' as well as the children's attention on the more intangible aspects of social development. And as members of the wider community, they can apply their efforts to increasing the appreciation of what people can do, even if this means decreasing the appreciation of "personality" as the chief focus of concern.

V.

VEBLEN AND THE BUSINESS CULTURE

THE FIRST OF THESE ESSAYS, "The Social and Psychological Background of Veblen's Economic Theories," follows the same plan as the Freud studies in the next section, for it is an effort to relate Veblen's ideas to each other and to his milieu. While, however, with Freud I kept as clear of biographical detail as possible, with Veblen I combined close textual analysis of his writings with reading what I could find, and talking with whom I could buttonhole, about the man himself. I'm not sure how much I would have guessed about Veblen from his writings alone, regarded as interview material for projective analysis, especially as Veblen took enormous pains to cover his tracks and hide himself in what he wrote—as compared with Freud's brave but unshowy effort to reveal himself through his dream-analyses and autobiographical writings. (Veblen, indeed, ordered all his letters and possessions destroyed—hardly any have been made public—and his last wish was that there should be no biography or even tombstone to recall him, a wish that reminds us of another ailing son of a strong-willed father: Kafka.) In this article, as well as in the book from which it is partly drawn, I offer some very tentative suggestions about Veblen's character structure and the relation this bore to his choice of profession, choice of intellectual weapons such as irony, and choice of topic. I am more concerned here with the sources of Veblen's ideas, and some of their consequences for intellectual history, than with whether they were right or wrong. That is, I am not here arguing with Veblen nor opposing him so much as trying to explain him.

My talk on "Relations between Social Progress and Technical Progress" was, *inter alia*, an effort to raise questions about the changing patterns and changing nature of the American business culture before a group of young technical people brought from all over the globe to attend a conference sponsored by M.I.T. students. These conferees, chosen mostly by twos from the various applicant countries, had been spending the summer at M.I.T. and were preparing for a bus tour of American industrial centers. As the discussion following my talk made clear, most of them were eager to adapt

American techniques for their home countries, while avoiding what they considered the debasement and vulgarity of American life; they were reluctant to admit that this country might be changing, and that their stereotypes about it were insufficiently complex. As one Dutch chemist rather aggressively said: "I am only in this country for a few months; I have *got* to see it in black and white!" Fortunately for him, other American speakers presented a not un-Veblenian view of the American business tycoon, his ruthlessness, raw empiricism, and lack of cultivation, which permitted him and others to feel I was seeing things which weren't there.

And to be sure, the question is left open in all my work as to how far and how fast the newer-model business values have spread: I have described a business typology without marking the boundaries and quantitative distribution of the several types. Certainly in my research in Kansas City I have found thriving exemplars of un-chastened enterpreneurship—businessmen who leave culture to their wives and ministers and remain untroubled by professionalizing tendencies within management. But these are small businessmen mostly, sometimes traders, wealthy but not economically influential; they are not "the transients" within large corporate businesses that William H. Whyte, Jr., has so imaginatively described in *Fortune*. With a strong hold on Congress and the state legislatures, on chambers of commerce and American Legion posts, on the businessmen's Bible classes which struck me in Kansas City as more energetic, optimistic, and bouncy that even small business itself, men such as those Veblen mercilessly satirized in his section on the country town in *Absentee Ownership* remain a potent political and cultural force, uneasily hostile to wealth and cultivation older and more secure than theirs.

However, theirs is not the only force and if I do no more in this article than raise questions for further searching, I shall be quite content. As Eric Larrabee remarked during the conference, the delegates were having trouble because American culture had become, in some ways, more sophisticated than they realized. I myself constantly feel that it escapes my efforts at interpretation, that I have a sense of only a very small fragment of what goes on, and that neither social science nor other forms of reporting are quite keeping up with the growing differentiation of our national life.

19. The Social and Psychological Setting of Veblen's Economic Theory*

In Veblen's own critique of other economists—and a major portion of his theory is just that—he relied securely on quasi-Marxist simplicities concerning causation. Other economists "got that way" because they were members of or sycophants of the kept classes, aristocratically disdainful of the actualities of production. Their theories, if they were classicists, were "superstructural" in the sense of being both above and behind the battle, for Veblen was one of the pioneers in the use of the cultural-lag concept which has done so much to confuse the understanding of the relations between technology and society. If they were *American* classicists, such as (in Veblen's view) J. B. Clark, they were likely to couple a pallid reformism with their "fine-spun technicalities," offering palliatives at the level of pecuniary theory for evils rooted in the very divorce of the pecuniary culture from its industrial base. And this reformism Veblen saw as a leisure-class product, along with female philanthropy, the arts and crafts movement, social work, and vegetarianism—the archaic by-products of the sheltered life of the better-off and the better-educated strata whose menial and hence life-giving work was done for them by others. Reformism was archaic because it was pre-evolutionary, pre-Darwinian; for Veblen, "A.D." meant "After Darwin." His emphasis on the datedness of economic theory—a charge to which Americans are especially sensitive since we like to be progressive and up-to-date—led Veblen to express recurrent hopes for the "younger generation" of economists, whom he wanted to make less literate and theoretical, less parasitic and less sanguine, less refined and more machine-minded. For Veblen as for Rousseau, what was young was not so likely to be corrupted and spoiled.

Veblen, however, never explained why some economists, himself included, were historically minded and literate in spite of being "younger." He admired Sombart and borrowed much from him; he had good words to say for Schmoller; and he attacked the German

* In the footnotes I have taken account of some of the points made in the discussion following the presentation of this paper to the Economic History Association, meeting at Bryn Mawr, September 1953. I gratefully acknowledge many helpful suggestions from Staughton Lynd.

Historical School only for not being completely free of chauvinism and reformism; for Karl Marx, in his role as economic historian and not in his role as prophet, Veblen had a good deal of sympathy. In his efforts to make economics a historically relativistic science, in his refusal to "take the current situation for granted as a permanent state of things," Veblen contributed to economic history rather than to economics proper (I happen not to share his bias that the classicists were all too proper), granted that his Morganatic anthropology was a kind of history, a Just So story of stages in a universal unilinear human destiny. And perhaps it can be said that Veblen's unremitting warfare with what he called "the guild of theoretical economists" opened up possibilities for a more historical or anthropological economics which later students, more cautious and less given to economistic explanations, have been exploiting.

§ I

BUT HOW, drawing from Veblen, are we to explain Veblen? In my forthcoming book, I make a very tentative effort to show how his theories reflect the conflict between his harsh, intrepid, and technologically adept father and his Bible-reading, softer, and whimsical mother.[1] Take, for example, his view that in the matriarchal past life was at its best, but that modern man is simply nostalgic if he dwells on this, for modern man must adapt to the discipline of the machine, its cold, impersonal calculus, or go under. Might we not say that this outlook, like analogous lost paradises, reflects the co-existence in his mind of periods of his own life: the earliest childhood, dominated by his mother, and the succeeding harsher if more productive phases, dominated by his father? Plainly, neither such a theory nor such a family constellation is idiosyncratic to Veblen; such families, indeed, peer out at us from Victorian portraits and memoirs—and, in fact, justify themselves by reference to ideologies of masculine work-mindedness and domination of nature, of masculine mathematics and calculation. Yet such correspondence between family and ideology, while fruitful for speculation, are not explanatory: they illustrate compatibilities but do not show why some children of ascetic fathers, like Samuel Butler, rebelled to become antagonists of the machine and admirers of luxury, while others, like Veblen, rhapsodized their fathers and defended their coldness, asceticism, and solemnity. In fact, a closer look at Veblen, while it shows the father portrayed as the philosopher-king of the future, the engineer, also shows the father attacked in the son's muted praise for "idle curiosity" and muted

1. *Thorstein Veblen: A Critical Interpretation.*

contempt for pragmatism—contempt expressed also in his unceasing and successful effort to make a failure of his own career.

Veblen's father, though notably progressive in his use of farm machinery and interest in science, never learned English; Rolvaag's statement is applicable to him: "We have become strangers—strangers to the people we forsook and strangers to the people we came to."[2] But Veblen's Norwegian heritage is important not only because it made him a marginal man, linguistically and intellectually cosmopolitan, socially awkward, and emotionally expatriate, but also because of certain specific values he seems to have acquired as a youngster. Blegen notes the fact that the Norwegian immigrants could not understand competitive sports and games. Recalling Schumpeter's observation that for the entrepreneur "economic action becomes akin to sport,"[3] it would seem plausible to connect Veblen's fear and distrust of the entrepreneur with his Norse peasant's sort of Puritanism which rejected sport.[4] Indeed, Rolvaag's novels show how the Norwegian immigrants viewed plays and dances as sinful; their ministers urged them to hold fast to their racial traits and not to emulate American ways. While Veblen emancipated himself from this piety in certain respects, sexually and theologically for instance, he remained in many ways a seventeenth-century sort of Puritan protesting against the more commercially minded and urbanized Yankee Puritans whose faith seemed to him as watered as their stock, whose expenditures appeared as wasteful as their wars and their agronomy, and whose Anglo-Saxon ideal of sport struck him as a form of juvenile delinquency.

Staughton Lynd, who has collaborated with me in the study of Veblen's background, has observed that Simon Patten was born on better, richer land than that of Veblen's parents—and Patten of course went on to emphasize American abundance and consumption whereas Veblen, ever fearful of scarcity, remained an ascetic and aesthetic enemy of consumption, above an efficient subsistence minimum. (Patten had studied in Germany and been impressed by *Gemütlichkeit*, by how well the Germans made use of their leisure.) Veblen did not feel, with Willa Cather, that "it took more intelligence to spend money than to make it,"[5] but rather that getting and spending were

---

2. Quoted in Theodore Blegen, *Grass Roots History*, p. 113.
3. *The Theory of Economic Development*, p. 93.
4. A genealogy of the Veblen family indicates that most of Thorstein's siblings married other Norwegian-Americans (judging from names, and the names given children) and apparently remained in rural areas: one brother, and his favorite nephew Oswald, entered academic life. Only in the next generation would there appear to have been widespread assimilation to American middle-class norms.
5. *One of Ours*, p. 102.

both frivolous pecuniary diversions from modern man's essential problem: habituation to the machine and its relentless logic. In turning in his own career from philology and Kantian philosophy to economics, he was not only converted, as his first wife later declared, by Bellamy's *Looking Backward*, but also seems to have wanted to immerse himself in the study of livelihood. But perhaps at the same time he was attracted as well as repelled by the almost philological intricacy the science of economics, in comparison with other social sciences, was beginning to attain.[6]

This last point is important, for it introduces us to the fact that Veblen did not remain a Populist or a Bellamy Nationalist: he outgrew both movements in part. Thus, while a good deal of his economics may be interpreted as a farm boy's stubborn empiricism—a show-me attitude toward theory and refinement, a dislike of classics and the classical, a fear of art and artfulness, a chronic suspicion of lawyers and financiers—Veblen is neither a Bryan nor a Dreiser. Soon after moving to Chicago in 1892, he ended his concern with agricultural economics and the price of wheat and began his lifelong preoccupation with the most subtle market and monopoly tactics of business enterprise. He was thoroughly aware that the future, not only of the United States but of the planet, lay with industry and not, by any fond hope, with the rural, the tribal, the fundamentalist. Though proud all his life long of his Scandinavian ancestry, and happier with farmers and Wobbly workers than with professors who could not chop a tree, make furniture, or saddle a horse, he nevertheless identified himself with the international world of scholarship and only on occasion with the more folksy and destructive vulgarities of Populism.[7] Indeed, as a self-proclaimed matter-of-fact scientist, he was able to conceal from himself (and from many of his readers) the extent of his animus against the rich and the scholastics who

---

6. To be sure, in Veblen's America economics was still often taught by divines and other amateurs, but Veblen, a gifted linguist, was familiar with the work being done on the Continent. On coming to Chicago, he translated Ferdinand Lassalle's polemical *Science and the Workingman*, and in the *Journal of Political Economy* he reviewed scholarly as well as socialist European economic literature. These reviews—some of them reprinted in *The Place of Science in Modern Civilization and Other Essays*—exhibit Veblen's skill in handling complex Marshallian types of argument in economic theory.

7. Neither Veblen's idealized engineer nor his footloose Wobbly hero has much in common with the masterful, muscular hero of Jack London's *The Iron Heel*. During the first World War, Veblen, though ferociously anti-German, was concerned about how international scholarship might be preserved through American aid. In this man of multiple and wavering identities, a concern for scholarship and especially economics—if not for particular scholars and economists —remained an abiding concern even when he became a "left-wing" journalist on *The Dial*.

neither toiled nor spun—save for spinning theories to justify their idleness and prestige. Through science he could sublimate his alienations and harness his hostility.

§ II

HE CAME LATE to economics, as he came late to the English language and the genteel tradition, to cities, and, in a way, to America. And this, too, is not idiosyncratic but reflects an era in which it was very difficult for the underprivileged young to get higher education, although it was also an era in which professors, secure in their own status, enjoyed polishing and bringing along those rare ethnics—a Veblen, a Bernard Berenson, a Morris Cohen, an Alvin Johnson—who did manage to get access to them. The zeal and enthusiasm of these newcomers for the classical culture was thus stimulated and preserved (as compared with the situation today in which professors and students, no longer so different from each other, are cool, sharing know-how rather than isolated excitement). The very backwardness of America then held certain advantages for the pioneers of scholarship who, even if like Veblen they turned hostile to classicism, came as individuals to a library with the same passion that whole nations have come to literacy when the printing press is first introduced. I should add, moreover, that but for this backwardness I doubt if we would be taking Veblen very seriously today; he stands out among turn-of-the-century thinkers in this country as he would hardly do in an international conspectus that took account of his great contemporaries on the European continent.

To return to Veblen as a late-comer: Trained initially in philosophy, the field in which he took his doctorate with a thesis on Kant, he turned his critical intelligence and linguistic acuity onto what he termed the "received homilies" of economic theory; his papers on Clark, Marx, Böhm-Bawerk, and others are magnificent forays in criticism. Often unaware of what he had learned from the men he attacked, he tested their theories for both internal consistency and relevance, not to "the economy" in the narrower sense in which that sphere is the province of a special breed of men called economists but to "the economy" in the broader sense which includes all human use of resources, political and cultural, tangible and intangible. By bringing the "state of the industrial arts" into the discussion of market relations, he forced attention to the cultural and technological prerequisites which many theorists of marginal utility had taken for granted. Likewise, he insisted on bringing into technical academic discussion the usages of the common man. Thus, in a review of Irving Fisher's *Capital and Income*, he argued that "capital" can only be defined by empirical observation of how businessmen use the term —there is no point in a more refined definition. Indeed, the study of economics becomes the study of businessmen's habits of thought; changes in businessmen's linguistic usage, therefore, reflect changes in what they do. Here the outsider speaks—or, in terms of his own theory (see *Imperial Germany and the Industrial Revolution*), the late-comer who takes over modernity without the encrustations of habit, sport, and dilettantism. In this and other papers, he stresses that price, interest, value, and other categories are conventions, not given in the nature of things or in human nature but through the institutional processes and social learnings we would today summarize as culture.

§ III

MOREOVER, like many outsiders and late-comers—including some of the most significant minds of the nineteenth century—Veblen employed the search for economic origins as a way of discrediting capitalism's claim to be sacrosanct and traditional, as well as the claim of particular capitalists to be innovators and contributors to welfare. In regard to the latter, when he did not charge them with usurpation and sabotage, he observed that they lazily engrossed the community's common stock of industrial understanding: they stole not so much surplus labor (a metaphysical concept Veblen derided) as a racial inheritance of instinctive workmanship (Veblen's racism was metaphysical, too, as he sometimes admitted). Concerning the former, Veblen pointed to the historically late entrance of substantial capital assets upon a population already somewhat crowded by growing scarcity of land, giving rise to the exceptional and unstable phenomenon of modern capitalism—a parvenu likes to pretend he has always been there. But the "assets," Veblen insisted (in line with single-tax thinking), are such only because the institutions so define them; thus when metals came into use, flint-beds were no longer assets, and in general "the maker's productivity in the case was but a function of the immaterial technological equipment at his command, and that in its turn was the slow spiritual distillate of the community's time-long experience and initiative."[8]

While Veblen was simply one of a number of nineteenth-century thinkers who, by ennobling earlier ages or submerged classes, challenged the capitalists' own lately attained patents of nobility, he was distinctly stimulating and original in his emphasis on the insubstantiality of capital, not only in terms of its historical uniqueness in its

8. "On the Nature of Capital," in *The Place of Science in Modern Civilization*, p. 339.

contemporary form but also in terms of its resting on interpersonal expectations and understandings much more than on plants and tools. Under Veblen's analysis the impressive physical apparatus of industrialism is separated from the interpersonal racketeering, the "intangible assets," the absentee ownership, the salesmanship and propaganda—all the vendible imponderables that truly dominate the business culture and constitute specifically modern "capital." His awareness of the role of propaganda, of confidence and confidence men, of "good will," is sophisticated, and links him with such political scientists as Harold Lasswell or such sociological economists as Pareto or Schumpeter, rather than with the classical or, for the most part, the institutional economists either then or now. Just as he saw socialism as grounded in large part on emulation, he saw capitalism resting on Kwakiutl-like motives of waste and display and on the airy romance of unstable hopes rather than on the solid substance of land, labor, and equipment. Indeed, one can trace anticipations in Veblen of Keynes's and Schumpeter's theories of crisis. And Veblen also anticipated their sense of the precariousness of future prosperity and the historically limited nature of the capitalist world of the nineteenth century.

§ IV

HE GOT THERE, however, I suggest, in part by the skeptical farm boy's route of distrusting the words, the promises, of city slickers, while being fascinated by them. His father, who had lost his first farm to a shrewd claimant, had been a man of very few words—and those in Norwegian; Veblen's own style is a conscious parody of the prolixity, pedantry, and legalism of the half-educated country lawyer or deacon. His distrust, moreover, is not only that of the farm boy who can never quite accept the reality of things beyond the palpable necessities of life but also a quite far-reaching distrust rooted in his character structure—a fear of being caught, made a fool of, taken in. This is one reason he was never willing to commit himself to a cause, a movement, a colleague, or a woman. All obligations seemed unstable to him. He was so ready to see the role of expectations in society in part because he himself was so fearful lest anything be expected of him; his whole academic career may be viewed as a sidling out of commitments, and his unfactual attitude toward getting the facts and unscientific attitude toward himself as a mere scientist may be seen as efforts to escape from amorphousness and to relate himself to something solid, if not to somebody. His crusade to get theory "down to earth" was thus in part the argument with himself of a refugee from the farm.

This fear of constraint and commitment, coupled with a fear of the freedom that would result from their absence, is one of the most distinctive themes of Veblen's character structure, visible in his writings as well as in other behavior. His writings, for example, have as a formal matter no principle of flow, of organization; they are endlessly repetitive in the large and in detail; sentences have style but little structure. Moreover, as we have seen, Veblen insisted on man's subordination to the machine, to the slow evolutionary drift of things, while at the same time he identified with the Wobblies, the less bemused portions of the underlying population, the masterless men who bowed to no authority save logic and to no rule save the slide-rule. This ambivalence we can relate once more to his parents, who thought him bright, expected much of him, but gave him little warmth—and these parents in turn provide a link with the tight patriarchal family and the no less tight ethnic group—a group who supported the post-doctoral Veblen while he loafed and read, read and loafed, because as a traditional culture they accepted the responsibility even for such kin as were deviants. And on the other side, we can relate Veblen's character structure to his choice of field, for I suggest that economics then, with its undefined boundaries and unmathematical, more or less speculative, often historical methods, attracted those who feared constraint, much as sociology and anthropology have more recently done. That is, economics may have appeared to Veblen to mix agreeable proportions of intricacy and openness, methodology and topicality. Veblen broke down the boundaries of economics even further: his very fluid definition led him to subtitle *The Theory of the Leisure Class* "an Economic Study of Institutions." The state of the art allowed him not to be cabined by his chosen discipline; and his eloquent pleas for opening it up to new areas of investigation—business practice, anthropology, psychology, as well as politics—have helped create such cadres of no longer quite marginal but also not wholly free men and women as yourselves, the economic historians.

§ V

ALL THIS ONLY BRINGS US to another paradox in Veblen's relation to his *Zeitgeist*, if this term can still be used. The psychology he went to school with, so to speak, was that of Peirce, James, and Dewey—a psychology that stressed, as indeed Kant's did, man's selective perception and active organization of the world, his adaptation of it to him, rather than his mere passive response to hedonistic drives. Again and again, Veblen states that man is an agent, an actor, shaping the institutions which in turn shape him; moreover, his concept of idle curiosity is a sort of instinctual basis for autonomy. He had some sympathy for Lester Ward, who drew humane implications from Darwinism; he was friendly with W. I. Thomas, who stressed the subjective nature of social life;[9] he even saw in animism a projection of the human will. And yet, because as already indicated he was afraid of his own fear of constraint, afraid too of the freedom he regarded, as his father might have, as soft and sentimental, he resisted the implications of his psychological affiliations for his economics. For him, Darwinism came as a discovery of mankind's submergence in blind, cumulative drift over which it would be naïve and vain to seek control. In counseling adaptation to the machine, he urged on men a ferocious surrender to the existent, even at the cost of distorting instincts which Veblen thought had been shaped for all time in a savage past. And in his aggressive scientism, no less deterministic than that of Comte and St. Simon and more so in some ways than that of Engels, he urged his fellow economists to give up their personal wishes for amelioration and to bind themselves, in fraternal anonymity, to become consultants for industrial managers, statisticians for project engineers (shall I say "policy scientists"?). In a famous passage, he criticizes Marx and his followers:

The neo-Hegelian romantic, Marxian standpoint was wholly personal, whereas the evolutionistic—it may be called Darwinian—standpoint is wholly impersonal. . . . The romantic (Marxian) sequence of theory is essentially an intellectual sequence, and it is therefore of a teleological character. . . . On the other hand, in the Darwinian scheme of thought . . . the sequence is controlled by nothing but the *vis a tergo* of brute causation, and is essentially mechanical. The neo-Hegelian (Marxian) scheme of development is drawn in the image of the struggling ambitious human spirit: that of Darwinian evolution is of the nature of a mechanical process.[10]

Indeed, I think William Graham Sumner, hard-boiled at least on the surface, had more influence on Veblen than his gentle colleague, John Dewey, with his, at least on the surface, more hopeful view of man. In making his choice among "influences"—and it will be seen

---

9. I have relied heavily, for information on Veblen's life and times, on Joseph Dorfman, *Thorstein Veblen and His America.* I am also indebted to a conversation with Professor Max Fisch concerning Veblen and Peirce. Since my address was written, an interesting essay has appeared comparing Veblen and William James: Lewis Feuer, "Thorstein Veblen: the Metaphysics of the Interned Immigrant," *American Quarterly,* V (1953), 99-112. Feuer, somewhat less sympathetic to James and more to Veblen than I am, stresses that Veblen was too close to a precarious personal existence to afford James's middle-class optimism about the human will.

10. "The Socialist Economics of Karl Marx and his Followers: II," in *The Place of Science in Modern Civilization,* pp. 436-37.

that I myself see men as having some leeway in choosing their influences rather than simply succumbing to tropisms—Veblen may
have been picking his father over his mother, his enemies over his
friends, his need to be restrained over his fear of restraint. Beyond
that, a certain personal passivity and shyness may have been at work
which made him dislike any theory or custom that gave renown to
individuals or brought them into the limelight. Veblen, having early
handed in his resignation to life and being in many ways a very
dependent person, seems to have felt that the "struggling ambitious
human spirit" could neither found a scientific system nor change the
world, even though, as in many fatalist schemes, this discovery heart-
ened him to espouse, with a very personal style, the claims of impersonality and, with a very unexpedient life, the mandates of expedient
adaptation and determinism.

§ VI

SUCH PSYCHOLOGICAL EXPLANATIONS, however, leave me somewhat unsatisfied, not only because I know all too little about the details of
Veblen's parentage and childhood but also because I know all too
well that men of very different background espoused quite similar
views of the economy—while of course other farm boys, such as
Alvin Johnson, differed from Veblen. Nevertheless, we must ask
how Veblen happened to select, among available careers and themes,
the particular contradictions that he made his own. The question is
in principle answerable even though others could achieve outcomes
similar in general, though never in detail, from different motives
and, of course, follow him for again different motives. And if we
then ask why so intelligent a man as Veblen did not go farther, why
he failed in so many ways appreciably to transcend his age, we are
once more brought back sharply to his biography. We see, for instance, that his country-boy late-comer skepticism and bitterness had
its opposite side in a certain gullibility. He was overimpressed by the
very captains of industry he derided. He gave them more power to
do damage, as saboteurs of production and Goliaths of consumption,
than they actually possessed; their personalities and even their success impressed him, in his shy, resigned failure, despite his Darwinist
defense. Their values impressed him even more. In making the canon
of efficiency the standard for judging all social life, he was able to
demolish much Victorian cant and pretense, but by the use of a
Philistine weapon borrowed from businessmen. Veblen contended
that businessmen were unbusinesslike, though only by insisting that
they were single-mindedly in pursuit of profits rather than production; this very single-mindedness, though some of the robber barons
came close to it, was for most of them an unachieved ideal. In his

own attempt to be single-minded, Veblen would have very little quarrel with the businessman today who wants government to be run like General Motors: if technocracy was a caricature of his gospel, it was not without his co-operation. Even the businessman who despises art, culture, and philanthropy finds something of an ally in Veblen, whose hatred for all archaic, inefficient, untechnological pursuits has at times a very militant quality. Believing himself a critic of his culture, he fell into some of its most characteristic nineteenth-century crudities and self-deceptions.

Even more striking, perhaps, is Veblen's unconscious acceptance of nineteenth-century rationalistic individualism. Veblen never seriously concerned himself with the problem of social solidarity: he assumed that men, once freed of the imposed incubus of pecuniary rivalry, would work together in obedience to both their instincts and their self-evident subsistence needs. While he spoke occasionally of the "parental bent" as a kind of instinct of social solicitude, he more typically took it for granted that "masterless men" would find in engineering mandates a sufficient basis for co-operation. During the same era that Durkheim and Freud, Brooks Adams and Sorel, Max Weber and Pareto were in one or another way preoccupied with centrifugal tendencies in modern society, Veblen saw the role of leaders and elites as sheer unnecessary swindle and expense. His preconceptions concerning human relations were those of a market economy —impersonal, rationalistic, calculable. Here again, Veblen is the very "American" efficiency expert, and paradoxically one who is attacking orthodox economics for its reliance on premises of hedonism and rationality. All of us suffer from the illusion that we are outside what we are criticizing.

To be sure, all this needs to be qualified by recalling once again that Veblen kept a kind of ikon corner for the impractical and the "un-American," the inefficient, the unbusinesslike, and the irrelevant, in the form of his concept of "idle curiosity." He called it an instinct, to give it a biological base beyond criticism—and obviously biology is the true nobility, coming first before all learned parvenus. But under idle curiosity he smuggled the university and research, his own vested interest and the one he cared most about. While everywhere else his mentality is that of the engineer or accountant, the Puritan and debunker, the person who has no truck with frills, frivolity, and nonsense—a mentality that drew him at once to the Bolsheviks in 1919—his design for the universities, and hence by implication even for economics, is impractical and indeed remains an attractive dream for many of us who are harassed by demanding students, repetitive committees, administrative chores, and foundation benevolence; we may be grateful here, as with other thinkers, for a certain lack of consistency.

§ VII

ONE MORE PARADOX and we are done. For reasons partly indicated, Veblen failed to account for modern capitalism in its specifically American variant—he gave the captains too much power, saw credit only as collusive and collapsible, and otherwise overestimated the destructive elements in the system; his asceticism prevented him from seeing the constructive role of waste and luxury on both the production and consumption sides.[11] In my judgment, he is a poor, if often amusing and provocative, guide to America.[12] But he really comes into his own when taken as a guide to the economics of underdeveloped countries—"underdeveloped" being our not wholly satisfactory semantic substitute for "backward." By simplifying and empiricizing economics, by putting it back into its cultural context and rejecting partial equilibrium analyses, by teaching us that every society draws on motives which are left over from previous epochs, he introduces an essential curriculum for Point Four missionaries. The new theorists of economic development, working where there is only a rudimentary market and not even a semblance of entrepreneurial ideology, may find Veblen's anthropological economics, with its iteration of the interrelatedness of everything, good and even inspiring reading. Someday we may be able to trace a United States Technical Assistance project in aid of Javanese home industry (tied to matrilineal descent lines) to a set of ideas set off originally by Veblen's own encounter

11. After the meeting, Mrs. Edna Macmahon of Vassar College told me the following incident, which occurred when she was a student of Veblen's: After a New School lecture, a pretty girl (a species usually able to overcome Veblen's defenses) presented Veblen with a gold clasp to substitute for the safety pin with which he attached his pocket watch to his clothes. Veblen declared, pulling out his pin, that it had true beauty, which he would not exchange for anything: that it could be bought at any five and ten, six for five cents; that the pin did not damage his clothes; finally, that if the girl could not grasp the functional aesthetics of the pin, she had learned nothing from the course!

12. For this judgment, I was gently chided by Professor Willson Coates of the University of Rochester and others who felt that to criticize Veblen in terms of developments since his time was unjust. The problem, of course, would not arise had Veblen not sought to transcend his times, both critically and prophetically; indeed, were he not to some degree original, there would be no point in seeking to understand him as an individual rather than simply as a type. It may well be that I expect too much illumination from Veblen, of a sort he is not equipped to give, and in this paper insufficiently stress his accomplishments. However, since many still move in evaluating contemporary America within the ambit of Veblen's rhetoric, it is important to emphasize that Veblen's America, to the extent it ever existed, predeceased him—while, to name a profounder guide, Tocqueville's America is in some ways more ours than his.

with a magisterial father and with a society which, for much of his life, insisted on defining him as impractical, even at times subversive, but mostly not good for much. And that would be the final ironic verdict on a man whose great discovery, in his own eyes, was the vanity of any human effort to oppose "the *vis a tergo* of brute causation."

20. Some Relationships between Technical Progess and Social Progress

THE REPORTS of previous conferences of this sort make fascinating reading. They suggest some of the ways in which certain American values and ideals are spreading throughout the globe at the same time that they are becoming devalued in this country. Technical progress is such an ideal. The MIT students who invited you here are not simply or single-mindedly devoted to it: they and many of their professors are increasingly concerned with *relations*—human relations, international relations; and with culture as a set of relations, including both the anthropologists' culture and the humanists'. The American ideal of social mobility takes all sorts of forms, in addition to the well-documented pattern of individuals moving upwards in a corporate hierarchy or an income bracket. One somewhat abstract form of the ideal is to move "up" from preoccupation with "merely" technical problems to preoccupation with social and psychological problems, with human relations. This is perhaps less a form of mobility for the individual scientist or engineer (though it may help groom him for higher position) than a form of mobility for the engineering profession as a whole. My very presence here may be taken as an indication that the tycoon of culture, the professor of social science or humanities, is beginning to rank with the tycoons of metallurgy or finance.

I have had several recent reminders of the increasing defensiveness of engineers—a group which, as recently as the Age of Hoover, had ranked comfortably high among the professions as the bearers of progress, hard common sense, efficiency, and other indisputably good things. On one occasion, an engineering society invited my colleague, Reuel Denney, and me to advise them about what could be done to make engineers more cultivated and more aware of interpersonal relations: the group felt very defensive about being good with sliderules or transistors but not with people or Shakespeare. On another occasion, students at the Sheffield Scientific School at Yale indicated their bewilderment and resentment at the fact that, when they spoke to their girl-friends, or to literary Yalemen, about jet engines they were accused of shop-talk, while the latter, when they chatted about Proust, Elizabethan poetry, or the future of the United Nations were thought to be unequivocally cultivated and fit for social gatherings! In each instance, the engineers rather mournfully asked what they must do to be saved. Surely, their misgivings do not spring from want of employment—as a glance at the glowing want-ads for engineers in any paper can establish. Rather, full or even overfull employment for engineers is part of that great wave of American abundance (which some of you, no doubt correctly, think we are far too ready to boast about), abundance which encourages the development of tertiary industries (the service, entertainment, education, and "culture" industries) and, within the secondary industries, an increasing concern with the supposedly higher things in life which can now be afforded. Indeed, if we want full employment without war, we cannot afford not to continue this development of turning out fewer tool and die makers and more museum directors and novelists.

It seems to me an open question whether there are such things as "higher things," apart from human meanings and cultural definitions. Is "Guernica" a greater work of the imagination than a telephone relay or a theory of nuclear fission? In the curious and paradoxical reversals of emphasis I am discussing, however, many of the less industrially developed countries seek immediate self-respect and status, as well as more obvious goals such as autarchy, by going in for steel plants and automobile assembly lines, despite the fact that improvement of agricultural techniques or distributive mechanisms might promise more immediate gains—gains, moreover, not requiring suffering severe deprivations in order to import heavy capital equipment. When at the 1952 meeting of this group Professor Walt Rostow pointed this out, he was criticized by representatives of "underdeveloped" countries for his emphasis on "mere" material well-being; he was put in one typically American position in international exchanges of having to reply that, while he wanted to put a practical base under ideals, he was of course not against ideals—he understood the Quixotic appeal of assembly lines. What also irked his questioners was his relative pessimism, his belief that the world could not be changed overnight. By contrast, his critics appear to me to have been somewhat reckless in their eagerness to hasten impressive industrial advance at no matter what human cost. Indeed, it was the Africans and Asians at the Conference who tended to be the eager-beavers, the romantic strivers after "efficiency," the unquenchable optimists, whereas the Americans were worldly wise, full of sober second-thoughts, and quite free of missionary zeal or cant. It was almost as if the traditional trans-Atlantic and trans-Pacific conversations had somehow got their labels switched, with the United States the age-old country and Europe and Asia the unexplored utopia, the millenary land!

I realize, of course, the complex processes of selection at work which might give one such an impression from last year's Conference. You who come from other countries are, I assume, not typical of your countries, not even typical of your countries' upper strata, else you would not be here. I remember the committee which met in this country from 1942 to 1944 to draw up an international bill of rights for presentation to some presumptive post-war official body. Representation was sought from all the Allied powers. It turned out that the non-Anglo-Saxons (such as Hu Shih from China) were often more "English" in their ways than the English: this was as true of the Hindu, who hated the English, as of the Egyptian, likewise Anglo-phobic, who had been co-opted to "represent" Islam.[1] I had greatly hoped in the committee meetings to learn something about the cultures of a number of other countries, but instead I mostly got one or another Westernized version of culture, often at the hands of men so bedazzled by the West that they could not help but be impatient with their native cultures, no matter how much they might chide us Americans for our lack of spirituality, our haste and hurry, our standardization. Many were marginal men, like the Hindu doctor in Orwell's *Burmese Days;* they could never really go home again even if, unlike Dr. Veraswami, they hid their admiration for the West under a superficial contempt. As is generally recognized, the mixing of peoples that industrialization has brought with it every-where (mixing of peoples from town and country, from East and West, from Catholic and Protestant and other denominational folds, etc.) involves a mixing also of values, and these 20th-century casual-ties among stranded, half-Westernized intellectuals are often as

---

1. No other remarks in my address provoked quite so much active and acrid rebuttal as my suggestion that the delegates were not "typical." None wanted to feel he was in any way different from "his" people to whom he would perforce return; the "Moslem bloc" was particularly vociferous in insisting that their cul-tures were as progress-minded as the American and that hence they themselves were in no way alienated from Islamic tradition; they denied that they were reinterpreting that tradition to find room in it for their own activities, their own ideologies. Most eager to rebut any inferences of his untypicality was an Egyp-tian who spoke perfect English, and who, it turned out, had been educated in England; not surprisingly, he saw England as the root of all his country's dif-ficulties in overtaking and surpassing American prosperity. Surely, the strength of nationalism, and often Communism (i.e., the new National "Socialism"), among non-Western intellectuals springs in part from the effort to submerge any doubts that one is a 200% Egyptian or Thailander or Nigerian in the face of one's knowledge of and desire for Western-model forms of technology, edu-cation, and values generally.

tragic as the more evident casualties among half-urbanized peasants whom Engels described in 19th-century Britain or as those among the detribalized whom Boeke has written about in modern Indonesia.

Conversely, as Americans begin to rise above the industrial evangelism of our own past, we make things very uncomfortable for those of us who are too much in love with older definitions of efficiency. Even in his best days, the efficiency expert, Frederick Winslow Taylor, had a terrible time trying to persuade Americans to work efficiently; he would raise productivity and real wages only to be hated by workmen and fired by management—and today the zeal he expended in trying to help workmen do their tasks with a minimum of strain is forgotten in easy denunciations of "Taylorism." It is men trained in the thinking of Elton Mayo, not of Taylor, who are now in demand—men who don't drive too hard, men who can create a happy atmosphere among companionable work groups, men who aren't too infuriated with waste. Sometimes I think that we tend to export our remaining zealots of efficiency, on Point IV or Ford Foundation missions, where they can speak for "American methods" as they never could at home! Don't mistake me: these men we send abroad are far more humane than Carl Peters, or the hero of Conrad's *Heart of Darkness*, and they are genuinely concerned with welfare; however, in their single-minded drive and energy, their dedicated willingness to fling themselves into what appear to be lonely and hopeless situations, they are true descendants of Taylor and the Puritan entrepreneurs. And of course, such people are not likely to be around here to address this Conference along with your panelists who (like myself) take a four-months summer vacation in New England!

It follows that we would expect recent immigrants to America and their immediate descendants to be today a principal locus of traditional American values. For these people, in their complex effort to become "Americanized," engage in some of the same misinterpretations of what that process means that foreign visitors are apt to accept: that is, they conceive America in terms already out of date among the better educated and more assimilated groups. They oversimplify America whether they resort to crime and competitive sports in order to get rapidly ahead, as good Americans are supposed to get ahead, or whether they resort instead to more unremitting (as well as more disagreeable) work than would have been appropriate in the old country. Just the other day I had a letter from a former student, now a private in the army, concerning the army's dependence on this latter sort of immigrant behavior; he writes:

"A great center of inner-direction [i.e., behavior in pursuit of a clear internalized goal] still exists—and it has particular strength among the rising second-generation kids. Several of our cadre around the Fort here are Armenians, Greeks, Italians, Hungarians, and Yugoslavs, etc.–and almost without exception they are great believers in the meritoriousness of 'hard work,' and 'principled behavior.' The Army depends on these plus the few Anglo-Saxon Puritan ethic people to get its work done. The Army requires such work-minded people who try to do a good job of whatever they're told to do no matter how odious the task, simply because it is 'wrong' and 'disgraceful' to do anything but a good job."

To be sure, the perspective of this letter is somewhat one-sided: it necessarily leaves out of account what the East and South Europeans have done to make Americans fonder of good food, good song, and the leisurely life generally. But at the same time, it is part of the evidence for the generalization that industrial development usually requires new sorts of people, just as kings and popes learned that commercial development required Hollanders or Jews or Lombards or Jansenists–part of the omen of what may happen to America for having virtually cut off immigration, a traumatic blow to world development both within and without this country.

In this connection, I was struck by the study of Knapp and Goodrich on the origins of leading American natural scientists. A disproportionately high number, they point out, come from small-town or rural backgrounds and attended small liberal arts colleges in the Midwest and Far West. One might plausibly interpret their data as follows: as youngsters, these men had known little luxury and less occupational diversity; hence their college science teacher could strike them as a figure of moment and if he invited them to work, let us say, on a carbon ring or a physics text, they were wedded to science (in a perhaps somewhat narrow and pragmatic view of it) for life. They had formed a work-minded character while young, but had not hitched it to a particular interest; the life of research seemed to them the pinnacle of service and ambition. By comparison, students from the cities, from the upper strata, attending larger and more cosmopolitan universities, would more often find such a career too narrow, and a college chemistry teacher too unexhilirating a model.[2]

---

2. In the light of a more recent study, *The Younger American Scholar: His Collegiate Origins,* by Knapp and Greenbaum, these comments must be somewhat revised, for more recent data indicate that the high-status, high-cost Eastern universities are now also producing a proportionate number of scientists. The authors suggest that this shift may be due, in part, to the increasing vogue of intellectualism among well-to-do Americans, but also think that the scientists turned out from these strata will be less pragmatic than those from the "grass roots." To complicate the picture, boys from the grass roots are now increasingly financially able to attend the more expensive institutions–migration within the country here replacing immigration as a source of talent, of novelty and enterprise.

What I have been getting at, in a number of different illustrative ways, is that American society, on the basis both of technological and cultural development, appears to be undergoing profound transformations at the present moment which are carrying us increasingly further away from those concerns which are still a matter of life and death in the countries where population presses heavily on food supply—countries which, now aware of other ways of life than their own, want the "technical progress" which for many educated Americans has either become a game or something towards which to feel snobbish and superior.[3] Is it any wonder the productivity teams that have come here from Europe to discover the "secrets" of American know-how have been often baffled: they cannot always tell which elements in our managerial and factory cultures are "scientific" and which are "magical"—the latter needed for American morale but not necessarily transportable. And of course we Americans do not understand our own system—I am much less sure of the things I am telling you than I may seem to be if you miss the ironies in my voice and the ambiguities in my argument. But we feel under pressure, both for the sake of our sanity and of our foreign relations, to discover ex post facto rationalizations for why we act as we do.

It is interesting that it was an American, Peter Weiss, at last year's meeting who asked Professor Rostow how non-American countries could without prior mechanization acquire the industrial *esprit* that could spark general economic advance. Machines, he felt, gave an air to a society, a heady and impetuous air, which somehow went together with high productivity—in my own terms, I would say that machines help educate and inspire, symbolize and socialize, at least once a proper cultural context is there for mediating and defining them. Certainly the enthusiasm and aesthetic sense of the Italians for modern machine design may be connected with their rapid post-war recovery: it minimizes the snobbery or strangeness traditional cultures sometimes feel towards the very machines they also envy and desire. Skill and competence in making machines that excite international admiration engender confidence: they have a halo effect. Athens and Venice in their commercial heydey had this confidence; many American industrialists and organizers have it now. But how can one borrow confidence from another country, especially

---

3. In extensive discussion, the delegates insisted that the "rest of the world" wants more factories, better medical care, and so on—but not American "mass culture" or "juvenile delinquency." Some appeared to want industrialization without urbanization, and perhaps without democratization. On the degrees of choice involved here, as illustrated by Mexican experience, see *inter alia* the work of Robert Redfield and Wilbert E. Moore.

when that confidence rests in part on the very achievements one is oneself seeking?

Equally perplexing for the borrower is the realization of how much American productivity depends on a casual yet calculated disregard or sabotage of standard operating procedures. The industrial sociologist William F. Whyte of Cornell tells the story of the workmen in an oil-cracking plant in Oklahoma who got angry because, in a collective bargaining session, the management had referred to them as semi-skilled. They proceeded to carry out literally the instructions of the chemist, instructions which they had previously treated as a good chef will treat a recipe—soon bringing the plant to a halt. It turned out that they understood the idiosyncracies of the machines better than did the supervisory staff—and they won a pay increase. Warner Bloomberg, Jr., a colleague of mine who has spent some years as a factory worker, recounts many similar experiences, including the important role workmen play in modifying a customer's requirements for accuracy according to their own knowledge of what is actually needed, thereby minimizing the number of rejected pieces. Such "corruptions" and "indulgences" mediate between the formally prescribed and the empirically provided elements of production—they comprise an invisible overprint on a blueprint.[4] I might add that similar practices, which many oversimple moralists regard as reprehensible, keep us from getting completely bogged down in the separation of powers our Constitution prescribes—I suppose that in any society the people who save other people from the pitfalls of their rituals are likely to be either notorious or unknown. All this again suggests that countries which think it is easy to install "American methods" by copying blueprints or our own copybook maxims may be in for serious disillusionment.

Let me choose, as one illustration, an American business practice which has impressed a number of the productivity teams—the willingness of businessmen to share their production methods with each other. Instead of trade secrets, kept in the family or in the business,

---

4. Mr. Bloomberg also cautions me not to take at full face value the extensive talk among managers concerning personnel practices and what I have sometimes called "mood engineering": at least in the heavy industries in which he has worked, an enormous concern for cutting down waste and increasing man-hour productivity hangs on, underneath the newer forms of talk. Even the labor force, he feels, is still productivity-minded, in spite of itself; as he reports workers as saying: "Give us a new machine and we'll end up making it do even more than the engineers thought it could. That's our trouble. We can't hold back forever. We're like a kid with a new toy." This is perhaps not so much work-mindedness as a game-mindedness which does not exhaust itself in factory loafing or in obstruction of management

our managers often cannot wait to tell other managers, through the appropriate journals or meetings of the American Management Association and other trade associations, what short-cuts they have discovered. This sharing of information and devices has perplexed European observers who had perhaps learned from American novelists, if not from Balzac or Dickens, that business was a cut-throat affair. To "explain" what they find, there is a tendency to rationalize this sharing as a conscious policy of tit-for-tat, a kind of Miltonian free trade in secrets, even a conspiratorial pool; and the Americans themselves, if charged with disloyalty within their own organizations, would very likely fall back on similar justifications. (I should add that the sharing might be even more extensive in some industries if it were not for fear of the anti-trust laws, though the spirit behind these laws is only one of a number of reasons why companies often pretend to themselves and to others that they are more competitive than in fact they are.) It is my impression, though of course very difficult to support, that the sharing of business information has more to do with the growing professionalization of management than with any conscious decisions to trade one secret for another. Officials who regard themselves as professionals find their fraternity, not among rentiers, but among people doing the same work in other companies as well as in their own company. They are tied to the company for which they work by that work, its interest and its perquisites, and not by stockholdings or family connections or tradition. . . .

Sharing of information can actually be quite expensive to individual companies, not only in "giving away secrets" but in the actual costs of distribution. It costs money to compile and publish reports, to send people to conventions, to receive visitors from other companies or (as you will discover when you go on tour) from abroad; yet all this is done by American companies without afterthought, uncomplainingly; neither the accountant nor the internal revenue agent is likely to object, any more than to the charitable donations or the "pure" research which corporations are increasingly going in for.[5]

All this, I suggest, is a facet of what I have elsewhere described as the shift from "conspicuous consumption" to "conspicuous production" in American life, in which our surplus is spent at the source, so to speak, in the very processes of production, rather than distrib-

---

5. Several M.I.T. students at the Conference objected that not all companies shared information or admitted visitors—proprietary drug houses were notably guarded. But others felt that the general point I was making was valid, although there was considerable variation among industries.

uted to stockholders or bankers and spent or hoarded according to private whim. Professor Walt Rostow observed last year that even in the late 19th century the American business leader was ordinarily at least as much concerned with finding an outlet for his social energies as with making a fortune—one that, in European style, he could use as a counter in acquiring status. Indeed, in retrospect it is sad to contemplate the vain struggle of the millionaires of that day for good repute: many pious ones sought to obey all the rules, and won only ridicule or antagonism; for a Carnegie or a Rockefeller there were few long-established, socially-approved roads to take. While today of course there are many Americans who want to make a fast buck and succeed, mostly in small business, in doing so, many big businessmen don't even dare spend a fast buck, but have their companies do it for them. If you want to find big businessmen still mightily driven by the entrepreneurial ethic in getting and spending, you may do best in the South and Southwest—or in Toronto: Canada already surpasses us proportionately in some indices of productivity, it has for generations exported many of its more enterprising French Canadians to the United States, thus keeping Quebec quaint for habitants and tourists alike.[6]

Since up-to-date American corporations now have to learn the arts of conspicuous spending, they need tutors—just as European princes did or American tycoons. Business schools (including very probably M.I.T.'s own school of management) play a part as such tutors; so do management consultants; so do industrial architects and designers. There are corporate officials who are addicts of one or another of the many fads—committee management, incentive systems, operations analysis, and a hundred other plans—and go about the country stumping for these devices and their morale-building and profit-building virtues. For these "muscular Christians" of enterprise, trade does not necessarily follow the flag and the Bible; these men act in obedience to their self-image as proper businessmen, no matter how strenuously they insist (as, depending on mood, most Americans will insist) that they act only out of self-interest. In this modern atmosphere of sharing, of geniality, of muted competition and unmuted conspicuous production, who would be the Scrooge who would hoard trade secrets, or hoard capital (like Sewell Avery, to the fury of his associates), or hoard time (very few top businessmen are actually as inaccessible as their secretaries like to pretend)?

In some ways, the Soviet Union is more "capitalistic" than Amer-

---

6. Cf. Everett C. Hughes, *French Canada in Transition*, on significant changes now occurring in this pattern—and for illumination of the general problem of the ways in which technical "progress" mixes different ethnic groups together.

ica; having learned what it could from American engineers in the Age of Hoover, it still plainly lives in an epoch of tight-fisted capital accumulation and secrecy—though it will be interesting to see to what extent its managers, as they become more professional, will begin to imitate American patterns of conspicuous production. Conceivably, this tight-fistedness may be one among many reasons why, beneath competing ideologies, Soviet agents have an appeal to "underdeveloped" countries which are even further away than the Soviet Union itself from the American plateau of opulence. Likewise, the wealthier parts of Europe do not appear to be captivated by the American example, even if they could afford it: a psychology of scarcity has become embedded there; and the state rather than the corporation is looked to for the appropriate spending of whatever surplus there is—while industrialists know what to do with profits, namely, buy land and a title and escape from "les mains sales."

The growing bureaucratization of business in America is one reason why a career in business no longer captures the imagination of our most gifted young people; as in Europe, there is a tendency to look down on business as demeaning. The tragedies common enough even a generation ago, of young men forced to go into their father's businesses when they would like to have become artists or scholars, are much rarer today. For one thing, it isn't father's business any more, but the corporation's—the kinds of taken-for-granted nepotism Douglass North has recently described for life insurance companies at the turn of the century are now frowned upon. For another thing, father has lost his easy confidence that his way is the only way. So we find that the talents which in the 19th century found their entrepreneurial outlet in building a railway, a department store, a foundry, now find it in building a diocese (what industrialist is a match for Cardinal Spellman?), a labor union (what tycoon is as fiercely individualistic as John L. Lewis?), a new university or foundation (what promoter could not learn from Robert Hutchins?)—all the "tertiary" areas of the economy.

One way of looking at this development is to see that the most extensive and radical social changes seem to occur when there is a sudden breakdown of old traditions—so sudden the traditions cannot recover quickly and develop new institutional and ideological protections. Thus, in this country there was a period of ten to twenty years when the movies, an altogether new industry, could experiment quite freely without successful censorship from the outraged fundamentalists or successful bureaucratization from the side of outraged bankers and investors; only much later was the "cancerous" growth halted and the industry forcibly routinized in its financing and management, and partially subjected to the popular mores it had previously succeeded in flouting and indeed in altering. In the same way the auto industry went haywire, so to speak, in its initial stages, before the settling down of union resistance, standardized consumer taste, and corporate "responsibility"—even that old-time new-style tycoon, Henry Kaiser, could not shake loose from the traditions. In sum, much of the economy consists of more and less stabilized ways of doing business. The more stabilized ways, the traditions, provide a cushion against the shock of new developments, just as precapitalist motives and ideas protected capitalism from its own destructive tendencies; the traditions at the same time invite radical new developments by their very inelasticity in the face of moderate reform. In this country after the Civil War it was the economy that appeared more open to innovation than the churches or the law, whereas today the economy appears to many people as the official or vested part of society, where change is likely to be very slow. Who would have heard of Henry Luce if, like other of his Yale classmates, he had gone into banking or the railroads or the plate glass business?

All these changes indicate that the United States may at the present time be an ambiguous model for countries wanting to be rich, or to be less poor. As you go on tour you may discover how inefficient Americans frequently are, how lacking in precise technical or professional knowledge, how inexpert and fuzzy our "experts" often are—a theme to which my own lecture might be an introduction in itself. Our industrial system is geared to, or around, this inefficiency; our amiability makes us put up with it; our concept of know-how is often a way of generalizing our amateur spirit into a confident mood. There may well come a time when we will be sending productivity teams elsewhere, having exhausted our immigrant and rural resources of painstaking efficiency and workmindedness prematurely—before, that is, having made production wholly automatic. At a recent *Fortune*-magazine-sponsored conference on the automatic factory (an abbreviated write-up appears in the magazine for Oct. 1953, vol. 48, p. 168), I got the distinct impression that very few American engineers and industrialists were capable of easily conceptualizing a factory without operatives; this blockage of imagination appeared to be limiting experimentation with full automatization (as against experiment with ever more specialized transfer machines and machine tools). The American technicians seem not to have been able to overlook the needs, at least for employment, of those who presently do the manufacturing—at any rate sufficiently to put their organized ingenuity behind the up-to-date "requirements of manufacture" that might lead them to automatization. They fear unconsciously, and often vocally, to go too far in replacing men with machines.

Perhaps on your travels you will be shown the new Ford engine plant in Cleveland, and be told that this is automatic. But you will actually find it designed in terms of operatives who, to be sure, do little physical work, but are attached to the highly specialized machines which move and shape material, whereas in a truly automatic factory a tape or other source of coded information would "instruct" far less specialized machines in the specialized procedures for handling the particular product. The Ford engine plant is a huge, new, proud investment in the antithetical procedure—possibly, an example of the hardening of the American industrial imagination at its allegedly most advanced.

There is, however, one problem connected with automatization which is not likely to come up on your trip, though it is highly relevant to what I have been saying about the image of American industry as efficient. Let me remind you here of Warner Bloomberg, Jr.'s observation that the work-force in large modern plants covertly mediates between the rigid specifications insisted upon by the customer or the supervisor and their own informal knowledge that much looser specifications will still do the job. They know the idiosyncracies both of the customer and of the individual machines—in general, they know much more about the industrial process than they appear to know or get credit for knowing. Literal fulfillment of all plant regulations and obedience to blue-prints would either halt production or make it excessively costly. How, Bloomberg provocatively asks, can a tape be taught to deceive itself or disobey itself? How can the engineer who gives information to the machine know all the factory folklore which is in the workmen's heads and which he has previously, often unknowingly, depended upon? Will not the punched tape become a form of red tape, snarling the plant by virtue of its very orderliness and clarity, with which machines without men cannot cope?

Given the kinds of gaps that exist in America between what we do and what we say we do, I have no good answer to these questions.[7]

---

7. Professor Richard L. Meier, who has had extensive experience with automatic processes, believes that they have become increasingly necessary for quality control as a counter to labor inefficiency and sloppiness. He agrees that one cannot keep two sets of books with automatic factories—one for the tax collector or the customer and one for an inner circle—but feels that large corporations, worried about how to control deviations in the lower ranks, would welcome precisely this assured clarity. And he does not feel it is impossible for engineers, observing skilled workmen, to build the latter's know-how into the automatic process itself and thus stabilize it.

Furthermore, he points out that the rise of automatic processes will, like any

However, when I speculate about the prospects for the automatic factory in less industrially developed countries, I can see certain compensating advantages that might make experimentation with it worthwhile. Hitherto, whenever industry has gone into a folk culture, a tribal culture, it has been necessary forcibly to disrupt that culture to provide workmen. They have had to be taxed (as in South Africa or Dutch Indonesia) or tempted (as in the Tata Mills in India or the textile plants that have migrated from New Hampshire to North Carolina). Everywhere, people have had to be forced off the land, off the "reservation," and almost everywhere new values—punctuality, for instance—are instilled into them. It is only in the very late stages that the questions arise of the American song: "How are you goin' to keep 'em down on the farm . . . ?"; earlier, the problem is how to get them off. The fully automatic factory could conceivably be installed with very little shift in values: it needs a tiny workforce—even less than an oil refinery. Speaking now not in terms of questions of investment and trade which I am not equipped to answer, such a factory, with its electronic brains, could obviate in some measure the historic process of having natives work under non-native supervision, or the supervision of members of a different ethnic and religious group; for once the prefabricated plant was erected, nobody except a few maintenance men would work within it. Conflict would occur over what it should make and what should be done with the product by whom, but no conflict would arise—or human beings be "reformed"—within its walls.

Perhaps such talk of a magic carpet may seem very remote to you, struggling as many of you are with exigent questions of heavy machinery import or unfavorable terms of trade. Or you may share the worry of some American engineers, about what would happen to millions of workers if factories needed them no longer—whether they could be shifted rapidly enough to such service trades of high labor utilization as teaching, barbering, poetry, or social research. But if you do harbor such feelings, it would be some evidence for my hypothesis that the way the Western world happened to achieve industrialization exercises great fascination as the only way. As generals typically prepare for the last war, so many prepare to imitate an American industrial plant that may already be obsolete. When it was suggested to some people from Asia that vitamin factories, which are

technological revolution, alter the character of the managers: they will have to become more statistics-minded, more adept at handling complex chains of information, but may need less skill than before in the executive leadership of a workforce and in decision-making on the basis of hunches. His forthcoming book on world technological development will deal fully and imaginatively with these themes.

relatively inexpensive, might rather rapidly improve diet and well-being, it seemed to me that objections were too quickly found to a project which lacked "weight"—which approached industrial development, not the hard way but the easy way.

A certain asceticism operates here to limit the imagination. There were cracks at the Cadillacs in Kuwait in last year's sessions. There was competition in appearing unmaterialistic. There was recognition of the undeniable virtues of British austerity in the post-war period. Yet I sometimes wonder if this asceticism and austerity provide the best climate for the kind of thinking we need if we are to experiment with other as yet untried roads to economic development, and if we are to subvert our principal vested interest: that in prevailing models and patterns. A certain luxuriousness, a certain lack of dutifulness, may stimulate the imagination, as against the portentousness by which some of you pay for your privileges in being here when so many of your countrymen are in want. In the past, Puritanism has accompanied industrialization, but now that the going concern of industry is here, and diffusable, I wonder if that ethic is still as essential.

That crazy, gifted traveling salesman, Charles Fourier, makes the point quite well in his book, *Social Destinies*. After referring to poverty as "that most scandalous of all social disorders," he asks:

"In what parts of the world, has Civilization made the most progress? In Athens, in Paris, in London, where men have been in no sense the friends of mediocrity or of truth, but on the contrary have been the slaves of their passions, and devoted to intrigues, to wealth, and to luxury. And where has Civilization languished and remained stagnant? In Sparta, and in primitive Rome, where the voluptuous passions and the love of luxury had but a feeble development."

Fourier's point is especially significant for those countries which are seeking simultaneously to bring about industrialization and the welfare state. The spirit of luxury and playfulness exerts its force when it provides contrast with the workaday world and its grim tasks and not, of course, when it simply reinforces a traditional idleness among a privileged caste. Economic and other development may require an increase of asceticism among some strata and a moderate diminution of it among others. At least, if it is to take new forms rather than those already exhibited in the West.

We should, in sum, be wary of assuming that there is only one pattern, that which Pirenne, Sombart, Schumpeter, Robertson, Max Weber, and a host of other scholars have sought to delineate. We do know from the work of these men that technology is not separate from the rest of culture, but is part of a climate which in the modern

West includes Bach and Newton, Descartes and Calvin, and the monk who invented double-entry book-keeping. But we cannot know that there are no other combinations capable of producing similar end-results in industrial plant. (We do know that similar behavior can come in individuals as the result of radically different patterns of motivation.) There is no reason to assume that we have exhausted human inventiveness in recombining cultural forms.

Nineteenth-century systems of thought tend to obstruct us here. Thinkers of that epoch were preoccupied by the search for origins, the search for the stages through which historical development was bound to pass. Linear thinking prevailed. It was ethnocentric both in putting the West at the pinnacle of progress (or, in rare instances of inverse boastfulness, of decay) and in a kind of point-to-point evolutionism consonant with Western teleological modes of thinking and speaking. Various forms of belief in monolithic inevitability fell in with the misleading analogy between societal development and the stages through which an individual organism must pass. Today, we have become more skeptical, but not always more creative. It is easier for us to break down the schemes of Malthus and Marx, Comte and Spencer, Veblen and Pareto, than to imagine potential alternative sequences.

An illustration of what I have in mind can be drawn from contemporary studies by anthropologists of the character structure of both small Pacific tribes and larger national entities. The studies seem to me to indicate that some character types are more adaptable to industrial civilization than others who appear to share a similar culture pattern. For example, the inhabitants of the island of Truk in the Pacific (an island occupied by the Japanese between the wars and then by the Americans) seem to typify the biting variant of what the Freudians term the "anal" character: they deal with the environment by seizing it, by active mastery and aggression. Not only did they take readily to machines, they took readily to those who could instruct them in technical matters. The American Navy found them adaptable and teachable; the Trukese even beat a Navy baseball team. Their adaptability led the Americans to encourage them to become mechanics and speed-boat operators, but by the same token little pressure was put on their culture as a whole to succumb to Western values. Because of this closeness of fit, the impact of occupation and mechanization on Truk seems not to have been destructive or revolutionary: characterological compatibility was sufficient to minimize the problems of cultural dissimilarity. Such compatibility, to be sure, need not always have this consequence; we deal here with highly complex and also controversial matters; Truk is described very differently by the anthropologists George P. Murdock and Edward Hall, both of whom have been there (my own interpretation is based on Hall's work and on Erich Fromm's analysis of Trukese character in a seminar with Murdock and Ralph Linton at Yale).

By way of contrast, let us look at one or another of the Caribbean cultures, such as that of Cuba or Puerto Rico, which the Fromm-Linton seminar characterized as "male vanity" cultures: in some strata, mothers early encourage their boys in exhibitionism and older males likewise encourage younger ones. The individual of this character type has difficulty in learning to master new aspects of his environment because vanity dictates that he already know it. Any discrepancies tend to be "resolved" by words, by quick and facile verbalization. Thus, a number of my colleagues who have taught at the University of Puerto Rico report how difficult they find it to teach young men whose vanity is humiliatingly wounded if they don't already know everything—who therefore are blocked in doing homework, or serious studying, or patient apprenticeship to new methods. (To be sure, among students everywhere there is a good deal of this —male vanity is not a Latin monopoly!)

A "male vanity" culture can inhibit industrialization on at least three counts. First, all work, certainly sweaty or evidently pedantic work, tends to be regarded as dirty work. Men talk or fight; they do not grease machines or even draw blueprints. Secondly, they take to teamwork, to the building of industrial harmony, rather angularly: envy (symbolized in the ability of women to force their men to fight on behalf of their honor) is too uncontrolled; narcissism, as represented in Sebastiano in *The Fancy Dress Party* and other Moravia male characters, is too unsublimated. Thirdly, along with these difficulties on the side of production comes the equally important role of vanity in dictating consumption so that, as I have already indicated, conspicuous consumption may be very powerful in such cultures. Bert Hoselitz' study of San Salvador for the U.N., for instance, shows that the wealth accumulated by the leading families there is either invested in showy, if stony, ground or in flashy purchases in San Francisco or New York, whereas the Jews of San Salvador re-invest their money in industry and commerce; traditional Jewish culture, though it favors the male, does not encourage the prickly sensitivity to masculine honor of Spain or Latin America. (I need hardly add that a male vanity culture imposes a considerable barrier to the spread of contraception—other perhaps than oral contraception—among wives.) Yet it would be rash to say that the male vanity character type is incompatible with economic advance; rather, such advance might proceed by seeing how the energies mobilized by this type could be harnessed to new forms of work, perhaps through nationalistic ideology.[8] Conversely, any steps that would alter the fear men of this type have of what other men think of them, might have cumulative consequences far greater than direct and often wounding efforts to teach them new industrial techniques. A map of the world in terms of character type would be useful to the harbingers of economic development, if only in saving them heartbreak and in pointing to those groups whose character is such that industrialism is unlikely to be adopted without very considerable dislocation; the Arapesh, as Margaret Mead describes them, whose men are too passive, too unaggressive either for vanity or for current forms of industrial work, might be an example.

The difficulties inherent in this approach must be fairly evident to you. While speaking of male vanity cultures, I could not help thinking of Spaniards I have known who can hot-rod with the best of our American young people; indeed, hot-rodding is a very male pursuit precisely in its use of machines. I thought, too, of the extraordinary renaissance of Italian industrial design typified by Olivetti. The characterological descriptions of peoples which we now have are crude. Furthermore, not every society can be usefully described in psychoanalytic terms, even apart from the problems presented by the character differences within any large and complex population—and we scarcely have other terms than psychoanalytic ones which possess the necessary inclusiveness. All the same, I think the approach worth working with, both for its intrinsic interest and for the light it might shed on the variable consequences of the spread of industrialization, accompanied by very different ground-rules, in Asia and Africa.

To conclude: while much of the rest of the world seeks ways of accumulating the capital, characterological and financial, on which to base industrialization, a great many of us in America, I have suggested, can find no good reasons for such accumulation. We have lost not only many of the motives impelling industrialization but many

---

8. Richard Meier, who has studied the "case" of Puerto Rico with this perspective in mind, believes that progress in any traditional culture, including a "male vanity" one, depends on deviant types; he has found one source of "inner-directed" types in Puerto Rico in exceptionally energetic "poor but honest" families in rural areas, all of whose children, irrespective of sex, get education somehow and move up in the society. Such families cannot be separated from their neighbors on any easily evident demographic bases—the educated children say they "owe it all to their mothers." These children, Professor Meier believes, are the backbone of rural economic and technological innovation. But of course just what it is in their families that spurs them on remains a problem for further research.

of the motives which gave structure and meaning to life itself. We have approached the accomplishment of one mission and are searching for another.

Very possibly, it will prove as difficult to find a moral equivalent for capitalism as William James discovered it was to find a moral equivalent for war. But I don't believe new goals are beyond human powers to invent. We Americans are tempted to extrapolate from our present situation rather than to invent, much as I have here suggested that other peoples are tempted to imitate Western industrial development rather than invent alternative patterns. I differ from many pragmatists in believing that one must go on imagining new goals, new aspirations, even if at any given time one cannot imagine their implementation; I hope you will feel the same way about such tentative and illustrative suggestions as that of the automatic factory even if you cannot quite see how to get from here to there. We know one thing for sure: that the future is going to be different from what we think, and probably more various. Among many reasons for this, our creativity, stimulated by such conferences as this, is one element. The M.I.T. students who brought us together dreamed up the whole idea, then found the means to implement it. They exemplify the new generation of American entrepreneurs who engage in team-work, are not profit-minded, and seek outlets in the world beyond our borders. It will be hard for you to understand their motives, but if you succeed in doing so, you will grasp a good many of the difficulties I have thrown your way this afternoon.

VI.

FREUD AND PSYCHOANALYSIS

THE ESSAYS in this section (and one on Veblen in the previous section) represent, as the rest of the volume does not, my abiding interest in intellectual history, especially in the relation between great thinkers and their milieu. I suppose in one aspect this is part of my preoccupation with individualism—with how some unique figure in the history of thought is able to arrive at and to maintain an independent view; I have touched on this earlier in the essays on utopian thinking and the "nerve of failure." However, I find intellectual history one of the subtlest of fields: I am skeptical of most accounts of "influences," and think that the road to or from Xanadu can be traced only with the greatest caution coupled with intense disquiet. Even when I speak, let us say, of the influence of Freud on middle-class marital relations or vice versa, I can not get rid of a sociologist's query as to how many were influenced by how much, and the "obvious" relations do not quite assuage me. All of history seems to me beset by similar pitfalls of causality and coincidence, and intellectual history is the more dangerous because of the delusive confidence its documents and texts, letters and journals, may engender.

In these essays, I have bypassed most of these issues in the history of ideas by concentrating primarily on the writings of Freud in terms of certain familiar dualisms: work and play, authority and liberty, heroism and weakness—I had also planned to include love and hate, reason and unreason (day and night), and others. My work on Freud, in which I profited from discussion with Philip Rieff and Murray Wax, was intensively carried on in 1946 and 1947 but, like the music project, was interrupted by my leaves of absence at Yale. Since these articles were written, a great deal of new information has been assembled on Freud's beginnings and the precise intellectual meteorology of his education has been carefully delineated—in articles by Siegfried and Suzanne Cassirer Bernfeld, in the Harvard doctoral thesis of Richard L. Schoenwald (done under Crane Brinton), and in the first volume of Ernest Jones' biography. In addition, the discovery of Freud's letters to Fliess has thrown unexpected and revealing light on the period of his greatest isolation—and greatest achievement—

the period after the break from Breuer and prior to the publication of the book on dreams. In reprinting my essays, however, I have taken no account of this accumulated learning which, to take an instance, shows Freud to have been somewhat less isolated than he leads one to think, even when he was most under the ban of traditional Viennese psychiatry. Nor have I taken account of the remarkable article of Erik H. Erikson, "The Specimen Dream of Psychoanalysis," which shows what a really skillful dream interpreter, familiar with the background, can do with Freud's own dreams.

One qualification, however, should be noted. The original context of these articles was an audience almost wholly sympathetic to Freud —students and staff in the College at the University of Chicago to whom I presented three lectures on Freud in the fall of 1946. Freud's writings had already been admitted there to the elite list of "Great Books," and a number of my colleagues were then rather orthodox adherents of Freud. Nor was Freud news to the majority of students; on the contrary, they seemed to me to be too inclined to swallow him whole as part of their progressivism. The situation was very different from my own undergraduate days when no course I took had Freud on a reading list and when the only classroom reference I heard to him was a sneering reference to "Saints Sigmund and Karl" who were presumably up to no good—days when my mother, an early and ardent admirer of Freud, hesitated to call my attention to him lest my father, a physician, object. In this context I did not have to worry lest I give cause for new sneers at Freud, nor was this a problem in the catholic, if often "Neo-Freudian," pages of *Psychiatry*. Here, let me state explicitly for the critical reader that what I know or think I know of Freud, I owe to Freud; that no one else has contributed so much to the vitality of the social sciences today; that my admiration, indeed wonder, at Freud's achievement remains undimmed by my criticisms of many of his views. These essays were not intended to please the orthodox, but neither were they intended to encourage glib dismissals of Freud, among those who know his work only through snippets and hearsay (as someone said when asked if he'd read a certain book: "not personally").

Schoenwald in his doctoral dissertation makes one serious criticism of these essays, namely that they regard Freud's work as if it had all been done at one time, not allowing for chronological development. This is correct: I rely primarily on Freud's early works, and I develop my themes irrespective of dates. But I think this is less of a drawback than would be the case were it my aim to state Freud's position on one or another issue of theory or therapy; rather, my central concern is Freud's outlook on man in society, and this changed I believe very little over the years, save for an obvious growth in pessimism. What is interesting is to find in a dream-interpretation of the nineties the germ of an idea that was not to receive the full treatment from Freud until a generation later when he turned to explicit philosophizing. While some distortion doubtless results from treating his remarks, spread over a long and active life, as if they had all been uttered in one breath, and while this may sometimes discover contradiction where there was dialectical development, I am inclined to think that no essential injustice has been done to a man one of whose principal claims to eminence was, as he once remarked, the courage of his prejudices—or, as we might say of him, the stubbornness of Moses.

These essays also deal, all too briefly, with one of the most interesting social movements of our day: the psychoanalytic movement of the last half century. In this aspect, the essays are to be compared with the one on the law in the final section, or on recreationists in Section IV, as studies of an occupational group and its vicissitudes as professionalization sets in. To survivors of an earlier analytic era such as Theodor Reik, this professionalization is as unwelcome as a settled grievance procedure is to the union militant who recalls the glorious and unsettling days of sit-down strikes; and perhaps my essays reflect a shade too critical and unperspectivistic a view of the contemporary regularization and "secularization" of analysis. For this stage of the movement has of course its positive sides. I am especially impressed with these after a recent visit to Winter Veterans' Administration Hospital in Topeka where a huge institution, of the sort which before World War II would have been a retreat for doctors on a permanent lost weekend, is now fired with the Menningers' enthusiasm for analytic therapy and their Foundation's enthusiasm for research.

"Freud, Religion, and Science," the final essay in this section, also deals with the contemporary situation of psychoanalysis, especially vis-à-vis organized religion. It was originally a wire-recorded lecture in a series on "Attack and Counter-Attack in Religion," which dealt with such figures as Nietzsche, Marx, Malinowski, Schweitzer, Niebuhr, and Toynbee—a series organized by the Unitarian student group at the University of Chicago. Excerpts have been published in *The American Scholar* and (under the title, "Freud: Religion as Neurosis") in the *University of Chicago Roundtable*. The remarks on American Catholicism in this address might well have been included in the section on Marginality, Minorities, and Freedom; they spring out of the interest I share with Everett C. Hughes in the sociology of American religious groups, a field in which a few of our students have been active. As the paper indicates, I believe Freud has done more than any other psychologist to stimulate the scientific study of religion—something that William James was unable to accomplish. (Max Weber and the anthropologists, if we include Durkheim, have probably done more.) But of course what I say about Catholicism remains at the most general and tentative level—a beginning of discourse rather than a terminus.

Students at Chicago sometimes ask why they are given Freud to read and not Jung, Adler, Rank, and other dissidents. Indeed, why should Freud rather than Jung be chosen in a series on religion? The answer must be institutional as well as individual: for a variety of reasons, it is Freud and his followers who have had the principal impact on American social science; it is they who have helped give direction to the new field of "culture and personality" studies, who have sent anthropologists to the field to study totems and taboos— if only to disprove Freud. Freud's followers were here first with the most, and no one can understand American cultural anthropology or social and clinical psychology or psychiatry without understanding Freud's work. Conceivably, Jung's theories or Adler's might have had this role; they didn't. One reason, I suspect, has to do with social status. Jung's theories, with their mystical flavor and racial emphasis, their "archetypical" focus, tend to appeal to the aristocracy—and indeed, humanists, often the aristocrats of academia, have been in some cases disciples of Jung. Adler's theories, with their common-sense flavor, their socialist humanitarianism coupled with underdog understandings, tend to appeal to the rare scientist who has a working-class identification; such men, in fact, working in clinics with poor patients and with an unequivocal therapeutic focus, are apt to have little time and resource for research and writing. By comparison, Freud is definitely bourgeois or upper-middle class; his theories have enough complexity to intrigue the highly educated, without frightening them by Jungian vagueness or offending them by Adlerian vulgarity; there may even be a connection between a certain compulsiveness in Freud's rationalism (a theme discussed in all these essays) and the ferocious industry of the Freudian adherents for whom, like Freud himself, therapy is not enough, but must be legitimated by research and by publication, despite the arduousness of the resulting daily round. While what I term in these essays the "third generation" of analysts is less preoccupied than Freud was with philosophic, religious, and generally "metapsychological" questions, they are no less research-minded and no less hard working bourgeois; their questions tend to be more technical, less "theoretical," more cautious—after all, they have been taught where Freud went wrong, as he did in his anthropology.

Very soon, I expect, the psychoanalytic movement will be hardly distinguishable from the broad front of research in personality—even now, psychoanalysis and psychiatry are in many institutions virtually interchangeable. (However, I also expect that there will continue to be men—cranky ones—who rediscover Freud with the freshness of first seeing, and who seek to lead reformation movements based on his books.) But of course such a sociology of intellectual movements must always halt before it pushes trend-thinking too far, realizing the importance of the role of single, unpredictable individuals. No one could have predicted the theories or the human accomplishment of Freud, or his first gifted disciples, even if one might have foreseen that, given a few energetic adherents, he would take hold in the United States as he has in no other land.

21. The Themes of Work and Play
in the Structure of Freud's Thought

THE PROCESS of incorporating Freud's thought into our living heritage of social and humanistic studies has moved bewilderingly fast, especially in America. But incorporation, as always with great thinkers, has been partial. There has been a tendency, among Freud's medical followers, to "empiricize" him, to forget about his philosophical interests and outlook in order to get on with the clinical job. Among nonspecialists, however, it is this philosophical side of Freud's thought that has often been most influential. In generally accepting it at face without an effort to refer it back to its base in Freud's own experience, people have neglected the very kind of reference he taught us to make. In my opinion, it is not possible to separate his technique from his cultural outlook and setting. It is sometimes said that he was a therapist and medical man in his earlier writings and a gloomy and speculative philosopher in his later writings. But we must be wary of such dichotomies by which, for many, the "good" Freud is separated from the "bad" Freud as, by similar measures, the "good" early Comte is separated from the "bad" later Comte, or the "good" Marx of *The German Ideology* from the "bad" Marx of the *Manifesto* or *Capital*. Though of course there are important differences in emphases, these men are of a piece—this, too, Freud would teach us—and their earlier writings contain the germs of the later views.

I have sought to establish this wholeness of the man in the light of certain important themes in Freud's philosophic and social outlook, by examining some of the implications of his early writings, making particular use of his own reported dreams. The later explicit statements in such writings as *Civilization and Its Discontents* or *The Future of an Illusion*[1] often merely confirm and elaborate a position that can be inferred from the "Dora" history, for instance, or from the book on dreams. I have, so far as possible, avoided coming into contact with biographical material or gossip about Freud, in order to see what the works themselves, so bravely revealing, have to say.

For my purposes here, it is not of very great importance to decide

---

1. *Civilization and Its Discontents* develops, *inter alia*, certain themes set forth in " 'Civilized' Sexual Morality and Modern Nervousness," *Collected Papers* 2:76, published in 1908, and the Clark University lectures of the following year.

at what point Freud's writings reveal him as a unique person—reveal, that is, his own deep affective involvement in an idea—and at what point he simply speaks, without much affect or individuation, in terms stereotypical of the general attitude of the era.[2] Certainly, his utilitarian and Philistine attitudes toward work and play were both central to his own view of life and a dominant note in his cultural environment. But what really matters for us is that by virtue of his greatness —by virtue, too, of the fact that he was on the whole a liberator of men—Freud has succeeded in imposing on a later generation a mortgage of reactionary and constricting ideas that were by no means universally held even in his own epoch. Like so many original thinkers, he was ambivalent; he provides the texts for the partialities of incorporation, and for contradictory life-paths and social policies.[3]

In this essay, I deal with Freud's basic attitudes to work and to play. They were formed in a society that was primarily job-minded; they circulate today in an American society that has much more chance to be leisure-minded and play-minded. While my preoccupation is with the social and cultural implications, it will I think be clear that the more technical contributions of Freud—for instance, his theory of dream interpretation, or his concept of the analytic transference—were to a very considerable degree shaped by his class and cultural outlook. This, of course, does not mean that the contributions are wrong; rather it helps us understand them, and puts us on the lookout for unsuspected pitfalls of ideological bias that may be hidden beneath questions of technique.

§ WORK: FREEDOM OR NECESSITY

FREUD VIEWED work as an inescapable and tragic necessity. Although he was no student of population problems, he implicitly agreed with Malthus' gloomy conclusion that men would be forever caught between the drives of hunger and sex—lucky to be one jump ahead of starvation. And sex, too, was for Freud a realm of necessity. He saw it, not as presenting men with a problem to be solved, nor with a

---

2. To decide this question, in each specific case, could be often highly speculative and difficult. Problems of the same sort arise when one seeks to interpret contemporary interview material, at least of a nonpsychoanalytic sort. There one must always ask: Does what the respondent reports say much about him as an individual, or is it mainly testimony—and, of course, that he gives this testimony says something about him—to the norm of his group, his social class, or the group or class to which he aspires? In Freud's case, we have the advantage of his reported dreams and associations, and many stray remarks, which it is sometimes possible to reinterpret by use of the method he discovered.

3. See Erich Fromm, "Individual and Social Origins of Neurosis," *Amer. Sociological Rev.* (1944) 9:380; reprinted in Clyde Kluckhohn and Henry A. Murray, eds., *Personality in Nature, Society, and Culture.*

game to be played, nor, coupled with love, as a road to human closeness and intimacy, but rather as a "teleological" prime mover, charged
with the task of socializing and civilizing men and thus preserving the
species. Sex could fulfill this task because of its ability to bribe with
an elemental pleasure and to appease with an elemental release. Work
was, then, the means by which the species maintains itself while performing its endless procreative mission.

This outlook, heavily influenced by Puritanism, took shape in the
early nineteenth century, in part as a reaction against the views of
utopian visionaries—men such as Condorcet, Godwin, and Owen—who
envisaged the possibility that, beyond this realm of necessity, might
lie a realm of freedom where work had social meaning and where the
economy would be our servant, not our master.

Needless to say, men are producing animals and must work in
order to live. Moreover, it is altogether likely, men being the creatures
they are and work being what it is, that some drudgery will continue to be associated with it. The question of the meaning of work, of
how it is experienced, is primarily a cultural problem; and cultures
differ enormously in the way work is interpreted in their value-
scheme. In some, work is not sharply differentiated from other aspects of life. It may be viewed as fulfilling religious duties; it may
have the pleasurable variety, creativeness, and interpersonal texture
which is associated with some kinds of farming, or artisanship, art,
or science. It may be viewed in other ways. Only, probably, in our
Western industrial culture, has work in fact the features Freud at-
taches to it; is it sharply set off against love, against pleasure, against
consumption, against almost every sort of freedom. Only here is it
a curse for most people, mitigated as such, often enough, not by its
own nature, but by the fear of boredom, which can be even greater
than the irksomeness of toil.

In the nineteenth century, dominated by scarcity economics and
Malthusian fears, work could nevertheless be given the rational meaning of the avoidance of hunger. And hunger and gain (ambition)
could be viewed as the self-evident motives of a market economy, the
former operating on the poor, the latter on the well-to-do.[4] In the
mid-twentieth century, in the countries of the Industrial Revolution
and especially in America, it is likely that with very little human
toil a full abundance can be assured to all inhabitants as the result
of the machine technology. But although the result has already been
a great lowering in the hours of work and vast improvement in physical conditions, work itself is still subjectively felt as a duty, without

4. Cf. Karl Polanyi, *The Great Transformation.*

meaning in its own terms. This is most striking evidence of the fact that the pattern of a culture can disguise, even distort, the inescapable problem of work. Neither the basic physiological drive of hunger, nor the basic equipment of production—man's brain and eyes and hands—instruct him in what meaning, what pattern, he shall give to work, any more than the basic drive of sex, and its genital equipment, tell him what meaning, what pattern, he shall give to love.

It is, as I shall try to show, the more pessimistic, middle-class, nineteenth-century attitudes that are reflected and elaborated in Freud's thought. I shall consider, first, his view of the "real," the workaday world, including his view of his own role in it, and, second, his attitude towards the subordinated world of play.

§ THE WORKADAY WORLD

FREUD, LIKE SO MANY scientists of a system-building cast of mind, was always in search of simplifying dichotomies, of polar opposites. As the "self" was the opposite of the "other," as the pleasure-principle and the reality-principle—or Eros and Thanatos—divided life between them, so the workaday world with its productive machinery, its markets, its other economic processes, was sharply marked off from the play-world, the world of fantasy and gratification. The former world, Freud took for granted as he found it; he reserved his insight and his unconventionality largely for the latter.

Freud regarded the world of business and professional life—of all areas where hunger and gain were alleged to hold sway—as unquestionably real. The views of critics, such as Veblen or Thurman Arnold, who see the mythical or fantastic elements of business enterprise,[5] are foreign to his mode of thought. It did not seem to occur to him that much work was obsessive busy-work, that businessmen often fled into work to avoid women, or that the seeming pursuit of business self-interest might be the sheerest rationalization for activities that were quite differently motivated. To be sure, the European businessman is more of an "economic man" than his American counterpart; his compartmentalization of work, separate from home and from play, is more complete; he *does* seek gain as his principal end, rather than friends, prestige, or an agenda. Nevertheless, Freud's attitude towards the work that men do in their occupations was almost that of a behaviorist who does not probe into motives.

Indeed, Freud concluded his book on dreams on the qualifiedly behaviorist note that "actions, above all, deserve to be placed in the front rank" in judging human character, since the dark and daemonic

---

5. See, for example, Thorstein Veblen, *The Theory of Business Enterprise;* Thurman Arnold, *The Folklore of Capitalism.*

psychic forces he had been describing had usually only the most limited consequences in the real, that is, the workaday, world.[6] In the
same volume, Freud described the dream-experiments of his colleague,
Dr. Schrötter, and concluded: "Unfortunately, the value of this important investigation was diminished by the fact that Dr. Schrötter
shortly afterwards committed suicide."[7] There was no note of sympathy or grief for this human tragedy: what mattered to Freud was
the work and not the man. Such behavioristic views seem to be a
reflection of the psychology of a market-economy: it does not matter
what men think or how they feel, but only that, overtly, they react
"appropriately" to the stimuli of hunger and gain.

Middle-Class Conventions Concerning Work

Freud's friends and patients, mainly upper-middle-class folk, were
not supposed to be motivated by the spur of hunger, but by the hope
of gain. Freud knew penury as a youth—financial needs drove him
out of the laboratory and into practice—but it was still the penury of
the rising student, not of the destitute proletarian. He assumed that
the individualistic motives of getting on in the world, the desires of
fame and success, were perfectly "natural"; it did not occur to him
that they might be culturally stimulated or produced, let alone that
they might be in themselves, neurotic drives. While he was apt to
minimize the extent of his own ambition, it did not trouble him to
avow his wish to be a full professor, to be famous, to be "an authority." With the exception of the cases where he had personal experience of bigotry or incompetence, he rather easily assumed that his
teachers such as Brücke or Meynert were "great masters," entitled
to "veneration";[8] there was nothing unreal about their attainments
and position. And, just as he assumed without question the conventions about greatness, he also assumed the other conventions of the
workaday world—for instance, about the great importance of priority
in scientific work. In one of his dreams he is anxious to "give Professor N. due credit for his diagnosis."[9]

The Playboy Classes

Three social groups seemed to Freud to be immune to the demands
of the workaday world. These were the aristocrats, who needed only

---

6. Freud, "The Interpretation of Dreams," in *The Basic Writings of Sigmund
Freud*, p. 548.
7. Reference footnote 6; p. 386.
8. Reference footnote 6; pp. 407, 409, 417. For a disavowal of ambition, see
p. 219, and cf. pp. 257, 446.
9. Reference footnote 6; p. 333.

to be born in order to be fed;[10] the professional artists and writers, who were privileged not only to live in the play-world of illusion but to draw from it the realities of fame and fortune;[11] and the monks and priests.[12]

The artist, as Freud viewed him, had the gift of being able to sell his day-dreams, his fantasy productions, even his megalomania, on the market; he could appeal to the hidden dreams and desires of his audience who responded by bestowing on him the admiration he could not have won in direct economic or sexual competition. The artist, moreover, was free from the arduous conventions of the scientist; by his gift, he could obtain a release from what others have to do and gain as direct an access to truth as to the hearts of mankind. While for the scientist, too—such as Freud—dreams and fancies might be real data, he must work and not play with them in order to make a profit.[13] But he must on no account "waste" his talents; Freud found Leonardo da Vinci infantile when, instead of turning his powers to account, he employed them in ephemeral toys and antic jests.[14] In a different vein, he also found Leonardo's passion for investigation neurotic: where one investigates the universe (instead of acting on it, or moving one's fellowmen by great art), one obviously misses real values for which a normal person would strive.[15] Naturally Freud applied to his own work a similarly conventional judgment: what helped him to cure patients was "real"; all else was "speculation."[16]

While, however, the artist had a privileged position in the native ease with which he won success, he remained, in Freud's eyes, a mere decoration upon the economic and political processes which mattered in the workaday world. Freud, the middle class patron of the theatre and collector of figurines, wrote of art as a monarch might speak of his court jester: "Art is almost always harmless and beneficent, it

---

10. See Freud's dream of Count Thun (reference footnote 6; p. 415).

11. "A kindly nature has bestowed upon the artist the capacity to express in artistic productions his most secret psychic feelings hidden even from himself, which powerfully grips outsiders, strangers to the artist, without their knowing whence this emotivity comes." Freud, *Leonardo da Vinci*, p. 84.

12. See, for example, Freud, "A Neurosis of Demoniacal Possession in the Seventeenth Century," in *Collected Papers* 4:436; see especially pp. 470-471.

13. However, even a scientist may sometimes be lucky; thus Freud writes: "From the reports of certain writers who have been highly productive, such as Goethe and Helmholtz, we learn, rather, that the most essential and original part of their creations came to them in the form of inspirations, and offered itself to their awareness in an almost completed state." Freud, reference footnote 6; p. 543.

14. Reference footnote 11; p. 108.

15. Reference footnote 11; pp. 42-43.

16. Freud, *A New Series of Introductory Lectures on Psycho-analysis*, pp. 207, 218.

does not seek to be anything else but an illusion. Save in the case of
a few people who are, one might say, obsessed by Art, it never dares
to make any attacks on the realm of reality."[17] Freud's attitude towards Count Thun, the aristocratic "do-nothing" Prime Minister of
Austria, was not very different: he, too, was a privileged idler.[18]

Work as the Man's World

Only in one respect did Freud deal with success as anything but
an obvious, self-evident goal which justifies the expenditure of immense efforts: he observed that in day-dreams men seek to throw
their laurels at the feet of beautiful women. Does it follow from this
that the real world, too, was in Freud's eyes subordinate to sex? The
question raises all sorts of ambiguities. On one level, Freud saw men's
libidinal drives, coupled in various harnesses with their aggressive ones,
as the source of all their productions: work was a channelling and
sublimation of these drives. But on another level, the nighttime sphere
of sex was clearly subsidiary to the daytime sphere of work, of accomplishment in the real world. For one thing, in Freud's eyes the
man of potency and means, unintimidated by cultural taboos, would
have no difficulty in finding appropriate sexual outlets. Achievement
—making a dent in the world—this was the problem. Indeed, women
were only trophies, to be tied, metaphorically, at the conqueror's
wheel: they were a by-product, pleasant enough, of his achievement,
but only incidentally an aim.

The workaday world then was clearly a man's world. Speaking
again of Leonardo, Freud referred to his "manly creative power"
prior to his homosexual, reflective and investigative stage;[19] Freud's
attitude towards Hamlet's indecision expressed a quite similar judgment. This "man's" world was threatened, not only by homosexual
tendencies, but by an excessive, uncautious interest in women. In
connection with one of his dreams, Freud tells us his fear that his
sons' talents will be "ruined by women," just as the great Lassalle was
killed in a duel over a lady.[20]

The place of women in this man's world was rather like that as-

---

17. Reference footnote 16; p. 219.
18. See Freud's dream of Count Thun (reference footnote 6; p. 415).
19. Reference footnote 11; p. 115.
20. Reference footnote 6; pp. 333-334. Freud does not see that Lassalle was
lured to his death, not by feminine wiles, but by his highly ambivalent ambition
for social status and fear of social humiliation. The plebian Jewish Lassalle,
despite his leftist views, was moved by the unconscious wish to prove his patent
of nobility; therefore, his real "folly" lay precisely in acceptance of the motives
and outlook which Freud took as the highest, most realistic wisdom. Cf. George
Brandes, *Ferdinand Lassalle.*

signed to them in Veblen's ironic *The Theory of the Leisure Class.*[21] Their very narcissism makes them desirable objects of display; their role is to be fed, tended, exhibited. But they must remain tractable in their gilded cage, and neither lure men to failure by giving them syphilis or otherwise draining their work-potential, nor, above all, enter the world of men as competitors.[22] Indeed, any effort of a woman to take part in the real world, in any capacity other than consumer of goods and libido, was interpreted as a desire to make up for her lack of a penis, the organ of power and creativeness. So strong were Freud's psychoanalytic rationalizations of the conventional Victorian—or, as Veblen would hold, predatory—attitude towards women, that they still impress many psychoanalysts, even women psychoanalysts.[23] Freud seems to have coped with the inconsistency, from his viewpoint, of his own daughter's entry upon analytic work by assigning to women analysts the field of child-analysis—very much as women in industrial management today are assigned the job of handling the morale problems, not of men and women, but of women only.

§ MAN'S NATURAL LAZINESS AND THE FUTILITY OF SOCIALISM

THE GRIMNESS of today's workaday world, as Freud saw and accepted it, is so great that it is understandable that men should exhibit signs of laziness, as if to justify the charge that they would not turn a hand, without the spur of hunger and gain. It is not surprising therefore to find Freud falling in with the hoary argument which seeks to derive the futility of socialism from the observed laziness of the working class.[24]

The Passive Paradise

This attitude Freud expressed in his interpretation of the myth of the Garden of Eden, which he saw as meaning that man longed for the idyllic idleness of the womb, or of childhood—the next-best in dependent passivity. But man was driven by his "original sin"—

---

21. Veblen, *The Theory of the Leisure Class.*

22. "We say also of women that their social interests are weaker than those of men, and that their capacity for the sublimation of their instincts is less." Reference footnote 16; p. 183.

23. Cf., for example, Helene Deutsch, *The Psychology of Women,* vol. I, chapters 7 and 8 .

24. Reference footnote 16; p. 246. Freud found socialism impossible on other grounds as well, namely man's natural aggressiveness, which departs somewhat from the conservative Malthusian pattern; but aggressiveness, too, comes down, though only in part, to the scarcity of possessions and men's desire to seize them from each other, rather than to work for them.

apparent in the sexual-aggressive Oedipus complex—to violate the conditions under which he might be taken care of in carefree bliss. Forced out of Paradise, he had ever after to work in the world, as sign and as penance; only in illusion could he momentarily return. Freud, who was accustomed to overturn many myths and see through them, accepted this myth as an historical truth, or rather as a primitive anticipation of the Victorian conviction that "life is real, life is earnest." A similar view is implicit in Freud's theory that man, as child and primitive, passed through a stage of belief in the omnipotence of thought. This magical thinking, in which wishes are automatically gratified, as they almost are for the infant, seemed to Freud to constitute one part of the charm of Paradise; men give it up for reality-thinking only under the pressure of frustration and pain. "If wishes were horses, beggars would ride"—or, more accurately, would fly. By a word, men would annihilate bothersome rivals, as Freud actually did in one of his most striking dreams.[25] The intensity of wishes and their violent ability to propel a dream thus arise from the fact that wish-fulfillment was once effortless, and that men never become reconciled to a workaday world in which this is no longer so. Freud assumed that men do not grow psychically, that nothing new happens to them in the course of development which might lead them to desire activity for its own sake.

Thus Freud had no doubt whatever that man needs to be driven into reality, by an angry God or his earthly deputies. Children, he felt, naturally did not want to grow up; they must be forcibly socialized, forcibly adapted to reality.[26] Parents who fail early to acquaint the child with pain, with what he must expect from the world, will create neurotics, recusants to their workaday tasks. Freud had no faith in his own children's talents as self-realizing, and he enjoined upon his wife the "training" by which these would be husbanded.[27]

In all this, I feel that Freud patronizes infancy and childhood. Even small infants seem to want to explore the universe—and not only in search of food and sex. Children—though, of course, like all of us, they have moments of regression—often are stifled in their wish to grow up, to accept responsibility and arduous tasks, by adult authorities who underestimate them. Conversely, adults, and children, too, forced to work at a pace that is not their own, react by rejecting work, in fantasy if not in featherbedded fact.

---

25. Reference footnote 6; p. 406. Freud says in the introduction to the second edition of the book on dreams that many of the dreams reported were connected with the poignant and emotionally significant period of his father's death.

26. Reference footnote 16; p. 201.

27. Reference footnote 6; p. 333.

§ FREUD'S ATTITUDE TOWARDS HIS OWN WORK

FREUD'S VERY DEFINITION of pleasure as release of physiological tension contains, in capsulated form, the essence of his attitude towards work. Even though he might, under certain conditions, regard work as a sublimatory release of tensions which are sexual in origin—which permits him on occasion to speak of "intellectual pleasures"—still he viewed these as only a poor second-best, purchased through a stunting of the primary, libidinal releases.[28] But if pleasure is release of tension, then toil—ordinarily the opposite of release—is by definition arduous. Nevertheless, despite the elaborateness of Freud's physiological and metapsychological explanations, despite all his talk about pleasure-principle and reality-principle, we must not forget the cultural setting: How could he as a self-respecting Victorian admit that his work was anything else but a chore? To speak of his job, as Americans today often do—usually with like conventionality—as "good fun," would hardly befit a practitioner of the Harley Streets of the world; we need merely remind ourselves of the unspeakable boredom from which even the most exciting case could hardly rescue the languorous Sherlock Holmes.

The Slave of Science

Freud's work, as I read his own account of it, seems to me of the very greatest intellectual interest; beside such detective work, even that of Sherlock Holmes is pallid and limited. But Freud seems to have found—or at least admitted to—almost no pleasure in it; on the contrary, his writings are full of references to his weariness, to the arduousness, rather than the ardor, of his unique intellectual adventure. "It is a habit of mine to run up two or three steps at a time"[29]—how blithely he speaks of "habit" rather than symptom when it is himself he is describing. His hurried days were almost incredible: ten or twelve hours of analysis—made especially anxious by the novelty of the task and the dangerously isolated position of the therapist—followed by writing up his notes on his cases;[30] then working far into the night on his writing, lectures, and correspondence; at night, writing and interpreting his frequent dreams, sometimes pages in length—only *once* did he not make "careful notes" on a dream;[31] finally, rousing himself in the morning with the greatest effort to begin another weary round.[32] Even when he suffered from the most

---

28. Reference footnote 11; p. 46.
29. Reference footnote 6; p. 290.
30. Reference footnote 6; p. 197.
31. Reference footnote 6; p. 349.
32. Reference footnote 6; p. 210.

painful boils, he refused to rest from "my peculiarly strenuous work."[33] until ordered to by the doctor. And of course in later life, his agonizing cancer of the throat gave him no excuse to slow the pace of his labor. Like other middle-class, self-made, self-driven men, he could only relax at the conventional times: on his vacation, or at the parties to which he infrequently went. He said of himself, characteristically, after a summer evening's lecture: "I was tired; I took not the least pleasure in my difficult work, and longed to get away from this rummaging in human filth. . . ."[34] But, even on vacation, Freud could not abandon his vocation. Just as he "amused" himself by examining starfish on his first visit to the Irish Sea at the age of 19[35]—how different his preoccupations from those of James Joyce by the Irish Sea—so he drove himself even in his beloved Italy, like any harried tourist.[36] Though he reproaches himself, or permits himself to be reproached, for his hobbies,[37] as for his other "vices" such as smoking which did not directly contribute to his work, he did in fact manage to turn most of his "play" to economic account, like a cook who saves her leftovers for a stew. He enjoyed jokes—and collected them for a book on wit; he loved Michaelangelo—and wrote a long analysis of his "Moses" statue; his wide reading of novels and poetry was automatically and unaffectedly ransacked for analytic clues. So in fact, nothing was "wasted"—nothing, that is, but Freud, who took for himself Claude Bernard's motto, *"Travailler comme une bête."*

In return for his Spartan zeal, Freud allowed himself to take pride in his conscientiousness, especially in cases involving no admixture of interest, like the twice-a-day injections he gave a cranky old lady;[38] while he scolded those "spoilt" gentlemen, the devout, who "had an easier time of it with their revelation."[39] And, indeed, the Sisyphus task of science, endlessly pursuing truth, becomes for Freud the very core of his personal philosophy of life.[40] Nevertheless, while Freud would agree with Spinoza that "the joy by which the drunkard is enslaved is altogether different from the joy which is the portion of the philosopher,"[41] still he would have insisted that there is little joy, but much enslavement, in the philosopher's quest.

---

33. See Freud's dream of not working; reference footnote 6; pp. 284-285.
34. Reference footnote 6; p. 441.
35. Reference footnote 6; p. 475.
36. Reference footnote 6; p. 414. Freud speaks of wearing out his brother "by rushing him too quickly from place to place, and making him see too many beautiful things in a single day."
37. See the dream of the botanical monograph; reference footnote 6; p. 243.
38. Reference footnote 6; pp. 204, 206 *et seq.*
39. Reference footnote 16; p. 237.
40. Reference footnote 16; pp. 236-238.
41. *The Philosophy of Spinoza*, edited by Joseph Ratner, p. 245.

"*Per Ardua ad Astra.*"

In one very important respect, Freud's Puritan attitude towards work in general, and to his own work in particular, had a profound influence on the whole psychoanalytic method. For he assumed, as a matter of course, that any answer to which one came without arduous toil must be wrong. It was this feeling, that truth must cost something if it is to be worth anything, which, among other factors, led Freud to feel that the more far-fetched and "difficult" the solution, the more probable its correctness. Thus, despite his reference, which we have earlier quoted, to the successful "intuitions" of his admired Goethe and Helmholtz, he distrusted intuition in psychoanalysis. Repeatedly, he attacked the "intuitive" method of dealing with dream-symbolism.[42] Moreover, not only in dream-interpretation, but in all his work, Freud played down the role of intuition, just as he distinguished between mere "speculation" and real scientific work. Again and again, he referred to himself as a sober-sided, meticulous investigator, who never jumps to conclusions, but constantly acknowledges his dependence in observation and theory, on "the real external world."[43] Understanding is the reward, not of the gifts of genius, but of the "expenditure of effort."[44] Undoubtedly, Freud expended tremendous effort, but of course it is not only this which led him to his genuine innovations. While he accused intuition of arbitrariness, the very logical, and often pedestrian, rigor of his own treatment of symbols led repeatedly to highly arbitrary, indeed quite fanatical, constructions. But, of course, these were "work"; they did not spring from an alerted, but at the same time unstrenuous, "listening" for what the symbol was attempting to convey, but rather from a forceful, categorical insistence that the symbol surrender its meaning to Freud's intransigence. Perhaps his relative disregard for his own imaginative gifts was not only a defense against the critical pettifogging researchers of his day, but also a rationalization of his envy for those whom he considered still greater geniuses such as Goethe, who appeared to him to have had an easier, sunnier path.

Every so often, however, Freud did refer to his pleasure in mastering difficulties.[45] But, like most political conservatives, he did not assume that men generally could share his own loftier motivations.[46] Among Puritans, such a hierarchy of toilsomeness is not uncommon. Compare the statement of Mrs. Gromyko: "Oh, Andrei does work

---

42. For example, reference footnote 6; pp. 369, 371, 374, 401.
43. Reference footnote 16; p. 239.
44. Reference footnote 16; p. 238.
45. For example, reference footnote 6; p. 275n.
46. *Civilization and Its Discontents;* reference footnote 1; pp. 24-25.

hard, yet not as hard as Mr. Vishinsky, and even that is not so hard
as Mr. Molotov works."[47]

Freud's Own Dream-work

A single, magnificent example illustrates Freud's method, and at
the same time these limitations. In his famous "Dream of the Botanical Monograph," Freud says:

> I have written a monograph on a certain plant. The book lies before
> me; I am just turning over a folded coloured plate. A dried specimen of
> the plant, as though from a herbarium, is bound up with every copy.[48]

His associations to the dream were manifold and revealing. Among
other things, Freud noted an association to his own monograph on
the coca plant. He has told us elsewhere of his frustration because
he did not become known as the discoverer of the anaesthetic properties of cocaine, the reason being that he let a friend continue the
research so that he (Freud) might take time out to become engaged
to his future wife.[49] He also made reference to the fact that his wife
often remembered to bring his "favourite flower"—the artichoke—
from the market where she diligently shopped, while he was less
"thoughtful" of her, seldom bringing her flowers.[50] The artichoke reminds him of a childhood scene where he tore up a book containing
"coloured plates" and of his later fondness for collecting books; he
reproaches himself, both for this expensive hobby, and for the "onesidedness" of his *Gymnasium* studies, which had led him close to
failing his botany examination.[51] In sum, after pages and pages of
examining separately each dream-detail, he permits himself in his analysis a slight awareness of his "thoughtlessness" towards his wife, of
envy and grandiose ambition, and a memory of destructiveness, safely
remote in childhood and in any case blamed upon his father. The
worst thing he can say about himself is that he has expensive and distracting hobbies! In fact, he calls the childhood memory itself a
" 'screen or concealing memory' for my subsequent bibliophilia."[52] A
curious "screen" in which he concealed the amiable and redeeming
veniality of a hobby for collecting books behind the less amiable vice
ot destroying them—perhaps the vice of destructiveness itself! But
play—that is, preoccupations and hobbies, especially if expensive, not

47. *Time*, August 18, 1947; p. 25.
48. Reference footnote 6; p. 241.
49. Freud, *An Autobiographical Study*, pp. 23-25.
50. Reference footnote 6; p. 242.
51. Reference footnote 6; pp. 243, 323.
52. Reference footnote 6; p. 243.

directly advancing one in one's profession—did appear to Freud as sinful.[53]

In his associations to the dream, Freud pushed aside his unconscious recognition of what the dream was about and disregarded the significance of flowers as a symbol. Instead, he tore the dream word-from-word like the leaves of an artichoke; he viewed the dream, not as a *Gestalt*, but in a series of concentric verbal associations. I would like to suggest another possible interpretation of the dream, on a fairly obvious symbolic level. Freud seems to have been aware in the dream that flowers—a symbol which he elsewhere recognizes as plainly sexual[54]—do not speak to him; his love has become "a dried specimen of the plant, as though from a herbarium. . . ." Is it not also correct to assume that he is unconsciously aware that he has sacrificed his wife's love to his ambition—that *this* is screened by the mild, and yet symbolic charge he elsewhere makes against her that, but for his devotion to her, he would be famed as the discoverer of cocaine? Indeed, he scarcely permits himself to realize that he is readier to buy himself a monograph—he speaks of his "fondness for . . . possessing books"[55]—than to buy flowers for his wife; this, although the dream commentary refers to his seeing at a bookseller's on the previous day a monograph on the cyclamen, his wife's favorite flower.[56] (His wife has, in fact, become "puffy," like a stuffed animal, while Mrs. "Gardener," whom he met the night before, is still "blooming," presumably from Mr. "Gardener's" care.)[57] Flowers are, by their very nature, a symbol of emotional feeling, even waste; in the act of "possessing" them, they dry up; the artichoke, on the other hand, is not a real extravagance—it is edible. Yet there is more than "possessing" involved; Freud has imprisoned love within the covers of an illustrated monograph; he has crushed it; in penetrating to the heart

---

53. In speaking of the absence of affect in this dream, Freud writes that the dream "corresponds to a passionate plea for my freedom to act as I am acting, to arrange my life as seems right to me, and to me alone." Reference footnote 6; p. 439. But the "freedom" he refers to is that of his collecting mania, against the reproaches of his own conscience and those of his even more puritanical friends like the eye specialist, Dr. Koenigstein, who had told him the evening before that he was "too absorbed" in his hobbies. Reference footnote 6; p. 243. He reproaches himself: for not inventing cocaine, for "neglect" of botany; but he answers "I am entitled to freedom for, after all, I am conscientious and have made some good monographic studies." Thus, he assumes that he must justify not driving himself 100 per cent—"allowing himself," as he says, some small vices. By his standard, even his meagre vacations from the workaday world were sinful, especially where he "missed something," such as the cocaine discovery, as a result. Reference footnote 6; p. 268.

54. Reference footnote 6; pp. 382-383.

55. Reference footnote 6; p. 243.

56. Reference footnote 6; p. 241.

57. Reference footnote 6; p. 245.

of the artichoke, he has a lifeless specimen in his hand. I strongly suspect that the mild scene of childhood destructiveness, which Freud treats as screening his bibliophilia and, on a deeper level, his sexual curiosity, actually conceals the way in which his own life and that of those around him is torn by his almost total incapacity for love and spontaneity—this is his true "onesidedness." It is like the Irish Sea, which means little more to him than the examination of a starfish and the recollection of its Latin name.

Dream-work and Entropy

The concept of "dream-work" attributes to the process of dream-formation the same economics of affect which Freud employed in the process of dream interpretation. He writes, "we take pains to dream only in connection with such matters as have given us food for thought during the day";[58] that is, the dream-work is the processing plant which prepares the material with an eye to the driving wishes behind it, the inspection of the censor, and the economical and convenient packaging of the imagery. Behind this concept, there lies again the assumption of man's laziness. If we had our way, Freud is saying, we would not even dream; we would lie in the blissful fetal state. But our wishes, and external stimuli also, prevent this; these create tensions in our otherwise flaccid state of rest; the *purpose* of the dream-work is to release this tension and thus, by permitting us to go on sleeping, to restore us to the workless state. As Freud divided his year between his workaday months and his vacation period, so he divided the day between the waking tensions and the night's release. But this is not the only way to live! A vacation may be restful, though strenuous, if it lends variety and enjoyment to life; likewise, sleep is not merely the opposite of waking tension. In fact, recent studies have shown that restful slumber is accompanied by frequent changes of position; motionless sleep is not nearly so refreshing. Dreaming, too, is assumed to be an almost continuous process, of which the dreamer is only occasionally aware.

This feeling of Freud's, that he needed to explain the fact of having a dream, and to find the energy-source for the amount of "work" involved, misled him in at least two ways. It was one factor in his insistence that every dream represents a—probably libidinal—wish-fulfillment, the wish being the primal source of energy; this insistence led him to over-elaborate explanations of those dreams, such as anxiety dreams, judgment dreams, and so on, which did not appear to fit his formula. Secondly, it made him suspicious of dreams which, by their

---

58. Reference footnote 6; p. 245.

baroque imagery, their eloquent speeches, or other luxuriance, seemed to have required much "work"; since work is unnatural to man, this effort must hide something, must cover up a most forbidden thought. Thus, when Freud recalls in a dream the formula for trymethylamin, he takes this as "evidence of a great effort on the part of my memory,"[59] and goes off accordingly on a long, interpretative search.

This attitude towards effort pushed Freud towards over-interpretation in his analytic thinking generally. Being a strenuously effortful man, his thoughts and dreams, even without further elaboration on his part, would naturally tend to be complicated and far-flung. Moreover, Freud's work-drive compelled him to go beyond even his initial reaction, towards sometimes over-intricate structures of thought—the *Moses* book is a final and brilliant testament of this obsession which was at the same time part of the drive which made him great and courageous. And yet, concealed beneath all this work, is it possible that Freud is occasionally "playing" with us, and with himself? Is it not likely that, outwardly denying himself any playfulness or frivolity as doctor and scientist, he may have unwittingly sublimated his play-impulses, so that they can be glimpsed only in an "unnecessary" metaphor, a fine-spun interpretation of a dream, a tenuous reconstruction of history?

However that may be, it would seem an important task to track down, in Freud's more technical writings, some of the over-interpretations that may have resulted from his attitude towards effort. Here all I can do is to indicate some of the implications of this attitude. It seems clear that Freud, when he looked at love or work, understood man's physical and psychic behavior in the light of the physics of entropy and the economics of scarcity. For him, life was not self-renewing, or self-producing; he viewed the process of life as drawing on the given natal store, as on a bank account. Hence, for him, effort, expenditure, was problematical: it needed to be explained; something must lie behind it.

One views dreams quite differently if one holds a different view of the nature of life itself. If one thinks that growth is characteristic of life, that life can unfold unsuspected potentialities and resources, one feels that it is not *effort* that needs to be explained—that is life itself—but the *absence* of effort. Then it is the absence which appears pathological. So, if one comes upon a dream which is rich in invention and the use of symbolic expression, or which exhibits indignation, or judgment, or wit, or other human faculties which one appreciates in waking life, one will not feel that this is strange and that the dream

---

59. Reference footnote 6; p. 203.

must *necessarily* be about something altogether different. Any dream ordinarily requires interpretation, but its prima-facie opacity need not be due to a censorship over malign or outrageous wishes; the necessity for interpretation may result from the fact that symbolic expression is simply a different language, often a more abundant one than the dreamer allows himself in waking life.[60] Or it may be due to the fact that the memories called up in the dream have not been pigeonholed into the dreamer's organized, waking categories and thus appear with a freshness and intensity of experience which he may have had as a child.[61]

§ THE WORLD OF PLAY

ALREADY, in order to talk about the world of work, as Freud saw it, I have had to picture in contrast the opposing world of play. For, indeed, Freud saw these two worlds as sharply separated as was the *Aussee* where he spent vacations, from the urban Vienna where he did his analytic work. Freud's world of play, as we shall see, is a world of children, of artists, and, only surreptitiously, of adults— that is, those adults who are real men and not idlers or escapists.

The Nursery Years

Freud regarded childhood as an auto-erotic haven where all one's pleasures are within reach. Nor is there any conflict between the drives of hunger and sex: "Love and hunger meet at the mother's breast." Soon, moreover, the child discovers the pleasures of onanism; these, too, require no work, not even the labor of object-choice. But this cannot go on; Freud writes:

> This age of childhood, in which the sense of shame is unknown, seems a paradise when we look back upon it later, and paradise itself is nothing but the mass-phantasy of the childhood of the individual. This is why in paradise men are naked and unashamed, until the moment arrives when shame and fear awaken; expulsion follows, and sexual life and cultural development begin. Into this paradise dreams can take us back every night. . . .[62]

But this view of childhood as not subject to the laws of the adult world of reality was only one side of Freud's position. He noticed that children liked to play at being grown up, and indeed wished to grow up;[63]

---

60. I have leaned heavily on Erich Fromm's lectures on dream interpretation. See his article, "The Nature of Dreams," *Scientific Amer.* (1949) 180:44.

61. See Ernest Schachtel, "On Memory and Childhood Amnesia," *Psychiatry* (1947) 10:1; also Evelyn T. Riesman, "Childhood Memory in the Painting of Joan Miró," *Etc.*, (1949) 6:160.

62. Reference footnote 6; p. 294.

63. Reference footnote 11; p. 107.

and he had a clear vision, unusual for his epoch, of the terrors, phobias, and conflicts which beset even the most protected child. Unlike most adults, he did not condescend to the battles and nightmares of the nursery; these he accepted as real. And with his usual pessimistic sense, he observed that "the excited play of children often enough culminates in quarrelling and tears."[64] Thus he saw the child as more adult, and the adult as more child, than was the conventional opinion.

This contradiction in Freud's thought can be reconciled if one observes that he saw through the current myths regarding "the innocents of the nursery" only insofar as sex and aggression or matters related to them were concerned—and, obviously, this was no small achievement but one of his most decisive contributions. He saw, clearly enough, the sexual elements in children's play, the onanist practices, the animistic fantasies.[65] But he was at one with his adult generation in looking down on play in general as childish; he did not entirely grasp its reality-testing and reality-expanding functions, its nature as a part of or an aspect of preparation for human adult existence, any more than he respected the creative functions of the playful moods which he criticized in Leonardo's life.

Indeed, even to talk about "functions" when discussing play runs the risk of catching us in an anthropological or psychoanalytic functionalism which means that human freedom is limited to being "unfunctional"—a privilege, paradoxically, most relevant to human existence when seemingly most irrelevant, as many great teachers of mankind have understood.

Play and Foreplay

This divorce between work and play which sharply separates the world of the adult from the world of the child is not reconciled by maturity. Rather, once the genital stage is reached, play becomes attached primarily to the sexual function and continues in an underground, often unconscious existence. In his utilitarian attitude towards sex, Freud was much interested in what he called "foreplay," the preliminary stages of lovemaking. Foreplay seemed to him a kind of come-on which tempted couples onto the path of biological fulfillment; by its tension-heightening nature, it seemed to violate the pleasure-principle and to demand ejaculative release. By this ambiguity, it impelled otherwise reluctant people to comply with the "laws of propagation."[66] (The term "foreplay," itself, seems to carry its

---

64. Reference footnote 6; p. 315.
65. See, however, his discussion of children's food wishes and disappointments; reference footnote 6; p. 214.
66. The phrase is from Freud's *Leonardo da Vinci*; reference footnote 11; p. 70.

own linguistic self-contradiction: if it is play for a purpose, it is robbed of most of its spontaneous, amiable, frivolous, or tender playfulness.) In other words, just as Freud "allowed himself" his book-collecting and other hobbies for their recreative functions, so he "allowed" mankind this apparent frivolity of foreplay for its procreative functions: in both cases, pleasure is not really free, it merely baits the trap. After intercourse, so Freud felt, there is sadness; after play, one pays by sorrow and work.

Dreams and Day-dreams as Play

Fantasy and art are among the secondary and derivative efforts of mankind to obtain sexual pleasure; they constitute a kind of bargain basement, in which a meed of pleasure is sublimated—no other pleasure could equal direct sexual pleasure in Freud's view—in return for a modification in the ensuing pain. The discovery of this *ersatz*, inexpensive pleasure is made by the child, Freud argued, in the form of a hallucinatory wish-fulfillment, a kind of mirage in which the hungry infant, for instance, can persuade himself that he is being fed.[67] In later life, the adult can restore this state in dreams and day-dreams.

Freud perhaps tended to exaggerate the extent to which one can actually escape reality, unless one is crazy, by means of these fantasies. For although he is correct in believing that in the passive state one can afford wishes which would endanger one in real life, by the same token one diminishes one's satisfaction: somehow one realizes that "it's only a dream"[68] or a day-dream—and that it will never come to pass. Moreover, our individual and cultural imagination sets limits to wishes; they are often as poverty-stricken as that of the woman in the famous tale, which Freud quotes, who used the first of her three fairy wishes to procure some sausages which she had smelled next door.[69] The "damned wantlessness of the poor," against which Lassalle protested, is not dissipated when they sleep.[70]

My conclusion here is that Freud was romantic about dreams, as he was about more overt sexual life. By his insistence that, underneath the manifest dream, there must lie a wish, and that this wish, in an adult, would have a dark, luxuriant, and forbidden quality, he avoided

---

67. Reference footnote 6; pp. 509-510.

68. This phrase is from Freud's "The Interpretation of Dreams"; reference footnote 6; p. 513.

69. Reference footnote 6; p. 520n.

70. In a recent *Fortune* poll, a cross-section of the American people was asked what income they would like to have, if there were no limits to their demands. The average person gave a figure less than 25 per cent above what he was at the moment making; the mean figure was less than $4,000. See "Portrait of the American People," *Fortune* (1947) 35:10.

seeing how flat and conventional, how sorrowful and anxious, many dreams actually are. There is, for example, little that is wish-fulfilling in his own "Dream of the Botanical Monograph." Actually the censorship, to which he himself called attention, is not so easily evaded as he supposed; the most daring, and therefore frightening, wishes do not even exist in our unconscious, let alone rebel in the night against the dictation of the censorship.

But though there is a romantic element in Freud's view of the dream, this did not prevent him from subjecting it, like every other psychic performance, to the laws of scarcity economics. One dreams, he says, in order to continue sleeping, for otherwise the ungratified wish or outside stimulus, would wake one—one continues sleeping, of course, to prepare for the labor of the following day.[71] Thus the dream represents an elaborate compromise, a deal between the psychic forces: with the censorship relaxed by sleep, the repressed wishes are able to go in search of pleasure, using the thought-residues of the day, but at the same time the dream-work "binds the unconscious excitation and renders it harmless as a disturber . . . of sleep," while satisfying through displacement and other devices of evasion the censorship's one open eye. This involves, Freud writes, a lesser "outlay of . . . work, than to hold the unconscious in check throughout the whole period of sleep."[72]

Art as Play and Display

So far, I have been discussing the play-world in its private aspects, to which one has access principally in sexual "play" and in dreams. There is also a public play-world; it has virtually the same economy as that of the dream. It is built on fairy-tales[73] and other folk-myths, on wit, and on art.

---

71. Reference footnote 6; pp. 518-519.

72. Anxiety dreams do not seem to fit in this economy, and their explanation caused Freud no end of trouble. He finally concluded that anxiety is the response of that part of the dreamer's psyche which is displeased by the forbidden wish; this part, at least, is pleased by the suffering the anxiety occasions, which is felt as punishment. Reference footnote 6; p. 520; Freud, *A General Introduction to Psychoanalysis*, p. 192.

73. Freud had the genius to see that fairy tales were *"nichts für Kinder,"* that they had an adult meaning though one which the adults did not permit themselves to see. He applied to them the same interpretative process he had used on dreams; he analyzed their symbolism; he tried to see what really happens in them beneath their decorative screen. He found it typical that the heroine, for example, Cinderella, marries the prince; he took the status-striving, as well as the sexual, even incest, elements, as "real"; naturally, every girl would want to marry a prince and lead the do-nothing life of an aristocrat. Reference footnote 6; p. 371. Moreover he held that in fairy-tales we commit the Oedipal offenses; we are the "great criminals"; we indulge in the totem feast, with its sacrilege. All this gives us pleasure whose true nature, like that of dream, is concealed from us by its apparently harmless, innocent garb.

The artist's job is that of giving public expression to his private fantasies, fantasies which others may share; his work is others' play. Moreover, art, as Freud viewed it, is not bound by the rules of the workaday world—it is free. Like religion, the other great operator in the play-world of illusion, it can dissolve the dichotomies of human existence; it can deny the fact of death, or, as in the Greek and Egyptian sculptures which fascinated Freud, it can unite man and woman.[74] The pleasure in art is, as one would expect, partly Oedipal and rebellious sexuality, partly narcissism, in which both artist and audience identify with the hero. Licit gratification of illicit wishes is secured by these projections.

The relative thinness of the role assigned by Freud to art is surprising, in view of the amount of attention which he gave the subject both in his own writings and in his "hobbies." Of art as critic of society, as transcending the given cultural divisions and definitions of work and play, as conscious creator of new values, Freud does not speak. His own tastes in art seem to have been conventional for his time, place, and class. Like so many nineteenth-century bourgeois, he admired the Renaissance, perhaps finding in it an age less cramped than his own. His great hero was Goethe, regarded as a late-Renaissance figure. He seems to have had little taste for music. Though he admired Ibsen, who was also a defier of sexual convention in his writings, he was not in general interested in "modern art." But it is modern art which has most strongly rebelled against being a plaything for rich patrons; sometimes it has done so by its very "ugliness" according to accepted patterns. Moreover, Freud paid little attention to the formal problems of art, being primarily concerned with its psychological causes and effects; when he thought about form at all, he said that the problem was insoluble.[75] Thus, his attitude towards art, as well as his taste, was conventional: by assigning it to the world of play, of regression, of sex, he patronized it, as a sober, cultivated bourgeois should. Perhaps one could say that he viewed it, as a modern city-planner views a zoo or park, as a territory zoned off from the workaday world, which is there to delight but not to be taken with full seriousness.[76]

The Play of Words

Somewhat the same attitude governs Freud's view of wit. He saw the role of language as a reality-instrument in a way that could hardly have been done before the development of his theory of dreams. For

74. Reference footnote 11; p. 96.
75. Reference footnote 11; p. 120.
76. See Freud's remarks on the uselessness of beauty, including parks, in *Civilization and Its Discontents;* reference footnote 1; pp. 54-55.

by means of words, one delays gratifications, and tests reality experimentally before, so to speak, setting foot in it. Though the infant, like the primitive, uses them as magic handles, in his phase of thought-omnipotence, they nevertheless become tools, not pleasures. By their nature, moreover, they are logical, un-autistic: they relate us to the world and to the other people in it; only children and lovers are permitted a private language. But even here, in this instrument of communication, there is a domain reserved for pleasure: this is word-play or wit. At one point in his dream-theory, he speaks of comical effects as a "surplus" which is discharged by laughter;[77] wit is, indeed, the theatre and poetry of the poor. But the pleasure which Freud found in wit is not only that of release of the tensions of obedience to the laws of language;[78] it is also that of direct rebellion. While he collected for study jokes and stories of Jewish humor, he enjoyed also the richness of its satiric and sardonic elements.[79] And even the sexual elements which Freud emphasized in his analysis of wit are not only pleasurable in their own right, but in their rejection of convention. Freud, so meticulously clean as a physician, was quite "rebelliously" fond of "dirty" stories, just as he enjoyed spitting on the stairs of an old lady patient whom he detested.[80]

§ CONCLUSION

I HAVE INDICATED that Freud's ascetic rationalistic dichotomy between work and play, and the very limited role he assigned the latter, belong to the work-morality of nineteenth-century Europe—to the years when the advancing industrial revolution had still not shown its potentialities for drastically shortening labor and expanding leisure horizons. The chances are, moreover, that Freud went much further in the direction of asceticism, of eliminating "waste," than did most of the members of his class and culture: he actually did what it was only their ideal to do. But when one looks at contemporary American attitudes towards work and play, one cannot be too critical of Freud —one can, indeed, see much in his view that is refreshing. Thus he never adopted the notion that work and play must alike be "fun"— and, more particularly, fun with people. This notion forces men in the American upper-middle class to merge the spheres of work and play, often without advantage to either. An anxious gregariousness and concern for the expression of appropriate consumer tastes can permeate a business or professional conference as easily as a cocktail

77. Reference footnote 6; p. 538.
78. Reference footnote 6; p. 332n.
79. Freud, *Wit and Its Relation to the Unconscious;* pp. 164 *et seq.*
80. Reference footnote 6; pp. 269, 272, 291.

party. To a degree, Americans have substituted fun-morality for work-morality. But this, among other things, makes it difficult to admit that one is tired: one has not done enough to "deserve" it. Conversely, one tends to exploit his vacations not, as Freud did—when he was not traveling or climbing mountains—by doing productive work, but by seeking to train oneself for advances in status or in the solution of vexing interpersonal problems.

I can put my point another way by saying that there are certain advantages to making fun and play surreptitious—even sinful. For then, play is less apt to be socially guided, less apt to be compulsively gregarious. Freud's view of play as a kind of underground in adult life protects it—gives it some of the same chaotic freedom that the carnival provides in Catholic countries. As against this, the contemporary social focus on recreation sometimes tends to leave no room either for whorehouses or for underground passages of any sort; everything must be out in the open. And while in a utopian society this would not be so bad, today it often means that play is exploited in fact—as it was for Freud in principle—for physical and psychic hygiene.

Indeed, Freud's own account, in a somewhat distorted version, is one of the factors which has shaped this modern view. Many women, for instance, indulge in sexual play not because they seek pleasure but because they have been told, and told themselves, that repression is bad. Men justify their vacations on the ground that they "owe it to themselves." Emancipated parents are anxious if their children do not masturbate, lest they become neurotic. Men who have stomach trouble feel that they must "relax," must have more fun, to avoid further psychosomatic disorder—the give-away clue of psychic imperfection. And those men who cannot play are robbed, both by cultural developments and by the loss of psychological innocence Freud helped bring about, of the older defenses provided for them in a work-oriented society. So it turns out that, under the guise of fun and play, we remain today almost as truly ascetic as Freud, often enough without the very real satisfactions which—in spite of himself and in spite of his views as to the supremacy of sexual pleasure—he derived from his intellectually demanding and adventurous work. The threat of work today is not that it is arduous, but—in the some ways far worse fact—that it boring and without meaning.

As against this, Freud, despite his skepticisms and reservations, had no doubt that work was worthwhile and that scientific work, whatever its uncanny "primal" sources in sexual or aggressive drives, had its own logic, its own convention, and its own tradition. Moreover, while he was a utilitarian in his attitude towards play, and, in a way, towards life in general, he was actually much less of a utilitarian about science than many of his successors. The pursuit of truth was for him self-justifying: man had every right to penetrate the secrets of nature without giving an account of himself to academic, priestly, democratic, or other moralizing authority. Although he thought the truth would set men free, he was, nevertheless, far from the mood of many "policy-oriented" researchers today, who hedge their curiosity about by all sorts of expediential considerations and concern for various good causes. One of the things that makes Freud such perennially exhilarating reading is the sense of the "play of the mind" that he communicates.

It may be a long time before middle-class people, in America, will feel themselves free to play when they are not free to really work—if their work has degenerated into sociability or featherbedding. Those who are excluded from meaningful work are, by and large, excluded from meaningful play—women and children, to a degree, excepted. The kind of passionate fondness and excitement about his work that Freud had, although he would seldom admit this to himself, is also a good base from which to learn to play. And people have to learn to play—or stop unlearning; in this enterprise they are faced with the whole long tradition of the driving and driven men who created Western industrial society, Western political organization, and Western scientific thought, including psychoanalysis.

Perhaps it is time now for the analysts, and for other social scientists, to pay more attention to play, to study blockages in play in the way that they have studied blockages in work and sexuality. Yet, in studying play, one must be aware of the ambiguities that haunt play, be aware of the elusiveness and privacy that are its main defenses. We have far to go before we move to a new integration of work and play unreservedly superior to the Freudian dichotomies—an integration allowing us more work in work and more play in play.

22. Authority and Liberty in the Structure of Freud's Thought

SUFFICIENT TIME HAS ELAPSED since Freud built his system—not perhaps in years but in the movement of thought—to permit and require critical re-examination of the sort undertaken here. Such re-examination depends for its very method on Freud's own work, and its aim is less to point to weaknesses in that work, which have already been sufficiently discussed, than to contribute to the sociology of knowledge and to the ongoing effort, both in psychiatry and in the other social sciences, to separate what is essential in Freud's thought from the garb, determined very largely by the time and the culture, in which that thought made its debut. The texts of Freud which I will primarily use are not those in which he himself spelled out his *Weltanschauung*, but rather those more technical writings in which his outlook on such problems as those of authority and liberty appears only inferentially, and often without his own full awareness.

§ THE MEANING OF HUMAN HISTORY

KENNETH BURKE OBSERVES, in a remarkable essay on "Ideology and Myth," that when historical thinking succeeded philosophical thinking in the West, writers who wanted to establish some thing or some authority as essential declared that it was temporally prior:

> Thus, whenever they wanted to say that man is "essentially competitive" or "essentially good," they said that the "first men" were constantly at war or that men were "originally" good but were later corrupted by society. They postulated such "firsts" in some hypothetical past time, their thinking in this regard often being much more mythical than they suspected, and no more based on actual scientific knowledge about the past than was the "mythical" doctrine of "original" sin (which, translated philosophically, would mean "essential" sin, that is, some ineradicable difference between individual and group which the individual, eager to socialize himself, might experience as a sense of guilt).

Freud was similarly concerned with establishing status-rankings between different orders of the given, either on the basis of temporal priority or on the basis of what essentially *belongs* and what is merely additive or artificial. For him the "essentially" human was the ur-human—one reason, perhaps, why the myth of the primal horde held such attraction for him. Likewise his view of original sin—namely, the primal crime of Oedipus which is both deposited in our racial memory and repeated by each of us in the modified form of childhood fantasy and feeling—fits Kenneth Burke's description.

A concept of original sin is typical of a view of life which makes the past an authority over the present, in which the individual is mortgaged to society, and both the individual and society are mortgaged to the preceding generations. All through recent history, one finds secular variations of this outlook, and secular castes who, replacing the priests, have the duty of collecting the interest on the mortgage. The most striking, because extreme, example of this is in the work of Auguste Comte who was so impressed with the legacy of past ages that he invented quantities of new holidays to celebrate a calendar of secular saints; immortality was, for him, the continuation of the hold of the past over the present. Though he did not believe in original sin, he did believe that the individual owed to his parents, and to all the past, so enormous a debt that it could never be repayed even by a lifetime of altruism. In Ruth Benedict's *The Chrysanthemum and the Sword*, there is a recent analysis of this principle in operation in Japanese society. In Japan too the individual feels that he must spend his life in repaying his debt to his parents, and to society—symbolized by the Emperor. Payment of the debt in all such cases is never a mere matter of contract; it is always a matter of morality, enforced by feelings of shame and self-abnegation.

Freud's metaphorical doctrine of original sin is, at first glance, emancipated from such rigors. He does not believe in altruism, nor, of course, does he give a literal meaning to original sin. Nevertheless, in his manifest thinking, he seems to stand on the side of the past's authority. The most striking illustration appears in *Moses and Monotheism*. He suggests there that anti-Semitism may be due at least in part to the "stubborn" refusal of the Jews to acknowledge their share in the primal crime, which in their case took the historical form of the killing of Moses, their "father." And he points out that the ascetic renunciation which he attributes both to Jewish ethics and theology —the bare bones of monotheism—are the consequence of unconscious guilt feelings for this consciously forgotten offense. But the reader may well ask: Does Freud not accept here the authority of those of the dominant majority who are hostile to Jews and rationalize their hostility by swinging the club of the past over the present? Freud took his own Jewishness very seriously, as shown in his well-known letter to the B'nai B'rith.[1] To some extent he seems to be renouncing the present claim of the Jews to equal and decent treatment, and justify-

---

1. "On Being of the B'nai B'rith," reprinted in *Commentary* (1946) 1:23.

ing this renunciation on the basis of the past as forcibly reconstructed by him.

In fact, Freud traced all authority back to this source of the original father; as he writes in his book on dreams:

The sovereign is called the father of his country (*Landesvater*), and the father is the first and oldest, and for the child the only authority, from whose absolutism the other social authorities have evolved in the course of the history of human civilization (in so far as "mother-right" does not necessitate a qualification of this doctrine).[2]

It is significant to see what short shrift he gives, here and elsewhere, to matriarchy. The possibility of the ur-existence of matriarchy is obviously inconvenient, if one wants to justify contemporary authority by throwing over it the mantle of the primal father. Freud takes this latter step explicitly in his *Group Psychology and the Analysis of the Ego*.

Freud had, however, to face the fact that some children do not know their fathers, or know them only as lenient ones; and the fact that it was not easy to find convincing evidence for the existence of repressed Oedipal desires in every adult whom he analyzed. One way in which he dealt with this problem was by the concept of racial memory: from this, no one can escape. This memory included a realization of the primal crime, which, however, needed usually to be revived by some symbolic repetition; it also included a kind of ur-language and universal symbolism.

The concept of ur-language and ur-symbolism is of particular importance in Freud's thought. For its implication is that language and imagery are prisons, set up in the long-distant past, from whose categories and modes of thinking man cannot free himself; it is a kind of phylogenetic rather than epistemological Kantianism. Since mankind originally thought dichotomously, with ur-words meaning two polar opposites, the implication is that all real or basic thinking continues to be of this sort; neither cultural diversity nor individual style can do much but add trimmings to the racially inherited pattern.[3] Even in our word-play when, according to Freud, we put aside adult reality for a moment, we fall back upon puns and images which are part of the racial stock; so, too, with symbols, whether found in dreams or works of art. A small number of these have a given, usually

---

2. Freud, "The Interpretation of Dreams" (Brill, tr.), in *The Basic Writings of Sigmund Freud*, p. 275n.

3. Freud, " 'The Antithetical Sense of Primal Words,' " *Collected Papers* 4:184; London, Hogarth Press, 1925. In his essay on "Ten Levels of Language," Albert Guérard has shown the differentiated richness of the lingual inheritance, which both groups and individuals are free to alter in many ways; no one level is superior. *Amer. Scholar* (1947) 16:148.

sexual, meaning: a tool or stick is always a penis; a lake or river signifies birth or the womb; a room or wood means a woman; a dream
of flying symbolizes sexual intercourse. No deviations are permitted;
the racial memory controls the individual or cultural experience.

Yet in Freud's position there is a concealed element which is not
at all authoritarian; this is the notion that, since all have the same
memory, there are no fundamental differences between classes of
men or between nations. The upper classes are subject to the same
crude unconscious memories as any peasant: "None is so big," he
writes, "as to be ashamed of being subject to the laws which control
the normal and morbid actions with the same strictness."[4] Underneath, he is arguing, men are, after all, the same. Thus the dialectic
of history is turned around so as to deny privilege as well as to defend it.[5]

The same mortgage which binds society to its past, and to the
reincarnation of its primal father, also of course extends to every
single individual. Freud's utilitarian teleology led him to see the individual as a piece of somatic tissue indebted to its own sperm or ovum
until released by death—"the common fate . . . which subdues us
all."[6] Everyone is bound to procreate;[7] that is his purpose on earth,
and all else is preparation. This task he inherits, just as he inherits his
unconscious memories and passions; the neurotic tries to subdue these
—to escape their domination—and falls ill as a result.[8] From this point
of view, Freud's attack on narcissism is quite understandable: narcissism is, so to speak, the last refuge of the individual from his credit-
ors, social and personal. And yet—here again we see the ambivalence
of his view—he was the inventor of a therapy designed to lift from the
individual his oppressive mortgage, or at least to provide for a stay
of foreclosure and a remission of payments long since due.

It is now necessary to see somewhat more particularly the ways
in which mankind is bound to its destiny, at once phylogenetic and
teleological. Just as all are guilty of the primal crime, even if they
did not participate in or even consciously remember it; so all are sad-
dled with the prospect of a future which is not capable of much voluntary change. Immutable laws limit man's control over his physical environment and over his own desires for aggression and nirvana. The most
that could be hoped for is the slight amelioration of the inherited

---

4. Freud, *Leonardo da Vinci*, p. 38.
5. Cf. Freud, "Wit and Its Relation to the Unconscious" (Brill, tr.), in *The
Basic Writings of Sigmund Freud;* p. 778.
6. Reference footnote 2; p. 411.
7. Reference footnote 4; p. 70.
8. Reference footnote 2; p. 520.

framework; no radical transformation of society has any chance. This is a curious position for a thinker who discovered whole areas of untapped human resources, richer than the wealth of the Americas, and who in his clinical practice actually assisted men and women to make abundant use of their own latent energies which had been crippled by conflict and repression.

Since this *is* an ambivalent position, it is not surprising that Freud's whole attitude towards history combines elements from both the progressive and the cyclical theories which were current in his time. The progressive theorists, both before and after Darwin, saw mankind's development as linear—up from the ape, up from slavery, up from animism, as the case might be. Thinking of this sort goes back to the Enlightenment, to men like Turgot and Condorcet; it was refined by nineteenth-century writers who, like Hegel and Marx, introduced dialectical elements—or, like Comte or Maine, conservative ones—without changing the fundamental pattern. That pattern viewed history not as a series of alternatives which were rather accidentally chosen, but as entirely "necessary": what happened had to happen in accordance with the progressive laws. In such a late thinker as Bergson, even the laws evolve; nothing is static; everything moves forward according to a vital principle or spiritual gyroscope.

Cyclical theories of history, though old, did not find favor until late in the century. Antibourgeois writers such as Brooks Adams and Pareto reacted against the optimistic assumptions of the linear theorists. Whether they spoke of the circulation of elites or of the rise and fall of civilizations, their cynical platitude remained: *plus ça change, plus c'est la même chose*. Moreover, increasing historical and anthropological knowledge made the simple progressive theories difficult to maintain. Despite the efforts of the nineteenth-century ethnologists, for instance, no single sequence of tribal social development could be discerned. Those who were attracted to cyclical theories were not only rejecting modern capitalistic society as the best of worlds to date or even the prelude thereto. They were also rejecting the parochialism which viewed the fate of the planet from the perspective of Western Christianity or even, as in Comte's case, from the perspective of a single country thereof; that is, these thinkers chose their illustrations from a wider range of cultures—seeing less to respect in their own, and more to respect in the others. Thus, with the assistance of such men as Sumner, they laid the foundations of cultural and historical relativism.

Freud picked and chose among these contrasting attitudes. His notion of the gradual development of a phylogenetic inheritance, of the linear change from primitive to modern times, as recorded both

in language and in social organization and as deposited in the unconscious—this borrows from the progressive theorists. On the other hand,
his conception, most explicitly set forth in *Civilization and Its Discontents*, that epochs of repression and refinement are always succeeded by epochs of explosion and barbarity,[9] and his further, more
implicit belief that, from here out, nothing new can happen in history
—these are reminiscent of the cyclical theorists. This ambivalence follows not only from Freud's ambivalence towards authority but also
from his feelings towards his own civilization. Sometimes he was inclined to view this, ethnocentrically, as the height of human attainment, and to accept without question the values of science and cultivation and the middle-class world generally. But, except for the value
of science—which he never questioned so far as I can find—he could
also be quite sharp in his hostility towards the culture in which he
lived, and admire, without condescension, earlier ages and earlier
civilizations, such as the Egyptian. About the shape of the future,
however, no such conflict was necessary: this was virtually governed
by the past. Under these circumstances, Freud advised mankind to
"submit to the inevitable."[10]

To a degree, this attitude towards the future may be closely related to Freud's acceptance of scarcity economics. Where scarcity
prevails, there will authority also be found—the authority of the generalized past and the more direct authority of the ruling class which
must control the distribution of the limited resources. Freud was quite
skeptical that there could be alternative outcomes or abundant ways
of organizing man's relations to nature and to his fellows. For where
history appears as a series of determined events—and historical writing
almost always makes it so appear—the future can hardly be regarded
as open: at most it will present a dichotomy, an either-or.

Today, we are all short-run pessimists. But Freud's long-run pessimism has also become fashionable, perhaps prevalent, though it is
often linked to a religious base which Freud explicitly rejected. How
radical it was when he first expressed it may be gathered from an
essay by Bertrand Russell on "Current Tendencies,"[11] written in 1920.
This essay attacks the "cosmic impiety" of such thinkers as Bergson—
their delusions of omnipotence, of automatic progress, which he felt
ignored or trivialized man's existential problems. In such a climate of
late Victorian evolutionary optimism, Freud's pessimism was chal-

---

9. *Civilization and Its Discontents* (first published in 1930).

10. *New Introductory Lectures on Psycho-analysis*, p. 221. Compare, however,
his high hopes for the spread of psychoanalytic modes of thought in "The Future
Prospects of Psychoanalytic Therapy," in *Collected Papers* 2:285.

11. Bertrand Russell, *Selected Papers*.

lenging. Today, we stand in need of more impiety, cosmic and other-wise. It is pessimism which has become complacent.

Freud's pessimism, furthermore, was strictly limited. In his day-to-day clinical task, he acted without question on two progressive beliefs: the unfolding nature of science, and the linkage of knowledge to therapy. At least once, moreover, in his published writings, he per-mitted himself to face the possibility of economic abundance and its social consequences, saying that "a fundamental alteration of the social order will have little hope of success until new discoveries are made that will increase our control over the forces of nature, and so make easier the satisfaction of our needs."[12] History, then, is not hopeless after all. From this it follows that man, far from bowing to the inevi-table, must imitate Prometheus; he must not only understand, but act: "He has the right to make an effort to change that destined course of the world. . . ."[13]

To sum up, it may be said that Freud's view of history is a com-promise among ambiguous and contradictory elements. On the one hand, there is evolution and advance; there are great men who "make an effort to change that destined course," men such as Moses. On the other hand, there are definite limits, now in all probability reached, beyond which neither man as a biological product nor society as a bio-historical product can move; the future holds neither miracle nor messiah.

§ INDIVIDUAL DESTINY

ONLY LATE IN LIFE did Freud begin to write on these general social and historical problems, although as early as 1900, in his book on dreams, his attitudes were already fairly explicit. For most of his life he was concerned not with social but with individual destiny. Some of his case records constitute what today would be called a "life his-tory," and what medical men in any case term a "history"; from analyzing these, one can see what Freud thought of as open in human history and what as closed.

The theory of the birth-trauma can be a starting point. If all of a person's life is viewed as determined by the one crucial event which commences his independent history, all later events have been reduced to mere repetitions or reminders, over which the person has no control. That is why the theory is so forcibly reminiscent of the strictest Calvinist predestinarianism; it has the same universal, uncon-trollable quality.[14] In this strict form, Freud rejected the theory as

---

12. Reference footnote 10; p. 248.
13. Reference footnote 4; p. 43.
14. The theory of the birth-trauma appears to be scientific, but it was never

it was developed by his disciple, Otto Rank; but he continued to believe that this trauma was the prototype, though not the source, of all later anxiety, while the womb became the prototype of the Garden of Eden. To the constitutional inheritance, the phylogenetic memory, and the birth experience, Freud added a fourth source of the later life-pattern—namely, the early years of childhood. Though "the development of the individual is only an abridged repetition" of the phylogenetic experience, it can nevertheless be influenced "by the fortuitous circumstances of life," particularly of the first five years.[15] It is in these "circumstances" that liberty lies, as against the authority of the past.

The childhood experiences, however, are not fortuitous in any extensive sense. The child has no more control over who his parents are —except in dreams where, Freud delighted in pointing out, children always create different parents for themselves, or in the myths of birth such as that of Moses—than over the manner of his obstetrical delivery or his sex. And in his early years, the child is unavoidably helpless, dependent for life itself on the surrounding adult world. Freud's great contribution was to relate these "obvious" facts to a dynamic theory of character. Character is determined, once and for all, in the childhood situation. Writing of Leonardo's illegitimate birth, Freud states: "the love of the mother became his destiny; it determined his fate. . . ."[16]

In Freud's theory of character, the final (genital) stage is reached with the physical and psychic changes of puberty. This is the terminal; beyond puberty there are no further stages; before it, lie the various way-stations—oral, anal, phallic—at which the destined neurotic or pervert lingers too long or to which he returns. Just as the sex role, given at birth, is unalterable—short of castration—so these childhood phases determine the interpretation of the events of adult life: choice of mate, of livelihood, of *Weltanschauung*. Even the most dramatic and unexpected experiences, such as those of war, serve chiefly to revitalize and repeat a childhood pattern; that is, the traumas of war and death are perceived within the characterological limits which are already set. After puberty at the latest, and probably much earlier, nothing new can be added; the life pattern is already fixed— short of psychoanalytic therapy.

The decisive importance of this concept of character for contemporary work in the social sciences can scarcely be over-estimated. In

actually tested, though as Freud pointed out it offers itself easily to empirical scrutiny. *The Problem of Anxiety*, pp. 94-96.

15. Reference footnote 2; p. 497.
16. Reference footnote 4; pp. 94-95.

our attempts to understand social and political movements, historical changes within a culture, conflicts of class and caste, and many other similar problems, the theory permits us to advance in our methods and hypotheses.

If all men are prisoners of their childhood character-structures, over whose formation they have had no control, it easily follows that all their later motives, tastes, and judgments are not, in any real sense, theirs at all. Men are viewed less as individuals than as the representatives of their sex-and-character roles. In what is perhaps his most famous case history, that of "Dora," Freud dates the onset of the patient's hysterical neurosis from her rejection of a sexual advance from an older, married man, a long-time friend of the family. Freud assumes that not to be excited by a reasonably presentable and potent male is itself neurotic, and some of his analysis is based upon this assumption. He scarcely grants Dora, or any other woman, the privilege of taste and idiosyncrasy even—indeed especially—in the most intimate relations of life: a penis is a penis, and that is enough for a "normal" woman who has physically attained, as 14-year-old Dora had, the genital stage. That Freud believes this, may be inferred from a footnote to his report on Dora's case, in which he remarks, as if in answer to possible critics, that he has seen the man who attempted Dora's seduction, and that he is attractive![17] Hence Dora's refusal must be neurotic. Of course, it *may* have been neurotic, though the man as Freud describes him seems rather a dubious character. Our quarrel is only with Freud's implication—to be sure, qualified by other arguments—that Dora had no freedom of choice, so to speak, in the matter: she *must* be neurotic since she refuses to "bow to the inevitable," the fact of being a woman.

But men are subject, in Freud's analysis, to an authority identical to that which women face in their sex roles. So when he finds a patient who, instead of visiting a girl about whom he has heard, takes a train in the opposite direction, this, too, *must* be neurotic—of course, it *may* have been. Freud insists that the biological equipment of men and women, rather than the cultural definition of that equipment, is determinative of normalcy.

Given the crucial importance of sex and sex-roles in the Freudian theory, little new can happen; whatever does happen will be explained as essentially a repetition or recombination of the past. The figures

---

17. "Fragment of an Analysis of a Case of Hysteria," in *Collected Papers* 3:38. The case of Dora is, of course, exceedingly complex, and Freud could argue that Dora was in fact in love with Herr K. Note also Freud's reference (in "Further Recommendations in the Technique of Psycho-analysis," in *Collected Papers* 2:377, 385) to "all the individual details of [a patient's] way of being in love."

created in dreams Freud compares to dragons or centaurs.[18] These composite creatures, like the unicorn, seem to me to symbolize man's difficulty in imaginatively transcending nature. Just as deterministic theories of history, whatever their differences *inter se*, put the historian in the position of an authority who, in the name of History, sets limits to mankind's future development, so the Freudian analyst makes himself into an authority in the name of Character or Sex. In his view, motives are without opacity, and actions, though often ambivalent, are without ambiguity. If a person cares about justice, that must be because he is essentially envious; if he shows pity, that must be because he is reacting against a basic sadism; he gives himself away to the observing authority in the very act of concealment. One can see that the same deterministic principle is at work here as in the concept of universal symbolism or as in some of the historical constructions—for instance, Freud's insistence that Moses *must* have been killed by rebellious Jews.

Now it may be argued that Freud in these instances is simply expressing the scientific postulate that everything is, in principle, capable of being explained, and that science has no room for the concept of freedom of the will or for accident. One might question so flat a statement of the postulate, by reference, for instance, to recent theories of probability; but that is not my purpose: it is not the fact of explanation but the nature of the explanation that I question. Just as in his psychic economics Freud applies the second law of thermodynamics and assumes that libido is indestructible, so he assumes in his analysis of the individual that one's childhood-formed character and role are indestructible; these form the real self, all else is trimming. His men and women are allowed little future, other than a repetition of the past; whatever happens to them is *"déjà vu."* Freud takes on himself the role which so fascinated him intellectually, the role of the Parcae; before him, as the representative of destiny, all men are humbled. Freud held that even in dreams man does not escape. He closes his book on dreams on this characteristic note: "By representing a wish as fulfilled the dream certainly leads us into the future; but this future, which the dreamer accepts as his present, has been shaped in the likeness of the past by the indestructible wish."[19] But even the predestining wish is not the person's own; it goes back to the childhood situation which was anything but unique and which in turn is merely a repetition of the primordial pattern. Would it be going too far to say that—for Freud—life itself, ever renewed in the individual, is subjected to the repetition-compulsion of the race?

18. Reference footnote 2; p. 350.
19. Reference footnote 2; p. 549.

§ THE STRUCTURE OF AUTHORITY WITHIN THE INDIVIDUAL

I HAVE POSTPONED consideration of the mechanics by which the person is, so to speak, held to his destiny, while being permitted a limited illusion of freedom. This is the function of the ego and the superego—the internal delegates of external authority.

The Walking Delegate from Economics: the Ego

The ego has the task of curing the child's addiction to the pleasure-principle and of encouraging his operation according to the reality-principle. This means somatic self-preservation—fundamentally coping with hunger; when that is taken care of, the ego can turn to its teleological duty of finding appropriate hetero-sexual objects, outside of the incest taboos, and thereby giving pleasure to the id. What is the nature of the "reality" to which the ego relates itself? It appears to be the given state of economic development in Freud's milieu, as interpreted by capitalist scarcity economics. The ego is concerned with survival, and with whatever happiness is attainable within this context. Thus from the viewpoint of the individual his ego is that part of himself which is charged with mastering reality; from the viewpoint of society his ego is merely the administrative organ which sees to the carrying out of the workaday tasks. In other words, the ego not only *develops* out of man's helplessness "in the presence of the great forces of life,"[20] but it exercises over the id the authority of those forces and administers their demands. It is an "official" agency, though of course on the lowest rung. But according to Freud it never achieves full control of its assigned internal territory.

The Walking Delegate from Ideology: the Superego

The ego, as the agent of economic or technical "reality," divides authority with the superego, which is the agent of parental and public opinion. This opinion is, in a sense, just as real a force as the other, for it depends on the given state of social ideals and patterns for identification. Nevertheless, Freud views the superego—as a Marxist might—as a sort of ideal superstructure. He does not credit it with the full power he attributes to the material base. Hence enforcement here does not spring from the ego's role of adaptation to life itself but rather from emotional, indeed irrational, pressures in the child's upbringing. While at one point Freud remarks, "When our student days are over it is no longer our parents or teachers who see to our punishment; the inexorable chain of cause and effect of later life has taken over our further education,"[21] it does not follow that the superego loses its

20. Reference footnote 4; p. 103.
21. Reference footnote 2; pp. 316-317.

function with adulthood. As an unceasing source of guilt feelings, it cooperates with external authority in subduing the rebelliousness of the id. By holding the individual up to his internalized ideals—ideals he can never attain—the superego sees to it that he does not violate the cultural taboos appropriate to his social station.

If one assumes with Erich Fromm that the function of parents and teachers in any historical culture is to see to it that the individual will *want* to do what, under the given social and economic conditions, he *has* to do,[22] further light is shed on the relation between ego and superego in Freud's thought. Freud seems to realize, half consciously, that "reality" itself, namely what *has* to be done, is actually not a sufficient spur to human performance. By the reality-principle alone, mankind could not be governed. What is required is an actual reversal within the personality of its native attitudes towards work and play, as Freud regarded them: it must learn to enjoy what is inherently painful—its workaday tasks; and to fear what is inherently pleasureful —satisfaction of the desires of the id. This transformation of the affects of pleasure and pain is carried out under the aegis of the superego; it is never left to matter-of-fact "cause and effect."[23]

How does this come about? Freud's account is exceedingly involved; I will oversimplify for purposes of this paper. The motive power for this change of affect is the child's dependence on the parents, not only for physical survival but for love. By using love as a reward for renunciation of pleasure, the child is trained in the way he should go; he becomes tractable, the word Freud uses in reference to his own sons.[24]

At first, this is an ego-adaptation; the parents represent "reality," and the child does what is necessary to manipulate them. But under the pressure of the parental demands for renunciation of instinctual gratification, this mode of adaptation proves economically inadequate. Some release for the suppressed impulses must be found. In this situation where the child is economically so hard pressed, torn between his need for further gratification and the necessity of not jeopardizing the margin of gratification that he does secure from his parents, he has recourse to the mechanism of identification. He internalizes the parental figures, particularly the one of the same sex, as part of his ego, and endows this new entity with his surplus of instinctual energy. So an outlet for the thwarted aggressive impulses is found—but at what a cost! For the superego now directs against the child the same

22. Erich Fromm, "Individual and Social Origins of Neurosis," *Amer. Sociological Rev.* (1944) 9:380-384.
23. Reference footnote 2; pp. 521, 533-534.
24. Reference footnote 2; pp. 333, 335.

aggression for which he could previously find no target. Continually the idealized parental figure is held before him as a norm, and every deviation in conduct or thought from this norm is followed by inescapable punishment. And since the energy for this punishment comes from the frustrated id, no actual conduct, no pure thought is satisfactory: the nobler the behavior, the less the id gratification, the more energy at the disposal of the superego, and the more the flagellation of the self.

To the historically-oriented Freud, the internalized parents were more than the child's idealization of his own particular parents. As well and beyond, they were historical figures, carried in the germ-plasm and evoked by the particular socialization process. The superego is not merely the precipitate of the particular Oedipus complex, but of the original Oedipal slayings. Thus, just as the child carries his ancestral germ-cell as both legacy and mortgage, so he continues in his superego a morality which springs not from his own direct experience, or even from that of his parents, but one which goes back into the phylogenetic past. This inheritance, Freud wrote, is only slowly altered in response to economic factors,[25] thus perceiving that the superego drives a person, in actual fact, not to the tasks required in his generation but to those required in the past. If there is rapid change in the economic environment, therefore, the superego and the ego would point in different directions; this, of course, is what actually happens when society moves from a technological economy of scarcity to a technological economy of abundance.

Ordinarily, and apart from neurotic outcomes, the ego and the superego divide between themselves the bureaucratic job of id-supervision, the role of authority shifting from one to the other depending on the balance of internal and external forces. Under conditions of civilization, this dual monarchy appears to grow very strong, while the original wishes of the id become more and more repressed or, with the transformation of affect, turned into their opposite. Moreover, with the transition to adulthood, the ideals of the superego undergo a change, attaching themselves no longer to the parents, but to outside powers—to God, to Public Opinion, and so on. Political leadership makes use of this mechanism; social groups are formed among people who have within themselves the same superego image. In this way, the internal bureaucracy and the external bureacracy remain in touch with each other, with the former able to supervise the execution of not only the parents' commands but also those of the parent-surrogates of later life.

---

25. Reference footnote 10; p. 244.

Mechanisms of the Internal Revolution

I rather doubt if any one would be as sensitive to the way in which authority actually operates within the individual as the foregoing shows Freud to have been, if he himself were not at least ambivalent towards authority. If Freud had been wholeheartedly on authority's side, he would have tended to overlook the extent of its power and the subtle infiltration of its operations, especially in modern society, into the very citadel of the personality. But beyond that, he would scarcely have been so aware of the seething rebelliousness which underlies outward conformity—of the civil war continually in progress within. For while many frightened bourgeois at the turn of the century were overanxiously afraid of socialism, few recognized, as Freud did, that the "revolt of the masses" was an affair not confined to the proletariat, and that hatred of civilization burned like an underground fire in even the strongholds of the *bourgeoisie*.

The fire burns in the id which, despite all efforts at repression, remains the stronger force—"the *daemonic* power," Freud calls it.[26] Indeed, the repressory forces must draw their energies from the great energy reservoir of the id, just as in modern society the masses supply the police force by which they are kept in check; the battle of revolution and counter-revolution—"cathexis" and "counter-cathexis," in Freud's terminology—goes on unceasingly. The proud ego and superego might be able to persuade both the outside world and the individual himself that everything is under control, only to be disestablished by the despised and rejected id.[27]

Thus in Freud's view the id is the great liberator, constantly struggling to overcome authority. The struggle is carried on according to the patterns familiar to us in a lenient, bureaucratic autocracy such as the Austrian Monarchy was in the nineteenth century: by sly evasion, by constant pressure, by satire, but rarely by open revolt. Freedom, then, is found in these interstices where the hierarchy is deceived or held at bay. Finally, the future lies with the oppressed id which will not take "no" for an answer.[28] This is one meaning of the well-known doctrine of "the return of the repressed." Let us see somewhat more precisely the forms taken by the internal fight for freedom.

26. Reference footnote 2; p. 543.

27. Cf. Freud, "The Origin and Development of Psychoanalysis" (Chase, tr.), *Amer. J. Psychol.* (1910) 21:181-218. Freud writes, in "My Contact with Josef Popper-Lynkeus," in *Collected Papers* 5:295, 297: "Our mind . . . is rather to be compared with a modern State in which a mob, eager for enjoyment and destruction, has to be held down forcibly by a prudent superior class."

28. It is interesting to compare John Dewey's view of the liberating role of impulse. See *Human Nature and Conduct*.

Because the ego and superego draw their energies from the id, they are forced to relax their hold in sleep. They feel, moreover, that they can afford to relax since they have, as Freud puts it, closed the gates to motility;[29] nothing very serious can happen to the workaday authorities. Thus, every night is *Walpurgisnacht* for the id; in dreams these revels are recorded. But since the dreams are on the record, since they are recalled during the working day, they cannot express openly the desires and the revolts of the underground; in Freud's metaphor, they evade the censorship by the characteristic devices of obscurity and concealment known to all underground movements. These devices lull the censorship—viewed by Freud as just as stupid as the Austrian bureaucracy—by flattery, *double entendre*, and the invisible ink of symbolic language. Under these conditions, anything can be expressed, provided only that it is properly veiled.

In Freud's own dreams, for example, as interpreted by him, no authority is safe from attack. Count Thun, the Austrian Prime Minister; Meynert, the great psychiatrist to whom Freud in his waking life deferred; Brücke, Freud's inspiring teacher; the Emperor; Freud's own father—all are accused in his dreams of the vilest habits, the greatest absurdities; but all accusations are safely disguised by distortion, caricature, and obsequiousness.[30] Thus dreams, as Freud explained, play the role of the court jester, or of the Hamlet who is "mad north-northwest."[31] The authorities can rationalize their leniency with the remark, "After all, it's only a dream."[32] But it is the id which has the last word, for it maintains an unrelenting pressure; and since it forgets nothing and never misses an opportunity,[33] it will someday catch the censorship unawares and present the authorities with really frightening demands. The censorship will ring the alarm, and the sleeper will wake, frightened and anxious, finally aware that underneath the seemingly placid surface of his life there flow deep and dangerous currents—the "daemonic power." The play-world, to which Freud assigned dreams in one part of his theory, turns out to be not so innocent after all; in fact, Freud believed that there simply were, for adults at any rate, no guileless dreams.[34]

While dreams evade the bureaucratic censorship through their elaborate concealments of style, jokes and artistic productions escape by their wit and charm; it was indeed through these qualities that the

---

29. Reference footnote 2; p. 510.
30. Reference footnote 2; pp. 269 (Count Thun), 417 (Meynert).
31. Reference footnote 2; p. 423.
32. Reference footnote 2; pp. 455, 513, 548.
33. Cf. reference footnote 2; p. 268.
34. Reference footnote 2; pp. 250-251.

Viennese often coped with their rulers and with the problems presented by the Empire's ethnic mixture. The id expresses its criticism by what Freud called tendency-wit, but then turns to its masters with a smile, saying, "After all, I don't mean it; it's only a joke." The censor is as humorless as he is stupid; he either misses the point of the joke or is tempted by it to let the villain through. To prove his point, Freud made an elaborate analysis of Jewish humor which, like so much of the underground humor which circulates in totalitarian states, is often a bitter attack upon authority. In the many jokes, for instance, which on their surface poke fun at the lies and sales talk of the *schadchen*, the Jewish marriage brokers, Freud saw that the underlying theme was an attack on the whole system of arranged marriage which put the fate of the young in the hands of the ghetto elders.[35] Similarly, in jokes of which poor Jews were the apparent butts, he saw that the real attack was on the dominant majority. Jokes, then, like dreams, are never guileless; they are skirmishes in the unending civil war within the individual and within the group.

Another evasion, in Freud's view, lies in the belief of adults that children's play is innocent and therefore need not be severely and closely supervised by the bureaucratic hierarchy. The "authorities" however are mistaken, just as mistaken as when they leave the dreamer, the jokester, the artist to their own devices. For children, Freud insisted, are naturally rebellious against authority; they hate their parents; they hate the sibling who displaces them; they have an eye, for which they are not given credit, for what goes on in their world.[36] When the individual child grows up, when his ego and superego take over their respective duties, a convenient amnesia covers over these early perversities and revolts. As Freud pictures the process, it is rather like the way in which American Negroes so quickly forgot their stirring history of slave revolts after emancipation. But the forgetting is only in the conscious mind. The id, which never forgets and never denies itself, is therefore constantly able to refresh its powers by harking back to these childhood perceptions and experiences. But as an adult, one is not aware on the conscious level of what one's own children are up to. Thus the internal authorities, despite their power, are not really able to suppress all claims for liberty, simply because they cannot get access to the claims; they are in the position of a jailer who has lost the records of his prisoners. No matter how he strives, the "liberation cannot be inhibited."[37]

Still another evasion rests on the fact that sexual activities, by

---

35. Cf. reference footnote 5; pp. 700-701.
36. Reference footnote 2; pp. 298-299, 499-500.
37. Reference footnote 2; p. 537.

their very nature, are carried on in private; the bureaucracy would have to have a far-flung network indeed to catch all evaders. Of course, as Freud saw, sexual intercourse is not quite free of bureaucratic regulation. He realized that a patriarchal society necessarily is an authoritarian one, since fatherhood, unlike motherhood, is not a palpable fact but must be inferred from circumstances. The inference is stronger or weaker depending on the amount of supervision—which in the Middle Ages took the form of chastity belts and in the Victorian Age of an overwhelmingly strong female superego. Even so, the civil war goes on. While virtually totalitarian pressures may limit illicit intercourse to a minimum, since interpersonal relations can be fairly well controlled, no pressures whatsoever can control the intrapersonal relations to the point of suppressing all sexual protests from the id. Masturbation, though carried out in private, and almost universally present in childhood, is too obvious to the waking self to escape censorship. But it was Freud's genius to see that in hysterical neurotic symptoms the sexual wish was, in spite of everything, expressed. To all appearances, and even in her own mind, a woman might seem most refined, but her gestures, her compulsions, her eating habits might betray an unmistakably sexual note.

Reference to the "refined woman" leads to still another area where the bureaucracy is easily evaded—namely, the lower classes generally, the peasants, the simpletons. While in the Marxian view these are the oppressed classes, in Freud's eyes they were freer from internal and external censorship than their "betters." Because they are not supposed to know any better, because their superegos are relatively weak, they can get by with assaults on the prison of language or the prison of sex; their transgressions will simply amuse the "authorities." In his book on wit, Freud explains that misuses of the language—obscenities, for example—which would make us indignant if committed on purpose, make us laugh if committed by a naive person; he is not dangerous, and we can afford to laugh. Such people are like children, except that they happen to be adult.[38]

But people of the upper and middle classes do not get off so easily.[39] A very few—the elite, the leaders—are strong enough knowingly to defy the hierarchy within and the hierarchy without; Freud admired them. The rest, however, adapt themselves as best they can to the world and its opinions as they find them, content to evade only in dreams and daydreams, and in jokes and art. Another residue are unable to adapt at all; they are too weak, the pressures are too strong; moreover, they do not know how to achieve even the per-

38. Reference footnote 5; pp. 766-767.
39. Reference footnote 14; p. 90.

mitted evasions. These are the neurotics; Freud pitied them. Yet even they are not entirely devoid of liberty. They have, so to speak, a choice among neuroses. Perhaps they will become hysterical, expressing a sexual rebellion in a physical symptom such as vomiting. Or perhaps they will choose a phobia, refusing, for instance, to go out on the street lest they encounter temptation there. Or they may become obsessive as in the remarkable case of Dr. Schreber whose homosexuality took the form of constant preoccupation with thoughts of God's getting into him.[40] These "choices" hardly strike one as the essence of freedom. But one must remember that Freud did not believe there was much freedom to be had, even for the "normal" man. The point is rather that Freud did believe that the id was, in the last analysis, ungovernable; that the bureaucratic structure of civilization rested on a precarious foundation, since its agents were at the mercy of the oppressed; and therefore that the last word lay with the revolution.

§ AUTHORITY AND LIBERTY IN SOCIAL RELATIONS

AS ONE MIGHT EXPECT from his acceptance, in part, of cyclical theories of history, Freud was a believer in the theory of elites: that society was inevitably divided between a small class of leaders and a large class of led. Unlike the Marxists, he did not attribute this to any particular form of property relations; even under communism of goods, he felt that there would still be an elite, and the course of the Bolshevik revolution seemed to him to confirm his claims. His views rested not only on his belief in man's natural laziness, his need to be pushed into reality-work, but also on the theory of the death instinct, that man's aggressiveness would dissolve society into atoms if leadership ties did not hold it together. Thus authority has two independent psychological sources in the modern world: In the first place, it must ration those goods for which men will work; it does not matter so much whether these goods are directly economic commodities, as under capitalism, or are such things as fame and love, under communism. In this respect, the leader merely takes over the function of the parent who, as we have seen, brings children up by withholding love; conditional "love" is always the method of authority. Indeed, Freud attacked progressive education, which he felt would spoil children by giving them unrationed love. In the second place, the authority must keep order; without it, men's passions, envies, greeds, and superstitions would atomize society. With it, these same passions can form the basis of relatively enduring institutions.

These views are remarkably similar to those of the great theorist

---

40. Reference footnote 3; vol. 3, p. 390.

of autocracy, Thomas Hobbes; for he, too, tried to build a social order on a psychology—and one emphasizing men's fears and passions. Just as Freud imagined that society began from a compact of the brothers who had slain their tyrant father and realized that only in union and renunciation could they avoid the war of all against all, so Hobbes saw men in the state of nature as engaged in ceaseless combat, with peace attainable only by renunciation of virtually all individual rights. But there are significant differences, as well as striking comparisons, between Hobbes and Freud. The former, writing in a period of chaotic civil war, believed that men could be persuaded to make this surrender by an appeal to their reason—in Freud's terms, to their ego; that is, to their quite rational fear of being killed since no one man could be—like Freud's mythical primal father—strong enough to stand off all the rest. Hobbes said to men: Look here, is not death the worst thing? Is it not sensible to surrender everything else—freedom of speech, of religion, and so on—to assure plain physical survival? Moreover, if it should turn out that the leader on whose behalf you have surrendered these things does *not* bring peace, then you owe him no obligation; go find a better one.

In other words, Hobbes saw men endangered by their rational self-interest, which led them to aggressive striving to attain and secure the good things of this world. But he also thought men could unite through appeals to this same self-interest—self-preservation being, after all, a rational business for any living thing. And he thought all men equal, not only in the state of nature, but in the possession of this fundament of reason which could lead them to unification in a national state. He distrusted illusion—which he called superstition—because it clouded men's reason and led them to do fanatical things which were not in the interest of self-preservation.

While, like Hobbes, Freud saw aggression as native to man, he saw it as fundamentally an irrational striving rooted in the death instinct. He felt, moreover, that men could not be persuaded to renounce any desire by reason alone; the id is altogether too strong. Most men, that is; for only the elite could learn to live on a plane of sublimation. But the masses, in Freud's view, could be led to renounce aggression only through authority and what today would be called ideology—the cement of emotional ties. Thus the elite, producers of efficacious illusions, could live without these illusions, but not the masses.

While Freud did not publish his *Group Psychology and the Analysis of the Ego*[41] until after the first World War, his belief that the

---

41. Both this book and *Beyond the Pleasure Principle* reflect the impact of the war on Freud.

masses needed to be subjected to the authority of forceful leaders can be traced in his earliest psychological writings. Like Hobbes, he was afraid of anarchy; but he did not live in a period of anarchy, but rather, up until 1914, in one of the most stable and peaceful epochs in Western history. One of his dreams is especially interesting in this respect. It shows his admiration for Szell, the Hungarian parliamentary leader, who knew the arts of "leading men and organizing the masses" and was able to cope with the "anarchy" of the Hungarian delegates.[42] While Freud admired the rebel Garibaldi, who unified Italy, he seems from this dream to have had a typical Austro-German's contempt for the rebellious national minorities within the Hapsburg Monarchy. To one of these minorities, the Jews, Freud himself belonged; but he repeatedly insisted on the need for scapegoats in order to maintain the national solidarity—outgroups and ingroups, in present-day terms. Indeed, notions of racial solidarity run through his work.[43] While Hobbes took the value of the nation for granted, he did not see it as the focus of sentimental ties.

For Hobbes, moreover, the leader had no special emotional qualities—no aura of charisma; he was simply the man who happened to take up the vacuum of power, and he was the leader only so long as he was powerful. Freud, following LeBon, saw the leader as having a quasi-magical influence on the mass. He was attracted to orators—such as Szell and Garibaldi—men who could cast a spell. In his article on the Moses of Michelangelo Freud seems fascinated by charisma, by the physical and psychic strength which emanates from the great man—both the portrayer and the portrayed. So it is with his other historical heroes, such as Hannibal and Napoleon. These are the men who are above illusion, but who create it; above fear, but who inspire it; above loyalty, but who demand it.

All this sounds familiar enough today. But at the turn of the century, it was a far less conventional view. Nietzsche, for whom Freud had profound admiration, stood almost alone. Other elements in Nietzsche's theory are also found in Freud: the attack on reformers, the ridicule of humanitarians,[44] and the contempt for the bewitched masses,[45] who look always for the "happy ending" in their fantasies.[46] Nor, obviously, did Freud much care by what ideology the leader secured the necessary mass submission; late in life, he expresses con-

42. Reference footnote 5; pp. 271, 411.
43. See reference footnote 10; p. 242. Cf. reference footnote 2; p 272. ("In the dream I am surprised at my German Nationalistic feelings").
44. Note, however, that Freud states that he was a member of the Humanitarian Society. Reference footnote 2; p. 240.
45. Reference footnote 10; pp. 194-195.
46. Reference footnote 10; pp. 220-221.

siderable respect even for the Bolsheviks who, he feels, have known how to organize the masses.[47]

This, as will be apparent, is only one side of Freud's view; perhaps it is the more conscious and explicit side. But before turning to the more libertarian themes, it is necessary to see how Freud, in his day-to-day writing and work, treated the powerless groups in his society. This will, I think, afford more insight into his personal authoritarian tendencies than will his writings on leadership. For the latter might, or so one could claim, spring from a realistic judgment of social needs; the former, while less explicit, had a more deep-lying effect on psychoanalysis itself.

§ THE HIERARCHY OF DIFFERENCES

I MENTIONED at the outset that Freud tended to view differences as implying relations of super- and sub-ordination; this, in fact, was my definition of authoritarian thinking. In comparison with man, for example, Freud saw the other animals as a powerless group, a down-trodden class. It is interesting that they never appear in Freud's writings, so to speak, in their own right; they are always the objects of phobias or the stuff of symbols. Where a little 5-year-old boy is afraid of draft horses falling down in the street, Freud cannot believe this could be pity, or any form of human sympathy; it is simply a sexual symbolism.[48] Of course, it might have been that alone, or that plus a special feeling for struggling horses in harness—a frightening sight to a sensitive onlooker. The point is that it seems hardly to have occurred to Freud that one might identify with oppressed and struggling animals, and that what might have been so frightening to Hans was seeing in these huge horses the same struggle that he felt himself engaged in.

Freud's attitude towards the lower classes of human society was actually not very different. Wherever servants, nurses, porters, and so forth, appear in his writings, they are viewed as dubious rather undifferentiated beings, scarcely credited with personality. Freud repeatedly warns parents against the damage that nurses can do to children; they are viewed as seductresses, rather than as persons who might give a middle-class child the love and stimulation withheld by his parents.[49] As one gets glimpses of his own behavior towards the few lower-class people he came in contact with, such as maids and

---

47. Reference footnote 10; p. 247.

48. "Analysis of a Phobia in a Five-Year-Old-Boy"; reference footnote 3; p. 149; but cf. p. 254, and also "Totem and Taboo" (Brill, tr.), in *The Basic Writings of Sigmund Freud;* pp. 906-907.

49. For young men, actresses constitute a similar danger. Reference footnote 2; p. 325.

cabdrivers, one finds a tendency in him to be exploitative, even mean. He spits on the stairs to annoy a particularly neat housekeeper. He drives cabbies too hard. He seeks bargains from shopkeepers. He upbraids the conductor of an express.[50] In all this, he is the nineteenth-century bourgeois gentleman, for whom the lower classes are not really people, scarcely seen as individuals, and not respected.

Another social difference is that between adults and children; and here, too, Freud is partly on the side of the powers-that-be, the grown-ups. He frequently refers to children's questions as a "nuisance";[51] it seldom occurs to him that adults' questions of children—"And how old are you, my little boy?" and, "What are you going to be when you grow up?"—may also be a nuisance. More seriously, he makes the famous charge that children are "polymorphous-perverse"—that is, that their sexual life is not confined to the genital zone. Despite all his qualifications, this seems to me to be the application of adult standards to child behavior. He does not see that our language patterns, to which he was so sensitive in other connections, are adult-oriented; the child is forced into them both as object and subject. Likewise Freud speaks of children as immoderate,[52] lacking the ego and superego controls by which the adult has learned to govern his behavior. In this way, he justifies the authoritative controls which are applied to them. But it is at least an open question whether children are as wanting in moderation as Freud supposed. Just as recent experiments have shown that children, left to themselves, will choose the foods that their particular metabolisms need, there is evidence that they are far from immoderate in satisfying their other desires where they have not already been cramped by adult interference.

"The child's ambition," Freud writes, "is not so much to distinguish himself among his equals as to imitate the big fellows. The relation of the child to the grown-up determines also the comic of degradation, which corresponds to the lowering of the grown-up in the life of the child. Few things can afford the child greater pleasure than when the grown-up lowers himself to its level, disregards his superiority, and plays with the child as its equal. The alleviation which furnishes the child pure pleasure is a debasement. . . ."[53] Does this not sound a bit patronizing? So a white man would talk about Negroes, or a colonial about the "natives." In all these instances, a civilization that is

---

50. Reference footnote 2; p. 269.
51. See, for example, reference footnote 5; p. 796.
52. Reference footnote 5; p. 796. But of course he also regards the adult demands made of children as immoderate. See, for example, "The Sexual Enlightenment of Children," in *Collected Papers* 2:36.
53. Reference footnote 5; p. 796.

different is judged by a kind of unconscious ethnocentrism. And of course a vicious circle is created. For the powerless do tend to imitate the powerful, and to "enjoy" degrading them.

Freud, as I have already noted, wanted "tractable" sons. So, in his psychoanalytic theory, he accused children of not wanting to renounce illicit goals—and emphasized less adults' reluctance to renounce their privileges vis-à-vis this helpless minority; in the same way, Freud viewed the Oedipus complex from the side of the adult who is the focus of the child's rivalry and love—more often than from the side of the child of whom the adult wants greedily to take possession.

That Freud sides with the authorities in this warfare is most sharply shown by his relative lack of indignation against the crimes parents commit on their children, even when those crimes have landed the children in his office. He takes for granted that that is how things are, and while he succors the victims he feels little fury against their oppressors. He never notes that the threat of castration is a more severe punishment than warranted even for the Oedipal crimes which he believes children would like to commit. Even in the most extreme case, when a patient is taken from him by her parents who fear she will recover, he records the fact with only a marginal protest.[54] On the other hand, where he does have some control over an upbringing, as in the famous case of little Hans, he is critical of the mother for "spoiling" the boy, but much less of the prying father who pesters the child with psychoanalytic questions and interpretations from morning to night—a father who, as the report implicitly reveals, had no respect for the child's integrity, privacy, and idiosyncrasy.[55]

The Analyst as an Authority

A further example of Freud's attitude towards the powerless, lies in his treatment of neurotics, a minority, as against the "normal" majority. On one level, Freud consciously accepted the standards and outlook of the normal man and branded the neurotics as weaklings, constitutionally and psychically inadequate. These attitudes find their way into psychoanalytic therapy in Freud's primarily one-way concept of the transference. "Transference" means that the patient transfers to the analyst the constellations of love, hate, and other affects, which developed in his childhood; he treats the analyst, in feeling, as if the latter were his father or another significant figure. The theory, obviously, contains a great deal of truth. And, while Freud

---

54. See Freud, *A General Introduction to Psycho-analysis*, pp. 400-401; and cf. "The Psychogenesis of a Case of Homosexuality in a Woman," in *Collected Papers* 2:202, 206.

55. Reference footnote 48; p. 207.

does deal with the "countertransference," in which the analyst's own resistances get in the way of his work, he does seem to set up an ideal in which only the patient is affected by the patient-analyst relationship, and where the analyst is merely a neutral figure.

But suppose the patient rebels, and refuses to accept the analyst's authority? Freud called this the "resistance," and set himself the methodical task of breaking it down. If a patient expresses a doubt about the content of a dream, Freud is apt to interpret this as a resistance.[56] If a patient is unable to give associations to a dream, Freud will supply the answers from the symbolic dictionary;[57] in other words, Freud, in effect, tells the patient, If you do not come across and reveal the mechanisms which I know to be at work within you, I will find them anyway. Once, he succeeded in producing from a patient the desired sexual key, after saying he would have to discontinue the analysis.[58] Though, theoretically, Freud called "resistance" anything which impeded the analysis, in practice he seems at times to have regarded such resistance as a personal attack: he said, in effect, to his patients, If you oppose me, that is your "resistance," your preferring to remain ill, and, perhaps, you wish to have me fail. In part, Freud thus avoided debate upon the merits of the case. A most striking single example of this outlook appears in the book on dreams. A patient knows Freud's thesis that all dreams are wish-fulfillments. Then she dreams of something so disagreeable—spending the summer with her mother-in-law—that it cannot be a wish-fulfillment, even in the most far-fetched interpretation. Freud replies that the patient wished to prove *"that I should be wrong, and this wish the dream showed her as fulfilled."*[59]

Though Freud insisted that the analyst should counsel and direct the patient as little as possible, he seems to have been not entirely aware of the degree of authority he exercised. In one of his earlier cases, he reports that he "expected her [the patient] to accept a solution which did not seem acceptable to her";[60] in the dream-associations he accuses her of showing him up by not getting well and responds by telling her that her symptoms are her own fault,[61] that he would prefer to have a more "docile" patient.[62] And, like God, there are no secrets from him; few things so engaged his efforts as attempts

---

56. For example, reference footnote 2; p. 474.
57. For example, reference footnote 2; p. 381.
58. Reference footnote 2; p. 334.
59. Reference footnote 2; p. 229.
60. Reference footnote 2; p. 195.
61. Reference footnote 2; pp. 196-197.
62. Reference footnote 2; p. 199.

of patients to hide something—this was "resistance" with a vengeance.[63] He prided himself that they could seldom, if ever, succeed. In this he had the advantage of a "phonographic memory";[64] if a patient got fuzzy about a dream, Freud could always catch him up.[65] Moreover, since not even the slightest error escaped him,[66] he must have given patients the feeling that they could not get away with anything.

This same congeries of attitudes towards the powerless—towards children, women, neurotics—is manifested towards the intellectual problems with which Freud was concerned; one might view this as sadism towards the (powerless) material of theory. Freud himself gives us, as one of his favorite quotations, a similar comparison which was once made by Lassalle:

> A man like myself who, as I explained to you, had devoted his whole life to the motto *Die Wissenschaft und die Arbeiter* (Science and the Workingman), would receive the same impression from a condemnation which in the course of events confronts him *as would the chemist, absorbed in his scientific experiments, from the cracking of a retort. With a slight knitting of his brow at the resistance of the material, he would, as soon as the disturbance was quieted, calmly continue his labor and investigations.*[67]

Freud's intellectual powers seem to have been excited by that very "resistance of the material," whether the "material" was the reception of his theories at the hands of the Vienna profession, the "resistance" of a patient in analysis, or the intractability of facts which he wished to order into a theoretical framework. "How many seemingly absurd dreams have we not forced to give up their sense!"[68] Freud says of himself with pride. And elsewhere he refers to a type of dream which "stubbornly refuses to surrender its meaning."[69] In such a case, he advises the analyst to turn the inexplicable symbol into its opposite— say exchange night for day, or wet for dry—a technique that sometimes led him to great discoveries and sometimes simply to victory over a stubborn fact. One might even suppose that Freud's great admiration for Moses, Hannibal, Michelangelo, and others, may have sprung in part from his identification with the effort to shape and hew the hardest materials, physical or human.

---

63. See, however, the benevolent attitude towards patients' denials Freud takes in "Constructions in Analysis" in *Collected Papers* 5:358.

64. Reference footnote 10; p. ix.

65. Reference footnote 2; pp. 472-473.

66. Cf. "Psychopathology of Everyday Life" (Brill, tr.), in *The Basic Writings of Sigmund Freud*.

67. Reference footnote 5; p. 682.

68. Reference footnote 4; p. 65.

69. Reference footnote 2; p. 352.

Many illustrations could be given of this effort of Freud's to fit everything into a comprehensive system, even at the cost of distorting. When he deals, for instance, with dreams, he establishes that they are all wish fulfillments—and if, later on, a dream turns up which does not seem to fit this system, Freud can become very ingenious in nevertheless finding a wish. When he deals with Biblical history, as in *Moses and Monotheism*, his arbitrariness in selecting as true those narratives which fit, and rejecting as "tendentious" those which do not, strikes me as a somewhat aggressive handling of the data.

Moreover Freud was particularly attracted by anything which savored of mystery or challenged his powers of unmasking.[70] He was fascinated by the uncanny, by the dark and secret springs of life. But he was not awed; on the contrary, he responded by attack, by an insistence on penetrating the secret, coming to the heart of the artichoke.[71] The sign "Keep Out" has attracted many great thinkers, some of them Jews and other "marginal men" for whom exclusion touched a sensitive spot. But here we see that the material on which a thinker works is only apparently powerless; though it cannot talk back, it "resists," and it is "protected" by all the categories of convention. Sometimes it seems as if a certain tendency to overpower is necessary for the creation of any radically new intellectual system; like Lassalle, the pioneer must be as deaf to the objections as the chemist to the cracking of his retort. Yet it is also this refusal to "listen" to the material which results in the distortions and overstatement of such a system.

§ FREUD AS PROMETHEUS

BUT ALL THIS is only one aspect of Freud's view. I have stressed this aspect because, for one thing, this hierarchical, reactionary side of Freud is just what attracts a number of contemporary intellectuals to him. Freud fits in with the current vogue of the "tough guy." And it is understandable that his tendency towards dogmatism should be admired by people who today force themselves to sound dogmatic even though they lack Freud's real self-confidence. However, in seizing upon the dogmatist in Freud, and upon the power-worshiper, they actually disregard his much more complicated view of things. In the remaining pages, I want to take up some of those themes in Freud that are liberating and equalitarian, and it will be seen, I think, that these themes are interwoven with their opposites. It is just such textures of ambivalence that Freud taught us to unravel.

---

70. Speaking of the occult, Freud writes that "prohibitions will not stifle men's interest in an alleged mysterious world." *The Question of Lay Analysis*, p. 104.

71. See the "Dream of the Botanical Monograph"; reference footnote 2; p. 243.

Liberating Underprivileged Reality

I have already indicated that another way of looking at the elements of sadism in Freud's handling of data is to see them as a source of the energy and drive needed to liberate those aspects of reality that convention had submerged or hidden. And it cannot fail to strike us that the same man who intransigently sought to organize the material of experience into the shapes of his theoretical constructions also "listened" to that material with a rare attentiveness and respect. And what he listened to particularly were the little things—the unnoticed words, gestures, silences, and so on—which previous thinkers had considered too trivial for notice. And not only little things but despised things too: "absurd" dreams, "debasing" perversions, "infantile" memories. Freud admitted them all into the structure of his thought and gave them all the credit of having meaning. Since, for Freud, these secret things are also the basic, the *Ursache*, they are even credited with an eminence over the more "powerful" and accepted data of experience. In other words, not only was no fact too humble to be lifted into the theoretical structure, but it might easily find itself outranking the more obvious and insistent facts which had been stressed by earlier thinkers.

Liberating Underprivileged Illness

It is the same with Freud's treatment of neurotics. Before his time, neurotics had generally been regarded as malingerers in whom no organic symptom could be found; or their ailment was credited to bad heredity. Instead, Freud insisted that psychic injuries ranked at least equally with the more obvious physical ones, were entitled to as much consideration, and were subject to the same causality. Everyone knows with what abuses the insane were treated before Freud's time, and how they are treated even today; the most innocent treatment for neurotics was to give them placebos, the harmless pills which swell the doctors' income. On the whole, medicine seemed to rank highest those specialists, such as surgeons, and eye, ear, nose, and throat men, who had the least close contact with the patient as a human being. And by and large when Freud started in psychiatric practice, only the hypnotists attempted to establish contact with the mentally ill; Freud soon rebelled against the authoritarianism of these men, with their inflexible "suggestions." He chose instead the far more respectful technique of "free" association. By this, he hoped to be able to listen to the voice of the id, freed from the supervision of the ego and superego, as well as from the surging noises of the external world.

Thanks to Freud, the powerless and despised neurotic finds himself, in the analytic situation, in a new relationship. Instead of being cursed out of the doctor's office with an accusation of malingering, or breezed out with a "why don't you just relax," or gentled out with a prescription for placebos, his every "thoughtless" word and act is taken with the utmost seriousness, and for a length of time—often years—unknown in any analogous professional relation. He can "make" the analyst listen to his stream of consciousness, his outcries, his silences, subject only to the injunction of sincerity, of keeping nothing back. But even this injunction bespeaks respect: not only the obvious respect for confidences, but the belief that what the patient seeks to hide is, after all, a human act or thought; and that, fundamentally, he has no thought or experience which cannot be matched among the dominant, the so-called normal.

Liberating Women and Children from Suffocating Piety

While in Freud's day the typical note in the treatment of the neurotic was brutality, the typical note in the treatment of women and children was sentimentality. In both cases, the powerless were treated with contempt; but in the second case the contempt, though it could be brutal enough, was veiled by hypocrisy and the assignment of angelic virtues to the group in question. Thus, Victorian middle-class womanhood—like the Southern white woman of today's romance—was put on a pedestal compounded of chastity, pity, and pretense. In showing up the falsity of this picture, Freud, despite acceptance of antifeminine bias, did much to put women in the same class with men. In the first place, his concept of bisexuality meant that women and men had come from the same original format—rather than from a male, as in the Adam and Eve myth; moreover, in the life of each sex, there existed elements from the other sex, one source of homosexual ties. In the second place, though Freud stressed the differences between the erotic and workaday roles of men and women, these after all are smaller than the similarities: both are subject on the whole to the same ontogenetic as well as phylogenetic destiny; both have the same internal structure of ego, superego, id; both may fall into the same characterological formations—both may fall ill of hysteria.

By similar leveling measures, Freud reduced the gap between the upper and lower classes of society. For him, the king was naked—with the ur-nakedness common to all mankind.[72] All women, of high and low degree, lost control of themselves in their destined labor of

---

72. See reference footnote 2; pp. 293-296.

childbirth. Freud liked to tell the story of the obstetrician who played cards with a baron while the baroness was in confinement. When the latter called out, "Ah, mon Dieu, que je souffre," the husband jumped up, but the doctor said, "That's nothing; let us play on." Later she called, "My God, my God, what pains," but still the doctor said it was not yet time to go in. "At last, there rang from the adjacent room the unmistakable cry, 'A-a-a-ai-e-e-e-e-e-E-E!' The physician quickly threw down the cards and said, 'Now it's time.' "[73]

Likewise, in rescuing children from sentimentality, Freud in one sense put them on the same footing with adults. As I have pointed out, he credited them with vices, with rebellion, with lust and hate and murderous intent. His ur-thinking made every adult at heart a child, by the very process of debasement he himself described as central to the process of wit. Even the first difference—the one between animals and men—was broken down in the pattern of Freud's thought; he viewed men as, at bottom, animals and found the source of their most human traits in the sexual instincts which they share with the mammalian phylum.[74]

Furthermore, whatever markedly ambivalent deference Freud paid to the temporal authorities of his day—the upper classes, the males, the distinguished—he retained more than most men the obedience of the true scientist to the truth and to the scientific tradition which the Renaissance revived and glorified. While he was forced against his will to quarrel with scientists, he never broke faith with Science. The things he rendered unto Caesar are trivial coin in comparison with the devotion he rendered to his fierce, yet fundamentally humane and passionately secular deity of Science.

Thus, we may compare his taking the side of the adult against the child in some of his views, such as the Oedipus complex, with his protest against adults who lied to their children. He realized quite clearly that children who can see through their parents' lies will become free of the parents, and he wrote that children who reject the stork fable begin their "psychic independence . . . from this act of disbelief. . . ."[75] Even more strongly, he denounced the "sadly antiquated" *patria potestas* which survives in modern society: "Even in our own middle-class families the father commonly fosters the growth

73. Reference footnote 5; p. 681.

74. Cf. Fenichel, *The Psychoanalytic Theory of Neurosis*, p. 213. "The child is not as arrogant as the adult person, who tries to believe in a fundamental difference between human beings and animals."

75. Reference footnote 4; p. 47.

of the germ of hatred which is naturally inherent in the paternal relation, by refusing to allow the son to be a free agent or by denying
him the means of becoming so."[76] And the mother, too, he added,
circumscribes her daughter when the latter's "budding beauty" reminds the envious parent "that for her the time has come to renounce
sexual claims."[77] More searching still is Freud's awareness that the
father's strictness evokes the child's criticism and the latter's close
awareness of every weakness in the authority, but that this criticism
is repressed and remains unconscious.[78] No truer statement as to the
operation of authority has ever been written than this: that criticism
is called into being by interest and need, and that the findings are then
repressed and remain operative in the unconscious mind. Ambivalence
towards the father, one may assume, is the inevitable outcome of this
process, with conscious love and admiration acting as a cover for
unconscious criticism and hate. Of this ambivalence, Freud's own attitude, which I have just reviewed, is an example; the phrases just
now quoted hardly spring from an unequivocal worshiper of authority.

As one would expect, Freud's reported dreams indicate his ambivalence towards his own parents. He reports, without apparent indignation, his mother's deceiving him, her strict middle-class restraints.[79] But certain dreams are polemics against his father; Freud
interprets these either to mean that the manifest father represents
some other authority—when it could more easily refer both to the
father and to the other authority—or by accusing himself, for example, of sexual curiosity, thus putting his father in the right.[80] Nevertheless, the dreams stand as proof that Freud rebelled against his
father, but, like so many sons, did not carry the rebellion through.[81]

Promethean and constricting elements seem to me similarly intertwined in the thought and heritage of many great thinkers throughout history, whether one thinks of Confucius or of Marx, of Plato
or of St. Simon. To be born is to be mortgaged; to live is to be
crippled; to be socialized is to be limited as well as freed. And, as
violent social revolutions have their Thermidors, so do violently original social thinkers look both forward and back. However, such an
attempt at generalization will be misleading if it obscures the profound differences among thinkers in the degree to which they blend

76. Reference footnote 2; pp. 303-304.
77. Reference footnote 2; p. 304.
78. Reference footnote 2; p. 416.
79. Reference footnote 2; pp. 266-267.
80. Reference footnote 2; pp. 416, 433. Cf. also the dream on p 411.
81. Cf. "A Disturbance of Memory on the Acropolis," in *Collected Papers*
5:302, 311-312.

the prejudices of their class and age with means of escaping from those prejudices. Moreover, elements in a thinker which may have been peripheral in his own time may turn out to be decisive in his reception by later ages.

One can already see in Freud's case the divergent streams of social philosophy that trace their origins, more or less justly, to his work. I have spoken of the fashion among certain intellectuals to use Freud—along with Dostoevsky, Kierkegaard, and others—as a spokesman of man's irrationality, his need for mystery and authority. Among some psychiatrists, Freud's stress on reality-orientation can be read as justifying therapies aiming to adjust the patient to society as given, whether reality happens to be deserving of such sacrifice or not. And among a large lay public, diluted Freudian interpretations are used by people to evaporate their own hostility; and to explain others' hostility to oppressive life-conditions as simple transfers of Oedipal rivalry to the social scene—or things of the same sort. There is a side of Freud that warrants these abuses of his contributions, just as there is a side of Marx that cannot completely disavow the atrocities committed in his name.

For Freud did share, in the ways which I have tried to trace, many attitudes which, in his epoch and in his class, were used to establish and support differences of value and rank. On one level, he sided with the authority and looked at the powerless through authority's eyes. But on another, and more characteristic level, he rebelled against authority. As in many such rebellions, his tactic was not to exalt the underdog but to degrade the top dog. "You are all the same," he seems to be saying, "princes and paupers, gentlemen and pimps, philosophers and babies." And, just as a lord has no secrets from his valet, so the illustrious could not dazzle Freud's eyes; in the very highest attainments of man—his art, his speculation, his juridical institutions—Freud found the cloven hoof of sex. As on the western plains the Colt revolver was called "Old Equalizer," so Freud saw the legacy each man carried on his person as the fundamental equalizer of the race.

23. The Themes of Heroism and Weakness in the Structure of Freud's Thought

Students of intellectual history tend to exaggerate, so it seems to me, the importance in contemporary life of the ideas whose derivations they trace. Since they are themselves intellectuals, for whom ideas are very important, they fall prey to the error of the specialist who sees the world from the angle of his own routines. Thus, one can find Nazism blamed on a congeries of alleged fathers from Machiavelli to Nietzsche, from Gobineau to Spengler or Carl Schmitt. Likewise, in much current discourse, William James and John Dewey are treated as the founts of all that is alleged to be shallow, manipulative, and complacent in American life. A whole school of critics, led by Van Wyck Brooks, blamed on the debunking writers of the twenties the cynicism and pacifism which they thought prevalent in the pre-World War II era. In this fashion, people whose trade is words cry their own wares even in the very act of claiming to be overwhelmed by the far more powerful words of their chosen enemies.

Obviously, it would be absurd to rush to the opposite extreme and to contend that words and ideas have only negligible influence on the stream of events. Indeed, a just appraisal in a concrete social context is always exceedingly difficult, as are efforts to isolate *any* single item in a cultural complex. We know well enough that institutions often come close to reversing their founders' intentions: that Christ was not a Christian, Marx not a Marxist (let alone a Stalinist), Dewey not a school principal in the Teachers College patronage network. And where a man's thought and action do not lead to creation of a new institution but mingle in a general climate of opinion, the tracing of the consequences of his work is even more a shadowy and impalpable task: no Mendelian law governs the unembodied transmission of ideas. Even when men acknowledge indebtedness, what does that prove? They often say they owe it all to their mothers. We are, I think, quite far from even knowing how to begin the job of evaluating the weight of any single person's ideas in the historical process. Conceivably, the sort of studies now undertaken by social psychologists concerning the impact of the mass media—radio, print, and film—on people will give us some clues as to the influence and social distribution of particular words and images.

Yet when all this is granted, it remains plausible to say that Freud has had tremendous impact on our popular culture. As radioactive tracers allow us to follow chemical substances in the physiologist's laboratory, so the verbal tags adopted by Freud and his followers give us some way of tracing the rapidity of the diffusion of his inventions. The number of psychoanalysts even today is a mere handful—in America, it would seem, less than 500—fewer than the number of "missionaries" who spread Marxist gospel as members of the International Workingmen's Association in the 1850's and 60's. And while the devotion, diligence, and productiveness of these analysts—who fill journals while treating patients and training the young—could scarcely be excelled by any band of missionaries, these qualities, without the aid of a powerful ideology, would not have given them their present place in popular discourse.[1]

It would be valuable to make a comparative study in detail, and to see how, in different countries and different social strata, Freud's thought has been received and modified, used and abused. Plainly, the process that Lasswell, with reference to political ideologies, termed "restriction by partial incorporation"[2] has also occurred with Freud. One would expect this process to occur when students in their courses read some watered-down or textbook version, but this process even occurs when students read Freud in his own words. For the revolu-

---

1. Freud, in one of his moments of sober self-judgment—at other times, as I shall try to show, he was overmodest—ranked his contribution alongside those of Copernicus and Darwin: he saw it as reducing man's stature and self-pride. So he found it easy enough to explain why he had enemies, and could defend himself by explaining the "resistance" he met with. But he made less, at least in his published work, of the fact that after 1902 or so he attracted friends and followers—at a time when it still cost something to be a friend of Freud—and that before the Second World War his thought had spread to all industrialized or even semi-industrialized lands. To be sure, in "The Future Prospects of Psychoanalytic Therapy," he allowed himself to speculate, as early as 1910, on the possibility that analytic thought would permeate education, would be made available to the poor, and would finally make therapy unnecessary by the progress of what would today be called preventive mental hygiene. (*Collected Papers* 2:285; London, Hogarth Press, 1925.) But he seems not to have realized that men were and would be attracted to his work, not only because it was socially useful, but because it was adventurous—that men would, in effect, trade their vanity for the pleasures of disinterested discovery and understanding. Indeed, it is striking that a number of the ideologies which are popular today, such as Marxism and Freudianism, cannot adequately explain the appeal they have for many of their devotees. A good many people embrace Marxism, for instance, in order to make sense of the world, or to contribute to it, and not only because of class consciousness; people embrace psychoanalytic thinking because it adds to the interest they find in observing human beings, and not only because of such motives as narcissism.

2. Harold D. Lasswell, *World Politics and Personal Insecurity*, p. 6.

tionary concepts of Freud can no longer have the same impact when they have their teeth drawn by the very nature of most classroom situations—when, moreover, students already come with some familiarity with major themes: the unconscious, childhood sexuality, the importance of dreams, slips and errors, and so on. But it follows from this that it makes little sense to blame Freud for the untoward consequences of some aspects of his thought as it is currently modified and received —if we find, for instance, "neurotic" used as a term of apology for the self and of vicious denigration against others. That certain elements in Freud's view of life were narrow, class-biased, and reactionary is one of the points made in the preceding two papers and in this one. But this must not blind us to the fact that Freud expressed his views at a time when, in many quarters, democratic sentiments were powerful and when the "common man" was, in America especially, given a great deal of lip service. His opposition to those dominant trends, even when the latter happened to be progressive, was stimulating and productive; and this is not altered by the fact that today some of his views on work, on authority, on heroism, may no longer liberate thought but, in the present context of Freud's reception, may confine it.

It is, then, up to each generation to read Freud as if it were for the first time, much as men in the sixteenth and seventeenth centuries sought—and even today such men as Schweitzer and Buber still seek —to approach the Bible anew. I would like to succeed in sending at least some of the readers of these articles back to Freud to see whether the themes I trace in his work actually exist and, if so, whether they can be stated in a more fundamental and searching way. By such ever-renewed readings, I hope that Freud can be saved from the fate of "partial incorporation," and that his power to challenge, inspire, and perplex can be retained. If so, we need worry less about tendencies to put his work to manipulative uses and his authority behind socially regressive ideologies.

In depicting Freud's view of human nature and social organization in the previous articles, I have already touched on Freud's ideal of human life—what he admired in people and, conversely, what he despised. Indeed, such ideals, explicit or implicit, are ordinarily part of that image of human nature from which everyone makes judgments as to the meaning of life and the value of, and possibilities for, social relations. Here I want to examine Freud's ideal and its counterimage of weakness in more detail.

Note that I have taken heroism and weakness—not heroism and villainy—to be polar opposites in Freud's view. Such a polarity ostensibly eliminates ethical considerations. It accompanies a view which sees men as divided into a strong elite and a numerous but vacillating mass. But here again one finds ambivalence in Freud's outlook. For while he shared with thinkers such as Nietzsche and Carlyle elements of an elitist position, he also emphasized, as I have indicated before, the fundamental similarity of all men, their obedience to the same instinctual laws and infantile survivals.

§ PORTRAIT OF A HERO

FREUD'S IDEAL MAN is harmonious within and successful without. He has conflicts and meets obstacles but they are all in the external world. Out of polymorphous infantile sexualities he has developed a definite gential supremacy; the hero neither lingers at the childhood way-stations of sex nor returns regressively to them. His potency is unproblematical and his choice among sexual objects is unrestricted by fetish or fixation. Freud, in commenting on a statement by Leonardo that "great love springs from great knowledge of the beloved object," declares that people in love "are guided by emotional motives which have nothing to do with cognition; and their consequences are rather weakened by thought and reflection."[3] In this light, "genital maturity" means for Freud lesser rather than greater complexity and differentiation of emotions. But one must qualify this by observing that such maturity involves a man's ability to make love to women of the same social class and refinement as his mother and sister; he remains immature so long as, hounded by the incest taboo, he can let himself go only with women whom he socially despises— that is, who do not forcibly remind him of the forbidden objects of his childhood. By implication, therefore, mature love involves more than mere ability to secure genital heterosexual release.[4]

Nevertheless, the course of the hero's sexual gratification, as one senses it from Freud's writings, takes the shortest line between the unconscious wish and the conscious gratification; there is no occasion for the procrastination of daydreaming nor, indeed, for the 'waste' of

---

3. Freud, *Leonardo da Vinci*, p. 40.

4. One must remember, moreover, that more was involved in such ability in the days before the advent of easy and reliable contraceptives and of easy and reliable women who were not courtesans. While at one point Freud pleads for the spread of contraceptive knowledge among married couples ("Sexuality in the Aetiology of the Neuroses," in *Collected Papers* 1:237-239), this is not inconsistent with his statement in which he speaks of nongenital forms of sexuality: "ethically they are reprehensible, for they degrade the love-relationship of two human beings from being a serious matter to an otiose diversion, attended neither by risk nor by spiritual participation." " 'Civilized' Sexual Morality and Modern Nervousness," in *Collected Papers* 2:95.

dream-stimulated emissions.[5] There is none of "the tendency to reflection and delay" that Freud noted in Leonardo's art.[6] Freud attributed a similarly uncomplicated quality to the dreams of the normal person. "Indeed," he writes, "the natural dreams of healthy persons often contain a much simpler, more transparent, and more characteristic symbolism than those of neurotics, which, owing to the greater strictness of the censorship and the more extensive dream-distortion resulting therefrom, are frequently troubled and obscured, and are therefore more difficult to translate."[7]

The hero, viewed economically, follows, without scruple, without hesitation, without doubt, the hedonistic calculus in his sexual life. Freud declares:

> The man who in consequence of his unyielding nature cannot comply with the required suppression of his instincts, becomes a criminal, an outlaw, unless his social position or striking abilities enable him to hold his own as a great man, a 'hero.'[8]

Moreover, the hero is a person of great energy potential: "psychic greatness like somatic greatness is exhibited by means of an increased expenditure."[9] Viewed topologically, this pattern means that the ego of the hero is in unquestioned command, and that conflict between the conscious and unconscious levels of the personality is at a minimum. As the wise statesman never veers too far from the demands of the mob he leads, but controls and channels them in the very process of carrying them out, so the hero's ego is in the closest touch with the wishes of the id, of which it is in one sense a most effective "public servant."[10]

Plainly, all this does not mean that the hero is as completely free of internal superego restraints as he is unintimidated by society's efforts at repression. While his ego does not cringe before an internalized father-imago, the superego functions to provide an ideal to which the narcissistic elements in the personality can aspire and to

---

5. The dreamer, Freud writes, "thinks in his sleep: 'I don't want to continue this dream and exhaust myself by an emission; I would rather save it for a real situation.'" "The Interpretation of Dreams" (Brill, tr.), in *The Basic Writings of Sigmund Freud*, p. 514.

6. Reference footnote 3; p. 116.

7. Reference footnote 5; pp. 381-382.

8. *Collected Papers* 2:82.

9. Freud, "Wit and Its Relation to the Unconscious" (Brill, tr.), *The Basic Writings of Sigmund Freud*; p. 777.

10. Even so, Freud pointed out that "the subjection of the *Ucs.* by the *Pcs.* is not thorough-going even in perfect psychic health; the extent of this suppression indicates the degree of our psychic normality." Reference footnote 5; p. 520. See also Freud, *The Ego and the Id*, pp. 81-83.

demand a high level of performance in line with that ideal. The restraints so imposed may perhaps be compared to the concept of
"noblesse oblige." For they are voluntarily accepted—even though
their original imposition may have been far from voluntary—as a
nobleman's code is supposed to be, rather than submitted to through
the operation of the bureaucratic internal machinery based on fear
of castration, of God, of public opinion. The hero has a certain
Spartan, uncomplaining attitude towards life, and a sportsmanlike adherence to the rules of good breeding. Freud's heroes are at farthest
remove from the spoiled Bohemian attitudes, seemingly free of
superego and of inhibition, which Freud detested.[11]

Nevertheless, there is, I feel, something romantic and parochial
in Freud's image of the ideal type of man as one who goes directly
at what he wants, including sexual objects, without getting lost in
the toils and discontents of thought.[12]

With a different outlook, one might describe neurotics as people
for whom life is insufficiently complicated; they over-simplify it by
seeing new events within the stereotype of old ones; they find nothing new under the sun. The ideal of a mentally healthy person would
then be someone able to differentiate his experience in every field; to
see other people, for example, in terms of subtle changes in them so
that they are never the *same* people. Such a person would make only
minimal use of the categories and conventions which culture provides
in order often to simplify life to the point of bareness.

We may make the comparison more concrete by another glance
at Freud's picture of genital love. For him, "two on an island" was
the ideal; he wrote in *Civilization and Its Discontents* that a pair of
lovers needed no one else to complete their happiness but wished to
withdraw their libido from the task of building civilization.[13] This is
an adolescent moviegoer's dream of love, but not something which
mature lovers actually seek: love rather leads them to widen and
complicate their dealings with other people, with art, and with other
civilized matters. In those cultures, whether 'civilized' or 'primitive,'
where human relations are marked by subtlety of feeling, sexual love
can become filled with overtones. Moreover, one may today observe,
among the groups where Victorian morality has waned, that love
can become even more complex and, if you please, more 'intellectual,'

---

11. Cf. his well-known remark that "revolutionary children are not desirable
from any point of view." *A New Series of Introductory Lectures on Psychoanalysis*, p. 206.

12. There is a similar note in Elton Mayo's critique, based on Janet, of "obsessive thinking" in modern industrial society. See, for example, Mayo, *The
Human Problems of an Industrial Civilization*.

13. Freud, *Civilization and Its Discontents*, p. 80.

precisely because it lacks the artificial spur of taboos and inhibitions.[14] Contrary to what many think, romantic love does not depend on delayed gratification but on gratification and mutuality which occur on many levels of the love relationship. Indeed, as Simone de Beauvoir has so well observed in *Le Deuxième Sexe*, such love can grow only when women are emancipated, when they no longer, as in Freud's day, have "only the choice between unappeased desire, infidelity, or neurosis."[15]

For other elements in Freud's picture of the hero, one may turn to his two loving studies of Moses. In his essay on "The Moses of Michelangelo,"[16] Freud describes the hero admiringly—his great frame and impressive beard, his noble brow and piercing, inscrutable glance, his fiery anger and his equally powerful restraint. In *Moses and Monotheism*,[17] Freud pays more attention to the hero's intellectual than to his physical qualities. The hero is shown to be a proud Egyptian nobleman, his monotheism the product of the kingly temper of Ikhnaton, which brooked no illusions and required no orgies of belief. This Egyptian Moses is undeterred by the resistance of the image-worshiping masses; he is unafraid of the fate of pioneers. This intransigence, so similar to his own, appeals to Freud. Likewise, as he indicates obliquely in his book on dreams, Freud admires "those powerful personalities who, by their sheer force of intellect and their fiery eloquence, ruled" the course of the French Revolution; and he also admired the eloquence and virility of Garibaldi.[18]

Views of this sort, largely implicit in Freud's pre-World War I writings, became of course much more explicit in his *Group Psychology and the Analysis of the Ego*, where he writes:

... from the first there were two kinds of psychologies, that of the individual members of the group and that of the father, chief, or leader. The members of the group were subject to ties just as we see them to-day, but the father of the primal horde was free. His intellectual acts were strong and independent even in isolation, and his will needed no reinforcement from others. . . .

---

14. Cf. Freud's remark that "the view may also be accepted that the differentiation of individual character, now so much in evidence, only becomes possible with sexual restraint." *Collected Papers* 2:91. It depends, of course, on what one means by "restraint."

15. *Collected Papers* 2:93. Since writing the foregoing, I have been glad to find the searching article by Edith Weigert, "Existentialism and Its Relations to Psychotherapy," in PSYCHIATRY (1949) 12:399-412, which takes much the same attitude as the text.

16. *Collected Papers* 4:257.

17. Freud, *Moses and Monotheism*.

18. See reference footnote 5; pp. 461, 410-411.

He, at the very beginning of the history of mankind, was the *Superman* whom Nietzsche only expected from the future. Even to-day the members of a group stand in need of the illusion that they are equally and justly loved by their leader; but the leader himself need love no one else, he may be of a masterly nature, narcissistic, but self-confident and independent.[19]

Evidently, there is a solipsistic tendency in this Freudian hero. In his contempt, in the style of his idealism, in his egocentric insistence on having his way, he reminds one of certain Hollywood types, or of the Hero Roark in Ayn Rand's best-selling novel, *The Fountainhead*, which was later made into a movie. This hero is tall, dark, handsome, and young.[20] But it would be manifestly unfair to push the comparison with Hollywood too far. Freud's hero is no rich playboy; his orientation is entirely toward reality, toward serious tasks in this world. He is in fact quite grown up; like Leonardo in his later years, he has attained "the resignation of the man who subjects himself to the 'Aváyxn, to the laws of nature, and expects no alleviation from the kindness or grace of God."[21] He has faced the fact that "dark, unfeeling and unloving powers determine human destiny," or, again, that "the world is not a nursery."[22] In other words, the hero is one who is able to live without illusions—but this includes an end to illusions about the self, an end to vain regrets, wasteful mourning,[23] feminine pity, and sentimentality.[24]

---

19. Freud, *Group Psychology and the Analysis of the Ego*, pp. 92-93. It is interesting to note, in this connection, one of the charges that Freud brings against the United States; namely, that in this country "leading personalities fail to acquire the significance that should fall to them in the process of group-formation." Reference footnote 13; p. 93. In other words, America in Freud's eyes lacked dominating leaders, through identification with whom the masses could be bound to one another and to the system.

20. Several of Freud's dreams or dream-associations refer to his feeling of aging. Reference footnote 5; p. 220 (his black beard turning color); p. 447 (growing grey); p. 446 (youth as a time of many loves).

21. Reference footnote 3; p. 105.

22. Reference footnote 11; pp. 229, 230. Perhaps it should be added that, in Freud's view, the nursery becomes very like the world.

23. Freud again and again returned to the problem of mourning and sought to explain its "wastefulness" in terms of mental economics. See, for example, "Mourning and Melancholia," in *Collected Papers* 4:152. It is typical of his outlook that he was baffled whenever men seemed to extend themselves, whether in grief, in love, or in work, without the pressure of apparently overwhelming need. With a different outlook, one would find a problem in an inability to mourn, as in affectlessness generally.

24. Finding that Leonardo was "kind and considerate" to his young male disciples, Freud regards this as a correlate of his homosexuality. (Reference footnote 3; p. 77.) Freud also notes his "exaggerated sympathy for animals" (pp. 114, 36). He may, of course, be right with regard to Leonardo; my point is that he seems to accept, though not without qualification, conventional definitions of masculinity.

This stern reality-orientation of the hero includes the related element of steadiness and practicality in the pursuit of goals. Subject to "storming passions of the soul-stirring and consuming kind"[25] though he may be, he is nonetheless able to hold his fire, even to sublimate if need be. While he seeks, by the exercise of his "manly creative power,"[26] to change the course of the world, he faces the delays and frustrations of his self-appointed task with stoicism. Freud admired the insouciance in the face of death of aristocrats in the French Revolution,[27] or indeed of any criminal who could go to the gallows with a laugh.[28]

But to enter Freud's Valhalla it is not enough to be brave; one must also succeed. Sexual achievement is, in fact, the sign of success as of maturity. Freud writes:

A man who has shown determination in possessing himself of his love-object has our confidence in his success in regard to other aims as well. On the other hand, a man who abstains, for whatever reasons, from satisfying his strong sexual instinct, will also assume a conciliatory and resigned attitude in other paths of life, rather than a powerfully active one.[29]

Freud agrees with those critics of Leonardo, the homosexual, who object that the latter did not finish all the work he started; and he comments on Leonardo's "lack of ability to adjust himself to actual conditions."[30] And yet in writing about Leonardo, Freud states that he himself "succumbed to the attraction which emanated from this great and mysterious man, in whose being one seems to sense forceful and impelling passions, which nevertheless evince themselves in a remarkably subdued manner."[31] There are, moreover, other heroes of

---

To be sure, Freud criticizes German Army leadership in the First World War as too harsh, resulting in a failure to create sufficient libidinal ties between officers and men, hence among the men *inter se;* but this seems really to be a critique not of harshness as such, but of unskilful manipulation of men. Reference footnote 19; p. 44, n. 1.

25. A phrase Freud uses in explaining why the over-ratiocinative Leonardo missed those loves and hates that "others experience [as] the best part of their lives. . . ." Reference footnote 3; p. 43.

26. Freud, reference footnote 3; p. 115.

27. Cf. reference footnote 5; p. 461.

28. Cf. reference footnote 9; p. 798.

29. *Collected Papers* 2:93-94. Freud goes on in the same passage to point out that since women are intimidated from sexual curiosity, they are likewise rendered submissive in other spheres of life: "the undoubted fact of the intellectual inferiority of so many women can be traced to that inhibition of thought necessitated by sexual suppression." Such observations on Freud's part must be taken as a counterpoise to what has been said earlier about the exclusively masculine qualities of the hero.

30. Reference footnote 3; pp. 101, 116.

31. Reference footnote 3; pp. 117-118. Cf. his reference to "the magic of his [Charcot's] aspect and his voice," in "Charcot," *Collected Papers* 1:15.

Freud who were in the long run unsuccessful; he admired Hannibal and Ikhnaton. Thus, plainly enough, the men whom Freud looked up to are not cast in a single stereotype. They must leave a mark on the world, but there are different types of marks which count.

Perhaps the most important evidence of this is Freud's lifelong reverence for "the immortal Goethe."[32] He writes that his decision to become a medical student came about through reading, at 17, Goethe's essay on Nature;[33] and quotations from Goethe, meant to illustrate the latter's psychological wisdom, are scattered throughout his writings. Moreover, with his own desire "to fathom with coldest reflection the deepest secret,"[34] he was preoccupied with the "secret" of Goethe's genius, as with that of Leonardo and of other artists. In "A Childhood Recollection from *'Dichtung und Warheit'* " Freud traced the early source of "that victorious feeling, that confidence in ultimate success, which not seldom brings actual success with it"[35] —that smiling destiny which Freud felt he himself perhaps lacked.

While Freud, not unlike Goethe, took for his subject matter all of human life and history, and many of the sciences, social and physical, while he wrote with the style of a novelist and ran the psychoanalytic movement with the style of a statesman, he continued to view himself as a restrained and plodding specialist. He speaks of "an inclination to concentrate my work exclusively upon a single subject or problem," and seems to accept, as I noted in a previous paper in commenting on his "Dream of the Botanical Monograph," the charge of being "one-sided."[36] In a way, this is quite fantastic: it is hard to think of anyone in the last seventy-five years who has roamed and rummaged so widely in so many different fields. Yet

---

32. See Freud's dream of Goethe, reference footnote 5; pp. 418-420, 352.

33. Freud, *An Autobiographical Study*, p. 14.

34. A phrase Freud quotes with reference to Leonardo. Reference footnote 3; p. 39.

35. *Collected Papers* 4:367. Freud, like many worshipers, failed to see the bitter tensions and surrenders in Goethe's life, which are dealt with in a fine, and to me convincing, essay by Ortega y Gasset, "In Search of Goethe from Within," reprinted in *Partisan Review* (1949) 16:1163-1188. Possibly, Freud was taken in by his envy of just those phases of Goethe's life that Ortega y Gasset finds suspect—his role as a courtier, his inability to commit himself to his art. Freud would not call this last an inability, but rather an ability to lead a well-rounded life. However, from this other point of view, Goethe's sunny freedom seems to be more apparent than real.

36. See reference footnote 33; p. 17. One may perhaps speculate as to what claims to grandiose versatility may lie concealed behind this self-image—or what truth in the sense of Freud's recognition of his unremittingly rational and intellectualized rhythm of life; that he did not care for music, an art whose meanings are difficult to seize by means of intellect, may be of some relevance here. Cf. *Collected Papers* 4:257.

this modesty, whatever its source, saved Freud from supposing that when he had analyzed the "family romance"—that is the Oedipal constellation—of a great artist, he had also fathomed the latter's gift for writing romances. Artistic gift and artistic technique Freud felt to be beyond the reach of psychoanalytic scrutiny. Since he had no similar hesitation in explaining other great human attainments psychoanalytically, one may suppose that his deference to the artist shows by implication that he retained to the end of his life what he felt at seventeen: unquestioning admiration for talent and achievement, such as Goethe exemplified for him. Whatever one may say of the limitations of the qualities Freud sometimes admired, the fact is that, in spite of his growing pessimism, he continued to be able to admire.

A further and quite remarkable example of this ability appears in Freud's *Festschrift* essay, "My Contact with Josef Popper-Lynkeus." There Freud quotes a story of Popper's, published in 1899, which described a man so pure and whole in heart that his dreams lacked opacity. He adds:[37]

> And if Science informs us that such a man, wholly without evil and falseness and devoid of all repressions, does not exist and could not survive, yet we may guess that, so far as an approximation to this ideal is possible, it had found its realization in the person of Popper himself.

Here we find Freud admiring, though not without a characteristic touch of irony, a utopian reformer, a mere scribbler of impractical plans for social amelioration! At the close of the essay, Freud refers to the disappointments he had suffered when great men whom he had "honoured from a distance" turned out to be unsympathetic to psychoanalysis. With such experiences, it is surprising that Freud did not become more soured on those heroes, such as Popper, who were his contemporaries.[38]

§ FREUD'S ATTITUDE TOWARD HIS OWN QUALITIES

THIS BRINGS US to inquire directly how far Freud himself, in his own eyes, measured up to his portrait of a hero. It is hard to say, but there are a few stray remarks which we may take as clues. Unlike Leonardo,

37. *Collected Papers* 5:300-301. It is interesting to recall that Edward Bellamy once described in his story, "To Whom This May Come," a society in which people would know each other's inmost thoughts, hence have no need for guile. See Arthur E. Morgan's *Nowhere Was Somewhere*; Chapel Hill, Univ. of North Carolina Press, 1946; p. 142. Cf. the pungent observations of Harry Stack Sullivan concerning an anthropological report about an isolated Malay tribe whose members engage in mutual dream interpretation. "The Study of Psychiatry," *Pyschiatry* (1949) 12:326.

38. Cf., for example, Freud's warm tribute to Romain Rolland, in "A Disturbance of Memory on the Acropolis," in *Collected Papers* 5:302.

he is not the son of a "great gentleman,"[39] and while in his dreams he compares his father to Garibaldi, or to the statesman Szell who leads the unruly Magyars,[40] his father seems to have been a somewhat small-minded and unsuccessful man who could not imagine great things for his son.[41] Freud's boyhood and youth, moreover, were anything but glamorous. Instead of killing insolent Egyptians, he was a "good boy" at the *Gymnasium;* later, in Brücke's laboratory, he was afraid of arousing the master's ire by being unpunctual.[42] In contrast with those of his heroes who were courtiers or leaders of great armies, Freud spent what he terms "this unfruitful and actually somewhat humiliating period of my student days" at the Chemical Institute.[43] Compelled to wait five years before he could afford to marry,[44] he settled down with a prudent *Hausfrau,* remaining, he implies, sexually "above reproach."[45] In his daily life, he trained himself to wear a mask of politeness.[46] Nor was his routine varied by wild drinking bouts or Dionysian orgies. Freud was plagued, as I have already noted, by aging; and also by the Job-like but quite unheroic afflictions of boils, swellings in the nose, rheumatism,[47] and finally cancer. He bore these painful afflictions, as he bore the approach of death, with an extraordinary stoicism, but one feels that he was far from thinking himself a hero on this account.

Despite his family's poverty, Freud appears, moreover, to have been a sheltered lad, educated among the professional and business classes. And this diligent student, though he went through medical school, seems to have been astonished at his later realization of the prevalence of sex and sadism. For it is with a certain recollected innocence that he tells us of his surprise that other highly esteemed doctors —Breuer, Charcot, Chrobak—knew about the sexual etiology of neu-

---

39. Reference footnote 3; p. 100. In fact, Freud notes that his very name— "*Freude*" means "joy" in German—is the butt of jokes. Reference footnote 5; p. 268.

40. Reference footnote 5; pp. 410-411. In another dream (p. 418) he makes his father "a professor and a privy councillor."

41. Cf. Freud's discussion of his feeling of guilt for having outdistanced his father, in "A Disturbance of Memory on the Acropolis," reference footnote 38; pp. 311-312.

Even as a student at the University, Freud felt that, as a Jew, he could look no higher than for "some nook or cranny in the framework of humanity" from which to make a contribution. Freud, reference footnote 33; p. 14.

42. Freud, reference footnote 5; p. 407 (see also p. 450): "What overwhelmed me was the terrible gaze of his [Brücke's] blue eyes, before which I melted away. . . ."

43. Reference footnote 5; p. 445.

44. Reference footnote 5; p. 418.

45. Cf. reference footnote 5; p. 221.

46. Reference footnote 5; p. 223.

47. See reference footnote 5; pp. 199, 201, 220, 284.

rosis all along;[48] they took for granted what for Freud was a discovery—one that landed him, as it were by default, into greatness and controversy. In one respect, however, these discoveries did not disillusion Freud. For he seems never to have shed the illusion, perhaps typically middle class, that there *are* people who experience the wildest sensuality, or who abandon themselves in orgies of destruction. In *Civilization and Its Discontents* there are passages about intense pleasures of this sort which culture has forced us to surrender.[49] Such passages remind me of the newspaper advertisements several years ago for the movie "Anna and the King of Siam": "A strange, barbaric world of unendurable pleasures . . . infinitely prolonged." This is language to arouse excitement, to suggest experiences from which we, a humdrum people in a workaday world, are inevitably cut off and can only share by sublimation. If such pleasures are to be won by the adventuring hero, Freud was in his own eyes no hero.

Yet such romanticism about sexual conquest is of course only one aspect of Freud's complicated view of things. Though there was no pleasure to compare with sexual excitement, Freud convinced himself that even this delight was fundamentally unsatisfying in the long run: it had to contend not only with obstacles in the external world but with the fact that in the civilizing process, sexual energy itself seemed, in Freud's view, to be diminishing. And true lasting greatness, Freud believed, was generally paid for by libidinal sacrifice. Indeed, the tragedy implicit in this outlook runs through his last long philosophic essay, *Civilization and Its Discontents*, in which he argues that since men can only be happy in a state of idleness and sexual gratification, no conceivable culture can meet their requirements: both biology and culture forbid. The reader is led to conclude that the earth is a trap, for it tempts men to have wishes which it cannot satisfy, and the adult's only realistic course is that of Odysseus: to stop the ears of others and tie oneself firmly to the mast of sublimation, until in old age and finally in death the wishes lose their power to torment.

Work, then, and especially science and art are surer bets than sex. But how did Freud regard himself in his chosen field of scientific work? One of his dream associations is quite poignant evidence of his unsatisfied wishes to be uncontroversially great and famous. He imagines himself going anonymously to be treated for glaucoma by a doctor in Berlin; the doctor applies cocaine which makes the operation pos-

---

48. "The History of the Psychoanalytic Movement," in *The Basic Writings of Sigmund Freud;* pp. 937-938; also in *Collected Papers* 1:294-296.
49. Reference footnote 13.

sible; and Freud takes pleasure in the secret knowledge of his share in discovery of the drug.[50] Thus Freud in this fantasy plays the role of a prince of science in disguise. Since he came close to being in fact the discoverer of cocaine's anaesthetic uses and never forgave himself for missing the opportunity, the fantasy, with its image of eye illness, is obviously touched with self-pity. Today, many people learn of the discovery of cocaine only through Freud!

One may find similar notes of self-pity based on a quite understandable feeling of isolation in Freud's long essay "On the History of the Psychoanalytic Movement."[51] Freud speaks there of those "lonely years" when he alone *was* the Movement—when he thought "science would ignore me entirely during my lifetime," though he believed that at a much later time his discoveries would be found and honored. While on the one hand he regards those years as "a glorious 'heroic era,'" on the other hand he seems to have been unduly impressed by his invitation to accept an honorary degree and to deliver lectures at Clark University, in Worcester. In his *Autobiographical Study*, he writes:[52]

As I stepped on to the platform at Worcester to deliver my *Five Lectures upon Psycho-Analysis* it seemed like the realization of some incredible day-dream: psycho-analysis was no longer a product of delusion, it had become a valuable part of reality.

Even as of 1909 this seems slightly excessive, as does Freud's overgratefulness for the Goethe prize bestowed on him by the City of Frankfort—"the climax of my life as a citizen."[53] When disciples came, he accepted them, by his own later avowals, somewhat uncritically, and he worked with them to give to the minuscule "psychoanalytic movement" those congresses, journals, reports from abroad which one might expect from a world-wide organization of many thousands.

How is one to explain this disparity between Freud's altogether

---

50. Reference footnote 5; p. 241. While Freud would himself tend to assume that, once we have found the wish that was motive to a dream we must take it at face value, I would prefer to argue that the dream- or day-wish may be of much less weight in the total personality than explicit conscious considerations. Dreams may represent the husks, rather than the vital centers, of one's contemporary life, and it is far from decisive proof of childish ambition that one has a dream or daydream, perhaps in a mood of depression, such as Freud here reports and interprets. Today, indeed, dream-interpretation often permits people to discount themselves unduly and to take a passing thought, whether libidinal or aggressive, as better evidence of their "true" selves than a lifelong commitment.

51. Reference footnote 48; *Basic Writings;* p. 943; *Collected Papers* 1:304-305.

52. Reference footnote 33; p. 95.

53. Reference footnote 33; p. 135.

extraordinary achievements, which in the main he evaluated justly, and these scarcely heroic concerns? I think that here again one is confronted with the problem of Freud's ambivalence toward authority. To the extent that Freud irrationally admired the powerful and illustrious of his day and had not completely freed himself from his "innocent faith in authority"[54] it was almost impossible for him to avoid viewing himself and his work through their eyes, even or perhaps especially where that judgment was a negative one. Thus, though Freud's own method gave him an exceptional weapon for understanding the hostility and irrationality with which he was surrounded, a weapon which, ironically, distracted him from seeing in equally full light the friends who flocked to him, he nevertheless seems to have felt to some slight extent: *After all, my enemies are right; I am, like so many other Jews, a disturber of the peace and it is only right if I am badly treated.* He was anything but the rebel who likes to *épater les bourgeois* and who consciously feels worried only if he has the admiration of conventional circles. In spite of himself, Freud could not help his preoccupation with questions of rank within the institutions of solid-seeming Vienna[55] and, beyond Vienna, solid-seeming 'official' German science and chauvinistically hostile but culturally reputed Parisian science.

Elsewhere, I have briefly discussed the problem of "the nerve of failure," by which I mean the ability of a lonely thinker, or other minority-figure, to remain unimpressed by the judgments passed on his views, his personality, his system of values by the dominant authorities of his day.[56] Some thinkers defend themselves by a kind of paranoia, as Fourier did; others minimize their deviations, as for a time Robert Owen did; still others, such as Marx or Rilke, take refuge in understandable but hardly amiable dependency on a few loyal patrons. Very few men seem to have been able to rest secure in the knowledge of their qualities and conviction of their achievement without some support from authoritative contemporaries. Freud possessed the nerve of failure in great measure. To sustain himself, he depended on his reason, on his ability to trust his own experience— even after this ability was temporarily shaken by the dramatic disproof of the stories of seduction his early patients had told him and he had

---

54. Reference footnote 33; p. 27.

55. Cf. his dream of the memorial at the University, reference footnote 5; pp. 407-408.

56. "The Ethics of We Happy Few," *University Observer* (1947) 1:23 *et seq.*; "A Philosophy for 'Minority' Living," *Commentary* (1948) 6:413-422; "Some Observations on Community Plans and Utopia," *Yale Law Journal* (1947) 57:173. [All reprinted above, in Section II.]

believed.[57] He thought, not that he was crazy nor that the authorities were, but that he was a laborious worker and discoverer, while they were bigoted, frivolous, and hypocritical. Freud wrote in 1921 that "he who knows how to wait need make no concessions";[58] such a man may also, with good friends and good luck, avoid the fate of a Semmelweiss.

Furthermore, Freud was able to discover in his own case how the oppression of the child by the authority of the father, or other parental figure, can be prolonged in the obeisance of the adult toward father-surrogates. He recognized, in connection with the memory on the Acropolis, his unconscious feeling that to become unequivocally great would amount to an act of impiety toward his own father.[59] Freud therefore had to laugh at himself when, in interpreting a dream, he found that he compared himself with Hercules, with a superman.[60] Even at the age of 40, with distinguished contributions to neurology and related sciences behind him, and well started on his unique psychoanalytic enterprise, he dared not think he had grown so big.

Nevertheless despite the great distances which Freud felt separated him from his heroes, it is clear that he never surrendered his quite justified hope that he would be as great as they. This may be one factor overdetermining the devotion of his last major work to the story of Moses. As Freud pictured him, Moses found his "clients" among the weak and alien tribe of Jews, as Freud found his among the neurotics who were treated as hereditary pariahs by the medical profession of his day. Moses, in Freud's view, sponsored an ego-deflating system—a tight, logical monotheism which made no concessions to human frailty by the route of superstition or animism; here again the parallel to Freud's own contribution seems clear. Moses, according to Freud's account, was reviled and eventually killed by those whose illusions and indulgences he attacked; Freud, as we have seen, was intensely and continuously conscious of an ever-widening area of hostility—from the infuriated psychiatrists of Vienna, to the wider reading and writing public,[61] and finally even including the

57. See Freud, reference footnote 33; pp. 60-62; also "My Views on the Part Played by Sexuality in the Aetiology of the Neuroses," *Collected Papers* 1:275-281.

58. Reference footnote 19; p. 40.

59. Freud, reference footnote 38.

60. Reference footnote 5; pp. 440-41.

61. For early references, see, for example, reference footnote 5; pp. 420, 429; for later ones, for example, reference footnotes 11; pp. 186-191. Note also the form of his book, *The Question of Lay Analysis* (Procter-Gregg, tr.; New York, Norton, 1950): the discussion proceeds, as so often in Freud's writing, by an

Austrian Church, the Nazis, and other bitter enemies of his science, his outlook, and his Jewishness. And while, in Freud's view, the killing of Moses by the Jews only fastened them eventually more fully to his teachings of grim renunciation, so Freud hoped for the eventual victory of the persecuted wisdom of science and truth, including psychoanalytic truth.[62] To the end, so far as his writings show, Freud was not for any length of time impressed by the seeming strength of his opponents; he did not come to think that his own soft voice would be *spurlos versenkt*.

At no point, indeed, was Freud's consciousness of his enemies that of a timorous man; perhaps it was rather that of an ambitious one. It was precisely the most exposed and criticized positions in his theory to which Freud ardently held. He refused, as he says again and again, to play down the role of sex, either in the life of children or of adults, whatever might be gained by the concession; and, after the "defections" of Jung and Adler, he felt even more committed to holding the fort. In his book on dreams, he wrote: "An intimate friend and a hated enemy have always been indispensable to my emotional life; I have always been able to create them anew. . . ."[63] In the same book he declared that it was decades since he had had any anxiety dreams,[64] and in all probability this did not change with the further passage of years.

Freud had the courage to pursue his way in the face of common opinion and of the in some ways more substantial obstacle of congealed scientific opinion paraded as common sense. He learned, despite his university training, to pay more attention to what was said by an hysterical woman patient than to what was said in books and lectures by professors of psychiatry. At the same time, he rejected neither the vested institutions nor the impalpable traditions of science; though he felt compelled in self-defense to found his own movement, he hoped eventually to rejoin the mainstream of scientific thought and communication. If one judges the heroes of mankind not in terms of the power they wielded over masses of men but in terms of their contribution to the control of nature, including human nature, and to the enrichment of the human spirit; if one adds consideration of the courage, the nerve of failure, needed to achieve that contribution in the face of obstacles, then surely Freud deserves to be regarded as

---

argument with an untutored critic and, with other evidence, makes me think that Freud constantly internalized the voices of his foes.

62. Cf. Freud, *The Future of An Illusion*, p. 93, quoted below, p. 400.

63. Reference footnote 5; p. 451.

64. Reference footnote 5; p. 522. He worried (see p. 420) about the future his own children would meet as Jews, but not about the hostility he himself encountered.

one of the great intellectual heroes of all time. It is not the least of his triumphs that he was willing and able to go on to the very end of his long life reopening questions and laying himself open to criticism by writing; perhaps his failure fully to see and foresee his laurels was in part a way to avoid any resting on them.

§ WEAKNESS AND NEUROSIS

IN SKETCHING Freud's portrait of a hero, I have already very largely indicated his portrait of the weakling; it remains only to review several cumulative themes. The weakling, as Freud depicts him, comes of "poor stock"; he possesses a quantitatively small libido and has other constitutional inadequacies.[65] This hereditary taint is magnified by a poor educational environment. The weakling is apt to be overgratified as a child: Freud traced one type of homosexuality in part to a boy's having "too much love" from the mother.[66] To at least some degree, he seems to have believed that only a rigorous training would produce a manly sexuality. And indeed one can agree that there is something to this view if the love of the mother is actually the smothering pseudo-love of overprotection, which neither gives the child a basic sunniness and security nor gives him the chance to free himself by fighting a patently oppressive parental authority.

At any rate, Freud felt that the combination of poor heredity with poor training or supervision in childhood expressed itself in adult sexual inadequacies which might take form either as neurosis (repression of libido from heterosexual object-choice) or perversion (wrong object for libido). In either case there is a failure to surmount the Oedipus complex, to break with the father and at the same time to identify with his masculine role, and this may show up in a Hamlet-like wavering as in a Leonardian overreflectiveness. This attitude of considering the unaggressive as weak appears with special clarity in Freud's famous letter to Einstein. There he writes:

Why do you and I and so many other people rebel so violently against war? Why do we not accept it as another of the many painful calamities

---

65. It is evident that, behind the argument over "constitutional" factors in neurosis, lurk many social struggles, just as most eugenic considerations hide class or ethnic bias; today a similar argument rages over William Sheldon's studies of delinquency but, thanks partly to Freud, the weight of scientific opinion has shifted and "hereditary factors" are viewed with great (perhaps excessive) skepticism.

66. Reference footnote 3; p. 73. Freud also believed, at least in his early practice, that strict watch should be kept over children to prevent "excessive" masturbation, as well of course as sexual assaults by relatives, nurses, and tutors. But cf. footnote 29.

of life? After all, it seems quite a natural thing, no doubt it has a good biological basis and in practice it is scarcely avoidable.[67]

He adds that the pacifists' attitude "is not merely an intellectual and emotional repudiation; we pacifists have a constitutional intolerance of war, an idiosyncrasy. . . ."[68] And while he ends on the note of hope that the rest of mankind, with the growth of culture, may become equally organically intolerant of war, the whole essay assumes that it is pacifists who need to be "understood," while warlike people can, on the basis of the death instinct, be taken for granted. We may compare with this Freud's essay on "The Taboo of Virginity,"[69] in which he seeks to explain on grounds of fear, and not at all on other possible grounds (such as culturally organized sympathy), those customs which in some tribes have a maiden deflowered before marriage by an instrument—again the point at issue is not the facts of preliterate psychology but the trend of Freud's mind.

Yet there is more to Freud's view of the matter than a mere criticism of "over-refinement" and a readier understanding for those who take easily to blood and thunder. As one can see by studying his essay on "'Civilized' Sexual Morality and Modern Nervousness," written in 1908, he was preoccupied with the loss of individual enjoyment as well as racial vitality that he felt accompanied Victorian sexual repressions. In this same essay he suggested that neurotics are those who only partially succumb to such repression:[70]

Neurotics are that class of people, naturally rebellious, with whom the pressure of cultural demands succeeds only in an apparent suppression of their instincts, one which becomes ever less and less effective.

The neurotics, in this view, were those who had too much libido to permit them to surrender completely to the cultural ideals of sexual restriction, and too little fortitude to resist the hypocritical social norms imposed on them by the beguiling authority, first of the father and later on of society at large. It is, therefore, not only out of weakness of will but out of strength of libido that the neurotic falls ill. It seems that Freud does not maintain a wholly consistent position regarding the source of the neurotic's inability to attain heterosexual success.

Later experience led Freud to considerable skepticism as to the

---

67. "Why War?" in *Collected Papers* 5:285; see also "Thoughts for the Times on War and Death," in *Collected Papers* 4:288.

68. Reference footnote 67; p. 287.

69. *Collected Papers* 4:217.

70. *Collected Papers* 2:76, 86. Cf. the development of the point by Erich Fromm, *Man for Himself*, pp. 22-23, 36-37.

ability of such people to overcome their dependence; instead, he saw that in the analytic situation they often only renewed it in a new form.[71] However, despite his awareness of the contrast between the neurotic's irresolution and stubbornness in remaining ill, and the mastery of self and others which he admired in his heroes, Freud never for a moment doubted that neurotics suffer, that they are oppressed, that society bears on them much more harshly than it does either on the elite who succeeded discreetly in getting their way or on the mass of men who have very little to get. In other words, Freud, in his daily work, took the neurotic with complete seriousness, and one must set this consistent behavior over against the passages in his writings where he glorifies the strong and ruthless males.

Indeed, I think that one of Freud's greatest contributions, though it is one he took more or less for granted, lay in his willingness to spend years if necessary with patients who were neither fatally ill nor important people,[72] without, moreover, any great confidence on his part that they would inevitably get well. To be sure, he declared that "a certain measure of natural intelligence and ethical development may be required of him [that is, the person amenable to psychoanalytic therapy]; with worthless persons the physician soon loses the interest which makes it possible for him to enter profoundly into the mental life of the patient."[73] Nevertheless, without a great deal of willingness to "enter profoundly into the mental life" of people who were very far from his image of the hero, he could easily have gotten rid of his "interminable" patients, as other doctors did. Today, it is just this 'luxury' aspect of psychoanalysis—its prolonged concern with individuals as such, and for their own sake—that is sometimes under attack. Popularly, analysis is often regarded as occupational therapy for wealthy women; hostility to the neurotic is easily disguised by charging him with the crime of being middle-class, or the double crime of being middle-class and a woman.

Unquestionably, efforts to hasten analysis, and to broaden its scope beyond the middle class and beyond the well-to-do, are desir-

---

71. See "Analysis Terminable and Interminable," in *Collected Papers* 5:317 *et seq.*

72. Erich Fromm takes a very similar position in *Psychoanalysis and Religion*, p. 98.

73. "Freud's Psycho-Analytic Method," *Collected Papers* 1:270-271. Since Freud's day, a number of his followers have been trying to widen the bounds of what they find "interesting" and endurable in patients. See, for example, Frieda Fromm-Reichmann, "Notes on the Personal and Professional Requirements of a Psychotherapist," *Psychiatry* (1949) 12:361, and the insistence of O. Spurgeon English that manic-depressives are not as insensitive as they seem and can be reached by therapy, "Observation of Trends in Manic-Depressive Psychosis," *Psychiatry* (1949) 12:125.

able, but I cannot conquer the suspicion that some psychiatrists—
not to speak, of course, of medical men who are not psychiatrists—
share to a degree the popular impatience, sometimes dimly veiled by
fascination, with the seemingly endless talkfest of individual analysis.
Among the many motives which impel the physician to resort to shock
therapies (and the community to consent to this), a lack of Freud's
generous concern with the well-being of a single all-too-human person may perhaps be one. Indeed, one cannot read Freud's article,
"Sexuality in the Aetiology of the Neuroses,"[74] written in 1898, as
well as other writings of this early period, without seeing how passionately Freud protested against injustice in the treatment of neurotics,
and the medical hypocrisy which veiled that injustice; he adds that
"the layman is deeply convinced inwardly of the unnecessariness, so
to speak, of all these psychoneuroses, and therefore regards the course
of the disease with little patience. . . ."[75] Nearly forty years later, in
one of his last papers, he recurs to a similar theme; he begins "Analysis
Terminable and Interminable," published in 1937, with these remarks:

> Experience has taught us that psycho-analytic therapy—the liberation
> of a human being from his neurotic symptoms, inhibitions and abnormali-
> ties of character—is a lengthy business. Hence, from the very beginning, at-
> tempts have been made to shorten the course of analysis. Such endeavours
> required no justification: they could claim to be prompted by the strong-
> est considerations alike of reason and expediency. But there probably
> lurked in them some trace of the impatient contempt with which the
> medical profession of an earlier day regarded the neuroses, seeing in them
> the unnecessary results of invisible lesions. If it had now become necessary
> to deal with them, they should at least be got rid of with the utmost
> dispatch.[76]

This outlook made Freud a "rate-buster" among his medical colleagues—a person, that is, who violated "production norms" as to how
much sympathy and time were to be given to patients; and it seems
not unlikely that hostility based on this ground may sometimes have
been rationalized as based on the *content*, especially the sexual content, of Freud's discoveries.

Conversely, one should expect that Freud himself, with his ambivalence toward authority, would be to some degree affected by such
medical attitudes. Just possibly, his tough, 'masculine' talk might
therefore be considered, among other things, as a defense mechanism
against so 'unmanly' a drain on his sympathy for the weak and oppressed as, on one level, he may have felt his therapeutic work to be
—a drain he could not, however, avoid as his experience with free

---

74. *Collected Papers* 1:220.
75. Reference footnote 74; p. 247.
76. Reference footnote 71; p. 316.

association and transference problems developed. In this interpretation, I suggest that he may have been frightened by the dangers for him of what he regarded as sentimentality, of identifying too closely with his patients. He justified his conduct to himself and others by stressing his preoccupation with research—research which, by his bad luck, had to be done with patients.[77] But that he was haunted by the problem appears in his discussions of the analyst's role, in which he concluded that complete neutrality and impassivity of behavior in the transference situation were not always tolerable.[78]

A number of those analysts who belong to what one might term the third generation from Freud are, perhaps especially in America, not much interested in his ethical concerns and 'metaphysical' explorations. For example, they dismiss the death instinct as a late aberration and do not inquire into the latent tragic import behind its manifestly dubious biology. They strenuously avoid 'jargon' or any other eccentricity and try to become indistinguishable from the other hard-boiled medicos from whose ranks they have sprung. By insisting on medical training, they tend to eliminate at the outset some of the more sensitive spirits who might seek careers in analysis. The *American Imago* struggles on largely supported by some of the old-timers; many of this new generation prefer to report clinical findings. This tendency among some analysts is part of the process of 'normalizing' Freud which I have referred to earlier. Such a development is perhaps inevitable when what has begun as a sect becomes an institution with a more approved and lucrative cultural niche.

But such analysts make a mistake if they suppose that they can avoid the metaphysical issues Freud raised by a matter-of-fact focus on therapy and clinical research. The words they use, to describe to their patients or to each other what is going on in the patients, are inevitably loaded with cultural meanings and ethical judgments. No matter how they may duck the issue of the goals of therapy, their own ideals of heroism, their own views of what is weakness, will affect whom they accept or seek out as patients, what they say to them,

---

77. Cf. also the following remarks from *The Question of Lay Analysis*: "Not every neurotic whom we treat may be worth the trouble of analysis, but there are many valuable personalities amongst them. The goal of our achievement must be to secure that as few human beings as possible are left to confront civilized life with such defective psychical equipment; and to that end we must collect much material, and learn to understand much. Every analysis is instructive and can be made to yield fresh elucidation, quite apart from the personal worth of the individual patient." Reference footnote 61; p. 78.

78. See, for example, "Observations on Transference-Love," in *Collected Papers* 2:377; and cf. "Recommendations for Physicians on the Psycho-analytic Method of Treatment," in *Collected Papers* 2:327, 331.

and the tacit models they themselves are for their patients. Since they want to be just like other doctors, they try to push all problems of ethical responsibility under the tent of 'professional [that is, medical] ethics,' an ethics which less friendly critics of the profession might see as principally a code of trade secret and trade association tactics.[79] In his writings on lay—that is, nonmedical—analysis, Freud showed himself fully aware of the dangers of medical incorporation and regularization of his work. As I have tried to show in this paper, he very much wanted official recognition—but not at the price of emasculation.

---

79. However, the therapeutic duty of the doctor was a strong support to Freud in his early days when he was attacked in medical circles for prying into sexual matters. See, for example, reference footnote 74; pp. 220, 221-224.

24. Freud, Religion, and Science

I WANT TO BEGIN by saying a few words about the social setting in which such a series topic as ours—Attack and Counter-attack in Religion —occurs. Then I want to say something about the use made of Freud in the religious counter-attack before turning more explicitly to Freud's own views. Finally, I shall touch on possible rapproachements between certain tendencies in religion and certain tendencies in psychoanalysis.

§ I

WE MAY TAKE IT as a principle of social observation that, when we find the words "attack" (or "counter-attack"), we must always ask, who is really hitting whom? If we listen to the rhetoric of Southern whites, they talk as if the Negroes, and Northern "do-gooders," were hitting *them*. The Nazis gave it out that the Jews were the attackers. Any child learns to say, "He hit me," to justify an attack. Obviously, we cannot accept at face value the clamor of many religious organizations that they are under attack from psychoanalysis, Marxism, secularism, and so on: we must examine the power relations actually involved. It may be that the very rhetoric of being attacked used by these groups is a sign of their crescence and of the weakening of the allegedly attacking groups.

In *Patterns of Culture*, written in 1934, Ruth Benedict discussed the problem of criticism of contemporary American institutions and how such criticism might be advanced and enlightened by anthropological and comparative studies. We have accustomed ourselves, she observed, to shedding our ethnocentrism when it comes to religion; nobody gets into trouble because he attacks religion; we have not done that, however, with respect to our economic institutions, with respect to capitalism. Here we have remained ethnocentric, and an attack may be dangerous.

Now I wonder if you will agree with me that, fifteen years after this book appeared, the situation is very nearly reversed. The massed social pieties which ranked themselves behind the economic order in the pre-Roosevelt era now seem to rank themselves behind religion and nation. The economic order is today nothing one has to be particularly pious about—unless one is a Communist and then, indeed, religion and nationalism are both involved. But one has to be (and, more important, feels one ought to be) considerably more careful about the religious order. To give an interesting example which comes to mind, the magazine *Commentary*, published by a secular and on the whole conservative group, the American Jewish Committee, has contained many profound critiques of capitalism, articles for instance by John Dewey and Karl Polanyi. These caused no trouble for anybody. But when the gifted novelist Isaac Rosenfeld wrote an article suggesting a psychoanalytic interpretation of Jewish dietary laws, noting a possibly sexual undertone in separating meat from milk, a violent storm broke out upon him and the magazine and it became necessary for the editors to print a disclaimer and apologia.

The movies, with their extraordinary sensitivity to pressure, provide another illustration. In the twenties or thirties there was a Lillian Gish picture in which a minister seduced a young girl who was his ward. I doubt if such a movie would be made, or could be made, today. Religion, much more than free enterprise, is sacred in the movies—many films are devoted to sentimental glorification of churchly figures—and in popular culture generally. Even capitalists enjoy going to plays and reading books which either make fun of business or, as in *Death of a Salesman*, make tragedy of it; and, so far as I know, no one has criticized the play, *The Madwoman of Chaillot*, for the silliness, let alone the offensiveness, of its handling of the bourgeois class.

If we wanted to give a psychoanalytic interpretation, we might think of the image of the rebellious son who carries out a partial, not wholly successful, rebellion against his father. Because of his ambivalence and partial failure, the son feels guilty; because of his partial success, the father gives in; and there is a reconciliation on a new level. Similarly, the revolt against the Hoover economic order (or, more accurately, the radical change in economic conditions) carried out since 1934 has been partly successful—too successful to allow the "father" to hope more than nostalgically for the restoration of "free enterprise." But father and son have come to terms on religion and nation, and the continuing and perhaps even increasing social anxieties and rigidities, displaced from economics, have found a new, "spiritual" fold. This shift permits religious organizations today, which in some ways are much stronger than in the thirties, to feel themselves aggrieved by any scientific and intellectual tendency which is at all outspokenly irreligious. Such a tendency can then be attacked as an "attack on religion," without violating the code of fair play.[1]

---

1. When I expressed this tentative view of the shift in power positions between "science" on the one side and "religion" on the other, in the course of my lecture, many in the audience questioned my interpretation. Some pointed to Blanshard's *American Freedom and Catholic Power* as evidence that the older Mencken atti-

We can recall that when the psychiatrist Brock Chisholm stated in a lecture to the Washington School of Psychiatry that the myth of Santa Claus was a swindle on children, the Canadian cabinet was forced to meet, and he very nearly lost his job as health minister.

I may be mistaken—and certainly there are counter-tendencies which indicate the weakening of organized religion. But assuming that I am right, how are we to explain this alteration in the climate of discussion concerning religion? Obviously, in this article I can touch on only a few of the many factors involved. One factor is the increasingly sympathetic attitude toward religion taken among avant-garde groups. Intellectual anti-clericalism, like anti-clericalism in the labor movement, is out of fashion; and it is not surprising that psycho-analysts—even those "orthodox" in other respects—seem to have fallen in with the general trend, and either stick to their clinical work or claim religion as an ally.

To be sure, the avant-garde has little social power and less political influence. Nevertheless, its loss of the barbed and merrily agnostic elan of a Mencken, a Veblen, a Haldeman-Julius is not without effect, especially among those who are or want to be young. The avant-garde had power enough during the twenties to put religion on the defensive among those upper-class and upper-middle-class Catholics and other communicants who wanted to feel socially and intellectu-ally accepted and up-to-date. Such people did not want to appear backwoodsy and bigoted. Today, however, it is "backwoodsy" to be anti-religious, and in fact I find among my students that only, on the whole, small-town, especially Southern, boys will go whole hog with Freud's view of religion. The revival of interest in religion (if not in church-going) among intellectuals means that many in the upper social strata who are affiliated with organized religion need no longer flinch in pressing the claims of religion and in attacking its few remaining outspoken foes. They can now accept without embar-

---

tude toward organized religion is still strong. A more important argument, in my opinion, was raised by those who contended that the *lack* of strong scientific attacks on religion today was caused, not by the strength of religion and the weakness of the scientific temper, but by its opposite: religion is no longer an issue which the young, emancipated by science, find worth arguing about. And to be sure, scientists now go their way with less worry than ever before about those theological issues which developed in the great battles between science and organized religion from the sixteenth to the beginning of the twentieth century; the turmoil in which such a man as the biologist Gosse was caught by Darwinism is today hardly conceivable. But one reason for this "peace of West-phalia" is that religionists are at last resigned to leaving natural science alone—it is only philosophers, humanists, and psychologists who, dealing with man, face even the possibility of jurisdictional dispute with organized religion.

rassment the anti-scientific position of the devout of lesser social standing.

This alliance of the classes in defense of religion is facilitated by a development much more important in its bearing on our topic than the altered mood of the avant-garde—namely, the rise in the social position of American Catholics in the last several decades. Everett C. Hughes, a very thoughtful and sympathetic student of church institutions and especially of Catholicism, has pointed out that one of the greatest sources of anxieties among middle-class Catholics is the problem of the relation between their church affiliation and their social mobility. Because they are mobile, these Catholics have looked for the definition of "good American" in the past largely to non-Catholics: to high-status Protestants, to Jewish intellectuals and mass-media opinion leaders, and (to a degree) even to the "leakage," as those are called who seep away from the Church. But as Catholics have increasingly moved into the managerial and professional classes, they have been able greatly to influence the definition of "good American," and have taken the lead, since they were among the "earliest arrivals" in the crusade against Communism, in defining the "bad un-American" as well. At the same time, non-Catholic opinion leaders, for the reasons given earlier, do not define the middle- and upper-class style of life in such a way as to exclude good Catholics—save, perhaps, for the still differentiating and hence exceedingly anxiety-provoking issue of birth control.

Yet, while the Catholics have risen substantially, they have not yet gained full social security on the American scene—and the same, of course, is true of the Jews, whose "religious" revival deserves a chapter to itself. Consequently, they are not yet able to laugh off such criticisms of religion as, despite religious censorship of the mass media, continue to crop up. It is unlikely that, fifteen years ago, a high Catholic churchman would have dared to attack an Eleanor Roosevelt after the recent fashion of Cardinal Spellman; it is unlikely that, fifteen years hence, a high churchman will find such a polemic fitting and needful.

So far, I have stressed the tendencies to censor science and intellectual discourse that are implicit in the new "united front" of religionists and intellectuals. But in this same development there are liberating aspects. The seriousness with which religion is now taken has made an interest in it respectable among many scientists who would earlier have considered an irreligious attitude—a village atheist's outlook—an essential mark of emancipation. While William James was considered by many of his professional colleagues to be a kind of nut for concerning himself with religious experience, especially of a mystical and sectarian sort, no such scorn would greet a similar student, for instance Gordon Allport, today. Nor do I think we should bemoan the passing of the village atheist, with his easy monotone of a debunking approach to questions of faith and morals.

§ II

IT IS IMPORTANT to realize, in the light of this changing political and social context, that Freud, when he wrote on religion, seems generally to have thought of himself as the attacked, not the attacker. In *The Future of an Illusion*, written in 1928, he showed his sensitivity to the charge that he was robbing people of their faith. He pointed out that *he* had no such faith in his own arguments: people, he said, were capable of great "resistance" to unacceptable thoughts; their emotional bonds had shown enormous tenacity which even the great Voltaire, let alone Freud, could not shake. Hence, Freud argued, he and his movement were the only ones likely to suffer from an attack on religion. Likewise, when he wrote *Moses and Monotheism* ten years later, he for a while did not dare publish the last chapters—though these raised no new points against or about religion—because he thought it would give the Austrian Church an excuse for closing down the psychoanalytic movement in Nazi-threatened Vienna. Beyond that, Freud felt that whenever it was attempted to put bounds on the inquiries of science—to confine it, for example, to the "material" universe—this actually constituted an attack on science's right to deal with everything. No matter how small the enclave which, like some Vatican City, was preserved against the inquiries of science, Freud felt a real challenge to the total claim and method of empirical investigation.

Now it is ironical that, in the continuing campaign of organized religious thought against organized scientific thought, Freud is today frequently thrown into the fray on the side of the campaigners. It is worth devoting some attention to this paradox, because it will help both to illuminate Freud and the kind of orthodoxy which currently makes use of him. We may consider four themes: the allegation that Freud has dethroned reason and crowned irrationality and mystique; the emphasis on anxiety in Freud's writings; his pessimism about man's fate; and his concept of original sin.

In thinking about these uses of Freud, I was reminded of the figure of Squire Gaylord in William Dean Howells' novel *A Modern Instance*, written in 1881. Gaylord is the crusty village atheist, and also the lawyer, of a small Maine town which Howells calls Equity. A cantankerous man, with a low opinion of mankind. "For Liberal

Christianity," Howells writes, "he has nothing but contempt, and refuted it with a scorn which spared none of the wordly tendencies of the church in Equity. The idea that souls were to be saved by church sociables filled him with inappeasable rancor; and he maintained the superiority of the old Puritanic discipline against them with a fervor which nothing but its re-establishment could have abated." There is something of the Squire in Freud. As he says in *Civilization and Its Discontents* (pp. 23-24), he is happier with, or at least more respectful of, the old-time religion than with its liberal variants which have pretensions to accommodate science. And yet, as we shall see, the "hard" religion which often appeals to Freud for support would be considered by him quite as comfortable and lacking in real strength as a church social.

The first such appeal to Freud is made on the basis that he dethroned the claims of rationalism and positivism and upheld those of the dark, irrational forces in man. The neo-orthodox today like to talk about such forces as a way of slapping down the liberals who are alleged to believe that man is good and his life a feast of reason. They cite Freud's findings as evidence for man's daemonic powers and also for his need for unquestioning faith. This view, I think, comes from a misunderstanding of Freud—and it is probably also a misunderstanding of the "liberals" such as John Dewey who are set up as straw men on the other side. Freud is fundamentally a rationalist—in fact, it would be difficult to find anyone in the Enlightenment who was more so. His whole effort as a scientist was to make the irrational understandable—to capture it for rationality—while as a therapist he had the same goal for the patient—that he should gain control over his irrational strivings by an understanding of them. To a degree (and perhaps we tend to overestimate the degree) the Enlightenment had overlooked and Victorian hypocrisy had buried the *materials* which Freud drew attention to; but the *method* of Freud was invariably the method of science, of positivism if you like, and the morality he demanded of himself and shepherded in his patients was a modified, but far from rebellious and Bohemian, Victorianism.

If we look at the whole body of Freud's work, we can see that he was attracted, like many great scientists, by puzzles, by mystery, by what was veiled and hidden whether by prevailing medical doctrine, by religious dogma, or by the uncanny and perplexing nature of the material itself. Yet always his effort was to order this material, sometimes with pedantic rigor, and he sharply criticized those who used "intuitive" methods in dealing with symbolic data. As other nineteenth-century entrepreneurs took upon themselves the white man's burden of subduing foreign customs and procedures which seemed irrational from the standpoint of Ricardian economics, so Freud sought to subject to laws—for which he often used the term "economic"—all the seemingly irrational phenomena he uncovered. In *Beyond the Pleasure Principle,* there is a typical passage where he expresses these scientific goals. He is arguing that the purpose of an instinct is the restoration of an earlier state in the history of the human race, and that since living matter was once inorganic, there must be an instinctive drive to restore that earlier condition; the goal of life must therefore be death. Yet in the middle of this highly speculative flight, Freud writes as follows:

"If what results gives an appearance of 'profundity' or bears a resemblance to mysticism, still we know ourselves to be clear of the reproach of having striven after anything of the sort. We are in search of sober conclusions of investigation or of reflections based upon it, and the only character we wish for in these conclusions is that of certainty."

Moreover, it is interesting to see that, when he dealt with religion —and he recurred to it again and again in his work—he analyzed only its more rational forms. Despite his discussion of the "oceanic feeling" in *Civilization and Its Discontents,* a discussion which ends in dismissal, he seems nowhere to have dealt with Western mysticism in its wide variety of expressions. Unlike William James, he was less interested in the religious *experience* than in the meaning of the rules and rituals laid down under religious auspices. (There are some partial exceptions to this, as we shall see.) In general, he looked for this meaning in terms of a disguised statement of an historical truth. Like an archaeologist, he asked, "what does this religion say about these people's past?" And he found the answer in, for example, a father-murder at an earlier point, followed by guilt and remorse, and the deification of the slain. Here, typically, we find Freud asking rational questions of, and giving rational answers about, data whose source lay in the unconscious of men and in their irrational feelings. The source of religion lay in the repressed, irrational childhood of the race. He was able to interpret it as he did myths and dreams in a rational way.

True, Freud was not very sanguine about reason. He thought that to trust it might sometimes be to trust in an illusion. But at least it was capable of disproof as an illusion, according to the canons of reason itself; and therefore it was superior to the illusion of religion which did not offer itself to proof or disproof. In other words, while Freud was skeptical about how much science could explain, he was far more skeptical about the claims to explanation of any other system, including occult practices and religion.

Another theme in Freud which makes him appealing to some of
the more sophisticated among the neo-orthodox is his repeated emphasis on anxiety. But here again, there is I believe a misapprehension
of Freud, some of it perhaps of a semantic sort. Freud's "anxiety" has
only a peripheral connection with the "anxiety" of the fear-and-
trembling school. Far from being a sign of potential grace or of any
religious significance, it is a sign of weakness and sexual inadequacy.
Freud did not admire those who trembled in contemplation of the
problems of living and dying. He himself did not tremble, but steeled
himself in Stoic fashion against isolation, illness, and impending death.
To be sure, he counselled resignation. But this was the resignation
of the strong and not the resignation of the weak—moreover quite
different in quality from the haughty self-abasement whose long religious tradition can be traced in St. Paul, St. Augustine, and their
successors.

There is even perhaps a certain Philistinism in Freud's view, like that
of the self-made man impatient with anyone unwilling to come up the
hard way. What Freud admired in the Jews—and it seems to me he gives
them just a bit too much credit—was their stiff-necked pride in the
face of the universe, in the face of persecution. Skeptical as he was
of religion, traces of his admiration for the tough, uncompromising
monotheism of the Jews appear again and again in his work. The Jews
in repressing the memory of having killed Moses, their "Father,"
could never enjoy the expiation of their guilt, as the Christians could
in the Son's atonement for their sins.

I think it follows from this that Freud would interpret the seeming toughness of Christian neo-orthodoxy as not tough at all, but a
new form of comfortableness: a refusal to defy the father, as all
must do who wish to grow up; a refusal to face uncertainty; a wal-
lowing in anxiety, rather than a resolution of it through action. Thus
he would find a secondary gain of surrender hidden under the only
apparent harshness of contemporary revivals of old-time religion.

Still another theme where some religious thinkers trace affinity
with Freud is that of pessimism. Freud was undoubtedly a pessimist,
but of a different brand from most religious writers. Not only did he
have little faith in social reform or in man's innate goodness, he also
had no faith at all in eschatological visions, let alone in any doctrine
of election. In this sense his pessimism is more thoroughgoing than
that of his new religious allies. Moreover, as we have already seen,
Freud did have a qualified confidence in reason; through strengthening of man's ego—the wise arbitrator seeking to balance and control
the passions—he hoped for a better future. More important, perhaps,

than these statements of *Weltanschauung* or ideology is the fact that one cannot read Freud's work without realizing the passionate and sanguine admiration he had for human achievement, for human curiosity, for human mastery. What delighted him in monotheistic religion was its intellectual achievement, even if he saw elements of illusion in it.

The final theme in Freud to which some religious people point is his emphasis on original sin. Somewhere Freud writes, "Psychoanalysis confirms what the pious are wont to say, that we are all sinners." Certainly, there is something here from which the orthodox may take comfort, but it is less than they think. Freud's thought is filled with paradoxes and ironies and we must use his own method to make sure that we do not take him at face value: his text, like that of a dream, challenges us to interpret it. When we do this, Freud's concept of original sin appears at best as an analogy to the religious concept. For Freud saw its origin in biology, rather than in a religious framework. Its biological base was the death instinct, followed by the primal crime, the killing of the father, but this chronologically original sin was for him the source of god-making rather than the result of God's prior existence. More meaningful, perhaps, than these differences in the nature of the concept are the differences in the metaphorical use made of it by Freud and by some of the neo-orthodox. The latter, as Arthur Murphy and Gardner Williams have pointed out with reference to Reinhold Niebuhr, in saying that all men are sinners are creating a preferential position for those who recognize this fact. For Niebuhr, those men are in some ways the worst who think themselves good; those the most arrogant, who think they understand society.[2] This position elevates those who abase themselves, who acknowledge man's intellectual and moral limitations. Freud, on the contrary, used original sin as a democratizer of men. He liked to

2. In correspondence, Dr. Niebuhr has pointed out that I have been unjust to him here, and I accept his criticism. Quoting Pascal's remark that "Discourses on humility are a source of pride to those who are proud," he declares: "I have again and again insisted that such are the powers of human self-deception that those who have what I believe to be a correct analysis of human nature may use it as a source of pride. . . . There is a sense of course in which everybody who strives for the truth gives implicitly a 'preferential' position to those who perceive the truth, as you do for instance, in your article. I cannot help but feel, though this may be quite unjust, that you had to make some critical remark like that in order to establish the preferential position of irreligion as against religion in the matter of truth, for it would be embarrassing to grant that any truth could come out of a religious position. . . ." Dr. Niebuhr referred me to statements in *Faith and History* and *The Children of Light and the Children of Darkness* to show how thoroughgoing a foe of pretence and arrogance, in and out of theology, he has been; I needed no references for his zeal on democracy's behalf.

see the symptoms of sex and aggression in the work of the high and mighty, and in the very good of the "good" men who scorned his theory. And not only men, but men and animals and men and gods were equalized by Freud's view: his interpretation of the totem animal as both a sign of the original crime and as destined to become a god may be thought of as the symbol for this. So we must conclude that for Freud the phrase "original sin" is tinged with irony—and beyond irony, compassion.

§ III

THE FUNDAMENTAL PREMISE of Freud's view of religion is that we can understand it, not in its own terms, but only by understanding men and their human situation. For him, then, religion is a shared neurosis, having its origin, like any neurosis, in the Oedipus complex, that is, in hostile and rivalrous attitudes towards the father which have been replaced by identification and submission. Equally interesting and significant, however, is Freud's idea that neurosis is a private religion. One of his most interesting case studies is that of Schreber, a German jurist who, at the end of the nineteenth century, developed highly elaborate and quite original religious views while he was confined in a mental hospital. Through his conversion into a woman, Schreber felt God would "get into him," and he would found thereby a new race of Schrebers. Schreber's religion was socially defined as paranoia because, unlike the great religious leaders of history, he could not make others renounce claims in favor of his God as he had offered to renounce his masculinity. (In the nineteenth century and since, as we know, many cults hardly less fantastic have flourished in America.)

Furthermore, both private religion and shared neurosis resemble each other for Freud in that both seek to escape from reality, and as we have seen he criticizes those who, by whatever route, try to avoid facing life and pressing their claims. Once he allowed himself to say of the priests: ". . . they are spoilt, they have an easier time of it with their revelation." What he meant was that he himself was a scientist, arduously digging in the murky, the disapproved, the controversial, while at the same time obedient to the traditions and procedures of science. As against this, the priests took the easy way out of *"ipse dixit."*

Freud's analysis of the monastic reports of the troubles of a seventeenth-century painter, Christopher Heitzmann, is revealing. It appears that, when Christopher was around thirty or forty his father died, and the son had tough going economically and psychologically. He could not work, could not paint, and was depressed. In a vision, the Devil appeared to him, and Christopher made a deal with him that, if the Devil would take him as his son for nine years, then he, Christopher, would belong to the Devil thereafter. When the nine years were up, Christopher wanted to welch (as Freud viewed it) on the bargain, and so hied himself to a monastery where he underwent conversion and was saved by the intercession of Mary. Much else is involved in Freud's essay, but important here is his position that Christopher-become-monk took the easy way out.

Freud had something of the same tough approach to the person who escapes through suicide and through mental illness—and even to the artist who, in Freud's eyes, deals with fantasy, not with the "real." Conversely, those whom he admired were those who were able to make others renounce, those who "civilized" others while remaining strong and unbowed themselves. Thus he admired Ikhnaton, the Egyptian monarch whom he credited with founding monotheism, the worship of an abstract sun god, and with forcing the Egyptians, at least for a time, to give up their comfortable beliefs in immortality and in a plenitude of gods. He admired Moses, whom he regarded as an Egyptian follower of Ikhnaton, who succeeded in imposing on the Jews the monotheism of his King. These were men who left an impress on the world, but for their followers—those who gave in to fear, to guilt, to remorse—Freud had scant respect.

Both the religious man and the neurotic in Freud's eyes are cowards who compromise the search for the meaning of life and the truth of social relations. The religious man is inhibited by the power of his racial memory, by collective authority. This blocks his inquiries in certain areas and this blockage spreads over other areas. Likewise, the neurotic is blocked in his search by his inability to rebel against parental authority. This inhibits his sexual curiosity; and this blockage, too, spreads over other areas. Similarly, Freud found analogies in obsessional ritual between religion and neurosis: the same compulsiveness, the same driven need to carry out acts the meaning of which had been repressed—meaning related in the case of the individual to his own childhood, and in the case of the religious man to the childhood of the race.

There is, however, in Freud's estimation an important difference between religion and neurosis, resulting from the fact that the former is *shared*. He speaks, for instance, of a compulsion neurosis as a caricature of a religion. It is this because it lacks the companionship, the close touch with others, secured by the religious devotee. The latter finds his way to others—and hence to a part of reality—through religion, while the neurotic is isolated by his very rituals, often practiced

in secret, which he cannot and dare not share with others. This ability
to share, even if it is only the sharing of a collective illusion, puts
the religious man on the same psychological footing as the successful
artist. The latter is one who, in Freud's eyes, is originally alienated
from reality but who, through success in selling his private fantasies
to the public, wins his way to fame, money, and beautiful women—
and so at least to the realities of social existence. Thus, the privacy of
neurosis endangers the individual escape, while the publicity of religion brings the devout into contact with others, even though reality
be mutually distorted.

Now we must stop for a moment to ask again, what kinds of religion is Freud talking about here, what aspects of religion? In the
first place, he is preoccupied with the search for origins that was so
characteristic of nineteenth-century scientific thought. In company
with the early evolutionary anthropologists, he was concerned with
tracing religion back to a presumptive starting point. This led him
to examine the beginnings of totemism and of monotheism—the latter
interested him mainly in its Jewish and Christian forms. When he
talks about modern religion, he seems to be referring to its more
puritanical Victorian versions. I have already pointed out that he
left out of account anything which might be called genuine religious
mysticism. In this latter tradition, in some of its Christian, Jewish,
and also Oriental forms, the religious man is placed on a footing of a
certain equality with God. He is made in God's image, and God in
his. They communicate with one another; the mystic may even talk
back to God—recall Joseph wrestling with the angel. This kind of
mysticism is, to be sure, rather individualistic, but its attitudes are
not unknown to some of the Protestant sects of the seventeenth century and later that emphasize love, such as the Dutch cult of the
Family of Love. Freud seems to have been unaware of these minority
phenomena and, indeed, in view of his system it is somewhat hard to
see what he would have made of them.

In fact, I am afraid that these kinds of religious experience are but
infrequently considered. Perhaps we have a kind of bias in the sorts
of religion we talk about, when we discuss the relations of religion to
science and philosophy. We are influenced by what is powerful,
rather than by what might teach us something.

However, that may be, Freud did not grant a great future to religion, in his own limited definition. This collective neurosis would not
last. For, if the individual can grow up, can overcome his Oedipal
ties, so can the race. He arrives at this conclusion after a magnificent
dialogue with himself in *The Future of an Illusion*. We may call his

alter ego in this dialogue the Grand Inquisitor, though Freud does not call him that.[3] When Freud suggests that perhaps the human race can grow up, then comes the Inquisitor and denies it. Religion is useful, the latter says, useful to force the mob to renounce and to console it for having renounced, and to reconcile them to the culture from which they reap so little gain. Moreover, the Inquisitor adds, religion has this great advantage over science, that high and low strata of society can come together in its folds, as in the Catholic Church, with the high strata making their own sublimatory refinements yet remaining in the same house with the low. Freud answers that we can hope that all men (not merely some) will become rational and face reality. The Grand Inquisitor returns and says, what is this reality? If you know it, you know that most men cannot face it, and that religion, though untrue, is useful and will if it passes be replaced by doctrine not calling itself religion but equally untrue, equally constricting for the masses, and equally consoling to them. Freud replies:

"You shall not find me impervious to your criticism. I know how difficult it is to avoid illusions; perhaps even the hopes I have confessed to are of an illusory nature. But I hold fast to one distinction. My illusions—apart from the fact that no penalty is imposed for not sharing them —are not, like the religious ones, incapable of correction, they have no delusional character. If experience should show—not to me, but to others after me who think as I do—that we are mistaken, then we shall give up our expectations."

And then he adds:

"We may insist as much as we like that the human intellect is weak in comparison with human instincts, and be right in doing so. But nevertheless there is something peculiar about this weakness. The voice of the intellect is a soft one, but it does not rest until it has gained a hearing. Ultimately, after endlessly repeated rebuffs, it succeeds."

So Freud ends the story.

We must take full account of Freud's tentativeness here. He is often criticized as a dogmatist, and I am one of those who have made this criticism of him. But concerning religion and its future, Freud says that he may be mistaken, and that the last word will be said by others besides himself. With this let us turn to look at some of the elements in Freud's view of religion that may be overstated or mistaken

§ IV

IN WHAT HAS JUST BEEN SAID, I have adverted to the analogy Freud draws between ontogenesis and phylogenesis, between the life-cycle

---

3. In his essay on "Dostoevsky and Parricide," Freud pays his respects to the great scene in *The Brothers Karamazov*, and points out that Dostoevsky, out of his neurosis, allowed his great intelligence to be humbled by the Little Father of the Russians and the Great Father of the Russian Orthodox Church. Nowhere does Freud make sharper remarks about the intellectual's "turn to religion."

of the neurotic individual who succumbs to the Oedipus complex and the history of humanity which has succumbed, in the form of religion, to the guilt of the prehistoric Oedipal crime. Obviously, all such "organicistic" analogies are as dangerous as they are alluring. Freud, though well aware of this, repeatedly resorted to such analogies and metaphors and, like many scientists, put more weight on them than was warranted. To be sure, when he came to study in *Moses and Monotheism* the history of the Jews, he abandoned the historical universalism which would have given all human beings the same phylogenetic experience and racial memory; instead, he traced those particular events of Jewish religious experience which, to his mind, gave the Jews a distinct national character and a distinct racial memory—one which the Christian world only repeated in considerably chastened and modified form. Those Jews who could not endure this guilt of the murder of the father, Moses, accepted Christ as the Messiah, the Son who came to atone for their racial crime, to expiate their guilt. It is plain, however, that Freud did not similarly differentiate between the historical experience of different social classes within a society, though in his day-to-day work he recognized of course that the lower classes suffered less from sexual inhibitions—and therefore should presumably have "inherited" a different set of Oedipal memories. Any attempt at racial, or "human-racial" interpretation of history, such as Freud builds on his analogy between individual and group, inevitably "de-classifies" societies and runs into trouble in dealing with the stratification and divisions of any complex social order such as that of the Western world, or even of the Jews of Biblical times. It follows, therefore, that Freud's approach to religion will prove unsatisfactory to the more sociologically-minded investigator.

To illustrate this, and to show the limitations in Freud's method, I should like to review briefly a discussion in the psychoanalytic periodical *Imago* concerning the development of Christian dogma. An orthodox Freudian position was taken by Theodor Reik; a more sociological view was taken by Erich Fromm, and it is from the latter's article on "The Origin of the Dogma of Christ" that I primarily draw.[4] Both Reik and Fromm were struck by the fact that there is a change in the image and symbolism of Christ in the early Christian era. He appears in early representations as a young man, sometimes a young man suffering on the Cross; in later representations He appears as a babe in the arms of His mother, the Virgin Mary, who had been very much in the background in the early period.

The orthodox psychoanalyst looks at this development and says,

---

4. On this problem I am indebted to Murray Wax for many helpful suggestions.

in effect: oh yes, we know all about such alterations; that is simply ambivalence; people cannot make up their minds whether they wish Jesus to be a man or a baby. Moreover, we often see such ambivalence in our patients; they, too, cannot make up their minds whether to be a man or a child. So again mythology confirms what we find in the study of the neuroses.

Erich Fromm's critique of this kind of psychoanalytic analogizing is, I think, sound. He points out that such a view does not take religion seriously enough, does not take society seriously enough, does not even take the individual seriously enough. For the development of Christian dogma can tell us much, not about the psychological complexes of individual men who may have been ambivalent in one respect or another, but about the social struggles which shook the Roman Empire at this period—struggles in which, despite their individual ambivalences, men took sides and developed important religious and social institutions. We cannot dismiss such struggles without examining them historically, any more than we can dismiss the tragedies of individual decision and indecision in a social setting by speaking only of ambivalence.

Thus, Fromm observes that the young Christ of the early decades represents the Messianic hopes of the peasants, of the oppressed classes. They identify with Him as a man, as a focus of social protest—and as a man who becomes God. True, He does not replace God—the movement is a Messianic one, not an actual and successful social revolution—but He joins God on high. Much later, when Christianity has become a state religion and when the Messianic hopes have evaporated, we find an entirely different image of Christ. He is the Son who is consoled and protected by His mother; moreover, He was God all the time, rather than attaining to Godhood by His own manly efforts. This shift is a sign, at one and the same time, of psychological regression among large social strata and of the defeat of these same strata. The peasants no longer challenge the Empire even in fantasy, and their religion mirrors their situation as earlier it mirrored their hopes for social change. Fromm notes that it is only with the coming of the Reformation that God re-emerges as a father-figure, while during the medieval epoch the challenge to the father, to authority, is muted and the mother-figure predominates. Thus the Reformation's change of Christian imagery presages new social stirrings and new possibilities of rebellion. In this analysis, the emphasis is on *social* authority, which is reflected both in the structure of the family and the structure of religious doctrine; whereas in Freud's or Reik's analysis, the emphasis is on the family—on the individual domestic constellation—from which the racial and religious imageries are developed.

I want, however, to warn you that Fromm's argument is a very complicated one—so, for that matter, is Reik's discussion of religious rituals—and I have only presented it in oversimplified form. I would not want to leave the impression that Fromm takes an entirely Marxist position, of saying that religion is a mere superstructure—a narcotic in the class struggle. Fromm criticizes Kautsky's view as to the origin of Christianity quite as sharply as he criticizes Reik's. For Fromm sees religion as playing an important part in social struggles, and not merely as a reflection or distortion of those struggles.

Taking religion seriously as a factor in man's long effort to free himself, Fromm also differs from Freud in the role he assigns religion within the individual's psychic economy. Freud, as we have seen, considers religion to be crippling for the individual, crippling to his intellectual curiosity and his emotional claims alike—and this holds for all religion which deserves the name. In contrast with this, Fromm sharply differentiates among religions in terms of their specific social functions. Some doctrines which are not *called* religion may be far more crippling than some which are called religion. That is, while all of us, by virtue of the socialization we have undergone, are crippled to some degree, we cannot differentiate the more crippled from the less crippled by the tags of church identification. If we look at the whole person and the interpretations he puts on his religion—the specific quality of his religion—we may very well find that a devout person is far more "free"—far less deluded—than a man who claims he has outgrown belief in God.

Religion, in other words, can tell us a good deal about the individual believer and the social system in which he exists. We can, in socio-psychological terms, interpret the part religion plays in the life of men and groups. But this part is seldom simple and monolithic. Paradoxically, Freud seems to have taken too much at face the religious opposition to science, and failed to see, at least in this particular, that we have not said the last word about a man's rationality when we have stamped him as a believer—his religion may be the very sign of his rationality, though a disguised one.

This leads me to a further criticism I would like to make of Freud's view of religion, namely concerning the problem of motivation. When Freud found a religious man, he was likely to assume that his altruism, for instance, covered something up—perhaps it was a reaction-formation to anal-erotic sadism. Surely, that often happens, and the time when Freud lived was particularly noted for its pious frauds, its hypocrites who concealed their meanness consciously or unconsciously under a cloak of fervent religious devotion or obsessive attention to ritual. But it seems to me that today we face an altered situation, in which the limitations of Freud's view have become more apparent. Partly as the very result of Freud's work, we have invented a new kind of hypocrisy in which we have to cover over anything decent in ourselves, and call it tough. If we do an altruistic or decent act, we don't dare admit it, even or perhaps especially to ourselves. We rationalize away what is good and genuine in us. The businessman, for instance, chalks it up to public relations if he does something generous. The student, if let us say he does not cheat or is not aggressive, will chalk it up to timidity, to his fear of what people might think—he will certainly not give himself credit for any nobility of impulse. This new hypocrisy strikes me as in some ways quite as displeasing, and socially perhaps considerably more dangerous, than the old.

It would seem to follow from this that we cannot regard religion as simply a method for controlling libidinal and aggressive drives in the interests of society or of some other ultra-individual power. Religion is not, as Freud thought it to be, a kind of tax collector that collects from everybody the energy necessary to power civilization, and to keep it going. Nor will we necessarily find in religious practices what Freud called "the return of the repressed," that is, the reappearance in distorted or symbolic form of the very tendencies that religion had served to inhibit. Freud's whole position here, while it contains much that is true for certain epochs and for certain social groups, rests on his "scarcity economics," his view of man as having only so much libido, so much benevolence, to go around. And if this structure of motivations, with its tendency to biological reductionism falls, with it does Freud's view that religion on its ethical side represents, in the individual no more than a reaction-formation, and, in the society, no more than a method of social control. As Freud saw an obsessional neurosis as a caricature of a religion, so we may regard Freud's picture of religion itself as a caricature of certain reactionary Augustinian tendencies within the Christian denominations—where the establishment comes close to being a method of social control and a reaction-formation against hatred and lust in whose very practices and doctrines hatred and lust reappear.

Furthermore, as I have already implied, there is in Freud's analysis of religion a somewhat pedantic treatment of religious symbolism. Freud does not, like Durkheim, study a religious ritual with the feeling that the ritual is trying to say something to him in another language —something which may be quite as rational as any scientific text. For example, he fails to see how a whole group, like the American Negroes, could guard their aspirations for liberation under a religious guise.

Though far less heavy-handed than some of his followers, he never-theless handles symbolism, whether in religion, in dreams, or in works of art, a bit too literally—not rationally so much as rationalistically. He wants to force it into a certain framework, and to pierce through the manifest symbol to its genetic origin. But the search for origins, which we have already seen to be characteristic of his approach to religion as to so much else, may tend to lead one to miss both artistry and overtones of contemporary meaning. In a way, the origins of a religious doctrine are relevant to contemporary men only insofar as they have incorporated those origins in their reinterpretations of what they do. Hence even if it were true that religion invariably arose out of men's fear and guilt, it would not necessarily follow that it is today propelled by fear and guilt.

§ V

HAVING MADE these criticisms of Freud's view of religion, I think we must grant his tremendous contribution to our understanding of it. As in so many other fields of his boundless curiosity and passionate moral courage, he succeeded in his effort to win a new territory for science, or at least a new angle of approach to the new territory. It is an approach which, when combined with other approaches, can be very fruitful, as I think Fromm's work indicates. Indeed, to make the study of religion (apart, of course, from Biblical criticism and other ongoing nineteenth-century efforts) respectable among scientists was perhaps as hard when Freud wrote as it was to make science re-spectable among religious fundamentalists.

Another contribution Freud has made to the study of religion leads me to introduce a kind of dialectic argument with the views of Malinowski. Malinowski takes a functional view of religion. This "functionalism" means that, if the investigator finds religion as an element in the life of a man or a group, he will assume it has a function, will seek to discover what it is, and will not consider it part of his task to criticize the function. Whatever is, functions; whatever func-tions, is part of the ethnographic picture. Many cultural anthropolo-gists—partly because of the almost inevitable contemporaneity of field work, the lack of historical data—will not assess the historical weight of anything that functions in the present, and will perhaps overinterpret functions which may, in fact, no longer matter very much. They may be simply relicts.

Freud erred in the other direction by putting his emphasis almost exclusively on origins and relicts. This, however, provides him with the perspective from which he says—whether he is right or wrong in his prediction is not the question here—that the religion which seems to have such a strong hold on mankind will very likely disappear with the adulthood of the race. For he can look back historically and conclude that the hold of religion was not always what it now is; that there have been decisive historical events, such as the reign of Ikhnaton, or the Jews' killing of Moses, or the Crucifixion of Christ, which altered the social and individual function of religion. Malinowski finds it hard to do this with the Trobriand Islanders.

But Freud's look forward is not only based on his look backward into history. He also looks into himself, and asks: do I need religion, can I get along without it; and if I can, why not all men? By assuming the unity of men's psychic constitution, he was enabled by self-analysis to subject social institutions to criticism, whereas an anthropology that follows functionalism literally cannot criticize what it finds, if it "functions." In other words, Freud found within himself a scientific *Weltanschauung* which transcended religion in its historical givenness, and from this base he could criticize religion and look forward to its demise while granting its functional role in the development and cementing of Western civilization.

§ VI

LET ME TURN FINALLY, in the light of what has just been said, to the question of possible meeting grounds between psychoanalysis and religion. . . .

Within both fields, within psychoanalysis and within religion, there is an increasing preoccupation with meaning, with values. We must be as careful not to confuse psychoanalysis with one brand of it as we must be not to confuse religion with one brand of it. Indeed, I think it fair to say that the differences in attitude towards fundamental questions *within* religion and *within* psychoanalysis are greater than the differences between like-minded schools of religion and analysis.

As I have said, religion is today for many no longer the formal, often hypocritical shell that it frequently was in the nineteenth century. Great numbers of people can no longer coast on nineteenth-century religious observances, and they have been driven by modern life out of the religious communities that once held them fast. In the name of religion, they therefore meet together to consider where they are. It should not disturb or confuse us that these people put their quest for meaning in religious terms; he would be a bold person indeed who would allege that these terms cannot hold and develop new meanings.

A number of analysts have come to the same conclusion by a different route. In his therapy, Freud rejected the notion that he was a moral or ethical guide; he thought this would be a concealed dictatorship and that his job was done when he had helped the patient to find his own ego-ideals, free from compulsive obedience to, or flight from, a parental imago. Actually, he could largely coast on the implicit ends of the nineteenth century, and assume that his patients were on the whole sensible people whose neurosis did not itself originate in a moral conflict. Moreover, he was able to solve most moral problems which came up in his research and therapy by one ethical principle we have already seen at work in him: passionate devotion to the truth. Psychoanalysis in fact constitutes a great ethical achievement in its invention of a human relationship whose cardinal principle is scrupulous, or if you please ruthless, honesty *on both sides.* Freud's early patients, at any rate, were hysterics or obsessional people who had obvious symptoms and who wanted to be free of them, in order simply to lead good Victorian lives.

Perhaps is was Jung who first saw, in the immediate generation of analysts after Freud, that this (or training) was not the only reason people came to analysis. His patients seemed to be mainly men of middle age who were "in search of a soul"—who asked the analyst, "What is the purpose of my life? What should I do with it?" Their neuroses seemed to be bound up with moral problems, problems of choice. Increasingly today, this new type of analytic work with people who are not obviously ill—whose "symptom" is their malaise, their whole way of life—people who are troubled about moral issues, or who ought to be troubled about them, forces analysts to become concerned with problems of casuistry, of values, as part of the very task of therapy. Neurosis then appears, not so much as a conflict between "natural" libidinal demands and society's restraints, but as a conflict among moral strivings within the individual himself—though these, of course, reflect the conflicts within society. And, in terms of technique, the analyst's task may no longer lie in coaching sexual frankness. The analyst may have to help patients confront repressed moral issues about which they ought to be, but are not consciously, troubled.

In two books, *Man for Himself* and *Psychoanalysis and Religion,* Erich Fromm has made an effort to grapple with these moral problems as they present themselves in analysis, within an evaluative framework that finds much in common with what he terms "humanistic" religion. He takes religion much more seriously as a source of illumination for psychotherapy than most psychoanalysts (including Jung) have hitherto done. At the same time, he employs the Freudian methods to understand the hold over men of both humanistic and "authoritarian" religion, and its value for them. Thus he regards himself, not incorrectly, as working in the tradition of Freud, but (like John Dewey) he regards certain elevated ethical attitudes and cosmologies as truly religious, which Freud, when he adverted to them at all, regarded as too highbrow to be given the name of religion. Fromm represents a number of contemporary analysts who are preoccupied with theological questions, not simply as Freud was—i.e., as "evidence" of human weakness and as sources of historical data—but on their merits and in their own terms. At the same time, theologians, turning the tables, can look to psychoanalytic developments for evidence concerning basic human "needs" and the psychic mechanisms which give rise to problems of an ethical and religious sort.

Such reconciliations, however, are not likely to get very far in the prevailing atmosphere where people are afraid of criticizing religion. For if the onslaughts of organized religious groups succeed in putting psychoanalysis, along with other inquisitive sciences, on the defensive, psychoanalysis—far from joining in the possible creation of new, syncretistic religious patterns—will either leave religion alone, as too hot to handle, or will form expedient alliances and make expedient obeisances and denials of any claim to ethical and religious relevance. If, in other and more "emancipated" circles, psychoanalysis, in the form of a diluted popular Freudianism, can still put people on the defensive who would like to know how to live decent lives, they will look to analysis only for debunking cliches and for symptom-therapy, not for its moral illumination.

Indeed, if we are to get beyond such sterility and defensiveness on both sides, we must abandon the misleading notion that there is such a thing as pure science or pure religion. All thought—that of religion and psychoanalysis alike—is impure, or, as Freud would say, ambivalent; all thought must be constantly removed from its wrappings of this time or that place. This is true of Freud's views concerning religion, as their paradoxical uses traced here would seem to indicate. It is also true, I venture to say, not only of our religious inheritance as a whole, but specifically of our traditional religious way of dealing with the temerities of science.

No doubt, future developments in the relation between psychoanalysis and religion (including Fromm's attempt to break down this distinction and to develop new ones) will depend rather more on such larger issues of social structure as the fate of the Catholic middle class than on the success of the intellectual adventure of a handful of theologians and analysts. But religious and scientific advance must usually occur as relatively powerless movements within a precarious setting. Freud, like other innovators, started as a minority of one.

VII.

TOTALITARIANISM

THERE WAS A TIME when intelligent people tried to interpret totalitarianism either in terms of the ideological smoke-screens of the totalitarians or in terms of some theory of class conspiracy. Thus, many intelligent people before and even during World War II saw Nazism as a combination of Rhineland industrialists and Junker landlords and officers, making use of anti-Semitism and German chauvinism to "fool the masses," smash unions, and maintain the *Osthilfe*, the much-attacked Prussian farm subsidies. Popular support was summed up in a reference to the *Lumpenproletariat*, or possibly by an allusion to lower-middle-class malaise. I had been briefly in Germany in 1931, and my colloquial German, learned from a nurse "just off the boat" who knew no English, was enough to allow me to talk with students and other young men who were Nazis. Many of them were very idealistic—indeed, it was their ideals, as well as their unconscious aggressions, which were betraying them. I thought it likely that Germany would fall to Hitler, and wondered at the complacency of the older people I saw, who felt, with the wisdom of experience, that, if Hitler did reach power, the responsibility would sober him—as it had sobered the Social Democrats.

When it turned out that power did not sober or stabilize either Hitler or the Bolsheviks, many people jumped to the other extreme —represented in such a book as George Orwell's *1984*—and saw the totalitarian ruler in the image of the mad scientist: vicious but rational, his dreams of omnipotence come true. The earlier simplistic and economistic explanations (I don't intend to suggest I was myself immune from them) were exchanged for literary, philosophical, and theological ones, notably in Hannah Arendt's brilliant and evocative *The Origins of Totalitarianism*. Looking back at the record, however, it is all too easy to say that the observers who interpreted Nazism and Stalinism by extrapolation from their own experience underestimated the wilfulness, the lust for power and destruction, of the totalitarian movements and hence the inevitability of "permanent revolution." Without the aid of France and England, and then of the Soviet Union, Hitler would not have managed to bring on a war, and without war

409

he could probably not have achieved his aim of full totalitarian domination—indeed, on taking over in 1933 he was in many ways quite inhibited and cautious. He himself was less confident of the outcome in the early years than many who now retroactively see a malign logic in all that occurred. Likewise, many Russian experts seem to believe that no move is made in the Soviet sphere without Politburo planning and approval—no move based on jurisdictional dispute, personal caprice and connection, or luck. Doubtless, the leaders wish it was like that! The real world puts limits—not enough, to be sure—on the wishes of even the most powerful and cruel men.

Today, however, those who think, for example, that McCarthy is bound to triumph in America, or that Malan and his party will succeed in their extremist program, appear to have "history" with them. In this new context, I feel we are witnessing an over-reaction against the earlier tendency to assimilate Nazi and Soviet phenomena to familiar despotic patterns: we have become extravagant in denying that these regimes had any imaginable connection with social structures of an ordinarily inefficient sort. My paper on "The Limits of Totalitarian Power," delivered at a meeting arranged by the American Committee on Cultural Freedom, gave me the opportunity tentatively to question this view before a group where there could be no danger of complacency towards the Communist countries—especially as I was on the program with such tried and true anti-totalitarians as Hannah Arendt, Bruno Bettelheim, and Nathan Leites. Even so, there was a tendency among some of my listeners to resent the suggestion that the Soviet regime could not completely cut the bonds of human solidarity and restructure human personality—not yet; there was a feeling that I, an unhurt outsider, was necessarily innocent, unable in my rationalistic liberalism to grasp the terrible monolithic quality of "the system."

Underneath some of these criticisms there lurked the belief which I have often encountered that social science, in its effort to probe and understand our times, must necessarily miss the basic evils and the deep irrationalities of totalitarianism and, besides, evaporate away our indignation and our will to fight. (The articles on intellectual freedom and on race relations in section III have of course come in for similar attack.) I think I recognize these dangers. We have all met people who diminish their sympathy with themselves by giving out parlor-Freudian analyses of their moods and conduct. When I have made myself read some of the literature on concentration and labor camps, I have been aware of my wish for mechanisms to put this terrible material at a distance, so as to diminish both my anxiety and my empathic suffering. Science can serve many concurrent aims—not only to disclose the truth but to give a safe-conduct pass to the scientist, an asbestos coating in hell. Yet at the same time I feel that an almost hysterical heavy-handedness can all too often cloak itself in righteousness and plead rank on the basis of more intense suffering; a refusal to use all available techniques for examination can also appear as a noble disdain for evil. I would hate to see the day dawn when intellectuals had to wear their piety (or their loyalty!) on their sleeves. We need both satire and sermon, both psychology and theology.

"The Nylon War" is a serious attempt, couched as satire, to suggest how the Soviet Union might be brought down short of war. Even if human beings have a good deal of unsuspected resistance to the totalitarian reformation of man, the regimes themselves are not likely to be destroyed from inside until one can make atom bombs in a bathroom; "The Nylon War" seeks to organize both American energies and Soviet limitations—it is a foray in Keynesian economics in reverse. I conceived the idea originally as something of a heuristic device to sharpen discussion among a group of social scientists meeting in 1947 under the auspices of the Harris Foundation for International Affairs to discuss "the world community." Two points of view had been vocal at the meeting. There were the self-proclaimed "realists," men like my colleague Hans Morgenthau, some of them geopolitically oriented, who thought in terms of the bipolar "big powers" and exchanged strategic details about Iranian oil or Skoda's output or de Gasperi's majority. Opposed to them was a smaller group, of whom the late Ruth Benedict was one of the more eloquent, who occasionally also sought the prestige of "realism" but did so in terms of psychology and culture rather than of steel plants or armored divisions. This latter group's theme-song was: "The Russians have a culture, too, and on this basis we can and must understand them." Although less patently nationalistic, this second group was no less devoted to the cause of the Western powers in the cold war, but it conceived of cross-cultural communication as a realistic possibility, once American ethnocentrism could be overcome. Some of them, to my mind, appeared to scant the fact that "the" Rusisans were not in charge, but had been conquered by a dictatorship, whereas some of the geopolitically minded were preparing to fight World War I over again with better military weapons—they assumed an enemy as rationalistic as they thought they themselves were; they missed the wild irrationality of a "people's imperialism" and underestimated the rational appeal of ideals to the West.

I recur to these events because the attitudes expressed at this conference are still so dominant, and especially the mood and method of realism. One limitation of this mood is that it robs academic life of one of its principal pleasures and functions, that of serving as a counterpoise to the life of statesmen and executives. My fellow-conferees tended to gravitate towards immediate policy questions—and to bind themselves to the alternatives the State Department might be willing or able to accept at the moment. Since we were a bunch of professors, and not the State Department, since we lacked its channels of information and misinformation, but also had less of an emergency mandate, I felt we should liberate ourselves from the conventions of thought which pass as realism. The notion of the Nylon War was intended to confront us with the very excess of realism in American domestic policy as well as with the fact the anthropologists sometimes understressed, namely that we Americans also have a culture, and one not capable of perennial patience or inaction. Thus, my satire sought to highlight some of the amiable qualities of the United States—industrial energy and romanticism, imagination, activism, generosity—as well as some of the salient qualities of the Soviets—inflexibility, cupidity, "projective" interpretation of the enemy, want, and fear.

I was encouraged by the Berlin airlift to revive the idea and write it up, and I was greatly stimulated by discussion of technical details with Kenneth Mansfield, then a graduate student in international relations at Yale and now a member of the staff of the Joint Congressional Committee on Atomic Energy. Many magazines rejected it—one on the ground that they'd "had enough articles on Russia"; for one thing, it was too long. After the Korean War began, I got it out again, cut it to a quarter its original elaboration, and published it in *Common Cause*, a tiny journal, since defunct. When after that it was picked up by *Etc.*, *The Christian Century*, and a Dutch monthly, I began to get letters and calls asking me if the "war" (whose fictitious date had by then been passed) had actually gotten under way! It was like a page out of *The Invasion from Mars* that people could feel so remote from the current of probabilities as to take my tale for literal fact. The still unresolved disquiet about flying saucers, coupled with the merely extrapolative and unfictional character of much "science fiction," are other indications that people often believe that anything can, and perhaps has, happened; the disorientation from reality that this misreading indicates is frightening.[1]

---

1. Since the above was written, I have had a letter from a man in Sydney, New South Wales, asking me for further references on the "war" on the assumption it has occurred and also whether *Common Cause* is not (as charged by a local representative of the U. S. Information Service) a "Commie magazine." In which case the war would not have occurred but would be "Commie propaganda." One hardly knows whether to laugh or weep at such a letter—and at so humorless and fearful an American representative abroad. "The Nylon War" has also

In a fine essay on "Democracy and Anti-Intellectualism in America,"[2] Richard Hofstadter has argued that intellectuals are characterized by both piety and playfulness—they care very much about what happens to truth, to ideas, and to their human carriers, and they also enjoy the play of the mind, the intellectual function, for its own sake. A dialectic must operate between these two contrasting attitudes, else one succumbs to fanaticism or stuffiness on the one side or dilletantism and debunking on the other. My own recent tendency has possibly been to err on the playful side and concentrate my fire against piety, perhaps as a counter to the relative asceticism and portentousness which seems occasionally characteristic of the University of Chicago. And certainly I agree with Hofstadter's insistence on maintaining the value of both attitudes, just as I feel that a tennis game should neither degenerate into "social tennis" and chit-chat nor lose its game-like quality in competitive ferocity.

When I was working on this manuscript, the June riots broke out in East Berlin, and filled millions of us with hopeful excitement. Even if, as seemed likely, the insurgency should be rapidly overcome, the reminder that totalitarianism could kill men and silence them, but not permanently crush them, cannot come too often—not only to us who stand by but to those Germans whose "Deutscher blick" (the furtive look out of the corner of the eye to see who is listening) has become a kind of totalitarian tic through twenty years of brown and red shirts. Thus, we are all of us fatefully indebted to the nameless ones who took the risks of the June days. And we are also indebted to the Americans whose energy overcome others' hesitations and provided food parcels for Eastern Germans who dared to "come and get it." If only we Americans had more faith in our own weapons, and the imagination to extend this operation into a full-scale "nylon war!" Perhaps we fear to be called materialists: no country was ever called this for its war materiel, but only for its consumer goods.

been reprinted in several anthologies edited by professors of English, where it has appeared as an example of satire; there at least, properly labeled, readers have not written to say that they've missed the papers lately and was the war over!

2. In *Michigan Alumnus Quarterly Review*, vol. 59 (1953), pp. 281-295.

25. Some Observations on the Limits of Totalitarian Power

Twenty and even ten years ago, it was an important intellectual task (and one in which, in a small way, I participated) to point out to Americans of good will that the Soviet and Nazi systems were not simply transitory stages, nor a kind of throwback to the South American way—that they were, in fact, new forms of social organization, more omnivorous than even the most brutal of earlier dictatorships. At that time, there were many influential people who were willing to see the Nazis as a menace but insisted that the Bolsheviks were a hope. And even today one can find individuals who have no inkling of the terror state—people who, for instance, blame "the" Germans for not throwing Hitler out, or for compromising themselves by joining Nazi party or other organizations, or who attribute Soviet behavior to the alleged submissiveness of the Russian character or trace it back to Czarist despotism and expansionism and whatnot. Yet it seems to me that now the task of intellectual and moral awakening has been pretty well performed, and stands even in danger of being overperformed; in pursuit of the few remaining "liberals who haven't learned," groups such as this [the American Committee on Cultural Freedom] may mistake the temper of the country at large, misdeploy their energies, and, paradoxically, serve complacency in the very act of trying to destroy complacency.

Intellectual communication, in this as in other cases, cannot avoid the ambiguities arising from the differing attitudes in the American audience at large. I know that I will be misunderstood. For one thing, those who have suffered directly at the hands of the totalitarians, and who can undoubtedly find many audiences where complacency still rules—where, for example, the Soviet Union is still sneakingly regarded as somehow on the right track as against "capitalist exploitation"—such people may feel that I take too lightly the domestic well-wishers of the Soviet Union, or the lethargic. No one likes being robbed of a well-earned agenda.

Yet I cannot help but feel that the telling of atrocity stories—undoubtedly true stories—may have ambivalent consequences and, after a time, may harm the very cause in hand. Let me give as an illustration the way in which many liberals today, in government service or in academic life, repeat tales of loyalty-probe incompetence or injustice, of school board and trustee confusion between liberals and "Reds," of stupid F.B.I. questions, and so on. Such tales are meant to arouse us against the dangers of domestic reaction, but they have frequently the consequence of leading a government employee to burn back issues of *The New Masses,* of a faculty to drop the *Communist Manifesto* from its reading list, of a student to fear getting involved with even Americans for Democratic Action lest it prejudice his employment possibilities. Then such tales are in turn spread, to justify still further concessions to an alleged need to conform to the prevailing climate of opinion. . . .

Now I want to suggest that something of the same sort may occur if we begin, after greatly underestimating, to greatly overestimate the capacity of totalitarianism to restructure human personality. During the last war, I talked with many people who were concerned with the plans for occupying Germany at war's end. Most assumed that there would be not only physical but organizational chaos and that it was necessary to have skilled civil affairs officers to take over tasks that the Germans, broken by Hitler and the war, could not assume for themselves. I felt that this was unduly patronizing of a great and gifted people, capable of spontaneous organization and of settling affairs with the Nazis if the occupying powers merely held the ring and supplied some necessities of life. I think we can make the same mistake—for I believe it was a mistake—about the Soviet Union and its satellites, and fail to see that even the terror is not omnipotent to destroy all bonds of organization among its victims.

Similarly, I think we can become so fascinated with the malevolence of Stalinism that we may tend to overestimate its efficiency in achieving its horrible ends; and we may mistake blundering compulsions or even accidents of "the system" for conspiratorial genius. Overinterpretation is the besetting sin of intellectuals anyway and even when, with Hannah Arendt, we rightly point to the need to cast traditional rationalities aside in comprehending totalitarianism, we may subtly succumb to the appeal of an evil mystery; there is a long tradition of making Satan attractive in spite of ourselves. And the more practical danger of this is that we may, again reacting from underestimation,[1] misjudge not so much the aims as the power of the enemy and be unduly cowed or unduly aggressive as a result.

---

1. I have had some fairly extended experience of this. I remember in 1931 talking with American engineers in the Soviet Union who thought the Russians too incompetent in the mechanical arts ever to build tractors, let alone planes; they failed, as it seemed to me, to realize how the huge friction of Soviet incompetence could be partly overcome by the even huger burning up of human resources if one cared not at all about them. Likewise, when some seemed complacent about the Chinese Communists on the ground that "you could never

Consequently, I want to open up a discussion of some of the defenses people have against totalitarianism. Not that these defenses—I shall discuss apathy, corruption, free enterprise, crime, and so on—threaten the security system of the Soviets; that system is a new social invention and there are as few defenses against annihilation by it as against annihilation by atom bombs. Indeed, in some ways totalitarianism is actually strengthened by these partial defenses people are able to throw up against it, which make it possible for many people to compromise with the system as a whole. But at least a few European thinkers may be perplexed by the readiness of Americans, lacking firsthand experience of people's capacity to resist, to assume that totalitarianism possesses the kind of psychological pressure system pictured by Orwell in that sadistic but symptomatic book *1984*: here is a fantasy of omnipotent totalitarian impressiveness which I think may itself, among those who admire efficiency and have little faith in man, be an appeal of totalitarianism for those outside its present reach.

For we must distinguish, first of all, between the appeals of totalitarianism when it is out of power and its appeals when in power; my concern here is mainly with the latter. Out of power, totalitarianism competes like any other party, only more so: it can be all things to all men, attracting the idealist by its promise to reform society, to clean out the swindlers; attracting the disoriented and bewildered by its simplistic "explanations" of their misery and of their world, and by promising to get rid of seeming anarchy by enforcing social co-operation; and attracting the sadist in the way the Berkeley study of the "Authoritarian Personality" has documented. (In the Moslem countries and the Far East, the Communists do not need even this much of an armory: a promise to drive out the foreign devils while promising Western-style commodities to everyone may be almost enough.) Most large-scale societies will offer a spectrum of people available for the high-minded, middle-minded, and low-minded aspects of totalitarian politics, though probably a crisis is necessary to convert their organization into a fighting revolutionary party with a real hope of capturing power. That is, the fact that totalitarianism has captured a country doesn't tell us as much as some observers have supposed about the character of its total population; the mass base necessary can be far less than a majority and it can include people of

organize the unbelligerent Chinese for aggressive war," I felt that this left out of account the awful weapon of systematic terror and utter ruthlessness about killing one's "own" people that is Moscow's first export to its satellites and "national" Communist parties.

profoundly non-totalitarian personalities who have been fooled—to whom the appeal has not been a very deep-going one.[2]

When the latter wake up to the fact that the God they followed has failed them, it is of course too late to change deities. For many years it seemed to me that the Soviet Union was more dangerous in this respect than the Nazis, let alone the Fascists in Spain and Italy, because the latter were so clearly corrupt that they could not help but disillusion their idealists rapidly. Thus, during the Nazi regime, while the concentration camps were more or less hidden, the power and pelf struggles within the Nazi echelons were not: Hitler might remain for some unsullied. but hardly the party bums and barons of lesser magnitude, struggling to build up private empires of business and espionage. The ideological trappings fell away speedily enough. To be sure, there remained some fanatics, especially perhaps in the SS, savagely incorruptible. But many Germans who were drawn to the Nazis precisely by their claim to eliminate corruption were quickly enlightened when they saw the even greater corruption introduced. As against this, the Communists have seemed more incorruptible—a kind of Cromwellian type, hard-bitten and ascetic—thus perhaps retaining ideological impressiveness as well as gaining physical oppressiveness even after being installed in power. And certainly that impressiveness remains even today for many of those outside the system. Inside, however, there is some evidence—and of course only tantalizingly little—that corruption, blackmarketing, crime, and juggling of figures are widespread; presumably this makes it hard for the idealistic young to be overimpressed with the system's ethical rightness. To be sure, we have had such "training" in contempt for bourgeois comfort-seeking and the dangers of the desire for wealth, that if a Communist is desirous not of wealth but of power he can more readily appear idealistic; perhaps we should learn that the *auri sacra fames,* the cursed hunger for gold, is not half so dangerous to the human race as the ascetic drive for power—a point recently remade by Eric Hoffer in *The True Believer.* Indeed, anyone who claims he wishes to eliminate vice utterly is declaring a very dangerous and antihuman heresy—one all too prevalent, I might add, in today's municipal and national politics in this country. We must teach ourselves,

---

2. What I have said here needs to be qualified by an understanding of the less conscious motives which attract people to a totalitarian party. The Nazis, for example, were not really all things to all men; they gave the wink to some men that, for instance, their legality was merely window-dressing, and the latter could use the window-dressing to satisfy their conscious inhibitions against what at bottom drew them to the party. See, for example, Erik H. Erikson's discussion of "Hitler's Imagery and German Youth," in *Childhood and Society,* pp. 284-315.

and the young, to distinguish between genuine idealism and arrogant, curdled indignation against behavior which falls short of some monastic image of virtue.

More generally, I have long thought that we need to re-evaluate the role of corruption in a society, with less emphasis on its obviously malign features and more on its power as an antidote to fanaticism. Barrington Moore in *Soviet Politics,* and Margaret Mead in *Soviet Attitudes Toward Authority* present materials documenting the Soviet campaign against the corrupting tendencies introduced into the system by friendship and family feeling—some of Mead's quotations could have come from Bishop Baxter or other Puritan divines, and others from American civil service reformers. While Kravchenko shows how one must at once betray friends in the Soviet regime when they fall under state suspicion—and here, too, the Soviets are more tyrannous than the Nazis who expected friends to intercede with the Gestapo—it would appear that such human ties have never been completely fragmented, whether by Puritanism,[3] industrialism, or their savagely sudden combination in Bolshevism. Actually, people have had to defend themselves against the Soviet system's high demands for performance by building personal cliques, by favoritism, by cultivating cronies; thus, an informal network has continued to operate alongside the formal one, whose extraordinary expectations can in fact only be met in this way. (Similarly, Petrov points out that no amount of indoctrination has persuaded the Russian people to like and admire spies and informers, or to extirpate from their own reactions the profoundly human emotion of pity.)

To be sure, corruption does not always and inevitably work as a solvent for ideological claims. Hannah Arendt, returning from Germany last year, described the way in which many middle-class, educated Germans, in order to justify to themselves within their rigid code the compromises they made with the Nazi system, had to exalt that system ideologically; they were trapped by complicity as they would not have been had they been more cynical. Incidentally, their wives, who had to hunt for subsistence on the blackmarket, were probably better off in this respect—they did the needful things to keep going, while allowing their husbands to remain deceived in their older morality. And it could at least be argued that women—as the Bachofen-Fromm interpretation of the Oedipus trilogy would indicate

---

3. While I think that there are many revealing analogies between theocratic Calvinism in its heyday and Stalinism, I do not think the similarities should be pressed too far; among many other differences, the Puritans—in any case, far less powerful—believed in law.

—are more immune than men to impersonal and abstract ideals; they are more conservative in the good and in the bad sense—more "realistic."

I am not, it should be clear, discussing what are called resistance movements, but rather what might be called resistance quiescences. I am talking about the quieter modes of resistance to totalitarianism, not so much in practical life as in mental obeisance, in refusal to internalize the system's ethical norms. I am, moreover, quite unable to say what *proportion* of people, either under the Nazi regime or the Soviet, succumbed or managed to defend themselves in this way; I cannot assign quantitative weights to one mode or the other. It is one of our difficulties as intellectuals that we cannot easily assign such weights. We are likely to overestimate symbolic behavior that appears to give deference to totalitarian power. And the testimony of intellectuals who once believed in totalitarianism and have now fled it is further indication as to the dangers of a totalitarian regime for the emotional life of people like ourselves: ours is in many ways the most exposed position since overt obedience to mere power is least habitual, and since we need—whatever our rational beliefs about men's irrationality—to justify and integrate our behavior in some fashion, perhaps especially so when we ourselves are wholesalers or retailers of ideology.

Myrdal, when he visited this country, commented on the "protective community" of the Negroes and of lower-class people generally who, vis-a-vis the whites and the authorities, "ain't seen nothing or nobody"; long training has made them adept in duplicity, evasion, and sly sabotage. (A similar phenomenon exists in Italian peasant communities, under the name of "*la omertà*.") True, this kind of protective community breaks down on occasion, even under the relatively mild pressures and promises of white or official society; the Soviets have much more violent and fearsome methods. Moreover, the Soviet secret police are facing a population most of which is new to urban life, ways and byways: industrialization always stirs the melting pot and throws strange peoples together who have little understanding of or sympathy for each other, or whose suspicion of each other can be easily aroused. Whereas the workers of Hamburg were already accustomed to the industrial revolution and its problems and prospects of social interaction, the Soviet Union is in a sense one vast labor camp where social organization has to start pretty much from scratch.[4] Even so, I think it likely that there are protective

---

4. There is no space here to go into the analogous problem of the concentration camps themselves. Kogon's and David Rousset's accounts would seem to indicate that in these camps some prisoner rule developed, and much corruption

communities in Russian farms and factories, which punish Stakhano-
vites and cope with spies.

In a brilliant article in *The Reporter*, Lionel Trilling has delineated the anti-social, anti-societal bent of a great deal of American
literature: Huck Finn escaping the well-meant civilizing clutches of
the Widow Douglas is a good illustration of his theme. But we may
raise the question whether such escapes—if not to the open spaces then
to a protective community or an underground institution like a blind
pig or a whorehouse—are not to be found in all the major cultures
which have any complex institutions at all, and possibly even in the
simplest cultures if we only knew where to look for them. We must
never underestimate the ability of human beings to dramatize, to play
roles, to behave in ways that seem contradictory only if we do not
appreciate the changes in scene and audience. A friend of mine, Mark
Benney, riding a train with peasants in Nazi Germany, was struck
by their impassivity of feature. When he and another stranger, a
Nazi, got off the train, he could feel behind him a sudden relaxation
of facial and postural tensions, and looking back he saw people who
were, in a sense, not at all the same people.[5]

By the block system and the other machinery of a police terror,
the Soviets can cut off many of the traditional underground institutions, and make others too hazardous for all but a few heroes. But
even in such a case, human ingenuity is not completely helpless.
Overfulfillment—literal obedience to extravagant Soviet demands—
can be another form of sabotage; I have heard tell of one group of
Moscow cynics who would go to meetings and joyfully accuse all
and sundry of deviationism as a sure way to break up the party. All
fanatical movements, I would suggest, are as threatened by the real
or pretended deviations in the direction of perfect obedience as by
the underground. Beyond all this, there remains the escape into the
self, the escape of withdrawal, of what Kris and Leites have termed

---

(reminiscent of the kangaroo courts in the worst American jails), with various
groups of prisoners fighting among themselves, and with guard allies, for hegemony. When I raised this problem at the Committee's meeting, Hannah Arendt
insisted that the camps described by Kogon and Rousset were exceptions, and
that in most no such prisoner ingenuities and defenses developed. Reliable evidence is hard to come by; see, however, Theodore Abel, "The Sociology of Concentration Camps" in December, 1951, *Social Forces*, vol. 30, pp. 150-155, which
offers some support for my own position; and see, also, David P. Boder, *I Did
Not Interview the Dead.*

5. In a letter, Norman Birnbaum has suggested that the peasants' uneasiness
was pre-political—due to their natural reserve with urban people (city slickers)
not of their kind. But he also points out that if this were the case it would
not change the fundamental fact: the ability of people to be "two-faced" and to
practice social concealment on the basis of minimal cues.

"privatization." The Soviet press, by its attacks on the practice, gives evidence that depoliticization tendencies are strong, and one would expect people to develop ritualized ways of handling their political exhortations without inner conviction.

In my 1931 visit to the Soviet Union, I talked with students who had decided to go into medicine or engineering, rather than journalism or writing, as more protected, less polemical and sensitive areas; doubtless, many of them were sadly fooled when, in the purges, they found themselves accused of sabotage and wrecking, or even theoretical deviations based on their seemingly unideological decisions. Ever since then, I have sought to find out whether young people were able to choose army careers, or skilled labor, as ways of avoiding such dangers; I have found some evidence that such escapes are extremely unlikely since bright boys are already spotted in high school and compelled as well as bribed to develop their talents and deploy them; they cannot hide their light under a bushel.

One of the reasons why young people are willing to assume dangerous responsibilities is of course that the rewards of success in managerial posts are very great. It has become obvious that Soviet managers are no longer held, as in the earlier years of the regime, to ascetic standards of living. It is possible that, among the abler cadres, an entrepreneurial risk-taking attitude towards life is encouraged, which makes the prospect of becoming a factory manager with access to women, dachas, power, and glory worth taking the risk that it won't last, and may even be succeeded by exile and still grimmer fates —a psychology which bears some resemblance to that occasionally found among professional soldiers for whom battles mean promotions as well as deadly dangers.

But monetary rewards have their own logic. The loose change in people's pockets tends to encourage free enterprise or, as it is known in the Soviet Union, the black market. The black market also enters when managers scrounge for goods in order to fulfill production quotas and so remain managers. And business as usual, like other forms of corruption, is a wonderful "charm" against ideologies, useful particularly because of its own ordinarily unideological character. Under the Nazis, both in Germany and in the occupied countries, business was often almost an unconscious sabotage of the regime: people in pursuit of their private ends violated the public rules without, so to speak, intending any resistance. They did not have to be heroes, any more than the scofflaws were who drank under American prohibition, or the fellow who wants to make a fast buck in the Western war economies. Guenter Reimann in his book *The Vampire Economy*, tells as a characteristic story the answer to a question as to what a permit from a Party member for a certain commodity would cost: "Well, it all depends on what kind of a Party member you have to deal with. If he no longer believes in National Socialism, it will cost you a hundred marks. If he still does, five hundred marks. But if he is a fanatic, you will have to pay a thousand marks."[6]

In the past, we have tended to interpret such signs of passive resistance in terms of our hope for an eventual overthrow of the system from within; we have been like the Marxists who thought contradictions would bring capitalism down. Now we know that it takes more to destroy a system than its own contradictions, and we have been apt to go to the other extreme and assume that the system was, therefore, since it didn't collapse, all-seeing and all-powerful over the minds of men. Two errors common to the social sciences have worked together to this end. The first error, as just indicated, is to imagine social systems as monolithic, and as needing to be relatively efficient to remain in power. Actually, systems roll on, as people do, despite glaring defects and "impossible" behavior. We have created an imaginary image of what it takes for an institution to keep going; in fact, it can go on with little support and less efficiency. One reason for this mirage we have is that when a revolution does occur, we explain it as a matter of course by pointing to the defects of the previous system—and we fall here into the error of supposing that what happened *had* to happen. Barring relatively accidental factors, the system might well have gone on for a long while. (Incidentally, this same historicist error is an element in the overestimation of the power of totalitarian appeals; we assume, for example, that these appeals were responsible for Hitler's victory in Germany as if that victory were a foregone conclusion and not a series of reversible choice-points.) Social scientists, having logical minds and being efficient themselves— even when they sing the praises of irrationality—seldom take a sufficiently perspectivistic view of a society to see it as rolling along in spite of all the things which should bring it to a stop. In this error, of course, they do not stand alone; most of us tend to overinterpret the behavior of others, especially perhaps when we are menaced by them.

The second error, which is perhaps historically older, is more

6. Dr. Arendt in her rebuttal criticized the relevance of this and similar incidents on the ground that they occurred prior to Germany's entry into World War II—prior, that is, to the descent of the iron curtain which protected and facilitated complete totalitarianism. Without the slightest doubt, the Nazis grew ever more ferocious as the war progressed—thus, mass genocide did not really get under way until then; nevertheless, just because of the iron curtain, it is all the more necessary to examine whether the system did ever become efficiently monolithic even when all possible restraints of a humanitarian or public-relations sort disappeared. Cf. Trevor-Roper's *The Last Days of Hitler*.

formidable. It assumes that men can be readily manipulated and controlled, either as the earlier utopians thought in pursuit of some greatly uplifted state, or as the more recent anti-utopians such as Huxley and Orwell have thought, in pursuit of vulgarity and beastliness. (Orwell, to be sure, exempts his proles from the ravages of ideology.) Social science is concerned with prediction, with categorizing human beings and social systems. So it has perhaps a professional bias toward cutting men down to the size of the categories, and not allowing them to play the multiplicity of roles, with the multiplicity of emotional responses, that we constantly show ourselves capable of. Thus we run into a paradox. On the one hand, we think men can be adjusted into some Brave New World because of fundamental human plasticity and flexibility, while on the other hand we do not see that men's ability precisely to fit, part-time, into such a world is what saves them from having to fit into it as total personalities. We have assumed—and in this of course we reflect our own cultural attitudes —that people must be co-operative in order to co-operate, whereas throughout history people have co-operated because to do so made realistic sense, because certain conditions were met, and not because of the psychological appeal of co-operation per se. We have, under the pressure of recent events, reacted against the older view of writers like Sumner that people and cultures can hardly be changed at all towards the view that they can not only be changed but can be easily destroyed.

Ever since the rise of the bourgeoisie and of public opinion and mass politics, people have been afraid of the seeming chaos created by the open fight of special interest groups. The fight is open because there is a press and because each group tries both to solidify its own members and to recruit others by universalizing its appeals. In the contemporary world, there are many influential men who believe that this war of vested interests, occurring within the framework of a democratic society, will endanger consensus and disrupt the entire social fabric. Totalitarianism, in fact, makes an appeal, less to people's special interests as, let us say, workers, than to their fear of all competing interests, including even their own as these are organized by lobbies and pressure groups. Having an image of society as it ought to be, as orderly and co-operative, they tend to welcome, especially of course when the going gets rough, a system which promises to eliminate all social classes and other vested interests which impede co-operation. Thus, on the one hand they are frightened by the ideal of a pluralistic, somewhat disorderly, and highly competitive society— still the best ideal in the business, in my opinion—while on the other hand, their view of men as plastic allows them to suppose that the totalitarians will change all that and transform men into automatically socialized creatures like the ants. When we put matters this way, we can see that there may be grandiose fantasies at the bottom of the fears of people like Orwell, deeply repressed fantasies of human omnipotence such as Hannah Arendt has traced in the totalitarians themselves.

For me, the most striking conclusion to be drawn from the state of Germany today, from the stories of the refugees from behind the Iron Curtain, even from the present behavior of former concentration camp inmates, is precisely how hard it is permanently to destroy most people psychologically. Once the terror is removed, they appear to snap back, ravaged as in any illness, but capable of extraordinary recuperative efforts. In extreme situations such as Dr. Bettelheim has described, people sink to almost incredible abysses or more rarely rise to incredible heights; but if they survive at all, they exhibit an astonishing capacity to wipe away those nightmares.

As the concept of social harmony and integration has misled us as to the amount of disorganization a going society can stand, so I believe that the concept of psychological integration has misled us as to the amount of disintegration and inconsistency of response that an individual can stand. Even in our society, we tell lies to ourselves and others all day long; we are split personalities; yet, with a minimum amount of support from the system, we manage to keep going. All our days we give hostages to history and fortune, and yet are able to call on self-renewing aspects of the ever-filled cup of life.

A certain immunity to ideologies seems to me to be spreading in the world, if not as fast as totalitarianism, at least in its wake. This immunity is far from perfect, even in its own terms. Totalitarianism can appeal to cynics in their cynicism just as much as to idealists in their idealism. An ideology can be fashioned out of anti-ideology, as totalitarian parties have been fashioned out of an anti-party program. And a world is certainly ill-omened in which we must fear the enthusiasm of the young, and prefer their apathy, because we have learned (a hundred and fifty years after Burke) to fear ideas in politics.

We simply do not know whether, over a series of generations, it is possible to rob people even of the freedom of their apathy. Very likely people need at least some ability to communicate disaffection if they are not to conclude that only they alone are out of step. And privatization implies accepting the given regime as part of the order of nature, not to be fought by the likes of oneself—only in that way can terrible guilt feelings be avoided.[7] There comes to mind the story of

---

7. We must be careful in evaluating evidence here. A group of people near

a German anti-Nazi who, shortly after Hitler's coming, had taken a job as stenographer to an SS committee. Everything went well for a while; his convictions remained unshaken, and he continued old Socialist associations. But then one day he had a paralysis of his right arm; he could not move it at all. He went to a psychiatrist, who came quickly to the source of the paralysis, namely that the stenographer could not resign himself to the constant Heil Hitler salutes.

And, indeed, many of the defenses I have discussed are little better than forms of paralysis which, by their presence, evidence the resistance men put up against seemingly implacable destinies. I would prefer to see men fighting back through paralysis than succumbing through active incorporation of the enemy. But this is hardly an optimum way to live one's life, and we cannot be—even apart from the danger to ourselves—unmoved by the plight of those now living and dying under Communist regimes. All we can do while we seek ways to bring those regimes down without war is to find our way to a more robust view of man's potentialities, not only for evil, about which we have heard and learned so much, not only for heroism, about which we have also learned, but also for sheer unheroic cussed resistance to totalitarian efforts to make a new man of him.

Frankfurt remarked to my colleague Everett Hughes, when he had won their confidence, "Unter Hitler war Es doch besser." This did not mean they had been or were still Nazis, but just the opposite, namely that they were making an unideological judgment, immune as well to Occupation, to democracy, as to Nazism.

26. The Nylon War

Today—August 1, 1951—the Nylon War enters upon the third month since the United States began all-out bombing of the Soviet Union with consumer's goods, and it seems time to take a retrospective look. Behind the initial raid of June 1 were years of secret and complex preparations, and an idea of disarming simplicity: that if allowed to sample the riches of America, the Russian people would not long tolerate masters who gave them tanks and spies instead of vacuum cleaners and beauty parlors. The Russian rulers would thereupon be forced to turn out consumers' goods, or face mass discontent on an increasing scale.

The Nylon War was conceived by an army colonel—we shall call him 'Y'—whose name cannot yet be revealed. Working with secret funds which the Central Intelligence Agency had found itself unable to spend, Y organized shortly after World War II the so-called 'Bar Harbor Project,' the nucleus of what, some five years later, became 'Operation Abundance,' or, as the press soon dubbed it, the 'Nylon War.' After experiments with rockets and balloons, it was concluded that only cargo planes—navigating, it was hoped, above the range of Russian radar—could successfuly deliver the many billion dollars worth of consumer goods it was planned to send. Nevertheless, when Y and his group first broached their plans to a few selected Congressional leaders in the winter of 1948 they were dismissed as hopelessly academic. America had neither the goods nor the planes nor the politics to begin such an undertaking. But in the fall of 1950, with the country bogged down in a seemingly endless small-scale war in Korea, Y's hopes revived. For one thing, the cargo planes needed for the job were beginning to become available. Moreover, a certain amount of overordering by the Armed Services, panicky over Korea, had created a stockpile of consumer goods. More important, the Administration, having locked up all known and many suspected Communists in one of the old Japanese relocation camps, had still not convinced the country that it was sufficiently anti-Soviet, though at the same time many Americans wanted peace but did not dare admit it. A plan which, in fact and in presentation, took attention away from alleged Far-Eastern bungling, and which was both violently anti-Soviet and pro-peace, appeared to offer the possibility of restoring the Administration's tottering position in the counry.

This is not the place to recount the political maneuverings that preceded Truman's success in securing a two billion dollar initial appropriation from Congress, nor the Potomac maneuverings that led to the recruitment of top-flight production and merchandising talent from civilian life. Our story begins with Truman going before Congress to secure authority to 'bring the benefits of American technology to less fortunate nations' by round-the-clock bombing, the day after the news of the first raids hit the American public.

The planners of the Bar Harbor Project had staked American prestige, their professional futures, and the lives of six thousand airmen on the belief that the Soviets would not know of these first flights nor meet them with armed resistance. When the opening missions were accomplished without incident, permitting Truman to make his appeal, Washington was immensely relieved; but when the second wave of planes met with no resistance either, Washington was baffled. It was at first assumed that the Soviet radar network had again simply failed to spot the high-flying planes—cruising at 48,000 feet and self-protected from radar by some still presumably secret device. We now know that what actually happened was a division of opinion in the Kremlin —we can piece the story together from intelligence reports and from clues in *Pravda*. A faction, led by foreign trade chief Mikoyan, maintained that the scheme was a huge hoax, designed to stampede Russia into a crusade against a fairy-tale—and so to make her the laughing stock of the world. He counselled, wait and see. And, indeed, it *was* a fairy tale for secret police boss Beria, who argued that the raids had never taken place, but that reports of them had been faked by some Social Democratic East Germans who had somehow gotten access to the communications networks. When this idea was exploded, Beria counselled shooting the planes down, on the ground that they were simply a screen spying out plants for an atomic attack. Stalin himself believed with repentant economist Varga that American capitalism had reached so critical a point that only through forcible gifts overseas could the Wall Street ruling clique hope to maintain its profits and dominance. Coupled with these divisions of opinion, which stalemated action, was the fear in some quarters that America might welcome attacks on its errand-of-mercy planes as a pretext for the war of extermination openly preached by some only mildly rebuked American leaders.

At any rate, the confusion in the Politburo was more than mirrored by the confusion in the target cities caused by the baptismal raids. Over 600 C-54s streamed high over Rostov, and another 200 over Vladivostok, dropped their cargoes, and headed back to their bases in the Middle East and Japan. By today's standard these initial forays were small-scale—200,000 pairs of nylon hose, 4,000,000 packs of cigarettes, 35,000 Toni-wave kits, 20,000 yo-yos, 10,000 wrist watches, and a number of odds and ends from P-X overstock. Yet this was more than enough to provoke frenzied rioting as the inhabitants scrambled for a share. Within a few hours after the first parcels had fallen, the roads into the target cities were jammed. Road blocks had to be thrown up around the cities, and communications with the outside were severed. The fast-spreading rumors of largess from above were branded 'criminally insane,' and their source traced to machinations of the recently purged 'homeless cosmopolitan Simeon Osnavitch (Rosenblum).'

But the propaganda of the deed proved stronger than the propaganda of the word. As Odessa, Yakutsk, Smolensk, and other cities became targets of aggressive generosity, as Soviet housewives saw with their own eyes American stoves, refrigerators, clothing, and toys, the Kremlin was forced to change its line and, ignoring earlier denials, to give the raids full but negative publicity. David Zaslavsky's article in the June 10 *Izvestia* heralded the new approach. Entitled 'The Mad Dogs of Imperialism Foam at the Mouth,' he saw the airlift as harbinger of America's economic collapse. 'Unable because of the valiant resistance of the peace-loving democracies to conquer foreign markets, America's Fascist plutocracy is now reduced to giving away goods. . . .' Taking another line, *Red Star* argued that to accept American consumer goods would make stalwart Russians as decadent as rich New Yorkers.

However, the Russian people who could get access, either directly or through the black market that soon arose, to American goods seemed not to fear decadence. Again, there was a change of line. Falling back on a trick learned during Lend-Lease, it was claimed that the goods were Russian-made, and *Pravda* on June 14 stated that the Toni-wave kit had been invented by Pavlov before World War I. However, Colonel Y's staff had anticipated this altogether routine reaction. On June 17, the target cities of that day—Kiev, Stalingrad, Magnitogorsk—received their wares wrapped in large cartoons of Stalin bending over, in a somewhat undignified pose, to pick up a dropped Ansco camera. This forced still another switch of line. On June 20 Beria went on the air to announce that the Americans were sending over goods poisoned by atomic radiation, and all papers and broadcasts carried scare stories about people who had died from using Revlon or Schick shavers. And indeed booby traps (planted by MVD) succeeded in killing a number of overeager citizens. For a while, this permitted specially-recruited Party members to gather up the goods and take them to headquarters for alleged de-radiation.

But here something unexpected occurred. We know from a few people who managed to escape to the West that a number of Party elements themselves became disaffected. Asked to turn in all American goods, they held on to some possessions secretly—there was a brisk underground trade in fake Russian labels. Sometimes wives, having gotten used to the comforts of Tampax and other disappearing items, would hide them from their more ascetic husbands; children of Party members cached pogo sticks and even tricycles. Thus it came about that when Party members were ordered to join 'decontamination' squads the depots were re-entered at night and portable items taken. By the beginning of July, all attempts to deceive the people had only made matters worse; things were getting out of hand.

Faring badly in the 'War,' the Kremlin turned to diplomacy. On July 5 at Lake Success Malik described the airlift as 'an outrage remindful of Hitlerite aggression' and, invoking Art. 39 of the U.N. Charter, he called on the Security Council to halt the 'shameful depredations of the American warmongers.' Austin replied that 'these gifts are no more or less than a new-fashioned application of ancient principles,' and the Russian resolution was defeated, 9-2. The next step occurred in Washington, when Ambassador Panyushkin handed Secretary Acheson a sharply worded note warning that 'should these present outrages continue, the U.S.S.R. will have no recourse but to reply in kind.'

Seattle was the first American city to learn the meaning of the Soviet warning as on July 15 a hundred Russian heavy bombers (presumably from bases in the Kuriles) left behind them 15,000 tins of caviar, 500 fur coats, and 80,000 copies of Stalin's speeches on the minorities question. When the Russian planes came, followed in by American jets, many were apprehensive, but as the counter-attack had been anticipated it proved possible to prevent incidents in the air and panic on the ground. Since then, Butte, Minneapolis, Buffalo, and Moscow, Idaho, have been added to the list of America's frontline cities. But in quantity and quality the counter-offensive has been unimpressive. Searing vodka, badly styled mink coats (the only really selling item), undependable cigarette lighters—these betray a sad lack of know-how in production and merchandising. In an editorial, 'Worse than Lend-Lease,' the N.Y. *Daily News* has charged that the Nylon War gives the Soviets free lessons in the secrets of America's success, but truly conservative papers like the *Herald-Tribune* see the comparative showing of Americans and Russians as a world demonstration of the superiority of free enterprise.

It is clear, at any rate, that free enterprise has not suffered much of a jolt—nor, indeed, has the mounting inflation been much reduced—

by the Russian campaign. To be sure, the massive air-borne shipments of caviar have made luxury grocers fear inventory losses and Portugal, heavily dependent on the American anchovy market, has been worried. But these pin-pricks are nothing to what is now becoming evident on the Russian side—namely the imminent collapse of the economy. For the homeland of centralized economic planning is experiencing its own form of want in the midst of plenty. Soviet consumers, given a free choice between shoddy domestic merchandise and airlift items, want nothing to do with the former and in a score of fields Russian goods go unwanted as the potential buyer dreams of soon owning an American version. Soviet housewives, eager to keep up with American-supplied 'Joneses,' pester their local stores, often to the point of creating local shortages—indeed, the American refrigerators have created demands, not only for electricity, but also for many foods which can now be stored (and hoarded).

Much of this disruption is the result of careful planning by the Bar Harbor Project's Division of Economic Dislocation. The Division, for example, early began studies of Russian power distribution, and saw to the landing of 60-cycle radios, shavers, toasters, milking machines, in 60-cycle areas; 25-cycle appliances in 25-cycle areas, and so on, especially with an eye to areas of power-shortage or competition with critical industries. In cooperation with G.E., methods were worked out by which the Russian donees could plug their appliances, with appropriate transformers, directly into high-voltage or street power lines; thus simply shutting off house current could not save the Russian utilities from overload. Similarly, drawing on the American monopolistic practice of tie-in sales, goods were dropped whose use demanded other items in short supply—oil ranges, for instance, were dropped throughout the Baku fields. Of course, mistakes were made and in one or two cases bottlenecks in the Russian economy were relieved, as when some containers were salvaged to repair a tin shortage of which the planners had not been advised.

But it is not only on the production end that the raids have been disruptive. Last Friday's raid on Moscow—when 22,000 tons of goods were dropped—may be taken as an illustration. For the first time General Vandenburg's airmen tackled—and successfully solved—the knotty engineering problem of dropping jeeps (complete with 150 gallons of gasoline and directions in simple Russian). So skillfully was the job done that half the three hundred vehicles parachuted down landed directly on the Kremlin's doorstep—in the center of Red Square. The raid was given wide advance publicity through the Voice and leaflets and when the great day came Moscow's factories were deserted as people fought for roof-top perches; in addition, an estimated

250,000 collective farmers swarmed into the city. In fact, as people drift from place to place hoping that their ship may fly in, the phrase 'rootless cosmopolite' at last assumes real meaning. Economists, talking learnedly of 'multipliers,' calculate that Russian output is dropping 3 per cent a month.

The Kremlin has reacted in the only way it knows, by a series of purges. Sergei Churnik, erstwhile head of the cigarette trust, is on trial for 'deliberate wrecking and economic treason.' Bureaucrats live in terror lest their region or their industry be next disrupted by the American bombardment, and they waver between inactivity and frantic Stakhanovite shows of activity. These human tragedies testify to the growing fear in the Politburo concerning the long-run consequences of the American offensive. The tangible proofs of American prosperity, ingenuity, and generosity can no longer be gainsaid; and the new official line that Wall Street is bleeding America white in order to create scarcity and raise prices at home, while 'believed,' has little impact against the ever-mounting volume, and fascinating variety, of goods and rumors of goods. Can the capitalistic gluttons of privilege be such bad fellows if we, the Russians, are aided by them to enjoy luxuries previously reserved for the dachas of novelists and plant managers? In an article in the *New Statesman and Nation*, Geoffrey Gorer has recently contended that the airlift serves to revive primitive Russian 'orality,' and that the image of America can no longer be that of a leering Uncle Sam or top-hatted banker but must soon become amiably matronly. It is thoughts along this line that most worry the Politburo although, of course, the MVD sees to it that only a tiny fraction of the mounting skepticism expresses itself openly or even in whispered jokes. But what is the MVD to do about a resolution of the All-Workers Congress of Tiflis that 'Marxist-Leninist-Stalinist democracy demands that party cadres install officials who can cope with the mounting crisis'?

Translated into plain talk, this means that the Russian people, without saying so in as many words, are now putting a price on their collaboration with the regime. The price—'goods instead of guns.' For Russia's industrial plant, harassed by the rapidly growing impact of Operation Abundance, cannot supply both, let alone carry on the counter-offensive against America. Intelligence reports speak of scheduled production cutbacks varying from 25 per cent on tanks to 75 per cent on artillery; it is symptomatic that washing machines, designed to compete with the American Bendixes which are being dropped in ever-increasing numbers, will soon start rolling off the assembly lines of the great Red October Tank Works—after its former manager

had been shot for asserting that conversion to peacetime production
could not be achieved in less than two years.

Meanwhile, diplomatic moves are under way—so, at least, the Alsop
brothers report—to liquidate the Nylon War. It is obvious why the
Russian leaders are prepared to make very considerable concessions
in the satellite countries, in China, and in Indo-China in order to regain
the strategic initiative in their domestic affairs. But on the American
side the willingness of many to listen to Russian overtures is based on
the success, rather than the failure, of the campaign. One sees a repetition of 1940 as the Washington *Times-Herald* and the *Daily Compass* join hands in attacking Operation Abundance, the former calling
it 'an international WPA,' the latter arguing 'you can't fight ideas
with goods.' Addressing the Stanford Alumni Club of Los Angeles,
Herbert Hoover spoke for millions in observing that the monthly cost
of the airlift has already exceeded the entire Federal budget for the
year 1839. Still another tack has been taken by Senators who want the
airlift to continue, but with different targets; some, insisting that
charity begins at home, have wanted free goods landed on their dis-
tricts; others have supported the claims of Japan, the Philippines, or
Franco. Still others fear that many of the air lift items could be recon-
verted in some way for use by the Russian war machine; they are
especially opposed to the jeep delivery program, despite reports it
is wreaking havoc with the Russian road system as well as with the
gasoline supply. And the House Un-American Affairs Committee has
charged that trade secrets are being delivered to Russian spies by
Red homosexual officials and professors disguised as plane pilots.

These are the obvious enemies, and against them stand some obvious friends of the Nylon War. Both AFL and CIO, now in their
eighth round of wage increases, vigorously support the program,
though it is rumored that the Railroad Brotherhoods have done so
only in return for a fact-finding board's support of a 14-hour week.
Farmers have become reconciled by the promise that bulk agricultural products will soon move over the aerial transmission belt—in
part to encourage the wanderings of Russian farmers. The business
community is divided, with the CED, Juan Trippe, and Baruch leading the supporters of the airlift.[1] But it would be a mistake to assume

---

1. It goes without saying that there are many fights within pressure groups as
to *what* the airlift shall carry—and ideological considerations are not confined to
the Soviet side. Thus, the Committee Against Juvenile Delinquency has reg-
istered strong protests against sending comic books. More serious issues revolve
around the Planned Parenthood League's campaign to get contraceptives included
in the airlift items. In addition to humanitarian arguments, the claim is made

that support of Operation Abundance springs only from hopes of material gain. The renewed fight against oppression and want, the excitement of following the raids in maps and betting pools, the ridiculousness of the Russian response—all these things have made many millions of Americans less anxious than they have been since the days in October 1950 when it seemed as if the Korean War would be quickly concluded.

Indeed, it is just this loss of tension which has given rise to much of the covert opposition to the Nylon War, as distinguished from the overt opposition already discussed. On the one hand, certain leaders are frightened that the Russian dictatorship may indeed be overthrown —as Colonel Y in his more optimistic moments had ventured to hope. This is thought to raise the possibility of all sorts of chaotic movements developing in Central and Eastern Europe, and even further west—Franco, for instance, feels threatened at the loss of his 'enemy,' and has offered to act as mediator in the Nylon War. On the other hand, it has become increasingly difficult for American politicians to frighten the American public about Russia: the once-feared monolith now appears as almost a joke, with its crude poster-and-caviar reprisals, its riots over stockings, soap, Ronsons, and other gadgets which Americans regard in matter-of-fact fashion. The sharp drop in war sentiment in the United States has resulted in psychological and even actual unemployment for a number of people.

What do the coming months hold? It is significant that this depends almost entirely on the outcome of the American domestic struggle: the Nylon War has altered the whole power-complex which, as the Korean War dragged on, still heavily favored Russia. It is now Russia, not America, whose resources are overcommitted, whose alliances are overstrained. In fact, Mao's visit to Moscow at the end of July seems to have been attended with apprehension lest he ask America to cut Red China in on Operation Abundance—at a price, of course. The possibility that this may redound to the credit of the Truman Administration in the 1952 campaign is not the least of the nightmares haunting many Americans, and at this writing it is impossible to predict whether the opponents of the program will win out.

Meanwhile, Operation Abundance marches on, solving technical problems of incredible complexity. The latest move is the perfection of an ordering system whereby Russians can 'vote' for the commodities they most want, according to a point system, by the use of radio-

---

that this will reverse the demographic trend now so favorable to Russia; the League's slogan is 'Give them the tools and they will do the job.' Walter Lippmann predicts a Rome-Moscow axis if the League should win out.

sending equipment, battery-run, with which we have provided them. The commodities available will be described over the Voice of America—now for the first time having something to 'sell'—by Sears Roebuck-type catalogues, and by dropped samples in the case of soft goods. The method making it impossible for the Russian government effectively to jam this two-way communication of distributor and consumer is still the great secret of the Nylon War.

VIII.

PROBLEMS OF METHOD IN THE SOCIAL SCIENCES

HOW OFTEN have I not sat with a group of lawyers and heard one of them say, "Of course, I know nothing about it, but . . ." The lawyer's feeling that he could master anything in a pre-trial two weeks, that there is no expertise but his own, is often arrogant and Philistine, and I used frequently to have to argue with my brethren of the bar that neither economics nor anthropology could be so easily encompassed. However, I suppose I did gain from my professional experience some of this confidence—for Justice Brandeis I became an "expert" in the making and shipping of berry boxes in one short spell, and in freight-rate making in another; for Lyne, Woodworth & Evarts, I learned how to cross-examine heart specialists in insurance cases, and learned something of paper-making for the reorganization of International Paper & Power. But it was not only the occupational mystiques of other people that I was encouraged to deflate, but of my own pro-fession: the essay herein on "Law and the Legal Profession" repre-sents my long-held belief that social scientists and other laymen stand too much in awe of the law, that its method of casuistry, its biblio-graphic techniques, and so on, don't take three years to learn. (I still have to find a profession, including medicine, that doesn't inflate its claims to the neophyte to some degree.)

At the same time, I know that in my writings on social science, I have often suffered from not studying under the guardian angels who would have kept me from treading where they rightly fear to; read-ing over my first forays into social science, made while I was still teaching law, I am in places abashed at my unwitting temerity. If the temerity survives in pieces written much later, at least it is witting; thus when I write now about the study of national character I know from long stewing that the term "character" in this context is filled with ambiguities, and that I have no satisfactory answer to problems with which writers I respect have struggled long before my time.

The article on the legal profession exhibits such temerity in the freedom with which it draws on my own exceedingly limited oppor-tunities to observe lawyers; it is rather a program for field studies of the practicing bar than a formal statement of research results—my own or others'. It was first presented, at the invitation of Robert Redfield, a lawyer turned anthropologist, to the introductory graduate course on "Culture, Society, and the Individual" at the University of Chicago, in 1947. In the following two years, while I was at Yale, I sought to introduce a group of law students to the study of their own profession, encouraging them to use summer vacations to interview members of the bar in their home towns. Many of these students lacked confidence that they, untrained in social science techniques, could actually do interviews—perhaps they had not yet gained the confidence of the lawyer I dwelt on a moment ago. They found, however, that they could use a questionnaire on the basis of very inadequate briefing sessions I gave them; their project broke down less, I suspect, because of technical difficulties than because many of the faculty and students at the Yale Law School were more eager to use social science to prove something about the virtues or vices of juries, bar associations, or other polemicized themes than out of curiosity about the daily work and mythology of the practicing bar—curiosity not aiming to pin anything on anybody.

These experiences were in my mind when I revised my 1947 lecture for the 1950 annual meeting of the Association of American Law Schools. One of the commentators on the latter occasion was Professor Everett C. Hughes, from whose recurrent Chicago seminars on occupations and professions I have learned much of what value there may be in this article. In introducing the version of my talk which appeared in the *Chicago Law Review* (also drawn upon for the composite article here presented), he stated:

"Sponsorship in medicine is certainly strong, and there are those who say it is important in the academic career. American culture has stressed individual effort and ability, but never to the exclusion of family, class, religious and ethnic affiliations. We have had a kind of mixture of nepotism with insistence on delivering the goods. It may be that the law, or certain branches of it, demands abilities less amenable to social inheritance than those which make people company presidents. . . ."

Such considerations led me to draw on my own recollection of *Harvard Law Review* days, and on intermittent observation of other law reviews since, for rather hypothetical suggestions as to the role of the reviews—a unique student institution—in breaking down ethnic and class barriers in much the same way the Army has done: by putting people of different breeds on the same firing line, subject to Authority (the brass in the one case, the Law in the other), and forcing them to spend most waking hours in each other's company. But of course this would only apply to law reviews which, like the major ones, use some impersonal method of selection; and all this rests on the fact that law schools themselves, being cheap to run and even highly profitable, do not ordinarily if ever discriminate in their admissions policy. There are some 60 law reviews in the country, and very likely the pattern which I here suggest is not omnipresent—what are the patterns would be one of the topics for an anthropological or sociological study of the profession, as well as a basis for comparison and contrast with other professions.

This article, like the one on the recreationist in a previous section, might perhaps have been placed in a section on professions. However, it is apposite to a section on method because it is so largely concerned with the ways in which social scientists are drawn to certain fields of study and are repelled by others, such as the law. I suggest why there have been so few studies of lawyers and law, and what some of the theoretical rewards of such studies might be—but I would hate to see this suggestion taken as one more agenda for my fellow scientists. I believe strongly with Michael Polanyi that scientists are their own best planners, once they are in communication through print and congress and know what others are in general doing. Not very much of benefit to a field can be done by laying out programs; more can be achieved by providing a model which stimulates one's colleagues in a variety of ways and even produces new colleagues by making the field seem worthwhile and challenging to undergraduates. At best, my article is meant to suggest that the law is not so forbidding an area for social scientists to enter as it may appear; my remarks are intended as liberation rather than exhortation.

And the same is true of "Some Observations on Social Science Research," which treats some of these general themes as part of an effort to appraise the current state of affairs in sociology and social psychology. I decided to write this piece after I had heard a graduate student report in a seminar on a revolutionary plot he had had the good fortune to witness during World War II; he was miserable because he could not fit what he had seen into Max Weber's theory of charisma. It had not occurred to him that the theory, a very ambitious one, might not be the best way of approaching his particular problem; it had only occurred to him that he must be a very poor sociologist. And his doubts actually served to interfere with his report of incidents where precise observation would have been invaluable to a later Max Weber. This student was a casualty of current sociological polemics, and my article was aimed to clarify his and like situations.

In general, factors of spirit and stance have a great deal to do with what a social scientist feels prepared to study. When the Carnegie Corporation gave the Committee on Human Development a grant for the study of old age in a community, the question whether the community should be Chicago, a small town, or what, immediately involved such considerations of attitude. Chicago itself, despite apparent accessibility, was ruled out because it appeared too big, too unencompassable, too amorphous; we did not feel ready for it. Bravely we ruled out smaller cities—Peoria, Racine, South Bend, Decatur, and others for which we did feel more or less ready. Hearing of our search, an alert group in Kansas City invited us there, and, despite the distance, we accepted the challenge of a city far larger than the Muncies and Newburyports that have been studied, if smaller than such a megalopolis as Chicago.

In the study of aging, our difficulties are hardly less. Aging is almost as large a topic as life itself. There has been some good medical and physiological work but, despite the current vogue of geriatrics, little effective conceptualization in terms of social-psychological factors. In our Kansas City research, we decided to interview only those people who were over 40—though of course we realize that aging, like dying, begins much earlier. But this gives us a spread from 40 to 80 and up: a variety of contexts of obviously enormous range.

"Some Clinical and Cultural Aspects of the Aging Process" is drawn from a memorandum in which I sought to grapple with this issue. Since it was written, our Kansas City staff has been doing many interviews seeking to sharpen the criteria for aging as these can be applied to an interview, but we still feel we are a long way from delineating ideas that can be quantified, or that are especially applicable to our community rather than to aging in America as such.

I have included sections of two articles, "The Meaning of Opinion" and "Social Structure, Character Structure, and Opinion," jointly written with Nathan Glazer. The first of these articles was written before the 1948 election and published soon thereafter, with some afterthoughts on the Truman upset. It was an outgrowth of our curiosity concerning the ways in which public opinion pollers handled the "don't know" vote—the person who claims to have no opinion in areas where most respondents in America do have opinions. We saw this "vote" as one possible avenue for exploring the cross-cultural forms of opinion-formation and opinion delivery both among social classes in the United States and among different countries with different traditions of rapport and privacy—countries, for instance, in which conscientious women, aggressive enough to get in a door and polite and pleasant enough to stay safely there, may not be readily available. The second article (which I have telescoped into the first) was a somewhat more technical report of our own program for analyzing interviews, included as part of a post-election post-mortem on the polls in the now-defunct *International Journal of Opinion and Attitude Research*.

These articles indicate my view that social science is not soon likely to have available to it the great talents necessary to fulfill its present ambitions. Even if a society which had time and money and personnel enough for all the demands of social science might be attainable, I am not sure it would be wise to draw too many away from physics or business or psychiatry into sociology or social psychology! What does make sense is to make use of amateur and part-time observers; indeed, national surveys and many other projects could not get along without them. In several of the essays in this volume—in the one on movies and the one on social science research —I deal with the potentialities of "mass observation" as a resource for research, when for instance one wants to monitor TV throughout the country or observe movie audiences or parades or other non-recurring phenomena. But such observation is also important for the individuals who do it, for whom it can be a way both of contributing to science and to their own adeptness as observers. Thus, undergraduate students whom I have encouraged to do interviews, even though they did not intend to become professional sociologists, have not infrequently learned new confidence in approaching people, new awareness of the nuances of conversation, as well as enhanced appreciation of the complexities and even treacheries of the data out of which generalizations about human behavior are developed.

27. Toward an Anthropological
Science of Law and the
Legal Profession

Examination of the barriers to the study of law and lawyers in the United States helps at least make a beginning, depressing as it may seem, in the direction of an anthropological science. Among other things, by seeing what we are up against, we may prevent the disillusionment which is bound to set in (perhaps has set in) because so little has actually been accomplished by the realist movement in American jurisprudence.[1] Many times, programs and exhortations have driven law professors and their social science allies into the breach between them, but no junction has been provided for the American culture comparable to the brilliant pioneering work on preliterate culture by Llewellyn and Hoebel in *The Cheyenne Way*.[2]

§ I

LET US LOOK first at the obstacles from the side of the lawyer who wants to take an anthropological look at himself and his role. He has been trained to move within a terminological system of abstractions which are (as Roscoe Pound has pointed out in his comments on the "ideal" or "normative" element) necessarily self-contained.[3] True, many lawers of recent years have moved away from abstraction toward a greater semantic hygiene. But law, however they define it, remains ethnocentric in the fundamental sense that it is the "law" of a particular jurisdiction, or bench, or board of officials. This ethnocentrism appears in many ways, among them the tendency to exaggerate the differences and underplay the similarities in the legal systems of Western society. Thus lawyers are brought up on dichoto-

---

1. Little, that is, in the domain of research; the realist movement has had a considerable influence on teaching and on actual practice and case law.

2. Karl N. Llewellyn and E. Adamson Hoebel, *The Cheyenne Way*.

3. A. R. Radcliffe-Brown (*Encyclopaedia of the Social Sciences*, pp. 531-34) points out: "If you examine the literature on jurisprudence you will find that legal institutions are studied for the most part in more or less complete abstraction from the rest of the social system of which they are a part." And he adds: "The system of laws of a particular society can only be fully understood if it is studied in relation to the social structure, and inversely the understanding of the social structure requires, amongst other things, a systematic study of the legal institutions."

mies between common and civil law: one is supposedly judge-made, the other statute-made—or one is supposed to rely on precedent, the other to disregard it. Such teaching may lead the lawyer to overlook the possibility that the use of precedent is not merely a legal game played in America and not in France, but is actually a human characteristic to be looked for everywhere.[4] (Pound's distinction between "Cadi justice" and "Western justice" also deprecates this possibility.)

If there is a touch of snobbery in the lawyer's trained ethnocentrism, there appears to be more than a touch in his focus on appellate litigation as the classical road to legal education. The rituals of the upper-court "opinion industry" are overt and impressive, and law students sometimes fail to observe that upper courts edit the "script" provided them by lower courts, much as a Hollywood producer edits his scriptwriters, in order to feel important and because institutional pressures compel him to assume this function and to give it weight in action. (Tammany has always known this and, one suspects, has made a tacit deal with the leaders of the bar to toss them the New York Court of Appeals, where the prestige lies, while holding on to the lower courts, where the money lies.)

To be sure, most lawyers today recognize that their most important work is done in the office, not in the courtroom; the elaborate masked ritual of the courtroom holds attraction only for the neophyte and the layman. Yet it is astonishing how strongly the image of the judge stands as the image of the lawyer-hero. While at the better law schools at least one and often nearly three years are spent in debunking upper-court opinions, in showing their largely derivative quality, their endless fallacies, their interminable self-confusion as to what they are "actually" deciding (as against what they *say* they are deciding), the better products of the better law schools want nothing more exciting when they get out than a chance to serve as clerk [as I did] to an appellate judge—the "upperer" the better. And as members of the bar they will move heaven and earth to get on the bench themselves (which is the source of much dirt in our political system, since many congressmen have partners who itch to be judges), although they know from practical experience how little power the judge has under the American system and how skilled lawyers are in emasculating that little.

---

4. Interesting light might be shed on this question by studying the adaptation to the United States of the refugee lawyers whom Hitler drove here. One surmises that they could draw on their European experience and therefore adapt most readily if they possessed an anthropological turn of mind and were inclined to look for institutional similarities under obvious—and often emotionally disturbing and distracting—differences; whereas they could not adapt if they capitulated too readily to the proposition that adaptation had to be a total, all-or-none process.

Why this is so would be a study in itself. We would have to find out why Holmes and Brandeis have been inflated to mythical proportions and have captured the imagination of the young law student, who is unlikely even to know the names of the brilliantly daring and inventive corporate and governmental lawyers who helped build our modern industrial society and its governmental stimuli and curbs. We would have to find out what there is in law practice, even in the most refined offices, which is felt as dirty work, from which the bench is an escape. We would have to find out whether the judge becomes an ideal before law school or in law school (certainly the federal circuit courts have a great attraction for law deans and professors!)—an ideal which later experience does little to influence.[5] And so on.

Moreover, we would have to draw class, ethnic, and regional distinctions in the image and appeal of the various levels of the judiciary. As Kentucky has its "colonels," so it, and the South generally, has its "judges": men of good family who represent the law as a scholarly, humanistic occupation and who, as R. L. Birdwhistell puts it, regard judgeships as their "natural right" by inheritance and early jurisprudential bent. In the big cities, on the other hand, judgeships become part of the system of ethnic brokerage by which the party machines keep the urban peace—the rise of the Italian judge is a recent illustration. Plainly, considerations of class and ethnic status influence the symbolic appeals of the robe to the profession and its lay audiences. Furthermore, is it not likely that, with the growth of concern for security as against risk, and for "plateau" positions as against achievement peaks, the judgeship, with its long tenure (even under elective systems) and fixed salary—and, save in rare cases, short hours—is preferred even to the most creative tasks in private practice?

The fact that law schools today spend their time in impious treatment of cases—this is what the "case method" means—is of course a tribute to the generations of lawyers who, especially since the time of Bentham, have reacted against the mystique of the law and have

---

5. It is not surprising that the public at large shares the lawyer's reverence for the judge: United States Supreme Court judges rated highest (doctors next) on a poll of occupation prestige, and the Supreme Court decision on racial covenants served to overawe a bunch of white Chicago hoodlums who had not been impressed by any other form of pro-tolerance propaganda. The hoodlums, indeed, are not so wrong. For, whether in general the judicial power is shadow rather than substance, there can be no doubt that in the field of Negro-white relations the Supreme Court has exerted enormous leverage, from *Dred Scott* to the *Civil Rights* cases to the latest decisions on segregation in education and transport.

sought to ridicule its fictions and ceremonies. Bentham did so under the banner of rationality: he wanted the law to make sense. The new-style debunkers, of whom Thurman Arnold is one of the most gifted,[6] are less sanguine about reason: indeed, they often come close to glory-ing in the claimed irrationality of legal myths, symbols, and rituals. This aspect of their work may be thought of as part of the general tendency of intellectuals to decry intellectuality wherever it appears to be overrationalistic while regarding more or less romantically those uneducated folk who are supposed to have not only more fun but also more common sense. This anti-snobbery is very clear in the writings of Judge Jerome Frank, who not only wants to elevate the study of lower courts to a position of academic respectability but attacks as snobbish and overintellectual antiquarians those who con-tinue to study upper-court verbalisms.[7]

Yet these contemporary legal critics of the law are not only amused by legal rigmarole and nonsense; under their wit they have hidden their anger at legal injustice, stupidity, and waste. While they may talk, as Veblen also did,[8] as detached observers, they are moti-vated by a profound concern for social policy, for the beneficent use of law in the public interest, and in this they remain the heirs of Bentham.

Yet this countermovement (which has captured the law school avant-garde) has had little concrete consequence in studies of legal process in America. A too immediate concern for public policy is perhaps one reason for this, for it tends to take away the curiosity and the patience of the observer: he is likely to assume that he has done his job if he has proved that a legal device is a myth or a fiction or a rationalization—though this does not even prove that it is irrational. The guilt of the more sensitive lawyers over the abuses and wastes of their profession—as these are seen in the Benthamite and the Veblenite view—may be one element in this preoccupation with "getting the goods on" the upper courts, the corporate bar, the bar associations (other than the Lawyers' Guild), as the case may be. Such guilt may even conceal a grandiose notion that the lawyers have a vocation, a "calling," to change the face of America.[9] In that case,

---

6. *The Folklore of Capitalism.* See also Fred Rodell, *Woe unto Ye Lawyers.*

7. E.g., in *Courts on Trial.*

8. Thorstein Veblen's chapter on the law in *Absentee Ownership,* pp. 40-68, is still a very stimulating classic.

9. Lasswell and McDougal's justly famed article on legal education, "Legal Education and Public Policy," *Yale Law Journal,* LII (1943), 203-95, suffers from such grandiose aims, which is perhaps one reason why it still stands as a huge land grant for research which has not yet found its occupants of quarter-sections, at least so far as I know. My own article, "Law and Social Science" (*Yale Law Journal,* L [1941], 636-53), suffers from the same high hopes.

guilt can become a vested interest which is hostile to research, even while it appears to invite it.

§ II

IF, WITH THIS ALL TOO BRIEF COMMENT, we turn now away from the legal profession and ask why the other social sciences have not, on their side, done more with the law, we find that some of the same explanations hold. Sociologists, for instance, have until quite recently been as much concerned with immediate social reform as their brethren of the bar; thus, they have looked at the law only where it impinged on the disadvantaged groups in society—on the criminal, the juvenile delinquent, the poverty-stricken seeker of divorce, etc. Like the criminologists still railing at the M'Naghten rule,[10] they view the law as unjust as well as irrational; their aim is to show up, perhaps to change, the law and the legal mentality rather than to understand it sympathetically. Furthermore, the sociologists who are theoretically inclined have concerned themselves with formal definitions of law (e.g., M. Georges Gurvitch) and with the problem of the origins of law—both perfectly valid enterprises but not good ways to bring the sociologist into actual contact with the legal profession as a going concern.

Meanwhile, anthropologists have been merrily analyzing some of the functions of law in preliterate societies—Sir Henry Maine's classic work may indeed be thought of as some sort of bridge between the study of legal origins and of functions. Malinowski, Hogben, Redfield,[11] and Llewellyn and Hoebel have tried, in Radcliffe-Brown's sense, to view primitive law in the setting of primitive social structure. They have not denounced legal myth and symbolism; rather, they have tried to see its function, sometimes with the admiration of one craftsman for the craft of another. Since they could approach primitive law with some knowledge of law in Western society, they needed no Rosetta stone to translate the symbolism which they found.

As soon as the search for origins lost its high priority, moreover, this anthropological enterprise could readily shed the ethnocentrism and snobbery which we have seen to be barriers on the side of the lawyer's study of law in our own culture; cross-cultural uniformities

---

10. Neither George Dession's paper, "Psychiatry and the Conditioning of Criminal Justice," *Yale Law Journal*, XLVII (1938), 319-40, nor the casebook of Jerome Michael and Herbert Wechsler, *Criminal Law and Its Administration: Cases, Statutes and Commentaries*, each with a very sophisticated approach, seems to have put an end to this sterile attack and counterattack between lawyers on one side and criminologists and psychologists on the other.

11. See, e.g., Robert Redfield, "Maine's *Ancient Law* in the Light of Primitive Societies," *Western Political Quarterly*, III (1950), 574-89.

as well as curious diversities could be looked for readily enough. By the same token, the anthropologist could be quite as interested in the law of a small group, lacking in political power, as in the law of a national state or "big power," and this very interest in what was intrinsically significant saved him from the frequent sterility of the "public policy" approach, which begins with what some other people (the officialdom, the liberals, the elite, etc.) think to be important in our own society, which is usually something pretty sizable in scope. Furthermore, the anthropologist's bias vis-à-vis institutions has in the past tended to be very different from the sociologist's: whereas the latter sees institutions as "vested," as restrictive, the former sees them (as united in the concept of culture) as fundamentally channeling and hence permissive. This leads the anthropologist to look for the channeling aspects of the law as well as the litigious and punitive ones —a point of view which, in Llewellyn's case, has governed his approach to American law as much as to Cheyenne law.[12] (Of course, this distinction between sociological and anthropological slants is rapidly breaking down; and elsewhere in this paper "anthropological," "sociological," and "social-psychological" are used as virtually interchangeable terms.)

Perhaps most important of all, the anthropologist is not likely to harbor the naïve assumption that the law, or any other institution, serves only a single function—say, that of social control—and that any other functions which in fact it serves are excrescences or "contradictions." The concept of ambivalence is part of his equipment; he tends to search for latent functions, transcending the ostensible.[13]

Yet despite this equipment and experience with primitive law, the anthropologist has still not turned back to American law with the *élan* he has shown in studying such other American institutions as the movies, child-rearing, and social class. My impression is that social scientists somehow believe that, since it takes three years to get through law school, law itself must be impermeable to them without long and arduous preparation. Many are willing enough to grant verbally with Thurman Arnold that the law is a set of irrational mystifications; but they feel nevertheless that the trained lawyer must "have something" that they could not possibly acquire in short compass. Men who are prepared, before going into the field, to learn a primitive language seem unready to tackle the hardly more difficult

12. See, e.g., Karl N. Llewellyn, "The American Common Law Tradition and American Democracy," *Journal of Legal and Political Sociology*, I (1942), 14-46.
13. Cf. Camilla Wedgewood, "The Nature and Functions of Secret Societies," *Oceania*, I (1930-31), 129-45, and the work of Robert K. Merton on manifest and latent functions in *Social Theory and Social Structure*.

semantics of American law. One of the few social scientists who has not been impressed, the psychologist Robinson, tried to explain matters as follows:

> The lawyers are a priesthood with a prestige to maintain. They must have a set of doctrines that do not threaten to melt away with the advances of psychological and social science. . . . They must, in order to feel socially secure, believe and convince the outside world that they have peculiar techniques requiring long study to master. In a way they have overplayed this card. Even laymen are coming to see that if The Law were as difficult to understand as the profession implies, nobody would ever be able to become a lawyer.[14]

What is the blockage which prevents other social scientists from doing what Robinson did? It seems to me that there *is* an irrational blockage, much like that among people who feel that they cannot handle simple mathematics or statistics—and so "prove" to themselves that they cannot. It is easy enough to see Robinson's point that the legal profession has an obscurantist interest at stake, but it is less easy to see why the social scientist falls for this. Has he at stake some self-image which his legal competence would threaten, in the same way that the girl who cannot read timetables believes her femininity at stake? I do not know the answer, but the blockage itself is a matter one can observe often enough—and not among social scientists only. Consider the manufacturer of soft drinks, a small businessman, who feels no awe of his chemist at all—there is no magic there for him—but who stands in terrible awe of his lawyer. Or the social scientists who, aware enough of specialization in their own fields, try to get free legal advice from a colleague with legal training about landlord and tenant law, divorces, wills, copyrights—even assault and battery! They assume, though they know he may not have practiced law for ten years, that he has some magic formula for them at his fingertips; moreover that there *is* a formula. They are astonished to find that he, as a lawyer, is much more casual about legal matters than they; that he goes on the principle (so often pointed out by Judge Frank) that the law in any given case is uncertain. In spite of their skepticism, they are surprised, for at bottom they believe in the certainty and majesty

---

14. E. S. Robinson, *Law and the Lawyers* (New York: Macmillan Co., 1935), p. 28. It would require a great deal of discussion to try to explain the one apparent exception to this, namely the group of political scientists who study and teach "public law." Many of these men treat Supreme Court cases with a reverence (even when they criticize them) that few lawyers would maintain; they are likely to be more literal than lawyers, for they have missed the three years of case-law debunking—training whose result is that the lawyer takes law less seriously than the typical educated layman. These teachers of public law do, however, share with law teachers the belief that cases on "public policy" are prima facie important.

of the law. But, again, this describes their attitude; it does not explain it.

Nor does it explain it to point to the over-reaction of many social scientists who, convinced that they cannot penetrate the opacity of the law, declare that there is nothing really there to be understood. The doctrine of Sumner and his followers that man-made law and legislation have minimal power to alter folkways and mores has influenced not only those who aver that law is fundamentally irrational but also those who aver that it is, if not wholly irrelevant, at best a cultural lag—or, in Marxist terms, an ideological superstructure. (An attitude basically not very different is to be found among those law teachers who see "the balancing of interests" as the formula of legal intervention and do not allow the law at any point a crucially innovating role—that is, they do not see law as an "interest" in its own right.) Despite the work of Max Weber, and, even more, his hints concerning the role of law in the development of Western "rationalization"; despite such a book as Commons' *The Legal Foundations of Capitalism;*[15] despite many other things which could be cited, the social scientists of this stamp believe that law is fundamentally a "secondary" or derivative institution—and thus feel they do not need to take a look to see whether and to what degree it is such.[16]

The American corporate bar played a decisive role in the development of our society, as Berle and Means have recognized.[17] Only lawyers had in the post-Civil War period the particular gift for the framing of corporate charters, security issues, and all the rest; the particular courage to work ahead of the cases and statutes in order to give powers to corporations which had never been tested (and often have never yet been tested) in court; the particular tradition to give body

---

15. John R. Commons, *The Legal Foundations of Capitalism.*

16. An interesting study of W. P. Webb's *The Great Plains* might be made from this perspective. Webb sees water law, manufactured in England and New England, as bowing to the rainfall pattern of the plains, and he attacks the doctrine of equal riparian rights as a bigoted and misguided "lag." Yet no one seems to have asked why, when it came to underground waters, and later underground oil, the developments in technique since *Acton* v. *Blundell* did not lead to compulsory pooling and a departure from *this* precedent. Was it simply the competitive ethos of Texas? Or the vested interests of the makers of oil derricks? I doubt it very much; I think that the law often cuts its own channel—in this case so deep that a court held a compulsory pooling law unconstitutional, although it would in 1846 have been quite conceivable to decide *Acton* v. *Blundell* the other way. This "watershed" role of developments within legal doctrine itself has been little studied, though obviously it has to be studied before we can dismiss law as mere ideology, superstructure, or lag. For a pilot effort of my own (which helps make me fully aware of the difficulties) see my examination of the development of libel law in "Democracy and Defamation: Fair Game and Fair Comment," *Columbia Law Review*, XLII (1942), 1085-1123, 1282-1318.

17. Adolph Berle and Gardner Means, *The Modern Corporation and Private Property.*

to such decisive inventions as the fiction of the corporation as a "person." This extraordinary achievement has neither created topics for the social scientist to study in close detail nor, as observed above, made heroes for the bar—perhaps because the social consequences have been so generally deplored among intellectuals;[18] perhaps, too, because the anonymity of office work—"paper work"—leads to its relative disregard.

Only relative disregard, however. Since the corporation is obviously important and glamorous for its friends and foes alike, students of the law from within and without the profession have paid some attention to its development. Such studies have been a junction point between law and economics,[19] or between law and political science, though hardly yet between law and anthropology. The place to begin the latter kind of junction is at a point which is neither glamorous nor obviously policy-oriented, but where the functions served by the legal process do not strike one at the first, and perhaps stereotyped, glance and need to be discovered anew.[20]

§ III

LET WHAT I HAVE TO SAY from here on be regarded simply as notes or prolegomena to some field studies of the functions of law and the lawyers in our culture, with an emphasis on those functions which perhaps have received less recognition than is warranted in view of what we might learn if we understood them. Here, as elsewhere in social research, curiosity does well to focus on what is changing rather than on what is more or less stable.

Take, for example, the apparent decline in the function of law as popular amusement or festivity. This decline may be viewed as a fairly good index of urbanization and the rise of modern leisure industries. But law still serves this function in the smaller country places. Here court sittings are seasonal affairs, not like a bank or a store which

18. Until the twentieth century it would seem that the truly inventive American lawyers and judges had been conservatives: Marshall, Field, Choate, for example. Since we like to think that inventiveness is a liberal monopoly, we do not find these men to be models for young lawyers today; Brandeis is a model, or Holmes—the latter thought to be both liberal and legally inventive, though he is neither.

19. Cf., e.g., the pioneering work of C. Reinhold Noyes, *The Institution of Property*. Noyes tries (in chap. vi) to treat the question as to the relation between property and social stratification in terms of politically enforced legal rules for the distribution of men and things upon land. And he sees that property may serve the function of stabilizing one's geographical location. See also the general framework of theory presented in *ibid.*, pp. 16-21.

20. Similarly, law and psychology will not really mesh while attention remains concentrated on the obvious junctions of insanity law, trial psychology, evidentiary rules, etc.

is open for business every day. James West, in *Plainville, U.S.A.*, is fully aware of it.[21] He describes the legal "party" thrown for Hobart Proudy, who shot his cousin, Mort Proudy, in the seat of the breeches with both barrels; a witness testified in Hobart's favor that he should be let off because "if he had intended to kill Mort, he would have, since Hobart won't shoot a squirrel down out of a tree, anywhere except in the eye." The legal "party" served thus to entertain the community and to throw a scare into Hobart—West is fully aware of compounding practices but sees them not as an excrescence but as an essential part of the legal order. He also describes the way in which an adultery suit between an undertaker and a garagekeeper over the affections of the latter's wife provided the town with an agenda for gossip: "The atmosphere was electric with spiteful talk for many months, though most people said 'Nobody will make any money out of that trial and it may break both men up.' " This remark leads West to comment on the ambivalent attitude toward law on the part of Plainvillers: they fear it, yet enjoy it; one suspects that they enjoy it, as one enjoys a roller-coaster ride, partly because they fear it. Even so, one of West's informants noted the decline of scandals as compared with her experience farther south: "The people here," she observed, "are either a lot better or a lot smarter." Perhaps it is only that they have increasing access to other amusements, such as the movies and radio.

But the word "amusements" does not convey the full significance of this function. "Amusements" are always more than individualistic escapes from monotony; they are, like the weather, an endless unifier of conversation and of attitude. The Plainvillers share a common focus for discussion, and politics and law may be seen in part as providing topics in this way, just as a high-school basketball team might do. By the same token, a trial may serve as a divisive point, not in terms of a factional split as between the friends of the garagekeeper and of the undertaker, but in terms of a moral turning point, such as is described in James Gould Cozzens' fine novel, *The Just and the Unjust*, or as the Western world experienced—perhaps for the last time?—in the trial of Sacco and Vanzetti.

It would be interesting to pursue these leads further and to inquire, as could be readily done by means of interviews, into the question as to what sorts of laymen talk on what occasions about what sorts of legal process today. One hypothesis is that in middle-class intellectual circles court cases play much less part in conversation than they did even twenty years ago; but that in labor and Negro circles they may

---

21. James West, *Plainville, U.S.A.*

play more part—certainly, many labor-union officials, in their upward intellectual and social mobility, seem to be quite law-oriented. Over all, there may be a general fading-out of law, not only of courts, from public view. But this remains to be seen.

§ IV

COULD THE AMBIVALENCE toward law observed by West be related to the possibility that the lawyer must do things the community regards as necessary—but still disapproves of? Hence, is the lawyer something of a scapegoat? Now, to be sure, this does not in itself distinguish lawyers from prostitutes, politicians, prison wardens, some doctors, and many other occupational groups.[22] What does distinguish lawyers in this role is that they are feared and disliked—but needed—because of their matter-of-factness, their sense of relevance, their refusal to be impressed by magical "solutions" to people's problems. Conceivably, if this hypothesis is right, the ceremonial and mystification of the legal profession are, to a considerable degree, veils or protections underneath which this rational, all too rational, work of the lawyer gets done.

Of course, this view of the matter is in plain contradiction to that of Thorstein Veblen, who, it will be recalled, saw the engineers and the skilled workmen as the bearers of the modern, skeptical, matter-of-fact temper, while the lawyers were typical for the archaic, predatory, pecuniary, and otherwise nonrational employments. Very likely, there has been a notable change in legal education since Veblen wrote, with the major law schools going ever more heavily into the systematic practice of skepticism concerning judicial authority. *Lawyers learn not to take law seriously.* They learn to make distinctions; they are trained in relevance—or at least in worrying about relevance—and they will discover when they get into practice that relevance is a concept which, to their chronic frustration, seems nearly absent from the mental equipment of most of the people they deal with.[23] While

---

22. I am greatly indebted to Professor Everett Hughes for my understanding of this occupational pattern.

23. Compare the following recollections from Lenin: "When I was in exile in Siberia . . . I was an undergraduate lawyer because, being summarily exiled, I was not allowed to practice, but as there were no other lawyers in the region, people came to me and told me about some of their affairs. But I had the greatest difficulty in understanding what it was all about. A woman would come to me and of course start telling me all about her relatives and it would be incredibly difficult to get from her what she really wanted. Then she would tell me a story about a white cow. I would say to her: 'Bring me a copy.' She would then go off complaining: 'He won't hear what I have to say about the white cow unless I bring a copy.' We in our colony used to have a good laugh over this copy. But I was able to make some progress. People came to me, brought copies of the necessary documents, and I was able to gather what their trouble was, what

teachers of evidence for several generations have punctured the absurdities of the rules of evidence, they may have paid less attention
to the fact that their students were, in the process of learning to
apply and criticize the rules, also obliquely learning what relevance
means. . . .

In the wartime Army and Navy bureaucracies, it was often the
lawyer-in-uniform who in my limited experience appeared prepared
to cut red tape and to walk indelicately over red carpets; he might be,
and generally was, out of his "field," but he was engaged in what may
be his occupational role of being unimpressed by authoritative rituals.[24] He seemed less impressed than the accountants, bankers, businessmen, and engineers in similar slots. But, of course, such casual
observations, while "relevant," are hardly "evidence."

More to the point, perhaps, are the observations of Ferdinand
Lundberg in his article on "The Profession of the Law":

> The lawyer comes to know society not as a tenant or owner knows a
> house but as the architect, building contractor, and repair men know it.
> And his knowledge of society extends beyond the knowledge these tech-
> nicians have of any building, for he is intimately acquainted as well with
> the servants that staff the structure. He either knows all there is to know
> about judges, public officials, business leaders, bankers, professional poli-
> ticians, labor leaders, newspaper publishers, leading clergymen, and the
> like, or through that informal clearing house of esoteric information, the
> bar association, can find out from colleagues. The lawyer is a vast reser-
> voir of actual or potential information about the social and political
> topography. . . .[25]

The layman is, however, not quite sure how he feels about such
a person, whose usefulness he may need and whose knowledgeability
may fascinate him: the more he needs him, the more he may be likely
to project upon him his own tendencies to cynicism about authority
and about procedure. Journalists also have this sort of knowledge
about the culture, but, despite the best efforts of schools of journalism,
they have not been able to turn their profession into a secret society.
Indeed, it is the lawyer's LL.B. which allows his client to delegate this
outlook, and the work it entails, to him: he can seek counsel from
lawyers without loss of face, although the matter in hand may not,

---

they complained of, what ailed them" (*Selected Works*, IX, 355). I am indebted
for this reference to Nathan Leites, *Operational Code of the Politburo*, pp. 13-14.

24. From this perspective, not the least shocking thing about the Korematsu
cases is to see the Supreme Court bowing to the claim of "military necessity." A
court which is unimpressed by patent cases, or by the accounting concepts used
in rate litigation, or by most other factual grist, here falls for the flimsiest and most
outrageous propaganda handouts General DeWitt's lawyers could dream up! Lawyers actually in uniform were less easily swindled by "military necessity" than
these men of the robe. For details see Morton Grodzins, *Americans Betrayed*.

25. *Harper's* CLXXVIII (December, 1938), 10.

in any technical sense, be "legal" at all. It is, then, the lawyer who
loses face on his client's behalf.

What is there, then, in the selection and training of lawyers that
readies them for accepting such a role? Doubtless, many elements are
involved, but an important one is the fact that the law schools throughout the country are still fairly wide open to "talent," irrespective of
class, ethnic, and kin lines. Thus, they attract the more ambitious,
the more mobile young people—the bright Grinnell graduate whose
political science teacher tells him to "take a crack at Harvard Law,"
or the intellectual hope of a Bronx family which feels he is cut out
to be a lawyer and sends him to Fordham. Law schools maintain a
highly competitive atmosphere, and the law reviews are almost
uniquely work-oriented institutions: they pay no attention to "personality" and concentrate on performance with a zeal as rare and
admirable as it is savage.[26]
So far as I know, there is nothing in any other professional group
which remotely resembles the law review, this guild of students who,
working even harder than their fellows, manage to cooperate sufficiently to meet the chronic emergency of a periodical. Indeed, this
cooperation often develops an island of teamwork in a sea of ruthless
rivalry. Law review students frequently have a note-taking agreement, so not all have to attend class; and in other ways they are likely
to cover for each other in dealing with the obstacles to their review
work, and often enough to their education, that the curriculum offers.
To be sure, the major law reviews have a rather amiable rivalry
inter se, as the boards of editors on the older reviews have a rather
amiable rivalry with the records set up by earlier and deceased boards
of editors. But there is little that is factitious about this school spirit;
it is not whipped up by coaches (though here and there faculty advisors, public-relations conscious, may play this role) or by cheer
leaders, but is self-perpetuating. The resulting standards often become so high that the contributed articles by law teachers and prac-
titioners are markedly inferior to the student work both in learning
and in style and, in fact, often have to be rewritten by the brashly
serious-minded student editors. As democracy based on ability to *do*
something (rather than that spurious democracy which is based on
ability to *be* a right kind of guy) is strongest in the high schools and
colleges in the field of sports, so in the professional world it appears
strongest in the competitive-cooperative teamwork of the law reviews.

26. On the historical connection between social mobility and the law see my
article, "Equality and Social Structure," *Journal of Legal and Political Sociology,*
I (October, 1942), 72-95.

For it is a notable feature of this teamwork that it is based on impersonal and objective criteria in the sense that it ignores social class and ethnic lines and, beyond these, "personality" above a bare minimum. In many law schools, election is not really election, for it is based on grades alone; in others, it is based on performance, judged almost as impersonally as the grades themselves are judged by the scrupulous fairness of the faculty. (It is perhaps no accident that one or two law schools, as at Yale and Chicago, contain some of the most fervent devotees of Henry Simons' utopian vision of a free, impersonal, unmonopolistic economy; law reviews are the very model of such an economy, a model which it would be hard to duplicate elsewhere in the society.) I think that studies might reveal that, not only cooptation to the law review, but the election of officers thereupon, is heavily influenced by an ideology of impersonal, objective performance in which "merely" social and ethnic considerations are not only frowned upon but actually eliminated, so far as may be. Jews, for example, appear heavily represented in the upper mastheads of all the major law reviews. (They do on college papers, too, but that involves other issues of motivation and selection.) A great camaraderie, sometimes of a kidding and sometimes of a tacit sort, appears to develop on the reviews between the Jewish and the non-Jewish members. In what is left of their time away from school and books, sociability is often a duplication of the law review cliques themselves, these being based more on interest and congeniality than on fraternity-type considerations.

I do not doubt that members of law review staffs are pretty fully aware of how widely their mores diverge from those of the wider world, whether collegiate or business and professional, nor do I doubt that these "outside" considerations are sometimes brought inside, but when this happens they are felt as scandalous. The divergence from medical schools in this respect is obvious and striking. Medical school students do not edit journals in which, as not infrequently happens in the law reviews, students rewrite or even reject the work of their teachers. Already in the first year of medical school, the student has entered into a network of personal ties which will be decisive for his professional fate; he is judged, and judges himself, by his "personality" and connections quite as much as by his more intellectual qualities. "Personality" and connections, of course, have helped get him in to medical school in the first place, whereas law school admission, like law school life, is almost devoid of these tariffs. (The mathematical formula by which Harvard Law School selects its entrants is only an extreme illustration of this pattern.) The medical school student attends a "clinical" school in the very real sense that the values which dominate the school also dominate later medical practice, though perhaps in a somewhat muted form. Medical school students, no matter how service-oriented on entrance, soon learn that they live in a patronage network whose unspoken rules will govern internships and the whole complex ladder of medical practice today. A Catholic Italian boy will have to decide, for example, whether he dare play in the big-Protestant league, because one of his teachers has taken a shine to him, or whether he should take the safer course of playing in the Catholic minor league; if he misses his bet, he may easily fall between two stools.[27] In sum, the medical schools are "true to life" or clinical in a sense which the law schools are not; their pattern of social relations puts very little pressure on the medical community at large precisely because the students are in effect socialized as interns from the very beginning. To be sure, with respect to such issues as "socialized medicine," the medical schools controlled by full-time men may put some pressure on their students for progressive attitudes which are anathema to the medical associations, and at these same schools there is probably somewhat more impersonality than in most forms of medical practice. But on the whole, medical students do not need to face much re-orientation of values when they leave medical school; their problem is rather whether they can face treating patients without the full package of big-hospital facilities.

In contrast with this, the member of a law review staff who goes into practice suddenly confronts many of the class and ethnic barriers that his own team experience had lowered. He may enter a big non-Jewish or a big Jewish office, all of whose partners are themselves law review trained men, but all of whom are willy-nilly engaged in segregated practice. In the government, offices are unsegregated, which, however, often means largely ethnic in composition. And what is true of race is also true of sex; many large offices do not accept women as associates, though the men who run them may have worked closely with women in their law review days.

Nevertheless, the capitulation of the law review graduate to "life" is seldom complete. If he takes sex and race into account, he takes social class and religion into account much less than is the case in many other professions (e.g., architecture). It is partly this that permits the law to remain one of the careers open to talent, so that a railroad conductor's son from Altoona, who has done well at a name law school, may end up as head of a big manufacturing or utility com-

---

27. Hall, "Informal Organization of Medical Practice," 12 *Can. J. Econ. & Pol. Sci.* (1946); also, by the same author, "The Stages of a Medical Career," 53 *Am. J. Soc.* (1948).

pany, or a government agency, when he would never, without connections, have made the grade within the particular company or agency hierarchy. The career of the West Virginian, John W. Davis, is an excellent instance.

Furthermore, it may well be that a comparison of legal with medical practice would show that the former has been influenced, in its recent limited inroads on the barriers of race and sex, by the law school and particularly its law review ethos, as well as by the more generalized FEPC type of pressure. Certainly when, in the Christmas holidays before graduation, law students looking for jobs are confronted with the ethnic "facts of life," they return to their law review jobs with some uneasiness, and they may welcome bar association and other activities in which the old law review camaraderies are to some extent restored. This may be one source of the fact that Italians, Jews, and women seem of late years to have been finding jobs in the big offices, though these are understandably reluctant to duplicate in their own makeup the ethnic composition, often so heavily Jewish, of the law reviews from which they draw recruits.

If I am right in these suggestions, the law attracts people who can stand a certain amount of impersonality and who are trained to be objective, in the sense of being relevant and orderly. The very "ivory-towerism" for which the law schools are often attacked allows them to emphasize techniques which are relatively unclinical. The law student, and especially the law review student, does not encounter clients and is therefore not likely to be judged for what we might call his "briefcase manner."[28] The whole drift of the law is, in this sense, democratic, competitive, and impersonal. The law reviews put pres-

28. In considering the social and psychological consequences of professional education, it is at least as important to examine what has *not* been learned as to see what has been taught in the three years at school. The removal of apprentice lawyers from law offices during those years may be more significant than the items of instruction which have been substituted. This may sound strange, but we can see the problem clearly in an analogous case. As we know, industry turns increasingly to college-trained foremen, rather than promoting from the ranks, while at the same time proclaiming that the college-bred trainee might as well get a general education in college since he'll have to learn his technology and know-how in the factory anyhow. It would seem that college serves primarily to keep him for four years from learning the (often outmoded) ways of doing things he would learn if he were in the factory; when he starts fresh he can learn newer techniques developed in the meantime, and will be less disposed to sabotage them since all are equally strange. And perhaps the need to learn fast, to justify his college training and status, will lead him to short-cuts—certainly true of the greenhorn LL.B. who must acquire savvy fast. But the savvy acquired fast will be different—more rational—than the savvy acquired "the hard (clinical or 'real-life') way." Since coming to these conclusions, I regret the fact that law students do not have a better time during the three years when they are spared the mislearnings of practice.

sure on the profession, and the profession in turn puts pressure on the society.

Let it not be assumed that I am convinced this pressure is a good thing. Its concomitant is the rather scarifying emphasis on grades which is characteristic of law schools, for if the law review is a stepping stone to a high position, the stakes are more than a penny a point of average. Nor can we sensibly be too self-righteous about the more nepotistic atmosphere of the medical school, unless we would just as soon be attended when sick by Mr. Economic Man; indeed, the medical schools may conceivably be criticized as not snobbish enough but as simply typifying petty-bourgeois petty prejudice. A whole society run on the principles of the law review, in which everyone read Consumer's Reports in choosing services as well as commodities, while it would appeal to Myrdal and other radical democrats, might be a somewhat uncomfortable place, with none of the hominess provided by mild degrees of segregation and corruption. But a whole society run on the principles of the medical profession would, if anything, be even more intolerable, with guild controls dictating all choices. The tensions between these two systems of value and their two historic roots is characteristic of our modern industrial society.

The law review, then, would seem to present a kind of paradigm of impersonality combined with teamwork, to be studied in its own terms and also as a yardstick for the legal profession and, by contrast, other professions as well. Investigators would have to go on to see what the pace-setter is among the law reviews in these respects, and the degree to which different reviews represent, exaggerate, or modify the attitudes of their own law school communities. Is it only at the "national" law schools, for instance, where there is little parochialism in the *topics* treated by student editors, that there is little parochialism in the *choice* of editors? We should expect some subtle interplays between the interpretations of what is "law" at a given institution and the pattern of social relations for which the law review stands. But only careful observation can discover what the interplays are in each case, and what generalizations may be safely made about "the" law review and "the" school.

To repeat: law schools attract the more hard-working, ambitious young men; they drill them to respect top performance; they furnish them with models of, and perhaps contact with, previous graduates who moved rapidly into positions of influence. Under this combined nurturing, lawyers tend, I suggest, to become hard-working isolates. They are less inclined than the average client to be or appear to be "big-hearted," "good guys," etc.—the vocabulary by which they would be seduced into accepting the normal archaisms of the business world. The teamwork of a law review is very different from the teamwork of other, more clubby, professionals; this same atmosphere continues in the larger offices. An interesting illustration is gleaned from comparing the corporate bar's admiration for the SEC registration statement filed for the Kaiser-Frazer Company some years ago—a statement which whizzed through in record time—with the distrust of Henry Kaiser felt by his business competitors who view him as too streamlined for their comfort.

In sum, lawyers tend frequently to become paid rate-busters, mobile men in every respect, who find in devotion to their work and in the esteem of their professional colleagues rewards for serving clients in ways of which the clients do not entirely approve—and, what is more, do not want to have to approve. The "mystery" of the law is here a protection for the client: under an inevitable ignorance of *part* of a technical field, he can throw virtually the *whole* moral burden on his counsel and excuse himself on the ground that he could not possibly know enough to have an independent judgment. The lawyer, usually unaware of the psychological roots of this division of labor, may sometimes vainly try to "educate" his client into the whys and wherefores of his actions.

§ V

THE SO-CALLED PARTISANSHIP of the lawyer provides an interesting illustration of some of these problems. It is frequently said that lawyers are particularly partisan people; this is part of the stereotype. And it may be that the ambition of lawyers to go on the bench may spring to some extent from a wish to air opinions. Yet it is a question if lawyers are more opinionated than most people; they are ordinarily less partisan than nonlawyers and could hardly do their work if this were not so.

Every client realizes this when he sees the fraternizing of opposing counsel. He may suspect that his lawyer cares more for the opinion of other lawyers (including the judge) with whom he has to do business every day than he cares for the momentary problem of the client. The "rules of the game" of the law are so set up that lawyers can appear to fight hard without irretrievably hurting each other; yet, as with other games when *anomie* sets in and rules become purely instrumental, this restraint can break down. For many reasons, lawyers are more willing to bear each other's hostility for the sake of a client than other professionals (e.g., doctors); this would again seem connected—as Durkheim might predict—with the openness of the law-school world to talent, without ethnic and class barriers; and one of the important areas for sociological investigation would seem to be to study differences in type of professional camaraderie (at the client's expense) in different types of law practice. It seems likely that the lawyers' training in objectifying social relations permits them to tolerate not only the hostility of the public brought upon them for the disrespect of the public's image of the law they must show in order to get the public's work done but also this considerable amount of hostility to colleagues, or the risk of it.

But if there are times when the lawyer is less partisan than he should be in the client's interest (and it is hard for him not to confuse his own interest with the interest of his other present and potential clients who will exploit him as a bearer of a certain amount of good will from bench and bar), there are other times when the client cannot tolerate a non-partisanship which is clearly in his own interest.[29] There have been cases of quite conservative, but unfanatical lawyers, accustomed as few engineers are to taking account of human stresses and strains, who have lost their jobs as labor negotiators because management wanted, not success in the labor bargain, but a ritual of expletives against those damned union bastards. Sometimes businessmen and others dealing with the government have been similarly unwilling to accept, even in scapegoat fashion, their lawyer's matter-of-factness; they have wanted to pay, not for success, but for resounding speeches. And since they could find other members of the bar who would do this for them, they were deprived both of their success and of their comfortable assurance that they were morally superior to lawyers. Sometimes, as Everett Hughes has observed, this problem is handled by symbiotic teams of lawyers, one matter-of-fact, the other a ham actor. Similar demands are made today on our diplomats—men, of course, often trained in the law.

The demand for partisanship comes, moreover, not only from the client, but from the lawyer's own desire to believe in the client as a cause. John Brooks, in his novel *The Big Wheel*, describes the revolt of the writers for a newsweekly against a pious editor who wanted them to believe their own stuff: they felt their intellectual integrity depended on their being able to divorce their private beliefs from their daily writing stint. The law has a long tradition of rationalizing that divorce by an ethic of "invisible harmony" which assures each

29. This conflict between lawyer and client over the proper degree of affect which the former is to bring to the affairs of the latter is one of those conflicts between client emergency and occupational routine which has attracted the interest of Everett Hughes. As he observes, the client wants his problem given priority—yet he would be uneasy with a professional for whom his case actually was "the first" and who had neither been trained on other people's emergencies nor could control his own emotions in the face of the client's loss of control.

practitioner that if he fights hard for his client within the rules the general interest will be somehow advanced. Though obviously the matter is very hard to document, it appears that this ethic is breaking down and that lawyers consequently feel either the need to be partisan or to be iron-clad cynics.

When this outer and inner demand for partisanship is coupled with the perhaps increasing psychological need of lawyers to be liked by their clients, the lawyer's usefulness may be impaired. We must ask, in this connection, whether it is really a good idea to train lawyers in psychology, if the effect of this is to make them more sensitive to their clients' moods and judgments? If it is to make them more "other-directed"?[30] If it is to break down the psychological defenses of the "secret society"? Perhaps the lawyer, or certain kinds of lawyer, has to be a person with a thick skin, not very interested in how other people feel or in how he himself feels?

To put this another way, if the lawyer should become very concerned with others' feelings, might he not become merely a competitor with another kind of client-caretaker, namely, the public relations man? While to be sure many public relations men are LL.B.'s, can the law schools eventually do as good a job in training this crew as, let us say, schools of journalism or of applied psychology?[31] May not the eagerness of some law-school leaders to "modernize" their schools, by incorporating much social science, have the consequence, if what they introduce takes at all with their students, of cramping those mobility drives which have pulled and pushed lawyers along the particular career lines they have followed in this country to date? Obviously, we can say very little about such questions without knowing much more than we do about who goes to law school, what happens to him there, and how this is related to what happens to him later on.

Equally obviously, law schools differ very much *inter se* with respect to the kind of rate-busting ethos discussed above. It is not every law school whose graduates will carry to the courts (at their clients' expense) a real crusading effort to prove Williston right as against Corbin or vice versa, as some Harvard and Yale graduates in big law firms are said to have done in the pre-social-science era.

---

30. *The Lonely Crowd*, chap. vi.

31. It is interesting to watch how this new type of business and government counselor seeks to develop a ritual of his own in his competitive effort to displace lawyers as those who profit, in Lundberg's terms, from keeping their clients "in a condition of permanent convalescence, always dependent upon the expensive advice of specialists in obscure, often nameless disorders, never thoroughly ill, never wholly cured" (*op. cit.*, p. 2). This new ritual is usually based on public opinion research techniques and on psychological jargon—which perhaps has still some way to go before it becomes as impressive as law-talk.

CONNECTED IN SUBTLE and still opaque ways with some of these psychological shifts is the shift of awareness in the legal profession itself concerning the nature of legal rights. Whereas law has been very greatly preoccupied with property, with the relation of men to things, it is only in the most unsophisticated circles today that it is thought there are true rights *in rem;* elsewhere, it is recognized that all rights come at bottom down to relations among men, including relations among men concerning things, and that all rights are therefore creations of social organization. In the past lawyers have tended to be people who, so to speak, reified social organization; they moved among their complicated networks of personal relations (corporations, domestic relations, administrative rules, etc.) as physicists might move among their models of atomic nuclei. Their eye was on the structure, not on the personalities who happened at any moment to occupy various niches in it. This cultivated blindness to people, this ability to insist on the reality of legal fictions, helped to make it possible for lawyers to erect in confidence and good conscience the elaborate organizational machinery of our society. True, they lacked or repressed current sociological learning about the importance of the informal organization, whether in the bank wiring room at the Hawthorne plant of Western Electric or the higher reaches of the telephone company as described by Chester Barnard. But Danielian's book on the A.T. and T.—incidentally, one of the few corporate biographies which pays any attention to the role of lawyers—indicates that the development of the over-all telephone organization owes much to legal invention—and not alone in the patent suppression field.[32]

But anthropological and psychological learning offers not only the truism that legal rights are creations of culture, of human relations; it penetrates somewhat further into the question of what these rights are actually made of, what their effective sanction is. This may be illustrated by reference to an experimental psychodrama developed by the Veterans Administration in order to test candidates for jobs in the VA in terms of aggressiveness. A psychodrama is a playlet in which people play roles whose barest outlines are assigned to them; in this case, one of the testers plays the role of a Chinese laundryman who cannot speak English. The candidate is not told this but is told simply that his tuxedo has been left at a laundryman's, that he needs it for a big date at 7:00 P.M., and that he will see his tux hanging,

---

32. See Noobar Danielian, *A. T. & T.*, p. 97.

fully pressed, behind the counter. The following is a typical conversation.

CANDIDATE: Here is my claim check; there is the suit hanging there.
LAUNDRYMAN: Don't speak English. Boss back at 7.
C.: But I need this before 7. There it is.
L.: Don't speak English. (*Sits down behind counter and picks up paper.*)
C.: (*Hesitates, moves toward the counter.*)
L.: (*Lowers paper, looks up.*)
C.: (*Halts.*)
L.: (*Raises newspaper.*)
C.: (*Starts to cross counter.*)
L.: (*Rises, says nothing.*)
C.: (*Gives up and leaves, but in two cases only:*) God damn it, give me my suit! (*Goes and grabs it and leaves.*)

Our own problem here is not so much the question of aggression—though this has been of great interest, as it bears on law, in the work of Malcolm Sharp and others—as in the question: What is the counter made of?

There is no reason to assume that the counter is simply a culture barrier between Chinese and Americans, nor has the counter been charmed by a disease incantation. Rather, the counter seems to be made of some kind of interpersonal field situation connected with property rights and the nuances of trespass. Among these "generalized others" a line is drawn between the suit and its owner by some of the same considerations which created the relation between owner and tuxedo in the first place. (There being, apparently, some connection between the origin of property and of patriarchal society—a society, that is, which rests on inference and reasoning about paternity—one wonders if the VA would have gotten the same results in the psychodrama had the actors both been women!)

There are many unresolved complexities in this experiment. It may, however, serve to illustrate a further point, namely, that social psychology has much to gain from a study of the operation of law. In handling such incidents, psychologists sometimes show a tendency to overestimate the importance of individual personality, or of the "field" created by a number of personalities, while overlooking the bearing of a long historical development of a structural and institutional sort, to which these personalities, unless quite crazy, will defer, at least up to a point. The strength of the VA's imaginary counter depends not only on the weakness of the VA's candidates but also on the long and luxuriant growth of legal forms and practices. These have proceeded historically without becoming entirely the product, at any given time, of the private personalities of those who then fill the institution's statuses and perform its duties.

§ VII

ANOTHER ILLUSTRATION may be drawn from my observations when I served a term in the Appeals Bureau of the New York District Attorney's Office. What struck me there was the fantastically unutilitarian character of many of the briefs we wrote. The head of the office, a law-review-trained man, felt that no case was too humble not to be loaded with all the erudition and art of brief-writing the whole staff could muster. There were open-and-shut gambling cases, for example, where our brief would draw, not only on Hawaii and the law reviews, but even on New Zealand reports and perhaps something from the French Court of Cassation! Now, who was the audience for this display of professional activity? It was not a make-work ritual such as James Caesar Petrillo might devise, for not only were we all high-minded men but we were in fact shorthanded and were actually more likely to lose men and even funds than to gain them by our tactics. For they were certainly not appreciated by the trial lawyers in the office who ridiculed us as some kind of fanatical brain trust, pointing out, as we well knew, that we won 98 per cent of our appeals anyway and that most of the judges did not, or perhaps could not, read briefs. Nor did we endear ourselves to defense counsel, often barely literate and often much too impecunious for such displays of irrelevant learning. Nor did our briefs come to the attention of members of prominent downtown firms, who might appreciate our standards and hire our people—for such members enter the criminal courts only, so to speak, by proxy.

Thus, after eliminating rational explanations for our activity— activity in which I found myself joining in spite of myself—I concluded that we were engaging in some sort of secularized religious activity by which the members of the Appeals Bureau exploited a long tradition of legal learning in order to lend meaning to their daily lives. (Recalling how legalistic many of the Puritans seemed to their more easygoing and worldly foes, we may think of the law as one of the secular equivalents of seventeenth-century theology.) On the face of it, these lawyers were worldly men, or at least worldlywise; behind their backs, in their unconscious, operated motives of an unworldly sort they would have done their best to deny. Perhaps something of what Veblen called "the instinct of workmanship" was also at work here, some desire to do a good job apart from any immediate audience. These nonutilitarian elaborations go on in the law—our office was not unique, though it may have been extreme— not in search of justice but in search of something which transcends even justice, some kind of quest of the Absolute, some kind of art for art's sake. Indeed, I am fairly sure that something of the same sort happens in all occupations, but the lawyer is perhaps less able than others to conceal his intellectual orgies. They are often a matter of record, or they exist in filing cabinets. At the same time this very openness of the lawyer's play with reasoning may be a factor in the way the profession operates (of course, in conjunction with other professions, such as teaching and the more intellectual branches of the ministry) to drain off some of the culture's more adept and avid reasoners, who might find themselves deviants if these careers were not open to them as external defenses and internal sublimations.

It follows that the lawyer's sense of relevance—often greater than that of other people—must constantly struggle in this way with his desire to use his very rationality for ends he cannot admit to himself. And this in turn may link up with the ambivalent roles of the lawyer in our society, who stands at once for reason and for an excess of it.

It may follow, if what I am arguing here is supportable, that the lawyer, the person to whom society assigns the function of being peculiarly rational and relevant, protects himself from his clients by his mobility and professional *élan* and from himself by such ritualistic overwork. That is, he encysts his reason both within layers of professional mystique (much as the Delphic oracles may have done, or shamans of many tribes and climes) and within irrational work patterns of his own.

But, of course, lawyers are not the only examples of such irrational use of rationality. Any true effort to see the functions for the lawyer of his own functions in society must proceed in terms of a more general view of occupations and professions—such a view as my colleague Everett Hughes is engaged in developing.[33] Many lawyers, like many other professionals, have to work hard to down the suspicion that their work lacks meaning, lacks "reality." Lawyers sometimes feel that all they live by is words, that they perform operations which have been taught them but which have no nonsolipsistic consequences. Watching lawyers at work, puzzled about the relation of that work to some larger and more embracing whole, one is reminded of the hero, Laskell's, attitude towards his fishing expedition, as Lionel Trilling describes it in *The Middle of the Journey*:

> Lack of practice made him awkward with his casting. He dutifully reminded himself of all the things he must think about—arm close to the body, wrist loose, the fly to touch the water before the leader. He did

33. See, e.g., his articles, "Work and the Self," in John H. Rohrer and Muzafer Sherif (eds.), *Social Psychology at the Crossroads*, pp. 313-23, and "Institutional Office and the Person," *American Journal of Sociology*, XLIII (November, 1937), 404-13.

not believe that it made any difference. He did not really believe there
were fish in the stream, or that he could catch them, or that fish had ever
been caught by this method. You equipped yourself expensively, you
learned the technique, you did everything the way you had been taught,
and even, for the deceptive pleasure of it, you debated the theory of flies
with other fishermen, arguing about just what it was that the fish saw
when the fly floated over its head. But nothing really happened, or whatever happened happened for quite other reasons and not because you did
what you did.[34]

Here, too, the more we find out about law, the more we will know
about the meaning of work as a mode of relating people to some sort
of physical and social reality, as culturally or existentially defined—
and as a mode also of alienating them from reality and from each
other.

§ VIII

ON ITS FACE, it seems not a difficulty but an advantage that the student
of the legal profession can have ready access to records, files, and
other materials accumulated by a diligently record-keeping lot of
men. To be sure, no profession likes to be studied (apart from the
public relations value of being professional and prominent enough
to have studies made), and Judge Frank in *Courts on Trial* reports
a striking example of judges' refusing to co-operate with would-be
investigators,[35] but on the whole the lawyers are used to being visible.
Perhaps, indeed, it is the very mass of material which is depressing
to a prospective student. For the social scientist who wants to get
beyond, on the one hand, generalizations about the unreasonableness
of the law and, on the other hand, these peripheral touchings at the
most obvious points of criminal justice and trial psychology, needs

---

34. Compare with Trilling's remarks the following observation by Llewellyn
and Hoebel in *The Cheyenne Way*, p. 292: "Thus each law-job, and all of them
together, presents first of all an aspect of pure survival, a bare-bones. The job
must get done *enough* to keep the group going. This is brute struggle for continued existence. It is the problem of attaining order in the pinch at whatever
cost to justice. But beyond this, each job has a wholly distinct double aspect
which we may call the *questing-aspect*. This is a betterment aspect, a question
so to speak of surplus and its employment. On the one side, this questing aspect
looks to more adequate doing of the job, just as a doing: economy, efficiency,
smoothness, leading at the peak to aesthetically satisfying grace in the doing of
it. On the other side, the questing aspect looks to the ideal values; justice, finer
justice, such organization and such ideals of justice as tend toward fuller, richer
life. It no more does to forget the bare-bones in favor of these things than it
does to forget these things in favor of the bare-bones." Cf. also Simmel's significant juxtaposition of art and play with law as activities which are purposeless
in the sense that they are self-determining and independent of the original
impulse that led to them (*The Sociology of Georg Simmel*, trans. Kurt H.
Wolff, p. 42.).
35. *Op. cit.*, p. 116.

to wade into the lawbooks themselves and into office files, as well as to observe, as James West did, the ceremonial and festive functions of Ozark court sessions. He has to sit in on sessions between lawyer and client, especially lawyer and corporate or governmental client, to see if he can observe ways of thinking that are peculiarly legal. Maybe he will have to make distinctions not only among various kinds of law practice but among various groups of law-school graduates. At the same time he may discover that the first and easiest place to observe these tendencies of the American legal mind in the making is in the classroom, on the law review, and in the social life and the myths of the law students. For surely one mode of beginning any serious investigation of the kinds of problems being discussed is to look at the ways in which, on the day of entry, first-year law students already possess a kind of legal culture and personality and by seeing what happens to this as they go through their rites of passage to the LL.B.

Does this mean, to be concrete, that the sociological investigator has to go to law school himself? The law has been made out as much too esoteric—the investigator can pick up what legal lore he needs with relative ease and speed if he has any kind of flair for technical vocabularies. But knowledge of the law and knowledge of the culture of lawyers are obviously two different things; to gain the latter probably requires participant observation. And it may turn out that the investigator who has the best chance of picking up this culture in all its nuances will be one who is sufficiently familiar with the counters of legal discourse to share some of the culture of the lawyers among whom he will move. If he knows some, by the usual journalistic rule, he can pretend he knows more (or, sometimes, less), and find out still more. He will know where to look, where to probe. He will not be so taken up with imbibing legal phrases and mechanics that he will assign to the lawyers he is observing as much affect in the use of these phrases as is necessary for him in the original learning process.

An illustration may be drawn from anthropological field work. Sometimes ethnographic reports give the reader the impression that the preliterate tribe spent most of its emotional energies preparing breadfruit, or casting spells, or hollowing out canoes. All these activities had the same fascination for the anthropologist who had never engaged in them himself as the visiting of factories, nurseries, or prisons, which had been left out of their education in their own countries, had for Western tourists to the Soviet Union. In much the same way, the student of an occupation may be misled by the beat of his own rhythms of attention. His own interest may, without his full awareness, evoke a greater interest among his informants, who can perhaps recapture an earlier enthusiasm for their own shop thereby.

But to put it this way puts the task of participant observation too mechanically—too much as a problem in "rapport" and nondirective interviewing. I am enough of a fly fisherman to believe the legal problems have intrinsic interest; that they are one way of structuring the world—not so bad a way as lawyers in the present mood of defensiveness are often likely to think. The student who wants to see what the function of law is for the lawyer—and hence at least one of its important functions in the society of which lawyers are a substantial part—has to fall for it, just a little bit. Doubtless, he could also learn something if he hated it bitterly. But since there are many things to be studied, anyone omnivorous enough to choose the law and the legal profession might as well have some dessert in a diet that will at best contain a good deal of roughage.

28. Some Observations on Social Science Research*

§ I

EVERY WORK OF SOCIAL SCIENCE today establishes itself on a scale whose two ends are "theory" and "data": that is, the great theoretical structures by which we attempt to understand our age at one end, and the relatively minuscule experiments and data which we collect as practicing social scientists at the other. In between are smaller schemes of generalization as well as larger and less precise observations. The relationship of the two ends of the scale to each other has never been completely clear, and all efforts simply to resolve the problem by comparisons with the natural sciences, or by drastic rejections of one or the other end of the scale, have failed to achieve general acceptance. Social scientists in pursuit of professionalization of their craft and of status as "scientists" are disturbed by this state of affairs, and are hopeful that, if not now, then soon the theory-data tension can be reconciled by some "operational" formula, and that there will then be no doubt as to what is social science. In this paper, I propose to indicate some reasons for skepticism as to these hopes, and some reasons for thinking that the tension is a productive one in the present state of the art, one we might as well enjoy.

To be sure, some deny there is any problem of reconciliation by arguing that only experiments and data are science while all the rest, though it may be produced by people who call themselves social scientists, is art or polemics, journalism or whatnot. Still others escape the problem of reconciliation by the opposite denial: they reject as pettyfogging make-work the meticulous technical operations of social science, and they use the club of late great essayistic thinkers to beat live field-workers into humiliation. Their trade-mark: did it take all this foundation money and all these IBM machines to tell us this, which Tocqueville already knew a hundred years ago!

What is today the most influential group of social scientists espouses neither of these extreme polarities. Rather, it hopes that the large visions of the "fathers"—of such thinkers as Marx, Simmel, Durkheim, Weber, Freud—can be broken down into smaller-scale parcels that could be subjected to empirical verification by contemporary researchers. In this way, it is thought, we should eventually be

---

* In collaboration with Nathan Glazer.

able to work our way from research projects testing rather small bits
of generalization to large theoretical structures, no less illuminating
than those of the past, but in their relation to data more closely parallel to the theories of natural science.[1] As yet, the hope that one can
thus ascend from the twigs of research projects to the main trunk
of social science theory remains only a hope—though one pursued
with ingenuity and devotion by some of the most competent and
gifted workers.

§ II

THE SHARPNESS of the polarity between theory and data varies with
the age: we live in a third period, succeeding one in which theory
reigned supreme, and another, data. Since the gospel of data is connected by personal, if not by inevitable intellectual ties to the concept
of a value-free social science, its supremacy has fallen with the present
self-consciousness of social scientists concerning values, and their desire to be useful in the formation of public policy; if we had to set
a date for this development, we could set it in 1939, when World
War II began and when Robert Lynd published his influential
Knowledge for What? In this third period, each side in the theory-
data conflict has strong defenders and the issue is joined with an
exigent sense of mission. Moreover, it is part of the conflict that ambitious philosophies of history, past and present, should be sent tumbling
down before some inconvenient facts energetically marshalled by the
"data"-wing. But it is no less a mark of the intellectual history of
our age that new philosophers of history, reacting against the slavery
to fact of most contemporary historians and many contemporary
social scientists, should be constantly exasperated by the paucity of
data and tempted to stretch their theories over larger ground than
those data allow. And in its turn this recrudescent temerity, especially
when as with Toynbee it attracts a large lay audience, distresses
many of the workers who prefer the data end of the scale, and then
seek to arm themselves with still more data, first, to demolish the
new philosophy of history, and, second, to build the pile of data high
enough to compete with it.

    In this climate of opinion, the theorist—and I speak here of the
scholar who theorizes, who tries to pull together many facts in a
large scheme of understanding, not of the person who is concerned
with the problem of theory as a methodological specialty—can hope,
at best, to be considered "stimulating," but irrelevant to the main

---

    1. It goes without saying that the "natural science" that thus serves as a model
is itself often a mirage: not natural science as it is actually practiced by its best
contemporaries, but an ideology often based on Newtonian models.

course of social science. His "intuitions," as they are half-enviously, half-patronizingly, called, if they are not exploded out of hand by facts, may be considered worthy of processing by other social scientists—we have thus arrived at the strange position where the most seminal works in the social sciences, if they were published today, would probably be denounced in many professional quarters as sheer talk, though talk which might, under a particularly broad-minded thesis committee, be considered as a quarry for graduate students seeking a topic. That is, works of the type that in the past were most significant for the development of social science would today be considered, charitably, as plausible and interesting, but not as starting points for serious intellectual discussion among social scientists trying to evaluate their meaning and value and even validity.

It is argued, of course, that with the rise of empirical techniques social science has outgrown the need to rely on the type of "impressionistic" work of its early formative years. And we cannot dismiss this view as sheer error, for contrary to what many of the "theory"-wing suppose, these techniques have an unexampled richness and promise. Any kind of formal use of interviews, for instance, was not known in the social sciences even thirty years ago; the projective psychological tests are for the most part still younger; the formal, systematic effort at controlled observation that we find in the community survey or the professional ethnographic monograph is less than sixty years old, and in this period works in this genre have become increasingly more precise and many-skilled in method. In their general form and in their possibilities for technical validation and for mathematical treatment, these methods suggest a new vision of social science: superseding social science as an only moderately specialized development out of history and common observation, the goal now looms of a systematically organized body of observation and strict generalization as taut and impressive as the structure of natural science. In my judgment, attainment of the goal is still a long way off, for reasons that I shall come to in a moment; but the impatience of those to whom the goal seems close at hand, with any social science enterprise which does not appear to move directly towards it, is understandable.

Indeed, there is one problem which no amount of improvement in research methods will ever permit us to overcome, namely the limitation of our knowledge of the past imposed by the unfortunate fact that we cannot interview or test the dead. Historiography and archeology can do remarkable jobs of reconstruction, but they can seldom satisfy the ambitious social scientist in search of quantitative comparisons—a point well made in Paul Lazarsfeld's presidential address to the American Association for Public Opinion Research on "The Obligation of the 1950 Pollster to the 1984 Historian." Thus, if we are comparing, let us say, religious affects today with those of a generation ago, there is no need to be markedly more precise at the near than at the far end. Frequently the consequence is, however, that social scientists bemused by the richness of contemporary method confine their studies to the contemporary scene. And they do so not only when they deal with preliterate cultures where historical materials are scanty (though, if one is not perfectionist, less scanty than sometimes supposed), but also when they deal with civilizations where historical materials are abundant but frustrating. Yet it hardly needs argument in these pages that we cannot assay the weight of any prevailing pattern of attitudes and institutions without appreciating their historical development, and that if we do not study permanence and change in a time dimension we might as well surrender altogether the effort to understand society.

This, then, is the dilemma created by the development of our new tools: that they suggest to us a strict form of social science, in which every generalization refers directly or by a process of unassailable deduction to objectively available bodies of data—these generalizations being as meaningful, useful, and interesting as those of natural science; but for the present—possibly, indeed, for the foreseeable future—such generalizations are impoverished and hobbled by these self-same scientific forms, and consequently social science becomes less interesting, meaningful, and useful—as far as permitting us to understand a sequence of development goes—and less attractive altogether as an intellectual enterprise.

§ III

IN THE PRESENT STATE of controversy, there is tremendous pressure on students of social science (including especially sociology, social anthropology, psychology, and political science) to take sides either in the "theory" or in the "data" camp; this is easy to observe at such an institution as my own, the University of Chicago, or at Columbia, where both camps are well-armed but hungry for more arms, and where both can call on the support of a great tradition. When these students in their own research discover the really extraordinary difficulties of linking any important generalization to measurable data, and thereby closing the gap between the camps, they are apt to conclude, not that there is something wrong with the warfare, but that they are themselves lacking in what it takes to be warriors. The students would be much better off if they could take a stand against taking a stand: if they could realize that the dilemma is at present irresolvable, and nobody's "fault," and accept it as such; that it makes no sense, on the one hand, to reject the new techniques as grubby and inartistic, or, on the other hand, to discard the humanly valuable essence of social science: its power, as seen in the impact of certain great works in the past, to illuminate and describe in some larger framework the experienced details of social life.

Yet I know how difficult it is to convince anyone that one has not, even surreptitiously, taken a stand for "data" or for "theory." Margaret Mead can publish Samoan house-descriptions and genealogies, or co-operate in a wartime study of food habits using the most advanced techniques, and still be dismissed by many professional colleagues as "intuitive," or belabored by the even more fearsome term "insightful." The late W. I. Thomas would today perhaps be startled to see his work viewed as a storehouse of social-psychological theory, when his own much greater preoccupation was with the facts and forms of social reportage. On a much smaller scale, I find similar misunderstanding of my own teaching and writing. *The Lonely Crowd,* which lies towards the theory end of the scale, aroused misplaced enthusiasm from some historians and humanists because of its lack of graphs and tables, and perhaps misplaced animadversions from some social scientists who viewed it as more biased towards the "theory" end than was intended. For the book is full of data, mainly but not entirely in the traditional form of observation from everyday life: I speak there of movies, comic books, magazines; of progressive schools and traditional schools; of the way parents think of children, and vice versa; of the way executives think of workers, and vice versa. Many humanists fail to realize that such data require supporting data, and a more formal and systematic effort to demonstrate that what they and the author refer to as matters of common knowledge are really so. Conversely, many social scientists, prematurely dazzled by the new techniques, fail to realize how far we still are from being able to prove what we "know" by them.

To put matters another way, I do not believe that one is surrendering the strict demands of science to a human but unscientific desire for understanding if one accepts the theory-data dilemma and works within its limitations, while recognizing that at some future date those limitations will greatly change. For science itself arises out of the desire to explain, to understand: the technical operations are subsidiary to this. If the natural sciences did not satisfy this desire by real accomplishments, it is unlikely that they would enlist creative minds to serve the hard discipline of the techniques—though as a paying and going concern they can enlist many unadventurous minds drawn by motivations other than those of the pioneers. So, too, social scientists who insist that we must serve the machines and the techniques regardless of the quality of understanding that emerges from that service—for that service alone is real science—fail to appreciate not only the history of science in general but also that social science is still too untried to enlist and retain large-scale support without large-scale accomplishment.

Undoubtedly, science requires sacrifices of its acolytes, but the nature of those sacrifices differs with the age. By and large, American social science no longer requires of its personnel the humiliation, poverty, lack of recognition that were the fate of Marx, Comte, Freud, and, to a degree, of Sumner, Sorel, Veblen. But field-work is still arduous and heart-breaking, research still filled with disappointments, blind alleys, and want of adequate resources.[2] It is a sacrifice of vanity to realize that one will never even approximate the glorious achievements of the fathers, not perhaps live to see the edifice constructed by the technical adeptness of the great-grandsons. It is a sacrifice of impatience to be charitable both to one's work and that of others when this work has the status of "pilot projects," as social scientists overoptimistically dub most of their present enterprises— overoptimistically, because they assume that there will soon be a whole plant engaged in the production of results. In this situation, the claim that we should make the sacrifices of scientific work without the hope of gaining a better understanding of society—indeed while ridiculing whatever understanding is achieved, for instance by novelists, without training and technique—is to make vain demands on our willingness to wait for "production miracles."

I am quite aware that this formulation does not solve the question of how we know that an understanding not established directly or by strict reasoning on a sufficient volume of empirical data is a true understanding. I don't propose to unravel this epistemological mystery here: it is enough to observe that the acceptance of the position that only the generalizations founded on irrefutable data are true leaves us to conclude that all understanding of society (other than in economics, the social science with the greatest achievements to its credit) established up till now is pure illusion; and that all sociology is simply hypothesis awaiting proof, for I believe it can be shown that with rare exceptions even the most up-to-date data support the most up-to-date generalization only as example, not as proof in any (even probability-theory) scientific sense. Yet at the same time, only a data-extremist would insist that the study of Weber, Durkheim, Sim-

---

2. The scientific workers in the field of "culture and personality" must endure a particular kind of sacrifice, namely to have to live with heightened self-consciousness of all personal relations and cultural phenomena, making it hard for them to separate their professional work from the rest of their lives.

mel and other great turn-of-the-century founders is irrelevant to our understanding of social processes: some light emerges.

And the reason for this is that we are ourselves men living in society; and, as the saying goes, we were not born yesterday. Many social scientists, worried about bias and struck by what natural scientists have achieved in studying stars and atoms, being neither one nor the other, feel that when they approach work in their field they should cultivate a complete skepticism, at least until the not far distant day when theories will be buttressed at every point by data; ironically, this wanton innocence is itself the cultural product of some of the very thinkers whose writings they would reject as unscientific. Natural science deserves tremendous credit for having achieved so much when so inevitably distant from its objects; social scientists, rather than trying to impose on themselves similar handicaps, should take full advantage of the fact that they are themselves part of their universe of study, and heirs to a long and not utterly noncumulative tradition of thinking about man.[3]

§ IV

DOUBTLESS, more social scientists will agree that the problem is to proceed from one end of the theory-data scale to the other, so as to encompass a suitable combination of thought and fact, than will agree on which end should be taken as the starting-point. My own belief, already indicated, is that there is no "right" end, no royal road, but that one can fruitfully begin at either end, or anywhere between. One must be willing to take seriously theories which are not established, and even theories which are, in some formal sense, "refuted," when they offer a real illumination and insight, which will undoubtedly turn out to be a partial illumination. Thus, it makes not very fruitful use of Weber's book on the Protestant ethic to ask whether it is true or false. To be sure, the book evoked a whole historiography of disproof, but the book still helps us understand our world and our place in it. Certainly, no theory can have this success if it is in plain opposition to many facts, for the theory itself is an effort to explain and order facts; yet agreement with some large and crucial facts may be more important than contradiction by them in details.

At the same time, social scientists should be more willing than

---

3. Crane Brinton, in *Ideas and Men*, sees social science as largely noncumulative—having to be learned over again for each worker and each generation—while natural science is largely cumulative. And there can be no doubt that the truths of social interaction—of psychoanalysis, let us say—have to be experienced by each individual before he can make important use of them in research; yet there is a cumulative tradition which makes it possible to learn noncumulative truths, helping new field workers, for example, to face the ineluctable hardships of their initiation.

many of the ablest are, to begin at the "data" end of the scale, though without the illusion that they can move immediately therefrom to the grist of theory. Our obsession with our image of the natural sciences tends to make us think of data as only verification, as supporting a theory or destroying it. Yet the value of data as simple reporting on the quality and details of social life has been a most significant part of social science: Booth's *Life and Labour of the People in London*, Thomas and Znaniecki's *The Polish Peasant in Europe and America*, the Lynds' *Middletown* volumes, the Allison Davis and John Dollard studies of the Deep South, and many other works that present full pictures of some social phenomenon, partake of many of the qualities of good reporting. The theoretical schemes which the reporting supports usually seem less and less important with the passage of time: the data remain valuable and stimulating, and as useful in support of the theoretical schemes of the future as of those of the original authors.[4] Important branches of social science are even more clearly reporting rather than theory: this has been true, at least until recently, of most public opinion research: the poll data gathered in the public opinion journals, in the recent Cantril-Strunk volume, and in the *American Soldier*, form a rich body of materials, which we would never have had if we had had to wait for a structure of the theory-hypothesis-data-new-theory sort to justify gathering it.

Likewise, the scorn so frequently heaped on "gadgeteers," from without as well as within the ranks of social science, fails to grasp how much we owe, in all the sciences, to sheer fooling around with methods and techniques, more or less for their own sakes. In many ways, Freud was a gadgeteer, first in his work on the staining of cells for histological purposes, later in his experiments with hypnosis and other therapies; we forget this, since he also used his techniques to make brilliant discoveries. True, "gadgeteer" is often applied to those who see in a device or machine a panacea for all ills, or at the very least a solvent for hitherto intractable problems, and here certainly

---

4. In the middle '30's a type of reporting developed which had much in common with social science: in those days, reporters took to crossing the country and asking questions of various people they ran into (James Rorty, Benjamin Appel, John Dos Passos, Samuel Grafton, and others), presenting pictures which can support a number of different interpretations. At the same time, *Fortune* began to give large scope to reporters—some of whom have become very interested in social science and its problems—who developed a new kind of "story" which often surpasses the work of professional social scientists in information and even, though perhaps without intending it, in "theory."

My understanding of the origins and present importance of the reportorial tradition in social science has profited greatly from discussions with Everett Hughes.

scorn is justifiable. But scorn is also levelled at gadgeteers who make no such grandiose claims, and here it seems to reflect attitudes of a very widespread sort: our hierarchy of skill and learning snobberies, our gnawing uneasiness about "materialism" and mechanical know-how, our ambivalence towards those aspects of American life that John A. Kouwenhoven, in his book *Made in America,* sums up as the "vernacular." Science suffers, however, when the gadgeteer must justify himself by association with some immediate and high-flown purpose, whether drawn from the realm of theory or of social action.

In sum, whatever end of the scale one begins at, one is likely to be under pressure to move rapidly towards the other end—"to link theory and data" as the phrase goes—by people who have insufficient respect for either end in its own terms, and who fail to appreciate all the intermediate and frequently indirect and unplannable steps in between. This leads to the most paradoxical results: on the one hand, scholars think they have "proved" their case scientifically when they are very far from it—for if their case were not, to their own satisfaction, demonstrated, they could have no respect for themselves; and, on the other hand, other scholars are reduced to despair when they discover that the petty data they have accumulated in a stretch of painstaking and mayhap costly work bears little relation to the grand hypothesis with which they began. In this situation, work which is very far from technical validation, let alone from proving anything important about society, is often desperately seized upon by the promoters and defenders of social science in order to convince themselves and others that they are in a good line of work, and, beyond that, that they could produce far more if they got the funds and the go-ahead orders. As the design engineers in an industry feel harried by the demands and expectations of the product engineers who want to produce, and the sales engineers who want to sell, so the design engineers of social science are under the pressures just indicated from the production and sales staff who insist on putting on the social science assembly line what is still necessarily in the handicraft and mock-up stage.[5] In many quarters, the promoters of social science have aroused such unfulfillable expectations as to risk a disillusioning bust of the whole enterprise. Thus, while at an earlier time social scientists may have been overtimid, "ivory-towerish," and afraid of responsibility,

---

5. It should be added that this is often done in the friendliest spirit. At times, the production engineer will show an overgreat deference to the design engineer —as the result of snobberies already touched upon—leading the former to premature attempts to use and sell the work of the latter to raise his own status. Obviously enough, novelists and other artists are subjected to analogous briberies and temptations, and in the relation between highbrow and middlebrow art one can find similar tensions.

they seem today more endangered by check-kiting (in terms of reports leading to "pilot studies," to more reports, and so on endlessly) than by reticence.

§ V

ONE CAN IMAGINE the relief with which some promoters of social science have greeted a few recent very successful efforts to link theory and data. I shall discuss briefly two such major efforts—*The Authoritarian Personality*, by T. W. Adorno, Else Frenkel-Brunswik, Daniel J. Levinson, and R. Nevitt Sanford; and the *Yankee City* series by W. Lloyd Warner and his coworkers—in order to show that the difficulties we have been discussing arise even on the highest and most sophisticated level of research, and to show some of the risks one runs in taking such studies as models for slavish imitation.

The Authoritarian Personality is perhaps the most impressive attempt in recent American social psychology and sociology to link a large-scale and important theory to data which would support and demonstrate it. This thousand-page volume is the outgrowth of many years of study, first by members of the (Frankfort) Institute for Social Research, later by an able and energetic group at Berkeley that worked for another period of years: it was not a project set up to pay quick dividends out of capital to attract further capital, but rather one which took its time about the study of the authoritarian personality and its role in modern industrial society—a large order, indeed. The thinking at the "theory" end began in the late '20's and early '30's in Germany; a large volume dealing with many facets of the problem—*Autorität und Familie*—appeared in the mid-'30's, at which time empirical research projects had already begun; the research work that *The Authoritarian Personality* itself reports was carried out over a span of five years or more in Berkeley, and incorporates the use of the most subtle and advanced of psychological techniques. Time to work and think and experiment is essential for serious investigation, and this long period of maturation makes *The Authoritarian Personality* as good and significant as it is.

But there is just the rub. Society does not stand still—American society perhaps least of all—and the problem of twenty years ago is not the problem of today, and the problem of Germany then is not the problem of America now. Events continually outdistance our attempts to understand them; social scientists, no less than other people, must structure the world while at the same time keeping up with it. Economists kept talking about our economy as if its problems were those of underemployment for years after this problem had disappeared, and under circumstances that made its recrudescence unlikely for years to come, if ever.[6] *The Authoritarian Personality* rests on the equally irrelevant fundamental premise—as it appears to me—that European-style fascism is the great danger hanging over America, as well as on the minor premise—to me not important for America, and dubious even for Germany—that authoritarianism in character structure breeds and is bred by authoritarianism in social structure. As to fascism: there is no room here to set out all my reasons for believing that this is not the principal American menace—among them, is the position, developed in *The Lonely Crowd*, that virtually all sectors of American life (including would-be fascists) have an "in" on the political and social scene which would be disturbed by a *coup d'état;* moreover, that American big business is not as unified, ruthless, or conspiratorial as the authors of the book suppose; finally, if there exists a danger of internal repression in America today, it ensues more from the threat of totalitarian Soviet expansion than from sources in American "authoritarian personality."[7] As to the minor premise linking character and society, I suggest that, in America and England, the Puritan character, which qualifies in many ways as "authoritarian," actually helped foster a democratic social structure under given conditions of seventeenth-century life; conversely, the pliable "democratic" personality can be molded and made use of, under other social conditions and institutions, in developing a rigid and authoritarian society.

These may seem like drastic criticisms, and they certainly go to the heart of the authors' aims and conclusions. Yet the by-products of the study are invaluable: never, for instance, have we had, on such a large scale, such brilliant and brilliantly-validated use of "diagnostic" questions arranged in scales to test underlying attitudes, nor such grasp of nuances of verbal expression as clues to character, nor such an interesting discussion of the political attitudes of criminals, nor so capable an appraisal of the possibilities of typological treatment in social research. Nor is the study of fascism itself all waste effort by any means: there are undoubtedly some millions of fascist-minded people in the United States, and we now have an unexampled look at

---

6. We run here, among other things, into the matter of the "self-confirming prophecy" discussed by Robert K. Merton in *Social Theory and Social Structure.* Since people on all levels of our society believe that depressions are controllable (some, as the result of the Keynesians; others, as a result of their interpretation of our war experience), while they do not believe wars are controllable, the government will be under great if not irresistible pressure to live up to these expectations—by a war economy if necessary. This seemed evident to a number of observers before economists became concerned with the problems of full employment.

7. For a similar view, see Paul Kecskemeti, "Prejudice in the Catastrophic Perspective," *Commentary* (March, 1951).

many sides of their outlooks and personalities. Nevertheless, the study itself, as an effort to understand America, does not carry us far; the very gift and social concern of the planners of the work, which led them to the problem of fascism, led them off on what turned out, two decades later, to be a false scent; and if the study contributes, as I think likely, to the understanding of society, it will be indirectly, through its by-products.

Other examples of the complexites introduced by the necessarily long process of data-gathering and publishing are the studies of social class directed and inspired by Lloyd Warner. His first work in this field was done in a New England town at the beginning of the depression; the same techniques and concerns that were used in "Yankee City" in the early '30's have been carried over, with minor systematizations and modifications, to "Deep South" and to "Elmtown" ("Jonesville"), with way stations in between. But in these later studies the question is not raised whether class remains the most fruitful concept for understanding American culture and personality in 1951; or whether people today are as concerned with social mobility as they were twenty years ago, and as the technique then devised nearly inevitably makes it appear that they still are—for the technique tends to confuse membership in a social class, as symbolized by a brilliant variety of indices, with consciousness of that membership and of its implications, honorific and otherwise. The technique is not neutral—no technique is; it was devised at a time when certain problems relating to class were pre-eminent, and when Warner's insistence on their importance was stimulating and heretical; the technique took years to perfect, but now that it is perfected (a much debated point among experts), and relatively easy for students to apply, it must be asked whether other problems—divisions within social classes, for instance, or cutting across classes—may not have become more significant, even though class is still of great and obvious significance. Professor Warner himself, in fact, not being committed to a large and expensive apparatus, seems in his most recent work to be as interested in comparing the fantasy life of people on what he calls the "common man" level with that of the "uncommon man" as he is with new applications of the Yankee City scheme.

We must conclude, then, that the effort to link theory and data, at the present pace of work, runs into a most important set of logistical problems. It is hard enough to modify one's own conceptions to take account of a changing world, and perhaps to help change it; it is harder, much harder, to overhaul a huge research project, planned over the many years required for work, evaluation, and publication, so as to fit these changing conceptions. In answer to such dejections, it is often argued that money is the only bottleneck to the spectacular advance of social science—and that, if only a quarter as much were made available as was put at the disposal of atomic scientists, there would be no important areas of ignorance left about the world, let alone the United States! Conceivably, if there were *enough* money, and *enough* personnel, monopolistic competition among even large-scale research enterprises would tend to keep them flexible and fast on their feet to a degree—yet even here the logistical problem would remain, for a country that could be brought to devote such enormous resources to its own self-scrutiny would obviously be a very different land from the present U.S.A., so different perhaps that social science would no longer appear as inviting or necessary! One is almost awe-struck with the lack of humor, if not of humility, on the part of those social scientists who feel their trade so all-important that they can make such requests of the national income and the national man-power, and one could greatly admire the implicit utopian faith so displayed, if one did not feel an underlying insecurity prompting the frequent use of the nuclear physicists as a reference group.

It is evident, moreover, that the large-scale theory-testing operation runs the risks of encouraging mere discipleship which are always present in intellectual and artistic enterprise. The easiest way to do research is to apply the beautifully-engineered models supplied by such work as that of the Berkeley group and Warner—though actually, partly because this work has many complexities and is highly controversial, much inferior models are usually chosen. But while a proved sire may be the best bet in cattle-breeding, proved paternities in the social sciences are not so satisfactory. The discipline has much less chance, generally, of adapting his conceptions to the rapidly changing course of social development than the originator—but even the latter may be trapped by fear of disappointing, or "disemploying," his disciples.

Since I am myself a practitioner of social science, as well as a critic thereof, I must guard against the possible implication that I consider my own writing and teaching to have escaped these pitfalls —on the contrary, it is from falling in that I have learned to locate some of them. But I do suggest that certain aspects of my work which appear to some contemporary social scientists to be simply defects— a somewhat casual and unsystematic approach, and a refusal to set up the grand money- and time- and man-consuming research projects that would demonstrate my hypotheses—are not only defects, and certainly not unintended ones: if what I have said hitherto is sound, there are also virtues in the handicraft approach which, not entirely committed to a major course of action, is able to shift and turn with the development of the thought of the researcher, as well as with the course of social development. Without any question, however, this unmethodical method is subject to its own hazards, most of which have been examined at length in the social science literature of the recent, method-conscious decades.

§ VI

IT IS INTERESTING to speculate about what American social science would look like today if journalism had had as much prestige in the late nineteenth and early twentieth centuries as natural science, though perhaps the drive towards professionalization has been more important in shaping social science than the fact that the professional model chosen has generally been physics or biology. In England an organization has grown up in the last fifteen years—Mass Observation, or MO for short—which deserves to be better known in this country, for in conception it is a frontal attack both on the natural science model and on professionalization. It consists of a group of animated and amateur social observers who are encouraged to send in reports on assigned topics—and to suggest topics—to a central office run by social scientists: they have studied such British institutions as the pub, church-going, the last Coronation Day, and what happens at "all-in" wrestling. MO attempts to reduce the distance between observers and observed by allowing the latter to participate in the processes of social study—to bring to it what they have in the way of gifts of observation and to receive in return instruction and information based on others' observation. In intention, though not in its rather sloppy execution, it is an adult education venture in the social sciences.[8]

American (and British) public opinion specialists have heaped scorn on the MO sampling methods or lack of them; and one could also criticize the raw empiricism of such a book as *May the Twelfth*, which reports, without interpretation or selection or preliminary training of the reporters, what observers noticed on Coronation Day in 1938; there MO forgot that the first duty of a reporter is to be interesting, a duty which demands both selection and interpretation.[9]

In the United States there have been a few developments similar to MO but, significantly enough, all of them appear to have been

8. There is, of course, a tradition of local history studies, and also of local linguistics and folk culture studies, which goes back a long way in Europe, and to a lesser degree in this country.

9. Fortunately, Robert E. Park never got over his training as a Sunday Supplement feature writer for the Detroit press; he never managed, in his late career as a sociologist, to stay away from interest or "human interest" for very long at a time. See his "Autobiographical Note" in *Race and Culture*.

motivated by immediate problems of social policy rather than, as in the case of the British organization, by this coupled with "idle curiosity" about the society. During World War II the OWI ran what were called Correspondence Panels: men and women throughout the country who sent in reports on such assigned topics as how the draft was going, the effect of price control, and morale, receiving in return instructions and commentary; under the direction of Elizabeth Herzog, many small businessmen, housewives, and others learned for the first time to look at their communities with the detached and inquiring air which is the hallmark of the good reporter and the good social science observer. (With the end of the war, the program, like so much else that had been painfully built up, was hastily demolished.) More widely known is the "action-research" approach of the late Kurt Lewin and a group of his followers; their idea was that it might be possible to enlist ordinary citizens to study their own community problems; more than that, this self-study, they believed, would help in the solution of these problems, while the very effort at solution would in turn invigorate research. Under the influence of this approach there have been, for example, a number of "community self-audits," in which citizens, under the direction of social scientists, have examined their community from the point of view of its failings and fulfillments, particularly as to race relations. The method has much to be said for it, both as adult education and as social action, but I have some misgivings about its usefulness for research and deeper understanding: usually the social scientists in charge already know, in a rough way, that they will find anti-Negro bias in housing in Montclair or discrimination in employment in Northfield (two cities where successful audits were made), and "self-audit" can become, despite the democratic sympathies of the leaders, little more than a new gimmick to spur community activity.

At any rate, America much more than England seems to me to need both the reporting technique and the enlistment of the amateur observer that characterize MO—to need them for the basic job of finding out what goes on, apart from any question as to what can be done about it. This country is so big, so varied, so almost if not quite unencompassable, that social research cannot have enough observers who will break down its momentary generalizations and open up new views. Something like MO would permit what might be called "research by exception," where a researcher would count on his "far-flung correspondents" to tell him where something he had taken for granted was not so. Indeed, there are many fields of social research which simply cannot be handled by existing techniques. If we want to know, for example, the reactions of movie audiences to a nationally-exhibited film, as this varies from showing to showing, we cannot learn this at present, nor can sampling methods tell us how an audience, a group en masse, responds; the whole wide field of American popular culture needs mass explorers and mass observers: for sports events, dance-halls, bookie joints, fairs, and countless other pastimes. By bringing these observers into our research organizations, moreover, we are likely greatly to amplify our conception both of the complexity of our country and of its newly emerging problems, for there will be no want of stimulating queries and reports.[10]

Certainly, a social science militia of this type would go far to complement, and perhaps to check, the social science army of professionals envisaged by the logistics discussed earlier. We would be overwhelmed with data: our poor schemes would have to be sturdy indeed to stand up to it—perhaps, afraid of drowning in data, we would become fonder of theory! We would also have to focus on questions that interested our militia—and work on the problem of easy communication with them—for they would be bound to us, not by professional ties, but by mutual needs for understanding. We may perhaps not be prepared for the new functions that would be forced upon us. But at the same time, accepting our function as reporters as well as systematizers, we might continue to be happy even where we were unsuccessful.

§ VII

IN A THOUGHT-PROVOKING essay on "The Art of Social Science," Robert Redfield has called attention to some of the ambiguities of current emphasis on method in social research, pointing out that Tocqueville and other great and gifted observers had added much to our knowledge while ignorant of or violating the rules laid down by men who have added much less. If what I have said in this paper makes sense, we may draw a further analogy with contemporary problems of art, especially literary art. For it would seem that social scientists, too, have their "New Critics" who have been laying down a canon which, in the minds of some, operates to intimidate creative work. The canon is actually more perfectionist than its literary analogue, since it is based, not on actual work, but on often brilliant

---

10. Thanks to the cooperation of the National Opinion Research Center, I once had the opportunity to go over many reports sent in by interviewers to accompany their formal schedules—letters, really, rather than reports, which touched on how hard the interviewing had gone or how easy, on what types of questions made for trouble or interest, and on many of the day-to-day events and encounters in the interviewers' rounds. Often, these reports were more stimulating than the content of the schedules, which dealt with ephemeral opinions: what do you think of the UN, of Truman, of Palestine partition, or whatever else were the "issues" of 1948.

extrapolation from our old friends, the "pilot studies." And whereas the new critics in literature frequently have a verve and elegance in writing, and a depth in understanding, which compensates for much that may be lacking in creative writing, the new critics in social science—while they would hardly agree with William F. Ogburn's paper on "The Folklore of Social Science" that the social scientists of the future will not be gifted with wit or originality but will publish merely statistical reports—seem to feel that their ascetic laboriousness and lugubriousness in the content of criticism should also be reflected in its style.

Both developments, moreover, in literature and in social science, are in part the outcome of the tremendous advance in university teaching in the humanities and in the social sciences in the last several decades. At many institutions, large and small, there has been a heightening of critical standards, and students are confronted, not with easy-going teachers using casual texts, but with able and energetic new critics, who can discover the flaws in the finest poetry and fiction, or in the most heralded works of social science. And in both areas, as a price for this advance, there is a temptation for students to become easily discouraged about what they could contribute to creative work; they have to bear in mind so many injunctions, each of them "correct," that they can no more start their own enterprises than could a businessman in a completely regimented state—for their vanity and ambition are already low, as the result of other social developments than the rise of the new critics.

In the art world at least, the battle of artists and critics is an old one. But it is a battle of a noncumulative sort, which must be fought over in every era, because of changes in the division of labor, and in the strength and self-confidence of the several sides. In American writing, those seem to fare best who pay no attention to critics— symbolized by William Faulkner calling himself aggressively a farmer, and not a literary man. In American social science, many of the best contributions have been made by journalists and others who were out of the circle of academic life and criticism. But surely this is not an optimum solution, for it lowers the intellectual level of creative writing, and leaves critics as the audience for other critics. And while in art there is an inexhaustible storehouse for the critics to draw upon, in social science there is not enough good work to occupy many critics for a full-time day. Marx was right when he wrote in *The German Ideology* that it should be "possible for one to do one thing today and another tomorrow—to hunt in the morning, to fish in the evening, to criticize after dinner just as I have in mind, without ever becoming hunter, fisherman, shepherd, or critic."

29. Some Clinical and Cultural Aspects of the Aging Process

IF WE OBSERVE the aging of individuals, in the period after middle life, it seems to me that we can distinguish three ideal-typical outcomes. Some individuals bear within themselves some psychological sources of self-renewal; aging brings for them accretions of wisdom, with no loss of spontaneity and ability to enjoy life, and they are relatively independent of the culture's strictures and penalties imposed on the aged. Other individuals, possibly the majority, bear within them no such resources but are the beneficiaries of a cultural preservative (derived from work, power, position, etc.) which sustains them although only so long as the cultural conditions remain stable and protective. A third group, protected neither from within nor from without, simply decay. In terms more fully delineated elsewhere,[1] we may have autonomous, adjusted, and anomic reactions to aging.

§ THE AUTONOMOUS

IN THE CASE of someone like Bertrand Russell or Toscanini, one feels an essential aliveness of spirit that reflexively keeps the body alive, too, in the face of the inevitable physiological catabolisms. Such men create something new every day through their own reactions; in their work as in their general style of life they exhibit what Erich Fromm calls the "productive orientation."[2] It is most important to realize that such men are not necessarily "balanced" or "well-adjusted" people: they may have terrible tempers, neurotic moods; they may be shut out from whole areas of existence; they may get along well with very few people, or prefer the "company" of dead people as historians or musicians; they may relate themselves to the cosmos more through an emphasis on objects and ideas than on social relations. One can see in such cases that a passionate interest or preoccupation which has remained alive since childhood—though perhaps newly justified or rediscovered in middle life—may matter much more than the roundedness of interests we are today inclined to encourage among our two vulnerable groups of "clients": children and older people. It might be valuable to study, for instance, professional chess players of dis-

1. See chapter 14 of *The Lonely Crowd.*
2. *Man for Himself.*

tinction; my guess would be that they suffer very little deterioration as a social-psychological process, however constricted their lives may appear to the therapist whose norm is a superficial integration of a bundle of diverse activities.

Such individuals, I repeat, are fairly immune to cultural changes, or to cultural definitions of their own physical changes: they carry their preservative, their "spirits," within. Freud could continue to live with vigor in the face of cancer of the mouth which made eating embarrassing and difficult; as his life went on, it seems to me that he grew steadily more alive and imperturbable—*Civilization and Its Discontents*, written when he was over 70, belies its pessimistic theme by the very vitality of its presentation. Likewise Franz Boas, though he suffered from disfigurement and though he was in many ways a cramped person, does not appear to have experienced any decline of powers. The misfortunes brought by Nazism could no more shake either man than the misfortunes brought by their own bodies. Men of this sort exhibit in a dramatic way the specifically human power to grow and develop on a super-physiological level (with, of course, physiological consequences); as long as the body does not actively prevent, these men are immortal because of their ability to renew themselves.

In lesser degree, anyone who can experience anything for himself —whether he is a "man of distinction" or not—staves off by so much psychological death. Paradoxically, the premonition of death may for many be a stimulus to such novelty of experience: the imminence of death serves to sweep away the inessential preoccupations for those who do not flee from the thought of death into triviality. It is apparent that we enter here a cultural dimension and raise the questions how death is regarded or disregarded in America, compared to how it is viewed, for example, in existentialist philosophy.

I can think of several reasons why we have not paid very much attention to these autonomous reactions to aging. Such reactions are rare, and a spurious democracy has influenced both our research methods (I am sometimes tempted to define "validity" as part of the context of an experiment demanding so little in the way of esoteric gift that any number can play at it, provided they have taken a certain number of courses) and our research subjects (it would be deemed snobbish to investigate only the best people). Moreover, the period of life I am describing and its attendant qualities do not last long: men react productively to waning physical and often social power, only to die shortly thereafter. And we tend to view individuals as we do entire cultures: while we can admire the Hellenistic period although it was weak and vulnerable and soon perished, we do not on the whole admire declining empires nearer to us in time. We read their future fate—death—into our present judgment of them.

§ THE ADJUSTED

I SHOULD, I SUPPOSE, always put quotation marks around my use of the term "adjusted," for I define this, not in terms of my own value judgments but in terms of given cultural definitions. For instance, we all know the type of American executive or professional man who does not allow himself to age, but by what appears almost sheer will keeps himself "well-preserved," as if in creosote. For the most part, he lacks inner aliveness of the sort just discussed; the will which burns in him, while often admirable, cannot be said to be truly "his": it is compulsive; he has no control over it, but it controls him. He appears to exist in a psychological deep-freeze; new experience cannot get at him, but rather he fulfills himself by carrying out ever-renewed tasks which are given by his environment: he is borne along on the tide of cultural agendas. So long as these agendas remain, he is safe; he does not acquire wisdom, as the old of some other cultures are said to do, but he does not lose skill—or if he does, is protected by his power from the consequences, perhaps the awareness, of loss of skill. In such a man, reponsibility may substitute for maturity.

Indeed, it could be argued that the protection furnished such people in the United States is particularly strong since their "youthfulness" remains a social and economic prestige-point and wisdom might actually, if it brought awareness of death and what the culture regarded as pessimism, be a count against them. In a way, nothing happens to these people, which leads them (save possibly in rare moments of self-doubt and self-questioning) to regard themselves as well-off. They prefigure in complex and often imperceptible ways the cultural cosmetic that makes Americans appear youthful to other peoples. And, since they are well-fed, well-groomed, and vitamin-dosed, there may be an actual delay-in-transit of the usual physiological declines to partly compensate for lack of psychological growth. Their outward appearance of aliveness may mask inner sterility.

Like the women of an earlier day who were held up by stays, such "adjusted" people of the middle and later years are held up by endo-skeletal (mesmorphic?) tensions. As I have said, they are literally held up: nothing advances, save their careers, their responsibilities. This sort of energy must surely be ranked among the world-conquering assets of Western man: it is impressive to Indians to find Englishmen, as well as mad dogs, out in the noonday sun—they are gods of a sort, who tell the sun to stand still. Only at night, perhaps, coming home from a party, does the mask drop or crack, to be ritualistically reorganized the following day. We who are the beneficiaries of such accumulated energies in the past cannot lightly scoff at their possessors.

Nevertheless, I am inclined to think that many of the geriatric suggestions currently made for improving the adjustment of the elderly are aimed simply at finding ersatz preservatives, not at any inner transformations that would allow self-renewal to occur. Thus, we may seek to persuade a retired doctor or executive to take up golf or fishing with the same undiscerning ferocity he once threw into his work and its social context; we may shift someone from the faculty club or the Kiwanis into the Golden Age Club; and so on. It would be unjust to criticize too severely these ameliorative measures in the absence of understood and institutionalized ways of assisting more basic transformation—ways it is often, one fears, too late to start with by the time of retirement. (We know, in principle, it is never too late; but, as with other therapeutic questions, it is a matter of available help, of the allocation of scarce resources.) Yet we may occasionally discover dilemmas in which too quick an effort to assure a smooth adjustment results in this merely substitutive activity, whereas allowing a person to be confronted for a time with nothingness might save him—or destroy him—depending on what inner resources he could muster in reaction to the challenge.[3]

And in this connection let me bring up reservations about our usual social-psychological discussions of roles and role theory—discussions which too easily assume that people *are* the roles they play, the willing or unwilling puppeteers of the social drama. In my own view, the ability to play roles not only involves, in a great many instances, some rewriting of the socially-provided script, but some saving grace of potentiality not bound up in the role; the role itself is what allows people to give to it less than their full selves; it clarifies one's economy of affects. Hence there are reservoirs of inner life in a great many individuals whose roles, almost by definition, do not wholly absorb them. (The same is true, as Toynbee observes in terms of world history, of many cultures and what had been thought to be their "roles.") We see in wartime or other socially-structured emergency the great efflorescence of unsuspected potentialities in people —unsuspected often enough by the very individuals concerned. Where do these potentialities come from? It is hard to say, though we are tempted to refer them, as we refer so many mysteries, to childhood,

---

3. I have just come upon the excellent article of Dr. Martin Gumpert, "Old Age and Productive Loss," *Bulletin of the Menninger Clinic*, vol. 17, pp. 103-109 (May 1953). Dr. Gumpert stresses that the very bodily defeats and impairments of the aging person may be and often are more than compensated for by inner growth.

and to say that the cultural preservative is a deep-freeze in the sense, too, that childhood potentialities, though long neglected, are seldom wholly crushed. (Very few projective test experts, in my limited observation, focus sufficiently on the discovery of such potentialities; the "deeper levels" they look for are ordinarily those that foreshadow trouble rather than liberation: they are understandably more worried that they will miss a hidden flaw than a buried asset.)

Professor Martin Loeb, the field director of our Kansas City research, in discussing these notions with me, has been inclined to question the making of such explicit value judgments, the positing of an ideal of aging as the basis for setting up a typology. He suggested that I might be in danger of projecting into a typology my own dream that the autonomous person does not "really" age, at least in any deleterious way. And he asked what was wrong with a grandmother's way of aging who had had a hard life and now preferred to sit passively on the porch and watch her grandchildren and the passing traffic? Who was to tell her she should be spontaneous?

I doubt if this was meant as a warning against value judgments as such, for we cannot avoid them, but rather against shallow and ethnocentric ones. Still, I sometimes feel that middle-class social scientists are today almost too ready to throw over their own values, as class-biased, while accepting values from groups whose life-conditions have permitted them fewer alternatives. Our circle of sympathy should not be too narrow—should even perhaps include the lower-middle-class grandmother who wears too much grease paint in a pathetic effort to look like a cover girl. And certainly a grandmother who decides out of her life-experience to observe her progeny and the passing show and who is capable of observing people as individuals and not entirely as stereotypes would strike me as making a productive reaction to aging—spontaneity and aliveness are of course not to be equated with activity and hep-ness. In general, I feel that we can sharpen our scientific awareness of what aging does to people, and vice versa, by bringing into play our preference for more creative as against more stultified ways of meeting the challenge of aging in individuals and in cultural groups.

As the Eisenhower Administration takes office, I think we shall have an unusual opportunity to observe the working out of some of these ways. Some of the military and business leaders newly drafted into government will be unable to grow and develop when robbed of the protective surroundings their social systems gave them; they may even appear to age rapidly, to decay. (Others, sufficiently high up, can try to recreate analogous protective systems, down to the secretary, the staffs, the shape of the desks and perhaps of the subordinates too—so as to avoid the need to leave "home.") Still others, however, will prove to have, or to gain, the quality of inner aliveness that enables one to adapt to radically new surroundings; fear does not prevent their seeing that these are new, or force them simply to curse the newness as "bureaucracy," "politics," or whatnot; rather, they will be stimulated.

One would want to watch, also, for the consequences of different occupational experiences before entering the government. Are the department store executives whom William E. Henry has described as having a tropism towards decision-making better off than bankers who are in the main accustomed to constrict decision-making? Is it a question of the nature of different preservatives in different occupational groups, as these mix or refuse to mix with the occupational experience of government officials? Can we develop tests that will help answer such questions, not for young people early in their careers, but for middle-aged people suddenly given a new lease on a new office, if not on a new life?

An illustration of how difficult it is to predict which of these several "careers of aging" an individual will pursue is presented by the notorious misjudgments teachers are apt to make about the prospects of their students. Some who appear to have spark and originality lose it very shortly. Then, retroactively, one can see that while young they were kept alive partly by physiological changes and that aging started for them at 25 if not before; nothing new has happened after that. In such cases, it depends hardly at all on the individual whether the culture keeps him going until death or does not prevent his obvious and grievous deterioration. In contrast, other individuals who in their 20s appeared to be quite set in their ways, without much ability to have new experiences, turn out to have been harboring reserves which slowly come to reshape their whole orientation. Whereas for some and perhaps most men the possession of power protects them from having to develop (others are compelled to adapt to *them*), there remain a number of men for whom power serves as a stimulant to late flowering.

Thus, it is plain that for the "adjusted" group it matters decisively what institutions they hitch or are hitched onto, and whether such institutions encapsulate them or awaken them or destroy them. Their one-and-only life-cycle gets fatally mixed up with the larger institutional cycles. And, to recur to our image of the aging business or professional person, it sometimes seems as if his tenacious efforts to keep himself from sagging into a flabby or relaxed age provide much of the motive power for our entrepreneurial expansion combined with institutional conservatism.

§ THE ANOMIC

REAL DECAY sets in when the physiological vitality is lost, and when the culture does not carry the individual onward but drops him. Here we get the sudden decompositions, as they appear, of some men who are forced to retire, where it becomes evident that the job and its emotional ambience kept the job-holder together: he held a job less than the job held him. Or we get the spouse who—though he or she did not greatly love the other spouse—cannot survive him or her, but dies shortly thereafter in a metaphorical Suttee. (We find the same pattern among the "quasi-families" of people who are not married, but are tied to each other in a similar symbiotic way.) Such people live like cards, propped up by other cards.

At first blush, they may look very much like the people who have a better cultural preservative, but the paths soon diverge, and their decay sets in earlier. They are not the lawyers and engineers and businessmen of springy step, but the prematurely weary and resigned. As against the person who, in a way, never grows up, never faces death, they sometimes appear never to have been young. But in both cases—the adjusted and the anomic outcomes—there is a truncation of the "seven ages of man," the variety and contretemps of the life cycle; there is an insufficient dialectic between physiological decline and psychological increment.

Moreover, both the autonomous and the anomic reactions to aging are alike in that the individuals concerned make little use of the standard cultural preservatives—the former because they transcend and reshape them, the latter because they cannot attain them or maintain them. If responsibility accompanies maturity for the autonomous, and takes the place of maturity for the adjusted, the anomic find their way to neither. Like a person who is afraid to overshoot the green when he drives from the tee (or, more probably, gives up acting as if he wanted to make the green at all), they start out in life with aims that will not carry them through a career. And they do not succeed in getting onto an institutional escalator that will define for them what it is to have a career.

Our research in Kansas City, having moved out of the clinic and into the community, will probably have to develop typologies less "universal" than this one I have proposed here. For the three types I have sketched have nothing to do with Kansas City as such—with its conflict of rural and urban ideologies, its history as an entrepot, its prospective future as an industrial base. Differences of sex (I have said almost nothing about women in this paper) and of social station have decisive consequences for the forms of aging felt to be appropriate—

but these differences, too, while illustrated in Kansas City as elsewhere, are not peculiar to it. Nevertheless, as we examine different occupational groups in the metropolitan area, we may find this typology useful as a critique of each group's way of aging. Thus the well-to-do and ceaselessly energetic medical men of Kansas City may buy a cultural preservative at the expense of being run ragged from the days when they did autopsies to the day when they are the subject of one—perhaps a bit raggeder because busier, more successful, and slightly more traditional, than medical men elsewhere. As against this, we may find the pattern Warren Peterson suspects to exist among Kansas City high school teachers, that they are "old maids" at 30 and for 40 years thereafter (they must retire at 70) do not appreciably age, being kept alive by their young charges, their community obligations, their summer school courses, and the rest of the diurnal round to which this helplessly exposed target of community hopes, fears, and envies is committed.

Even here, I doubt if we shall find patterns exclusively Kansas City's, or exclusively metropolitan. But it is in any case fortunate that our research objectives, and our setting in Kansas City, both force and encourage us to move back and forth between clinical and cultural considerations, in search of a typology, or a set of them, that encompasses both.

30. The Meaning of Opinion*

THE RELATION OF MANY SOCIAL SCIENTISTS—and of course of the public at large—to the failure of the polls to predict the American presidential election was itself an interesting social-psychological phenomenon. Some of the opinion researchers hope to find the cause of the failure in some simple "bug" in the polling machinery, such as a sampling error; possibly a good deal of their security has rested in their belief that social science is as "scientific" as they believe natural science to be. Others are worried about the reactions of potential clients, governmental and commercial, for applied social research; they are troubled that the pollers may have done a bad job of public relations; they feel let down in their task of selling social research; they, too, would like to see some quick and simple explanation emerge. Perhaps these responses indicate some doubts as to the value of social science as a human enterprise of curiosity and self-understanding, doubts which need to be assuaged by "success," both in terms of accurate prediction and of public usefulness and approval.

Many other social scientists had a positive reaction to the failure of the polls. Something interesting and new had happened. Here was a chance to justify re-examining old routines, and to test others which had not had much of a hearing—and perhaps to learn something. We take it that this is the spirit in which this Symposium has been called together. A reaction of ours was that the judgment of the polls in terms of success and failure of prediction—that is, not in terms of percentage of error, but in terms of picking the winner—was a striking indication of the success-ethos of America. (Gallup was just as far off in 1936, but having picked the winner, it hardly mattered.) In social research, if not in life, however, it is better to be right than to guess who will be president; that is, better to understand what goes on in society than to predict, empirically, what will happen if one doesn't know *why* one is right. And good public relations can be a menace to social research, in terms of forcing or encouraging scientists to work on trivial tasks or even on serious ones which the culture, rather than they, think are important. Likewise, success, and the craving for it, can be constricting for social research, as indeed for any scholarly or creative work, forcing it to go through routines with ever greater technical proficiency and ever greater boredom; while failure can be liberating in its challenge.

---
* With Nathan Glazer.

We make one or two technical suggestions as to why the polls may have "failed." But our principal concern in this article is with the further expansion of the use of polls in public opinion research, to garner not only opinions but also the less accessible situations and feelings which underlie opinions. Public opinion pollers have, of course, been moving in this direction, aware that their delicate apparatus, though designed and originally used to measure surface reactions, needs to be perfected not only for this purpose, but also to be adapted to new and even more demanding uses, if it is to help us understand social change. The election is another reminder, if any were required, that these two tasks—measurement of opinion, and discovery of its roots in social structure and character structure—are fundamentally interrelated. This interrelationship exists, we suggest, not only on the level of predicting political behavior but also in the day-to-day practice of political polling, which cannot help, in the process of gathering opinions, gathering also a good deal of information which might locate the opinions in a more meaningful context. At present, much of this information is thrown away, as a residue or by-product—or indeed, as an obstacle getting in the way of the true opinion. Partly, the problem is a practical one: keeping the residues, and analyzing them, is in the present state of the art a most expensive and time-consuming operation. In the first instance, however, the problem is one of intellectual clarification: it is one of tracing the relationship between the opinion which is reported as such and its residues, and of suggesting ways of viewing the complex totality as a *Gestalt.*

To avoid misunderstanding, we should make clear at the outset that we are not making a plea for polling conducted by "depth" interviews. We do not believe that the longer and more "freely" someone talks, the more truth he necessarily tells, nor that psychological probing is as useful as, say, study of group affiliation and activity in predicting an election. We agree with most of the penetrating remarks of Paul F. Lazarsfeld[1] on the problem of open-ended versus structured interviews: namely, that virtually all the functions for which intensive interviews are used today can be met by different types of conventional poll questions, if intelligently constructed. Our point is rather that new functions, at the moment perhaps best met by intensive interviews, must be taken on by polling, if it is to serve as an effective tool in "mirroring" the public mind.

---

1. "The Controversy over Detailed Interviews—an Offer for Negotiation," *Public Opinion Quarterly,* 8, No. 1 (1944), pp. 38-60

§ SOME ASSUMPTIONS WHICH UNDERLIE POLLING

TO DIVIDE THE TOTAL POPULATION on any given question among those who are for, those against, and those undecided, gives an inadequate report of the state of public opinion on most types of issues; and this remains so even when the report is complicated by the use of such devices as George Gallup's quintamensional plan,[2] Roper's multiple-choice, or the various types of intensity thermometers. All these reports assume, in the first place, a qualitative equality among all those who select the same alternative, an equality reflected in the expectation that people in all social classes, and of all character types, will be equally habituated to the style of thinking which "makes up its mind" in terms of such stateable alternatives. These methods generally assume, in the second place, that the most significant division of opinion on any issue is between those who are for and those who are against, and between both of these and the "don't knows." But this simply reflects the structure of opinion as our political-legal tradition supposes it to be, with each view having its partisans and its "independent voters." This tradition is in turn supported by the way the mass media handle opinion, which is again in terms of a dichotomy or trichotomy, or in terms of categories and degrees of partisanship. Public opinion research comes along and confirms the existing ideology about opinion, both in its interviewing methods and in its manner of presenting its findings.

The scientific study of public opinion is thus today in the hands of neither the poll-takers nor the respondents: both are caught in an historical process which has not only set the questions to be investigated but also the form of the answer. We should at least assume that another structure of opinion may exist, in which every question has many sides, and many perspectives in which it may be viewed, each tinged with varying degrees of meaning and affect; we should try to work with models of opinion other than the conventional two- or three-sided one now in use. One such model, for example, might divide the population into those who had grounds for an opinion and those who did not. Among others, the National Opinion Research Center (NORC) has done much work along this line. Another model might divide those in whom the answer was deeply rooted from those to whom the answer was, so to speak, lightly attached. One might experiment with this by having the interviewer challenge or argue with the answer—contrary to the convention, which advocates of both structured and open-ended methods share, of "non-directive" interviewing.

2. "The Quintamensional Plan of Question Design," *Public Opinion Quarterly*, 11, No. 3 (1947), pp. 385-393.

Present-day polling, in its main assumptions, exemplifies the 19th-century liberal's approach to the individual as a social atom. By a convenient fiction, polling tends to treat its subject, in every social stratum, as a "responsible citizen"—one who considers the world in terms of "issues" and considers these issue in the terms in which they are discussed in the press and on the radio, holds a position in a political spectrum which runs in such single dimensions as left-right, or Republican-Democrat-Progressive, and feels it his duty to take sides on public issues both when polled and when called upon to vote.

To be sure, one can still find people like this—often people in the upper and upper middle classes, and many older persons of varying class position for whom opinion grows out of a feeling of responsibility, and out of a feeling of potency to affect political events which responsibility implies. Such people think that their opinion, and their vote, matter very much, and the mass media and the polling process encourage them in this belief. Maybe this is a good thing for society. But it unquestionably handicaps public opinion research to operate with assumptions which are no longer, if they ever were, a useful abstraction from the social reality of a mass society. The type of 19th-century citizen, whom we have characterized—a type we call "inner-directed"—becomes increasingly rare under the pressures of our era.

For most people in modern society, there is no such direct relation between responsibility for having an opinion and responsibility for action. They can see no relation between their political opinions and the actual course of political life—particularly those developments, such as war, which are most crucial to them. On the contrary, the obscurity and remoteness of the more decisive national and international political happenings, the general feeling that instead of "we" (the common people), it is some alien "they" (the distant powers) who manage events (among those social groups who assume events to be manageable at all)—these developments have made politics an anxious and frustrating topic. And this leads either to an obviously apathetic reaction to politics or to attempts (functionally no less apathetic) to view politics in some more tolerable framework, such as sports (the election as a race), chit-chat (the election as gossip), or the more amiable aspects of the American past (clichés about democracy). People today seem to us to be increasingly concerned with the opinions of others rather than with what they themselves think, and use their own opinions not so much to orient themselves in responsible action as to please, entertain, or simply get along with others. This psychic state increases their subjective feelings of powerlessness to affect the course of political events.

Yet the great majority of people, while they are actually powerless and while they feel as alienated from politics as from the other
major foci of modern life, are called upon, in our democratic tradition, to act as if they had power. They are called upon to vote, and
to expose themselves to information and exhortation from the mass
media and to discussion in their clique groups about political affairs.
The public opinion polls play a part in this call, though perhaps a
minor one, not only in the way their results are presented, but also
in the specific contacts between poller and pollee. The public opinion
interviewer is a pervasive symbol of the demand to be opinionated.
Most polls assume that people will have—and subtly therefore, that
they should have—opinions on the "issues of the day" or "news of the
week," though occasionally Gallup asks people "Do you have a cold?"
or "Are you happy?" or some similar question which does not come
straight out of 19th-century politics.

The fact is that people do respond, in overwhelming numbers, to
this social demand that they have an opinion. Perhaps 10 per cent of
the population refuses to be polled at all; another 10 per cent or so
gets into the no-answer or undecided box; all the rest "have an
opinion." If we took this evidence of the polls at face, we might
conclude that politics had in fact not changed since the last century,
that the masses who had entered the historical process had not with-
drawn from it. Maybe so. But we think that the polls conceal as much
as they reveal on this subject, and that if we look at the polls in
unorthodox ways, we can even now see that the meaning of opinion
is in flux.

§ HOLDING AN OPINION

THOUGH HARDLY MORE THAN HALF the electorate votes, a much larger
fraction of those approached by pollers have opinions on whom they
will vote for.[3] Asked to have an opinion, many people for whom the
opinion has no significance—other than to proffer on demand like a
password—produce one in accord with their station in life. And who
has not at some time delivered himself of an opinion stronger and
more pronounced than one he "really" held—as part of the conversation he holds with himself and with other people?

The poll interviewers (on the more cursory survey, where some
form of area-sampling or other careful counter-measures are not

---

3. Of course the polling agencies eliminate from their sample Southern
Negroes, and use relatively smaller percentages of certain social groups than
their proportion in the general population in order to get a first approximation
to the voting population. But even taking this into account, we think it is
undeniable that many more people say they will vote than do vote; and this
disparity is only partly accounted for by those who plan to vote and are prevented from doing so by technical accidents.

insisted on) can hardly help getting in on this conversation, subtly selecting as respondents the articulate and over-opinionated as against the recusant and under-opinionated. The interviewers can sense, even if they stick to their socio-economic quotas, who will be susceptible to the opinion-holding frame of the interview (and the interviewer) and who will not; in our culture, the opinionated are visible, while the under-opinionated, like our cripples and deformed people, are not visible. (The under-opinionated in the last election would probably have been, in the main, for the underdog candidate, Truman. But the over-opinionated would not necessarily have been conservative; they might also have been the more extreme and aggressive Jews and Negroes who were for Wallace. If this is so, then a quite unconscious bias—a bias, indeed, of the middle class, and of our culture generally —in favor of the opinionated might be one factor in the overestimation both of the Dewey and the Wallace vote; the interviewers simply "happened" to bump into more people who *held* opinions— this being the commodity they were looking for.)[4] . . .

These and many other sorts of variation in the style of response are important because a superficially identical answer coming from persons with different styles of response may well have very different meanings. We cite one instance, conceivably relevant for election polling, which was suggested to us by our study of files at NORC. It seems possible to differentiate between two, among many, styles of response: a *non-committal,* in which good rapport is not established; the respondent gives only as much as he has to, is not "friendly." And an *embarrassed,* in which, whether or not the respondent has answers for questions, he feels in a warm human environment permitting him to show and even enjoy his embarrassment (by gestures, giggles, coyness and laughter), and, often, his incompetence. We think that one might discover, if one were to rate respondents as embarrassed or non-committal, significant differences between them as to the sticking power of opinions. The embarrassed person is, we suggest, using his opinions more as a social device than the non-committal: he is trying to shift the encounter from one involving the transmission of information into one in which both parties get personal satisfaction;

---

4. Those who had "no opinion" were then handled by the home office with, perhaps, a similar psychological bias; they were treated as if they had had opinions, being divided up pro rata among those who had opinions, like wallflowers in a school tug of war. Since this had "worked" in earlier election polls, inadequate attention was paid to the latent meanings of the "no opinion" style of response. Similarly, the Elmira 1948 Election Study, mentioned hereafter, discovered after the election that those who had dropped out of the Panel, or refused—and probably also those who weren't at home despite several callbacks—formed a different group, in terms of vote, than those who were easily enticed onto the Panel and stayed with it throughout.

the personal satisfactions tend to become paramount, and the opinions to lose their factual importance. On the other hand, the non-committal person is "close" with, and to, his opinions: even when they can be pried from him, they remain his: they are not cooked to conversational short-order.

We would, moreover, expect the non-committals to decrease, and the embarrasseds to increase as the more socialized styles of response become more widely spread. Some indirect evidence on this may perhaps be gleaned from the study of refusals—the 10 per cent or so "hard core" who don't want to give the pollers any answers at all. NORC was able to get a few "foot-in-door" questions asked of those who refused on one survey, and a tabulation was made by Dr. Herbert Hyman (of NORC) as to who they were. A sizable proportion of the refusals gave explanations or said things that indicated they would chronically refuse to give answers, largely because of feelings of inadequacy. Significantly those who refused—in this survey—were generally older people and women, people whose style of response had, we suspect, been little affected by the currents of opinion and opinion-giving that circulate in contemporary culture.

§ THE FUNCTIONS OF OPINION IN THE UPPER CLASS

INDEED, THE UNRECORDED EXPERIENCE of observant poll interviewers seems to us one of the most important sources for discovering the meaning of opinion in the several social strata. This belief is confirmed by the opportunity given us by Herbert Hyman to read over some of his extraordinarily searching interviews with interviewers, and to interview several of these people ourselves. There is some evidence here, of course quite unsystematic, that the upper-class person—the pollers' "class A"—does not find emotional satisfaction in *voicing* an opinion to an interviewer, who is generally of lower social status, as distinguished from having and voicing an opinion at the dinner table, on the commuter train, and in clique groups generally. Perhaps the interviewer, according to the view of this social level, falls into the category of the cab-driver and the elevator man, with whom one exchanges seasonal pleasantries about the weather and the election, but with whom one is also reserved and close-mouthed.

We may interpret this reaction to the interviewer psychologically by saying that many of these upper-class respondents do not feel alienated from their opinions; they do not need to make either conversation or capital with them. Though in recent years they have often talked as if they felt politically frustrated, as if they could make no headway against "that man in the White House," or, indeed, against politicians in general, the premise of this apparent frustration is that they are not really powerless, but that they feel temporarily out of the seats of power. Actually, politics is a malleable domain for them, whether or not they feel responsibility for it. Yet even they tend to overestimate their power, and therefore the social importance of their having an opinion, and it is often this feeling which allows the interviewer to get by the doormen and secretaries at all.

§ ILLUSIONS OF OMNIPOTENCE IN THE UPPER MIDDLE CLASS

IN BOTH THE UPPER and upper middle class there is a high proportion of response on polls, particularly from men. People in these groups have been brought up to make choices and to consider their opinions significant. . . . In the working class, politics does not generally become a focus of interest, if ever, until after formal education is complete and the individual has entered on his work career, but in the upper middle class young people often begin to attend to political discourse earlier, in high school and college. Public opinion polling, and the election itself, meets such people on their own ground; they think about men and issues in the way that the polls, the mass media, and their clique groups all require of them. . . .

Such people are also tempted by their social situation to over-estimate their actual power. They are in contact with political "insiders" both in print and in person; this helps them to identify with the political world. In our interviews we often find such people to be possessed of a relatively high level of information about politics and a stock of opinions like a well-furnished wine-cellar, but lacking in any genuine affect about opinions which would lead them to discriminate between those opinions which have meaning in today's world from those which are mere opinionatedness.

The upper middle class tends to have an "inner-directed" ideology about politics, so that there is much talk and action in terms of responsibility. But the trend seems to us to lie with those whose opinions are lightly attached—hence easily secured by a poller—and yet who need opinions, for clothing, conformity, and comfort.

§ MAKING CONVERSATION BETWEEN THE SOCIAL CLASSES

AS ONE GOES DOWN the status ladder, one still finds an astonishingly high proportion of response on polls, both in permitting oneself to be interviewed and in having an opinion which can be fitted, without too much gerrymandering, into the dimensions of current polling work. In a sense, this is only another way of saying that America is a middle-class country and that middle-class values and styles of perception reach into all levels except perhaps the fringes at the very top and the very bottom. The study of polling, however, suggests two perspectives on this well-accepted statement: one is that people who are actually powerless and voiceless grasp at straws of participation, and the other is that the upper and lower levels of our culture converse with each other across status lines by means of the polls and, of course, also by means of the mass media and many other forms of exchange.

In the lower middle class, there often seems to be considerable satisfaction in voicing an opinion to the interviewer, even if it has to be manufactured on the spot for the purpose. Respondents in this group are not so often consulted as they might wish—"I told that fellow from the Gallup Poll . . ."—and at the same time, they do not want to be taken for ignoramuses who do not know, and consequently are quite happy to have a chance to show that they do know. And, of course, they *do* know. For, like the upper social levels, they have been trained to exercise consumption preferences, and they are willing, if not avid, cash customers for opinions on political issues. Through national and international affairs are for them mysterious realms, though they have no way of grasping what a political figure actually does, they can listen to Walter Winchell. . . .

Since such people have, however, no actual experience of potency in meaningful life situations—but only the imitation of potency in the consumption of goods and opinions—they will tend to be over-impressed by "public opinion." Frightened as they are of being taken for suckers, they assume public opinion to be much more given and set than it actually is, and, if anything, underestimate what *they* might do to change opinion by taking a strong stand against a current trend. Truman, no inside-dopester, was not impressed by the massive public opinion structure which the mass media talked about. Rather, like the self-made, inner-directed man of earlier generations, he thought it was up to him whether he got to the top, and his naïveté encouraged him where other-directed types would have despaired.

Added to the desire to participate on the part of the lower middle class is the cultural pressure, felt by both interviewer and interviewee, in favor of giving someone an answer rather than no answer. The situation is said to be different in France and some other countries, but the American attitude is summed up in the expression criticizing those who "wouldn't give anyone the right time." An opinion is considered a free gift in a culture where privacy is at a minimum, and people will feel that the interviewer is entitled to an opinion irrespective of whether they also try to guess which of several possible opinions he may want of them. Even the people who seem to enjoy slamming the door in the interviewer's face may be taking advantage of a rarely-given opportunity not to live up to expectations and to lord it over the (usually female) interviewer. It is not that they so value their privacy. And indeed, why should people not give their opinion freely when the opinions were often only created for this purpose in the first place? Opinions are not felt as part of one's underlying self; on the contrary, people have been so invaded, the threshold of personality has become such a highway, that they have very little private self left anyway. . . .

In this perspective, the polls may be thought of as a kind of political market research. Like most commercial market research, the effort is not really to find out what people might want under quite different social conditions, but rather to offer them a monopolistically-limited range of alternatives: just as they can choose between the four big weeklies. They can be for or against Truman, for or against Taft-Hartley, even for or against the United Nations, but they cannot be, in the given spectrum, in favor of trying to start a revolution within Russia, as against fighting or appeasing her. And probably they have been so conditioned that they would not know what to do with any radically new alternatives, but would try to fit them into the style of viewing "reality" which the existing polls reflect.

§ RAPPORT AND OPINION IN THE LOWER CLASS

EVEN THE LOWER CLASS participates in this "conversation between the classes." Some are left out, as indicated by the fact that the proportion of "don't knows" rises sharply in the lower class, particularly among women. Many of the "don't knows" and refusals in the lower social strata are actually frightened; frightened of authorities in general, of the FBI in some places, and of the Communists in others (as we found last summer in rural Vermont). Yet even among this group it is surprising how many respond.

There are few illusions of omnipotence here, as one finds them among the upper middle class; nor is there, we suspect, as much need as in the lower middle class for verbal aggression against interviewers —telling "them" (the powers) off, through the interviewer. Why, then, do people respond? Partly, of course, it is a matter of simple courtesy and needs no complicated explanations. But we think that the emphasis on rapport which dominates so much discussion of interviewing shows that there are other elements involved. The concern for good rapport as a requirement of good interviewing seems to us partly a reflection of the need of modern middle-class people to be liked by everybody. At any rate, rapport serves to insure the success of the "conversation of the classes" when it is conducted between the middle-class interviewer and the lower-class respondent. Thus great care is taken that the lower-class individual is approached sympathetically, and the polls try to use an interviewer of his own ethnic group, though they are rarely able to use one of his own class. This is not wholly pointless if one's goal is to maximize the number of responses, since rapport, by providing some interpersonal though usually spurious warmth, helps to repress unconscious feelings of powerlessness and distrust. But this is artificial; life-situations for the interviewee in the lower class are not typically suffused with rapport, and he is rarely treated with the consideration the interviewer shows him. Thus a false picture of the actual extent of political involvement is created, though it might be argued that it is a picture which would disappear under depth-interviewing and still greater doses of rapport. This needs testing, but it seems clear that the same culture which insists on "service with a smile" can also get answers with a smile—up to a point.

§ DOES THE ELECTION CHANGE THINGS?

THE FOREGOING OBSERVATIONS were sketched out by the writers in a memorandum written a year ago; naturally, we have had to ask ourselves whether Truman's victory does not show the power of the allegedly powerless. This may be. No doubt the union locals who put Truman over in the cities have a feeling of potency and elation, though coupled with misgivings they will be "sold out." Winning an election against odds, it may be argued, is different from merely having an opinion: affect is aroused and competence learned in the very process of getting out the vote. But even in the case of the union vote, many of the rank and file were simply pressured into going to the polls by a leadership which felt threatened by the Taft-Hartley Act; and while undoubtedly for many millions of Americans—somewhat more perhaps than we believed—opinion is formed by a realistic evaluation of alternatives, for these same persons, and for many others, the social and psychological meanings of opinion we have discussed become increasingly prominent. Whether we are interested in predicting elections or in understanding what is happening in America—and while the former may be hit by dint of sheer luck, ultimately it involves the latter—we must go past the level on which opinion research is now concentrating. Individuality and idiosyncrasy of response, up to now "processed out" of the polling process, is, we feel, the key to this next stage.

§ NEW APPROACHES IN INTERVIEWING AND ANALYSIS

A POWERFUL TENDENCY in current public opinion work is the attempt to stabilize and standardize the interview; idiosyncratic interviewing is another residue which is extruded as "bias." This effort is, in part, the necessary consequence of the methods of handling interview material in the home office, where the effort at standardization begins, ramifying out from there into pre-coded field techniques. For assembly-line work on a national cross-section, with an army of interviewers and coders to supervise, these methods are inevitable: their aim is to make interviewers, and the responses they obtain, virtually interchangeable on the verbal plane; as the skill grows of those who plan the survey, the interview and the interviewer are, in Karl Mannheim's terms, subjected to "functional rationalization." Opening up the interview to a wider ambit of human interaction cannot be done, therefore, without going back to handicraft methods in the analysis of the results. . . .

In our work we have tried to study first, the different types of interviews produced by different types of interviewers; second, the different types of responses to a challenging interview, using many difficult "why" questions, some "absurd" questions and unanswerable dilemmas, and, where possible, argumentative questions. Our effort was directed at confronting the respondent with a very large range of interpersonal meanings and styles in a single interview, as against the method now generally favored, which seeks to confront the smooth, middle-class side of the respondent with the smooth, middle-class side of the interviewer. The monotone of amiability called rapport, in which the interviewer must assume that all opinions received are equally valuable, equally inoffensive, undoubtedly finds out things which could be learned in no other way. But also one runs the risk of creating an unreal situation and of tapping a level of rationalization which may appear deep and intimate but which may actually be phony.

The Harvard Opinion Study has been making use of the "stress interview," in which a group of professors badger the respondent, to see how his political opinions stand up under pressure, and how he deals with contradictions in his views brought out in a series of interviews.[5] Arnold Rose has suggested other, somewhat less arduous techniques.[6] And as Hyman and Sheatsley have pointed out,[7] public opinion research can learn a good deal from Kinsey who, for example, excoriates liars and fixes interviewees with a steely eye, not a polite one. A fascinating range of possible interview techniques is suggested by Allen Funt, who conducts the "Candid Mike" radio program. Mr. Funt talks to people in all sorts of situations, and records the

5. We are indebted to M. Brewster Smith and Jerome Bruner for helpful information on this work-in-progress.

6. "A Research Note on Experimentation in Interviewing," *Am. J. Sociology*, 1945, 51, 143-144.

7. Herbert H. Hyman and Paul B. Sheatsley, "The Kinsey Report and Survey Methodology," *Int. J. of Opinion & Attitude Research*, 1948, 2, 183-195.

conversations with a concealed microphone for later rebroadcast: he has, for example, imitated a market researcher, but one using a meaningless double-talk in his interview instead of typical questions. His own style of talking to people is extremely interesting, in contrast to the current stereotype of rapport: he is in no ways charming, and has a dry, rather ordinary tone of voice, combined with a skeptical and even semi-hostile approach. Yet he has managed to get people to reveal themselves in ways—some of them outrageous—that no interviewer schooled in ordinary poll techniques could.

Obviously, there are ethical problems involved in more drastic interview procedures—as, indeed, in all social research which makes contact with human beings; and there are practical limits to what one can ask of interviewers and interviewees. But such problems are not avoided in conventional interviewing. A rapport-filled interview in which, while it lasts, the respondent is encouraged and assured that he is "doing all right," may leave him with a feeling of inadequacy, even perhaps trickery, if he should become aware of its lack of content. And conversely a challenging interview might actually give the respondent a vital experience, from which he learns something, as well as providing us with data.

We would like to cite an incident which indicates both how new techniques might plunge through the surface layer of opinion, and the practical difficulties in using these techniques. A panel study of the 1948 election campaign was made in Elmira, New York, a kind of follow-up to *The People's Choice* by Lazarsfeld, Berelson, and Gaudet. At one point questions were used which pointed out contradictions in the respondent's attitudes—for instance, asking him, if he were a worker and thought Truman was for the workers, why he was planning to vote for Dewey. Such questions would involve a loss of smooth rapport, but might reveal, in the very embarrassment of the respondent, something of his real feelings; and the authors urged that the interviewers be instructed to take note of the way the interviewee reacted to such questions, as well as of the words he uttered: to note, for example, whether he was embarrassed or at ease. The interviewers themselves balked on the pre-test, finding that they could not bring themselves easily to ask such questions, or to make much sense of the mode of reaction by the respondent. They were, naturally enough, too insecure psychologically, too drilled in obtaining rapport (especially in this study, interviewers were concerned over losing members of the panel, who would then be unavailable for subsequent waves of interviewing), and too eager to seize on easily-recorded and easily-classified replies to be able to experiment with more impolite and perhaps more fruitful types of interviewing. Despite the discomfort of the interviewers, the questions were asked. It is only with such approaches that one had a chance of discovering that, for example, those who were for Dewey, against their consciously understood class interests, might in the end turn to Truman.

Perhaps all we are doing here is suggesting that there may be other kinds of rapport than the conventional type. For to keep in human contact with an interviewee, while also making the interview a faceted and, at moments, barbed encounter, seems to us to require getting across to him that one is genuinely interested in the content of the interview, and in his reactions to it as an individual: we gather that this is Kinsey's conclusion, too. If one likes, one can call this less artificial footing rapport also—at least until it becomes too hard to take and the interviewer runs for it. . . .

§ DO WORDS HAVE A MEANING?

MUCH CURRENT SOCIAL RESEARCH proceeds on the assumption that if one wants to tap idiosyncratic meaning one must dispense with interviews altogether, except perhaps the psychoanalytic interview, and substitute projective tests such as the Rorschach, or the TAT, where the stimulus is non-verbal. A number of psychoanalysts, for instance, have said that Kinsey could not possibly have discovered anything veracious by his rapid-fire poll-type questionnaire. Indeed, some of the more orthodox Freudians, occasionally joined by some extreme semanticists, tend to take the position that people *never* mean what they say, and that the manifest replies to a question are inevitably a facade to be pierced rather than anything to be taken seriously.

We think that this outlook in social science is, among other things, an over-reaction against an earlier, naive reliance on the manifest content of answers to questions in personality inventories and other types of questionnaires. But today the best pollers no longer fall into such simplistic pitfalls; by pretesting with intensive interviews and converting these results into interlocking sets of questions, they try to follow the lead of Professor Lazarsfeld in the article already cited. We think it most unlikely that the failure to predict the election could have been repaired by depth interviewing in its present stage of development. On the contrary, we think it most likely that a better job of prediction might have been done by a conventional interview, had it dealt with such matters as group affiliation. . . . Let us move away from this sterile dichotomy between over-rational belief in words per se and over-skeptical nihilism about them, and see precisely in what direction public opinion research can advance if we believe that words do, sometimes, possess their rational manifest meaning, while being also projective of underlying character structure. . . .

Our own quite tentative hypothesis is that it is possible to work with answers to a relatively structured interview as if the interview itself as a whole, rather than as a set of separate questions, were a projective test. Our interviews are not long, nor do they probe for intimate data; skill in administering them helps, but is not essential. The problem is in interpretation, not in administration. For we handle the entire interview as a unit—a record of an experience—which we try to translate into a set of latent meanings which may in any given case include some of the literal, manifest meanings, too. This is done before any single answer is coded for purposes of correlation and comparison. That is, each single answer gives clues as to the latent meaning, the plot, of the interview, and as the latter develops, so it colors the meaning of the single answer, which must frequently be reinterpreted in the light of other answers and of the whole. Eventually, in a dialectic process, we come to a point where the latent, character-based meanings of answers are consistent and are seen to spring from a total personality, no matter how seemingly contradictory the surface answers are. The method we use thus resembles that used by the more "intuitive" and less quantitative workers with Rorschach and TAT. Moreover, to get beneath ideology, chit-chat, and rationalization that are always part of the manifest responses, we must look at and rely on the way things are said, and when they are said in the sequence of answers, and on what the interviewer can tell us as to non-verbal modes of reaction to a question. (Of course, we must know something of the interviewer, too, in order to evaluate the report.) . . .[8]

§ THE FEAR OF THE LATENT

LATENT MEANING—either of an answer or of no answer—may be understood if we grasp the socially structured interpersonal situation between poller and pollee, and search it for the residues, verbal and non-verbal, which now in our haste we throw away. But it is not only haste which often steers the academic, as well as the commercial poller, away from reliance on latent meaning. In our daily life we all

---

8. How much can be done by less elaborate analyses of less elaborate interviews is indicated by Babette Samelson's article, "Mrs. Jones' Ethnic Attitudes: A Ballot Analysis," *J. of Abn. & Soc. Psych.*, 1945, 40, 205-214. Taking a single NORC poll ballot—an ingenious ballot, with a number of open-ended questions —she has analyzed the full responses somewhat in the manner of a case history, to bring out a pattern of prejudice which purely extensive analysis of the whole set of returns would hardly have disclosed.

know that a gesture, an inflection, a nuance of phrase, may show a latent meaning which is the opposite of the patent one. In our working life, however, we fear to rely on such human knowledge because of the difficulties of proof, of standardization, and of validation. We fear to be called unscientific by our colleagues. The failure of the polls to predict the election should give us a kind of back-handed courage, by demonstrating that the alternative, highly-quantified methods may at times be equally fallible.

Depth interviewing, it is apparent, does not avoid the problem of interpretation of latent meaning. One cannot assume that the interviewee's self-revelations may be taken at face, especially if they are intimate and of the sort usually hidden. For these, too, may be as spurious as any surface rationalizations; the excellent rapport which produced them may merely have served to encourage boasting or aggression by the respondent. What we want is the whole personality, and neither what is on the surface nor what is covered up will alone suffice. There is, we conclude, no escape from the social scientist's own judgment. He must train himself to hear, and to understand, latent response, even though the whole culture, as well as the demands of his training and his colleagues, make this difficult.

At the same time the rewards of even a fragmentary approach to latent meaning are great. The election shows—as did the British Labor Party victory of 1945—how little we know, polls or no polls, about what is going on in our society. We do not know what the election meant to people in different social classes. We know almost nothing about the underlying forces in American life which are not visible—forces which cannot fit themselves into the pollers' opinion-grid. . . . Now, by virtue of our proven ignorance, we can justify staving off demands for quick results, and can occupy ourselves with discovering what is fundamental and how to get at it.

Place of Original Publication

1. "Values in Context" was first published in *The American Scholar*, Vol. 22, No. 1, 1952.
2. "Individualism Reconsidered" was first published in *Religious Faith and World Culture*, ed. by A. William Loos, Prentice-Hall, 1951. It was later reprinted in *City Lights*, Vol. 1, No. 3, 1953.
3. "The Ethics of We Happy Few" was first published in the *University Observer*, Vol. 1, 1947.
4. "A Philosophy for 'Minority' Living" was first published in *Commentary*, Vol. 6, No. 5, 1948.
5. "Some Observations on Community Plans and Utopia" was first published in *The Yale Law Journal*, Vol. 57, December 1947.
6. "The Saving Remnant" was first published in *The Years of the Modern*, Longmans, Green and Co., Inc., 1949.
7. "Some Observations on Intellectual Freedom" was first published in *The American Scholar*, Vol. 23, No. 1, 1953.
8. "The 'Militant' Fight Against Anti-Semitism" was first published in *Commentary*, Vol. 11, No. 1, 1951.
9. "Some Observations Concerning Marginality" was first published in *Phylon*, Vol. 12, No. 2, 1951.
10. "Marginality, Conformity, and Insight" was first delivered as a lecture at Smith College, March 12, 1953, and later revised as an address to the Mental Hygiene Society of Greater Baltimore, May 26, 1953. It was published in *Phylon*, Vol. 14, No. 3, 1953.
11. "Listening to Popular Music" was first published in *The American Quarterly*, Vol. 2, No. 4, 1950.
12. "Movies and Audiences" was first published in *The American Quarterly*, Vol. 4, No. 3, 1952.
13. "Some Observations on Changes in Leisure Attitudes" was first published in *The Antioch Review*, Vol. 12, No. 4, 1952. It was later reprinted in *The Antioch Review Anthology*, ed. Paul Bixler, World Publishers, 1953, and in *Perspectives, USA*, No. 5, Fall 1953.
14. "New Standards for Old: From Conspicuous Consumption to Conspicuous Production" was given as a lecture in the Barnard College series on "The Search for New Standards in Modern America," March 10, 1953, and is here reprinted with the permission of Barnard College.
15. "Recreation and the Recreationist" was first delivered as a lecture at the Chicago Conference on a Federal Department of Welfare, February 27, 1953. It was published in *Marriage and Family Living*, Vol. 16, No. 1, 1954.
16. "Football in America: A Study in Culture Diffusion" was first published in *The American Quarterly*, Vol. 3, No. 4, 1951. It was later reprinted in *The University of Chicago Magazine*, Vol. 45, No. 2, 1952.
17. "Bookworms and the Social Soil" was first published in *The Saturday Review of Literature*, May 5, 1951.
18. "How Different May One Be?" was first published in *Child Study*, Vol. 28, Spring 1951.

19. "The Social and Psychological Setting of Veblen's Economic Theory" was first delivered as a lecture to the Economic History Association, Bryn Mawr, September, 1953. It was later reprinted in *The Journal of Economic History*, Vol. 13, No. 4, 1953.

20. "Some Relationships Between Technical Progress and Social Progress" was first delivered as a lecture at the Foreign Student Summer Project of MIT, August 28, 1953. It was later reprinted in *Explorations in Entrepreneurial History*, Vol. 6, No. 3, 1954.

21. "The Themes of Work and Play in the Structure of Freud's Thought" was first published in *Psychiatry*, Vol. 13, No. 1, 1950.

22. "Authority and Liberty in the Structure of Freud's Thought" was first published in *Psychiatry*, Vol. 13, No. 2, 1950.

23. "The Themes of Heroism and Weakness in the Structure of Freud's Thought" was first published in *Psychiatry*, Vol. 13, No. 2, 1950.

24. "Freud, Religion, and Science" was first delivered as a lecture to the Channing Club of the University of Chicago, January 9, 1950. It was later (as "Freud: Religion as Neurosis") reprinted in part in the University of Chicago Roundtable on *Psychoanalysis and Ethics*, No. 638, June 18, 1950, and in *The American Scholar*, Vol. 20, No. 3, 1951. It was later reprinted in full in *The Chicago Review*, Vol. 8, No. 1, 1954.

25. "Some Observations on the Limits of Totalitarian Power," was first published in *The Antioch Review*, Vol. 12, No. 2, 1952.

26. "The Nylon War" was first published in *Common Cause*, Vol. 4, No. 6. It was later reprinted in *The Christian Century*, Vol. 48, No. 18; in *Etc.*, Vol. 8, No. 3; and in *New Problems in Reading and Writing*, ed. H. W. Sams and W. F. McNeir, Prentice-Hall, 1953.

27. "Toward an Anthropological Science of Law and the Legal Profession" was first given as a lecture to the introductory graduate course in sociology and anthropology at the University of Chicago, December 1947, and a revised version was delivered at the meeting of the Association of American Law Schools, December 1950, and was later reprinted in *The University of Chicago Law Review*, Vol. 19, No. 1, 1951, and in *The American Journal of Sociology*, Vol. 57, No. 2.

28. "Some Observations on Social Science Research" was first published in *The Antioch Review*, Vol. 11, No. 3, 1951.

29. "Some Clinical and Cultural Aspects of the Aging Process" was first published in *The American Journal of Sociology*, Vol. 59, No. 4, 1954.

30. "The Meaning of Opinion" was first published in part in *The International Journal of Opinion and Attitude Research*, Vol. 2, No. 4 and in part in the *Public Opinion Quarterly*, Vol. 12, No. 4.

Bibliography

1 9 3 9
"Possession and the Law of Finders"—*Harvard Law Rev.*, 52:1105-1134.

1 9 4 0
"Government Service and the American Constitution"—*Univ. Chicago Law Rev.*, 7:655-675.

"Legislative Restrictions on Foreign Enlistment and Travel"—*Columbia Law Rev.*, 40:793-835.

1 9 4 1
"The American Constitution and International Labor Legislation"—*Internat. Labor Review*, 44:123-193.

"Law and Social Science: A Report on Michael and Wechsler's Classbook on Criminal Law and Administration"—*Yale Law J.*, 50:636-653.

"Government Education for Democracy"—*Public Opinion Quart.*, 5:195-209.

"What's Wrong with the Interventionists?"—*Common Sense*, 10:327-330.

1 9 4 2
"Civil Liberties in a Period of Transition"—*Public Policy* (Harvard Graduate School of Public Administration, Carl J. Friedrich and Edward S. Mason, eds.), 3:33-96.

"Democracy and Defamation: Control of Group Libel"—*Columbia Law Rev.*, 42:727-780.

"Democracy and Defamation: Fair Game and Fair Comment I"—*Columbia Law Rev.*, 42:1085-1123.

"Democracy and Defamation: Fair Game and Fair Comment II"—*Columbia Law Rev.*, 42:1282-1318.

"The Cash Customer"—*Common Sense*, 11:183-185.

"Equality and Social Structure"—*J. Legal and Pol. Sociol.*, 1:72-95.

"The Politics of Persecution"—*Public Opinion Quart.*, 6:41-56.

1 9 4 3
"An International Bill of Rights"—*Proc. Amer. Law Inst.* 20:198-204.

1 9 4 4
"The Present State of Civil Liberty Theory"—*J. Politics*, 6:323-337.

1 9 4 7
"Some Observations on Community Plans and Utopia"—*Yale Law J.*, 57:173-200.

"The Ethics of We Happy Few"—*Univ. Observer*, 1:19-28.

1 9 4 8
"A Philosophy for 'Minority' Living"—*Commentary*, 6:413-422.

1 9 4 9
"Social Structure, Character Structure, and Opinion" (with Nathan Glazer)—*Internat. J. Opinion and Attitude Resch.*, 2:512-527.

"The Meaning of Opinion" (with Nathan Glazer)—*Public Opinion Quart.*, 12:633-648.
"The Saving Remnant: An Examination of Character Structure"; pp. 115-147. In: *Years of the Modern;* ed. by John W. Chase, New York, Longmans, Green & Company.

1 9 5 0

"Do the Mass Media 'Escape' from Politics?" (with Reuel Denney). In: *Reader in Public Opinion and Mass Communications;* ed. by Bernard Berelson & Morris Janowitz, Glencoe, Ill., Free Press.
"Criteria for Political Apathy" (with Nathan Glazer). In: *Studies in Leadership;* ed. by Alvin Gouldner, New York, Harper & Bros.
"The Themes of Work and Play in the Structure of Freud's Thought"—*Psychiatry,* 13:1-16.
The Lonely Crowd: A Study of the Changing American Character (with the collaboration of Reuel Denney and Nathan Glazer), New Haven, Yale Univ. Press.
"Langdon Narbeth"; pp. 121-135. In: *Social Sciences 2, Syllabus and Selected Readings,* Vol. II, Chicago, Univ. of Chicago Press.
"One from the Gallery: An Experiment in the Interpretation of an Interview" (with Nathan Glazer) (Part 1)—*Internat. J. Opinion & Attitude Resch.,* 4:515-540.
"Listening to Popular Music"—*Amer. Quart.,* 2:359-371.
"Authority and Liberty in the Structure of Freud's Thought"—*Psychiatry,* 13:167-187.
"The Themes of Heroism and Weakness in the Structure of Freud's Thought"—*Psychiatry,* 13:301-315.

1 9 5 1

"The Nylon War"—*Common Cause,* 4:379-385. (Reprinted in *Christian Century,* 48:554, & *Etc.,* 8:163-170, & in *New Problems in Reading & Writing,* ed. by H. W. Sams & W. F. McNeir, New York, Prentice-Hall, pp. 480-488.)
"Some Problems of a Course in 'Culture and Personality' "—*J. General Educ.,* 5:122-136.
"How Different May One Be?"—*Child Study,* 28:6-8, 29-30.
"The 'Militant' Fight Against Anti-Semitism"—*Commentary,* 11:11-19.
"One from the Gallery" (with Nathan Glazer) (Part 2), *Internat. J. Opinion & Attitude Resch.,* 5:53-78.
"Bookworms and the Social Soil"—*Sat. Rev. Lit.,* 34:7-8, 31-32.
"From Morality to Morale"; pp. 81-120. In: *Personality and Political Crisis;* ed. by Alfred H. Stanton & Stewart E. Perry, Glencoe, Ill., Free Press.
"Individualism Reconsidered." In: *Religious Faith and World Culture;* ed. by William Loos, New York, Prentice Hall.
"Two Adolescents"—*Psychiatry,* 14:161-211.
"Comments on the Jewish Student"—*Commentary,* 12:524-525.
"Football in America: A Study in Culture Diffusion" (with Reuel Denney) —*Amer. Quart.,* 4:309-25.
"Freud, Religion and Science"—*The Amer. Scholar,* 20:267-276.
"Some Observations Concerning Marginality"—*Phylon,* 12:113-127.
"Some Observations on Law and Psychology"—*Univ. of Chicago Law Rev.,* 19:30-44.

"Some Observations on Social Science Research"—*Antioch Review*, 11:259-278.

"Toward an Anthropological Science of Law and the Legal Profession"—*Am. J. Soc.*, 57:121-135.

"Leisure in Urbanized America" (with Reuel Denney), pp. 469-480 in *Reader in Urban Sociology*, ed. by Paul K. Hatt & Albert J. Reiss, Jr., Glencoe, Ill., Free Press.

1 9 5 2

Faces in the Crowd: Individual Studies in Character and Politics (with the collaboration of Nathan Glazer), New Haven, Yale Univ. Press.

"Some Observations on the Limits of Totalitarian Power"—*Antioch Review*, 12:155-168.

"Ambassadors to the Machine"—*Griffin*, 1:6-11.

"Some Observations on the Study of American Character"—*Psychiatry*, 15:333-338.

"A Lecture on Veblen"—*J. General Education*, 6:214-223.

"Values in Context"—*Amer. Scholar*, 22:29-39.

"Our Country and Our Culture"—*Partisan Review*, 19:310-315. (Reprinted in *America and the Intellectuals, Partisan Review*, 95-100).

"Leisure in an Industrial Civilization" (with Reuel Denney). In: *Creating an Industrial Civilization: A Report on the Corning Conference*, ed. by Eugene Staley, New York, Harper & Bros.

Introduction to *Commentary on the American Scene*, Elliott Cohen, ed., New York, Alfred A. Knopf.

"Some Observations on Changes in Leisure Attitudes"—*Antioch Review*, 12:417-436.

"Movies and Audiences" (with Evelyn T. Riesman)—*Amer. Quart.*, 4:195-202.

1 9 5 3

Thorstein Veblen: A Critical Interpretation—New York, Scribner's & Sons.

"Some Observations on Intellectual Freedom"—*Am. Scholar*, 22:3.

"The Social and Psychological Setting of Veblen's Economic Theory"—*J. of Econ. Hist.*, 13:449-461.

"Marginality, Conformity, and Insight"—*Phylon*, 14:241-257.

"The Study of Kansas City: An Informal Overture"—*Univ. of Kansas City Review*, 20:15-22. (Reprinted as "The Study of the City"—*City Lights*, No. 4, Fall: 3-9.)

"Conspicuous Production"—*The Listener*, 49:1009.

The Lonely Crowd—abridged edition, New York, Doubleday.

"Psychological Types and National Character: An Informal Commentary" —*Amer. Quart.*, 5:325-343.

1 9 5 4 *(forthcoming)*

"Some Relationships Between Technical Progress and Social Progress"—to appear in *Explorations in Entrepreneurial History*, Vol. 6, No. 3.

"Some Clinical and Cultural Aspects of the Aging Process"—to appear in *Am. J. of Soc.*, 59:379-383.

"Veblen's System of Social Science"—to appear in *Explorations* I.

"Recreation and the Recreationist"—to appear in *Marriage & Family Living*, Vol. 16, No. 1.

"A Career Drama in a Middle-Aged Farmer"—to appear in *Bulletin of the Menninger Clinic*, Vol. 17.

Index